GRIT

C.D. HOWE SERIES IN CANADIAN POLITICAL HISTORY
Series editors: Robert Bothwell and John English

This series offers fresh perspectives on Canadian political history
and public policy. Its purpose is to encourage scholars to write
and publish on all aspects of the nation's political history,
including the origins, administration, and significance of
economic policies; the social foundations of politics and political
parties; transnational influences on Canadian public life; and
the biographies of key public figures. In doing so, the series fills
large gaps in our knowledge about recent Canadian history
and makes accessible to a broader audience the background
necessary to understand contemporary public-political issues.

C.D. Howe Series in
Canadian Political History

*The series originated with a grant from the
C.D. Howe Memorial Foundation and is
further supported by the Bill Graham Centre
for Contemporary International History.*

GRIT

THE LIFE AND POLITICS OF PAUL MARTIN SR.

GREG DONAGHY

UBCPress · Vancouver · Toronto

25 24 23 22 21 20 19 18 17 16 15   5 4 3 2 1

Printed in Canada on FSC-certified ancient-forest-free paper (100% post-consumer recycled) that is processed chlorine- and acid-free.

Library and Archives Canada Cataloguing in Publication

Donaghy, Greg, 1961-, author
  Grit: the life and politics of Paul Martin Sr. / Greg Donaghy.

(C.D. Howe series in Canadian political history, ISBN 2368-9080)
Includes bibliographical references and index.
Issued in print and electronic formats.
ISBN 978-0-7748-2911-3 (bound). – ISBN 978-0-7748-2913-7 (pdf). – ISBN 978-0-7748-2914-4 (epub)

  1. Martin, Paul, 1903-1992. 2. Cabinet ministers – Canada – Biography. 3. Politicians – Canada – Biography. 4. Canada – Politics and government – 1935-. I. Title.

FC621.M37D65 2015   971.064'3092   C2015-901304-6
                                                    C2015-901305-5

Canadä

UBC Press gratefully acknowledges the financial support for our publishing program of the Government of Canada (through the Canada Book Fund), the Canada Council for the Arts, and the British Columbia Arts Council.

This book has been published with the help of a grant from the Canadian Federation for the Humanities and Social Sciences, through the Awards to Scholarly Publications Program, using funds provided by the Social Sciences and Humanities Research Council of Canada.

UBC Press
The University of British Columbia
2029 West Mall
Vancouver, BC V6T 1Z2
www.ubcpress.ca

FOR MARY

CONTENTS

CONTENTS

FOREWORD

The C.D. Howe Memorial Foundation was created in 1961 to memorialize the work of Clarence Decatur Howe, an internationally renowned engineer and a senior cabinet minister in the governments of William Lyon Mackenzie King and Louis St. Laurent. Among Howe's accomplishments as a public servant was the mentoring of a generation of Canadian business and political leaders who shared a profound interest in public policy debates and in the importance of understanding the nature of historical change.

In the more than fifty years since his death, the Foundation has played a central role in furthering this rich public debate on important Canadian political and economic issues. Howe family members and leading business and political figures, including Robert Fowler, Bill Howe, Mary Dodge, Adam Zimmerman, W.J. (Bill) Bennett, Raymond Garneau, and John Turner, have done much to shape the Foundation's policies and its legacy, reflecting their own experience in a lively public forum in which business leaders, politicians, and educators have actively participated. In the 1970s, for example, the Foundation commissioned a series, Accent Québec, which made a major contribution to the debate about the economic consequences of Quebec separatism. The Foundation also gave special importance to practical economic analysis, which, with the aid of an outstanding staff of young economists, led to the formation of the independent C.D. Howe Institute.

One of us, Bob Bothwell, was the co-author of the official Howe biography, while the other, John English, wrote a biography of one of Howe's most eminent colleagues, Lester Pearson. After the publication of those biographies, the trustees invited us both to become members of the Howe board. That invitation reflected the Foundation's commitment to the importance of Canadian history and biography in the education of young Canadians and in the framing of Canadian political debate. This commitment was further affirmed by the Foundation's support for the C.D. Howe Series in Canadian Political History, for which we are series editors.

Grit: The Life and Politics of Paul Martin Sr. is the first volume in the series. We were fortunate enough to know Paul Martin Sr. personally and developed a deep admiration for a politician who read history and philosophy with enthusiasm and who enjoyed debating the past and present with academic historians. His library was impressive in size and focus; when one took a volume from the shelves there was always evidence that he had read the book. There was also a less serious side. As Greg Donaghy's book shows, he had a lively wit, a strong sense of fun, and frequently entertained his guests with his mimicry of people he had known and with his caustic opinion of the events of the day. We can recall enjoyable evenings spent around the dinner table at home with his wife Nell, his equal and partner in both wit and hospitality. One of his most notable traits too was a willingness to engage with younger people. "He was a downy old bird," a young British reporter commented after a post-midnight session in Martin's living room in London. Martin, he added, was a man of "real quality," who compared favourably with the British politicians he interacted with during his tenure as high commissioner in London.

Political history was a much more common intellectual pursuit when Paul Martin was a major public figure. It is now much neglected in Canada, and English Canada has fared badly in comparison with the rest of the Western world and with Quebec. The last (and only) biography of Prime Minister Louis St. Laurent was published in 1967. Pierre Trudeau's National Energy Program of 1980, which still convulses national politics, has never received serious historical analysis and lives on mostly in the fulminations of its opponents. The Free Trade pact of 1987 got plenty of attention at the time, but the literature on the subject – written within a few years of the event – is sadly dated. The result is that contemporary

Canadians, even those with an interest in history, know less than they should about the history, distant or recent, of their own country.

It is for this reason that the C.D. Howe Foundation decided to endow a series in Canadian political history. Not only was Howe a pre-eminent political figure who deeply influenced the shape of modern Canada, he also flourished at a time when history books were read by more than just specialists. Canada was then a country where biographies of figures like John A. Macdonald and George Brown were bestsellers and where history informed government policy through the work of royal commissions on such subjects as federal-provincial relations or the functioning of the Canadian economy. The point is that history was considered relevant, and history informed public debate.

We cannot make that claim today. Too many contemporary politicians either reject history or reinterpret it to serve their own short-term purposes – adding a new meaning to the term "political" history. When this happens, most Canadian historians remain mute. Often they do not understand what is happening or how to reply to or refute this new kind of history-on-demand.

It is our hope that this series will make a difference. We are aiming at more than an academic audience. To reach Canadians other than academic historians, the books in this series will exclude professional jargon and intellectual obscurantism. We also value clear English and sound argumentation. Finally, we do not wish our books to be uncontroversial, and in every case we want to help contemporary Canadians to connect their present to their past.

Robert Bothwell and John English

PREFACE

P aul Martin's office was in an uproar. In the fall of 1956, the veteran
minister of health and welfare was at the top of his game. He could
boast of recent triumphs at the United Nations in New York and
over polio at home, and he aspired to succeed fading prime minister Louis
St. Laurent as head of the ruling Liberal Party. But in October, the celebrated
political journalist Blair Fraser dismissed Martin's chances in *Maclean's*,
the country's most important news magazine. Fraser suspected Martin's
ambition and disliked his liberal politics. The next leader, insisted the influential Liberal columnist, must be a Protestant from English Canada,
ruling Martin out. Not for the first time, Paul Martin railed against the
ugly realities of race and religion in twentieth-century Canadian politics.

Martin's politics and ambitions were anything but simple. He matured
in an era when the Catholic Church, particularly the French Canadian
church from which he hailed, represented a conservative bulwark against
modern liberalism. Yet the youthful Martin evolved into an unusual sort
of Catholic politician. As a university student, he shed the conservative
faith of his childhood and embraced a transformative Catholicism that
was deeply rooted in the broad Western philosophic tradition. He drew
on nineteenth-century British liberalism and the contemporary social
teachings of the Catholic Church and its key thinkers, Pope Leo XIII and
John Henry Newman, to craft a politics that enjoined government to defend
its citizens against both the excesses of free-market capitalism and the
depredations of the authoritarian state. He emerged from his youth as a

Catholic idealist, professing progressive, even radical, notions of workers' rights and global order, of an activist state supplying pensions and health care, enhancing peace and international security.

Building this new order was the business of politics, which Martin joyfully embraced as his life's vocation, a professional calling from God. A French-speaking Catholic in a world largely run by and for English Protestants, he was an "outsider," who learned early on to treasure tolerance, compromise, and accommodation as democracy's most vital political virtues.

Martin was an unshakeable Grit, who inherited a strong Liberal partisan identity rooted in the reform traditions of the "clear grits" of pre-Confederation Ontario. The nickname referred to the fine sand valued by Upper Canadian masons – "all sand and no dirt, clear grit all the way through." It was echoed in the American "true grit," conveying pluck and determination. Martin embodied both meanings. He resolutely practised a tolerant and civil politics that sought to unite Canadians in their shared struggle for a more just and equitable social order.

His critics, both Liberal and otherwise, questioned his ambition and willingness to compromise, and denounced his nakedly political tactics, often disparaging him as an unsophisticated ward-heeler. But there was nothing cruel or dishonourable about Paul Martin's politics. Dialogue and discussion, sometimes endless but always earnest, were key to brokering the alliances and bargains that were required to bring Canadians together in search of community and compassionate nationhood. His political imagination conjured pathways in the 1940s to new meanings of citizenship, pension reform, and health care.

Martin's politics reached beyond, and broke down, borders. This was true within Canada, where, he believed, accommodation and compromise could reduce barriers between French and English Canadians, dissolve divisions among ethnic and religious groups, and even bridge differences between Liberal and Conservative in aid of a greater good.

This was equally true for the world beyond Canada. Based in Windsor all his adult life, perched on the edge of the United States, Martin paid little heed to borders. From the bitter legacy of the First World War and the recurring crises of the interwar years, he drew a dynamic faith in the inevitability of world government and the international rule of law.

Neither the Second World War nor the brutal nuclear Cold War that followed dented his strong and active internationalism. Through the 1950s and into the turbulent 1960s, he harnessed his capacity for hard work with his patient faith in the value of dialogue and set out to build a better world, one free from war and want. He took a generous view of Canada's obligations to the world, savouring his wins and finding inspiration in his setbacks. "It only means we have to work harder to be more effective," he said of one reverse.[1]

Paul Martin was a complicated man. His faith, politics, and burning ambition remained inseparable. His career signals the best that politics can be: a tolerant dialogue bringing citizens together in search of active, compassionate government, at home and abroad.

GRIT

1

SWEET PAUL, 1903–30

Race, religion, and class defined the young Paul Martin. His paternal grandfather, James, was the youngest son of Irish immigrants who settled around Beauharnois, Quebec, during the early decades of the nineteenth century. Born in 1833, James was married in 1858 to a francophone, Emma Lemaire, who gave birth to Paul Martin's father, Joseph Philippe Ernest Martin, in Ottawa in 1876. Philippe, as he was commonly known, was raised in Thurso, Quebec, before leaving home to attend Rigaud College. Armed with the school's short course in commercial studies, he returned to Ottawa in 1896 to work as a clerk in a furniture store and later as a bill collector.[1]

Strong and athletic, standing almost six feet tall, Philippe was a "relaxed and easy going" man who "never worried about a thing." His children, who called him "Daddy," absorbed his love of sports, his obvious warmth, and his steadfast good humour. They delighted, too, at his speech, a kind of "broken French and broken English" that Martin would later wryly describe as "perpetually bilingual."[2] When chided in French by his wife, Lumina, for wasting the family's money on a cigar – "Le voici, avec un cigare dans sa bouche!" – his cheerful retort in English became a family favourite: "Well, where do you want me to put it? In my hass?"[3]

Martin's mother came from different, tougher stock. Lumina Chouinard hailed from a sprawling Quebec City family, which had spread to Ottawa in the mid-nineteenth century to take advantage of its booming lumber industry and post-Confederation prosperity. The Chouinards were a close-knit family of small-town lawyers, priests, and storekeepers, whose feet were planted precariously on the lowest rungs of the middle class. A petite woman, who barely reached five feet, Lumina was born in 1880 and raised amid a network of aunts, uncles, and cousins who occupied a warren of small, cheap dwellings that stretched from Bronson Avenue to Booth Street in Ottawa's LeBreton Flats district.

Lumina inherited the upward aspirations of the Chouinards. Employed before marriage as a schoolteacher in rural Embrun, just east of Ottawa, she spoke "beautiful English and beautiful French." Unlike Philippe, she fretted constantly about the family's finances and impressed forcefully upon all her children the vital importance of an education for getting ahead in this world. She was, her son Paul recalled candidly, "a very aggressive woman ... the activist in the family." Above all, he added, she was "very ambitious for her children."[4]

Lumina and Philippe Martin were married in February 1901 and set up house at 63 LeBreton Street, one in a row of small red-brick houses near the southeast corner of Somerset Avenue in Ottawa's west end. Their early married life was not easy. A first-born daughter died tragically at nine months in 1902. The young couple had other burdens to bear, as Lumina's father, Guillaume, and then her young cousin Thomas, moved into their cramped accommodations. Their responsibilities grew even heavier on 23 June 1903, when Lumina gave birth to their second child, Joseph James Guillaume Paul Martin. Eight months later, finding it hard to make ends meet, and perhaps grateful to escape the confining house on LeBreton Street, the Martins left Ottawa for Pembroke. Generously described by a popular tourist guide of the time as "an industrious little town" of almost six thousand souls, Pembroke was, in reality, a rough and ready lumber town, 120 kilometres up the Ottawa River, propped on the edge of the vast and sparse Canadian Shield.[5] There, Philippe found work as a clerk in the small grocery store owned by his sister's husband, Isidore Martin.

The Martins prospered in Pembroke. When Isidore's store collapsed in 1909, Philippe quickly found similar work with J.B. Kemp, which provided the family with a steady income for many years and ensured that Paul's childhood passed in what he later described as "relative tranquility." The family expanded quickly as devout Catholic families usually did: Paul was joined by a brother, Emile, in 1906, and then by five sisters; the twins, Lucille and Marie, in 1909; Aline in 1912; and a second set of twins, Anita and Claire, in 1915. A second brother, Charles Henri, was born "a blue baby" and died in 1914 at just two months.

The Martin family stood "very close to the Church in devotion, belief, and association," fasting and attending daily Mass during Lent and normally ending each day with the rosary.[6] Although such devotions were not unusual, their significance was reinforced in the Martin household by more immediate evidence of divine intervention. At the age of four, Paul contracted a severe form of polio that was sometimes fatal and often left even its surviving victims badly crippled. The prognosis was poor. "Goose oil and prayer," recommended the local doctor, "that's all that can help that boy."[7]

Martin's mother, Lumina, trusted in prayer. When Paul recovered enough to travel, she bundled him onto the train and set off for the popular shrines of Sainte-Anne-de-Beaupré and the new chapel of St. Joseph on the slopes of Montreal's Mount Royal, where Brother André Bessette prayed with the faithful. Paul's recovery was slow, and for the next few years his father and brother pulled him around Pembroke in a small wagon. Eventually, however, he walked again, but he was permanently burdened with a weak left shoulder, an impaired left arm, and a partially blind left eye. Lumina was steadfast in her belief that "it was Brother André, who made other cripples walk, who made it possible for Paul."[8]

During Martin's childhood, the family lived in a number of houses clustered close to Pembroke's St. Columbkille Cathedral and rented from the local Catholic bishop. Neither the house on Moffat Street, with its low-slung veranda, nor the dwelling at 329 Isabella Street, where the family moved just before Paul left for secondary school, were luxurious. But neither were they impoverished by local standards. The house on Isabella, to which Martin frequently returned as a young adult and recalled most clearly, lacked running water, depended on a wood stove for heat, and was certainly cramped, with the nine family members squeezed into two bedrooms. But the upright Heintzman piano in the dining room – bought on credit for two dollars a month – sounded a distinctive note and signalled Lumina's ambition and middle-class yearnings. "We were not rich," recalled Martin's youngest sisters, "but we were happy."[9]

Life in Pembroke was unsophisticated and isolated. "I cannot recall ever seeing a stranger having a meal at our house," Martin recalled with obvious wonder.[10] Life revolved around the family, and the Martins were close-knit. Encouraged by Philippe, who flooded the yard for an ice rink in winter and umpired local ball games in Dominion Park, the children enjoyed plenty of outdoor play. Philippe and Emile often managed some of Pembroke's lower-tiered sports teams, reflecting a family interest that Paul also embraced. Paul and Emile swam together in the nearby Ottawa River and were very good friends. Martin doted on his sister Lucille, to whom he was particularly close. All his siblings remembered him as "a great tease," who would provoke his little sisters into giggling fits during silent retreats and roar laughing at their roughhousing during Mass.[11]

His relationship with his mother was most significant in shaping the young Paul. His polio set him apart and reinforced his isolation, perhaps making him, as he later mused, "lonely by nature."[12] It left him with a craving for company that persisted throughout his life. He had few close friends of his own age in Pembroke, and because of his illness, he spent a great deal of time with Lumina, absorbing her fears, her faith, and most importantly, her strong ambitions. Like his mother, Paul worried about the family's finances and considered himself poor, a haunting insecurity that he never entirely escaped. Even as a teenager, he greatly resented the differences in wealth and influence that divided Pembroke's affluent mill-owners from its poorer citizens, and he recalled being deeply affected when his own father lost his job in 1921: "He was a strong man physically, and I can see yet the agony, the frustration, the sorrow, the disappointment, the bitterness that he experienced."[13] This sensibility fuelled a progressive social and economic outlook that grew stronger as Martin matured.

He was something of a "worrywart" too. School exams were "nightmares," and his good humour was frequently offset by a solemn seriousness and sense of purpose. Lumina often spoke to her children about "the nobility of public life," and even when Paul was a small child, his family told reporters in the 1940s, he wanted to be a politician. Mostly, however, Lumina spoke about the priesthood, and she was deeply gratified when Paul showed early evidence of a priestly vocation, daily rising at the crack of dawn to serve as an altar boy at the 6:30 Mass at the local Convent of Mary

Immaculate. When Pembroke bishop Patrick "Paddy" Ryan offered to pay Paul's secondary school fees to follow his calling, a time-honoured route upward for ambitious and devout Catholics, Lumina and Paul seized the chance. Paul was just fifteen when he left home in September 1918 to study at the Collège Apostolique St-Alexandre de la Gatineau in the small Quebec town of Ironsides, just a few miles north of Ottawa. When his father dropped him off on the gravel drive amid the college's lush green fields and imposing red-brick clock tower, Paul, who would always struggle to conceal his emotions, burst into tears.

He did well at St-Alexandre over the next three years, though he was never at home there. Nicknamed the "Holy-Ghost-Up-the-Gatineau" after the Spiritian fathers who ran it, St-Alexandre was a bilingual "petit seminaire," training priests for English- and French-speaking parishes on both sides of the Ottawa Valley. Run by a tough and athletic Alsatian priest, Joseph Burgsthaler, college life was meant to be shaped by a driving "thirst for a disciplined liberty."[14] There was lots of discipline but little liberty. The clock tower bell tolled the passing of each monotonous day: prayer, study, meals, play. Students, confined to the isolated campus on the banks of the Gatineau River, rose at six o'clock for daily Mass, breakfasted on porridge, toast, and jam, and ate dinners of pea soup, meat, and pudding.[15] This was not the life that Martin wanted, and when he encountered a former teacher decades later, he was unusually bitter in his reminiscences, telling his wife that "we all thought he was a son-of-a-bitch."[16]

The school's impact on Martin's politics was much more fundamental. By 1918, his attachment to the Liberal Party and its leader, Sir Wilfrid Laurier, was already firmly in place, inherited from his father. St-Alexandre, however, would sharpen Martin's identity as a French Canadian. Like many communities in the Ottawa Valley, Pembroke was deeply divided along linguistic lines between its French- and English-speaking inhabitants. Endless conflicts with the larger anglophone population and provincial restrictions on French-language education, embodied in the infamous Regulation 17, created pressures that made assimilation almost inevitable. The Martins were headed in that direction. Neither of Paul's two youngest sisters spoke much French, and the family often recited its daily rosary in English. Martin himself was educated in English at the local separate school and learned to read at Pembroke's Carnegie Library, where he was introduced to Mark Twain and Gladstone's collected letters. The outbreak of the First World War in 1914 and the imposition of conscription in 1917 in the face of fierce opposition from Laurier's Liberals and their French Canadian supporters sparked a crisis in Canadian unity.

The crisis echoed through Pembroke and in the Martin household on Isabella Street. When Grandmother Chouinard was refused Holy Communion at the Irish Canadian church of St. Patrick's in downtown Ottawa, the family was scandalized and unsure how to respond. "I can remember feuds around our family table," Paul recalled, "meal after meal, month after month." His father preferred discretion and raged against his Ottawa relations, who joined the local riots. Martin's mother was less accommodating and more determined to see "the French fact recognized and furthered."[17] This "nasty" division was doubtless uncomfortable for young Paul, and St-Alexandre represented an avenue of adolescent escape and self-definition. There, like most of his French Canadian classmates, he embraced the wave of nationalist enthusiasm that swept through Quebec's classical colleges in the wake of the First World War. The students he met "were very Quebec ... They were very French, very nationalistic." "I was a Nationalist in those days," he later boasted, and "prejudiced against English-speaking people."[18]

The school's curriculum served Martin well, and his studies were both broadly based and useful. Traditional Catholic theology dominated, as did Latin and Greek composition and literature. He also devoted much time to English and French grammar and literature, and to Ancient, British, and Canadian history. After his third year, when he changed his mind about joining the priesthood, the college generously added arithmetic, algebra, and geometry to his program to meet the admission requirements for St. Michael's College at the University of Toronto.[19]

In June 1921, Martin returned to Pembroke for a summer of work in the mills. Three months later, he boarded the train for Toronto. The product of an isolated rural parish, he left his childhood home for the last time, driven by a conscious and striving ambition, instilled early by his mother and reinforced by his miraculous recovery from polio. He carried with him a devout Catholicism, vague notions of social justice, and an unfamiliar

and untested identity as a French Canadian nationalist. All these characteristics would be enlarged and refined in the coming decade.

IN THE EARLY evening of 25 September 1921, Martin disembarked from the
train at Toronto's Union Station. Marvelling at the grand Eaton's Department Store, where his mother shopped by catalogue, he rode the tram
north along Yonge Street toward St. Michael's College. The deliberate result
of a sustained policy of "scholars before buildings," the unprepossessing
set of spartan buildings huddled between Queen's Park Crescent and
Bay Street to the east, in a small block extending south from St. Mary's to
St. Joseph's Streets.[20] Above the campus loomed the towering neo-Gothic
spires of St. Basil's Church, erected in honour of the patron saint of the
Basilian fathers, the Catholic teaching order that ran the college. The City
of Toronto was just beginning to widen Bay Street, tearing down the
college buildings on the eastern edge of the campus and transforming St.
Michael's, which had so far enjoyed the "quiet seclusion of a Muskoka island," into a construction site. Disgruntled students and faculty dubbed
campus, "the sand heap."[21]

The college's intellectual pedigree was more impressive. Founded in
1852 as a joint Catholic high school for boys and a seminary, "St. Mike's"
had joined the much larger University of Toronto in 1910 as a semi-
autonomous, federated college. Nevertheless, it remained profoundly
Catholic in inspiration and outlook. It was staffed almost exclusively by
priests and religious, and continued to enrol significant numbers of students who were headed for religious life, even in the 1920s. Many pupils,
including Martin, regularly attended daily Mass, and a three-day silent
retreat during the Lenten Holy Week was compulsory for all college members. Women students, admitted only in 1911 and housed in the nearby
Loretto and St. Joseph residences, were segregated and generally took their
classes by themselves. "It was," an early female student recalled bitterly, "a
man's world."[22]

The masculine Catholic environment eased Martin's transition from the
rural, bilingual St-Alexandre to the urbane and English-speaking St. Mike's.
"It was very foreign to me," he admitted. "It was all very strange, but very
exciting. I was happy almost from the first day I put my foot on the grounds

of St. Michael's."[23] He delighted in the college's more liberal discipline – enjoying the freedom to go out at night and to choose courses – and at the prospect of expanding his horizons. In this respect, the outward-looking college he encountered in 1921 fitted him to a tee. Increasingly confident and ambitious, Toronto's English-speaking Catholics were actively shedding their immigrant Irish past and embracing a modern identity as loyal, upwardly mobile, and civic-minded Canadians.[24] Under the guidance of Father Henry Carr, a young and liberal-minded Basilian, St. Mike's worked hard to embrace the Protestant university and the city around it. Carr, who became superior and college president in 1915, encouraged his students to pursue sports, especially football and hockey, and other intra-university activities as a means of breaking out of the Catholic ghetto.[25]

St. Mike's welcomed Carr's ambitions for a Catholic elite that was prepared to lay siege to the exclusive social and economic bastions of Protestant Toronto. Although the United States was making its cultural presence felt through magazines and movies, Toronto was still an Anglo-Canadian city. Eighty percent of its 522,000 people were of British heritage, with more than a quarter born in Britain.[26] It was city of stolid conservative values, favouring temperate tea dances at the King Edward Hotel and private home ownership. The Protestant Orange Lodge, feverishly loyal to Britain and intolerant of Catholics, dominated its political culture. But a new generation of Irish Catholic Canadians tested that orthodoxy. Led by Archbishop Neil McNeil, Canadian-born Catholic community leaders, priests, and educators advocated denominational peace, Catholic-Protestant reconciliation, and greater civic participation by Catholics. Conscious of their minority status, they shied away from doctrinal purity and embraced pragmatic compromise, adaptation, and accommodation to ensure the continued prosperity of their faith.[27] These values would mark Martin deeply.

Federation, too, was changing St. Mike's. Under pressure from the university, the college was moving away from the rigid and authoritarian Catholic theology that had dominated its curriculum since the mid-nineteenth century. Carr delighted in the change, pressing his younger staff to pursue the growing interest among Catholic theologians in the thought of St. Thomas Aquinas. Thomism flourished at St. Mike's. Pope Leo XIII, a scholar and intellectual, had championed the ideas of St. Augustine and St. Thomas to construct a modern philosophy of state that was robust enough to tackle the false philosophies advanced in defence of laissez-faire capitalism and socialism. Under Leo XIII, Catholic social thinking embraced a "centralist" position that was intended to maintain individual rights and freedoms within a communitarian social framework. Among the results was Leo's 1891 encyclical, *Rerum Novarum,* on capital and labour, which offered Catholics a worldview that legitimized the state's role in protecting private property, while strongly defending the principles of a right to a just wage and labour's right to organize.[28]

As he built up the college staff, Carr looked to Europe, where these ideas were being worked out most fully in a range of movements, including distributism, solidarism, and personalism. In 1919, he lured the Thomist philosopher Maurice DeWolf from Louvain, a leading centre of liberal Catholic thought. Prominent Catholic thinkers Sir Bertram Windle, the outgoing president of the National University of Ireland, and Fathers Léon Noël and Gerald Phelan from Louvain followed. Philosophers Jacques Maritain and Étienne Gilson joined them in the 1920s, eventually helping to found the renowned Pontifical Institute of Medieval Studies. The work of Maritain and Gilson on the right relationship between state and individual, the vital importance of Christian social responsibility, and the centrality of individual freedom represented the "finest flowering" of Leo's Thomistic legacy and gave St. Mike's the country's most vibrant department of philosophy.[29] "The intellectual temperature here," recorded one faculty member, "rises ten degrees when these men are around."[30]

Martin was unaware of these currents when he encountered Father E.J. McCorkell during his second day on campus. Facing tuition and residence fees of $350, the new student had only $40 in his pocket. He needed help, and he got it from McCorkell, St. Mike's amiable and imperturbable registrar, who found him a part-time job at a local student hang-out, the Bluebird Cafe, and arranged for a loan.[31] Martin cleaned furnaces, too. And during the summers, he flogged magazine subscriptions in northern Ontario and took bets at horse-racing tracks in Windsor, whose Catholic community was closely tied to St. Mike's.

McCorkell, who became a mentor and life-long friend, had a more significant role to play, steering Martin toward the study of philosophy. By the early 1920s, St. Michael's saw philosophy as essential for the education of a "cultured Catholic gentleman." Its "creative potential" was also viewed as especially good preparation for the rigours of law school, which St. Michael's graduates entered in increasing numbers each year, and which Martin already planned to attend. It had the added advantage that one could proceed from the first year pass arts course directly into the second year honours philosophy course without having to take an additional first year's honours course, an important consideration for poorer students like Martin.[32]

Martin's undergraduate courses were a fundamental part of his education, and they profoundly shaped his politics, his faith, and his identity. In sharp contrast to the otherworldly Catholic orthodoxy at St-Alexandre, the philosophy program at St. Michael's was broad ranging and comprehensive. It began with the Greeks, Plato and Aristotle, and moved steadily forward through the early church fathers, St. Thomas Aquinas, and mainstream Western thinkers such as Descartes, Mill, and Kant. McCorkell's lectures on nineteenth-century thought introduced Martin to the liberalism of John Stuart Mill and gave an intellectual foundation to the Laurier Liberalism of his childhood.[33]

The Thomism instilled by St. Mike's was equally bracing and just as lasting. Martin was especially drawn to Cardinal John Henry Newman, the "slippery and often elusive" English divine whom the Anglican historian Owen Chadwick shrewdly labelled a "conservative innovator."[34] Newman's reverence for authority and tradition suited Martin's particular heritage and his cautious personality. "One generation," Martin sometimes insisted, "had no right and no capacity to pass judgement on the traditions of mankind."[35] But mostly he was inspired by Newman's demands for an order in which Christianity – changing "to remain the same" – retained its force as a "governing factor in society."[36] Thomism provided Martin with a theological justification for challenging authority, secular or religious, rationally criticizing the existing order, and proposing reforms. Engaged in the world about him, Martin's Newman was a liberal reformer, whose probing, critical mind forged new tools for new problems, ever guided by Christian revelation. In an increasingly secular age, when many progressives were shedding their religious faith, Thomism gave Martin grounds to hold tight to his.

Outside the lecture hall, he threw himself into college life. During his four years at St. Mike's, he lived in its grey-brick residence, spending two years in the "Jews flat" on the fourth floor before moving to better digs on the second floor, or the "Irish flat." Unlike most of his classmates, Martin arrived on campus knowing precisely what he wanted to be: certainly a politician and government minister, and possibly even a prime minister. He chose his extracurricular activities accordingly. From the start, he was active in the college drama club, winning a seat on its executive and acting throughout his undergraduate years. He was also an executive member of the college literary club, which invited local worthies to discuss contemporary literature with high-spirited and romantic undergraduates, who cheerfully denounced modern novelists for their "ruthless realism."[37] A voracious reader whose tastes ran mostly to history, philosophy, and biography – subjects from which he could draw practical lessons – Martin never developed a genuine interest in imaginative literature, to the regret of his classmate, the novelist Morley Callaghan.

Sports were important for a well-rounded college career at St. Mike's, whose tiny student body of just over 140 men fielded thirteen "rugby" teams in 1928.[38] Martin, whose polio excluded him from the sports field, managed an intramural hockey team in 1923-24, losing the Jennings Cup final to a team of medical students. At least, Martin's crew consoled themselves, it wasn't "a very big cup."[39] He enjoyed more success the next year, when he managed the intermediate intercollegiate football team, which captured the S.J. Shaw Trophy.

Martin directed most of his extracurricular energies to student politics and debating, whose prestige rivalled athletics at the college. Earnestly focused on his future ambitions, he rounded up a handful of "politically inclined" students in his second year to form a new college discussion club, the pretentiously named Quindecim. Limited to fifteen carefully chosen members, the club hoped to introduce them to prominent political figures. Its reach consistently exceeded its grasp, however, and its guests, who included a Toronto rabbi, the Cuban consul general, and journalist Sir John Willison, were typically local celebrities or political has-beens.[40]

More important, and much more fun, was the college's mock student parliament, which Martin joined in December of 1921, standing as a Liberal. The following year, he played the part of the Liberal premier in the kind of rollicking session that undergraduate politicians have always loved, losing his government on a confidence vote but re-emerging triumphantly in the end.[41] Mock parliament was the springboard to a debating career at the college and at the University of Toronto, where Martin developed and honed the rhetorical skills that would become a prominent part of his political arsenal.

Although he was not the best speaker of his class (that honour went to Morley Callaghan), he was nonetheless a "bewilderingly formidable" opponent, armed by his philosophy classes with a quiver of memorized quotations from Aristotle, Augustine, and Aquinas. What he lacked in polish, he made up for in energy, enthusiasm, and volume. In a fictionalized account of his undergraduate days, The Varsity Story, Callaghan fondly recalled Martin's energetic style: "The St. Mike's man, speaking vehemently, was having trouble with his boiled shirt, which kept billowing out from the black vest. He kept pounding it in with his fist as he talked."[42]

Martin's enthusiastic approach, which established him as a presence on campus, delighted his listeners. In his second year, he won a college prize, the Gough Trophy, "for most consistent oratorical effort," and he joined Callaghan on the college's inter-faculty debating team in their third year. They lost to Law, beat Victoria College, and won coveted spots on the University of Toronto's intercollegiate team. As part of that team, Martin represented Toronto against McGill in February 1923, when he "fairly carried his audience away by his earnest and convincing style."[43]

His success as a debater reinforced his standing at St. Mike's, where he was admired for his maturity, judgment, and "intellectual balance." Callaghan later wrote that "his vast amiability made him popular."[44] His friends called him "Sweet Paul," a teasing reference to his fondness for desserts perhaps, but also an acknowledgment of his friendly disposition and self-confident manner. In his final year, Martin won that traditional measure of student popularity, election as St. Mike's student council president, using the position to rally student support for the college's first activity fee.[45]

His larger political ambitions, which were common knowledge on campus, marked him out among cynical undergraduates as unusual. As a student recalled, they saw through his "quasi-political techniques" and sometimes derided him as a "serious, somewhat plodding classmate."[46] Behind his back, aware of his pleasure when the campus press noted his successes, they tagged him "The Great One."[47] Persuading his contemporaries of his sincerity would be a lasting challenge for Martin, one that cast a shadow over his entire life.

Martin's professors and teachers, more worldly and more experienced, were less inclined to question the motives of an ambitious young under-graduate. They quickly took him up and happily opened doors for him when they could. Joking with a classmate (though only half in jest) that "influence is a great factor in the so-called successful Career," Martin courted his professors' attention.[48] In letters to his mentors, he was lavish in his flattery and his expressions of gratitude. They responded as well to his guileless and genuine "capacity for admiration," qualities that he re-tained throughout his life.[49] Like McCorkell and Carr, many at St. Mike's were impressed by his "honest simplicity and true humility."[50]

Martin's network was broadened further through his close friendship with Burgon Bickersteth, the warden of Hart House. His most influential mentor at the University of Toronto, Bickersteth was the son of a leading English Anglican family. Educated at Charterhouse and Oxford, he quali-fied as a charter member of the British establishment. A decorated vet-eran of the First World War, where he fought with the Royal Dragoons, Bickersteth was en route home to England after teaching in Alberta when businessman Vincent Massey offered him the warden's post in 1921.[51] Funded by the Massey family, Hart House was intended to introduce Toronto undergraduates to the best Oxbridge traditions and to serve as the university's cultural centre.

The charismatic Bickersteth was an inspired choice for warden. Just thirty-three years old, he was intensely interested in youth, who responded warmly to his "open-handed manner."[52] When he overheard Martin dis-miss him as a "damned Englishman," a story that Martin polished to a gem over his lifetime, he invited him for tea.[53] The effect was magical. Hart House overwhelmed Martin. It was, he recalled, "an unforgettable institu-tion – the library, the lovely dining room, the music room, the paintings – all those things young Canadians never saw at home."[54] Bickersteth lectured the French Canadian Catholic on the virtues of tolerance, and the two soon became friends. Martin copied the warden's dress and social mannerisms, and turned to him for career advice.

Like McCorkell and Carr, Bickersteth took Martin's political aspira-tions seriously. As he later wrote his parents, he derived a unique joy from "watching young freshmen, green, underdeveloped, narrow and restricted in their outlook ... beginning to play their part on the Dominion [national] stage."[55] Anxious to bridge the French-English divisions left by the First World War and conscription, he was drawn by the kind of ideal Canadian politician that Martin might one day become. "It's satisfactory to feel that this [Hart] House did something for him," Bickersteth wrote Prime Minister William Lyon Mackenzie King, "and that whereas he came here as an undergraduate with sharply developed racial and religious prejudices he has now got rid of those."[56] In due course, as one of Martin's professors put it, the bilingual Martin "may very well find a useful role in mediating and interpreting between us and our French-Canadian brethren of the Province of Quebec, for the promotion of mutual understanding and cooperation for the general good."[57] Bickersteth made sure that Martin met his Liberal friends, including Prime Minister King.

Four years as an undergraduate at St. Mike's and the University of Toronto gave some form and substance to the undefined liberal ideas that Martin had held on his arrival. During the summer of 1925, soon after his graduation, the Pembroke Kiwanis Club invited him to give a youthful perspective on the pressing issues of the day. As his sponsors had hoped, his French Canadian nationalism, though by no means entirely extinguished, had been smoothed over, replaced by a new attachment to tolerance as the central virtue of Canadian democracy. The University of Toronto, he told his audience, had many religions, but it functioned "as one harmonious body" and "teaches us that the solution to our difficulties lies in tolerance."[58]

The youthful Martin could still be provoked, however, especially in debate. Amid a throng of jeering students who were attached to the university's palpable British imperial heritage, he was sometimes tempted to revert to dramatic shorthand. "Canada first and England second!" he baited his audience.[59] But his real views on the imperial connection were more refined. His French Canadian doubts about the subject mixed easily with the dominant views of St. Mike's postwar Irish Catholic majority, most of whom had grown up in Toronto's separate school system, with its dual emphasis on a "love of God and country."[60] Like them, Martin consciously carved out a civic identity that was deliberately and proudly Canadian but not anti-British. In thoughtful moments, he was less inclined to distinguish sharply between the two nations. Although Canada needed its own national ideals and traditions, he insisted that "full and independent nationhood was in no sense an act of disloyalty to the British Empire."[61]

These views placed Martin on the left wing of his Liberal Party. His other central ideas on leaving St. Mike's were even more progressive. He flirted with proportional representation and denounced the suffocating grasp of party discipline, which stripped individual voters of "independent thought and decision" and replaced them with "the party spirit." That kind of compulsion, he warned, led to Bolshevism and the socialist nightmare that was sweeping across Soviet Russia. While young progressives throughout Canada were embracing fashionable collective doctrines, Martin grounded his economic ideas in his liberalism and Catholic faith. "I believe the only way to remedy conditions [of poverty]," he told Pembroke's leading citizens, "is the adoption of the spirit of Christianity and the acknowledgement of God." He forcefully reminded the town's factory and mill-owners that their "moral duty" as employers was to create the conditions of life that would make people happy.[62]

The virtues of tolerance, liberty, and economic justice animated Martin's talk. They were all values that his studies and experiences at St. Mike's and the University of Toronto had nurtured and reinforced. He was far less sophisticated in addressing the problem of war. Like many of his generation, exposed to the carnage of the First World War, he condemned conflict as "an insult to the intelligence." He embraced the League of Nations, created at the end of the war, simply – perhaps even skeptically – as evidence of a "determined effort for peace and the elimination of war." His remarks on the league lacked idealism and conviction, and reflected a parochial worldview that Toronto had done little to overcome. That was about to change, and during the next five years, as he rounded out his education, Martin's world expanded steadily outward.[63]

MARTIN'S UNDERGRADUATE experience extended his horizons and bred new ambitions. With encouragement from Bickersteth and McCorkell, he applied for a Rhodes scholarship in the spring of 1925 to study at Oxford. Distracted by his extracurricular activities, however, he had achieved just a "B" average and stood little chance. Instead, he was forced to resume his earlier plans to pursue legal studies at Osgoode Hall Law School in September 1925. Run by the Law Society of Upper Canada, Osgoode Hall was a relaxed and uninspired institution in the 1920s, where the "prevailing spirit was friendly."[64] The full-time academic staff was small and over-shadowed by the part-time teachers, who taught the dreary technical subjects – wills, contracts, torts, mortgages – that dominated the curriculum. Martin attended two dull lectures every morning from nine to eleven, then headed off to complete his professional articles in the "dirty, dusty, ill-decorated" law offices of Henderson and McGuire. He absorbed the practical minutiae of his chosen profession, but Osgoode "was not a happy place."[65]

During the three years that Martin studied law, he found his inspiration elsewhere. Like several other Osgoode students, he pursued a concurrent master's degree, writing a thesis at St. Mike's under Father Gerald Phelan on Cardinal Newman's *Essay in Aid of a Grammar of Assent*. Newman's seminal work on the importance of personal faith over reason alone in confronting the world reinforced Martin's Thomistic view of contemporary Catholicism and its continued relevance. Indeed, as he told a University of Ottawa conference that marked the 1945 centennial of Newman's conversion from Anglicanism, faith retained its engaged, liberating, and re-forming role in modern society. "The interior world, physical and historical, is but the manifestation to our sense of realities greater than itself," he insisted. "These Christian realities must again, as always in time of crisis, be reasserted with their eternal spirit, always dynamic and progressive, always coeval with the human soul and needs."[66] The graduate experience, which included a paid stint as a sessional lecturer in 1927-28, reinforced Martin's view of himself as an intellectual, a status he treasured.

He remained active in campus affairs. During the winter of 1926, he captained the Varsity debating squad in its successful contest with an Oxbridge team; the *Toronto Globe* called his performance a "triumph of eloquence."[67] In the spring, he was elected president of the university's Newman Club, the focus of Varsity social and religious life for Catholic students outside St. Mike's. His campaign was marred by bare-knuckled tactics – the Martin camp tried to close nominations early to exclude his opponent – that bordered on the illegitimate and did his reputation on campus little good.[68]

Martin used the club's speaking program in 1926-27 to enhance his own network, inviting prominent Liberal cabinet ministers Ernest Lapointe and

Fernand Rinfret to speak at its Sunday evening lectures. At the same time, he became increasingly active in Liberal Party circles. After campaigning in the Pembroke riding of North Renfrew during the 1925 federal election, he was elected vice-president of the University of Toronto's Gladstone Young Liberal Club for the 1926-27 academic year and served as its president the following year, his last on campus.

No one was surprised when Martin decided to seek the Liberal nomination in the June 1928 by-election to fill the vacant provincial riding of North Renfrew, which included his hometown of Pembroke. He had flirted with Ontario politics since arriving at St. Mike's, and he had become friendly with the provincial Liberal organizer, Nelson Parliament. In January 1926, he began to compile a carefully indexed clipping file on Ontario politics.[69] He was clearly ready for battle and was at least as determined to run as the party's organizers, W.H. Moore and Senator Andrew Haydon, were in having him contest the election during the summer's slow political season.

Renfrew Liberals were more doubtful. North Renfrew was a Conservative riding, and the Tory candidate, E.A. Dunlop, was a leading employer in the region and a prospective member of Premier Howard Ferguson's cabinet. Outside Pembroke, as one executive of the Liberal riding association explained, there was "quite a sentiment" to allow Dunlop to stand unopposed.[70] Martin's parents were skeptical, too. His father was particularly uncomfortable with the idea of his son challenging the region's leading industrialist. "I remember having a real row," Martin recalled, "getting up from the table and I was in tears – the idea that he would not support the position I was taking."[71] Martin and his Toronto backers forced the issue, and on 4 June he was selected the Liberal candidate. Next day, a *Toronto Globe* editorial attacked the unpleasant murmurs already circulating that Martin was acting from narrow self-interest, and it praised the young candidate for setting "an example for others of his fellow students to follow."[72]

Martin discovered how tough and nasty a real campaign could be, a lesson he never forgot. He confessed to his diary that the slow start and empty halls were "somewhat disheartening," and after wandering through the small towns and hamlets of the Ottawa Valley, he complained of being so tired that he could barely remember what he was doing.[73] In his campaign stops, he spoke about the daily struggles of the average worker, whose welfare, he insisted, ought to be the primary focus of government. He promised to support old age pensions, and he attacked Dunlop and other mill-owners for their low wages and selfish refusal to allow the provincial power company, Ontario Hydro, to develop the Ottawa Valley for the good of the community.[74] He promised a minimum living wage to reflect the Christian commitment to justice (while en route, he read Jesuit economist Father F.A. Walker on a livable wage for moral sustenance). The working-man, Martin reasoned naively with his audience, "if he cared to better his condition, could not consistently vote against me."[75]

But elections are rarely about ideas, and Dunlop's response was swift and unforgiving. The Tory attacked the provincial Liberal Party and its mor-alistic leader, W.E.N. Sinclair, for supporting temperance, an unpopular platform in much of the province. Dunlop savaged Martin's speeches as part of a "whisper campaign of slander" and dismissed his wage proposals as "foolish, childish, [and] juvenile."[76] The charges stuck. The North Renfrew Liberal-Conservative Association bought a full-page ad in the *Pembroke Standard-Observer* to remind voters of how much they owed Dunlop, who had brought the Eddy Match Company, the Shook Mill, and the steel equipment plant to Pembroke.[77] Townsfolk, who nicknamed the Liberal candidate "Paul-Who-Does-He-Think-He-Is-Martin," flocked to the all-candidate debates to see him mocked.[78] Dunlop pummelled his opponent, winning the election by a majority of 2,201, a historic margin of victory.[79]

Martin later claimed that the defeat hit him "hardish" and convinced him not to run again for a long while.[80] Yet he observed in his diary that "the experience was worth the effort," adding that "I have no regrets in hav-ing become a candidate at all."[81] The vote established his credentials as an aspiring politician. The right people noticed when the *Ottawa Journal* praised his initiative and assured its readers that "Mr. Martin will be heard from again. He has youth, he has ability and energy, and what is far more finer, he has the true sporting spirit."[82] He boasted to contemporaries of the cam-paign, even claiming that the Tories tried to bribe him not to run. Within a year, he was already hinting to friends about contesting a federal seat. Meantime, armed with a two-hundred-dollar parting gift from Moore, he caught the westbound train from Toronto in early July 1928 and set out to discover his country. He spent a week in Windsor, renewing contacts he had made as a summer student, and then headed west to Vancouver, working through a long list of Liberal contacts. It was a joyous trip, Martin luxuriating in his well-earned holiday. "Sleep," he sighed, "is a wonderful thing."[83]

He returned from his western tour with renewed energy, determined to pursue a graduate degree at Harvard Law School. The obstacles were daunting. He could not afford to fund the venture and was forced to beg from his political connections. Senator Haydon found him a six-hundred-dollar scholarship, but Toronto senator Frank O'Connor, the wealthy Catholic candy manufacturer whom he had hosted at the Newman Club, rejected his request for a loan of eight hundred dollars, offering him instead a job in his Boston plant. The encounter left Martin embarrassed and cautious about the sympathies of his fellow Catholics from English Canada. "I can't say that the Irish appeal to me very much," he rationalized in retelling the story, adding that "I never felt myself as a representative of the Catholics or the Irish in particular."[84]

Admission to Harvard was far from certain. Martin's sessional work at St. Mike's and the Renfrew campaign had taken time, causing him to fail a course in his final year and forcing him to write a supplemental exam. But he could be persuasive, and he convinced Donald MacRae, one of his Osgoode law professors and an acquaintance of Harvard dean Roscoe Pound, to back his application. MacRae's help did not rest solely on Martin's scholarly accomplishments. These did not, as the professor dryly put it, "enable me to say much in support of his application." Instead, MacRae emphasized his student's growing "tolerance" as a French Canadian, his active role in the Liberal Party, and his political ambitions. These "unusual qualifications" promised to create a public figure who could bridge the country's French-English divisions.[85] Martin would be "at least an interesting experiment," promised MacRae, "possibly a very successful one." Dean Pound hesitated but finally agreed "to stretch a point" and admitted the aspiring Canadian politician, whose case was clearly "exceptional."[86]

Martin thrived at Harvard, whose atmosphere was certainly different from Osgoode's. As he reflected later, it was "a workhouse ... Everybody worked very hard there, and everybody vied with one another. There was no leisure time."[87] His enthusiasm for the law school filled his letters home: it was "truly great," he gushed soon after he arrived, "a great educational environment."[88] Even his first "lonely" Christmas away from home, mostly spent catching up on his reading in a deserted library, failed to diminish his fervour. "Everything is proceeding smoothly," he assured Bickersteth. "Much work and enthusiasm is still the order of the day."[89]

Harvard's strong faculty inspired Martin. He described Dean Roscoe Pound, with whom he studied jurisprudence, as "brilliant and informative to a degree almost phenomenal."[90] He was equally pleased with his professor of administrative law, Felix Frankfurter (a future US Supreme Court justice). "I like him one of the best," he remarked ungrammatically.[91] Harvard's scholarly and academic approach to graduate law played to Martin's strengths. He liked Pound's philosophical turn of mind and Frankfurter's sociological understanding of administrative law. Most of all, he enjoyed the seminar in international law offered by Manley Hudson, whom he judged "a superb teacher, articulate and theatrical."[92] Martin's engagement was reflected in his results. At the end of the year, he ranked a very respectable sixth out of twenty-nine students, with marks ranging from a low of fifty-nine in Roman law to a high of eighty-four in international law.[93] His Toronto sponsors were pleased. Bickersteth told King that Martin had "done extremely well," and MacRae declared himself "entirely justified."[94]

Harvard represented the most rigorous legal training that Martin experienced, and it strengthened his exposure to international law. It also reinforced his determination to continue his studies abroad. "I wish I could express adequately the strength of my desire to study in England," he wrote Bickersteth in early 1929, asking for help. "That has always been one of my ambitions."[95] For much of his second term at Harvard, he was preoccupied with finding the money to follow Manley Hudson, who was leaving on sabbatical, to Trinity College, Cambridge. After failing to secure funding from the National Research Council, Martin refused to consider approaching Toronto Catholics and enlisted Bickersteth in an appeal to Vincent Massey, now Canada's chief diplomatic representative in Washington.[96] Though Martin consulted Bickersteth, he drafted the plea himself, stressing his "simplicity and gravity," playing up his radical French Canadian heritage, and reminding Massey that a year in England would "tend to make me more tolerant still."[97] Massey was unmoved, but a similar appeal from Bickersteth to Toronto financiers William Gundy and Percy Parker produced $1,500 for Martin. "I am happy beyond bounds of expression," he wrote Bickersteth on learning the good news.[98] On 5 October 1929, leaving his father dockside, Martin boarded the RMS *Doric* in Montreal and headed for Liverpool on a third-class ticket.

Cambridge suited him. "I feel perfectly at home," he wrote his St. Mike's classmate Frank Flaherty a month after his arrival. It was not Harvard, he sniffed, but at least initially he considered his tutors "top-notch," describing Pearce Higgins, his international law professor, as "the living Grotius."[99] Although he subsequently revised this assessment downward – Pearce Higgins, it turned out, "read his way dryly through texts he had presented dozens of times before" – Cambridge offered compensations that more than made up for the shortcomings of its faculty. The leisurely pace gave Martin time to enjoy all its offerings, and he delighted in its steady diet of debate and discussion. "Hardly a day passes without fulfilling an engagement for tea, breakfast, lunch or dinner in the rooms of some don or some student," he observed. "More talk goes on here in an hour than in Mrs. Kelly's backyard during an entire day."[100]

He passed his time reading in the Squires Library or attending lectures on campus. He joined several local discussion groups whose mandates embraced contemporary international affairs, including the Royal Empire Society and the Seeley Club, where he chaired its study group on British Empire and Commonwealth affairs.[101] He naturally joined the Fisher Society, Cambridge's Catholic chaplaincy, and the Union Club as well. There, he debated the merits of independence for India and of religious education, favouring both. His style drew applause for its "great vigour and lucidity," but he was an infrequent participant.[102]

His contacts with his British hosts were mostly fleeting, and his closest friends in Cambridge were Canadians. During the Christmas vacation, he and Frank Mallon, a fellow student from St. Mike's, travelled to Brussels and Paris, where life was "cheap and 'sweet,'" and students could dine on potatoes and bread for twelve cents a day.[103] At Easter break, he joined Torontonians Wynne Plumptre and Jack Beer, another "bosom-buddy" from St. Mike's, on a trip through Italy. "We all had the curiosity of students," he later reminisced, adding that "I can't emphasize how happy I was."[104]

One of his few British friends at Cambridge, the undergraduate law student Wilfred Jenks, had a profound influence on Martin. A brilliant scholarship boy, Jenks, who eventually headed the International Labour Organization in the 1960s, was an inspiring idealist whose faith in the possibilities of the League of the Nations touched Martin deeply. "No man in my life," Martin wrote, "so captivated me by his knowledge and zeal for a new international order based on law and justice."[105] Though he needed little persuading, Jenks convinced him to attend the Geneva School for International Affairs, a summer seminar on world politics run by the British historian and political scientist Sir Alfred Zimmern. Martin described Zimmern as a "cautious idealist" and as his "intellectual hero." With his French wife, he ran a quixotic eight-week course comprised of week-long multi-disciplinary sessions infused with his ardent faith in public opinion and international cooperation.[106] In the summer of 1930, the school offered seminars on world geography, sociology, the United States, education, economics, Asia, history, and law. The course ended with a visit to the opening session of the Assembly of the League of Nations.

Martin briefly returned to Pembroke during the fall of 1930, well rested and very pleased with his year abroad. "I have grown intellectually and corporally," he joked with his friends, who were already amused by his increasing girth.[107] "My year at Cambridge has been most successful and memorable," he wrote Prime Minister King, whose interest in the young Liberal politician had been carefully primed in his absence by Bickersteth. "There has come to me much experience and happiness," added the former French Canadian nationalist, now transformed into a devoted anglophile.[108] "I grew to like the English people and their country," he observed later. "I felt that perhaps there is no higher form of civilization than you find in the best Englishmen. They really are top people. They are strong and superior people."[109]

Cambridge and Geneva cemented Martin's attachment to international law and his commitment to the work of the League of Nations. His education abroad built on his experiences in Toronto and gave him the necessary tools to shape a sophisticated and idealistic philosophy of internationalism (and indeed, of government itself). It reflected the recent and varied influences on his thinking, embracing St. Thomas Aquinas and Zimmern in equal parts. He rejected Hegelian notions that the state was the highest form of association: "History proves the falsity of this idea. Political theory denies its worth. Ethics deplores its recognition." Citing Aristotle and

Aquinas, he based his case on natural law and argued that man was a social and political animal with inherent rights. "Since men have the same human nature," he asserted, "their natural equality gives them title in equal measure to the fruits of the earth." Man's social nature encouraged him to seek peace through cooperation in ever larger communities.

Reverting again to Aquinas, Martin reiterated his view that the proper function of government was to enhance this cooperation to maintain and promote the natural rights of its subjects. By providing justice – the right division of the fruits of the earth – government created the conditions for peace, order, and unity. By extension, world peace would be possible only when the international system and all its member states were subject to laws and legal norms that were capable of delivering justice. In the final analysis, Martin continued, half measures, such as Kant's federation of sovereign nations, would never work. Instead, states must ultimately surrender their sovereignty and join in world government.

He used Zimmern to demonstrate that this step would not diminish individual nations. Real internationalism would reinforce an "ordered nationalism" that preserved the "corporate inheritance" of each nation and formed a bulwark against the worst forms of twentieth-century materialism. "True unity does not involve the obliteration of all the diversities ... Internationalism will not affect the diversities seen in individuals and in nations, but through this diversity will come the realization of its thesis ... Mere uniformity is not unity; variety is wealth."[110] Bickersteth could not have said it better than the former nationalist he mentored.

2

THE YOUNG POLITICIAN, 1930-39

There were good reasons for Paul Martin to settle in Windsor on his return from Cambridge in the fall of 1930. The worst years of the Great Depression were yet to come, and the city he recalled from his visits in the late 1920s was still a dynamic metropolitan centre. Tucked into the northern end of sunny Essex County, the "Border Cities" included Windsor, with its vital port and rail facilities, and its three nearby communities: long-established Sandwich, affluent Walkerville, and gritty, polyglot East Windsor (or Ford City). They were amalgamated in 1935. Fuelled by Henry Ford's investments in automotive manufacturing, Windsor's population had soared from 15,000 to 100,000 in just twenty years.[1] Local horse-racing tracks on the major North American circuits and distilleries pumping booze into prohibitionist America spawned a culture of easy money and gangster glamour. Rumrunners Harry Low and James Cooper showcased their wealth in Walkerville mansions, and notorious Americans Al Capone and Bugs Moran came to visit.[2] Gambling, prostitution, and "blind pigs" flourished, giving the city a reputation as "a relaxed place of easy virtue."[3] What it lacked in size or sophistication was supplied by gleaming Detroit, which lay just across the river, spanned by the magnificent Ambassador Bridge, completed in 1929. Drawn by the endless parade of new technologies and riveting popular culture that defined twentieth-century America, Martin loved Detroit, a sprawling town of 1.6 million. It was a "fabulous city," he once remarked. "A big city. It has great institutions."[4] Windsor was just the ticket for an ambitious young man anxious to succeed.

Windsor also made political sense. It had strong local Liberal organizations, which had welcomed Martin when he visited the city at the start of his western tour in 1928. With its sizeable population of French Canadian Catholics, who settled the rural townships around Windsor in the 1740s, the region seemed tailor-made for an aspiring politician of Martin's bicultural background. It was a vital part of a familiar Catholic network, sustained by the Basilian fathers, who ran Martin's former college in Toronto as well as Windsor's Assumption College. For Martin, who always liked to have familiar friends nearby, the strong Basilian presence was comforting. In October 1930, he tucked a rail pass borrowed from a friendly reporter into his pocket and headed to Windsor, where he had lined up a job with the prominent law firm of McTague, Clark, Springsteen, Racine, & Spencer. He was twenty-seven years old.

Recalling his move to Windsor, Martin later confessed that he found the "adjustment to adulthood to be a little difficult."[5] His life in an Oak Street boarding house was a lonely affair, and within a few weeks, he gratefully accepted an offer of room and board in the familiar setting of the men's residence at Assumption College in exchange for teaching a course on political theory.[6] He settled in more quickly as junior counsel at Charles P. McTague's law firm. On the seventh floor of the old Security Building in downtown Windsor, he worked at a variety of tasks for thirty dollars a week. "Everything is going well with me," he assured a college friend after just a few months in Windsor. "I have become quite accustomed to my work and my environment. Truthfully, I am enjoying the practice of law very much."[7]

During the next two years, Martin remained pleased with the progress of his career, apart from his salary, which was a constant preoccupation. "I am working hard," he summed up his first year for an old classmate at the end of 1931. "While very poor, I am quite contented, plugging away with the great goal in mind."[8] McTague's modest demands left Martin with plenty of time to develop his political interests, and he took full advantage of his freedom to pursue "the great goal." Inspired by his recent visit to Alfred Zimmern's international school in Geneva, he began by devoting his spare energies to establishing a local branch of the League of Nations Society to promote the league and its brand of internationalism.

Over the winters of 1931 and 1932, Martin, who served as the branch's first president, marched a parade of high-profile speakers across the stage of downtown Windsor's imposing brown-brick Prince Edward Hotel. Professors, cabinet ministers, diplomats, and international civil servants preached the virtues of peace and international cooperation. Martin welcomed all comers, and his guests included Conservative justice minister Hugh Guthrie, Tory historian W.L. Grant, British high commissioner Sir William Clark, prominent Liberals Newton Rowell and Vincent Massey, and the feminist and socialist MP Agnes Macphail.[9] Martin underlined the importance of international affairs for Windsor citizens by also arranging a model league assembly, mounting a school-based campaign to "Teach Peace," and leading a local study group on world affairs.

The branch's activities reflected well on Martin. The *Windsor Daily Star,* which reported on most speakers, praised the young lawyer and his organization. The society, insisted a November 1931 editorial, "deserved great credit for the splendid list of speakers it has been able to present to local audiences."[10] Branch events introduced Martin to Windsor elites, established him as an expert on foreign policy and global affairs, and generated invitations to address a range of groups, including branches of the Women's International League for Peace and Freedom, the Ontario Labour Party, and the fledgling Canadian Institute of International Affairs, whose local wing Martin soon headed.

In the early 1930s, as the global economic depression and totalitarian governments in Germany, Italy, and Japan chipped steadily away at the fragile peace in Europe and Asia, Martin's reform-minded audiences provided him with welcome venues to defend his views on world politics. Like many young liberals of his generation, he was deeply influenced by British economist John Maynard Keynes's 1919 polemic, *The Economic Consequences of the Peace.* He campaigned against the economic reparations and war-guilt clauses of the Treaty of Versailles. He scoffed at those who responded to the turmoil that accompanied Nazi Germany's efforts to restore its global status by advocating either military rearmament or isolating Canada within North America. These were a guaranteed prelude to war.

Peace would be found only through the application of international law to sovereign states and the resolution of conflict through league-sponsored economic and military sanctions and collective security.[11]

Martin's growing prominence as a liberal peace activist did no harm to his standing as a lawyer or to his income. When McTague turned him down for a partnership in early 1932, he struck out on his own, eventually joining forces with Keith Laird in October 1934. The son of a prominent and affluent Windsor family, Laird remained his partner and close friend (as well as his main fundraiser and a major campaign organizer) for the rest of his life. Working independently, and then as half of Martin & Laird, Martin increased his legal profile and salary substantially between 1932 and 1935. As a young lawyer hustling cases, he could not afford to be picky in his choice of clients. Processing routine real estate deeds and wills, and defending Windsor's criminal class – local bootleggers and drunk drivers, small-time thieves, and corrupt municipal clerks and wrestling promoters – dominated his working life and established the character of his firm. In his first six months of independent practice, his income slowly increased to average forty dollars a month.

Next year, his financial progress improved. In 1933, Brantford alderman John Reycraft, a former classmate at Osgoode Hall Law School and a fellow Liberal, persuaded city council to hire Martin as its independent counsel during a probe into corruption charges involving its streetcar service. Retained at the rate of $50 a day, Martin stunned council when he submitted an $8,000 bill for only twenty-one days in court, insisting that the extra funds covered his preparation time. Reluctantly, Brantford paid up, pushing his income to $4,000 in 1933 and over $5,000 in 1934, and allowing him to clear most of his outstanding debts. However, with its barely suppressed accusations of sharp practice, newspaper coverage of the case, which was widespread in southwestern Ontario, cast an unfortunate shadow over Martin and hinted at his growing profile as a political lawyer and fixer.

This uncertain reputation was confirmed for many observers in early 1935, when Martin intervened briefly in the case of the Dionne quintuplets. The birth of the famous "Quints" in May 1934 ignited a firestorm of worldwide interest. When a shady American promoter convinced their impoverished and illiterate parents to put the girls on public display, Liberal premier Mitch Hepburn stepped in and placed them under provincial guardianship. Encouraged by their local Catholic bishop in Pembroke, Elzire and Olivia Dionne asked Martin for help in securing access to their children and to the potential proceeds from their commercial endorsements. Martin agreed, but the public reaction was swift and hostile. The Tory Opposition at Queen's Park feared for the Quints' safety in the clutches of "political lawyers from Windsor and Detroit."[12] Even Martin's Liberal friends greeted his news by pledging to defend the five infants against "racketeers, chiselers, and promoters," clearly slotting Martin into that group.[13] After arranging a meeting with Hepburn, he beat a hasty retreat and dropped the case.

Martin's ready access to the Ontario premier underlined his mounting stature in Liberal Party circles by the mid-1930s. Since returning from England, he had continued to nurture his ties with Liberal leader William Lyon Mackenzie King. His relationship with King, however, was complicated by sharp divisions within the party over policy. After their resounding defeat in the 1930 federal election, many Liberals, especially young activists like Martin, were keen to reform the party's organization and finances. They also wanted to update its social and economic policies to address the Depression and the rise of a dynamic new party on the left, the socialist Co-operative Commonwealth Federation (CCF). King and the Liberal establishment were doubtful. Though he welcomed organizational reform, King was sublimely confident that voters would return to the Liberal fold in due course, and he remained fiercely opposed to changing party policy.

The tense internal discussion over Liberal renewal unfolded fitfully after 1931. Vincent Massey, recruited by King as the first president of the National Liberal Federation (NLF) with generous promises of a voice in party policy, lobbied hard for change. To help him, Massey recruited a number of young Liberals, including Raleigh Parkin, his brother-in-law, Brooke Claxton, a Montreal lawyer, T.W.L. MacDermot, the McGill history professor, and Martin. Flattered by the attention, Martin accompanied Massey on a political tour through Western Canada in early 1932 as his part-time secretary. The patrician Liberal Party president repaid the favour the following year when he visited Windsor at Martin's invitation. He used the occasion to defend his "New Liberalism" and passionately offered an "advancing program of social legislation ... to see the abuses and evils of primitive capitalism checked and controlled."[14] King sputtered with indignation at the interlopers' cheek.

Martin was a regular visitor to Massey's Port Hope home to discuss politics throughout this period, and he was invited to sit on a committee that was planning an informal conference of liberal thinkers at Trinity College School in September 1933. With his soft bulk squeezed into a student desk several sizes too small, King squirmed uncomfortably as Massey forced him to listen to Canadian and British intellectuals, as well as prominent American "New Dealers" Raymond Moley and Averell Harriman, extol the benefits of a regulated, planned economy. Martin listened with delight. "It suited my book completely," he said.[15]

However, he played only a minor role in the reform campaign, and his commitment to the struggle was always a little ambivalent. Yet King noted his presence with malevolent suspicion and linked him with Massey, whom he increasingly treated as a "noxious rival."[16] "Massey & Paul Martin come [sic] on the scene a little too recently to direct affairs," he fumed in his diary.[17] When a Windsor journalist described King as a "forgotten man," he spied an assault on his leadership, complaining of "Paul Martin & Massey's efforts to have me out talking all the while, an endeavour to drive [me], like some modern slave master."[18] Martin may have sensed King's doubts. He congratulated him on by-election victories won with his current policies and praised his defence of his stand-pat Liberalism. King rebuffed these efforts with cold formalities.[19] Encountering Martin a few years later, he dismissed him as "self-important" and "lugubrious."[20]

King had another reason for his wariness of Martin: the lawyer's burgeoning ties with Ontario Liberal Party leader Mitch Hepburn. A successful and charismatic farmer from St. Thomas in southwestern Ontario, Hepburn was elected to Parliament in 1926 but left to seek the leadership of the Ontario Liberal Party in 1929. King opposed the move. He was appalled by Hepburn's womanizing and drinking, and jealous of the younger man's self-confidence and easy camaraderie with his supporters.[21] Ignoring a warning from King, Martin backed Hepburn at the December 1930 leadership contest, for sound policy and pragmatic political reasons. Hepburn represented change, not least with his promise to liberate the Ontario Liberal

Party from its crippling endorsement of prohibition. Just as importantly, Hepburn enjoyed overwhelming support from younger party members and Windsor Liberals, who were Martin's natural constituency.[22]

With Hepburn as leader, Martin was drawn back into provincial politics. At the November 1932 Ontario Liberal convention in Ottawa, he moved an important resolution that the "curtailment of socialistic and commun- istic thought by methods of direct coercion is ill-advised, and with a view of arriving at political and social truth, a free and unrestricted discussion of these and other questions is desirable."[23] Adopted unanimously, this liberal and pro-labour motion signalled a sharp swing to the left for the Ontario party. At a Hamilton Liberal "smoker" the following spring, Martin attracted province-wide attention when he described Conservative premier George Henry as "honest but stupid" and hinted that the Liberals had evidence that cabinet ministers held bonds in Abitibi Power, a company slated for provincial takeover.[24] Outraged Tories demanded proof, but a blushing Martin had none to offer. Liberals, however, were elated, and called him the "best of the Liberal propagandists in the province."[25]

When Premier Henry called a provincial election for June 1934, Martin stepped up his involvement. He suspended his law practice and cam- paigned for Hepburn in Lucan, Stratford, London, and Sault Ste. Marie.[26] He played a small but lower-key role in helping to organize the Italian vote in Windsor, Hamilton, Welland, and Niagara Falls.[27] In Windsor, he was a poll captain for James Clark and he supported Mayor David Croll, both of whom were elected as Hepburn swept the province. Ontario was the sixth province to vote Liberal since the Depression began, and the lesson was clear. On election night, Bill Tubman, a local Liberal worker, turned to Martin and remarked, "Your turn is next. These are Liberal times. You must not lose the chance."[28]

During the summer of 1934, Martin left Assumption College, moved into an apartment in the federal riding of Essex East, and gradually began to campaign for the area's nomination. One of three ridings that together represented the Windsor region in Ottawa, Essex East was divided be- tween an English-speaking and multi-ethnic urban and working-class core, which was badly dislocated by the Depression, and a surrounding French Canadian farming community. By the spring of 1935, there were no fewer than six candidates for the nomination: Martin, Dorothea

Robinson, Leo Sylvestre, Ulysse Reaume, Gabriel McPharlin, and Dr. Percy Gardner, the early favourite. To the delight of watching reporters, it was obvious that the "competition will be keen to the point of bitterness."[29] They were not disappointed.

The main differences between the candidates were not over policy, though they were real enough and certainly mattered. Robinson was the most reform-minded candidate, gleefully excoriating big banks and big business, while promoting free trade, unemployment insurance, and women's rights. Gardner, the establishment candidate, took a more conservative stance and was careful to defend the rights of industry. Martin positioned himself closer to the centre, occupying the ground to the right of Robinson. He was quick to distance himself from Hepburn and Croll, demanding more provincial money for local schools and attacking the provincial government for its unpopular plan to amalgamate the several communities of Windsor into one city. He was an active supporter of tariff reform, and he promised to allow voters to recall him if they wished. He was also among the most sensitive to labour's needs and explicitly outlined a platform of federal social programs that were of direct interest to workers, including minimum wage laws, unemployment insurance, old age pensions, and a mother's allowance. "The industries are making money," he thundered, "they have to share it. If they are not willing to share it, they will be forced to."[30]

The contest turned on personality and organization. Martin won on both counts. In 1934, Liberal candidate Gardner had mysteriously withdrawn from the provincial campaign, a move that fed rumours, almost certainly spread by Martin himself, that he had done so in exchange for $1,600 and the guarantee of the federal nomination. The mud stuck. Gardner retaliated, charging that these were the tactics of "the ordinary gangster and hijacker" and denouncing Martin as "a party henchman."[31] In reply, Martin stood primly aside, noting that Windsor voters were "not interested in cavilling and mud-slinging."[32] Mrs. Dunlevey, whose home on Riverside Drive hosted a campaign tea, threw both candidates out of her house in disgust.[33]

Martin was better organized than Gardner. Richard Benoit, a key ally, was president of the Essex East riding association, whose executive was dominated by close Martin supporters George Scott, Alfred Morrell, and

Alice Renaud. In late March, Renaud was asked to organize an association meeting at Belle River, a semi-rural corner of the constituency that was far removed from Gardner's urban strongholds. The large Martin majority in attendance voted to hold an "open" nominating convention on 8 June and to locate it in Belle River. Both decisions favoured Martin.

The nomination convention was a riotous affair. Martin supporters chartered a CPR train, the *Martin Booster*, to ferry five hundred supporters from Walkerville to Belle River for the Saturday afternoon meeting. The heat, the alcohol, and the queues to vote shortened tempers. When a Martin supporter was found with thirteen ballots in his pocket, the convention erupted and "an exchange of hot words ensued."[34] Gardner's supporters tried to recess the convention but were ruled out of order by Benoit, with Martin exclaiming, "For God's sake, be a Liberal."[35] After three ballots and four hours of voting, Martin was declared the victor, with 739 votes to Gardner's 517. McPharlin, who declined to drop out, tallied 177. He and Gardner refused to make the selection unanimous or to congratulate Martin, which bothered the young candidate. Had he known that Prime Minister King declined to send congratulations, he would have been even more upset. The Liberal leader thought the nomination "dubious," sent party secretary Norman Lambert to investigate, and set aside his unsigned draft letter of congratulations.[36]

The federal campaign of 1935 lacked the bitter drama of the Liberal nomination battle. Prime Minister R.B. Bennett's ruling Conservative Party was in full disarray, weighed down by the burdens of the Depression and divided by a secessionist movement led by former cabinet minister H.H. Stevens. Martin was more fearful of the unknown potential of the CCF, whose socialist program seemed likely to reverberate throughout Windsor's working-class neighbourhoods. He shaped his campaign to counter that threat. Shrewdly, he refused to debate with Ben Levert, the sharp-tongued CCF nominee. Always remaining just beyond Levert's reach, Martin accused him of "throwing mud," and he attacked the CCF for its "tie-up" with the local Communist Party. "If I can do anything in this election," he promised the anti-communist Catholic voters of Windsor, "it will be to deal this community the most crushing blow the Communists have ever received."[37]

His campaign was youthful, defiant, and reformist. His speeches and flyers emphasized his age, his own aggressive struggle to get ahead, and his independence. Even as King and Massey travelled to Windsor in support of Essex candidates, Martin insisted that he would refuse the "party whip" and often ended his stump speech with a casual but determined "you can like it or lump it."[38] In the rural districts, he savaged the government's British Empire trade agreements that exposed local corn-growers to brutal South African competition. Instead, he offered a program of liberal free trade that would benefit farmers and auto workers alike by tapping into the vast American market.

There was more. Martin promised to work to repeal section 98 of the Criminal Code, which governments and employers regularly used to deport unwelcome labour and union activists. He would also press for a commission to investigate the recent decline in job opportunities for Windsor residents in nearby Detroit. A Liberal government would certainly end the secret machinations of war-mongering millionaire arms manufacturers, a popular conspiracy theory in progressive circles since the First World War. He promised a commission to investigate unemployment insurance and assured his audiences that Ottawa would not hesitate to "conscript wealth" from industry to generate the necessary funds for public works and relief. "Industry must realise that it has some responsibility for the welfare of its workers," he stated. "That is not socialism. It is just social justice."[39]

The sitting Conservative MP, Dr. Raymond Morand, was popular and well respected, and he fought back with the weapons at hand. He mocked Martin for his youth and constantly referred to him simply as "Paul." He reminded voters of Martin's close ties to Croll and Hepburn, his recent arrival in Windsor, and his overweening ambition. "Where was he when Liberalism was being built up here? What right has he to represent this constituency?" Morand asked. "He lands here and suddenly and ruthlessly pushes aside others and by manipulation ... he is given the nomination."[40] These thrusts hurt, but Morand's policies were those of an unpopular government and a reviled prime minister. He stoutly defended his party's protectionist principles and its ineffectual response to the ravages of the Depression. He attacked the Liberal platform for its vague and unfulfilled promises that dated back to 1919, and he tried to make sense of his own leader's sudden conversion to New Deal–like economic and social policies.

It was almost enough. By the time the polls closed at 7:00 p.m. on 15 October 1935, the contest was too close to call. Martin visibly shrank as the early returns from affluent Walkerville gave Morand an imposing lead, but the balance shifted as the evening wore on and East Windsor and the rural sections of Belle River, Maidstone, and Tecumseh reported. With 51 of 108 polls tallied, Martin pulled ahead by 192 votes. His lead eventually stretched to 1,163. Amid "screaming youths and cheering crowds," he and his supporters piled into a convoy of cars for a tour of his riding, heading downtown to the offices of the *Windsor Daily Star* to accept Morand's congratulations.[41]

By the end of October, Paul Martin was packed and headed for Ottawa, and a backbench seat in the ranks of Prime Minister King's new Liberal government. En route, he stopped in Port Hope to celebrate Thanksgiving with Vincent Massey, who hosted "a little party" in his honour.[42] Appropriately, the two men were joined by a third, Martin's University of Toronto mentor Burgon Bickersteth, who caught the train down from Toronto for the occasion. They spent an uneventful weekend, basking in a sense of quiet satisfaction and anticipation. Martin's "life so far has been a wonderful achievement," Bickersteth wrote his parents that month. "I am convinced he will make his mark on the House."[43] Two weeks later, Martin was sworn in as a member of Parliament and headed back to Windsor.

Aware that his margin of victory was not large, he worked hard from the start of his parliamentary career to consolidate his local standing. For the next few decades, when the House of Commons was in session, he commuted from Ottawa to spend his weekends in Windsor, boarding the "damn pool train" to Toronto on Thursday or Friday afternoon and then taking the overnight to Windsor, arriving at seven o'clock in the morning. "Weekend after weekend, how the hell one ever survived that I don't know," he later wondered.[44]

On Saturday mornings, he held court in his Martin & Laird law offices, sorting out his constituents' difficulties. "They come to me with their problems, their marital problems, their medical problems, their worries and concerns," he complained, recalling the endless requests for help with everything from jobs to passports, visas, and housing.[45] The work was tiresome, and he loathed it, a sentiment he expressed freely to his skeptical campaign workers.[46] Nonetheless, he took it in stride. "I would like to see you and say hello and discuss your problem," he assured a desperate job-seeker in 1937. "A member finds it very difficult to satisfy all the demands ... I always try to do my best, however, and never refuse to discuss a man's problem with him. That is my duty and I shall be very pleased to do so with you."[47]

Martin kept in close touch with his riding. He cultivated relations with Windsor's ethnic leaders, especially among the local clergy, with whom he developed a close and easy rapport. On Sundays, he sometimes attended two or three Masses, reportedly sitting in the back pews so that parishioners would see him as they went to and from Communion.[48] He quickly developed the habit (which persisted long past his retirement) of marking milestones in the lives of his Windsor constituents, and later, in the lives of his growing roster of political contacts across the country. Births, graduations, weddings, and funerals generated a short note from Martin. Once, he even sent his congratulations to a street of Windsor residents when the City paved their road, by implication claiming a role in this municipal largess.[49] Hardbitten journalists and political opponents claimed to see through the notes and letters to the ambition behind them, and tended to dismiss them as "a bit of a joke."[50]

That was unfair. Martin himself would have been hard pressed to say where calculated artifice began and ended. He was effective at the constituency level because he genuinely liked people and wanted to help them. If they could vote for him, so much the better. Gordon Robertson, who worked with him during the mid-1940s before rising to become cabinet secretary, summed up a common view: "He was a very decent person. There was nothing cruel or harsh in Paul."[51] People, young and old, sparked his curiosity, and he took the time to ask them questions and listen to their answers. As a long-time campaign worker put it, Martin "asked people their opinion because he wanted to know, and he wanted to make them feel that they were part of a larger whole."[52] His attention to retail politics would ultimately cut two ways: supporters delighted in his growing reputation as an "outstanding constituency man," whereas detractors saw his fondness for Windsor and its people as damning evidence of his limitations as a typical "parish-pump politician."

This aspect of Martin's reputation was burnished by his canny use of local patronage to reinforce his ties with key Windsor Liberals. The records regarding this quiet subject are understandably spotty, and Martin himself downplayed his use of patronage in his memoirs, insisting that its value was already fading by the 1930s, replaced by more non-partisan mechanisms for allocating government jobs and contracts. Nonetheless, patronage remained a useful means of rewarding party workers and cementing alliances.

Martin was painfully conscious that patronage created both winners and losers, and he was inclined to spread the risk by involving the riding executive in the distribution of favours.[53] But not always. He determined which local companies were placed on the "patronage lists" of federal government departments and Crown corporations, and which were invited to bid on contracts for goods ranging from renovations to the Windsor Federal Building to supplying lightning rods to the Department of Agriculture. Introducing Windsor businessman Charlie Gordon to Minister of Transport C.D. Howe, Martin forthrightly described him as "a good friend of mine and a good friend of ours ... [He is] an important person politically in these parts and [a contract] will help me materially."[54]

Contracts also gave Martin access to local jobs, and he was careful to insist on his prerogatives. "No one should be employed for this work except Windsor people," he warned a contractor, "and as one of the Federal Members, I must insist on this."[55] He was involved in federal projects to dredge the many local waterways and to repair the public docks near his riding. He worked closely with H.F. Bennett, the Department of Public Works district engineer in London, to decide who won the jobs and to see that his supporters were hired as inspectors and foremen. And he supervised the list of men whom they hired to work on the projects, often fearful that he might lose as many friends as he won. "I want Adrien Tellier to get as much of the trucking as possible," he wrote Bennett on one occasion, "and whether or not Frank Labute gets any more I suggest that that be a matter for your discretion. I don't want to displease him, but on the other hand I do not want to displease Adrien Tellier."[56]

The tricky business of nominating postmasters, postmistresses, and rural deliverymen was just as worrisome. Martin received his first letter on the subject before the polls closed on election day, from a Liberal who had been removed as Belle River postmaster following the Conservative victory in 1917 and who now wanted the job back.[57] But removing the efficient Tory incumbent proved difficult. Unfamiliar with the complicated rules governing dismissals and the bidding process, Martin failed. He made no mistake the following year when a postal delivery job opened up in Maidstone, and Alice Shanahan, the local Liberal matriarch and a key Martin supporter, expressed her interest in tendering for it. Working with the post office's chief superintendent in London, Martin became skilled at making "arrangements" and launching "special inquiries" by the district inspector to disqualify unwanted candidates, however low their bids.[58] Shanahan got the job.

While Martin shored up his support in Windsor with jobs and contracts, he also demonstrated his determination to address the policy issues that he had raised during the campaign. Here, too, he focused on local issues. He helped to create a fuss when rumours surfaced in November 1935 that the Liberal government's new liberalized trade agreement with the United States would roll back the high tariffs that Bennett had imposed on automotive imports. After contacting ministers in Ottawa, Martin and neighbouring MP Norman McLarty assured Windsor auto workers that the King government would retain the tariff. They even convinced cabinet to move up the January Tariff Board hearings by several weeks to examine additional barriers to other American industrial imports.[59] The *Windsor Daily Star* was delighted and applauded the local members for "having done their part."[60]

The most troublesome item on the new MP's personal agenda was corn. Within weeks of the vote, he confronted fifty angry Essex and Kent corngrowers in a meeting to discuss the challenges created by stiff South African competition and low prices. He raised the matter with the minister of trade and commerce, the dour William Euler, persuading the government to send J.H. Grisdale, a former deputy minister of agriculture, to assess the region's corn problem. Grisdale discovered that the corn's high moisture content made it unsuitable for high-value industrial purposes and depressed its price. This finding offered little short-term help for either Martin or his farming constituents, though it did suggest a strategy for improving drying and storage facilities, which Martin and his rural allies could press on the government in the months and years ahead.[61]

Once settled in office, and with his home front secure, Martin was keen to demonstrate his broader national perspective. The Italian invasion of Ethiopia in October 1935 and the firm initial response from the League of Nations, where Canadian delegate Walter Riddell briefly headed a movement for economic sanctions, had raised the hopes of league supporters everywhere. These were dashed a month later, when Ernest Lapointe, King's minister of justice, repudiated Riddell's actions, sparking a national debate over Canada's policy at Geneva.

A strong league supporter, Martin was dismayed by Lapointe's position and disheartened by the support he enjoyed in the Liberal caucus, which he attributed to the average member's woeful ignorance of international affairs. This, he explained to an angry Brooke Claxton, a rising Liberal lawyer in Montreal, had tied King's hands. The prime minister, added Martin naively, "undoubtedly does support the League and the principle of collective action, but does not wish to take the initiative in matters that might lead to political as well as other difficulties."[62] From Martin's perspective, there was clearly scope for a modest initiative from the backbench, one that might bridge the gap between King's furtive support for the League of Nations and the government's inaction.

He decided to tackle the issue in his maiden address to the House in mid-June 1936. His speech was humble in tone and modest in length, appropriate for a young new member. It opened by suggesting small reforms to the mechanics of Canadian policy making: better briefings for delegates abroad, more discussion of international affairs in the House, and an improved division of labour in the Department of External Affairs. These were all the rock-solid certainties of Canadian liberalism during the mid-1930s.

Martin, who had waited to speak until King himself had outlined his own views, offered a pragmatic and hard-headed defence of recent government policy. Like King, he stressed the "realities of the moment" and Canada's very limited stake in European affairs. Canadians obviously wanted peace and collective security, he argued, but these could not be secured through league sanctions that might lead to war. He explained that it would be "the extremity of folly for a country like Canada, having but nine millions of people separated from Europe by thousands of miles, having no direct regional or local interest ... to urge the continuance of sanctions."

He ended with a litany of ideas, commonplace in liberal and progressive circles, for enhancing the league. Canada could help it develop new machinery to resolve the economic tensions that might lead to war. The country could help revise international treaties that strained the peace, removing the war guilt and Anschluss clauses from the Treaty of Versailles. The government could negotiate new global accords to limit immediately national armaments. The League of Nations could strengthen its power "to implement – not to enforce" these new treaties, recognizing that regional realities would determine the obligations of each nation. As Martin explained, "A country in the North American sphere or region cannot hope, if Europe in her region is not prepared to do her share, to keep the European house in order. It simply is not practicable." His carefully worded speech ended on a provocative note. It was time for Canada to offset its historical connection to the British motherland by embracing its own North American destiny and joining the Pan-American Union that united the other states of the hemisphere. Placing Canada firmly first, he argued that "internationalism through nationalism should be our ideal."[63]

His address was well received. The *Windsor Daily Star* welcomed its isolationist twist, which echoed its own views, and warmly congratulated Martin on his "brilliant maiden speech."[64] Prime Minister King was pleased with his support for his policy, describing the speech as "splendid." It made "a fair impression and an equally fair contribution to the most perplexing and important of all problems in the field of government activity."[65] CCF member Agnes Macphail was more perceptive, and she archly underlined Martin's clever ambiguity. "Good stuff Paul," she wrote him, "tho' I am not sure any one is clear or can be clear while he holds onto the League with one hand and onto the continent of North America with the other."[66] Martin was invited to reprise his address at the Canadian Institute of International Affairs annual conference on public policy at Lake Couchiching later that summer, signalling his arrival on the national stage.

IN THE FALL of 1936, Martin fell in love with Eleanor (Nell) Adams, whose family had deep roots in southwestern Ontario. Her father, Edgar, was born in Langton, on the shores of Lake Erie, and shared the region's early Methodist heritage, converting to Catholicism upon marrying her mother, Amelia. A Conservative who argued politics with Edgar "ad nauseam," Amelia was "the powerhouse of the family," and his success rested heavily on her efforts. They ran the general store in McGregor and moved to Windsor in 1916, where they opened a drugstore. Eventually, there were two stores and a farm back in McGregor, and by 1922, a treasured cottage in Colchester, on Lake Erie.[67]

The couple had two daughters, Roxalena Mamie and Nell, who was born in 1913. Nell was frantic, fun loving, and attractive. Educated at Windsor's St. Mary's Academy and Walkerville Collegiate Institute, she obtained an associate diploma from the Royal Conservatory of Music in Toronto and completed the one-year pharmacy diploma program at the University of Toronto. She and her sister, Roxie, her best friend, helped manage the family drugstores during the late 1930s. Nell and Paul were married on 8 September 1937 at Immaculate Conception Church, by his St. Mike's mentor, Father E.J. McCorkell.

Like many of the central events in Martin's life, the courtship became a finely honed story that he and Nell often presented to illustrate their public persona. Bowled over by Nell when he visited her store in search of a cigar, the cocky young MP later called for a date but was surprised to discover that she was unaware of (and unimpressed by) his political role and growing stature. Humbled, he eventually won her over, but he proved a dilatory suitor, forcing her to close the deal. "Look, Paul," Nell said, "we're either going to get married or we're not!"[68]

The story pulled aside Martin's too serious public demeanour, giving a glimpse of the personal humility and self-deprecating humour of the genuine man. Having Nell propose also seemed to signal a particularly modern marriage of equals, subverting traditional gender roles and reinforcing Martin's claim to represent young Canadians and the country's future. However, the story's use in political profiles of Martin, whose core masculinity is signified by the cigar that initiated the courtship, suggests a different, and more accurate, reading, with Paul looking after the nation's business, while Nell tended the home fires. From the 1930s to the 1950s, this safely gendered division of labour perhaps reassured Canadian voters, who were anxious to reinforce traditional family values in the face of the disruptions of the Depression and the Second World War.

An old-fashioned, almost Victorian marriage, it was by all accounts a happy and wonderful one. Nell's family in Windsor made room for Paul, warmly embracing him as a man on the rise, but her reception in Pembroke was perhaps cooler; Paul's mother, Lumina, never liked Nell much, resenting her Protestant heritage and relative affluence. The young couple proved companionable and well matched, becoming increasingly close during their first years together and trying out pet-names for each other: Darling, Snug, Pot, Dearest Pal, before eventually settling on Mother and Papa. Paul promised to learn to dance and teased Nell about her ignorance of politics. She teased him right back, reminding her "fat husband" of the extra fifty or so pounds that he now carried.

Married life revolved around Paul. Though profoundly devoted to Nell, he could be a clinging and difficult husband, who sometimes astounded outside observers with his petulant demands. When they were apart – Nell would always prefer Windsor and her family's cottage in nearby Colchester to Ottawa – he missed her terribly and relentlessly pressed her to join him. "I get so lonesome for you I could almost cry," he wrote in 1938. "We must not be separated again."[69]

He relied on Nell to manage all the minor domestic problems in his life and to provide him with a restful refuge. "I miss you awfully," he confessed. "My hair needs a trim. I need a shave. I require someone to look after me. I wish you were here to baby me, to sssshhhhh me ... Yes, I have it bad and I am not ashamed to say so."[70] When thwarted, he was quick to flare up and equally quick to seek forgiveness: "My little outburst of impatience was as unnatural as unnecessary ... Please forgive your impatient child." At home, he gladly surrendered his responsibilities to Nell. "Is it not wonderful how we have grown together?" he asked in June 1938. "You are part of me. I let you boss me. In fact, I love it."[71]

Nell provided the domestic sanctuary that Martin sought, but the bleak advice she later offered to the wives of young MPs hinted at the price she paid:

You will feel sorry for yourself. You will feel depressed. Save yourself some of this – just become resigned to it. It's his life, accept it. You're going to raise the children, run the house. Keep your complaints to yourself, because when he comes in, he's so exhausted and so pre-occupied, he's not going to listen to you anyway. So, you may as well have your house a haven, a refuge for him, and he'll always come home.[72]

The bargain was not one-sided. Nell escaped much of the drudgery that was expected of political spouses. She had a strong network of friends in Windsor and "stayed as far away from politics as she legitimately could."[73] When she did become involved with Martin's professional life, it was on her own terms. She appeared on stage beside him only rarely, with her hands clasped demurely in her lap, and made fewer appearances as the years passed. In more intimate settings, her natural good humour and grace helped smooth Martin's relations with voters, journalists, bureaucrats, and other politicians. Nell even charmed the irascible prime minister King when they first met in the late 1930s:

"My husband thinks you're a very great man," she told the prime minister.

"And what do you think, Mrs. Martin?" King asked.

"I'm going to take some convincing," she replied with a twinkle.

King was delighted and invited her for a stroll through Ottawa's Sandy Hill district the next afternoon.[74] More than once, CCF leader M.J. Coldwell mused ruefully, he had refrained from attacking Martin due to his regard for Nell, who had graciously nursed Coldwell's sick wife when he was away.[75]

Nor were reporters immune to Nell's earthy charms. When *Canadian Business Magazine* gave Martin one of his first national profiles in 1943, she was presented as an integral part of the package. "She is an attractive Irish girl," it wrote, "bubbling over with life, gifted with a delightful sense of humour, and is just the antidote the serious Paul needs. She kids him when he needs it most."[76] In the 1940s and 1950s, accompanying Martin to New York for UN meetings, she impressed a generation of Canadian dip-lomats by joining them on the dance floor long after he had retired to bed.[77] "None of us had much money," she recalled. "There wasn't much drinking. It was just sheer gaiety."[78] As his deputy minister once explained to Martin, "You have a natural interest in things political, social, and economic ...

Nell supplies a welcome relief from that on all occasions."[79] The marriage flourished.

There were other, less happy, changes in Martin's life during the late 1930s. In 1935, as he turned his attention exclusively to politics, his legal income diminished precipitously, dropping by more than 50 percent to just over $2,000 annually. Once again, as he explained to an insistent income tax collector to whom he owed money, he was left "rather hard-pressed for funds."[80] At the same time, his burdens were substantially increased as he assumed financial responsibility for his wife, his parents, and his two youngest sisters. Though his yearly income rebounded after 1936 with the addition of his $4,000 parliamentary indemnity, he practised law only sporadically for the rest of the decade, and his total income remained below $5,500, dipping to less than $4,500 in 1938. Of his combined legal and parliamentary incomes, he used more than $1,000 annually between 1937 and 1939 to cover the tuition and board required to send his sisters Anita and Claire to St. Mike's and to nursing school.

Martin accepted this burden as his family duty but was not always gracious about it, and he grumbled about the expense. His mother was unsympathetic. She reminded the family of the sacrifices that had been made for Paul, for whom she had a simple message: "Let him live according to his means."[81] Yet Paul remained ambivalent about his responsibilities and his growing role as head of the extended Martin family. "Oftentimes I take secret looks at Mother," he scribbled hastily during a visit home in mid-1938. "The passing years have been so kaleidoscopic that this fact is realised almost accidentally. The hair is grey, but the same maternal qualities are ever present. The Dad too, who works hard, he is growing old ... It makes me melancholy. It's the sort of feeling I get almost every time I leave Pembroke for Ottawa or Windsor."[82]

DURING THE LATE 1930s, Martin developed into a shrewd and effective parliamentarian. He was already a skilled debater, and the House of Commons provided the kind of familiar masculine environment in which he had operated comfortably since his years at the junior seminary of St-Alexandre. He was sometimes a bit pompous or too serious or long-winded, but his fellow MPs liked him and forgave him his shortcomings.

He flirted easily with the very few women members and kidded around with the older, more experienced MPs, who teased him about his well-known prime ministerial ambitions. Employing the timeless and legitimate tactics of backbench politicians who sought notice and advancement, he was judiciously partisan in defending government policy and shamelessly ready to flatter cabinet ministers.

Martin continued to divide his attention between local matters and a few carefully chosen national themes. He intervened in Commons debates to pin down the minister of transport on help for Windsor's local airport and pressed Windsor's case with the minister of finance for more aid under the Housing and Municipal Assistance Acts.[83] He was sensitive to populist currents in his constituency, chiding the government for its high radio licence fees and demanding greater oversight of the small-loan companies that charged his voters usurious rates of interest. He was also an effective voice for local industry, using committee proceedings to amend the revised Food and Drug Act to address a local manufacturer's worries and to defend high excise taxes for the automotive industry.[84] In a rare initiative that was even more important for Essex East, he sponsored a House of Commons resolution to make the government improve its drying, storage, and marketing facilities for southwestern Ontario corn.[85]

His speechifying was noticed but not tiresome. He enjoyed debating broad legal and philosophical issues at the national level, which gave him scope to show off his legal training and voice his progressive views. On nationalist grounds, he supported the effort to abolish judicial appeals to the British House of Lords, and his sound liberal values prompted him to oppose outlawing the distribution of communist literature by mail.[86] In principle, he endorsed the right of workers to freedom of association, but he hewed to the government line in rejecting CCF proposals to amend the Criminal Code to permit such associations. They were likely to interfere with provincial rights (and certain to disturb Liberal fortunes in anti-labour Quebec).[87]

Martin was most forceful and persistent when personal interest combined with a larger national cause. He continued to lead the campaign for a federal university scholarship program for poor students, drawing from his own experiences to make his case. This garnered him national coverage in 1937 and convinced him of the value of engaged public opinion in forcing government action, an insight that carried profound implications for his later approach to governing and policy making. He was outspoken, too, in support of a national unemployment insurance plan, beginning in 1938 when job losses suddenly spiked in the slumping Windsor auto industry. He belittled existing relief and public works programs as inappropriate in a modern, largely urban, national economy, and he decried Ottawa's misplaced emphasis on rural rehabilitation. He pressed the government to introduce a contributory plan, even unilaterally if that were needed to overcome the opposition of provinces that remained wedded to the outdated constitutional division of responsibilities in the BNA Act of 1867. Although he was not in the vanguard of this fight, his voice was raised and heard, and it confirmed his standing as a member of the Liberal Party's progressive wing.

It was harder to find the right balance between self-expression and party loyalty in the realm of foreign affairs, which remained Martin's principal interest as global tensions steadily escalated after 1936. Foreign policy was the well-guarded preserve of Prime Minister King, who was also secretary of state for external affairs. Though he liked King and admired his acute political sensibilities, Martin remained frustrated by his inability to make a positive impression. "If ever there was a man that was remote, it was Mackenzie King," he later observed. "You know, if Mackenzie King said hello to you, God, you got home and you put that in the book."[88] In the fall of 1936, both men headed to Geneva. Martin travelled as the Liberal Party representative to the World Youth Congress, a league-sponsored gathering of young people from thirty-six nations. King was there as head of the Canadian delegation to the annual meeting of the League of Nations Assembly, where he intended to reiterate Canada's firm opposition to league sanctions and collective security, a step designed to keep the country from being dragged into a European war.[89]

Over tea in his hotel room, King invited Martin, diplomat Georges Vanier, and other members of the delegation to listen to his draft speech. Convinced during the spring that King supported collective security, at least in principle, Martin was surprised at how far his leader had apparently retreated. He urged him to go "a little further along conventional League lines and along sanction [sic]."[90] King refused. As Martin left the room, he later told historians with relish, he overheard King remarking, *sotto voce,* "And I thought that young man had a future."[91]

The story is probably apocryphal and Martin's bravado overstated. King's account presents him as a slow-witted and wayward pupil who changes his stance after being properly tutored: "When read in part more slowly to him, he approved of it [the speech] in its entirety."[92] After hearing King deliver the address the next day, Martin (and Vanier) were fulsome in their praise, assuring him that "it sounded much better than it did last night. They were in every way better satisfied [and] ... quite pleased."[93] When Martin left Geneva at the end of the week, he tried to make his peace with King, thanking him for "so much kindness" and assuring him that "seeing my leader under Geneva shadows has meant much to me."[94] King's reply was polite, even warm, but it ended on a sharp note. "Opinions will, of course, vary and change," he reminded his backbench colleague. "It will be seen that having regard to Canada's present and future positions in intraimperial and international affairs, what I said was right and that it was said at the right time and in the right place."[95]

The differences with King over sanctions were worrying, but the trip to Europe, his first in five years, provided Martin with more substantive reasons for reassessing his views on Canada's place in the world. An excursion to Rome exposed him to Mussolini's militaristic Italy, fresh from its Ethiopian triumph, and the "frightening spectacle of a never-ending parade of young fascists."[96] He also encountered the complicated ideological crosscurrents of the Spanish Civil War, where General Francisco Franco's fascist and pro-Catholic insurgents were trying to overthrow the Republican government. Like many Catholics, Martin saw the Republicans and their communist supporters as threats to church authority, and he backed Franco. At the least, this compromised his relations with other progressive Canadians who were interested in their country's foreign policy. They favoured the Republican, anti-fascist cause. Spain drove home the point that it was a complicated world, one perhaps best avoided.

After his return to Canada, Martin's declarations on foreign policy and the looming crisis in Europe exhibited a good deal less starch. "Mr. King's speech in terms of the current European scene seems unanswerable," he scolded the Liberal editor J.W. Dafoe, who mauled the government's anti-league policy in his *Winnipeg Free Press* editorials of October 1936. Without much conviction, Martin added that perhaps King might have addressed the "positive side" of the league and "what we were prepared to do to bolster machinery not now functioning."[97] Martin declined to make a full statement on foreign policy during the 1937 session, intervening only briefly to congratulate the prime minister on the strength of the delegation sent to Geneva the previous fall.[98] When Dafoe attacked King's league policy at a Queen's University Conference on Canada-US affairs in June 1937, Martin was sharply critical in his remarks and pointedly drew them to King's attention.[99]

He finally addressed the House of Commons at length on foreign policy during the spring of 1938, but his effort was lacklustre. His speech drew heavily, and without attribution, on an influential article by Escott Reid (for which he was roundly teased), whose major elements had been endorsed a year earlier by King himself. Martin laid out the principles that guided Liberal policy: national unity; the overwhelming importance of relations with the United States and Britain, not the league; a backseat role for Canada in European and Asian issues; no advance commitment to league sanctions or the defence of the British Empire; and a willingness to help improve international trade.[100] King was enchanted, and he praised the speech in his diary as "very good from the Liberal point of view."[101]

The speech may have helped offset any irritation that King felt later that spring, when Martin inadvertently became caught up in the prime minister's ongoing feud with Ontario premier Mitch Hepburn. Since the election in 1935, Martin, like most Ontario MPs, had carefully avoided taking sides in the quarrel. His offhand comment to the press in April 1938, downplaying the dispute as evidence of Liberal Party vitality, provoked King's wrath.[102] It was, the prime minister noted acidly, "a childish & fool remark, missing the whole essence of the situation."[103] But Martin understood the situation as well as King, and when he met the prime minister a few days later, he made it clear where his loyalties lay. He fingered provincial ministers Colin Campbell, Patrick Dewan, and Gordon Conant as most opposed to King, and he ventured the view that Hepburn feared the "trained minds" of federal cabinet ministers Norman Rogers and James

Ilsley. Aligning himself with King's allies, he added that Hepburn "had the same feeling towards him."[104]

Appeased, King's anger faded, though another small test of Martin's loyalty was soon coming. In mid-July, he informed King of his plans to join a Canadian Institute of International Affairs (CIIA) delegation that would attend an August conference in Australia.[105] In response, King promptly asked him to join Canada's delegation to the next League of Nations Assembly in Geneva, which was scheduled for the same time. The offer put Martin in a very difficult position. King callously made things worse by assuring CIIA president E.J. Tarr that Martin was free to make his own decision, while simultaneously advising Martin himself to go to Europe.[106] Martin wisely capitulated and joined the Canadian delegation headed by Justice Minister Ernest Lapointe.

The trip was awkwardly timed. Having endured a difficult first pregnancy, Nell was approaching her August due date. On 28 August, it was decided to induce delivery, giving Martin just enough time to greet his son, Paul Jr., before catching the train to Montreal and boarding the *Empress of Australia* for the voyage to Europe.

In Geneva, he had nothing to do. During the spring of 1938, Hitler had marched into Austria, absorbing the German-speaking state into his new Reich. On 12 September, he demanded "self-determination" for the German-speaking parts of tiny, democratic Czechoslovakia. For two weeks, the world held its breath and prayed for peace. Martin was swept up in the historical drama. "The feeling is very tense here," he wrote Nell. "Families are moving out. Wives and children are going to safe places … There is not the slightest reason for being concerned about me. As a matter of fact, it is proving to be a great and paradoxically enough thrilling experience … I miss you terribly and love you awfully."[107] When British prime minister Neville Chamberlain, shuttling between London and Germany, eventually reached an accord of sorts in Munich, Martin shared the general sense of relief. "It was welcomed the world over," he wrote to Nell. "I hope it means a real and relatively permanent peace."[108]

Munich would mean very different things for Martin and for Canada. For him, September 1938 was a moment of personal accomplishment. Membership on Canada's delegation to the League Assembly, he hoped, signalled political advancement. As he thanked King earnestly on his return, "I shall certainly always remember your expression of confidence, and I will regard it as one of the deepest sources of encouragement a younger member could expect to receive from his leader."[109]

For Canada, Munich marked the start of the slow and steady descent into the Second World War. At the height of the crisis, cabinet agreed to follow Britain into war, though in public King held firmly to the line that Parliament would decide. Throughout the following year, he carefully prepared Canadian opinion to accompany Britain into hostilities. When the Munich agreement collapsed in mid-March 1939 and Chamberlain finally rallied to contain Hitler, promising aid to Poland if it were attacked, King and Lapointe acted in concert to preserve the unity of French- and English-speaking Canada. At the end of March, they announced that Canada would back Britain in a war with Hitler's Germany. At the same time, they insisted that Parliament would determine Canada's course in the event of war and that there would be no conscription for overseas service. Avoiding a rush to premature commitments, King's ambivalence pleased most Canadians, who stood resolutely behind him.

There was other reassuring evidence of the nation's unity in the spring of 1939. In late May, King George VI and his queen disembarked in Quebec City for a tour across Canada and the United States, quietly gathering North American supporters. Martin lobbied hard to have Windsor included in their itinerary, and to his satisfaction, it eventually was. But the visit passed quickly and was too soon replaced on the front pages of the country's newspapers with the grim news that Nazi Germany and the communist Soviet Union had signed a non-aggression pact, clearing the way for war in Eastern Europe. On 1 September, Hitler's forces swept over the border into Poland. When Britain responded by declaring war two days later, King summoned Parliament to meet on 7 September.

During that last summer of peace, Martin looked backward, not ahead. A law practice established, a political career well launched, a family started. "We have so much for which to be thankful," he reminded Nell in June. "We have one another – and truly we have had great experiences – among them the incredible impression of the King and Queen. How delightful it has all been."[110]

3

A CONQUERED WORLD,
1939–45

The special 7 September session of Parliament saddened Paul Martin. "My heart has been heavy," he wrote Nell. "Parliament has made its decision. We are now at war."[1] Exactly what this would mean, however, was not fully settled before Parliament adjourned on 12 September, two days after Canada declared war on Germany, and Martin hastened back to Windsor. Despite his physical disabilities, he wondered about enlisting, unsure where his personal duty lay.[2] He also fretted about the anti-government sentiment that was already brewing among French Canadian Liberals, who feared a repeat of the bitter conscription battles of the First World War.[3] What, Martin mused during the long train ride home, would the war mean for him?

The government's program was clear. Prime Minister King favoured a policy of limited commitments, and it was assumed in September 1939 that Canada's main contribution would consist of "food, raw materials and munitions."[4] The prime minister repeated his pledge of the previous March: there would be no overseas conscription. When he and his policies came under attack during the static "phony war" that followed Hitler's quick victory in Poland, he prepared for battle. In Quebec, nationalist premier Maurice Duplessis – "a little Hitler," thought King – called an election in late September to protest the centralization of power in Ottawa that accompanied the declaration of war.[5] In English Canada, King faced growing demands for a national coalition government, an idea backed by Conservative leader Robert Manion and Toronto financiers, armed with a campaign chest said to total $3 million.[6] The crisis came to a head in January 1940, when King's arch-enemy, Ontario premier Mitch Hepburn, introduced a resolution at Queen's Park to condemn Ottawa's war effort. When the House of Commons reconvened on 15 January 1940, King struck back. The MPs had barely taken their seats when the Throne Speech announced that the government would immediately seek a renewed mandate.

The clever move stunned Canadians, including Martin, who had skipped the speech to attend to an outstanding case in the Supreme Court of Ontario. Justice George McFarland interrupted his cross-examination to tell him the news. In Windsor, the election campaign was fought on a mixture of local and national issues. Martin ran scared. "I am working hard these days and will be until the last minute," he wrote a campaign worker. "Yes, things look good, but we must take no chances."[7] He reminded voters that he had crusaded since 1935 for scholarships, aid for corn-growers, and unemployment insurance. The Conservative and CCF candidates, once again Raymond Morand and Ben Levert, respectively, scored these as unfulfilled promises.

Martin heaped scorn on the Tory cry for national government, sneered at Manion's weak backbench – who, he echoed King, would form this national government? – and defended the government's war policy: "There have been no soaring food prices, no men getting rich on the sufferings of others, no pork and bacon barons, no Ross rifles in this war ... as in the last."[8] Voters across the country shared this favourable (if modest) assessment of the government's accomplishments. On 26 March 1940, they returned King with 181 seats and just over 50 percent of the popular vote. Martin rode back to Ottawa on the prime minister's coattails, winning 9,274 votes to Morand's 7,998 and Levert's 2,924.[9]

The spring parliamentary session, which opened on 16 May 1940, was difficult for Martin. The reasons were partly personal. When Hitler resumed his triumphant march across Europe, overrunning the Lowlands and France during May and June, Martin responded to the growing tension with deep longing for the comfort and security of his young family, which remained in Windsor. "The situation is very grave," he confided to Nell. "I miss you terribly. This business of being separated is no good."[10] A few weeks later, he added mournfully, "I miss Paul [Jr.]. It seems like a long time since I have seen him. And it is too."[11]

But his discomfort was mostly political. Amid the tense and exciting bustle of wartime Ottawa, there was little room for either Martin or his reformist views. With Allied forces retreating in disarray to Britain, King removed the early checks on the country's war effort, conscripted Canadians for military service at home, and emphasized winning the war above all else. A handful of progressive Canadians, Martin among them, hoped for more. In mid-July, they assembled at the Chateau Laurier Hotel to urge the prime minister to state Canada's war aims and pledge to achieve "a greater degree of human welfare, freedom and security."[12] King was doubtful. Instead, Liberal "whips" were laid on heavily, silencing government backbenchers with a strict "gag" order that was intended to reinforce party unity.[13] To Martin's chagrin, he was denied a place on the House of Commons committee that was charged with introducing the government's unemployment insurance scheme, a measure he had championed in the late 1930s. As he wrote of his isolation in the summer of 1940, it was "almost like being sent to Coventry."[14]

When rumours of a cabinet shuffle began to circulate in July, Martin joined other Franco-Ontarian Liberal MPs in pressing King for a post of their own. The prime minister ignored them. Martin's frank and generally disapproving assessment of his choices reflected disappointment: "Bill Mulock is in (no comment). Gibson from Hamilton is the new minister of National Revenue (no comments). Jim Ilsley goes to Finance, and this is good."[15] But he was wrong to feel aggrieved at his exclusion from cabinet. Despite its weaknesses, and there were many, it had real strengths. In addition to Ilsley, it included the formidable minister of defence, J.L. Ralston, the ubiquitous "minister of everything," C.D. Howe, and an outstanding troika from Quebec: Chubby Power, the minister of defence (air), Ernest Lapointe, minister of justice, and J.P.A. Cardin, minister of public works. In his classic study of Canadian wartime politics, historian J.L. Granatstein rightly judges it "one of the strongest Cabinets Canada ever had – if not the strongest."[16]

Lacking a role in Ottawa, Martin withdrew to Windsor and focused on rebuilding his flagging law practice, which had generated less than $900 in income in 1939. By 1942, his earnings at Martin & Laird had rebounded sharply and totalled over $8,000. Combined with his $4,000 parliamentary indemnity, this sum made for a comfortable living despite wartime inflation. The young couple had bought a modern six-bedroom home on Roselawn Drive in 1939 – Martin naturally thought it "one of the best houses in Windsor" – and Nell spent much of the war whipping it into "tip-top shape."[17] They had enough money for small luxuries, a trip for Nell and Paul to Florida in early 1940 and a new silver-grey Buick in 1941.

It helped that Martin was no longer supporting his two sisters, who had finished school. By the middle of the war, he had saved enough money to begin producing a tiny but regular stream of dividend income. As one of his later financial counsellors put it, "he loved to make money, and he loved to accumulate it."[18] An instinctive saver and conservative investor, he kept most of his money in Dominion of Canada bonds and in safe stocks. From 1940 to 1942, he invested solely in government bonds and the Industrial Acceptance Corporation, a long-established consumer finance company owned by the respectable Montreal firm of Greenshields.[19] In early 1943, he struck out more boldly, seeking professional investment advice for the first time and moving his money into a range of solid blue-chip stocks, including Canadian Celanese, Montreal Light, Heat & Power, International Nickel, British-American Oil, and the Consolidated Mining and Smelting Company.[20]

In the tense months of 1940–41, when Canada stood as Britain's ranking ally, Martin remained an active, if not particularly happy, member of Parliament. He intervened in only a few House of Commons debates and spoke at length just twice: in November 1940, despite his private views, he defended the government's refusal to define its war aims and the postwar world that Canada wanted until the present crisis had passed; and in June 1941, he urged the trade minister to honour the pre-war promises made to Ontario corn-growers to improve regional facilities.[21]

He continued to respond to local issues, waging a successful campaign in April 1941 to force the minister of national revenue to withdraw an "obnoxious" wartime customs form that was deterring American tourists from visiting Windsor.[22] With Windsor mayor Art Reaume at his side, he tackled Howe in October 1941 over inadequate federal housing for the families of Windsor servicemen.[23] And as the local MP, he dutifully tramped around southwestern Ontario, selling victory bonds, promoting recruitment drives, and exhorting members of service clubs and church groups to ask themselves, "Am I doing everything I can?"[24]

For Martin, the answer was a resounding "No!" Most of his tasks amounted to busywork, and he made no secret of his growing resentment. After one of his efforts, a worthy speech to grey-haired librarians on the value of public libraries to the war effort, his friends at the *Windsor Daily Star* bemoaned his enforced idleness: "With [Martin's] oratory and lucid mind, he could be a tower of strength ... The Government is missing a bet in not making greater use of the members of Parliament who are irked at the little they have here to do."[25] Arriving in Ottawa for the session that began in November 1941, Martin wrote Nell, "Not a full day has elapsed, and I am almost fed up already."[26] Just a few hours later, as he listened to the prime minister drone on, he scribbled a second woeful note from his Commons desk: "There is not much likelihood of anything unusual taking place. Already I have the sense of frustration. How effective it would be if only there was some encouragement. Perhaps, all I can do is wait for the opportunity – if ever it will come."[27]

But his chance was coming. During the session, he was nominated for membership on the House of Commons Special Committee on Reconstruction and Re-establishment, whose task was to think about the shape of a renewed postwar world, at home and abroad. This played to his progressive strengths, and he made sure that the prime minister was aware of his thinking. He backed freer world trade and stronger international banking mechanisms, and defended labour's demands for a voice in the war effort and for bargaining rights as part of its grand "partnership in industry."[28] As he hoped, King noticed and responded warmly, perhaps with encouragement: "I have read your article with the greatest possible interest, satisfaction and pleasure ... [It is] an excellent contribution of immediate practical value."[29]

Martin emerged from the government's conscription crisis in 1942 with his standing in King's eyes further enhanced. The issue of conscription for overseas service had remained dormant during the first two years of the war, but it resurfaced late in 1941, when former prime minister Arthur Meighen took over as Conservative leader and promised to fight for conscription amid army demands for more manpower. Pressure grew after 7 December 1941, when Japan attacked Pearl Harbor, the United States entered the war, and the conflict became truly global. King responded with a plebiscite, asking Canadians to release the government from its promise not to impose full-scale conscription for overseas service. He gambled that this incremental step might garner enough support in Quebec to avoid a polarizing rift in the country. He was wrong. English Canada voted overwhelmingly to give the government a free hand, whereas Quebec remained unalterably opposed.

The 27 April vote split the country and cabinet. King temporized. He decided to bring down legislation, Bill 80, to allow conscription for overseas service, but he would not introduce conscription itself until it was needed. J.P.A. Cardin, King's leading Quebec minister, insisted that no bill was required until conscription was absolutely necessary. King had gone too far to reverse course, and Cardin resigned on 9 May. Backed by Ilsley and Navy Minister Angus Macdonald, Minister of Defence J.L. Ralston insisted that the plebiscite result meant conscription, and they resented King's implication that Parliament would have to debate the issue twice. Ralston offered his resignation on 12 June. Though King convinced him to stay, the "wobbly" Liberal government hung in the balance through the early summer of 1942.[30]

The crisis put Martin in a difficult situation. As an adolescent, he himself had been emotionally seared by the debates over conscription in 1917, and he was deeply opposed to it. However, his riding followed the trend in English Canada, voting massively in favour of releasing the government from its promise. Yet the rural, mostly French Canadian, polls in Essex East, where Martin had done so well in 1935 and 1940, voted solidly "no." King was acutely sensitive to the pressures on caucus members who had large numbers of French Canadian constituents, and when Martin telegraphed his congratulations on a "great speech" just days before the plebiscite vote, he responded by drawing him in for a chat.[31] Martin remained committed to King, casting his vote loyally and decisively for his leader. "The situation continues to be acute," he wrote Nell. "The only way out is for us to stick with Mr. King. In this way, we will weather the storm."[32] The prime minister welcomed the support and took strength from it: as he recorded, Martin "thought if we could go to the length suggested ... we would be able to keep most of our own Quebec following ... Martin told me that ... I only needed to assert myself and the country would follow."[33]

MARTIN'S STEADY SUPPORT for the prime minister did not go unnoticed. In September 1942, after three long years of war, King canvassed a few of his ministers about the prospect of appointing parliamentary secretaries.[34] Although the position had been used in Canada during the First World War, he hoped to introduce a more permanent reform to the machinery of government. He saw the role as an opportunity for younger members to learn about the inner workings of government departments and cabinet. He was careful to say that it did not mean automatic advancement to a cabinet post, but he felt that it "would be a help, undoubtedly – probably, over a period of time, a very great help."[35] The plan was announced in the Throne Speech on 28 January 1943 and approved by the House of Commons in April. With exquisite cruelty, King casually delayed making the final appointments for several weeks as ambitious backbenchers, Martin included, sweated their future.

Ottawa pundits quickly agreed that Martin was an obvious choice for one of the new jobs.[36] He was already one of the prominent politicians of his generation, and his standing with King had risen during the conscription debate of the early summer. He enjoyed strong regional support, and two leading papers in southwestern Ontario, the Liberal *Windsor Daily Star* and the Conservative *London Free Press,* ran editorials advancing his candidacy. "He has qualifications and capabilities that should make him a valuable official," the hometown *Star* insisted in April 1943.[37]

Martin surely helped his own cause with a well-timed intervention from Toronto, where he was attending the Ontario Liberal convention in early May. The despised Hepburn and his cronies were finally on their way out, replaced by King's favoured candidate, Harry Nixon. "It was a King-Hepburn battle," the prime minister gloated, "with a complete routing of all the Hepburn forces."[38] As the gathering ended, Martin rushed to send King the good news in a hurried handwritten affirmation of loyalty. "The delegates insisted that the new leader would be one who would be loyal to yourself as Prime Minister," he gushed. "Throughout the entire deliberations, it was evident that the Liberals of Ontario wanted to show that they honour your statesmanship and leadership. For this reason, I hasten to offer you my congratulations."[39] King was gratified, welcoming Martin's letter "like the ozone of the sea to one who has been longing to glimpse again the open sweep of the sea."[40] Three days later, on 7 May, he summoned Martin to his office and offered him the position of parliamentary secretary to the minister of labour.[41]

King suspected that Martin wanted the External Affairs portfolio, and he was probably right. Nonetheless, Martin was grateful for the promotion and even offered to work for nothing. The role, he recalled in his memoirs, combined a "satisfying mixture of high-flown idealism and practical politics."[42] The few observers who noticed his appointment thought it a good one. *Canadian Business Magazine* considered it long overdue and predicted that Martin would "bring new energy, new zeal, and new knowledge to the Department." Toronto-based *Saturday Night* magazine echoed this sentiment, labelling Martin "a very interesting figure to watch."[43]

The position exposed Martin to the nuts and bolts of government policy making, to senior bureaucrats, and to labour and industry leaders in central Canada. He soon learned to handle routine House of Commons questions and to process simple parliamentary returns when the genial and aging minister of labour, Humphrey Mitchell, was absent. Though cordial enough, Martin's relations with Mitchell, who resented the younger MP's appointment as his permanent understudy should he ever trip up, were not warm. Departmental work brought him into closer contact with Arthur MacNamara, the very able deputy minister of labour, and Eric Strangroom, chief inspector of insurance with the Department of Labour and an expert on social security legislation in Europe. Martin's relationship with Strangroom, who proved particularly adept at supplying him with a steady stream of speeches and written material, effectively introduced him to the bureaucracy.

Martin's appointment also exposed him to the complicated business of government policy making, though he enjoyed little real influence. This became apparent in August 1943, when he tried to intervene in a looming dispute between factions of the National War Labour Board (NWLB) over how far Ottawa should go in acknowledging labour's rights. During the summer, the King government had grown worried by mounting labour unrest, which was prompted by the wartime ban on strikes and tight wage controls. The surging popularity of the CCF, which had stunned the country in early August by sweeping the reform vote and taking thirty-four seats in the Ontario provincial election, only four less than the governing Conservatives, heightened Liberal anxiety. The Gallup poll for September 1943 pegged the CCF's national support at 29 percent, a point ahead of both the Liberals and Progressive Conservatives, whose new name (adopted a year earlier) reflected the nation's shifting consensus.[44] Reacting to this demand for reform and more forward-looking policies for the postwar period, the NWLB asked Martin's old boss, Justice Charles P. McTague, to report on labour rights by the end of August.[45]

McTague recommended compulsory collective bargaining, enforced by a national labour code, relaxed wage restraints, and more labour representation on regulatory bodies. For NWLB member J.L. Cohen, a labour lawyer, that was not enough. He prepared a minority report to argue for more labour freedom, threatening a split that was likely to harm the Liberal Party's standing with unionized labour. After reading both reports, Martin urgently reminded the prime minister – who was bemused that he had earnestly labelled his recommendations "confidential" – that compromise was possible, was in the best interests of labour, and was important to revive fading Liberal fortunes. King welcomed the emphasis on compromise, which he shared, but ignored Martin's other recommendations, adopting instead the advice on timing and tactics tendered by Deputy Labour Minister MacNamara.[46]

As the Liberal Party shaped its postwar reform agenda during the fall and winter of 1943–44, King relied on other young men for new ideas and support, especially Jack Pickersgill, who was becoming one of his closest political advisors, and Brooke Claxton, his parliamentary assistant. They, rather than Martin, took the ideas for postwar reform that were bursting forth in the Committee on Postwar Reconstruction (which included Principal Cyril James from McGill University and the McGill radical social scientist Leonard Marsh), and channelled them into the Liberal mainstream. They pushed the Liberal Party on the road to reform and organized a key policy meeting of the National Liberal Federation's advisory committee in late September 1943. That gathering culminated in the Throne Speech of January 1944, which assured war-weary Canadians that "the postwar object of our domestic policy is social security and human welfare," promising a family allowance, a monthly financial supplement for their children. A month later, cabinet issued PC-1003, which endorsed McTague's main recommendations and backed union demands for compulsory collective bargaining.

Martin cheered from the sidelines, where he was busy carving out a significant and high-profile (but undervalued and less weighty) role for himself as a spokesman for reform. As parliamentary secretary, he spent much of his time explaining and defending the government's wartime labour policies in Ontario and, to Pickersgill's relief in King's office, in French-speaking Quebec.[47] Public advocacy was his genius. Over the summer of 1943, he tackled the Canadian Congress of Labour, the Montreal Metal Trades Council, and the Confédération des travailleurs catholiques du Canada. He assured working men and women that industry was a partnership between management and labour, which must be allowed to organize and bargain collectively. And the Liberal government, he promised with just the right touch of partisanship, was there to ensure that it happened.[48]

He repeated the message to the Board of Trade Club in Toronto that fall, pointing out that the war was democratizing the workplace whether employers liked it or not, that economic planning worked, and that "workers are not trash."[49] In the spring of 1944, he told audiences in Montreal, Hamilton, and Windsor that the Liberal government was alive to labour's needs, and he produced the statistics to prove it: union membership had grown by 61 percent since 1939, had seen 90 percent of its wage hikes approved, and had increased its overall wage package by $150 million.[50] More was coming. Like other Canadians, Martin looked ahead to the end of the war. Government postwar planning, he declared, would provide economic security for workers, full employment, and social security measures, including family allowances and health and unemployment insurance.[51]

He maintained his lively interest in international affairs during this period and spoke often on the importance of re-establishing some kind of world league after the war.[52] His post at the Department of Labour gave him his first substantial taste of international diplomacy and buttressed his standing at home as a foreign policy expert. In April 1944, he joined Humphrey Mitchell and Brooke Claxton as Canadian delegates to the twenty-sixth session of the International Labour Organization's (ILO) conference in Philadelphia. When Mitchell and Claxton were absent, he played a key role in managing the subcommittee charged with the conference's main challenge, defining relations between the ILO and whatever world assembly emerged after the war. After eleven meetings, Martin convinced government, labour, and employer representatives to forward the problem to a working group that would report at the next meeting of the ILO's governing council in January 1945. It was a narrow technical victory, but Martin was pleased, and he insisted on going to London in January to finish the job.

Conservative critics complained that he was "too statesmanlike" in his defence of labour and too casual with the figures that he tossed about in debate, which often proved unsubstantiated.[53] And superior foreign service officers in External Affairs, which was close to King, already disapproved of his immodest ambition. When he reported on his election to the chairmanship of the ILO's constitutional committee, the influential undersecretary of state for external affairs, Norman Robertson, sneered, "This is meant to be modest, I've no doubt."[54]

None of this seems to have bothered many Liberals or their prime minister, who noted with approval the solid research that underpinned Martin's House of Commons defence of the new family allowances.[55] Other influential voices echoed King's judgment. After a speech over the radio in late May 1943, for instance, the Montreal daily *La Presse* remarked with evident enthusiasm that the talk was "a magnificent and too rare effort ... Mr. Martin has shown himself to be a parliamentarian of considerable value."[56] The *Montreal Standard,* a popular illustrated weekly, declared Martin its "Man of the Year" in May 1944.[57]

Labour also awarded high marks to its parliamentary secretary. "He thinks in human terms of human welfare," wrote the *Montreal Labour World.* "The workers trust him; they know that he will leave nothing undone."[58] Radical labour activist J.L. Cohen, who represented the United Auto Workers when Ford locked out its members in April 1944, praised Martin's efforts to find a settlement as "most helpful and public spirited."[59] Word of Martin's diplomatic "skill, fairness, and good humour" followed him home from the ILO meetings in Philadelphia and London.[60] One journalist insisted that his success in London, where he negotiated passage of a resolution to bring the labour body into the postwar United Nations, meant that his "selection to a cabinet post ... is almost assured."[61] Perhaps it was, but one thing was even more certain: Paul Martin was not about to leave that decision entirely to chance.

Rumours of a major cabinet shuffle had circulated all fall, heating up after King appointed Brooke Claxton to the new Department of National Health and Welfare in October 1944. Martin worried that early 1945 was not a good time to be out of the country and out of sight. This was especially true after Secretary of State Norman McLarty, who represented Essex West, announced in February that he planned to retire before the next election, opening a cabinet seat in southwestern Ontario. En route to the ILO meetings in London, Martin confided in a short note to Nell "that I want not to be forgotten by my public (only to you would I say this)."[62] Nell had already taken matters into her own hands, sending the most important member of Martin's public – the prime minister – a charming letter in which she acknowledged his yearly Christmas greeting. In passing, she slipped in a few words of praise. "Our Prime Minister," she wrote, "is a truly great man with enduring patience under duress, an appreciation of the right time and right place – I believe him a most wondrous person altogether apart from the convictions my husband has for him." King was very pleased.[63]

Martin and his backers had other opportunities to advance his cause that spring, and they took advantage of them all. When King was feted at a London banquet honouring Churchill and Roosevelt, Martin immediately telegraphed him with the good news, "so thrilled was I."[64] He also made sure that King received a copy of his new booklet, *Labour's Post-War World,* which pleased the prime minister with its generous references to his own statements.[65] The Western Ontario Liberal Association, which represented the region's twenty-four ridings, wrote as well, urging King to appoint Martin to cabinet as McLarty's replacement.[66]

Claxton threw his considerable weight behind Martin, determined to secure another liberal ally at the cabinet table. He arranged for Martin to be given a prime speaking spot in the Commons debate over Canadian membership in the new United Nations.[67] He also outlined for King a compelling case in favour of Martin's membership in cabinet. First, the Windsor MP would strengthen the Liberal Party's support among labour. "Next to yourself," Claxton insisted, "no one is better known or stands higher ... They like him and he can speak to them. It would mean tens of thousands of votes here alone." Second, Martin's appointment "would recognize all that's *young and progressive* in the Party and Canada," resonating with millions of new voters. Third, Martin would reinforce the party's standing in vote-rich western Ontario, where he would become its main cabinet representative and campaigner. "He is one of the most powerful political speakers in Canada," Claxton observed. "One of the few equally at home on the hustings or in a debate or discussion, and in French and English."[68]

King fussed. On the morning of 13 April, he told Parliament that the long-delayed federal election would fall on 11 June 1945, still without finally deciding who would be in his cabinet. Late that afternoon, he summoned Martin for help with a campaign biography written by Ontario politician Ray Lawson. Unwilling to be obligated to Lawson, he wanted Martin listed as the author. Martin agreed, but only if he were not expected to support Lawson's claim for preferment.[69] Yet King continued to dither about Martin. He needed little persuading of his merits, and he instinctively liked his reformist instincts and valued his hard work as Mitchell's parliamentary secretary. Above all, he trusted his personal commitment, although he remained wary of his overly serious personality. Mostly, King was fearful of upsetting cabinet's careful religious and linguistic balance. As he shuffled his ministers, he was forced to acknowledge that the dour Irishman from the Ottawa Valley, James McCann, was a much better representative for Ontario's English-speaking Catholics, even though he himself felt "very strongly" that "Martin was preferable as a man."[70]

That left the bicultural Martin as a candidate for the vacant seat set aside for a French-speaking Catholic from Ontario. The other contender was Lionel Chevrier, a genial and debonair lawyer from Cornwall. A classmate of Martin's at Osgoode Hall Law School, Chevrier had entered Parliament in 1935 and had become one of the government's first parliamentary secretaries in 1943. In King's view, the two men were closely matched. Chevrier had "a more attractive personality" and might be more useful in nearby Quebec, but Martin was "very good with labour – somewhat ponderous but forward looking with ideas."[71] King leaned toward Chevrier. On 14 April, he told Doug Abbott, whom he planned to make defence minister, that he would bring the Cornwall MP into cabinet. He recognized that this left cabinet without representation in western Ontario. After sounding out Howe, who thought "this was the wise thing to do," he finally decided to offer Martin a cabinet seat. He justified including an extra French-speaking Catholic from Ontario by noting that Martin would offset the loss of a French Catholic seat in New Brunswick created by the departure of Transport Minister J.E. Michaud.

Deeply moved by King's offer, Martin quickly accepted it. The following day, a cold April morning, he was sworn in as Canada's secretary of state. This was a minor and insignificant portfolio, and most of Martin's young cabinet rivals occupied more senior posts: Claxton at Health and Welfare, Abbott at Defence, and Chevrier at Transport. Nevertheless, as he later recalled ironically, he left Government House "full of smiles and satisfaction. The world had been conquered ... and I was about to become one of the most important men in Canada."[72]

THOUGH HE LATER bragged that he never changed a diaper in his life, Martin enjoyed fatherhood. "Every act of Paul now interests and captivates me," he wrote of his son to Nell in 1941. "His progressive growth escapes my notice only when I am away. When I return I seek to notice changes ... Yes, we have a great little fellow."[73] He appreciated the role more deeply following the sudden death of his own father, Philippe, during a church service in October 1943, and the arrival in January 1944 of his second child, Mary Anne.

Throughout the war, he boarded with a few other MPs on Cobourg Street, while Nell stayed in the Roselawn Drive home. He missed her and the children. "I growingly find it more difficult to be away from you," he once wrote. "How nice it would be if you could come with me more often – really you can if you would."[74] Without Nell, he was prone to bouts of unhappiness and loneliness. But despite repeated coaxing, she clung to her life in Windsor, and the question of where the Martins would eventually live remained unsettled at the end of the war.

With Martin so often away, holidays became an important focus for family activities. In the summer, Nell and the children, her sister, Roxie (known to the children as Aunt Mame), and her son Michael Maloney, as well as a host of local aunts and uncles and cousins, headed down to the simple cottage in Colchester. Constructed from scrap lumber salvaged from an abandoned church, it had been in Nell's family since the early 1920s. Its most unusual feature was the rough clay tennis court out back, strung with old streetlights from Chicago. When the House recessed, Martin joined them. It sometimes took a day or two for him to settle in, but when he did, "he would be fun for the whole time."[75] He loved to swim before breakfast and enjoyed tennis on the homemade court, playing awkwardly but competitively. He was happy fishing, or joining Paul Jr. and Michael in a game of "British Battleship," sprawling across an inner tube in Lake Erie, while the two little boys, aged five or six, tried to overturn him.

In wintertime, the family gathered for Christmas at the Martin house. Martin almost always returned from family events in Windsor rested and bubbling with enthusiasm. "What a grand Christmas," he wrote Nell in January 1946. "Rarely have I been as happy ... You were, as usual, adorable. The children are such great additions. The house was heavenly. Thanks for such a lovely holiday."[76] Nell was equally content. "Little Paul and Mary Anne are just adorable," she replied. "You have every right to be proud. God was good to give us such lovely, handsome children."[77]

THE WAR YEARS seasoned Paul Martin. He weathered the sharp disappointment of being passed over for cabinet in 1940, and despite his frustrations during the next two years, he carried on dutifully in his riding and in the House, a loyal member of King's team. That was amply confirmed during the conscription crisis of 1942, when he cast his lot decisively with his prime minister. In his position as parliamentary secretary to the labour minister, Martin demonstrated yet again those qualities that had always impressed his superiors: his unflagging capacity for hard work, his intelligence, and his enthusiasm. He used the role to articulate the kind of progressive and forward-looking vision of postwar Canada that had sustained many Canadians throughout the long conflict. In doing so, he made himself too important for King to overlook when he rebuilt his war-weary cabinet in April 1945. With the country standing on the edge of peace, Martin was given his chance to shape the future. For him, it had been a good war.

4
APPRENTICE MINISTER, 1945–48

It was a triumphant Paul Martin who returned home to Windsor in the pale sunshine of April 1945 to seek his party's nomination for the federal election in June. For the riding convention, he donned a grey suit, which became increasingly battered and torn as the campaign wore on. Playing "Happy Days Are Here Again," a breezy celebration of the rum running and blind pigs that were already fading into nostalgia, the South Essex Associated Boys Band marched down Tecumseh Road to St. John the Baptist Hall. The hall was packed and a throng of rowdy Martin supporters milled about outside, where extra speakers had been erected. Inside, Ozias Dupuis, vice-president of Local 195 of the United Auto Workers (UAW), nominated the new secretary of state as the Liberal candidate for Essex East. The motion was seconded by Charles O'Brien, president of the Essex-Kent Corn Growers Association. The presence of these two men, worker and farmer, francophone and anglophone, sent a strong signal of the candidate's commanding reach that was punctuated by the roar of laughter when the chairman asked if there were any additional nominations.[1]

On election day, 11 June 1945, Canadians chose their third consecutive Liberal government, giving Prime Minister King's party 41 percent of the popular vote and a slim majority of 125 of 245 seats. The Tories took 67 and the CCF 28 seats. Though the Liberal total was down 53 seats from 1940, after six years of war and hardship, it was still a splendid victory. Campaigning on the "New Social Order" unveiled in their January 1944

Throne Speech, the Liberals reminded voters of their popular family allowances and their ambitious postwar reforms, aimed at economic and social security. The threat from the left-wing CCF, which had frightened Liberals since 1943, collapsed in the face of these promises, aided by a savage assault on social democrats by rabid right-wing anti-communist propagandists. The sudden end of the war in Europe on 8 May rendered Tory demands for unlimited conscription pointless, and the party irrelevant. Quebecers, grateful for King's careful handling of the conscription crises in 1942 and 1944, voted solidly Liberal.[2]

In Windsor, Martin made much of family allowances – he called them "the greatest act ever put on the statute book" – and the wartime gains of labour and farmers, and he insisted that there would be no postwar retreat. He again enjoyed vigorous backing from the *Windsor Daily Star,* whose columnists admired his hard constituency work and his frank defence of the virtues of politics. "I am not afraid to be called a politician," he declared. "Next to preaching the word of God, there is nothing nobler than to serve one's fellow countrymen in government."[3] As a minister, he was expected to campaign more widely, and he did. He swung through the major centres of southwestern Ontario and also spoke in Owen Sound, Hamilton, Toronto, and Kirkland Lake. He even spent a few days in Saskatchewan, campaigning for his prime minister, who was busy leading Canada's delegation to the UN founding conference in San Francisco.

When the ballots were counted in Essex East, Martin had 15,099 votes, giving him a majority for the first time. The Progressive Conservative candidate, Jim Byrne, polled just under 8,000 votes. The pro-labour CCF, which was expected to do well in Windsor, where the UAW had grown from nine thousand to fifty-one thousand members since 1939, won fewer than 4,000 votes.[4] But for Martin the victory was bittersweet. During the campaign's final stages, Byrne accused him and the Liberal Party of concluding an electoral alliance with the communist Labour-Progressive Party to defeat the CCF. Communists feared that social democratic support for labour rights, including the right to strike, might delay the production of supplies for Stalin's Soviet Union and impair the war effort.[5] The charges, certainly true, had little effect on the election, but they reinforced Martin's reputation as a backroom ward-heeler, a politician who was determined to win at all costs.

King's post-election frostiness was more worrying. Perhaps feeling especially bruised and sensitive after losing his own seat in Prince Albert, the prime minister was alarmed at the loss of six of seven possible seats in the tobacco belt around London. He blamed Martin.[6] It was an inauspicious start for the Windsor minister and a sharp reminder of the perils of membership in King's cabinet.

THE DEPARTMENT OF Secretary of State, one of the oldest departments of government, was a ramshackle affair with a broad range of disparate duties. It was responsible for the federal archives, state visits and protocol, bankruptcy, confiscated enemy property, and government publications. For much of his first year, Martin wrestled with the ticklish business of awarding civilian honours to Canadians for their wartime service as friends, bureaucrats, and ministers, and King himself nudged him toward their favourite nominees.[7] He was also responsible for the working conditions of the civil service, a job he enjoyed much more. He lunched with staff, visited their recreational facilities, and won their support when he lopped off the extra hour per day that wartime regulations had demanded of them.[8] Martin, observed journalist Austin Cross, who covered the federal bureaucracy beat just after the war, "worked harder for the public service than any other cabinet minister within memory."[9] Like pre-war progressives across North America, Martin was a firm advocate of a professional and merit-based public service, and he scored an early victory by persuading King to appoint the first permanent civil servant, S.G. Nelson, to the Civil Service Commission.[10] Nelson was a vocal champion of promotion by merit, and his appointment signalled the transformation of the commission into the professional administrative body that it eventually became.

Martin was much less successful in his campaign to reduce the size of the federal bureaucracy. Like most of King's ministers, he was fiscally cautious. Instinctively favouring small government, he worried that the civil service had grown too large and too quickly since the end of the war. In September 1945, he proposed a drastic reduction in the permanent establishment, suggesting that ministers cut more than a third of their departmental staff.[11] His efforts put him at odds with liberals such as Defence Minister Brooke Claxton, who thought the public service was already among the world's smallest, and the prime minister himself, who shuddered at the prospect of a public scrap over the cuts. "It was impossible," King insisted, "to do anything of the kind."[12]

As secretary of state, Martin also had a number of political duties. He was the political minister for his corner of southwestern Ontario, though most significant patronage appointments in the province continued to run through the office of the minister of reconstruction, C.D. Howe, who represented a riding in northern Ontario. Martin kept a close eye on Opposition motions and resolutions, and brought them to the attention of his cabinet colleagues. With Claxton and Pickersgill, he sat on the informal committee of ministers and advisors that increasingly ran the Liberal Party, and he doled out speaking assignments on CBC Radio's free-time political broadcasts.[13]

As Claxton and King had anticipated, Martin emerged as an informal labour spokesman at the cabinet table. "I find Martin a help in the cabinet in defending labour's position," King reflected in July 1945.[14] This was important for Liberal fortunes with working-class voters as peace beckoned and the economy struggled to find its postwar footing. During the summer of 1945, labour unrest swelled across the country. The wartime settlements imposed by the National War Labour Board unravelled as workers sought pay hikes and union security, and companies prepared to roll back the gains of their workforces. In Windsor, UAW Local 200 had a long list of demands for the Ford Motor Company of Canada, the city's largest employer in its most important industry. The UAW wanted wage and benefit increases, union recognition, and the compulsory check-off (collection) of union dues. Notoriously anti-labour, Ford refused to recognize either the union or its demand for a closed shop in the bitter and futile negotiations that had dragged on, unresolved, since April 1944. On 12 September 1945, when the plant whistle sounded the mid-morning break, ten thousand Ford employees in Windsor walked off the job.

The rookie minister found himself on uncertain ground. These were his voters on strike, but labour relations did not fall within his purview. They were the responsibility of Humphrey Mitchell, the slow-moving and indecisive labour minister, and Martin's manoeuvrability was constrained by the conventions of cabinet solidarity. It was a thorny situation, but he initially managed to get out in front of the growing wave of local anger. He was the first minister to intervene in the strike, arranging for Mitchell and Ontario's Progressive Conservative labour minister, Charles Daley, to meet with Ford and union representatives in early October. His luck changed, however, when Daley, a company supporter, withdrew from the meeting, which collapsed in disarray.[15]

The setback turned the union sharply against Martin. Roy England, the genial but tough president of Local 200, recalled his support for the striking UAW in April 1944 and charged him with "not working in the same manner he did before."[16] Not for the last time, Martin's position was weakened by whispered accusations that his search for a negotiated compromise was driven by self-interest and unbridled ambition for power.[17] He fought back, but his weapons were limited. He hinted at progress, he accused Ford of trying to break the union, and he appealed to its management to negotiate. Most importantly, he made sure that everyone knew where his sympathies lay. "These industries," he told the House with just the right touch of indignation, "will have to learn that they cannot treat their workers as bits of steel on the cement floors of their plants."[18]

But words were not enough. Already short of funds and driven onto relief, strikers demanded that the government force Ford to the table, a step that cabinet declined to take. When Windsor police escorted Ford security guards across the picket lines in early November, the 8,500 members of UAW Local 195 who worked in Windsor's automotive parts industry joined the strike illegally. Panicked aldermen summoned the provincial police and, to Martin's great distress, the federal Royal Canadian Mounted Police (RCMP). Ford workers responded by jamming over two thousand buses and cars, many of them hijacked from unfortunate passersby, into the streets surrounding the Ford plant, bringing downtown Windsor to a standstill.[19] The crisis evoked memories of the 1937 General Motors strike in Oshawa, when Dave Croll, Martin's old ally in the battles of the Depression and now a Liberal MP for Toronto, left Hepburn's cabinet to support the workers. "Act or quit," UAW boss Roy England demanded of Martin, who was stung by the comparison to Croll and visibly upset by the ultimatum.[20] Unlike Croll, he refused to step down. In the House of Commons and through his friends at the *Windsor Daily Star,* he issued a heartfelt plea for public support, insisting that he could do more to resolve the crisis from inside cabinet.[21]

He was right. The looming violence, which exposed communist influences in the Windsor UAW and undermined the union's support across the country, drove both sides back to the bargaining table. When Mitchell failed to convince the union to accept federal proposals for settling the strike, Martin recruited senior and more moderate union leaders from the Canadian Congress of Labour (CCL) and the UAW's American headquarters to pressure local UAW leaders England and George Burt. By late November, the labour minister had persuaded retreating union leaders to remove the picket lines around the plant's vital power station, provided that Ford agreed to resume negotiations.[22]

When the Windsor UAW hesitated to accept Ford's demand that the issue of union security and recognition should be sent to an arbitrator selected by Ottawa, Martin interceded again. Despite opposition in cabinet from Acting Prime Minister J.L. Ilsley and C.D. Howe, who thought the two sides should resolve their differences without government involvement, he backed the appointment of Supreme Court justice Ivan Rand as arbitrator. At the same time, he reassured CCL vice-president Pat Conroy that Rand had "progressive ideas."[23] This proved persuasive. "Conroy came up and gave us to understand that the government would pick a strictly impartial person sympathetic enough," recalled George Burt. "They almost told us they would give us some kind of union security."[24] The divisive strike, which lasted ninety-nine days and cost the Windsor economy $6 million in lost wages, finally ended on 20 December. After a week of hearings, Rand issued his report at the end of January 1946.

Rand's binding formula rejected the closed union shop, though it required that all employees in a unionized workplace pay union dues. This clear victory for Canadian workers established union security as a basic principle of postwar labour relations. The consequences were more ambiguous for Martin. He had managed competing cabinet and union pressures, and survived his first real test as a minister. Local labour representatives and the international UAW even publicly acknowledged his "splendid assistance ... [which] contributed greatly to the settlement."[25] Windsor union leaders were less generous with their thanks, however, and even in retirement, Martin fulminated about their failure to appreciate his pro-labour efforts, "when they damn well knew their best friend was me."[26]

MARTIN ENJOYED MUCH greater success on other fronts during the busy summer and fall of 1945. The war, which ended abruptly in August with Japan's defeat, had transformed Canada from an insular, rural backwater into a modern industrial nation. United as rarely before, or since, Canadians basked in the glory of their civilian armies, victorious in Italy and Northern Europe. They poured into the country's booming, overcrowded cities and marvelled at the vast new smelters and factories that had spewed forth a steady stream of tanks, ships, and munitions. Many were aware, however, that their raw-boned homeland still lacked the basic symbols of nationhood, including a national flag and a clear definition of Canadian citizenship.

Who was entitled to claim Canadian citizenship and what exactly that meant had been worked out earlier in the century in an imperfect patchwork of laws and regulations. The Immigration Act of 1910 included a limited definition to determine who had the right to reside in Canada for immigration purposes. Ottawa created the status of "Canadian national" in 1921 so that Canadians might be recognized by the League of Nations and appointed to its agencies. The Naturalization Act of 1914 determined the conditions under which a resident of Canada could be naturalized as a British subject, a neo-colonial status that was shared across the British Empire and reaffirmed at imperial conferences in 1930 and 1937. The three definitions were contradictory and a nightmare to administer. With war's end, many Canadians felt that the time had come to define their own citizenship.

It was not Martin's idea to define Canadian citizenship. King initiated the process in January 1945, before Martin returned from the ILO meetings in England, telling cabinet that he wanted to introduce the necessary legislation as soon as possible, a policy he made public during the spring election campaign. Once in cabinet, Martin embraced the challenge as his own, and he soon mastered the file. Other ministers left him largely alone. He relished the freedom, although he later sniffed with a hint of disapproval "that most of my colleagues had other priorities."[27]

He was wary of falling captive to his department, worried that its views reflected the suspect influence of its older and more experienced undersecretary (deputy minister), E.H. Coleman. He dismissed Coleman, who was born in 1890 and who spoke with the clipped accent of a fading Anglo-Canadian elite, as "a man who clung tenaciously to the past."[28] He convinced King to lend him instead the services of Gordon Robertson, a bright young foreign service officer who worked in King's office. The two got along well. Robertson found Martin "a joy to work with ... He was intelligent, perceptive, appreciative, and all association with him was leavened by his delightful sense of humour."[29] With Martin as chair, the two men created a working group of youthful policy-makers that included David Mundell from Justice and A.L. Jolliffe, the well-respected director of immigration.

In the summer of 1945, Robertson and Mundell handled much of the heavy lifting, pacing across the lawn on Parliament Hill as they hammered out the legal difficulties and bringing ideas and solutions to the minister for decision. As the summer passed, the new bill and its four main elements took shape. Two were not controversial. Martin, who was impressed by the pomp that accompanied the swearing-in of American citizens, was determined that his bill would inspire similar formalities. He believed that new Canadians ought to be encouraged to learn something of their country's history and its traditions, and that the state should mark their change in status with due ceremony. The group also seized the opportunity to recognize the changing status of women in Canada, replacing provisions in the Naturalization Act that forced women to assume their husband's citizenship after marriage. Under Martin's revised bill, women were free to choose their own citizenship.

The provisions on obtaining citizenship for immigrants were more politically charged. After lengthy discussion, Martin's working group decided that all immigrants, including British subjects, must apply to a judge to become citizens and must reside in Canada for at least five years before doing so. Finally, to appease the fiercely pro–British Empire contingent that still lurked in English Canada, the bill included the statement that a "Canadian citizen is a British subject." Martin believed that this "left Canada with a mark of inferiority," but he doubted that the bill would pass without this political compromise.[30]

By the end of the summer, the bill was ready for cabinet. Nervous about its reception, Martin was not inclined to take chances. In late August, he leaked it, first to the *Windsor Daily Star* and then to Torchy Anderson, a stringer for Southam News, which gave the story national coverage. The reaction was perhaps more muted than he might have wished. Nonetheless, the articles closely identified him with the bill and were generally positive, giving any skeptical colleagues little ground for concern. Cabinet approved the bill with virtually no debate in early September and made it an important element in the government's Throne Speech.[31]

While he waited for Parliament to open, Martin fretted about the British reaction to his bill. British Dominion Office officials were deliberately not consulted during the drafting process. Consequently, they were justifiably upset when they were handed an advance copy of the bill in mid-September. Their viewpoint was shared by their Canadian counterparts in the Department of External Affairs.[32] The British were further distressed when Martin flatly refused their request for a delay so that they could study the new law. Britain's Labour government fumed at Canada's "unilateral action" in proposing "a radical alteration" of existing arrangements, but there was little it could do.[33] Concerned that his bill might be compromised by public indications of British irritation, Martin returned to cabinet in October to seek its agreement to proceed, "even though there may be reasonably strong opposition from the UK authorities."[34]

He presented his Bill 20 to the House of Commons on 22 October. Both his speech, which one observer described as "moderate, graceful, constructive," and the bill itself were warmly applauded inside and outside the House.[35] The crowded parliamentary agenda, however, delayed second reading until the spring and freed Martin to join Louis St. Laurent, the minister of justice, and Jimmy Gardiner, the agriculture minister, on Canada's delegation to the first UN General Assembly, to be held in London early in 1946. Worn down by the Ford strike and the nerve-racking effort of getting his first piece of legislation into the House, he was ready for a break. After an enjoyable Christmas in Windsor, he headed overseas aboard the *Queen Elizabeth,* just restored to peacetime service, where he relaxed, "sleeping every afternoon, eating much, and ... doing little."[36]

Six weeks apart from Nell rekindled but did not resolve his simmering disagreement with her over where they should live. No sooner had he arrived in New York to catch his ship to England than he wrote Nell, expressing his optimism that "we will soon be together and I hope together in Ottawa."[37] Unpersuaded, Nell replied firmly that "I have definitely made up my mind I am not moving to Ottawa."[38] As always when he travelled, Martin missed his family, and his response was equally emphatic. "I have made up my mind that we must never be apart," he insisted. "And this means Ottawa."[39] A week later, in early February, he added a forlorn postscript: "Never again will I leave unless you can come with me."[40]

London kept Martin busy. When Canada failed in its bid for a seat on the new UN Security Council, he happily served as the country's leading representative on the less important Economic and Social Council (ECOSOC). The issues interested him, and he was cheered by the thought that it "might prove to be the more important body."[41] He was busier still when St. Laurent went home early, leaving him in sole charge. As he explained to Nell, with a touch of self-importance, his day began early and ended late:

> Our day starts with a talk with someone at breakfast (generally always official about some point in the conference.) At 9:30 a.m. in my suite (the largest) we have a delegation conference. Then at 10:30, we are off to the UN. At one there is a luncheon ... At 2:30 I went to a meeting of the ECOSOC, where I made an important speech on China's proposal for a World Health Organization. I then had tea with Cardinal Griffin of Westminster. I had to attend two cocktail parties ... At eight o'clock I had to attend a dinner given by Chile. You will agree, a full day.[42]

Obviously, he enjoyed his work.

It was cold that winter in London, and the Serpentine froze solid by mid-January. At UN meetings, any remaining warmth in the wartime alliance between Stalin's Soviet Union and the American-led democracies quickly disappeared. Public revelations that a cypher clerk at the Soviet embassy in Ottawa had defected with evidence that Moscow was running a spy-ring in Canada plunged East-West relations into an icy Cold War. The London trip gave Martin a ringside seat on the crisis, which he viewed calmly, unlike most of the professional diplomats in the Department of External Affairs. He was struck by the "doubt and cynicism" that he encountered, but he saw them as a good thing. "It may keep us in a realistic vein," he wrote Nell. "Much better this than over-optimism followed by another world cataclysm."[43]

The London sojourn also gave him a chance to squelch growing British pressure for a full-scale imperial conference to consider a joint approach to citizenship. This would surely rile the British Empire lobby in Loyal Protestant Ontario and complicate passage of the legislation. After consulting St. Laurent, Martin met with Home Office officials in January, forcefully telling them that Ottawa simply would not delay the bill.[44]

Martin presented his bill for second reading in April 1946. Encouraged by its broad popularity in the fall, he was bolder now than he had been in October. The act, he declared, provided "an unambiguous definition of the status of Canadian citizenship."[45] The Opposition endorsed Bill 20 in principle, suggesting that Martin had framed the kind of political compromise that Canadians valued. The CCF readily backed the bill, and though its spokesmen wondered about some of its provisions, they left that fight to others. Saskatchewan Progressive Conservative John Diefenbaker attacked the bill for treating British subjects like all other foreigners and accused Martin of striking at the unity of the British Empire. Tommy Church, the foaming imperialist from Toronto, was more strident. He denounced it as "a Tower of Babel bill" designed to keep British immigrants out and to appease Quebec. Nationalists from that province were just as hostile and just as extreme.[46] Liberal Maxime Raymond described the bill as "a step backward," characterized by a demeaning "colonial spirit."[47]

Martin had anticipated his critics. He had warned Gordon Robertson that the government would face "considerable opposition" to treating British subjects like other aliens, and he briefly considered dropping the proposal. In a refrain that would become familiar in official Ottawa, he leaned on Robertson. "I am counting on you," he begged, pleading for arguments to defend the policy.[48] He was counting on Jolliffe as well, turning to him for endless statistics to refute the notion that British subjects who emigrated to Canada should receive special treatment.[49]

Well armed with facts and figures, Martin handled the debate with skill. With patience and humour, he moved the discussion along quickly, deftly using House rules to contain Opposition speakers during second reading, when they controlled the floor and he was at a disadvantage. By the end of April, the bill had passed second reading, with support from all parties. During third reading, Martin judiciously retreated before Conservative pressure and agreed to amend section 10 so that British subjects could apply directly to the secretary of state for citizenship rather than endure the supposed indignity of appearing before a mere judge. This was a small gesture, but it reassured the Opposition that its concerns were not being ignored, and it helped calm the debate. Indeed, when the CCF later tried to remove the status of British subject from the bill, Martin did not even need to speak. After a few MPs made their points, the amendment was defeated, and the bill easily passed third reading on 18 May. King, who had followed the debate closely, awarded his minister "great credit for having piloted the bill through the House."[50]

The spring of 1946 gave Martin a short respite from the grinding pace he had followed since the election. He had been on the road almost constantly from September to March but could now spend more time in Ottawa and Windsor. Essex County turned out in force for a testimonial dinner in March to mark his tenth anniversary in the House. Hometown Pembroke declared 7 March "Paul Martin Day" and served cold turkey and baked ham in his honour. Thrilled by the recognition, he kidded friends from his youth in the Ottawa Valley that "I am still the same Paul Martin of yore."[51] By late April, he was back in southwestern Ontario, marching in the Easter Parade in downtown London. Nell celebrated his return by purchasing a deep-wine boucle with a white fox collar and a pair of nylons, her first spring outfit since 1939.[52]

The easy pace lasted until August. On holiday at the cottage in Colchester, Paul Jr. was struck down by polio in mid-August, the same disease that had devastated his father's health and would kill or cripple thousands of Canadian children each year until the mid-1950s. Martin heard the news by telephone from Nell while sitting in cabinet and rushed home to Windsor on a government plane arranged by his colleague C.D. Howe. During the next four "very anxious" days, he and Nell hovered beside Paul Jr.'s hospital bed, worried that he "would likely die or spend [his] days in an iron lung."[53] Fortunately, young Paul rebounded quickly, and within days, Martin was back in Ottawa, preparing to join Canada's delegations to upcoming ECOSOC and General Assembly meetings at the temporary UN headquarters in Flushing Meadows, just outside New York City. But he never forgot his son's crisis, which fuelled his commitment to activist government and provided his politics with a wellspring of deeply personal inspiration for the next two decades.

The Windsor MP had only a small role to play at the two UN conferences. He led the Canadian delegation to the ECOSOC session in September, where elections to its many commissions were the major item of business. On his toughest decision, choosing between election to the commission on human rights or statistics, he deferred to the minister in Ottawa, Louis St. Laurent, who favoured numbers over rights.[54] Martin returned to the General Assembly in October, but he was overshadowed by King, St. Laurent, and Andrew McNaughton, the charismatic general who spoke for Canada on the UN Atomic Energy Commission. As Cold War tensions with the Soviet Union worsened during the fall of 1946, they made sure that Canada hewed tightly to a policy of "moderation and restraint."[55]

Martin still found scope for individual initiative. He backed an unsuccessful move among the delegation's more progressive members, including M.J. Coldwell, the CCF representative, and diplomats Hugh Keenleyside and Escott Reid, to convince the Liberal government to vote with the UN majority in isolating fascist Spain. The effort failed to convince the skeptical deputy foreign minister, Lester B. "Mike" Pearson, or his more conservative Catholic boss, St. Laurent, the new secretary of state for external affairs.[56] Martin did better with his work on refugees and relief. St. Laurent was "very pleased" with his pragmatic efforts to work around the scrappy Cold War debate that threatened a solution to global relief problems and to find a way to keep international aid flowing when wartime arrangements were wrapped up at the end of 1946.[57]

Martin found his UN experiences hopeful and inspiring, but in this he was virtually alone. King, for instance, returned from New York in a gloomy frame of mind, warning his cabinet of "inevitable conflict ... with Communism versus Capitalism ... a sort of Armageddon."[58] For Martin, the meetings confirmed the views he had reached in London. After the "evasions of Geneva," he told reporter Blair Fraser, he was excited by the UN's willingness "to bite into everything." He was particularly impressed by the General Assembly's decision to condemn South Africa for its racist treatment of Indian nationals. Though Canada abstained on a technicality, Martin relished the debate as "fresh, forthright, and healthy, a speaking out against injustice no matter whom it might embarrass."[59]

New York that fall also provided a rare and important chance for Martin and Nell to enjoy some time on their own. They had honeymooned in the quintessentially American city in 1938, revelling in that "pulsating, dynamic, and unbelievable place."[60] Nell joined Martin at the Biltmore Hotel, and the break restored both their spirits after Paul Jr.'s illness. "She has represented the family in the night club circuit, while I have gone to bed early," Martin reported happily to Claxton. "She has enjoyed every minute of her stay and has been unofficial chairman of the delegation this last week."[61] Nell and Paul resolved the family's most important issue. In the new year, the Martins would finally move to Ottawa, living at 22 Goulburn Avenue for a few years before settling a few streets over, at 448 Daly Avenue. For the next decade, this modest red-brick house in Sandy Hill, a solid middle-class neighbour-hood just east of Parliament Hill, would be home for the Martins.

Martin's success as secretary of state fuelled his ambitions. He had hoped to become secretary of state for external affairs when the aging prime minister shed this heavy portfolio in September 1946. He was disappointed (but hardly surprised) when King asked Justice Minister Louis St. Laurent to succeed him.[62] The promotion made a larger cabinet shuffle virtually certain, and the rumours that swirled about insular Ottawa attested to Martin's rising political stock. The press labelled him one of King's "bright young men" and speculated that he might soon go to Labour or possibly External Affairs, if St. Laurent left early in the new year.[63] Blair Fraser even argued that Martin made a credible compromise candidate to replace King, whose retirement was surely imminent now that he had surpassed Sir John A. Macdonald as the country's longest-serving prime minister.[64]

Martin figured prominently in King's plans for remaking his govern-ment, and King considered him for several possible positions, including Justice, Labour, and Health and Welfare.[65] From King's perspective, Health and Welfare seemed a natural fit. Martin was demonstrably interested in social issues and had worked out well at the ILO and ECOSOC.[66] On 12 December, King called him in New York and told him of his promotion to minister of national health and welfare. Though Martin later claimed that he took the job on the condition that he enjoyed King's full support for an expanded department and deeper commitment to social security policies, this seems unlikely.[67] He accepted the offer with such alacrity that the prime minister cruelly mocked him in the privacy of his diary. "Mr. King," he mimicked Martin, "anything that you wish will be all right as far as I am concerned."[68] As he observed with breathtaking hypocrisy, this was exactly how ministers ought to behave.[69] Martin was justifiably hurt and angry when he read King's published diary thirty years later.

MARTIN'S NEW DEPARTMENT was just three years old when he took over on 12 December and moved into his offices in the Jackson Building. An ornate structure of alternating bands of brick and stone at the corner of Bank and Slater Streets, just four blocks from Parliament Hill, the department's headquarters had settled into a state of shabby disrepair. The ministry itself, however, was in much better shape. It was already large by early 1947, with 1,928 employees spread across the country and a budget of almost $290 million. It had two main branches, Health and Welfare, and two deputy ministers. The Health branch operated eighteen Native and four quarantine hospitals, as well as twenty-nine smaller medical clinics. It provided medical services to immigrants and Aboriginal Canadians, promoted public health, regulated food and drug safety, and controlled narcotics. Its smaller Welfare counterpart managed the vast family allowance program – it was already processing 1,588,465 cheques monthly – and old age pensions.[70]

In tackling these tasks, Martin was fortunately able to draw on an accomplished group of key political and bureaucratic advisors. Don Emerson stood closest to the core of his operation. A rough and ready Windsor native, Emerson served as head of the Ontario Young Liberals in 1944-45 and helped organize Ford office workers as vice-president of UAW Local 240. Martin recruited the labour activist as his private secretary in August 1945. Emerson quickly became his "alter ego and political strategist extraordinaire." Even Jack Pickersgill, who would emerge as the Liberal Party's leading backroom operative by the mid-1950s, was said to admire his political judgment.[71] Emerson spent much of his time in Windsor, mending political fences, doling out patronage, and standing in for the minister at local events. During the two decades that he worked for Martin, he developed a remarkable personal following in Essex East.[72]

Martin had an executive assistant in Ottawa, too. Dan Wallace attended Oxford on a Rhodes scholarship during the mid-1930s and taught English at Dalhousie University before the war. He learned about Ottawa and politics during the war, when he served as secretary to the National Film Board, where he honed his communications skills and political smarts.[73] He was replaced in 1954 by George Carty. Smart, funny, and affable, Carty enjoyed a reputation around Ottawa as a "good fixer." Both men were young, smooth, and well educated, and were responsible for drafting letters, writing speeches, and arranging Martin's appointments. They were assisted by an able secretarial group. This included the lively Betty Neill, who could forge Martin's signature so well that she often signed his letters home to his mother, and Marjorie Frank. Frank remained with Martin until 1968, eventually managing both his office and his household operations and budgets.

Though Martin inherited his two deputy ministers from Claxton, the fit was almost perfect. Donald Cameron, the deputy minister of health, hailed from progressive middle-class stock in Peterborough, Ontario. Born in 1899, he was the son of a country doctor who established the region's first collective medical clinic in 1905. A veteran of the First World War, Cameron graduated from Queen's Medical School in 1927 and the University of Toronto's School of Hygiene in 1928, with a diploma in public health. He was calm and precise, "a man of independence and fairness, who spoke forthrightly."[74] Most of his career was spent as a federal public servant, which left him a little "conservative-minded" and skeptical of fads, which he dismissed with sarcasm and good humour.[75] Claxton, who promoted Cameron from director of medical services to deputy minister of health in July 1946, described him as being "of modest character[,] wide knowledge [and] ability and undoubted acceptability."[76] He got along well with Martin, carving out a niche for himself as the team's voice of moderation.

Cameron was nicely offset by his younger colleague, George Davidson. The deputy minister of welfare, who was only thirty-seven in 1946, was much more of a policy activist. Like Martin, he had pulled himself up from a modest background through hard work and had devoted his career to social reform. The child of a general-storekeeper in rural Nova Scotia, whose working life was cut short in his late twenties by illness, Davidson attended the University of British Columbia and Harvard University on loans and scholarships, graduating in 1932 with a PhD in classics. His dissertation, on the Greek playwrights Euripides and Menander, was written entirely in Latin.[77]

Davidson returned to the West Coast in the midst of the Depression and worked at directing a series of local social and welfare agencies. He was head of the Canadian Welfare Council from 1942 until 1944, when Claxton recruited him to serve as the first deputy minister of welfare, responsible for implementing the Liberal government's family allowance promises.[78] Handsome, hard-working, and intelligent, Davidson was a skilled administrator and a charter member of the elite group of bureaucrats, or "mandarins," that seized control of Canada's public service during the world war. But he had qualities that set him apart from his peers. His early years with non-governmental welfare councils left him with sharper political antennae than most deputy ministers, which suited Martin perfectly. His progressive views also distinguished him from the financial whiz kids whom Deputy Minister of Finance Clifford Clark had recruited to manage Canada's wartime and postwar economy. He disparaged "Clark's boys" as "an imposing line-up of money economists with hardly a drop of humanitarian blood in the lot of them."[79]

Martin's office was youthful and tight-knit, united by a shared conviction that government should be mobilized to secure the well-being of the most vulnerable members of Canadian society. But working for Martin was not easy. His day began as early as 5:30 a.m., often with a swim to exercise his crippled arm, and lasted well into the evening. "He pushed himself very, very hard, all the time," recalled an advisor from the 1950s, and he expected his staff to do the same.[80] He could be brusque and cranky, especially when stressed, and he rarely thanked his staff for their efforts. Instead, he often responded to their memoranda and papers with endless demands for more detail, leaving them resentful and feeling that they had somehow failed him.

He treated his staff almost as family, and he made the same kinds of "extraordinary demands" on them that he sometimes made of Nell. His reluctance to let good staff leave for better jobs was legendary, and even Lester B. Pearson, who thought of making Davidson his deputy minister of external affairs in 1954, declined to tackle Martin regarding the issue.[81] He loved the telephone and routinely called public servants at home – early in the morning, late at night, through the weekend, bypassing the normal chain of command. He hated being alone, and he dragged junior officers to meetings and events, where they carried his bags and lit his cigars. And everyone who ever worked for him resented his habit of assigning two or three officers individually to draft the same speech or statement. They saw this as wasteful and duplicitous, evidence of a lack of faith in their abilities. It diminished Martin's standing among public servants.

For those who could endure the pace, working with Martin was rewarding. His office was a hive of activity, enlivened by a current of humour and punctuated by the constant flow of visitors on government, constituency, and Liberal Party business. Martin's heavy demands were more than balanced by his generous interest in the people around him. He frequently surprised staff with gestures of personal kindness, dropping by their homes with warm regards or interrupting business trips to visit parents, assuring them what a good job their son was doing in Ottawa, Washington, or New York. These men found working for Martin to be a profoundly "human experience," and they hoarded stories of his essential humanity. They remember rushing to a northern airport with the minister's dentures frozen in a cup left overnight on the hotel windowsill, or briefing him in a hotel room as he paced barefoot across the floor. "That," recalled one senior advisor, "was the earthy Paul Martin from Pembroke."[82]

More importantly, Martin was a consummate professional. He had strong views on the proper division of labour between politicians and civil servants, for whom, in fact, he had a great deal of respect and admiration. "It is not for the public servant to govern or to appear to govern," he insisted in his memoirs. "That is the job of those chosen by the people."[83] He worked hard to familiarize himself with departmental business, but he left day-to-day operations in the competent hands of his deputy ministers and their professional administrators. Writing in the mid-1950s, Claxton described the Department of National Health and Welfare as "one of the smoothest running outfits I have ever seen ... It could run on its own without much ministerial interference or guidance."[84]

In the mornings, Martin arrived at work prepared to govern, his briefing books read and understood. He made it clear that he was there to take initiatives, and he looked to his advisors for help. These were powerful incentives for public servants, who enjoyed a real voice in policy making under Martin. "The people around me," he told an interviewer, "had a great deal of influence. This is inevitable. Why have them there if they didn't?"[85] Davidson, who worked closely with him until 1957 and held several other deputy minister posts during his career, summed up the experience of working for Martin in the decade after 1947. As he told Martin, he was "the most difficult and demanding Minister I ever worked for and at the same time the most worthwhile, the most rewarding ... I have never ceased to believe that the best work I ever did – and ever will do – was done with you."[86]

AT THE END of 1946, the immediate prospects for Martin and his team were not bright. The broad-ranging program for postwar social security that King's party had adopted under pressure from the CCF during the winter of 1943-44 was badly stalled. The detailed proposals from the federal government, bound in a pale-green pamphlet that was inevitably dubbed the "Green Book," included a national health insurance plan and a universal contributory old age pension. Funded by Ottawa, these were to be run mainly by the provinces. In exchange for a free hand with provincial taxes and duties, Ottawa promised provincial governments a hefty annual per capita grant. When the proposals were presented at the Dominion-Provincial Conference on Reconstruction in August 1945, there were howls of protest in defence of free enterprise and provincial rights from conservative premiers George Drew of Ontario and his Quebec colleague, Maurice Duplessis. The conference adjourned. By the time it reconvened in April 1946, the Green Book proposals, chewed over by officials and repackaged by Drew and Duplessis, were in tatters.

A shift to the right among cabinet ministers and senior finance officials in 1946-47 made it difficult for Martin to pick up the pieces. Many had been skeptical wartime converts to bigger government and had backed increased social expenditures only as a means of forestalling the widely anticipated slide into a postwar depression. With labour already in short supply and inflation running at 8.5 percent by early 1947, the postwar economy was clearly booming. A chorus of voices was beginning to resist the further expansion of government.[87] The bespectacled and brown-suited Doug Abbott, who was promoted to finance minister in the December 1946 cabinet shuffle, was certainly no reformer. "His instincts were on the right," argued R.B. Bryce, then an assistant deputy minister of finance, and Abbott favoured tax cuts. So did his deputy, Clark, and other key economic advisors Sandy Skelton and Mitchell Sharp.[88] By the winter of 1946-47, cabinet was increasingly divided as influential ministers tilted to the right, convinced the Liberal government should slash high wartime taxes and shed its "socialist" hue before becoming trapped in the growing anti-communism of the early Cold War.[89]

Martin's most pressing priority in early 1947 was the old age pension. Canada's pensions rested on legislation passed twenty years earlier, which provided for a monthly stipend of just twenty dollars for Canadians who had reached the age of seventy. Ottawa paid 75 percent, and the provinces contributed the balance. The small pension was administered on the basis of a means test, which limited a recipient's total allowable annual income to $365. To meet wartime inflation, pensions had been raised by a 1943 Order-in-Council to twenty-five dollars a month, and the yearly income allowance was increased to $425. In addition, under wartime regulations, provincial supplements were no longer counted as part of the allowable income. During the federal election campaign in 1945, King promised legislation to incorporate these improvements into the Old Age Pensions Act. With the Order-in-Council of 1943 set to expire in the spring of 1947, speedy action was required.[90]

Martin used the opportunity to press the government for more than the minimum promised by King, though his proposals were not as generous as they might have been had he been a more experienced and confident minister. He tackled King first, reminding him that the government, which enjoyed only a two-seat majority, was "vulnerable." He contended that the Opposition, and many Canadians, would demand a larger pension, a re-duced qualifying age, and the abolition of the intrusive and deeply un-popular means test. The government might even fall on the issue. Martin recommended amendments to raise the old age pension from twenty-five to thirty dollars a month, with Ottawa continuing to pay its 75 percent share, and to increase the allowable annual income to at least $485. These changes would cost the government an extra $14-15 million annually. This was a sizeable increase, he acknowledged, though it fell far short of the $217 million envisaged in the Green Book proposals for a contributory universal old age pension.[91]

King himself introduced Martin's proposals to cabinet in late January, underlining his own interest in the matter. Nonetheless, they encountered resistance. St. Laurent objected, suggesting that the annual allowable income be raised to $600 and that the additional portion of the thirty-dollar pension be shared equally with the provinces. These changes would reduce the cost to the federal treasury and encourage greater initiative among the provinces, which ought to bear more responsibility for social programs. After two days of debate, cabinet remained deadlocked. Ministers agreed to increase the pension rate by an undetermined amount but asked the Departments of National Health and Welfare and Finance to reconsider the proposals from Martin and St. Laurent.[92]

Martin and his officials, Davidson and J.W. MacFarlane, the director of old age pensions, did well in the interdepartmental talks. When the figures were reviewed, it was clear that St. Laurent's formula would yield much smaller savings than anticipated and did not merit the political costs that were involved in shifting the burden to the provinces. The discussions also allowed Martin's department to liberalize the Old Age Pensions Act by removing restrictive citizenship requirements and relaxing the twenty-year residency rule. Although the evidence is sketchy, it seems likely that for a brief moment in early March, emboldened by Gallup polls that showed substantial support for increased pensions and several resolutions in the House calling for fifty-dollar pensions, Martin tried to convince Finance Minister Abbott to go even further. He proposed reducing the qualifying age for a blind person's pension from forty years to twenty years and either increasing the old age pension to thirty-five dollars a month and/or reducing the qualifying age to sixty-five.[93] Abbott was unpersuaded. In late March, cabinet agreed to a thirty-dollar pension with a $600 income allowance, shared with the provinces on the existing 75-25 percent basis.[94] This was better than Martin had initially hoped.

However, his success in cabinet was not repeated in the House of Commons, where he was handled roughly. It was his own fault. Throughout the session, he had boasted in the press of coming improvements in the pension program, including better pensions for the blind. By mid-April, Opposition MPs were impatiently demanding to see the legislation, denouncing the delay as a "disgrace to the country and to Parliament."[95] When the bill finally appeared in mid-June, the reaction to the thirty-dollar pension, which fell short of expectations, was sharp and hostile. Eighteen speakers lined up during the first day of debate to attack the legislation as "puny, disgraceful, miserable, unjust, and iniquitous." The critics included outspoken Liberal backbenchers George Cruickshank, David Croll, Tom Reid, and James Sinclair. The Vancouver North MP, Sinclair, denounced the bill as "a great disappointment to me ... [and] a bitter, bitter disappointment to the pensioners of B.C."[96]

Rising to respond to his critics, Martin made matters worse by losing his temper and charging Tory leader John Bracken with colluding with Ontario premier George Drew to embarrass the government over pensions. The Opposition benches erupted with cries of "Dirty Politics!" and quickly forced Martin to retract his unsubstantiated charges.[97] A drafting error in the resolution that introduced the bill created more trouble. The CCF's wily tactician and long-time pension advocate, Stanley Knowles, unearthed an obscure procedural rule that allowed him to insert into the resolution a provision for a fifty-dollar pension. The clever move forced embarrassed Liberals into a formal vote against raising the pension to this amount. The furor did generate one positive result, however: Martin secured cabinet's support for a last-minute amendment to reduce the qualifying age for a blind person's pension to twenty-one, recovering at least some initiative in the parliamentary debate.

Undaunted by his difficult debut in the House as health and welfare minister, Martin immediately began to cast about for a strategy to revise the government's entire approach to social security. In July, he hired Harry Cassidy, a professor of social work at the University of Toronto, to conduct a thorough rethink of the Green Book proposals. Cassidy was well suited for the job. After earning his a PhD in economics at the Robert Brookings Graduate School of Economics and Government in 1926, the Vancouver native established himself as one of Canada's leading experts on issues of poverty, social welfare, and public health. During the 1930s, he was active in the CCF and worked as director of social welfare for British Columbia, where he became friendly with George Davidson. Teaching at Berkeley and Toronto during the 1940s, he moved easily between the worlds of scholarship, politics, and government. Ambitious and dynamic, Cassidy favoured research and modern management techniques, pursuing "practical, efficient solutions to social problems."[98]

Over the next few months, Cassidy and the department's research division conducted a series of studies on the state of social security in Canada. The work was quietly presented at weekend workshops in October, when deputy ministers Davidson and Cameron and their senior staff joined what was, in effect, a graduate seminar in social policy, run by Cassidy. Uninvited, the rest of official Ottawa looked on from afar and wondered at the "strange things happening in the health department."[99]

Cassidy's conclusions were ready by December. The Green Book model envisioned that Ottawa would act on the package of promised welfare measures only when tax agreements were signed with a majority of provinces containing a majority of Canadians. With Drew of Ontario and Duplessis of Quebec refusing to negotiate tax accords, progress was impossible. To resolve this deadlock, Cassidy swept aside the Green Book model and proposed that Ottawa act alone, arguing that immediate priority should be given to moving ahead with federal health grants to the provinces, which were technically and politically possible. These had formed part of the Green Book proposals on health insurance and were seen as essential to allow the provinces to build up their health services and hospital beds as necessary prerequisites for a full health insurance program.[100] Cassidy insisted that these ought to be accompanied by measures to improve welfare, to extend unemployment insurance, and to introduce benefits for sick workers. A contributory old age pension plan (and other related benefits for the aged), he thought, could wait for two or three years, given the tricky constitutional questions involved, the complex bureaucracy required, and the income security already supplied by the existing means-tested program.

Martin welcomed Cassidy's emphasis on the health grants and made them his priority as well. But his ambitions were larger. He also decided to urge Prime Minister King to pursue a contributory old age pension plan immediately. A federal statement in support of such a plan, provided that the provinces agreed to a constitutional amendment giving Ottawa jurisdiction, would mobilize public opinion, isolate the stubborn provinces, and force them to negotiate. Martin outlined his ideas in a January 1948 letter to King. He wooed him with flattery, reminding King, who had recently indicated his intention to retire in late 1948, of his "long and distinguished service" in pursuit of humanitarian goals. He urged him to crown his career by acting decisively in favour of health grants and a universal contributory old age pension during the forthcoming parliamentary session.[101]

Martin's motives for pursuing such an expansive and ambitious program at that time were complex. Obviously, he was convinced that it would benefit Canadians and their postwar society, and that it would redound to the credit of the Liberal Party.[102] A legitimate element of political self-interest was involved as well. His deputy, Davidson, thought so, and he told friendly reporters off the record that "the only reason Martin was doing this was to win prestige," part of a strategy to position himself as a successor to King's likely heir, St. Laurent.[103] Moreover, he was worried about the cabinet's increasingly conservative outlook, which he feared would become more pronounced with King's departure. "Martin felt he could make more yards with King than he could do with St. Laurent," argued R.B. Bryce, who watched him manoeuvre from his perch as Treasury Board secretary. "Martin," he added, "was a student of tactics as well as social affairs."[104]

But Martin's plan was far too ambitious for King. The conciliatory prime minister was not about to end his career by risking a public spat with Ontario and Quebec over the Constitution. He rejected the notion of moving ahead with a universal contributory pension plan. He was also skeptical of elements in Martin's proposed health program, especially his plan to attack Canada's high maternal and infant mortality rate through free maternal hospitalization. He was appalled by the $40 million price tag attached to the overall health program. Davidson was told to pare it back for cabinet review.

The revised program still totalled $30.0 million, which would be spread across the provinces on a per capita basis. It included annual grants of $625,000 for health planning, $4.4 million for public health, $3.0 million for tuberculosis, $4.0 million for mental health programs, and $3.5 million for cancer. There were smaller contributions of $500,000 each to tackle venereal disease, help disabled children, train health care workers, and conduct public health research. Another $13.0 million per year, slowly declining after five years, was set aside for hospital construction grants.[105] Martin brought his scheme to cabinet on 21 April and 6 May but failed to secure a decision from his cautious colleagues. They sent the plan to a committee of senior officials for review.[106]

Unsurprisingly, the committee favoured the "money economists." Cameron and Davidson faced off against Mitchell Sharp from the Department of Finance, Sandy Skelton from the Department of Trade and Commerce, and J.R. Beattie of the Bank of Canada. They agreed on the small grant for health planning, if its name were adjusted to remove any implication that it was a precursor to national health insurance. The group also agreed on the health grants themselves, which Skelton had helped frame in 1944-45, but most were opposed to the hospital construction grants. The economists worried that building subsidies would be inflationary and that they might end up supplying a demand for beds that was generated by the private-sector insurance industry. The Department of Finance had other concerns: there was no evidence that the grants would lead to new hospital beds that would not otherwise be built; the program crimped the government's capacity to cut taxes; and the construction grants would raise popular expectations that Ottawa would carry forward other expensive Green Book proposals, including a public works program and expanded unemployment insurance.

This opposition disturbed King, who was growing anxious about Martin's ability to push the health program through cabinet. The canny prime minister thought that Martin relied "far too much on inspiring the press" and "loses his influence by talking too much outside cabinet."[107] He also felt that Martin lacked grace when fatigued or under pressure, later complaining that "he gets too impatient and is at times inclined to be rude."[108] On the lumbering train home from Toronto, where he had gone to bury the great Liberal activist and newspaper baron Joseph Atkinson, King decided "to make a strong fight" for the health program, and he took over the file as it headed back to cabinet.[109]

By the time King's ministers met on 12 May to reconsider the health program, his strategy was firmly in place. He met individually beforehand with Martin, Abbott, and St. Laurent, assigning each one a specific role in the cabinet discussion. King himself opened the debate, placing the program in its right historical context as the culmination of his life-long efforts as Liberal leader to advance social security in Canada. He warned his ministers that they should act quickly or they would find themselves trying to catch up to the Opposition parties. He turned then to Martin, who reviewed the three elements of the program in detail and explained the division with Finance. Abbott was next. Acknowledging that "he was defeated before he had begun," he outlined his resistance to the hospital grants. King later reflected with satisfaction that he "did his duty as a Minister of Finance."[110] St. Laurent then played his part, intervening as scripted to support the entire health program, including the hospital construction grants. Taking care not to "rush the pace," King delayed the final decision until the following day, 13 May.[111] Cabinet's approval for the health program was unanimous.

RUMOURS OF KING'S retirement and potential successors had circulated for most of 1947. Claxton, Abbott, and Martin figured on almost everyone's list as the representatives of the next generation. Aging Saskatchewan warhorse Jimmy Gardiner, the minister of agriculture, was also expected to run. Many pundits thought that Justice Minister Jim Ilsley might stand, but he was worn out by his wartime duties as finance minister, doubted his chances, and wanted out of politics. That left External Affairs Minister Louis St. Laurent, whom King favoured, as the likely victor. King respected his judgment and competence as a minister, and valued his loyalty during the war, when he had backed him during the conscription crises. St. Laurent, the prime minister hoped, would be a "new Laurier," bridging the divide between French and English Canada.[112]

Sixty-six-year-old St. Laurent was ambivalent about staying in Ottawa and often dreamed of rejoining his lucrative law practice in Quebec City. But by early September, King and a group of wealthy supporters had convinced him to remain in government and succeed the prime minister.[113] King discouraged potential candidates from seeking the leadership, and by mid-October the field stood virtually empty. As he interviewed Liberal cabinet ministers to confirm this story, *Winnipeg Free Press* journalist Max Freedman told his editor that the "final tip-off (from Paul himself) is that Martin is no longer in the race. He told me he had only consented to make a bid himself because St. Laurent promised to support him. Now St. Laurent is taking it himself. Paul, who is very fond of St. Laurent, expresses his satisfaction with a certain wry grace."[114]

According to a contemporary account, Martin had urged St. Laurent "most strongly" to stay in Ottawa and promised "to swing behind him ... to get him in as leader."[115] Both men understood the implications for Martin of a victory by St. Laurent, a French-speaking Catholic. "Do you realise, Paul," the older man asked, "that this would mean that you would not become leader, neither at the present time, nor at any time in the future; that, in fact, you could not follow me as leader?"[116]

Confident that his chosen successor's victory was safely assured, King announced his retirement at a National Liberal Federation meeting on 20 January 1948, promising a party convention to select a new leader in August. Over the next few days, Claxton, Abbott, and Martin, last and most reluctantly, indicated that they would not run against St. Laurent.

Observers of Martin remained dubious of his intentions. "I don't think Martin is completely resigned to giving up the leadership," Ralph Maybank, his parliamentary secretary, noted in late January. A veteran of the First World War, disgruntled Winnipeg South MP Maybank had damaged his career by opposing King over wartime tariffs and conscription. Martin kept his distance, and the two men were not close. But Maybank was right, though it remains unclear what Martin's ultimate strategy might have been. "Is it possible," Maybank wondered, "that Paul is counting upon other aspirants sowing seeds of dissatisfaction with St. Laurent because he is so old and then having St. Laurent say to Quebec 'Choose Martin'?"[117] Maybank certainly thought so. In any event, Martin made no secret of his profound unhappiness with King's interference in the leadership and with St. Laurent's "royal succession."[118] On St. Laurent's part in the charade, he later commented bitterly, "I never knew any man except perhaps Mackenzie King and Mike [Pearson] who was capable of devising the most amazing excuses for doing something that was downright dishonest."[119] As winter passed into spring, Martin looked for a chance to jump back into the race.

That opportunity flickered briefly during the summer of 1948 as the leadership campaign took on the trappings of a genuine contest. Quebec MP and former cabinet minister C.G. "Chubby" Power entered the fray to denounce the Liberal Party's attachment to "government by boards, committees, crown companies and commissions, all headed or controlled by the same person: Howe."[120] Gardiner, who had nurtured ambitions for the top job since 1935 and enjoyed wide support in rural Western Canada, joined in as well. With solid support from most cabinet ministers, St. Laurent remained well in front, but he no longer seemed quite so invincible. This seemed more apparent after his ineffective intervention in the Quebec provincial election of 28 July, when incumbent Maurice Duplessis trounced the Liberal opposition, winning eighty-two of ninety-two seats.

The prospect of an actual contest, however one-sided it might be, encouraged Martin and his backers, mostly younger members who were dissatisfied with the party's conservative leadership. In June and early July, Ontario Liberal riding associations in Brantford, York West, and Kent selected convention delegates who pledged to back Martin for the leadership.[121] In Essex East, BC MP Jimmy Sinclair, swept along by the emotions of the hometown crowd, declared that Martin was the man to succeed King, while the Windsor MP himself beamed happily on the stage beside him.[122] Martin's office was in direct touch as well with Young Liberals in Vancouver and Toronto, where draft-Martin "boomlets" had emerged by mid-July.[123]

Martin mishandled the pressure on him to run. Most observers realized that he had no chance. His friend and cabinet ally Brooke Claxton was appalled at the idea that he might join the race. "If he does," he wrote a friend, "of course, he will get nowhere, and will make an ass of himself."[124] Painfully anxious not to miss his chance, Martin fatally delayed making a decision. In mid-July, he coyly told his Toronto Liberal supporters that he was "giving the leadership a great deal of thought" but regarded St. Laurent's entry into the race "with great respect."[125] In private, he was just as ambiguous about his intentions. "As to my own personal position," he wrote one supporter, "what more can I say than that I will have to be guided by what I believe to be in the best interests of all concerned."[126]

On the eve of the convention, he continued to send mixed signals. Harold Dingman, an Ottawa-based syndicated journalist with close ties to him, reported that he "still wanted to stand behind St. Laurent ... [but] has told intimate friends that if the pressure gets too great, he will stand alone." Dingman added, "Martin is a worried man; he is jittery about the decision he must make; he is afraid to say yes, afraid to say no."[127] Blunt though it was, this judgment was fair and accurate. As Martin later tried to explain to one of his promoters, Lum Clark, a columnist with the *Windsor Daily Star,* as "long as it seemed there was a good chance he [St. Laurent] would win, I could not move."[128]

As Liberals from across the country assembled in Ottawa on 4 August, there was still no word from Martin. His supporters arrived from southwestern Ontario, telling the press that they would draft him when the convention opened the next day and that they expected him to stand.[129] King, who had managed every aspect of the convention, down to the balloons at the Young Liberal Dance, was alarmed to see Gardiner, Power, and now Martin lining up against St. Laurent. Indeed, he was "shocked" that Martin was not only prepared to run, but that he was "using the press to further his ends and getting a section of Western Ontario worked up in his interest."[130] King feared that the Catholic vote might be split among the three French Canadian candidates while Gardiner retained the sizeable, solid Protestant bloc. The result could be a genuine and divisive campaign, fought on religious and ethnic lines.

King promptly attacked on two fronts. He asked Howe and several cabinet colleagues to join the leadership contest and to publicly withdraw their nominations in favour of St. Laurent. He also asked Pickersgill to intervene with Martin and to persuade him to issue a firm statement that he was pulling out of the race and backing St. Laurent. Martin acquiesced, though the retreat was difficult for him. When King beckoned him over to thank him, he was stiff and ungracious, muttering only, "I have done it."[131]

His humiliation was not yet complete. Next day, as King rose to bid farewell to his party, sixty Martin supporters, including his law partner and close political associate, Keith Laird, left the Chateau Laurier Hotel and marched to the convention site in Lansdowne Park. Led by a kilted piper and waving large pink placards, they tried to burst into the Coliseum as the prime minister spoke. As one sharp-tongued Ottawa "player" observed, their effort was "cruelly inept, so preposterously vulgar."[132] Martin rushed offstage to the back of the hall. "Please fellows," he begged, "if you want to help me, don't do that. I appreciate your attitude and your loyalty, but please don't do this to me."[133] The group was quickly hushed and the convention wrapped up as scripted. St. Laurent was elected by 848 votes to Gardiner's 323 and Power's 56. A few days later, Martin and Nell slipped out of Ottawa, retreating to the cottage in Colchester.

Martin consoled himself, then and later, by reflecting on his successful convention speech, which had impressed many delegates. It echoed with the dynamism and liberalism of the apprentice minister who had recently given Canadians a new citizenship, larger pensions, and better health care prospects. His talk outlined a program of social security reform, including health insurance, and he hoped that its warm reception would commit the party and its new leader to its implementation. But he knew the struggle for liberal reform would be harder now. For many ministers, the convention had weakened Martin's standing in cabinet and done him "serious damage." As columnist Blair Fraser of *Maclean's* quipped, most ministers thought "he stood too long under the mistletoe for a girl who was supposed to be engaged."[134] The convention confirmed, yet again, Martin's driving ambition, suggesting to his critics that he would allow personal goals to overwhelm his political judgment.

5

A LIBERAL IN A HIGH-TORY CABINET, 1948-52

On his return from the Colchester cottage, Martin was dogged by rumours that he would soon abandon Ottawa for the leadership of Ontario's troubled Liberal Party, floundering again under another of Mitch Hepburn's forgettable successors. There is no evidence, however, that he was ever really tempted by the lure of Queen's Park. Instead, he spent October 1948 dutifully campaigning in federal by-elections in northern Ontario and rural Saskatchewan. He tramped through Algoma East for External Affairs Minister Lester B. Pearson, his rookie cabinet colleague, and rallied Liberal voters in the riding of Rosthern, a long hour's drive north of Saskatoon. "I have never yet seen a political figure make a finer impression on the university student body," one grateful host later wrote Allan McLean, secretary of the National Liberal Federation. Martin savoured the compliment.[1]

Martin, whom Prime Minister Louis St. Laurent kept on as his health and welfare minister, also impressed University of Toronto students the next month, when he was the honoured guest at a Hart House debate on the adequacy of Canada's social security program. His side lost, but Martin hardly seemed to mind. As the audience gathered around him in the student centre, so familiar a part of his own school days, he relaxed and joked about his recent loss at the leadership convention in August. "When I was a young man, I wanted to be prime minister or a cardinal," he recounted, adding with a sly grin, "Well, I now know, I can't be a cardinal."[2]

His resurrected confidence in his future goals reflected the country's buoyant mood in the final months of 1948 and early 1949. News that Canada, the United States, and their West European allies were making steady progress toward a North Atlantic Treaty, a new kind of democratic partnership to halt Soviet Cold War aggression, was greeted with relief and optimism. The country was cheered when Newfoundland signed the Terms of Union with Canada, clearing the way for it to join Confederation as Canada's tenth province in the spring of 1949. The postwar economy hit its stride that year, boasting full employment and stable prices. "Canadians as a whole have continued throughout the past year to enjoy higher standards of living than ever before," crowed Finance Minister Doug Abbott, as he presented his spring budget on 22 March.[3] The "sunshine budget," as it was dubbed, cut high wartime taxes, increased personal exemptions, and delivered an $87 million surplus.[4]

At least some of that surplus, Martin thought, ought to go toward improving Canada's social security programs, especially old age pensions. The pension problem was twofold. First, though Ottawa remained wedded to its wartime proposals for a national contributory pension plan, it had made no progress toward that goal since federal-provincial talks had collapsed in 1946, leaving itself exposed to criticism. The time had come, Martin encouraged Prime Minister St. Laurent in March 1949, for Ottawa to seek the constitutional amendment required to establish its plan, setting aside the program's details until later. If certain provinces refused to permit federal encroachment on their pension responsibilities, movement on this front would at least demonstrate to Canadians that they, not Ottawa, were responsible for the unsatisfactory aspects of the pension system.[5]

Second, there was an immediate problem with the current monthly pension. This had been raised in 1947 to thirty dollars a month, of which Ottawa paid 75 percent and the provinces the balance. But that amount was proving insufficient, after almost two years of inflation. Martin wanted to increase the basic pension to thirty-five or even forty dollars a month, adjusting as necessary the amount of additional outside income allowed under the means test. He also wondered if the government should not reduce the age eligibility from seventy to sixty-five, bringing Canada's pensions into line with those of most English-speaking nations. Though he favoured this step, he warned that the additional costs of a thirty-five-or a forty-dollar pension would be enormous.

His views, which exceeded the recommendations of his departmental advisors, failed to convince his boss. St. Laurent was reluctant to court trouble with the provinces over the Constitution, especially because a federal election was due later that year. This ruled out progress on contributory pensions.

The prime minister was almost as skeptical of Martin's recommendations for more generous pensions and asked him to review his proposals. Ottawa's hand was forced in April, however, when Ontario's Progressive Conservative government raised its pension contribution from $7.50 to $10.00 per month, noting tartly that this would represent a 25 percent share of a joint monthly pension of forty dollars. In addition to recommending a forty-dollar monthly pension to keep up with Ontario, Martin's revised proposals urged St. Laurent to reduce the female eligibility age from seventy to sixty-five, adding 71,200 pensioners to the rolls.[6]

St. Laurent remained unconvinced. Even so, he allowed his minister to bring his recommendations to cabinet. The political imperative to respond to the pension hike in Tory Ontario was overwhelming, and ministers quickly approved a forty-dollar pension. They declined to increase the level of allowable outside income, thus diminishing the impact of the elevated pension, and refused to reduce the age of eligibility for women, citing difficulties in administering a gender differential.[7]

Martin's pension increase was before the House of Commons by late April, when the prime minister finally called the long-anticipated federal election for 27 June. Determined to avoid Liberal charges of obstructionism – the Progressive Conservative House leader urged MPs to "show the old people what we can do in half-an-hour" – the Opposition parties scrambled over themselves to ensure the pension's speedy passage before the House dissolved.[8]

Martin was well prepared for campaigning. He had leased campaign offices in December and had since been busy speaking at Liberal nomination meetings across southwestern Ontario, where he was the responsible minister. In the run-up to the election, he escorted cabinet ministers C.D. Howe and Brooke Claxton through the region. In mid-March, he laid on a "flamboyant" reception in Windsor for St. Laurent, who delighted audiences with partisan attacks on the Tories for their "two-faced" approach to the North Atlantic Treaty, which they framed differently in pro-alliance Ontario and isolationist Quebec.[9] Locally, at least, Martin and the Liberal Party seemed invincible.

The *Windsor Daily Star* tried to spark some interest in the local race. It reminded voters that redistribution had adjusted the borders of Martin's Essex East riding, reducing his sympathetic French Canadian vote.[10] It played up the strengths of his challengers, heroic Dieppe veteran Russ Turnbull for the Tories and Windsor alderman William Riggs for the CCF.[11] It was still no contest. On 16 May, sitting in the back of an open sedan, Paul and Nell followed the Tecumseh Band and a dozen drum majorettes down Esperance Road to St. John the Baptist Hall, where four thousand voters turned out to nominate a Liberal candidate for Essex East. When the nervous chair closed nominations prematurely, Martin himself interrupted. "No, no, no," he remonstrated, "Have you anyone to nominate beside me?" The crowd roared its approval.[12]

Throughout the campaign, locally and in a series of national broadcasts, Martin highlighted Liberal accomplishments: pensions, family allowances, health grants. And more was coming, including contributory pensions without a means test and a national health insurance program. In the week after his nomination, he brought the message to Newfoundland, where he and Premier Joey Smallwood signed an agreement that extended Canadian pensions to impoverished Newfoundlanders. In June, Martin headlined Liberal rallies in North Bay and Sudbury, and then swung through Belleville, Newmarket, and Oshawa. Making as many as six speeches a day, the veteran campaigner attacked Tory leader George Drew for relying on support from Quebec premier Maurice Duplessis and his Union Nationale. The two arch-conservatives had been most responsible for derailing Liberal social security plans in 1945-46. What, Martin demanded, were they up to now, with their secret "tie-up"? He spent the last two weeks of the campaign in western Ontario, where he welcomed visits by Howe and St. Laurent, and in Windsor, where large crowds at campaign events confirmed the unbeatable Liberal tide.[13]

On election day, St. Laurent's Liberal Party swept to victory, winning 192 of 262 seats, and just under 50 percent of the popular vote. Martin polled over sixteen thousand votes, an outright majority that was almost double the tally of his closest rival. Liberals took 18 of 24 seats in western Ontario, defeating nine Conservative incumbents. The *Toronto Star Weekly*, which had backed St. Laurent, was optimistic. It celebrated the victory as a clear "people's mandate," calling on the Liberal government to continue with a progressive program of national development and social security. Pension reform and health insurance were at the top of its list.[14] The *Vancouver Sun*, however, feared the large Liberal contingent from rich, established Ontario, and fretted that perhaps Canada had elected "a Tory government without Drew."[15]

The Vancouver paper was closer to the mark. Like most ministers, Martin liked and respected the well-mannered and considerate St. Laurent, who unfailingly acknowledged birthdays and significant events with fatherly notes and warm telegrams. They differed over policy, however, and St. Laurent's cabinet, largely inherited from King, favoured the status quo. Sixty-nine years old and increasingly subject to bouts of depression, St. Laurent was inclined to resist the changes in Canadian society that Martin wanted most. A corporate lawyer who had spent his successful career catering to Quebec's insular and well-to-do establishment, St. Laurent believed that families and provinces, especially Quebec, were better equipped than Ottawa to provide for an individual's welfare in hard times, sickness, and old age.

He was impervious to the flattery and calculations of partisan political advantage that had worked so well with King. Martin tried this approach once or twice and gave it up. The cabinet's oldest and most senior ministers shared St. Laurent's conservative outlook. His second-in-command, Trade Minister C.D. Howe, was certainly no fan of government welfare; he sometimes hailed his younger Windsor colleague with a scornful, "Well, here comes Paul, the savior of mankind."[16] St. Laurent also heeded the advice of his cautious and skilful finance minister, Doug Abbott, who rarely lost a cabinet battle. These powerful voices of restraint were echoed by Jimmy Gardiner from Saskatchewan, James MacKinnon from Alberta, and Fisheries Minister Robert Mayhew of British Columbia. Behind their backs, Martin ridiculed them as "Howe-ites."

Martin's allies were younger and less influential. Defence Minister Brooke Claxton was an important supporter, but his attention was increasingly drawn elsewhere by the Cold War and his personal struggles with alcohol and depression. External Affairs Minister Pearson was helpful as well, but he was often away, and his views on domestic issues were discounted, to his great distress. Other sympathetic backers, including Veterans Affairs Minister Milton Gregg and Revenue Minister James McCann, were weak and ineffectual. As a journalist once quipped, Martin stood almost alone as "a Liberal in a sometimes high-Tory cabinet."[17] Clearly, if he hoped to reform Canada's social security system, he would have a fight on his hands.

SUMMER BROUGHT A welcome break for Martin and the annual holiday at the Colchester cottage with Nell, young Paul, and Mary Anne. The holiday was cut short in mid-August, however, when Martin was named vice-chairman of Canada's delegation to the fourth UN General Assembly, representing the country at the Economic and Social Council. This minor role quickly assumed an unexpected profile. Soon after arriving at the temporary UN headquarters in Lake Success, just outside New York, the delegation head, Lester B. Pearson, was elected chair of the Assembly's political committee, which left Martin as the main Canadian UN spokes-man. He made the most of this chance to demonstrate his foreign policy credentials.

In the fall of 1949, the United Nations was more deeply divided than ever. The Cold War became more fraught every day, intensified by the North Atlantic Treaty, signed in April, the summer's crisis over Western access to occupied Berlin, and Soviet atom bomb tests in September. In China, the insurgent forces of communist leader Mao Zedong finished their long march to power. At the United Nations, the clash pitted the Moscow-led communist bloc against the United States and its allies in a series of increasingly acrimonious debates. Martin defended the world body as humanity's "best available hope," citing its social and economic work, and pointing to its successes at reducing conflict in Palestine, Indonesia, and Kashmir. "I have been impressed with this conviction," he assured Can-adians over CBC Radio from New York, "that though so many of our agenda items involve the threatening split between East and West, the important thing is that both East and West are here to discuss them."[18]

At the same time, Martin, the former varsity debater, thrived in the rough-and-tumble of the Assembly's debates and its Cold War atmospherics.

Sensing that the Western democracies, their citizens, diplomats, and states-man alike, were tired of Soviet bullying, he resolved not to be cowed. He emerged as the lead speaker behind a Western resolution that accused Soviet satellites in Eastern Europe of curtailing religious freedom, and he won headlines across Canada for his assault on their "ruthless arbitrary measures."[19] He baited the Soviet Union's UN ambassador, Andrei Vishinsky, and scolded him for his tiresome speeches. "I think another hour and a half of Mr. Vishinsky twice within two days," he quipped, "is perhaps something more than human endurance can tolerate."[20] The Department of External Affairs billed the emerging East-West confrontation as "Mr. Martin versus Mr. Vishinsky."[21]

The bitter quarrel between the two men climaxed in mid-November. When Vishinsky attacked the North Atlantic alliance and Western dis-armament proposals, Martin responded with an unusually frank con-demnation of Soviet faults. For forty-eight minutes, switching between English and French, he confronted Vishinsky straight across the UN conference table and explained why the Western world feared the Soviet Union. He outlined the frightening implications of communist notions about the inevitability of East-West war, and he described deep Western concerns about a totalitarianism that crushed and isolated "the free play of moral, intellectual and spiritual forces upon which the Western world has grown."[22]

When he finished, Western diplomats crowded around to offer their congratulations. The Canadian delegation's switchboard lit up with more than a hundred telephone calls, all but two supporting Martin. At home, there was plenty of editorial backing, though most of it lumped Martin and Pearson together. The *Victoria Daily Times* described Martin's speech as great, but its approval was qualified. "It will be understood, of course," wrote the *Times* disdainfully, "that Mr. Martin was taking up the cudgels on behalf of the Hon. L.B. Pearson."[23] The *Toronto Daily Star* was gener-ous in its praise. "Martin stole the show," it declared, insisting that his "speech was of exceptional importance and confirmed Canada's reputa-tion as one of the principal exponents of the Western powers."[24]

Despite the Cold War raging in New York, security and defence were not yet the watchwords they would soon become. The Liberal government remained preoccupied with economic and domestic issues. There was little reason for Martin to return to Ottawa while the General Assembly dragged on from September to December, and he rarely did. He made sure he was home, however, when the ad hoc cabinet committee on the federal-provincial conference gathered behind the green baize doors of the Privy Council Office's committee rooms in late October. Weeks earlier, the prime minister had invited his provincial counterparts to meet in January 1950 to discuss a made-in-Canada amending formula for the Constitution, striking a cabinet committee to undertake the preparatory work. Whereas St. Laurent was anxious to limit the talks to constitutional issues, Martin saw the meetings, the first federal-provincial gatherings since the Green Book proposals were killed in 1946, as a chance to reinforce Canada's social security efforts. He warned that restricting the agenda would be "extremely difficult." The premiers, especially the CCF leader in Saskatchewan, would want to discuss social security questions, and Ottawa ought to be ready with its policies defined.[25]

He was persuasive. With his backing, Health and Welfare officials overcame the lingering skepticism of Norman Robertson, clerk of the Privy Council, and by late November, three senior-level committees were examining unemployment insurance reform, old age pensions, and health insurance. A standing Interdepartmental Committee on Social Security was created to supervise their efforts in late December, when it became apparent that the work would not be completed for January's constitutional conference. Operating under this administrative structure, with Martin hovering in the near background, officials began to overhaul Canada's social security program, hoping to have a federal package to replace the 1945 Green Book proposals by the fall of 1950, when a second federal-provincial conference, on tax sharing and fiscal questions, was to be convened.[26]

Martin's mood soared. Although cabinet did nudge defence spending upward in the new year despite his opposition, this was not the victory claimed for Claxton by his biographer.[27] The increase was small, and keen-eyed officials, keeping careful score, acknowledged the strong demand in Canada for more social security spending.[28] Off the record, Martin confidently assured journalist Bruce Hutchison that Ottawa was moving "into the big social security field. It has scrapped all its Green Book ideas … [and] proposes to advance into old-age retirement and health insurance in stages." Questioned carefully, he admitted that cabinet had not yet reached a final decision, but he "had no doubt about approval because ... St. Laurent already approved his plans."[29]

Martin was overstating his case. Progress on the three working committees was uneven. Arthur MacNamara, the capable deputy minister of labour, and his committee made quick work of plans to extend unemployment benefits, which cleared the House of Commons in February. The committee on health insurance, under deputy health minister Donald Cameron, made some headway as well. The committee, which included Mitchell Sharp from Finance and economist Sandy Skelton from Trade and Commerce, met every few weeks between December and February. Its initial efforts concentrated on probing estimated per capita costs for health insurance, forcing Cameron to revise his annual costs upward from $25.95 to $28.30 per person.[30] It also tackled the tough problems associated with determining which health services should be offered when, weighing national standards against anticipated provincial demands for flexibility.[31]

Persistent unspoken tensions regarding the cost of the program divided Sharp and Skelton from Cameron and his officials. Even so, by spring, the committee had agreed on a possible program for health insurance, which Martin reviewed carefully and approved as it moved through the committee. In its first stage, provinces could choose from a menu that included diagnostic, general practitioner, and hospital services. Diagnostic services, alone or in combination with either of the other two, would have to be part of the initial offering. All three elements would have to be available within five years, though the plan allowed provinces to implement the program on a regional basis. Ottawa's share of the bill, to be divided with the provinces on a fifty-fifty matching basis, was estimated to be $128.4 million. The proposed health insurance plan was sent to the senior interdepartmental committee in early June for its approval.[32]

There was less progress on old age pensions, under George Davidson, the deputy minister of welfare. He favoured a simple universal pension without the hated means test, which was difficult to administer, humiliated the elderly, and discouraged individual thrift. Others, including Martin and Finance mandarins such as Mitchell Sharp, wanted a national contributory plan. This, too, would eliminate the means test. It would also link contributions to payments, which, it was hoped, would put a brake on rising expenditures. However, it would require a costly administrative apparatus and would exclude the 40 percent of Canadians who were non-wage-earners.[33]

The deadlock left the government without firm plans when the House of Commons gathered in February 1950 amid mounting popular opposition to the existing means-tested pension. This was especially unfortunate for in the winter of 1949–50 Canadian trade unionists wanted access to the big industrial pensions that were increasingly available to American workers. With help from church groups and CCF associations, the Canadian Congress of Labour flooded the capital with a million postcards demanding its abolition. Anticipating the Opposition's onslaught, Martin and St. Laurent pondered the wisdom of referring the matter to a parliamentary committee, a decision they reached in February. Martin chose the Liberal representatives on the joint committee of twenty-eight MPs and seven senators, and St. Laurent nominated one of its co-chairs, the ambitious backbencher from Montmagny-L'Islet, Jean Lesage. The other chair, from the Senate, was J.H. King, the former labour minister who had guided Canada's first pension bill through the House of Commons in 1926.[34]

The committee was hard-working and effective. Its main Progressive Conservative spokesman, Donald Fleming, later recalled with satisfaction that it "toiled long and arduously, and ... constructively."[35] Veteran Winnipeg MP Stanley Knowles of the CCF thought it was "the best committee he had yet served on."[36] The reform-minded David Croll, Martin's old Windsor ally from the 1930s, emerged as the group's leading Liberal. Between 3 April and 23 June, it held thirty-eight public and fourteen private hearings, and reviewed 1,334 pages of testimony from the country's main business, labour, and welfare bodies, as well as from several provinces. Officials from the Department of National Health and Welfare described the current plan and its shortcomings, and presented detailed studies on state pension plans in eight other countries.[37]

Davidson and Sharp were assigned to work with the committee, where they clashed over the merits of their preferred options. Davidson's arguments in favour of a universal pension gradually won out over Sharp's vision of a contributory pension with a small universal supplement. Behind the scenes, Croll sought CCF backing for a universal scheme and pushed Knowles to moderate his party's demand for a pension of fifty dollars a month at age sixty-five. Knowles retreated, but in exchange demanded government help for impoverished retirees who were between sixty-five and sixty-nine years of age. Under the watchful eyes of Martin, St. Laurent, and Abbott, whom they consulted, the two men traded figures and nailed down the details, confident that any accord would garner the support of the other parties.[38]

The result was a unanimous report that recommended a universal pension of forty dollars a month at age seventy, to be paid by Ottawa, and a means-tested pension of forty dollars a month at sixty-five, to be funded equally from the federal and provincial treasuries. The scheme would cost as much as $338 million in its first year; Ottawa's share of this would be $256 million, a substantial increase over the $100 million or so that it was already spending on old age security. Although the new pensions would be paid from general revenues, St. Laurent insisted during his talks with committee members that the plan include provisions for a special contribution, or dedicated tax, from employees and employers to maintain the contributory principle.

With plans for health insurance and pension reform safely winding their way through the system, Martin could ease into his summer break with a deserved feeling of accomplishment. After packing Nell and the children off to the Colchester cottage in time for the summer's first weekend, he travelled to Dalhousie University to receive an honorary degree, the kind of joyous award that he was beginning to collect with some frequency. When troops from communist North Korea suddenly marched over the border into South Korea on 25 June, he saw little reason to change his plans. US president Harry Truman rushed to provide fighter cover for South Korean forces, which were already in full retreat, but cabinet reacted with less urgency. Half-convinced that South Korea was lost, Canadian ministers dispatched a token force of three navy destroyers in late June before quitting town for the summer. Martin spent the first lazy weekend of July in Pembroke, with his sister Anita and his mother, and then joined his family in southwestern Ontario.

Over the next few weeks, a sense of foreboding gathered as South Korea grimly held on and pressure for a stronger reaction to communist aggression mounted in New York and Washington. The crisis finally erupted on 14 July, when UN secretary-general Trygve Lie issued a public call for

UN members to contribute ground troops to the US-led effort in Korea. St. Laurent summoned his ministers back to Ottawa, only to find them divided and uncertain. Many, like Defence Minister Brooke Claxton, favoured doing nothing, worried that the Korean conflict was only a "side-show," a communist effort to divert Western attention from the real prize, Europe. Pearson, more aware of the strength of American feeling and anxious to reinforce the UN role in the crisis, urged a more forthcoming response. Ministers struggled for compromise, eventually sending Pearson to Washington to seek assurances about American Cold War strategy.[39]

Martin's focus lay elsewhere. He flew back to Ottawa with Nell by his side, acutely conscious that his plans for social security reform were now threatened by the crisis in Korea. The *Winnipeg Free Press*, the steely voice of pragmatic Prairie liberalism, was already warning that "these are not normal times. They are times of shooting war and mortal danger ... The Federal and Provincial Governments would be wise, under these conditions, not to embark hurriedly on a costly pensions scheme and a sharp increase in taxes until the immediate military situation has clarified."[40] On 19 July, when cabinet gave Claxton permission to expand Canada's Armed Forces, stuffing an extra $40 to $50 million into his budget, many observers concluded that war had "tipped the scales against further advances toward the welfare state and old age pensions."[41]

Martin fought back in public and private. Alarmed at newspaper stories that buried the joint committee's plan for a universal pension, George Burt, the Canadian director of the United Automobile Workers, asked Martin for public assurances about the scheme and its impact on recently won union pensions. He promptly got them.[42] When Pearson returned from Washington on 2 August with news about American grand strategy and proposals to raise a brigade group for use with either NATO or UN forces in Korea, Martin dug in his heels. Pearson won the round, but he privately criticized Martin as the "big obstacle ... who fought hard against doing anything in Korea." Canada's top diplomat mocked the health minister for "always making eloquent speeches on collective security but want[ing] to do nothing about it in a pinch."[43]

Martin was unrepentant. He returned to the fray in mid-August as cabinet wrestled with the rapidly rising bill for its defence budget, which was now expected to top $1.447 billion for 1951-52, an astronomical share of the total federal budget of $3.759 billion.[44] "There would be considerable feeling," he reminded his colleagues, "that, if large new expenditures could be undertaken for defence and to discharge international obligations, something could also be done for old age security."[45]

The fate of social security spending remained undecided as cabinet turned its attention to the special parliamentary session that opened on 29 August to address Korea and a crippling national railway strike. The diversion was short-lived. Ministers revived discussion of social security amid preparations for the upcoming federal-provincial conference in mid-October. The debate pitted Martin against Abbott, the finance minister. On health insurance, the fragile peace between Martin's department and Finance, which had supported the June proposals, shattered under the impact of the war in Asia. Finance officials insisted that the plan's figures were uncertain estimates at best and implied that the scheme relied on the self-serving judgments of medical experts in Health and Welfare. They even charged Health and Welfare officials with being unsure about which services should have priority, a damning indictment that was partly true.[46]

Finance's opposition to pension reform was just as strong and deep-rooted. Abbott and his deputy, Clifford Clark, confided to sympathetic journalists that they were both "dead against the committee plan to raise pensions."[47] New taxes to pay for pensions would "throw the whole budget into chaos," throttling economic growth. Pensions would drive up inflation, channelling cash to those Canadians, the poorest, who were most likely to spend it and stoking a "semi-war" economy already running close to full tilt. The two Finance men were confident that the pension scheme would be delayed, with Ottawa "kidding the public and exercising masterly footwork." Just to be sure, they enlisted the help of the *Winnipeg Free Press,* which targeted social security spending in a biting editorial on the "crying need for stern government economy."[48]

Almost weekly, from mid-October to mid-November, Martin gathered his deputies and senior officials in his Jackson Building office to plot strategy. His first priority for the federal-provincial conference, he told them, remained agreement on old age pensions. He was certain of success: "If the present war situation does not badly deteriorate, he did not see how we can fail to go ahead."[49] The group rehearsed the case against Finance's warnings about the inflationary dangers of the parliamentary committee's pension scheme, asserting that the impact would be much smaller than estimated. Most of the pension money, some $250 million of the proposed $385 million expenditure, was already being spent in one form or another on pensioners. The extra funds would not be ready for distribution until the end of 1951 at the earliest, delaying the onset of any inflationary pressures. Moreover, failure to implement the universal pension would force Ottawa to bump up its current pension to forty-five or even fifty dollars to cover recent price hikes. Davidson and Martin pressed these views on their deputy minister and cabinet colleagues but without much success. Abbott, Clark, and their allies squirmed uncomfortably and sought compromises to make the scheme less costly and more palatable. They gave little ground. As mid-November approached, the outcome remained uncertain.[50]

Martin had plans for health insurance as well, though he acknowledged that its approval was now unlikely. Taking a long view, he insisted that "health insurance ideas should be brought out so that we could get a high priority for them immediately after the decline in our defence needs."[51] At a minimum, he hoped to establish a federal-provincial committee to work on health insurance and advance his agenda. He also wanted provincial backing for new legislation to place the 1948 health grant program on a statutory basis, with a more flexible set of governing procedures.[52] To achieve these two objectives, he kept health insurance on the cabinet agenda. When St. Laurent told ministers on 23 November that "there was not yet sufficient hospital accommodation or qualified personnel to implement a national health scheme at this time," Martin demurred and promised fresh proposals before the next meeting to overcome these objections.[53]

Cameron, whose staff was hard at work shaving pennies off cost estimates, bundled the health grants legislation and a revised insurance scheme into a single package. This included a novel bid to introduce health insurance on a province-by-province, rather than national, basis. Since only Newfoundland and the Western provinces were likely to join in the next few years, the cost would be a mere $15.0 million in the first year, rising to $30.5 million in year two.[54] Cameron unveiled this cheaper and more flexible scheme before a very surprised group of deputy ministers on 27 November. Unfamiliar with its substance, they avoided specifics. Sharp grimaced with disapproval on procedural grounds. The surprise *démarche* left Norman Robertson, the cabinet secretary, "somewhat at a loss."[55] In the end, he suggested that Martin himself raise the matter with the Cabinet Committee on Federal-Provincial Relations when it met to finalize federal policy before the premiers arrived in early December.

In two meetings, on 28 and 30 November, St. Laurent's cabinet committee speedily resolved the stalled debate over the short-term future of social security in Canada. Martin was not disappointed. He pitched his newest health insurance proposal but quickly pulled it from the table. Given the government's other financial commitments and policy worries, he would not "press" for approval. Nevertheless, he hoped that cabinet would instruct the Interdepartmental Committee on Social Security to keep the proposals under study so that Ottawa would be ready to move forward on health care when the time came. This seemed sensible, and ministers promptly agreed. There was not much debate over pensions either. The politics were compelling, and taking the chair at the second meeting, St. Laurent simply declared that Ottawa would tell the provinces that it was willing to implement universal pensions as outlined by the parliamentary joint committee if they agreed on the necessary constitutional amendment.[56]

Martin was pleased with his pension victory, and he joined the federal delegation that greeted the premiers as they arrived on Parliament Hill on 4 December. Yet compared to Claxton, Pearson, and Abbott, who set the tone for the gathering with grim statements on the global crisis and its financial implications, he played a small role. Down the hall from the main proceedings, in the Centre Block's historic Railway Committee Room, he chaired a subcommittee of provincial ministers who were charged with reviewing the technical issues associated with the proposed pension changes. He parried their questions skilfully, but the main business lay elsewhere. No province dared oppose the popular federal scheme, though Quebec, Alberta, and Nova Scotia were still uncommitted when their premiers left town three days later. St. Laurent himself brought them round over the next few months, clearing the way for a constitutional amendment in the spring.

THE PENSION FIGHT left Martin exhausted. Just after Christmas, which the family spent with Nell's sister in Windsor, he set off on a long-anticipated holiday to Jamaica with an old Windsor friend, drugstore owner Fred Holmes. Nell, who returned to Ottawa with the children, hoped the trip would revive his spirits and encourage "the stirrings of ambition again or a much better perspective."[57]

Soon after arriving in Montego Bay, Martin and Holmes were summoned to stay with the Canadian-born British press baron and former politician Lord Beaverbrook. This was Martin's first encounter with the fading Conservative, whose enormous wealth, influence, and worldly experiences overawed him. His high regard and deep affection for the "Beaver" echoed his youthful attachment in the 1920s to Hart House warden Burgon Bickersteth. "He was in every way a remarkable man," Martin recalled in the 1970s. "One of the most intriguing and able men that ever lived."[58]

He was genuinely fond of Beaverbrook. "I don't want to be too fulsome," he told staff as they drafted a note to his friend, "but I like the man. I think he is a genius and I want to say so."[59] Martin made no secret of his unabashed admiration. "You will never fully appreciate what knowing you has meant to me," he gushed to Beaverbrook in 1952. "Living under your roof, conversing with you, and meeting so many of your guests, will always be among my most pleasant experiences."[60] "I miss you terribly," he wrote after one visit. "Is this too boyish a thing to say? Your talk, your company – is the most stimulating thing I have ever experienced and I wish you were close by so that it could be repeated often."[61] Beaverbrook responded warmly to Martin's fondness, and over the next decade or so, he treated Martin and Nell to annual winter trips to his Bermuda estate of Cromarty and welcomed them to his home in Fredericton and his suites in New York's renowned Waldorf-Astoria Hotel.

That first Christmas encounter gave Martin's spirits a badly needed lift. The holiday also gave him time to take stock of his life and career. At forty-seven, he was content: "1950 has been a busy one, and very happy one too," he wrote Nell from Bermuda. "You have been painstaking and understanding. How much I have to be thankful for. A family to be proud of, a wife to hold up as the best a man can have."[62]

Martin's family was changing and growing. The household at 448 Daly Avenue, where they had moved during the hectic summer of 1950, included Paul's sister Anita, who supervised the children when their parents were away, and sometimes a live-in domestic. Paul Jr., twelve years old, was "fighting adolescence," laughed Nell, adding that "with a husband at one end of it, and a son starting something, Mama walks on eggs."[63]

She thought that a dog might help, and Togo the Boxer joined the household.

Nell grew more devout as she aged, and religion retained an important role in family life during the early 1950s. The children attended the local French Catholic school, École Garneau, run by the Oblate fathers, and the family normally headed down Stewart and up Cumberland Streets to St. Joseph's Church for Sunday morning Mass. Like her mother-in-law, Nell was fond of reminding her children that there were only three vocations: religious life, teaching, or politics.[64]

Easygoing Paul got on well with his parents. Even as a young adolescent, subject to fluctuating bouts of "tears, temper, sensitiveness & laughter," he responded to Nell's efforts to nurse him through a minor illness with a card earnestly addressed to "the greatest Mom in the world."[65] He later recalled that Nell's lively presence "created the glow of good fortune around my childhood that I still feel today."[66]

He was close to his father, too, and took his frequent absences in stride. He was old enough to travel with Martin to Windsor and to visit him, unaccompanied, at work. Martin was delighted when Progressive Conservative leader George Drew noticed his son, "a fine looking lad ... I was glad to meet him and see his bright-confident-young face so full of hope for the future."[67]

Mary Anne was different. She was still very young, barely seven, and she found her parents' increasing absences tougher. More introspective than her brother, she had a strong and "exuberant" personality of her own. "Mary Anne," Nell wrote her husband dryly in January 1951, "pursues her own inimitable way."[68]

Martin was home for the parliamentary session that opened at the end of January 1951. As they assembled in the Commons, the MPs were reserved, and their wives attended the Throne Speech dressed mostly in black, as if to emphasize the country's seriousness of purpose faced with the continuing war in Korea. China's intervention in the war, and ham-handed American efforts at the United Nations to brand Beijing an aggressor, threatened to escalate the conflict into a general war. The international crisis meant more trouble for Martin. In late February, officials in National Defence convinced cabinet to transfer responsibility for civil defence planning from their department to his. Leery of civil defence's desperate need for money, just as their military requirements exploded, defence planners argued that Health and Welfare, which enjoyed close relations with the provincial and municipal authorities that shared responsibility for this file, was better placed to ensure welfare services in the event of a war with the Soviet Union or a civil emergency.

The press, acknowledging Martin's strong leadership skills, welcomed the change. *Saturday Night* magazine thought that giving this important file to Martin, with his "remarkable energy," was "clearly sensible."[69] Initially, he embraced the assignment. When Federal Civil Defence Coordinator Major-General Frank F. Worthington briefly encountered his new boss, he wrote to a colleague with obvious satisfaction of Martin's "very active interest."[70]

Underfunded and disorganized, civil defence was a troubled dossier. The Federation of Mayors and Municipalities was already upset at Ottawa's unwillingness to find the necessary dollars to stockpile emergency supplies, train police and fire-fighting services, and build shelters against a possible attack by Soviet bombers. Delegates to the Dominion-Provincial Conference on Civil Defence, where Martin's role was unveiled, muttered quietly about Ottawa's lack of support. Ontario premier Leslie Frost and Provincial Secretary Arthur Welsh were less reticent, and as Martin settled in, they lashed out. "Ottawa kicks civil defence around and clearly implies it is unimportant," Frost protested. "Yet it then tells us to tighten our belts and dig up five billions for the defence program."[71]

Martin hoped that demonstrable progress would blunt the criticism. In April, he pressed officials at a meeting of the interdepartmental Civil Defence Coordinating Committee to begin deploying air raid sirens in cities across Canada. He opened the new Civil Defence College in May with a rousing high-profile call for Canadians to take up their civil defence duties, delighting Opposition MPs, who dubbed him "the Windsor warrior."[72] Later in the summer, on his return to Ottawa from a meeting of the Joint Canada-US Civil Defence Co-ordinating Committee, he summoned Worthington, Davidson, and Cameron to his office for a scolding. "For God's sake," he told them, "let's get these damn sirens going so that we can give the people ... some indication that we are doing something. We are doing a great deal, but people do not know it, and one reason is that they do not hear these loud noises."[73]

With little funding and continued sniping over who was responsible for what, progress was elusive. When Montreal produced an elaborate civil defence plan in August, with a cost pegged at the fantastic figure of $363 million, Martin was dragged into another spat with local authorities. He was similarly embarrassed when Ontario municipalities, including Windsor, endorsed a resolution demanding that Ottawa assume the full cost for civil defence. Frustrated by the lack of political support, Worthington erupted during a press conference at the end of the summer when asked by reporters why Canada's effort had stalled. Pointing toward Parliament Hill, the general growled, "The trouble lies behind you!"[74]

Martin quickly rebuked Worthington, parading him before reporters to assure the country that the Liberal government was "doing all that it can."[75] Canadians were unconvinced, and Martin's efforts to persuade them otherwise met with a cool, even hostile, reception. "Mr. Paul Martin has come and gone without adding much to the sum of everyman's knowledge of civil defence," carped the *Victoria Daily Colonist* after a civil defence visit to British Columbia. "There is nothing in what he said to set at ease the feeling that Ottawa takes civil defence in a rather casual fashion."[76]

Martin, who later described his experience with civil defence as "a frustrating assignment" and "a real headache," increasingly ignored both it and Worthington, who became the butt of staff jokes in the office.[77] For his part, Worthington complained to his diary that consulting Martin was difficult, that his Treasury Board submissions lingered unsigned, and that he no longer enjoyed his minister's confidence.[78] Despite Worthington's objections, in early 1952, Martin and Davidson crafted a $1.4 million program for shared federal-provincial civil defence grants, a funding effort designed to remove the sting from criticism of Ottawa's inaction in a time-honoured way. "The federal government can now back out very gracefully and throw the owness [sic] on the province," Worthington noted bitterly, "but that does not solve our problem, nor foster better progress in civil defence."[79]

CIVIL DEFENCE WAS not merely a source of frequent and unfamiliar criticism – it was a drain on Martin's time and a distraction from the real business of building the welfare state. Since the spring of 1951, he had completely immersed himself in Ottawa's efforts to roll out the new pension program.

He met twice with his provincial counterparts to iron out administrative details and forestall their carping. He guided the first pieces of legislation through the House in June and took an active hand in managing the successful (and politically sensitive) drive to register the 400,000 applicants for the universal pension. The effort won him scarce credit, though he was attacked for tying himself so closely to the distribution of government funds. Using the fictional persona of Mrs. Noggins, journalist Bruce Hutchison mocked him, unfairly but with deadly effect: "Yes sir, Paul is my favourite statesman. And 'e don't need no public relations, 'e don't need even to talk because the money talks for 'im."[80]

During the summer, Martin was also embroiled in a renewed dispute with Finance Minister Abbott over how to fund the expanded pensions. By July, Abbott faced a huge surplus of over $500 million (out of an overall budget of $3.8 billion), and he proposed to dip into it to pay for the pensions. This little expedient would allow him to balance his budget and avoid imposing the social security taxes recommended by the parliamentary joint committee. Martin was appalled. With good reason, he was convinced that pensions could survive only if they reflected the contributory principles implicit in a dedicated tax. He favoured raising the money through a supplemental income tax, and he opposed Abbott's plan.[81]

Relations between the two men were further strained by Abbott's refusal to ease his anti-inflationary restrictions on consumer credit, which were killing the country's auto industry. As Canada boomed, twelve thousand Windsor workers were handed pink slips, and their city slid into recession. The outraged mayor, Martin crony Art Reaume, had a curt message for Ottawa: "You're not going to flatten Windsor."[82] Martin understood, and he organized a series of meetings with union, industry, and civic leaders during August.[83] These culminated in a summit with Abbott, Howe, and sympathetic labour minister Milton Gregg, whom Martin convinced to establish a special committee of deputy ministers to tackle job placement in Windsor and to reduce barriers to re-employment elsewhere. And if that didn't work, Martin promised, Ottawa would ease its credit restrictions. Abbott was "very annoyed."[84]

The two ministers remained at odds for most of September, jostling for tactical advantage. Martin tried to force Abbott to bring his plans for financing pensions to cabinet, where he himself enjoyed some support.[85]

Abbott insisted on keeping them private, confident that the prime minister would side with him.[86] He was right. St. Laurent favoured a contributory system, but he worried that Martin's funding model would be "expensive and extremely cumbersome." He backed Abbott's compromise proposal to earmark 2 percent of the existing 10 percent sales tax for pensions, and to add 2 percent levies to income and corporate taxes, with any immediate shortfall coming from general revenues.[87] With the funding disagreement resolved, Martin's bill for universal pensions sailed through the House with all-party support and passed third reading on 8 November. Mitchell Sharp, one of social security's great skeptics in Finance, offered Martin his congratulations. "Mitchell," he replied earnestly, "that wasn't my objective. My objective is medicare."[88]

That goal seemed tantalizingly close. In June of 1951, the prime minister had mishandled a question on the government's attitude toward recent proposals by the Canadian Medical Association (CMA) for a national voluntary health insurance plan run by private industry. St. Laurent's qualified support for the scheme ran counter to the Liberal Party's long-standing promise of a public plan, prompting Opposition demands for a statement of government policy. It fell to Martin to reply. As he and St. Laurent walked to their seats in the House of Commons, they hastily agreed that Martin might disarm their critics by indicating the government's willingness to "consider" a second joint committee, this time to look at health insurance.

A joint parliamentary committee on health would lead inexorably to public health insurance, and cabinet split over the question of striking one. The debate raged during the autumn and into the winter of 1952 as ministers prepared their legislative agenda for the coming session. Waging an "extensive campaign" for cabinet support, Martin was confident.[89] So were his deputies, Cameron and Davidson. Cabinet might stall for a year, Davidson insisted with quiet confidence, but "we shall certainly have it in time."[90] By February, Martin and his staff were outlining the committee's structure and tasks, and drawing up a timetable for the introduction of national health insurance in 1953.[91]

Martin's conservative opponents were "astonished" that St. Laurent had conceded so much, and there was "strong opposition" in cabinet to the proposed committee.[92] They cited the hefty cost of health insurance and recent pension expenditures. One "high level source," possibly from Finance, speculated that the plan was doomed because of its inflationary impact.[93] Martin's anonymous critics found willing allies among the staff of the *Winnipeg Free Press*, whose editorials were intended "to persuade Parliament to think hard on this subject before plunging into another gigantic and incalculable cost."[94] The views of the shy and inarticulate fisheries minister, Robert Mayhew, were important. A close but often underestimated confidant of the prime minister, Mayhew warned St. Laurent that "the country had bitten off more than it could chew" and could afford "no more gigantic new commitments like health insurance."[95]

As the opposition mounted, St. Laurent wavered. "He had made a mistake," he confessed to Mayhew, "and had wrongly given the impression that he intended to go ahead with [health insurance] in the near future."[96] In late February, the prime minister himself raised the question in cabinet. He made two points. The government simply did not have the money for an expensive health program, which would have to be left to the provinces. Moreover, as the country still lacked sufficient hospital capacity to meet even current demands for care, offering health insurance to Canadians would just not be right. The government would have to tell the House that it had considered but rejected the idea of a committee on health insurance.[97]

That unpopular task was assigned to Martin. Although he accepted St. Laurent's judgment as "realistic," it hurt nonetheless, and his brief account of the episode in his memoirs conveys his lingering bitterness at his betrayal and public defeat.[98] "So far as health insurance is concerned," the clerk of the Privy Council, Jack Pickersgill, gloated with his friends at the *Winnipeg Free Press*, "I would hand it back to the Indians."[99] The retreat signalled a halt in the growth of Canada's postwar welfare state, and it gave Canadians a chance to consider the unfamiliar and enormous changes of the past decade. Under Martin, federal spending on health care and pensions alone had mushroomed from roughly $97 million in 1947 to $443 million in 1952.[100] For the first time in many years, Martin had no major initiatives in his sights.

THE LEGISLATIVE HIATUS promised an uncommonly relaxing spring and summer for Martin, a promise that was fulfilled – at least initially. At

St. Laurent's request, he spent a few days in February at Vincent Massey's Port Hope estate, welcoming his early mentor home from England as the first Canadian-born governor general. It was a joyful reunion of old friends, which Martin marked by teasing Massey about his distaste for the press and poking fun at his own well-known fondness for publicity. "There will be," he promised, tongue firmly in cheek, "I hope, no fanfare of any sort, but should there be others present ... we will all accept the situation happily."[101] Photos of a beaming Martin shaking Massey's hand were soon splashed across the front pages of Canadian newspapers.

There were other small pleasures that spring, including honorary doctorates from the University of Ottawa and his alma mater, St. Mike's, which marked its centennial by honouring its most successful graduates. Martin's family was pleased by the recognition, whose significance they appreciated at its most profound level. "I shivered a wee bit (with pride)," his mother, Lumina, wrote feverishly. "Who knows! *but with humility also* because God had willed it that you should have done as well."[102]

Canada continued to boom through the spring and summer of 1952. Glib Madison Avenue publicists, planning a series of talks on Canada for Americans, enthusiastically subtitled their program "Nation on the March."[103] Immigrants poured into the country: 74,913 in 1950; 194,391 in 1951; 164,498 in 1952. The gross national product exploded, increasing from $15.5 billion in 1948 to $24.6 billion in 1952, and unemployment declined from 3.6 percent in 1950 to 2.9 percent two years later. Industrial workers saw their annual weekly wage package keep pace, growing from $45.08 in 1950 to $54.41 in 1952.[104] "From Coast to Coast," boasted the *Financial Post*, "Dynamic Growth."[105] An April Gallup poll gave the Liberal government the support of 48 percent of voters, mainly due to the old age pension.[106] Governing was fun. When the Tory member from Eglinton, Donald Fleming, attacked Martin for including his name on departmental publications, the minister twitted his former law school classmate from the fastness of the government benches. "It's just like the old days in college," he laughed. "Donald does not like to see Paul's name ahead of his. Unfortunately, Paul is the minister and as long as he is the minister, he must accept responsibility ... If he accepts the responsibility, he has to have his name on all the pamphlets."[107]

In June, Martin turned forty-nine. From his daughter, Mary Anne, he received a heartfelt "spiritual bouquet," a litany of devotion and self-denial offered up to God for his benefit. Over nine days, the young girl attended fourteen Masses and received Communion and recited her prayers twelve times. She obediently completed all her chores and finished eleven homework assignments.[108] Her neat, handwritten card was eloquent testimony to her parents' exacting standards. However, Martin's doctor delivered less pleasant tidings. He warned Martin, whose five-foot-seven frame carried almost two hundred pounds, that he badly needed to lose weight. Over the next several months, the minister dropped forty pounds and was rewarded with a spot on the list of Canada's best-dressed men for 1952, under the cruel headline "Fat Man Makes Good."[109]

There was time that summer for a long holiday, which began in July at the Colchester cottage and extended into mid-August, when Paul and Nell joined Ontario lieutenant governor Ray Lawson on his luxury yacht, *Osceola,* to cruise Georgian Bay. The trip had barely started when Martin's world was suddenly knocked awry. On 9 August, headlines across the country broke the story of a fake immigrant visa ring operating in Windsor, teasing readers with intimations that a prominent local family was involved.[110] Four days later, when Martin's sister Aline Wald was tied to the scandal, he braced for the assault.[111]

As a private member in the 1930s, Martin had been allowed to carry on his law practice, though the line between acting as a lawyer and acting as an MP could be thin, and determining when it had been crossed was often difficult. At least once, he and partner Keith Laird had accepted a relatively large sum, at least $800, in exchange for their help in obtaining visas and related legal work.[112] The line became clearer when Martin joined cabinet in 1945, and he asked his partners, Laird and the newly recruited Robert Easton and William "Bill" Cowan, not to accept immigration cases for remuneration.[113]

Immigration remained a sensitive topic for Martin. In March 1948, CCF MP Alistair Stewart had mysteriously obtained two letters from his files, hinting at his pre-war work, and deep in his cups one night, had threatened to use them. Martin and Laird hastened to cover their tracks, and a sober Stewart decided not to release the material, which had apparently been stolen from Martin's offices.[114] At about the same time, Martin learned that Aline had set herself up as an immigration consultant in Windsor, trading off the family connection. As each incident would tend to raise questions about the other, Martin was livid. Terrified, Aline turned for help to a local priest, who urged Martin to give her "proper supporting direction," using "discretion and brotherly understanding."[115]

This was asking a great deal. Martin tried unsuccessfully to convince his sister to cease her activities and even used his influence, slashing through government red tape to set her up in a legitimate business. In the end, he severed contact with her in August 1949 and made it clear in writing to American consular authorities in Windsor that her visa work was entirely unauthorized.[116] But rumours continued to dog Martin. They echoed the allegations of sharp practice from the 1930s and were undoubtedly reinforced by Windsor's early 1950s reputation as a city of easy virtue. In the spring of 1952, the Conservative newspaper editor Grattan O'Leary, angry with the way in which Martin had used one of his editorials to attack Drew, warned the minister that he was "preparing a dossier on you and your connection with – curiously enough – immigration, whatever that may or might have been."[117]

Don Emerson, Martin's sure-footed aide, handled the crisis as it unfolded. By 15 August, the *Detroit Times* had linked Aline Wald to Martin, and within a day, it had located an affidavit that described her efforts to help clients obtain false statements of their net worth to circumvent American visa rules. Groaning that "the worst has happened," Emerson insisted that Martin stay out of town and keep his mouth shut.[118] And he made sure that Martin's friend Harold Vaughan, publisher of the *Windsor Daily Star*, remained supportive. He positioned Martin ahead of the breaking news by promising the *Star* an inside track on his side of the story, as well as his 1949 correspondence with the American consul general on Aline's activities. Returning to Windsor on the evening of 17 August, Martin gave the *Star* its interview, which ran the next day alongside the first stories confirming US Justice Department interest in Aline. Martin was treated with warmth and sympathy, which set the tone for much of the coverage that followed.[119]

The Canadian press was largely forgiving, and several old friends rallied. Burgon Bickersteth, Mitch Hepburn, and Art Reaume sent their warm wishes. Only Quebec City's *Le Soleil* asserted that Martin was guilty of an "indiscretion coupable."[120] The personal cost was heavier. "It's humiliating for us all," Anita wrote unhappily.[121] Family ties with Aline were broken, and she felt forced out of Windsor. "We will, as far as we know," she told her sister Marie, "go to Vancouver – over 3,000 miles – surely that will be far away where it can't hurt Paul."[122]

THE IMMIGRATION SCANDAL and the health insurance setback cast a shadow over Martin during the fall of 1952, which he spent with Lester Pearson at the United Nations in New York. In the great American metropolis, he sensed the restless mood rattling North America as the continent turned its back on years of crisis-driven reform and settled into a new norm. Change was most evident south of the Canada-US border, where the farmers and workers who benefited most from the Democratic Party's New Deal and Fair Deal marched to the polls in November and voted in their millions for Republican Dwight Eisenhower and a cheap tax cut.

Some observers detected a similar stirring in Canada. The Liberal Party, which had not lost a single by-election between 1945 and 1951, lost three seats in May 1952 and had its vote totals trimmed in three other contests. Martin's friend, the businessman and movie magnate Paul Nathanson, linked the party's shaky fortunes to high taxes and the war in Korea. Journalist Bruce Hutchison thought the change was more deeply rooted and argued in a year-end review that Canadians had turned on the welfare state, tired of costly government programs in an era of high defence spending.[123] His view was echoed among the Liberal elite, whose conservative-minded cabinet representatives had fought Martin over universal pensions in 1950 and defeated his plans for health insurance in the spring of 1952.

Martin, who won five dollars from his secretary by betting on Eisenhower, thought otherwise. Liberals, north and south of the forty-ninth parallel, he argued, had simply forgotten their fundamental reform values. "We cannot be content to stand on past laurels or to sound the bugle for wars already won and forgotten," he told Nathanson. "The Liberal Party has to be dynamic, changing its program to meet changing needs and changing conditions."[124] As 1952 passed into 1953, he worried whether St. Laurent's party was capable of the dynamic renewal that he hoped to see.

6

THE GREATEST COUNTRY
IN THE WORLD, 1953–56

Louis St. Laurent's government seemed tired as the new year dawned, justifying Martin's apprehension. His own winter and spring were busy but not very productive. From February to April, he bunked at the aging Drake Hotel in midtown Manhattan, minding Canada's UN delegation and restlessly flitting back and forth across the border. There was little to do in New York but stand by as Beijing digested an Indian resolution on Korea, against a backdrop of endless Cold War bickering. Martin waited patiently, his faith in the United Nations undiminished. "I can appreciate how such a slow-moving, talkative body must disturb a man of action," he wrote Lord Beaverbrook. "I am disturbed too ... But it is the beginning of something which some day will be as permanent a fixture on the international level as law and its institutions are in national communities. This observation may infuriate you. But it is my conviction, and I know you would want me to say so."[1]

There was even less to interest Martin in Ottawa, where the Liberal government was tidying up its legislative agenda in anticipation of an election, now rumoured for June. Finance Minister Doug Abbott produced another "sunshine" budget that balanced the books and trimmed the tax bill. Nell's judgment, delivered in a scribbled note to Martin from the parliamentary gallery, reflected the national consensus (as well as the country's deep postwar yearning to carry on with normal activities): "Pappy dear ... The children alone. Come on Home. Budget a huge success."[2]

The only significant blemish on the government's record was in the defence ministry, where reports of corruption and mismanagement were slowly destroying the political career of Martin's friend and rival, Brooke Claxton. "It was my impression," reporter Grant Dexter joked grimly, "that Paul had sufficient to bear any trouble that might overtake Brooke. But hurt to the government was something else again."[3]

Martin contributed his own small measure of progressive policy to reinforce Liberal fortunes. Denied access to additional revenues, he persuaded the prime minister to let him retain the money from the hospital construction grants program, which was set to decline from $13.0 million to $4.5 million annually between 1953 and 1958 under the terms of the 1948 health grants. He proposed using this money to fund new grants for maternal and child health work, diagnostic facilities, and rehabilitation services, just in time for a spring vote.[4] The measure struck the sort of judicious balance between fiscal responsibility and progressive government action that appealed to postwar Canada. It sailed through cabinet and guaranteed the health minister smooth passage through the House of Commons debate on his departmental estimates when he unveiled the plan in mid-May. A month later, on 12 June, St. Laurent called an election for 10 August.

Martin was unsure that this was the right call. He worried that ten thousand Ford workers in Windsor would be on holiday in August and not around to vote.[5] There was no need for concern, however. The Canadian economy remained strong, buoyed by the incoming flood of American dollars and riding the final wave of the postwar commodity boom. Soviet dictator Stalin's death in March and a Korean armistice in early July signalled a welcome easing in global tensions. Canadians, many of whom were British in origin and outlook, basked happily that summer in the reflected splendour of Queen Elizabeth's coronation. "It would have been nice to attend," Martin sighed wistfully as senior colleagues abandoned Ottawa for London's Westminster Abbey. He settled instead for a long weekend of fishing at Frank Ahearn's place on 31-Mile Lake in the Gatineau Hills, before heading back to Windsor, where he led his neighbours in Tecumseh in three cheers and a blessing for the queen.

The evening the writ was dropped, Martin kicked off his campaign in Dave Croll's downtown Toronto riding of Spadina before taking a seven-day tour through the Prairies. He was back by mid-June to help St. Laurent launch his party's national campaign with a rally in Windsor, chosen as a "typical" Canadian community. As Liberal organizers had hoped, the visit was a hallmark Martin event. Nothing was left to chance. Long before the party leader arrived, the Windsor arena was stuffed to overflowing with three thousand Liberal activists, and a local high school teacher warmed up the eager crowd with practice cheers. With sirens screaming, a police escort whisked St. Laurent's motorcade through the city to the arena, where he was greeted by fair-skinned beauties, black railway porters, and kids from Windsor's tiny Chinese Canadian community. During the rally, which was broadcast nationally, the live audience was prompted with placards reading "loud applause and cheers" and "quiet in 15 seconds." For many visiting Liberals, it was all a bit much. Jack Pickersgill recalled being "staggered" by the hoopla.[6] Martin's "American electioneering methods," one Liberal worker later reported, "shocked us." Worse, they shocked the members of the staid Canadian press, who "were not impressed" and who criticized the "Martin machine."[7] Like so much else, the rally set Paul Martin apart as different.

"Uncle Louis" floated above it all, delivering a stately, if uninspired, speech that ignored Tory leader George Drew and focused on the litany of Liberal achievements since 1945 – family allowances, health grants, old age pensions, peace and security, and so much more. He left the politics to others. Martin was a popular campaigner and he spent mid-July criss-crossing Ontario, from Windsor to Belleville, and north to Pembroke and Sault Ste. Marie. As Liberal strength grew, Tory promises mushroomed, prompting Martin to mock George Drew for changing his tune from "Anything You Can Do I Can Do Better" to "Oh, Promise Me."[8] He delighted in pointing out the obvious contradictions in the Tory platform: "They claim they can ... spend more and save more, up budgets and down taxes, go into the red and yet stay in the black."[9] The attacks hurt. With three weeks to go, Claxton summoned Liberal ad men to Ottawa, declared that "the election was in the bag," and reeled in the party's campaign budget.[10] Martin cancelled plans for a swing through the Maritimes and focused his energies on re-election in Essex East.

His campaign in Windsor followed its usual course. On 29 June, almost 2,500 constituents milled about Tecumseh's St. Jean Baptiste Hall as Nell and Paul pulled up in an open convertible. A union worker and Woodslee farmer nominated the candidate, and the Leamington Town Band banged out "For He's a Jolly Good Fellow." There were new twists in 1953. Martin toured his riding on a truck with a self-contained stage, offering music, dancing, and a variety show alongside "old time politics." In the bars that dotted the Windsor waterfront, the Paul Martin Singers, sixteen young entertainers – the men wearing tight gabardines and flowery shirts, the women in shorts and "halter-bras" – serenaded bemused patrons with "Our Paul Is the Only Man For Us."[11]

As always, Martin himself remained at the core of his effort, and he relentlessly sought out voters whenever he was in town. One July Sunday, with the temperature soaring to ninety-one degrees, he made fifteen campaign speeches. Asked why he pushed so hard, he grinned, wiped off the sweat, and grunted, "Have to, it's a matter of prestige."[12]

His principal opponent was a tough-talking Progressive Conservative alderman, Al Kennedy, who had grown up with Martin in Pembroke. Kennedy flailed away at Martin for providing "milk for the Hottentots and igloos for the Eskimos" but doing little for Windsor. The charge played on local feeling that Martin spent perhaps a little too much time at the United Nations, but it was so demonstrably false that he did not bother to respond.[13]

A desperate Kennedy finally resorted to unproven allegations that Martin's main aide, Don Emerson, had taken a 5 percent cut from a government contract awarded to a Windsor company. Martin's reaction was swift and forceful. He tied Kennedy directly to the company partners who were circulating the charges and attacked their credibility by forwarding their criminal records for fraud and theft to Harold Vaughan, publisher of the *Windsor Daily Star*. He also produced a letter from their lawyer John Reycraft (the same Osgoode Hall classmate who had arranged his own contract with the City of Brantford in 1933), which cast doubt on their story. The tale nevertheless set Liberal tongues wagging in Ottawa, where it fuelled doubts about Martin's integrity. If any St. Laurent minister was taxing contracts to fund his political campaigns, Pickersgill suggested later, it was Paul Martin.[14]

The story had little currency in Windsor, where the facts were known and doubts were few. On voting day, 10 August, Martin polled 19,711 votes, a remarkable 67 percent of the ballots cast in Essex East. His three competitors lost their deposits. These results reflected the national trend. St. Laurent's government was swept back into office with 171 seats and a comfortable majority. Martin was jubilant, and with almost a hundred cars in tow, he left his campaign headquarters early and toured 125 miles through Essex East, finally arriving, near midnight, at the Maidstone home of his early backer Alice Shanahan. Standing on a chair under a single porch bulb, puffing on his eleventh cigar of the day, he surveyed his two hundred workers and sighed, "Canada is the greatest country in the world. Make no mistake about that."[15]

MARTIN DESERVED TO take some well-earned pleasure in his decisive victory. By 1953, his political organization – he bridled at the term "machine" – had given him a commanding presence in Windsor and restored his standing as a plausible contender for the federal Liberal leadership. In the wake of the 1953 election, John Bird, the syndicated columnist for Southam News, surveyed the recent careers of five rising stars from the cabinet of August 1948. Abbott, of course, remained the favourite to succeed St. Laurent. Three of the others – Claxton, Transport Minister Lionel Chevrier, and Justice Minister Stuart Garson – had been bruised by scandal and unpopular policies, and were out of the race. Bird considered Martin, whom many had written off after the disastrous 1948 leadership convention, as the cabinet's "surprise success story."[16]

Martin's strong suit remained retail politics at the local level. Despite his heavy ministerial duties, he kept in close touch with his voters, marking the milestones in their lives with phone calls, cards, and letters. They responded in kind, sharing their hopes and worries, confident that they would receive a careful hearing. "It comes in handy knowing that we can write you like this," confided Mildred Roberts, who told him of the challenges she faced in dealing with a badly burned eye and the difficult birth of her first child. "We appreciate it very much, and if you ever need a favour, I'm sure we'd be glad to help."[17]

For his most important backers, there were small gifts, often the semi-exotic detritus of diplomatic and political life: ticket stubs, faded invitations, old programs. In 1956, shortly after his twentieth anniversary as a parliamentarian, Alice Shanahan, to whom he had sent a rose plucked from atop King's casket in July 1950, recalled an exchange with profound satisfaction.

"Alice," Martin had said to her when first elected, "if you ever see me getting the big head, tell me about it." "Well Paul," she wrote twenty years later, "I have never had to say anything pertaining to you getting the 'big head' … You will be [sic] the same Paul Martin as in 1935."[18]

As a cabinet minister with staff, Martin used structured and sophisticated methods. He broadcast bimonthly reports of his activities on Windsor radio station CKLW, which were second in popularity only to the classic Sunday evening sitcom *The Great Gildersleeve*.[19] Each fall, beginning in 1945, his supporters organized the Young Liberals Dance at Lakewood Golf Club, a massive undertaking that attracted as many as two thousand patrons. As the music blared and couples swirled, Martin worked the room, shaking hands and assuring folks that "I wouldn't have missed it for the world."[20] The dance was the single event on Martin's political calendar that Nell never missed.

By the mid-1950s, Martin's staff maintained a list of eight thousand active backers and kept close tabs on the ethnic and civic groups that defined Windsor life.[21] He opened the German Club, toured the Jaycee Transportation Show, laid the cornerstone for St. George's Romanian Orthodox Church, and marched each May through the streets of Windsor with the thirty-thousand-strong anti-communist Blue Army of Our Lady of Fatima. He also made sure that the choir in Maidstone's thirty-member Negro Congregational Southern Baptist Church enjoyed appropriate accompaniment, buying it an old upright piano that cost him thirty dollars.[22] His message to these groups was upbeat and deeply rooted in his own experiences. He preached above all the value of civic tolerance, in Canada and abroad, and celebrated individual human spirituality as the elixir that would defeat the Godless materialism of Soviet communism.

He stayed in touch when he travelled. From UN headquarters in New York, his staff sent a steady stream of personalized letters to "every doctor, lawyer, and Roman Catholic priest in Windsor."[23] His mailing lists, which carefully targeted local opinion makers, included poll captains, labour leaders and bishops, rabbis and ministers, and small-town editors and high school principals across southwestern Ontario. The letters typically assured recipients that Martin was working hard, offered a candid glimpse into UN operations, and affirmed his faith in their continued value. Whatever happened, he promised earnestly, he would do his best.

He did his best for Windsor's general welfare, too, and by the mid-1950s, there were new post offices in Walkerville, Tecumseh, and Belle River, with an extension tacked onto the main Windsor post office for good measure. "It was after the insistence of your Member of Parliament, the Hon. Paul Martin, and your senator [Gustave Lacasse]," Postmaster General Edouard Rinfret told a small group of Windsor voters as he stood beside a smiling Martin in a cold March wind, "that we finally agreed to give you this wonderful building."[24]

He fought Abbott and Chevrier through 1951-52 for changes in the Municipal Grants Act to permit Ottawa to pay East Sandwich a grant in lieu of municipal taxes for land that was occupied by the federally owned Windsor airport. He returned to the fray in 1954, extracting another $135,000 from the Transport Department to relocate a road that had been disrupted when the airport expanded. He lobbied the Canadian National Railway for a modern train station, and he convinced the transport minister to pay for breakwaters and dredging to reduce flooding and improve the region's harbours at Belle River, Puce River, and Pike Creek.[25]

Patronage remained part of his political arsenal, one that is largely inaccessible to historians. As health and welfare minister, he enjoyed access to a number of minor offices. His department certified pilots as fit to fly, giving him the authority to appoint the local doctors, invariably Liberal, who conducted the examinations.[26] Working with regional ministers, he managed appointments to the various medical review boards that qualified the blind and the disabled for their federal benefits.[27] He directed departmental work to the Cockfield-Brown advertising agency, which returned the favour by supplying the national Liberal Party with publicity help during federal elections in 1949, 1953, and 1957.[28]

There were richer patronage pickings in Windsor itself, especially following the 1953 decision to expand its airport. Martin's office was deeply involved in the project from the start, overseeing the influx of federal dollars. He spent the spring of 1954 sorting out a tricky dispute over the value of the land expropriated for the expansion, eventually securing hefty settlements for local farmers – and jobs for Windsor land appraisers and lawyers. He made sure that Bud Odette's Eastern Construction company won the bid for the airport's administrative building, and the company and union leaders arranged jobs for key Martin supporters. When Leo

Ryan won a subcontract from Cart Construction, Martin insisted that he share the work with his friends at Sterling Construction. That was just for starters. There were contracts for electrical work, parking and road work, and air conditioning, and for a tenant to run the airport's restaurant and lounge.[29]

Martin's growing influence across Canada did not rest on his patronage operations, but on his extraordinary outreach and information activities. He had always valued good publicity, and as health and welfare minister he had access to the necessary administrative machinery to realize his ambitions. His department's efforts to educate and inform the public and the media exploded during the 1950s under his stimulus. He added staff to its small Information Division, which grew by 50 percent between 1948 and 1956. When its aging director, Lieutenant Colonel C.W. Gilchrist, retired in 1954, Martin replaced him with the more dynamic Harvey W. Adams.

In Martin's first full year as minister, the department distributed its three main periodicals to 126,000 subscribers and sent out an additional 2 million pieces of literature.[30] By 1956, the Information Division was dispatching almost 900,000 periodicals annually and over 10 million pieces of literature, each issued under the minister's name or title.[31] Martin's name, and possibly an encouraging "envelope stuffer" on some aspect of his department's work, arrived monthly in millions of Canadian homes along with their pension and baby bonus cheques. "He is the government's Santa Claus," wrote a journalist, "its good fellow who helps the sick and the aged and the needy. He is the housewives' 'sugar daddy.'"[32]

Martin's portfolio, along with his UN and foreign policy duties, gave him ammunition and opportunities for publicity, outreach, and public speaking. Hundreds of annual grants from his department for hospitals and laboratories, civil defence projects and public health initiatives were accompanied by sheaves of press releases. He shocked Canadian diplomats during one trip abroad by insisting that "every time I get on and off the plane, there's to be a press release, with Canada, Liberal, and Martin, front and centre. And I don't care if you reverse the order."[33]

He crossed Canada, addressing the health professions – doctors, nurses, and public health workers – ethnic and civil defence groups, and labour unions. He enjoyed talking to students of all kinds and was in constant demand as an "A-List" speaker at Liberal rallies. Mostly, he featured his department's current health and civil defence concerns, but many audiences were ready to hear him speak on tolerance and faith and on handling communism, and as a determined advocate for the United Nations. He was easily the most prolific speaker in cabinet, delivering more than 150 speeches every year. The *Montreal Gazette* estimated that he gave more speeches during the 1954 summer recess "than any three other cabinet ministers combined."[34]

He remained, as he had been in his youth, a fluent and effective public speaker, with a "deep resonant voice."[35] His thoughts were clearly organized and substantive. He had grown into his ministerial role, developing "an amazing facility" to take a speechwriter's text, rework it until the words "rolled," and deliver the final product as if it were entirely his own. His staff made a point of recording who drafted his best speeches.[36]

Margaret Aitken, the Toronto columnist and Progressive Conservative MP for York-Humber, described him as the most "adroit" minister at handling probing Opposition members. "He manages to turn the question around so it becomes a plug for his department or for the government," she complained. "Every answer is a miniature speech."[37] As a senior parliamentarian, Martin was courteous and good-humoured, much less prone to erupt into the bad-tempered outbursts that marred some of his early ministerial performances. From 1953 onward, he took his seat in the government's front benches, ever more confident, perhaps even slightly smug and arrogant, about his abilities to turn back Her Majesty's Loyal Opposition. When Pearson apologized for leaving him "stuck" in the House, answering critics at the tail end of the Suez Crisis, he quipped in reply, "Not stuck, Mike, not stuck, because I'll have the answers."[38]

Martin's outreach activities kept him in the headlines. It helped that he worked hard at cultivating friends in the Parliamentary Press Gallery. His contacts at the *Windsor Daily Star,* especially Maurice Jefferies, kept him abreast of developments in the lives of gallery members, and he acknowledged them all with short notes and telephone calls. He understood how the press worked, ensuring that reporters had what they needed to do their job. He was almost always ready to talk, to share tidbits of information and leak secrets to advance his causes. When External Affairs issued his UN statements in "miserable, single-spaced [mimeographs] that are very difficult to read," he had his office retype them for journalists, adding helpful headings and highlighting key passages.[39] Similarly, landing in Ottawa from a trip abroad, he assured the gaggle of reporters who were racing against a deadline, "Don't worry boys, it's all right here in a press release." As one journalist remarked, Martin "has helped create good publicity for his department – and himself – industriously and intelligently by being genuinely helpful."[40]

Martin's success with the media was mixed. He could usually count on a stable of second-tier journalists, often syndicated in smaller papers, to fight in his corner. These included Norm McLeod, Alex Hume, Austin Cross, Gerald Waring, and Charles Woodsworth, as well as Conservative reporters Richard Jackson and Patrick Nicholson. "I often feel I would like to do more for you," confided Cross, "and perhaps put in a plug here and there for your work."[41] Nicholson often contended in print that Martin was a possible successor to St. Laurent, despite the popular view that the Liberal leadership should alternate between French and English Canadians. "I hope," he wrote Martin after one piece appeared, "this is only the first note of a clarion calling delegates away from a pointlessly hidebound alternation."[42] Some, such as Alex Hume of the *Ottawa Citizen*, almost begged for Martin's favour: "Did you not see, or hear about, my by-line Wednesday afternoon saying Paul Martin, by qualification & experience is considered on Parliament Hill to be a natural for External Affairs if, as expected, Pearson goes to NATO etc? My reference was much better & fairer than the Globe editorial."[43]

Martin attracted support from heavier-weights such as I. Norman Smith and Peter Stursberg, but Canada's most influential journalists remained impervious to his charms. Blair Fraser, editor of *Maclean's*, Grant Dexter, editor of the *Winnipeg Free Press*, and Bruce Hutchison, who left the *Free Press* to become editor of the *Victoria Daily Times* in 1950, despised him. Like Pickersgill and Manitoba Liberal senator T.A. Crerar, with whom they were very close, they distrusted his vaunting ambition and doubted his integrity. Though Liberals, they opposed his progressive views on expanding government's role in contemporary life. More importantly, they favoured Abbott and Pearson in the undeclared race to succeed St. Laurent. Martin was initially upset and puzzled by their hostility, a reaction that gave way to anger and scorn. With friends, he made no secret of his dis-like for Fraser, whom a confidant derided as being "at the beck and call of your colleague [Pearson]."[44] He dismissed Hutchison's best-selling books as "repetitive" and irredeemably spoiled by their "purple prose."[45]

His extensive outreach activities brought unwelcome scrutiny. Questions from the post office and the Opposition benches forced him to rein in his mail for a short time, and the Treasury Board probed the activities of his department's Information Division.[46] External Affairs even refused in 1954 to stamp any letters from Martin's UN delegation that were destined for Windsor. "Doesn't it get you going," his staff flared, "when insinuations are made that all the letters Mr. Martin writes are personal?"[47] It bothered him more when the press joined in the laughter that resulted when the unruly Progressive Conservative member for Restigouche-Madawaska, Charles Van Horne, nicknamed him "the Kodak Kid" and berated him as a "two-bit publicity seeker."[48]

Critics found his "practised" speaking style a little flamboyant and thought that he tended to charge ahead "monotonously" without varying his pace.[49] Worse, he proved unable the shake off the earnestness and touch of pomposity that had marked his first speeches at the University of Toronto, flaws that invited teasing and parody. Writing for the *Toronto Telegram*, Margaret Aitken playfully lampooned his style:

> When I asked Mr. Martin what consideration was being given to a request from the Health League of Canada for a larger grant, he answered in typical Martinian fashion.
>
> First he established his martyrdom ("I was in Toronto last Monday and you know what that means!") Then he stressed how hard he worked. (He had received a deputation from the Health League). Finally, he wound up with a well-rounded plug for the Health League – a worthy organization, doing good work, etc.
>
> "But what consideration was being given ...?"
>
> "I am in the throes of consideration," broke in Mr. Martin expansively. And that was that.[50]

MARTIN'S RESPONSIBILITIES AS health and welfare minister began to weigh on him in the fall of 1953. During the election campaign of that spring,

Liberal backing for health insurance seemed to slip, with St. Laurent's unilateral announcement that the party would support provincially administered health insurance only "when most of the provinces are ready to join in a nationwide scheme."[51] For Martin, this was an embarrassing reversal, though he retained his office in the new ministry. As the big causes that animated his first years in the portfolio became more remote, what remained were difficult and frustrating policy challenges with few decisive victories.

This was certainly true, for instance, in the case of extending pensions to disabled persons, a task that St. Laurent, touched by a young Quebecer's heartfelt plea for help, handed him in August 1953.[52] Drafting the legislation – the rules regarding who got money and when – was technically difficult, and Martin struggled with it for the next year. The pensions got him into difficulties with his senior officials over departmental priorities, trapped him in ceaseless haggling about cost sharing with the provinces, and worried his cabinet colleagues, who sensed political trouble ahead.[53] When the new act came into effect in January 1955, backbenchers and ministers protested that the provinces, especially Quebec, claimed too much credit for the joint program and that the pension's conditions, which were too narrow, were angering voters.[54] By the end of 1955, Martin was tired of the pension. "We are taking a lot of stick for the Disabled Act," he told his officials, pleading "is there anything we can do before it comes up at the session?"[55]

Civil defence was also proving a tough nut to crack. Martin had largely ignored it since 1952, when the deadlock in Korea reduced popular fears of immediate global war. Disputes with the provinces over funding and jurisdiction persisted, however, making civil defence an especially difficult file just as news of the hydrogen bomb began to leak out in early 1954. The weapon's enormous power, evident in now familiar images of Pacific atolls dissolving beneath clouds of radioactive dust, revolutionized civil defence. Simply put, "duck and cover" was no longer enough.

Martin summoned a federal-provincial conference for March 1954 to kick-start civil defence planning in the thermonuclear age. The role played to his strengths, and he handled the conference well, communicating Ottawa's resolve to evacuate Canadians from their targeted cities. But over the longer term, he struggled to meet surging public and parliamentary interest in the bomb and its implications. The *Toronto Globe and Mail* identified him as the main reason why "there is still no blueprint for an integrated civil defence program in Canada" and the *Regina Leader-Post* blamed him for "too much dallying."[56] He was badly embarrassed in October when Victoria dissolved its civil defence board and quit the program. "We think [it] … just plain stinks," said an unhappy city councillor.[57]

Spring brought further political woes: probing about nuclear tests and radioactive fallout over Canada. The CCF member for Winnipeg North Centre, Stanley Knowles, always a challenge, began the assault in early March, when he asked if Ottawa would back a request by American scientists for a UN study on H-bomb tests.[58] The question was followed by a flurry of queries from CCF members M.J. Coldwell and Colin Cameron, as well as Liberal backbenchers Tom Goode and F.A. Enfield, all seeking assurances that fallout from US atmospheric tests over the Pacific would not harm Canadians. Martin stalled for more than month before finally assuring the House that his department was aware of the problem and working hard on it. His reply fooled no one, and critics assailed him for his "non-committal" remarks.[59] Moreover, the comments were only partly true. The department did have plans to establish a laboratory to examine nuclear safety, but they had stalled in Martin's office. When Defence Minister Ralph Campney refused to co-sponsor the plan and Finance officials insisted that Martin seek cabinet approval for the project, he had refused to act. He was unreasonably and unaccountably worried that he might be defeated in cabinet. Only after Cameron exerted considerable pressure did he relent and seek cabinet's blessing for the lab in May.[60] He had handled the issue poorly, and he knew it. As the House debated his estimates in steamy July temperatures that topped a hundred degrees, he confessed to a friend that "I managed to get every item through but the last one, and it may be the most difficult of all, as it is the item for civil defence."[61]

But not all the news was bad. In the spring of 1955, Martin helped score a signal victory in the war against polio, which he and his son, Paul Jr., had both contracted as children. By the early 1950s, due to better public health records and tracking, the public perceived polio as a "runaway epidemic," and it became the subject of an extensive North American research effort.

By 1953, Jonas Salk of the University of Pittsburgh had achieved promising results in early tests with a vaccine that consisted of a dead, inactive virus. With help from the University of Toronto's Connaught Laboratories, which developed both a medium to grow the polio virus in quantity and a process for doing so, Salk planned to try his vaccine in large field trials during the summer of 1954, with production to begin the following year.

This presented a problem for Canadian policy-makers. If it were to meet the anticipated demand for a proven vaccine in the summer of 1955, Connaught Laboratories, Salk's Canadian producer, had to begin production in July 1954, six months before the results of the trials were due. Connaught raised the question with the country's deputy health ministers at the Dominion Council of Health meeting in May 1954 and offered to start making serum in July for $1.50 per dose. The deputies agreed to consider the plan, but the provincial reaction was hardly enthusiastic. Anxious to encourage the provinces to take up the offer, Cameron persuaded Martin to share the vaccine's cost with them on a fifty-fifty basis for the fiscal year ending on 31 March 1955.[62]

This did the trick, and by October, when Salk's preliminary results confirmed the safety and efficacy of his vaccine, Connaught Laboratories had already started to make 1.5 million doses in time for next summer's polio season. While officials awaited Salk's final results, expected in April, the vaccine's success created a new dilemma for Martin. Would Ottawa, the provinces asked, continue to share the cost of the vaccine into the new fiscal year? Martin hesitated, intimating that provincial authorities should take over the program "in the usual way." Cameron insisted, however, that the public health benefits were paramount and again persuaded him to find the money.[63] Thus, on 12 April, when Cameron telephoned from the University of Michigan with news that the field trials were a success, Ottawa found itself on the side of the angels. Canadian children lined up in orderly rows for their government-funded inoculations.

South of the border, where the vaccine's distribution was left to the private sector, there was trouble. In a desperate scramble that was marked by shortages and bidding wars, parents rushed to secure shots for their children. Worse, on 26 April, California reported that five children had come down with polio after receiving vaccine prepared by a small American supplier. Assured by Cameron that "properly made and administered Salk vaccine does not produce polio," Martin issued a statement to declare that Canada's supply was sound.[64] Two weeks later, as additional cases of vaccine-related polio emerged, the US secretary for health, education and welfare, Oveta Culp Hobby, suspended the entire American effort while her scientists determined whether the vaccine was safe. Across North America, parents, whose hopes were pinned on Salk's vaccine, panicked.

Martin was always a careful decision-maker, who often consulted widely before acting. He did so now. After learning of the American suspension at 8:00 a.m. on 7 May, Cameron gathered his top public health officials – Drs. D.B.D. Layton, L.I. Pugsley, and Louis Greenburg – in his modest Bank Street office. George Carty represented the minister. Their confidence in the safety of Canada's supply, which was independently tested by both the producer and the federal Health Department's Laboratory of Hygiene, was bedrock solid. (The US product was tested only by the manufacturer.) They consulted with American authorities by phone, spoke with the drug industry, and polled provincial deputy health ministers, who were "unanimous" in agreeing to go ahead with the immunization program.[65] Backed by this phalanx of expert opinion, Martin held his breath, swept aside the prime minister's doubts, and issued a courageous lunchtime statement that endorsed Canada's program.[66]

Going ahead with the program was undeniably the right call. The American media, happy to seize any stick to beat the US government, was kind. "Canadian Paul Martin showed imagination," declared *The New Republic*. "Mrs. Hobby did not."[67] The *New York Post* enthused, "No snarls, no doubts, no delays ... And it's cheaper too."[68] The *Nation Magazine* quietly applauded Martin's "vision and courage."[69] Canadians were pleased to be noticed. "Nothing this country has done in recent years," bragged the *Toronto Daily Star*, "has evoked such widespread American praise as has our government's handling of the polio vaccine."[70]

This was heady stuff, but Martin's joy was offset by the summer's long and onerous parliamentary session. The House droned on into late July, its collegial atmosphere poisoned by the heat and a Tory filibuster over Howe's unwise demand to extend the emergency powers granted the government during the Korean War. Bored and lonely, Martin yearned to be at the family cottage in Colchester. "I am going to do my best to spend a little time with the family," he resolved to a friend in July. "I am beginning to forget what Nell and the children look like."[71]

HE MADE IT to Colchester early in August, but his short holiday was interrupted by local speaking engagements and a cabinet meeting in mid-month. A week later, he was back at work full-time, preparing to fill in at the United Nations for Pearson, who was visiting the Soviet Union. Through the mid-1950s, the United Nations (and New York) increasingly provided Martin, and Nell, too, with a welcome break from the frustrating grind of departmental business in Ottawa. At the United Nations, Martin felt he could still make a difference, securing the national recognition that would reinforce his claims to the Liberal leadership.

He arrived in New York in September 1955, more confident than ever of his diplomatic skills. He had worked alongside but independently of Pearson at the UN General Assembly during the fall of 1952 to close the gap between American and Indian policy-makers regarding the fate of prisoners-of-war in Korea.[72] For the first time in his career, he had played a key role in shaping Canadian foreign policy and tactics, even acting autonomously at the foreign minister level. He had impressed Canadian journalists Norman Smith, Mark Harrison, and Walter O'Hearn with his strong performance and was profiled in a syndicated feature that ran nationally under the pleasing headline "Martin Emerges as Seasoned Negotiator at UN Meetings."[73] Jules Léger, the rising diplomat who would become deputy minister of external affairs just two years later, was a senior advisor on Canada's delegation, and he, too, liked what he saw. In a letter to Martin, he remarked warmly that working with him was "one of the most enriching experiences of 1952 ... I was deeply touched by the friendship that you kindly showed me."[74]

Martin took sole charge of Canada's UN delegation for the first time in 1954, while Pearson was in London for NATO talks on West German rearmament. He described the experience as "exhilarating."[75] It became even more enjoyable when he found himself thrust to the centre of renewed efforts to advance the quixotic Cold War quest for disarmament, a campaign that offered liberal internationalists new hope after Stalin's death in 1953. When Soviet ambassador Andrei Vishinsky, Martin's old UN adversary, proposed an agenda for negotiation that met several key Western objectives, he moved quickly. Sweeping aside doubts from the experts in External Affairs, he tabled a motion to get the talks moving.[76] Western support was automatic, and even Vishinsky made encouraging noises, proposing only minor textual amendments, most designed to give the Soviet and Western plans equal billing.

Martin was thrilled. "I hardly slept a wink," he later wrote.[77] But Washington did not share his enthusiasm, and its representative dug in his heels, insisting that any revision must also mention a recent American disarmament proposal. For ten days in October, Martin shuttled between the two sides, urging both to compromise. Pearson watched nervously from Europe. "I do not think," he warned Martin at one point, "that the effort should be continued to the point where it would cause trouble between us and the US."[78] But Martin persisted, his friends urging him on. "Stick to your principles," wrote Cameron, as word of Martin's labours spread. "I believe you are bound to be proved right."[79] In the end, both Washington and Moscow bent a little, and UN Resolution 808(IX) was unanimously adopted by the General Assembly on 4 November 1954.

The vote was more important than its simple procedural status implied. This was the first time since 1946 that East and West had co-sponsored a disarmament motion, and it gave Canadian diplomats, recalled scholar-diplomat John Holmes, a helpful infusion of "encouragement and satisfaction."[80] Holmes also noted that the initiative reinforced Canada's standing in New York, helping to create a climate for further diplomatic successes.

It was important for Martin, too. As he makes clear in his memoirs, Pearson had succumbed to "cold-feet," but he had not. He had pressed ahead over the objections of his professional advisors and won praise from UN secretary-general Dag Hammarskjöld, who thought he "had done an admirable job."[81] The approving nods strengthened his confidence in his diplomatic skills and judgment, and in his capacity to act independently. Moreover, the experience encouraged him to embrace a more moderate view of the Soviet Union. He insisted on Western preparedness and a strong NATO, but he pointed to the UN resolution as proof that negotiations were possible. Perhaps, he told a London audience on his return home, "the USSR has come to recognize at last the frightful significance of a third world war, which would be unprofitable for victor and vanquished alike."[82] He was quick to see his views confirmed in Moscow's willingness to sign a peace treaty with Austria in May 1955.[83] Following a July summit of "Big Four" leaders in Geneva, Cold War tensions eased further, and as Martin left for New York in the fall of 1955, he was primed for action.

New York was fun. Martin took up residence in the Beekman Tower Hotel, scruffier than the Drake but closer to UN activities, and hosted a parade of visiting Canadians. Claxton, more relaxed since leaving politics in June 1954, was in town, as was Howe, and he spent time with both. He also spent time with Roland Michener, the neophyte Tory MP for Rosedale, and his philosopher wife, Norah, who shared his interest in Jacques Maritain. Nell came down as well, of course, her second visit ending abruptly when she rushed home to be with young Paul, who was hospitalized with appendicitis in November. *Damn Yankees* played Broadway, and the Yankees played Brooklyn in the World Series (the damn Yankees won). Martin took in both.

But work came first. He toyed with an initiative on disarmament, a familiar file, but soon turned his attention to the deadlock over the admission of new UN members. Under the UN Charter, membership in the world body was reserved for sovereign "peace-loving" states, and applications to join could be vetoed by the permanent members of the UN Security Council. As the Cold War intensified during the 1940s, both sides deployed the sanction with happy abandon to exclude applicants whose political sympathies lay with the opposition. By 1955, twenty-two countries had lined up to join, and many smaller nations, including Canada, were growing tired of waiting for the great powers to find a solution. "Something could be done," Hammarskjöld insisted, "if some governments or some men had the wisdom to find the right formulas and the courage and guts to carry them out."[84]

Canada was an unlikely candidate. Neither Pearson nor the diplomats in External Affairs were keen to sponsor a solution. They knew that a deal would carry enormous benefits – it would signal a reduction in Cold War tensions, enhance waning UN prestige, and validate the UN claim to be a genuine world forum.[85] Yet there were dangers. The British and French were cool to the idea of a compromise, and the Americans were downright hostile. They strongly opposed admitting Soviet satellites, especially Outer

Mongolia, which was hardly a state in Washington's eyes.[86] There would also be headaches over earlier US statements that rejected "package deals" as immoral, and endless pressure to seat communist mainland China.[87] And so, as Pearson told cabinet in mid-September, there would be no Canadian initiative.[88] When a Soviet diplomat hinted that Moscow might back a move by Ottawa, Pearson consulted the American secretary of state, John Foster Dulles, who scuttled the idea.[89]

Martin took his own soundings in New York, where the results were more promising. The Soviets remained interested, and he guessed that the British, though reluctant to fall out of step with Washington and wary of adding anti-colonial states to the United Nations, might come on board.[90] His opening speech to the United Nations, which invited his audience to defy the great powers if that was required to "advance towards universality," produced another encouraging development. Spain applied for membership soon afterward and persuaded the Latin American republics to support an initiative. Martin decided to act.

With help from Geoff Murray, the delegation's most junior member and a lasting supporter, he drafted a resolution to embarrass the Security Council into action by asking it to reconsider states whose previous applications had been rejected. In late October, after meeting resistance in External Affairs, he appealed to Jules Léger, now deputy minister, for permission to circulate his motion. Sensitive and scholarly, Léger was a self-described *homme d'équipe*, who was normally accompanied by his assistants when he dealt with ministers. His reservations were overridden by the determined Martin, who circulated the Canadian draft to the Australian, New Zealand, Indian, British, and American delegations.[91]

In Martin's view, these discussions suggested two general conclusions. First, Canada could probably count on the reluctant support of both London and Washington, though as a matter of principle neither was keen on encouraging the General Assembly to beat up on the Security Council. Second, Martin's consultations had reinforced his conviction that, if Canada didn't act, no one else would. Though the major powers were ready to see the membership problem resolved, none was prepared to press the issue forward. What was needed, Martin concluded, was a resolution "designed primarily to have the Assembly express with the largest possible vote its views in favour of the admission of the largest possible group of new members." From then on, as he announced bluntly to Ottawa, this "aim was foremost in our minds."[92]

His views were greeted with dismay in the East Block headquarters of External Affairs. In giving Martin permission to circulate his resolution, the department explained, it had never imagined bringing the motion to a vote. As the exercise was designed merely to "bully" the major powers into finding a solution to the membership problem, the Canadian delegation needed only to keep the resolution in the background, maintaining interest and increasing the pressure by widening the circle of states consulted. Canada would not even begin to consider introducing its resolution until the great powers, whose foreign ministers were to meet in Geneva later that fall, had failed to take action. Meantime, Martin was to sit tight and do nothing.[93]

Disappointed by these instructions, Martin decided to overcome Ottawa's reluctance to put his resolution into play. He leaked news of his efforts to Peter Stursberg, one of his stable of friendly syndicated reporters.[94] The story, which broke nationally on 2 November, proudly revealed that Canada was heading UN attempts to "open the doors ... to all those clamouring to get in."[95] Unaware of Martin's role in engineering the article, diplomats at External Affairs fretted that it exposed him to stepped-up pressure for action at the United Nations. As he had hoped, Léger responded by increasing the pressure on Paris, London, and Washington, warning them that Canada would have to act if they did not.[96] Although the *démarche* produced no useful result, it cleared the way for Martin to insist on taking the next logical step: enlisting co-sponsors for his resolution. Without much enthusiasm, Léger agreed.[97]

Martin's single-minded determination and expanding search for co-sponsors generated a sharp reaction from Canada's closest allies. Selwyn Lloyd, the British minister of state for foreign affairs, complained that his disarmament successes "had gone to his head" and dismissed his diplomacy as "very tiresome."[98] Sir Pierson Dixon, Britain's sharp-tongued UN ambassador, compared the unstoppable Martin (whom he described as "messianic") to "a man playing a hunch at a gambling table." He added that "this was not what one would expect from the representative of Canada, given the traditional Canadian policy of keeping in line with United States and United Kingdom policy."[99]

Washington's response was stronger. For several weeks, the American UN ambassador, Henry Cabot Lodge Jr., had warned Dulles that the US position was eroding as word of Canada's resolution circulated. He demanded a flanking American effort to seat all outstanding applicants except Outer Mongolia. Reluctant to beat too hasty a retreat, Dulles hesitated.[100] But now he ordered Lodge to work. "Quickly get out our own 17 power proposal," he instructed and "rally enough support for it to nullify the Canadian proposal."[101] Lodge released his plan on 13 November and tried to halt General Assembly consideration of the membership issue by asking for an early meeting of the Security Council on the same subject.[102] As one observer put it, "Lodge and Dulles, in effect, had declared war on Paul Martin."[103]

While Lodge reinforced the weak American position and dissuaded potential co-sponsors, Martin had not been idle. He revelled in political campaigning, and with his initiative out in the open, he gleefully urged his delegation to gather co-sponsors. "Better get moving, boys," he told them, promising "a cigar for every co-sponsor you get."[104] Within days, Canada's diplomats had lined up twenty-seven supporters, drawing support from Asia, the Middle East, Latin America, and Europe. Soon afterward, Martin replied to Lodge's opening salvo by tabling the Canadian resolution in the General Assembly.

With this, American objectives shifted. Resigned to Martin's package of eighteen new members, Washington was increasingly concerned with what would transpire if Nationalist China carried out its threat to veto Outer Mongolia. The State Department's worries were twofold. First, observers would accuse Washington of engineering the veto and blocking the admission of friendly states such as Ceylon, Japan, Italy, Austria, and Spain. Second, a veto might result in such a backlash against the Nationalist government that the General Assembly might very well try to assign the Chinese seat to communist Beijing, a serious blow to US policy in Asia. As the General Assembly prepared to take up the Canadian resolution, American efforts at the highest levels in New York and Washington to persuade China not to use its veto proved futile. Anxiously, Lodge asked Martin for a week's delay to give the United States time to convince China to forgo its veto. Suspicious of American intentions, Martin refused to commit himself.[105]

His skepticism, unreasonable in American eyes, enraged the Eisenhower administration. In Washington, Dulles called in George Glazebrook, minister at Canada's embassy and the senior officer in the absence of the ambassador. He berated the hapless diplomat for failing to consult the United States and accused Pearson of cutting a deal with Moscow "behind the backs of the United States."[106]

Lodge met Martin that afternoon in New York. When the US diplomat repeated the American plea for a delay, Martin claimed that the matter was "out of his hands" and rested with the General Assembly. His assertion was disingenuous and the tactic unwise. Lodge reacted angrily, accusing Ottawa of bias against the Republican administration and threatening retaliation against Canadian oil exports if the resolution were not withdrawn.[107] When this failed, Lodge implied that Martin's initiative did not have Pearson's support.[108] Martin was not intimidated. Lodge had once reminded him that "when I speak, I speak for the Government of the United States," to which he had replied with a short lesson on cabinet government: "Cabot ... when I speak, I AM the government of Canada."[109] This time, too, Lodge's bullying proved counter-productive. Far from changing Martin's mind, it convinced him to press ahead, certain that Washington was adopting "diverting tactics that will have the result of avoiding Assembly consideration."[110]

The testy confrontations with Dulles and Lodge set alarm bells ringing in Ottawa. In late November, Pearson flew to New York to refute the notion that Martin's initiative did not have his full support. At the same time, he softened Martin's opposition to Washington's requested delay and agreed to give it time to convince Nationalist China not to veto Outer Mongolia's application.[111] Final debate on the membership issue was delayed until December, when the General Assembly adopted Martin's resolution by a vote of fifty-two in favour, two against (China and Cuba), and five abstentions (including France and the United States). Some jockeying occurred in the Security Council – Japan and Outer Mongolia were vetoed – but the major powers agreed to seat sixteen new members, establishing the principle of universality of membership.[112]

As the new members took their seats, the General Assembly rose and gave Paul Martin a rare – and much deserved – standing ovation. His efforts helped revitalize the United Nations and set it on the road to universality. This admittedly would make the General Assembly less tractable as dozens of post-colonial states in Africa and Asia thronged aboard in the late 1950s and the 1960s. Though some lamented this fact, Martin knew that the United Nations could not be an effective forum for world issues unless its membership reflected global realities. As John Holmes, an assistant under-secretary at external affairs, wrote to him, "this gesture of faith and confidence in the world as it exists, which you personified, will do more than anything to stop the rot."[113] The initiative was good for Canada as well. It demonstrated a capacity to conduct multilateral diplomacy independently of its major allies, broadened its contacts in New York, and reinforced its standing with the smaller UN powers.

The new members initiative was a personal triumph for Martin. Against the advice of the professional diplomats and the inclination of Pearson himself, he had made this issue his own. He treasured the outpouring of praise, especially from old friends. "You have done something at the United Nations which has made your friends very proud and countless people in Canada and elsewhere very grateful," wrote Governor General Vincent Massey, one of his earliest backers, "so as one of those both proud and grateful I wanted to say so."[114] Success yielded other rewards. Justifiably, it increased his standing as an international figure in his own right and made him a more credible candidate to succeed St. Laurent. Writing in the *Montreal Herald*, Gerald Waring asserted that Martin had become "immeasurably stronger."[115]

MARTIN HURRIED BACK to Ottawa in December, excited by the possibility of finally shifting cabinet's policy on health insurance and scoring his most important domestic victory since universal old age pensions in 1951. The change in his domestic fortunes had been dramatic. Twelve months earlier, few would have expected him to make the slightest progress on the tough health file. Indeed, by March 1955, he had seemed to be in full retreat regarding health insurance, squeezed between an obdurate cabinet and provincial and popular pressures for headway. Ottawa's strategy of withholding its aid until "most provinces" were ready to join a national plan (and thus pinning delay on the provinces) had started to collapse. Four of the provinces – Newfoundland, Saskatchewan, Alberta, and British Columbia – already had some form of health insurance, and they resented the attempt to blame them for the impasse. More worrisome, the shrewd and pragmatic Leslie Frost, Ontario's Progressive Conservative premier, had moved into the field in late 1954 as his voters became disenchanted with their privately funded health care, which left a third of Ontarians without hospital coverage. By early 1955, Frost was pointing an accusing finger at Ottawa.[116]

Despite the looming provincial challenge, there was little give in cabinet, which applauded when Pickersgill told Kitchener Liberals in March that "you'll never get health insurance in Canada until you get rid of Frost."[117] Martin's isolation was apparent when ministers met that month to consider the coming Federal-Provincial Conference on fiscal relations. St. Laurent had invited the premiers to Ottawa for a preliminary meeting in April to set the summit's agenda, which he hoped to restrict to taxation and aid to the unemployed without benefits.

Health was excluded from the start, and Martin was excluded from the restricted cabinet committee that oversaw federal policy, though aid to the "employable unemployed," or welfare, surely fell within his portfolio.[118] Unsure of his footing, he said nothing, even when he was asked to review St. Laurent's opening statement.[119] When publicly pressed on health insurance, he retreated to impregnable territory: three times in early 1955, he indicated that either provincial unanimity or a constitutional amendment might be required to implement health insurance, a stance that reinforced Ottawa's battered strategy of delay.[120] His supporters were baffled and alarmed. "If the cabinet shifts its health insurance plans to the constitutional amendment basis," observed the Liberal *Ottawa Citizen,* "it will, in effect be abandoning the project for the visible future."[121]

The premiers gathered in Parliament Hill's neo-Gothic Center Block on 26 April to decide their agenda. The prime minister's opening statement was calm and judicious, the speech of a man in complete control. He carefully explained why the broad social security and tax proposals of 1945 were no longer needed in the booming 1950s, and he argued that the best chance for improved federal-provincial relations lay in an agenda that focused on two manageable issues: fiscal arrangements and help for the long-term unemployed. Frost countered that the country faced too many problems to restrict the agenda so tightly. He listed six issues, citing health insurance as among the most important. This view was strongly endorsed in the public opening statements of the premiers from British Columbia, Alberta, Saskatchewan, and Manitoba. Watching reporters remarked that St. Laurent was "obviously annoyed."[122]

Next day, the debate was renewed more forcefully, when the premiers assembled behind closed doors. Frost doggedly continued to insist on adding health insurance to the agenda. He reportedly tossed clippings of Pickersgill's Kitchener speech onto the table and growled that it was time for Ottawa "to put up or shut up."[123] He was backed again by his four Western colleagues. By lunchtime, they had forced St. Laurent to call for a break to reassess the federal position.

The national delegation, which included Martin, Finance Minister Walter Harris, and Justice Minister Stuart Garson, gathered in the prime minister's office. As Martin wrote in his memoirs, "I told [St. Laurent] that I could not carry on as minister of health and welfare if health insurance was not put on the list of issues for full discussion."[124] It's unlikely that this threat alone swayed St. Laurent, who once observed "that most of the ministers have a habit of wanting to resign from time to time."[125] But Martin's view was embraced by other ministers on the delegation, and St. Laurent was forced to retreat. When the premiers reconvened that afternoon, he agreed to include "Health and Welfare Services" on the agenda for the next meeting. The premiers scheduled their plenary for October and handed the preparatory work to a committee of deputy ministers. When asked by the provinces for his views, Martin promised federal proposals by October.

Federal policy slowly came together during the busy summer of 1955. In July, Cameron hosted a meeting of provincial deputy health ministers, securing a technical consensus on what kind of health program might be possible.[126] This was reflected in a Health and Welfare position paper that was disseminated in late July with Martin's blessing.[127] Though parts of Canada remained "under-doctored," the deputies agreed that the country (with ratios of 1 doctor per 948 people and 6.5 hospital beds per 1,000 people) had the necessary facilities to support a modern health care program, thanks in part to the national health grants.

There was agreement on the scope of the program and the order in which it should be introduced. Dental and pharmaceutical care were ruled out from the start as impractical and too costly. The full package would encompass hospital care, diagnostics (laboratory and radiological care), medical services (GPs and specialists), and visiting nursing services, and it ought to be introduced in roughly that sequence. Ideally, provinces might establish the services gradually, at rates reflecting their unique circumstances. The complete program would take ten years to establish, adding $30 to $35 million annually to the federal budget, until it reached $600 million. Ottawa would pay half.

Reaching an agreement with the bureaucrats in Finance and the Treasury Board was more difficult. The top economists were polite, even friendly, and the results of their August encounter gratified Cameron and his gang of doctors. "I was very pleased indeed at their attitude," Fred Jackson of the Health Services Division wrote Martin. "They seem to think, apparently, there is no financial reason why the Government should not go ahead with the program."[128] This was true, but the government's financial advisors were hardly eager converts to the cause. Economist John Deutsch, the powerful Treasury Board secretary, remained highly dubious. He feared that Canada could not afford health insurance over the long term, and he complained to friends of "our budget becoming rigid; hard times running us into heavy deficits (he speaks of billions); inflation; balance of payments difficulties; controls; loss of freedom and so forth."[129] There would be more meetings, the "money men" promised Cameron as they exited his boardroom, but none was ever offered. Instead, Bryce and Deutsch were increasingly drawn to proposals for catastrophic insurance, a cheap half-way measure favoured by Frost, with whom they and St. Laurent were flirting dangerously.[130]

Martin appealed to Finance Minister Walter Harris, even though the two men were not close. Smart, accomplished, and hard-working, Harris hailed from Baptist temperance stock rooted in small-town Ontario. His shy and unassuming style – he liked to crack, "Don't try to make a statesman out of me; I am just an Ontario farm boy" – hid a strong ambition that legitimately aimed at the top job. Though constrained by his role as finance minister, he was inclined to favour health insurance, and he understood, as perhaps only an Ontario minister could, the importance of outflanking Frost.[131]

Martin's pitch was political. Convinced that Frost would take the initiative at the October meeting, he insisted that the Liberal Party could not afford to be the only one in the country that was afraid to move forward with health insurance. He argued on humanitarian grounds as well. Canadians wanted and needed protection from the crushing costs of illness; voluntary private-sector insurance plans, such as Blue Cross, with its deductions and restrictions, were not working, especially for lower-income families. These Canadians required insurance whose cost was pegged to their income, a progressive scheme that would have to operate under government auspices.[132]

Recalling his department's July paper, Martin urged Harris to back two of its key components. First, Ottawa should offer to fund at once the extension of diagnostic services to the whole population. Second, the prime minister's opening statement to the coming premiers' meeting should indicate that when a majority of the provinces, representing a majority of the people, were ready to proceed with hospital insurance, Ottawa would contribute its share, up to 50 percent of the cost. Harris cautiously threw his support behind Martin. In late September, cabinet endorsed Martin's "double majority" formula on the understanding that Ottawa would pay half the cost of an extended diagnostic program and contribute an undefined share to hospital insurance.[133]

This makeshift compromise still left Ottawa on the defensive at the federal-provincial summit in October. St. Laurent's opening statement pledged support for diagnostic services and hospital insurance, provided there was agreement on a plan by "a substantial majority of provincial governments, representing a substantial majority of the Canadian people."[134] Even with the addition of the adjective "substantial," Martin and his advisors were pleased with the statement, which Davidson judged "good and strong."[135] St. Laurent was much less impressed, dismissing his own statement as "only *verbiage* anyway, and the more of it the better."[136] This assessment was echoed by the premiers, who wondered what "substantial" meant. Six provinces? Eight provinces? Sixty percent of Canadians? Seventy-five?[137]

Unlike St. Laurent, Frost was precise and persuasive. He distributed five specific proposals, emphasizing the need to act quickly. Ontario favoured the plans for diagnostic services and comprehensive hospital insurance, but it was willing to consider alternative schemes for home care, catastrophic insurance, and maternity care. Frost finished his presentation by urging the premiers to strike a committee of health ministers to consider these, and other plans, in detail. The effect, recalled Ontario advisor Malcolm Taylor, was "electrifying."[138]

Handcuffed by the cabinet compromise and unable to negotiate, Martin fled to New York before the premiers left town. With his absence, no work was done on fleshing out the federal position, even as Frost prepared hospital insurance legislation for Ontario, and Carty warned Martin of "the urgency of the situation."[139] The delay was not unwelcome. Provincial health ministers, whose committee was to meet Martin in late January 1956, would expect additional details on the federal offer, which meant renewing the cabinet debate on health insurance. Martin seemed unsure of his chances, and he weighed his next step carefully. In December, he suggested to Harris that the government strike a joint parliamentary committee on health insurance. This measure would allow him to postpone the cabinet debate, while generating the parliamentary and public support required to compel recalcitrant ministers into line.[140]

Harris was not convinced, and he told Martin sharply to bring the issue to cabinet, which still had to determine the precise federal offer and a cost-sharing formula. Bristling at the finance minister's presumption in urging their minister to open the cabinet discussion, Cameron and Davidson advised him to set his own pace.[141] He certainly tried. He waited patiently while Cameron, Davidson, and Deutsch, meeting on 6 and 13 January, sorted out the rough details of the hospital insurance program. The deputies agreed on benefits covered under diagnostic services and hospital insurance. They excluded hospital depreciation and current debt from the program, and they whittled the funding formulas down to two. Both departments envisioned a federal share of 50 percent. Option A, which focused on per capita costs, would pay more to the poorer provinces, whereas Option B, which addressed actual costs, would send more federal dollars to the high-spending provinces.[142]

Martin himself was undecided regarding which option he favoured when his cabinet colleagues surprised him by raising the issue on 18 January. After an inconclusive debate, the decision was held over until cabinet met on 20 January. By then, Martin had made up his mind. Compensation for non-participating provinces, he began firmly, was not part of his plan. He reviewed the historical Liberal commitment to health insurance, insisting that there was no room for retreat. At the coming health ministers' meeting, he planned to wait out the provinces, holding back Ottawa's offer until their views were known. But a federal offer must come. Ottawa, he proposed, should pay up to half of the program's costs, with a contribution made up of 25 percent of the national per capita cost plus 25 percent of the provincial per capita cost. "This method," he ended, weighing the votes around the table and across the country, "was particularly advantageous to the Maritime provinces."[143]

The debate split cabinet. Ministers were divided over the timing of an accord, with some proposing that it be delayed until after the next federal election. They also differed over compensation for non-participating provinces. It would not be fair, argued Pearson and St. Laurent strongly, to tax all provinces for a program that operated in just a handful. Harris also fretted about the wisdom of "going the limit" and backing a program that might eventually cost as much as $250 or $300 million. Perhaps, he and others suggested, Ottawa might leave the initiative to the provinces or contribute a smaller share.

Martin fought back fiercely. With Pickersgill's support, he opposed compensation for non-participating provinces, correctly pointing out that this would remove a vital incentive to join a national program and might even halt the creation of the magic majority. If money were a problem, he snapped at Harris, cut defence; anything less than 50 percent was simply "insufficient" and likely to spark accusations that Ottawa was "sabotaging" the health deal. Cabinet adjourned early in the afternoon, asking Martin, Harris, Davidson, Deutsch, and Bryce to sort out the final details and report back.

The hospital insurance package that emerged was a triumph for Martin. There were few surprises. Hospital care and diagnostic services were in; capital costs (debt and depreciation), as well as TB and mental patients already under provincial care, were out. Provincial schemes would have to be universal, and any extra charges levied on patients must be limited to 10 percent of the cost. Once these conditions were met by six provinces representing a majority of Canadians, Ottawa would contribute amounts equal to 25 percent of the national per capita cost plus 25 percent of the provincial per capita cost. Cabinet agreed that Martin would present the federal offer to his provincial counterparts when they gathered a week later in Ottawa, taking care not to mention compensation for non-participants. At the same time, Martin added shrewdly, St. Laurent should outline the proposals in Parliament, engaging his own prestige in their realization. They weren't verbiage now.

7

DISAPPOINTMENT AND
OPPOSITION, 1956–63

There was one more victory to savour. On 23 January 1956, provincial health and finance ministers assembled in the House of Commons Railway Committee Room to hear the federal offer on health insurance. Martin was optimistic. Flanked by a contingent of cabinet colleagues, whom he wanted to expose to the provincial perspective, he presided over an agenda that was designed to bolster his chances. For three days, he drew from provincial ministers the details of their existing health care operations and their proposals for health insurance, highlighting shared priorities and the political case for action.[1] His confidence grew steadily. At one point, he strolled out of a session, arm-in-arm with Dana Porter, treasurer of Ontario's Progressive Conservative government. "Mr. Porter and I," he smiled at the press, "just want to say the conference is proceeding very well."[2]

On the final day of the talks, he unveiled the federal offer to pay half the national average cost for hospital insurance on a sliding scale that favoured the poorer provinces, provided that at least six provinces with a majority of Canadians agreed. The three Western provinces made optimistic noises and rich Ontario confined itself to restrained muttering. A deal seemed certain. The Liberal press was generous in its praise. A *Toronto Star* editorial called it "another giant step on the road to complete social security."[3] The *Hamilton Spectator* added that the "plan is packaged so attractively that it would appear to leave little room for criticism."[4] Even the Conservative

Toronto Globe and Mail acknowledged that the federal offer was a "cleverly-designed package that will be difficult for individual provinces to turn down."[5] Martin seemed to have scored a signal triumph.

But the federal offer was much more contentious than he had anticipated. The decision to exclude psychiatric and TB patients under provincial care attracted widespread criticism. Although these patients already received free health care, the provision seemed illiberal and unprogressive just when new drugs and therapies made it possible to imagine a world free of mental illness. The Canadian Mental Health Association denounced Martin for "discrimination of a most vicious and immoral type."[6]

Provincial support was slow to materialize as well. Many of the poorer provinces thought that Ottawa ought to pay more, perhaps as much as the 60 percent it had promised long ago in the original Green Book proposals of 1945. "It's a little like being offered a Rolls-Royce at 50 percent off list price," a provincial finance minister complained. "It's a bargain, alright. But it doesn't do you much good if you don't have $500 to your name."[7] By the end of May, among the smaller provinces, only British Columbia, Saskatchewan, and Alberta had grudgingly indicated that they would back the plan.

Ontario's hesitations were especially disturbing. Since nationalist premier Maurice Duplessis of Quebec had rejected the federal plan as infringing on provincial jurisdiction, Ontario's support was vital if the program were ever to cover a majority of Canadians and take effect. Premier Leslie Frost supported health insurance in principle, but as the spring advanced, it became clear that he had deep reservations about the federal offer. He believed that the plan shortchanged affluent Ontario, and he wanted Ottawa to pick up the costs for psychiatric and TB patients and to contribute to administrative and capital expenses. He also wanted assurances that federal money would flow as soon as Ontario launched its plan, even if there were not yet six participating provinces.

Most importantly, Frost rejected the federal demand that the plan be "universally available" from the outset. He hoped to move toward universality, but for political and philosophical reasons, he preferred to reach this goal gradually, without undue compulsion. He proposed immediately enrolling payroll employees in the plan, leaving the self-employed free to join or remain with their private insurers. He was convinced that most

Ontarians would subscribe to the provincial plan and that coverage would eventually be universal. Martin met with him in early June but was unable to persuade him to soften his position.

The standoff was a blow. With Prime Minister St. Laurent fading and a leadership campaign in view, Martin's failure to deliver on hospital insurance, which he had sold as a surefire winner, reduced his standing in cabinet at a time when he was already tired and discouraged. The winter and spring of 1956 had been a tough slog. Martin had spent much of his time on the road: he had toured Toronto and southern Ontario in February, Western Canada in March, and northern Ontario in May. He was frustrated by Ontario finance minister Louis Cecile's "cheap, carping criticism" over means tests for old age and disability pensions, and by a spat with Alberta premier Ernest Manning over residency requirements for welfare recipients. He could do nothing about either.

It irked him that few Canadians, and fewer still in Windsor, where he spoke in April, seemed to care much about his UN work, especially his new members initiative. "If Pearson had done this, boy-oh-boy," he later complained, "it would have been all over the map."[8] Throughout the spring, he was also burdened by the lesser crises that characterized life at the sprawling Department of National Health and Welfare. There were production delays with the Salk polio vaccine, an uproar when the lunatic fringe discovered fluoride in Canada's tap water, and a tainted cheese scandal. "This is no way to run a department for the benefit of public health," jeered the *Edmonton Journal*.[9]

On top of it all, St. Laurent's government tottered on the verge of collapse. The prime minister was tired and withdrawn, and Trade Minister C.D. Howe, grown autocratic and ill-tempered, ruled. Desperate to push through a bill to finance his dream of a trans-Canada pipeline carrying Alberta gas to central Canada, he schemed with Finance Minister Walter Harris to limit debate with closure. From the moment that Howe's bill was introduced on 14 May until it passed on 1 June, "Black Friday," the House was in constant uproar. Martin doubted the value of closure – he called the measure "draconian" – and he sat glumly in his seat as the House erupted around him, only occasionally joining the raucous debate. The Opposition dug in its heels, resorting to endless procedural challenges and histrionics. The Speaker waffled, and the prime minister, tossing his hands into the air, wailed, "We're drifting, we're drifting."[10] Perhaps, Martin wondered that summer, it was time he quit.

Nell was doubtful. She thought he'd be lost without politics, and she asked St. Laurent to find him something to do. At the suggestion of diplomat Escott Reid that Martin be sent to Asia, Pearson proposed a Far East good-will tour.[11] Though he feared that this was simply a make-work project, Martin agreed to go, drawn by the chance to encounter the teeming vast-ness of postwar, revolutionary Asia. He made sure that his trip would be purposeful. "I hope you will plan for [my] time to be fully occupied," he cabled Reid in Delhi. "I do not want to take a lot of time off for rest."[12]

An extended ministerial trip across the Pacific was still an unusual event in 1956, and during the fall, Martin's office and home buzzed with excited preparations. St. Laurent offered the RCAF's C-5 Hercules transport plane, a lumbering and noisy craft that was nonetheless considered luxurious. Martin filled it with his delegation. Nell was certainly coming. She spent October getting shots and wrapping Christmas gifts for the children, who would spend the holidays in Windsor. Mrs. Martin, the *Toronto Globe and Mail* assured its readers, "would do Canada no harm at all as a representa-tive of Canadian wives and mothers."[13]

Martin recruited a sympathetic group of journalists to accompany him. Robert McKeown from *Weekend Magazine* and Doug Leiterman of Southam News Services, who represented the Ottawa press gallery, were joined by stringers from British Universal Press and Montreal's *La Presse*. His friend Paul Nathanson, who owned Associated Screen News, sent along a cameraman. Martin was irritated that *Maclean's* declined to send a reporter, but he was delighted to include his friend Dick Graybiel, son and heir of the *Windsor Daily Star's* publisher.

For help on the voyage, Martin brought along his executive assistant, George Carty, and the liveliest secretary in his office, Betty Neill. Policy briefings and advice were provided by Arthur Menzies, whom Martin had first met as a young foreign service officer stationed in Windsor during the Second World War. Skittish and cautious by temperament, Menzies was the son of Presbyterian missionaries, a "mish kid," who had grown up in pre-war China and risen through the ranks to become the well-regarded head of the Far Eastern Division in the Department of External Affairs. It was a happy reunion.

The group left Ottawa's Rockcliffe Airport on 11 November. During the sixty-three-day tour, they crossed the Pacific to Indochina, visited Australia and New Zealand, and then turned north to Singapore, India, and Pakistan. They returned to Canada across the Atlantic. Martin set an exhausting pace. During flights, he devoured briefing books and telegrams, and dictated a stream of reports. "Minister carries on as usual," Neill scribbled in a note to her office mates, "writes to all the newsmen ... to the prime minister every two or three days, [deputy foreign minister Jules] Léger, and everyone he can think of in Windsor. Of course, with no mail coming in and no phones to use and no transportation problem, Minister has nothing left to think about but letters so it gets rather rugged."[14] Driven and focused, he often left Nell, who was "white-knuckled" with fright during flights, under the care of Menzies, insisting that she "pull herself together."[15] She did, but it was not always easy. "Was I ill!" she wrote home spiritedly from Indonesia, "& if you want to feel at low ebb, try being sick so far away from home & know you have to pull yourself together for a long flight."[16]

Martin kept up his tireless pace on the ground. During a typical stop, he met with Canadian diplomats and held official talks with host ministers and heads of government. He visited local hospitals, Canadian aid projects, and missionary stations, as well as rural villages and urban slums, determined not to miss genuine Asia. He was "visibly shaken" by his tour of the slums of New Delhi.[17]

Working especially hard at generating the "goodwill" that was the point of his trip, he would alight from his car and thrust his hand toward a village farmer with a cheery, "Hello, I'm Paul Martin from Windsor." The newsmen grinned cynically, but Menzies was impressed by his efforts and his countless speeches. By the end of the day, he was often so excited but overtired and unable to sleep that Nell would ask Menzies "to slip him a pill" and put him to bed.[18]

Martin had not ventured beyond North America (and the Caribbean) since 1946, at the dawn of the Cold War in Europe. His passage through Asia, where the East-West conflict raged most fiercely, shaped his understanding of contemporary world issues in several critical ways. He had always enjoyed meeting historical characters, and he found it useful to spend time with many of the continent's leading post-colonial figures, including Ngô Đình Diệm of Vietnam, Sukarno of Indonesia, and Jawaharlal Nehru of India. The trip helped him appreciate Asia's enormous scale, its vital standing in any calculus of world peace, and its impassioned claims to be judged on its own post-colonial terms. The experience gave Martin the same confidence in his independent judgments about Asia as he had in his views on the United Nations or the Commonwealth.

He drew specific lessons from the voyage as well. His encounters with Asian poverty cemented his support for Canadian foreign aid. He visited Canadian soldiers who were serving with a truce supervisory mission on a "god-forsaken" hill in Laos, and returned a strong backer of peace-keeping. "I am sure that we have done a useful service in the cause of peace," he wrote St. Laurent en route to Bangkok, adding that "this is certainly one of our most effective endeavours."[19]

The trip also shifted his view of communist China. Following Washington's lead, Ottawa had refused to recognize the communist regime when it seized power in 1949 and had helped the United States block it from occupying China's UN seat. Counting anti-communist Catholic voters in Quebec, Martin had endorsed this policy, even as Pearson challenged it during the mid-1950s. However, as his Asian hosts reminded him, from their perspective, China – looming over Burma, pressing down on Indonesia, meddling in Indochina – was a force that must be acknowledged. Encouraged by Menzies, he slowly admitted the "logic" of recognition.[20] His conversion was probably not as complete as his memoirs suggest, but he knew that Canadian policy would have to change.

His visit to Vietnam, whose brutal civil war would threaten world peace and confound Canadian-American relations for the next two decades, was equally significant. Vietnam was already a global hotspot. When its French colonial rulers abandoned Indochina in 1954, an international conference in Geneva divided Vietnam into a communist "democratic republic" in the north and a non-communist "republic" in the south. An international control commission (ICC), a tripartite commission of Canada, communist Poland, and neutral India, was asked to oversee the peace, settle refugees, and help with elections to reunite the country. In early 1956, American-backed president Ngô Đình Diệm repudiated elections that he could not win and set about building his own state in South Vietnam.

Martin arrived in Saigon as Diệm's state-building experiment gathered momentum. Vietnam excited the Canadian visitor. He was charmed by Ngô Đình Diệm, a fellow Catholic, and impressed by his successful efforts to absorb a million Catholic refugees from North Vietnam. The president's familiarity with Catholic philosopher Jacques Maritain, whom Martin had known as a student, surprised and delighted him. Clearly, he wrote St. Laurent, there was a "community of spiritual interests." He described Diệm as a "dedicated, honest, and courageous leader," who offered the prospective of a modern, independent state in South Vietnam. Surely, he deserved Canada's help.[21]

As his friends had hoped, Martin returned to Ottawa "exhilarated" by his experiences. "I have never had so much fun in all my life," he told the House of Commons in January 1957, taking up the business of running his department.[22] Health insurance topped his agenda. During his absence, Premier Frost and his key advisors had visited Ottawa to discuss the deadlock. There was some good news. George Gathercole, Ontario's principal economist, and Malcolm Taylor, its leading health expert, hinted to Donald Cameron, deputy minister of health, that the province would probably cover the costs for psychiatric and TB patients and certain ancillary items. On the two main issues, however, Frost refused to bend. He told the prime minister in December that Ontario hoped to reach 85 to 90 percent enrolment, but that he would not guarantee the figure or make the insurance plan compulsory. He also insisted on access to federal funds before the program started to operate. Cabinet deferred its reply until Martin's return.[23]

Martin scented success. As he told cabinet, even provinces with universal plans did not achieve 100 percent enrolment. If Ontario promised to cover at least 85 to 90 percent of its population, that would meet the federal criterion.[24] Finding a basis for those assurances proved tricky but not impossible. Though Frost declined to give ironclad guarantees, he promised to make every effort to secure near full enrolment, and he told his ministers to provide Martin with sufficient information about Ontario's plan to satisfy Ottawa that the provincial scheme was likely to attract enough subscribers to meet this target.[25] For its part, Ottawa agreed to make federal money available as soon as six provinces had reached funding agreements with it rather than waiting until the six insurance schemes were operational.[26] This was a reasonable compromise, and Ontario accepted the federal offer in March, clearing the way for Martin to push the necessary legislation through Parliament and to recruit two more provinces, Newfoundland and Prince Edward Island. But implementation would have to wait. The House was prorogued in April and an election called for 10 June.

Liberal hopes for election victory were high. St. Laurent was a popular figure, and polls taken during March 1957 put his party ahead: 48.1 percent of decided electors planned to vote Liberal, compared to just 31.4 percent for the Progressive Conservatives, campaigning under their recently chosen and untested leader, John Diefenbaker.[27] But trouble stirred beneath the placid surface. Across the country, business investment was down and unemployment inched higher. The spring budget hardly met the economic challenge. Despite a surplus of almost $400 million, cabinet refused to stimulate the economy with more spending. Martin had campaigned loudly for higher pensions and family allowances in December and January, but his was a lonely voice. St. Laurent, Harris, and senior Finance officials feared inflation and opposed additional welfare expenditures. The March budget bumped up family allowances only slightly and limited an overdue pension increase to just six dollars. The Opposition had a field day, dubbing the finance minister "Six-buck Harris" and asking "How small, how despicable, how mean, how low can a government get?" As one Liberal minister told a friend in the press, "$6 is all wrong. Now $10 would have been great. Even $5 dollars would have been better. But $6 is cheese-paring. We would have been better off to have left it alone."[28]

Martin's seat was certainly safe, his popularity undiminished in Windsor. He spent the first few weeks of the campaign on the road, combining leftover departmental business with vote getting in Montreal and Toronto. During the last week of April, he toured the Maritimes, where he spoke to fourteen political rallies, twelve hospital groups, and five student bodies. After a short stint in Ontario, he hopped a plane for the West. He impressed Tom Kent, the young editor of the *Winnipeg Free Press*, with his stump speech, a broad appeal for support built on the government's record for managing social security, federal-provincial relations, and foreign policy. His audiences were unmoved, however. In Winkler, Manitoba, "disgruntled farmers" gave him a "hot" reception.[29] On the coast, in Vancouver and Victoria, audiences heckled or stayed away as Liberal support evaporated. Diefenbaker, who drew crowds of four thousand in Victoria and six thousand in Vancouver, laughed when he bumped into Martin in the Saskatoon airport. "Might as well go home, Paul," he crowed, "you can't win."[30]

As Martin flew back to Ontario, he knew that Diefenbaker was right. Howe, the government's most powerful minister, had retreated to his Port Arthur riding in mid-May, prey to rumours that he was about to be defeated. By early June, other ministers were racing home to shore up their support. "There's nobody here but us candidates," wailed one Liberal backbencher.[31] Almost alone among his colleagues, Pearson continued to campaign widely, laying down political markers for the future. Martin returned to Windsor, a decision that prompted whispered accusations that he had abandoned his party to save his seat. These were not entirely fair: he had always planned to spend the last week of the campaign around Windsor, where St. Laurent was scheduled to speak at a major rally on 6 June. He stuck to his plans.

On polling day, 10 June, the news in Essex East was good. The Tory vote was up by several thousand but not enough to matter. Martin garnered more than twenty-two thousand ballots, his largest total yet, and easily retained his majority. Elsewhere, the results were grim. Diefenbaker's Progressive Conservatives had won 112 seats against 106 for the Liberals, 25 for the CCF, and 19 for Social Credit. Nine cabinet ministers had lost their seats, including Howe and Harris. St. Laurent immediately summoned his ministers to Ottawa and prepared to turn over the government to Diefenbaker on 21 June. In the grimy cafeteria of the Jackson Building, the Department of National Health and Welfare bid farewell to its minister. As Martin left his office for the last time, many staff members broke into tears.

Defeat forced St. Laurent out, kick-starting the simmering race for the Liberal leadership. Diefenbaker's triumph had reduced the field of viable candidates to Martin and Pearson, who was the odds-on favourite. Pearson enjoyed enormous support from the quarters that mattered. The country's leading Liberal journalists, Bruce Hutchison, Grant Dexter, George Ferguson, and Blair Fraser, had long favoured his ambitions and urged him to run. Their job now, Dexter wrote privately, was "to help Mike shine."[32] And they did. Pearson's supporters also included the party's youth, who were gathered in convention at Presqu'ile, Ontario, when St. Laurent's resignation was announced. They greeted Pearson's call for a modern liberal charter with a standing ovation and chants of "We want Mike, we want Mike."[33]

The party's senior wing was at Presqu'ile as well, manifest in the shadowy presence of Senator W.A. "Bill" Fraser. A former Ontario whip, Fraser was a wealthy Trenton farmer and businessman, with memberships in the Granite Club and the Royal Canadian Yacht Club. He worked the party's backrooms, fixing problems and raising funds, and he spoke with Howe's authority. At Presqu'ile, he met with Martin and Pearson several times, together and individually. His talks with Pearson were conclusive. "I can say without any question that Mike Pearson can be assured of being chosen at the convention," he reported to Howe, adding that "he is by far the best in sight and is enthusiastic about taking on the job."[34]

The message for Martin was different. Fraser pulled aside the ambitious Windsor MP to persuade him not to run. "He would start with two strikes against him," Fraser warned, "i.e. French and a Catholic following a French-Canadian Catholic Prime Minister."[35] Though Martin was noncommittal, Fraser left town confident that he was "reconciled to the fact that the leadership is not for him at this time." But the senator had misread Martin; within weeks, both he and Pearson were "campaigning actively" for their party's top job, to be awarded at a national convention in January 1958.[36]

Why Martin decided to run despite the overwhelming odds against him remains unclear. He was probably driven by a complex combination of practical, idealistic, and emotional considerations. Pickersgill told journalist Bruce Hutchison that Martin was running to enhance his "post-Convention power in the party."[37] That seems one likely motive. Martin was certainly capable of the long strategic view, and many of his advisors were encouraging him "to play along with Mike ... If the Grits happen to make it, Pearson as leader and Paul as External Affairs would make a pretty strong team. Then Paul would be the natural successor."[38]

There were less tangible motives as well. Soon after the contest, Martin told his old Hart House mentor, Burgon Bickersteth, that he had run for "the good of the party." It was important to show Canadian voters that the Liberals were headed by "capable and strong" men and that the leadership was not "pre-arranged in any way."[39] His genuine idealistic attachment to Liberalism and all its works makes this a plausible part of the explanation.

The searing anger that he clearly felt at the injustice of having his ambitions thwarted by race and religion, factors over which he had no control, played its part as well. "No one," he insisted in his memoirs, "had a vested right to be leader. I wanted the job as much as Pearson."[40] In his middle age, he refused to be cowed by the intolerance and prejudice that he had encountered and overcome as a university student and a young MP.

Finally, he may have felt trapped by the expectations that his strong and long-held ambitions had created among his closest supporters, his family and friends, and his backers in southwestern Ontario. He dared not disappoint them. Even when it was announced in October that Pearson had won the Nobel Prize for his UN diplomacy, boosting his stature enormously, Martin persisted. When his friend Paul Nathanson advised him to withdraw, his negative reply expressed a deep sense of helplessness. "There is really nothing else I can do," he wrote miserably.[41]

He still hoped to win, and he fought hard. He tried to enlist the support and prestige of former colleagues and party leaders. For his own unfathomable reasons, Jimmy Gardiner of Saskatchewan pledged his support, but the others declined. Though an effective minister, Martin was not popular or well liked in the party's senior ranks. His ambition made him seem selfish and unprincipled. "Martin was always out for Number One, first, last and always," recalled a contemporary.[42] After helping Martin fund his hospital insurance, Harris complained bitterly that "Paul wasn't grateful, because he never is."[43] They recalled his brushes with scandal and questioned his integrity. They nodded knowingly when McGill law professor Maxwell Cohen later quipped, "I worry about Paul Martin's soul."[44]

Martin's canvass of his former colleagues could not have been easy. He had known Lionel Chevrier, with whom he shared a Franco-Ontarian heritage, since law school in the 1920s. He had anticipated his support and clearly "felt badly" when he learned that Chevrier was committed to Pearson.[45] His request for help from Harris was equally awkward. "Walter," he began, "I never liked you." The answer, of course, was no; Harris recounted the exchange to his friends, "shaking with merriment."[46] Martin also approached Howe, with a "tearful" plea for support on the grounds that his bicultural background would enhance relations between French and English Canada. The emotional outburst simply confirmed Howe's view that Pearson ought to be leader.[47]

Obtaining cabinet-level support was not central to Martin's strategy. Many Liberals blamed party brass for their defeat in June, and he hoped to tap into their anger. A small team of advisors provided most of his help. He recruited Jim Brown, the defeated Brantford MP, as his campaign manager. Toronto lawyer Fred McDermott drafted publicity material, and businessman David Fingard handled the money. Martin campaigned quietly during the fall, an effort that culminated in swings through the Prairie provinces during December and higher-profile trips to Vancouver and Quebec early in the new year. He soft-pedalled his ambition, refusing to declare his candidacy until nine days after Pearson had done so, and when he acted, on 13 December, he indicated only that he would be "available" if the party wanted him.[48] The tactic fooled no one.

Martin's grassroots campaign faced another challenge – access to the delegates, whose names were not available until late December. Once they were identified, he redoubled his efforts. Shortening his hours in the House of Commons, he returned home early, slipped into his pyjamas, and worked the phones, with a tray of sandwiches and his beloved House of Lords Panetela cigars beside him. By the time he was done, he had spoken to half the 1,527 delegates, and during the final weekend before the convention, he was so active that Bell Telephone gave him his own operator.[49] The intensity of his effort surprised Liberals, who were used to gentler manners, and they complained of his aggressive tactics. The young Toronto delegate Keith Davey recollected his call from campaign headquarters. "Paul Martin calling me was like the Pope calling," he recounted with mock awe. "And he spoke to me as if we were old friends, and he obviously had the book on me because he said, How's that new baby?"[50] Davey voted for Pearson.

Martin picked up a trickle of supporters. Many, like the young Jim Coutts, who later worked for Pearson, wanted a tough politician who could "rally the party and do the work that had to be done."[51] Others were drawn by Martin's command of policy. He won all five delegates from the University of Saskatchewan Liberal Club, whose members compared him to Pearson, concluding that he possessed a more "intimate knowledge of domestic as well as foreign affairs."[52] Some delegates were determined to ensure a vigorous race for the sake of the party. "I'm going to help Martin," one explained, "simply because we can't have Toronto unanimously for Pearson."[53]

"In hindsight," Martin wrote disingenuously of the convention, "it was all so friendly and low-key."[54] It was indeed a simple affair, at least by the standards of later conventions, but it was not particularly friendly. As delegates gathered in Ottawa on 14 January, Nell transformed the Daly Avenue house into a way station for Martin's friends and workers, stocking the freezer with minute steaks and washing loads of linen.[55] Between trips to the train station to meet supporters, Pearson and Martin lingered in the lobbies of the nearby Chateau Laurier and Lord Elgin Hotels, shaking hands and answering questions. Pearson's crowd sported his signature bowtie and cardboard hatbands, dubbed "Pearson's haloes." Martin's smaller delegation wore buttons promising that "We can win with Martin," and "The swing is to Paul."

In the evening, the action moved to hospitality suites in the Chateau Laurier. The press contrasted Pearson's suite, "spacious, gracious – and dry," with Martin's "smoke-filled backroom, small, intimate – and wet."[56] It seemed the perfect metaphor to capture the essential difference between the two candidates. Pearson hid his political ambitions. Even as a cabinet minister, he nurtured his image as a public servant and diplomat, beyond politics. He cultivated an air of genteel respectability and the casual manner of the gifted amateur. Martin's ambitions were always clear, and he was easy to caricature as a hard-driving professional "pol." Justifiably, he resented the metaphor as profoundly misleading. Pearson, he liked to say, "was more political than I ever was."[57]

Both men campaigned equally hard, and the mood soured in their two camps. Pearson supporters charged their opponents with appealing to Quebec on the basis of race and religion. Enraged by Martin literature that quoted them out of context and without permission, Jack Pickersgill and Senator Dave Croll, Martin's old ally from Windsor, issued statements criticizing his aggressive operation. Jim Brown countered with an attack on Liberal leaders. He implied "that 'the brass' in the Liberal Party is opposed to [the] Hon. Paul Martin's bid," and he urged delegates to back "new leadership with an ear to the ground and an eye to the future."[58] Asked to comment, Martin stood by Brown's statement. The convention, Pickersgill later noted, "cast a shadow over relations with Paul Martin for some time."[59]

The vote took place on 16 January. As most expected, Pearson won overwhelmingly on the first ballot, securing 1,074 votes to Martin's 305. According to his backers, Martin had hoped for much better and was unaccountably surprised. He rallied his spirits to move the traditional motion to make the selection unanimous. "I'll let you in on a secret," he said graciously, "I voted for Mike."[60] But it was hard to hide his deep disappointment. As the convention adjourned, he was unusually short and sharp with the press. His family and friends echoed his bitter feelings. "I hope he quits," sputtered Dave Fingard. "I never want to see him hurt again."[61]

But he had no time to recover. The House of Commons assembled on 20 January to debate a government motion to resolve the House into a Committee of Supply, a resolution that the Opposition usually sought to amend with a non-confidence motion. Committed to opposing the government aggressively, yet leery of Prime Minister Diefenbaker's sustained popularity, Pearson was reluctant to defeat the government and fight an election. Tired from the leadership contest and uncertain of his tactics, he turned to the clever Pickersgill for advice. The two men concocted an ingenious scheme in which Pearson would appear combative but manage to dodge an election. He would denounce Diefenbaker for his poor economic leadership, urging him to resign and return the job of running the country to the more experienced Liberals.

The strategy backfired. "The arrogance and stupidity was breathtaking," marvelled Progressive Conservative Erik Nielsen.[62] Catcalls arose from the government benches – "Of all the nerve," shouted the decorous minister of public works, Howard Green – and laughter erupted in the press gallery.[63] Brandishing confidential government documents proving that the Liberal cabinet had long anticipated impending economic trouble for Canada, Diefenbaker leapt to the attack as Pearson slumped in his seat. Martin, who was not consulted on the Liberal strategy, watched with professional admiration as the prime minister, a consummate politician, savaged the hapless Pearson. "It was Diefenbaker's greatest hour," he acknowledged. "It was one of his best speeches, and he just tore us to pieces."[64] After battering the Opposition for another two weeks, Diefenbaker asked the governor general to dissolve Parliament. Election day was set for 31 March.

Martin knew that this campaign would be different. For the first time in years, there was a real battle for the Progressive Conservative nomination in Essex East. Roy Hicks faced a formidable challenger, Georgina Montrose. A well-connected Conservative who had sat on Windsor City Council since 1943, Montrose was judged capable of beating Martin. The weaker Hicks eventually won – it was rumoured that Liberal workers tipped the scale in his favour – but the contest forced Martin to keep a close watch on Windsor.[65]

Nevertheless, he was one of his party's strongest campaigners, and he spent much of the campaign on the road. After securing his own nomination, he flew to Halifax and worked his way back to Windsor. The weekend at home was followed by a week in southern Ontario and another in Western Canada. He toured eastern Quebec in March. In public, despite his convention loss, he was vintage Martin – outrageously partisan, hard-hitting in his attacks, and good-humoured. He denounced Progressive Conservative plans to divert Canadian trade from the United States to Britain, which harked back to the Tory protectionist policies of the Great Depression, crying "Bennett over again."[66] He reminded audiences that "Tory times [were] tough times back to the 1890s!"[67] He told friends that "I have never worked as hard on an election. Perhaps because I am tired, I feel it more than usual. I have been working all over as well as in my own constituency."[68]

It was not enough, could not be enough. Diefenbaker prowled the country, blue eyes glinting, jowls quivering, fingers pointing. Martin sensed disaster in the smaller, restless audiences that he encountered. As Diefenbaker's tide swept the country, he hunkered down in Windsor. During the last two weeks of the campaign, he was up every day by five o'clock "to shake on-and-off hands" at the auto plants and small factories that dotted the city landscape. He was said to have made five thousand telephone calls himself.[69] The struggle for Windsor was too close to call. Loyal constituents, who had once hailed him with promises that "You don't have to worry about us, Paul," turned away, murmuring a more non-committal "Good Luck, Paul."[70] As polls reported through the evening of

31 March, his headquarters were glum and silent, the loudest sounds coming from the chalk as it scratched results on blackboards.[71] By the end of the evening, Martin had pulled ahead of Hicks by just over 1,500 votes, his smallest margin since 1935. Across Canada, the situation was worse. Much worse. Diefenbaker had won a staggering 208 seats, reducing the Liberals to a rump of 49. The CCF retained 8 seats, and Social Credit was shut out.

THE TRANSITION TO Opposition was hard. Martin lost his office staff and advisors, except for his secretary Marjorie Frank. Don Emerson, his most important political aide since 1945, returned to Windsor to search for work, a difficult task that strained their relations. "Martin doesn't like to be bothered," he scoffed, complaining that "I'm just trying to do people favours and am left holding the bag."[72] The ex-minister missed governing. He told a fellow parliamentarian that "over there (on the Treasury benches) it is always exciting. There is always something important to do."[73] For months, he hung around the House of Commons library and reading rooms, and "wandered about the halls ... like a lost child." He nagged senior officials in the Health Department for news of their work until they came to "despise" him.[74] He was so discouraged that he wondered to friends whether he should "drop out of politics." Over the next few years, there were regular reports that he was about to quit, and periods of "self-analysis" and "indecision."[75]

Part of the problem was financial. Without his cabinet stipend, Martin's annual salary dropped from $25,000 to $10,000. "I worried myself sick," he recalled. "How was I going to get along?"[76] He consulted widely and endlessly about the problem. "It is not for me to say whether I think you should retire from politics and that you address yourself to the job of making things financially secure for Nell and the children," Frank Ahearn, an old friend, finally snapped in frustration.[77] Though it concerned him deeply, money was not likely to become a genuine problem. His conservative investment portfolio, heavy with bonds and the blue-chips of twentieth-century Canadian and American business, was handled by the most respectable stockbrokers in Montreal and Toronto. His savings had grown steadily during Canada's commodity boom in the 1950s, almost doubling in value from $117,761 in 1950 to $223,925 in 1953. By 1957, despite recently losing $60,000 on Irish Copper and other mining stock, his investments totalled $300,193.[78]

His financial success reflected the help of his close friend Paul Nathanson. The two had met during the late 1930s, when Nathan L. Nathanson, a wealthy Liberal donor and president of Famous Players Theatres, hired the Windsor lawyer for a small local job and introduced him to his son, Paul. The younger men were close in age and became unlikely friends. Nathanson was shy and introverted – he was once described as "Canada's Howard Hughes" – but he had a gift for making money.[79] In the 1940s, he had plotted with his father to establish a second national cinema chain, Odeon Theatres, to challenge Famous Players for control of Canadian audiences. By 1946, when Nathanson sold his stake in Odeon, the two chains had agreed to split Canada's market. An architect of the informal duopoly, Nathanson emerged as the rich and powerful president of Sovereign Film Distributors, which enjoyed exclusive Canadian distribution rights for two of Hollywood's top studios, Columbia and Universal.[80]

Martin often turned to Nathanson for financial guidance, and he did so in the summer of 1956. Their discussions convinced him that his investments "ought to be getting more income" and that "real estate provides much of the answer."[81] He loathed the risk involved with shifting his resources into real estate, and the process was protracted. In October 1956, Nathanson offered to sell Martin the Drysdale Building in downtown Vancouver, a small battered office complex that he acquired when he took over Associated Screen News in 1954. If Martin assumed the heavy mortgage of $178,000, he could have the building for a small cash payment of $60,000. He weighed the deal carefully. Worried that most of the building's leases would soon expire and expose him to market risk, he shrewdly complained to Nathanson that his rate of return would be between only 6 and 7 percent, well below the 13 percent he had been told to seek on real estate deals. He declined the offer in the spring of 1957.[82]

Nathanson soon produced a second asset for sale – four cinemas in downtown Vancouver, rented to Odeon Theatres, stable tenants that Martin could count on. But this was a much larger venture, which required him to invest $175,000 of his own money, with Nathanson and the banks holding a mortgage for the balance of $150,000.[83] He hesitated. Nell, whose family had strong entrepreneurial roots, was ready to take the risk. She put great faith in Nathanson's financial acumen, reminding her husband that his moods were so finely tuned that they "fluctuated with the markets."[84] She begged him to complete the deal, but Martin was unmoved. Finally, he asked Ralph Campney, a defeated Liberal cabinet minister from Vancouver, to arrange for an independent evaluation of the property. When he learned that the price fairly reflected market conditions – it was actually slightly less than the appraised value – he agreed to the purchase in October 1957.[85]

Other ventures beckoned. He helped Nathanson in a thrilling but futile race for a share in Canada's budding second TV network in 1959–60. He dabbled in penny mining stocks with the colourful prospector W.A. "Wild Bill" Richardson, trading legal work for shares in high-risk syndicates. He held a handful of corporate directorships, too, but not in the major-league boardrooms that he wanted, and part ownership of a franchise in a chain of TV repair schools. Nathanson would suggest other real estate deals, including an office building in Montreal and a string of gas stations in the Ottawa suburb of Eastview (Vanier), but Martin demurred. All these money-making schemes faded into insignificance when compared to the Vancouver investment. Its impact, which was almost immediate, boosted Martin's income sharply in the late 1950s. During his last full year as a minister, 1956, he had earned just over $33,000; his income for 1959 soared to $58,800.[86] By almost any objective standard, he had achieved a real measure of financial security and independence.

His other major worry during the early years in Opposition centred on his uncertain standing in Pearson's Liberal Party. The awkwardness began at the top, with his relations with Pearson. For the first time in his political career, Martin's leader was not a distant father-figure, feared and respected. Pearson was just six years older, a near contemporary. Their paths had crossed during the 1920s at the University of Toronto, when Martin was a student and Pearson a young history instructor. Though they moved in different circles, their friends and colleagues often overlapped. They met again in London in 1936, when Martin, a first-term MP, accompanied his prime minister to Europe, and Pearson, a rising diplomat, was posted to Canada's high commission. Over the next decade, they kept in touch with offhand notes of congratulation to mark professional milestones, each man recognizing a talent worth cultivating.

Their casual friendship changed in 1948, when Pearson left External Affairs to join cabinet as foreign minister. Martin had wanted that job, and he viewed Pearson as an unwelcome interloper and a rival for the party's top post. The rivalry was easily contained by St. Laurent, who treated his cabinet as family and expected his ministers to get along. On the whole, Martin and Pearson did, even becoming political allies in cabinet. Martin shared Pearson's postwar internationalism and regularly filled in for him in Ottawa and New York. Pearson was one of the few ministers who backed Martin's efforts to strengthen Canada's social security system. The two valued their reciprocal support, but they were not close.

The leadership race complicated their fragile relationship. Martin recognized Pearson's political appeal and the legitimacy of his victory, yet defeat still rankled. He seethed with jealousy, and he resented Pearson's easy rise to prominence, particularly when contrasted against his own struggle for a seat and a cabinet post. "He was the beneficiary of the establishment," Martin insisted. "He took advantage of this, perhaps unconsciously, but he took advantage of it and it helped him considerably."[87] Quite simply, as their colleague Paul Hellyer later explained, "Martin felt that Pearson had his job and [Martin] felt that he could do it better."[88]

Pearson managed Martin with care and skill. He disliked his ambition and often suspected his politician's reflexes. In his memoirs, he gently mocked Martin's "parliamentary debating skill – never using one simple word when fifty were needed to confuse and frustrate our political foes."[89] But with only forty-nine members of Parliament led by a decimated front bench, the Liberal leader knew that he needed Martin's political strength, both in Ottawa and across the country. This was especially true since many Canadians questioned Pearson's own political smarts and his ability to defeat Diefenbaker. Pearson treated his defeated colleague "with kid gloves and showed him lots of consideration."[90]

He wooed Martin with small favours and gestures. He celebrated Martin's victory in the general election of 1958 with a warm note "from the bottom of my heart."[91] Martin became the party's foreign affairs critic and was sometimes asked to stand in for Pearson at meetings with the prime minister or at public events. When Martin toyed with a private-sector job offer in late 1959, Pearson "urged [him] to stay."[92] Martin told reporters that

Pearson "wanted me by his side," hinting that he had been promised the External Affairs portfolio in a future Liberal government. Pearson did not contradict him, and there were hints of other futures. With Pearson's blessing, party insiders reminded Martin of "the value (for the future) of him being 100% behind his Leader in thought as well as in word ... These friends do not think the future actually belongs to Paul, but I guess they will talk to him that way."[93]

Martin remained "totally loyal" to Pearson.[94] His behaviour reflected convictions that were undoubtedly shaped by his experiences in the King and St. Laurent cabinets. "To work well with others," he explained, "one must be part of a team." Since its members would be imperfect, given human nature, there must be prior agreement "that you are not going to expose these weaknesses at the first opportunity ... There is nothing worse than disloyalty."[95] Even as Martin's deep-seated ambitions stirred again after 1960, they were accompanied by public affirmations of support for his leader. "Mike Pearson and I," he assured a reporter, "are friends of long-standing ... I am working with him to bring our party back to power."[96] It suited both politicians to establish a basis for mutual cooperation, though neither let go of the resentments and suspicions that lay at the heart of their uneasy partnership. Grant Dexter, no lover of Martin, came away from a talk with Pearson in April 1962 spitefully cheered by the thought that he "really has no illusions about Paul."[97]

Martin's relations with the Liberal Party in Opposition were equally ambivalent. Defeat, insisted Chubby Power, the old Liberal warhorse from Quebec, meant that "the course of Canadian liberalism should now be leftward. It will take some time to shake out the financial moguls and the orthodox Gladstonians. But left we must go."[98] Pearson agreed. He was attracted by new ideas and young people, and when he set out to rebuild his shaken party, he looked beyond its established structures for both. He started with newcomers Tom Kent and Walter Gordon. Kent was a young, razor-sharp, progressive Englishman who had come to Canada in 1954 as editor of the liberal *Winnipeg Free Press*. He convinced Pearson that "liberalism must 'mean' something if it was to survive."[99]

Gordon, a Toronto businessman, was older but no less influential. He had helped raise funds to ease Pearson's transition into politics in 1948 and organized his leadership campaign. He had chaired the Royal Commission on Canada's Economic Prospects of 1956–57, sharpening his critique of American postwar investment in Canada and its harmful implications. Gordon was close to a group of young party activists who were centred in Toronto, dubbed Cell 13, which included Keith Davey, Barney Danson, Paul Hellyer, Phil Givens, David Anderson, Royce Frith, and Richard Stanbury. Affluent, urban, and modern, they were determined to "sweep out" the old guard.[100]

Over the next few years, Kent, Gordon, and their young allies, including Quebec economist Maurice Lamontagne and Cape Breton politician Allan MacEachen, redefined Canadian Liberalism. They embraced the gospel of economist John Maynard Keynes and dreamed of eradicating unemployment and poverty through greatly expanded public-sector spending. There would be money for regional development to improve the country's resource and manufacturing sectors, and to renew its neglected cities. Economic progress would come with a slate of enhanced social programs, including full medical and sickness insurance, better vocational training, and educational reform. Increasingly skeptical about Washington's foreign policy, Gordon added a nationalist twist with proposals to reduce the flow of American investment.

The ambitious agenda was debated at the party's Study Conference on National Problems in September 1960, a conclave of liberal and progressive thinkers that was modelled on Vincent Massey's gathering at Port Hope in 1933. Much of it was translated into policy at the 1961 National Liberal Rally. "The overwhelming impression that emerged for public consumption," observed journalist Christina McCall-Newman, "was one of newness, vitality, and progressivism."[101] To ensure that the party retained this focus, its main, unelected, architects – Gordon, Kent, and Davey – joined the Leader's Advisory Committee in early 1961, challenging Martin and other members of the party's parliamentary wing for their leader's favour.

These new activists ought to have been part of Martin's natural constituency. He was not unsympathetic to many of their progressive social initiatives, though they reached ahead further and faster than any similar proposals under St. Laurent. But he held back. He distrusted their lack of real political experience, and he opposed the party's national study conference for including so many people who "were not real supporters."[102] His hometown of Windsor was highly dependent on American investment, and he was suspicious of the nationalist tinge that coloured Gordon and the party's younger wing. Like other experienced politicians, he worried about tying the party's fate to an activist agenda while in Opposition, saddling a future government with a heavy program that it could not implement. He did little to hide his doubts. As a journalist remarked at the conference, Martin "could almost be heard to mutter, 'Enough of these bloody ideas – let's get back to the politics.'"[103]

The party's younger members were equally dubious of Martin, whom they were inclined to dismiss as a simple "old pol." They laughed aloud when one of the crowd's newer converts, the Albertan Jim Coutts, a skilled mimic, recounted the tale, doubtless apocryphal, of Martin touring his riding:

> "And how is that fine woman, your mother?" Martin asked one youthful voter, implying that he knew her well.
>
> "Much the same as she was this morning when you asked," the constituent replied. "Still dead."[104]

A decade later, Martin would privately admit that "I was out of touch, especially with the younger people. I was unaware of the generation problem."[105] That gap opened in the late 1950s and yawned wider over time, as a gulf was fixed between Martin and Pearson's youthful party. Though overblown, there is considerable truth in Tom Kent's claim that after 1958, Martin "really withdrew from a major role in the party."[106]

MARTIN UNDERESTIMATED the impact that Pearson's recruits and their left-leaning policies would have on the Liberal Party's evolution during the next decade. For him, the party's future remained where it had been throughout his political career – in the House of Commons. His House differed from the one encountered by his principal colleagues on the Liberal front benches, Pearson, Chevrier, and Pickersgill. Pearson was never truly comfortable in the parliamentary setting and grew less so as his relations with Diefenbaker soured. Pickersgill, admired as a tactician but feared for his wit, was deeply disliked by Conservative ministers and MPs. Martin, however, was one of the boys, "a House of Commons man," and that mattered in making him one of the Opposition's outstanding critics.

MPs valued his sense of humour and his willingness to join in their games. He laughed at their boyish jokes, at the puerile notes warning him that his fly was undone when he rose to speak, at the efforts to ply him with alcohol before important speeches.[107] As a cabinet minister, he had undertaken countless favours for his fellow MPs, creating friendships on which he could draw. "The huge Conservative majority will sit still," marvelled political journalist Richard Jackson, "and from this well-regarded friend take such abuse as would be tolerated from no other member of the Opposition. It makes him the Liberals' fightingest member. He can carry and finish an attack that no other Liberal or CCFer could even start."[108]

It helped that his relations with Diefenbaker were good. The two men were unyielding political foes but had been friends since the 1940s. Martin never forgot that Diefenbaker was "extremely kind" to him when Paul Jr. was stricken with polio in 1946; as health minister, he reciprocated, rushing supplies of an experimental drug, aminopterin, over the border to treat Diefenbaker's first wife as she fought leukemia in 1951.[109] The two men were joined by their shared resentment at having had to fight hard for every success against their respective parties' privileged establishments. Martin was quick to cable his congratulations to the prime minister-elect in June 1957, joining him a week later for a tour of his office with its newly hung image of Sir John A. Macdonald. The visit was heavy with significance.[110]

Martin was the only member of the Opposition whom Diefenbaker feared. Indeed, as he remarked, "Paul is the only parliamentarian the Grits have."[111] Diefenbaker admired his keen tactical sense. "Ahhh," he would chuckle as the Opposition executed a tricky parliamentary manoeuvre, "that's Paul."[112] Martin sharpened his talent for needling ministers and drove the prime minister to distraction by running roughshod over the obliging Speaker, Roland Michener. He would rise slowly in question period, his face wreathed in smiles for "my friend the minister," and pose an innocent-sounding query. His follow-up question would be sharper, with his body turned so that he could not see Michener. As it gradually dawned on Martin – after his point had been made – that his words had moved the Speaker to object, his mood would switch from assertiveness to humble cooperation. The effect was immediate: "When the members on both sides of the House start yammering and pounding their desks, and Mr. Speaker Michener is bobbing up and down on the Commons 'throne' like a be-robed Jack-in-the-Box, it's the signal that Paul Martin is up and at it."[113]

Martin's debating and speaking skills rivalled Diefenbaker's own. Arthur Ford, the veteran editor of the Conservative *London Free Press,* thought him "the best orator in the present house."[114] Most contemporary observers rated Diefenbaker more highly, but the difference was slight. "When it came to play-acting," claimed Associate Defence Minister Pierre Sévigny, "Martin was second-best only to Diefenbaker. He could look sad or gay almost at will, sound happy and delighted for a moment, then appear sorry and mortified a few seconds later."[115] Conservative journalist Patrick Nicholson, who liked both men, wrote that Diefenbaker "towers above all others in today's House" and can "play upon his audience as can no other orator in federal politics today." Martin, he added, was the Opposition's most "colorful politician."[116]

Martin served as the main Liberal critic for foreign affairs, agriculture, and labour. Though his semi-rural riding included a large farming community, he had learned little about agriculture during his two decades in Parliament. His friends at the *Windsor Star* kidded him that he "did not know a soybean from a summer fallow."[117] They were probably right. The job of agriculture critic fell to him by default. He was a willing but ineffectual farm spokesman, happily stepping aside when Hazen Argue, the displaced CCF leader from Saskatchewan, defected to the Liberals in 1962.

He was better versed in foreign policy, but during the first years in Opposition, it was hardly a vote-getter. The Progressive Conservative government hewed more or less to the policies established by St. Laurent, and Martin was reluctant to be too critical. He genuinely liked both of Diefenbaker's external affairs ministers, Sidney Smith, whom he had known as a student at university, and his idealistic successor, Howard Green.

Martin specialized in labour and unemployment. The plight of the jobless appealed to his populist instincts and his traditional Liberal prejudices. His interest reflected the political imperatives of his industrialized and heavily unionized constituency. He was particularly aware of the threat

1 The grade seven class at Pembroke Separate School in 1915. Paul Martin, third from the right in the middle row, has his arms crossed.

2 "A thirst for a disciplined liberty." After three unhappy years at the Collège Apostolique St-Alexandre de la Gatineau, Martin arrived at Toronto's University of St. Michael's College in 1921. He thrived amid its progressive Catholic ethos, graduating in 1925.

3 Martin speechifying in Windsor in the early 1930s.

4 Progressive Conservative Gordon Graydon, Justice Minister Louis St. Laurent, and Martin arrive for the first meeting of the United Nations General Assembly in London, January 1946. A committed internationalist, who had watched the League of Nations collapse during the 1930s, Martin remained a steadfast champion of the postwar UN.

5 "If Mackenzie King said hello to you, God, you got home and you put that in the book." Prime Minister W.L.M. King and Martin, whose skilful work on the Canadian Citizenship Act impressed his boss, share a word before the first Citizenship Court ceremonies, Ottawa, 3 January 1947.

6 Promoted to minister of national health and welfare in late 1946, Martin was responsible for the costly range of shared federal-provincial social programs, including old age pensions, that epitomized the expanding postwar welfare state. He is shown here at a meeting of the Interprovincial Old Age Pension Board in January 1948. Left to right: C.H. Green, Ontario Old Age Pensions Committee; W.A. Goodfellow, minister of public welfare for Ontario; Martin; B.W. Heise, deputy minister of public welfare for Ontario.

7 "The people around me had a great deal of influence ... Why have them there if they didn't?" As national health and welfare minister from 1946 to 1957, Martin assembled a strong team of advisors. Among them were Dr. Donald Cameron, deputy minister of health (left), and Dr. Fred Jackson, director of health insurance studies (right), in Martin's office, Ottawa, 1950.

8 "For God's sake, let's get these damn sirens going." Cabinet handed Martin responsibility for the country's lacklustre civil defence effort. Despite his high-profile publicity work, Martin failed to convince Canadians that Ottawa took the underfunded program seriously, and he was criticized for its inadequacies. Maj. Richard Bingham, chief of civil defence in the civil service, Martin, and Brig. J.C. Jefferson, deputy federal civil defence coordinator, are shown here at a launch for a civil defence display, c. 1952.

9 "A seasoned negotiator." A regular member of Canada's postwar UN delegations, Martin played an important role in advancing a Canadian initiative in 1952 to restart deadlocked talks on ending the Korean War. He is shown here addressing a meeting of the Political Committee at the UN on 3 November 1952.

10 "A family to be proud of, a wife to hold up as the best a man can have." Mary Anne, Martin, Nell, and Paul Jr., September 1953.

11 "I think he is a genius." Martin admired accomplished, charismatic, and unconventional men, including the British press baron and former politician Lord Beaverbrook, whose friendship he nurtured through the 1950s. Shown here are Martin, Nell, and Lord Beaverbrook sailing in Montego Bay, Jamaica, in January 1954.

12 By 1955, their bitter Cold War rivalry had prompted Washington and Moscow to veto the membership applications of twenty-two nations anxious to join the UN. When UN Secretary-General Dag Hammarskjöld pressed for progress, Martin, head of Canada's UN delegation in the fall of 1955, responded with a  dramatic diplomatic initiative that ensured the UN's universal character. In this photo, Martin consults with Hammarskjöld during debate on the admission of new members at the UN in New York, November 1955.

13 "Hello, I'm Paul Martin from Windsor." After a decade as national health and welfare minister, Martin was growing frustrated with political life in Ottawa. He left Canada on a goodwill tour through Asia in November 1956, determined not to miss the teaming vastness of revolutionary Asia. In this photo, Martin shares a hookah with a villager at a sugar mill in East Punjab, India, on 17 January 1957.

14 "In close shots, his glasses are distracting and his eyes unmistakeably look two different ways." Martin was gifted at public affairs and easily handled Canadian journalists during the 1940s and 1950s. He understood the importance of the new medium of television, seeking advice on his make-up and performances. But he did poorly on TV, and during the 1960s, a younger generation of reporters grew skeptical of his public pronouncements. Shown here are Martin and Alan Hodges on the set at CKCO TV Kitchener in 1957.

15 On the eve of the Liberal leadership convention, Martin and former prime minister Louis St. Laurent (right) greet Lester B. Pearson on his return from Norway, where he received the Nobel Peace Prize.

16 "I wanted the job as much as Pearson." Despite the overwhelming odds against him, Martin challenged party favourite L.B. Pearson – a long-time friend, and rival – for the leadership of the Liberal Party in January 1958. Insiders were surprised by Martin's aggressive tactics in a campaign, which he lost by a tally of 305 votes to Pearson's 1,074. In this photo, Martin supporters carry him around the hall during the leadership convention on 15 January 1958.

17 "The result was especially gratifying." The Liberal Party rebounded in the 1962 general election, which reduced Prime Minister John Diefenbaker's Progressive Conservative government to minority status. To Martin's delight, the Liberals added two new seats in the Windsor area. Shown here are Martin (right) and new MPs Herb Gray of Essex West (left) and Eugene Whelan of Essex South (right) shortly after the June vote.

18 "I don't think the Lord himself could beat Paul Martin here." The candidate listens as Gabe Renaud, a voter in Martin's Essex East riding, complains about access to Highway 401. The 1963 election campaign returned the Liberal Party to power with a minority government. Martin won his seat in all ten federal elections held between 1935 and 1965.

19 "Books are my one extravagance." Martin and Nell in the renovated library of the Lowe-Martin House in Windsor, 1963.

20 "It was very clear that there was a chord." Soon after becoming secretary of state for external affairs in April 1963, Martin realized that handling the complications arising from French president Charles de Gaulle's determination to inflame Quebec nationalism would be one of his most important tasks. He relied on his close friendship with de Gaulle's foreign minister, Couve de Murville (right), to get the federal point of view across to the Élysée. At their meeting in Paris on 16 January 1964, the two men agreed to regular bilateral encounters.

21 A product of the Great Depression and the Second World War, Martin remained a staunch liberal internationalist and strongly backed collective security at the UN and NATO. Shown here are Martin and Prime Minister Lester B. Pearson flanked by Ambassador George Ignatieff (left) and NATO Secretary General Dirk Stikker (right) in Paris, 17 January 1964.

22 "We cannot act like shopkeepers." On 12 March 1964, as Greek and Turkish Cypriots rioted on Cyprus, and Greece and Turkey edged closer to war, Martin hurried to New York to admonish UN Secretary-General U Thant for failing to create a UN peacekeeping force. On his return to Ottawa, Martin played a key role in cobbling together an international force and defusing the crisis.

23 "I had as much to lose politically as anybody." Martin and US Secretary of the Treasury Douglas Dillon at a meeting of the Canada–US Joint Ministerial Committee on Trade and Economic Affairs in Ottawa in April 1964. The two delegations skirmished over Canadian export incentives for automotive parts, part of the process that eventually led to the Auto Pact, a key preoccupation for Martin in 1964–65.

24 Martin admired US Secretary of State Dean Rusk, who was always ready to hear him out. Here, the two men, who enjoyed a friendly relationship, chat informally at the spring ministerial meeting of the North Atlantic Council in The Hague, Netherlands, 11 May 1964.

25 "An intriguing and powerful personality ... LBJ was a strong president." In contrast to Pearson, who was disconcerted by their January 1965 visit to President Lyndon B. Johnson's Texas ranch, Martin delighted in the Texan's easy informality and frank political talk. The difference in perspective between the two Canadians mattered and would shape their views on the escalating American engagement in Vietnam. In this photo, Martin bids farewell to the US president at his Texas ranch as Pearson looks on.

26 Paul Martin had always aimed for the top job in government. Once the front-runner to succeed Prime Minister Pearson as Liberal leader, the aging minister faded as the Liberal leadership campaign unfolded in the spring of 1968 and Justice Minister Pierre Trudeau roared ahead. When he did poorly in the early voting, Martin graciously retired from the race. He is shown here waiting for the results, seated in the stands and puffing a cigar with his son Paul Jr. at his side.

27 "Complaints from less developed countries and polite waffling from developed countries." In April 1968, following his leadership defeat, Martin retired from the House of Commons and joined the Senate as Government Leader. His new job was much less demanding, and he became a popular choice to lead official Canadian delegations abroad. In April 1972, he joined Marc Rochon of the Department of Trade and Commerce (left) and Ambassador Don McPhail (centre) at the UN Conference on Trade and Development, Santiago, Chile.

28 The family cottage in Colchester, constructed from lumber salvaged from an abandoned church, had been in Nell's family since the early 1920s. It remained a valued refuge, where Martin returned each August. Martin and Nell are shown here at the cottage in August 1976.

29 "The young people of today are certainly different." Martin, who always enjoyed talking to young people, addresses a political science class at Wilfrid Laurier University in March 1986.

30 Martin and Paul Martin Jr. at the Lowe-Martin House in Windsor, c. 1990.

posed by the CCF, which reacted to Diefenbaker's success by reinventing itself in 1961 as the New Democratic Party (NDP), with formal ties to Canadian labour.

Martin failed to distinguish himself during the 1958 parliamentary session, which opened in May and dragged on through the summer. Diefenbaker's popularity made it risky to attack either him or his government too forcefully. Martin was happy to escape in August, when Pearson, in one of the small gestures he used to woo his support, suggested that he represent the party at a conference of parliamentarians in Geneva, combining the excursion with a tour through the Middle East. It was a chance to get away with Nell, to whom he had promised a European vacation long before. The Martins stopped in London and conferenced in Geneva before finally heading to Rome. "The trip is just wonderful," Nell wrote home. "We get very tired and are apt to spit at each other, but just when we get fatigued."[118] The devout Nell was overwhelmed by the Vatican and their glimpse of Pope Pius XII. "I was speechless with emotion," she recalled, "the most dramatic time in my life, when His Holiness came in the door ... Oh, how happy I was."[119]

The Middle East held greater attractions for her husband. This was his first visit to the region, where the simmering Arab-Israeli conflict and the Suez Crisis had pushed it near the top of the global agenda. Like many Liberals of his generation, Martin was a strong supporter of Israel. He had backed Jewish demands for a homeland in the wake of the Holocaust and had embraced the UN role in its creation, views that were doubtless reinforced by his networks at home. Unlike many French Canadian Catholics of his age, he was free of anti-Semitism, and the emphasis he placed on tolerance as the central civic and political virtue made him a welcome and frequent speaker at such interfaith groups as the Canadian Council of Christians and Jews. He also had a circle of close Jewish friends, which included Paul Nathanson, the Montreal lawyer Lazarus Phillips, and the suave Michael Comay, Israel's ambassador to Canada from 1953 to 1957. The emotional highlight of Martin's trip was undoubtedly the day spent on a kibbutz at the edge of the Negev, discussing philosophy with David Ben-Gurion, Israel's first prime minister. The young country was "indeed a miracle," Martin told friends and colleagues, "an unbelievable place."[120]

He spent time in several Arab countries, which was an even more forma-
tive experience. He was impressed by Egyptian president Gamal Abdel
Nasser, "a charmer ... gracious ... tremendous personality ... fully in
control of everything he does."[121] Iraq, where the regime had erected kan-
garoo courts to rid the country of its previous rulers, repelled him. Nell
called it "gruesome."[122] In Lebanon, which was gripped by crisis, he met
outgoing and incoming presidents Camille Chamoun and Fuad Chehab,
and then mischievously slipped away from his Canadian handlers to meet
with insurgent rebels. The Middle East was a dangerous place, he concluded, one marked by instability, tension, and Cold War intrigue, much
of it plotted by the American and British diplomats on whom Canada still
depended for news of the region. That needed to change, he told senior
officials in External Affairs on his return. Canada ought to have more of
its own missions in the Middle East and should play an independent role,
one more focused on the United Nations, even at the risk of alienating
Washington and London.[123]

Martin's mother, aged seventy-eight, died in September. As he recalled
simply, her death was "a very sad blow."[124] During the final years of her life,
they spoke almost daily. "The telephone would ring at 8 in the morning,"
recalled her daughter Lucille, "and my mother would say, 'That's my son
in Ottawa.'"[125] For the rest of his life, Martin faithfully marked the deaths
of his parents, Lumina and Philippe, with annual memorial Masses in
Pembroke's St. Columbkille Cathedral.

His spirits revived in the new year. Canada's unemployment rate touched
7.0 percent in January 1959, up from 4.6 percent in 1957, giving the Opposition its first real target. Pearson, Chevrier, Martin, and Pickersgill – the
"Four Horsemen of the Apocalypse," as Tories dubbed them due to their
negative criticism – were a formidable team. Martin led the attack on
unemployment and the gnawing inflation that diminished the wages and
purchasing power of Canadians. His assault on government economic
policy in his respone to the Throne Speech was judged the best performance in the House since Diefenbaker had savaged Pearson a year earlier.[126]
"Canada," he thundered later, "has a higher percentage of unemployed
workers than any other country in the western world."[127] There was more
trouble, as there had been in the 1940s, over Martin's careless use of statistics. Justice Minister Davie Fulton described his figures as "fabrications,

pure and simple." Doug Harkness, the minister of agriculture, scorned the "Martin bureau of statistics," or Martin BS.[128]

Martin persisted in his attacks, prompting another uproar in committee and winning national headlines for his fight against the heavy-handed tactics of the Conservative chair and his large majority of young MPs. "Don't lose your temper now," he teased in a "fatherly" voice. "A man who loses his temper loses his mind."[129] He gloried in the notoriety and the bruised feelings on the government benches.

The session demonstrated that the Liberal front bench could handle Diefenbaker, and party morale soared. When the House of Commons reconvened in January 1960, with the unemployment rate touching 8 percent, the Liberal Opposition resumed its attack on the government's economic policy. Martin again hammered away at unemployment. He daily characterized the issue as "alarming," "an emergency," and "a disaster," denouncing the government's "relaxed" and "laissez-faire" approach.[130] Dropping his voice, he explained for insensitive Tory ministers that unemployment "makes a man feel useless, not wanted; it makes one live out of fear; and from fear ... springs hate."[131]

He hounded the sincere and unassuming labour minister, Michael Starr, in pursuit of the precise number of jobless. Why, he probed, did Starr indicate that there were only 504,000 unemployed Canadians, when his own figures showed that 782,542 Canadians were actually drawing unemployment insurance?[132] By March, when the Labour Department estimates were up for debate, the Speaker had lost control of the House. While Liberal members prolonged the tortuous debate, government backbenchers shouted them down. The government's confusion and bungling were evident. "This has been a good session," Martin reflected, "I feel we are making great gains. Bit by bit, the public are beginning to realise this is basically a weak government."[133]

Poll results suggested that he was right. Progressive Conservative support had declined from a high of 59 percent in January 1959 to 48 percent in May 1960. "I venture to suggest," Martin predicted in July, "that because of the way the government has handled the problem of unemployment in particular the next Gallup poll ... will show that the hon. gentlemen have lost still more support from the Canadian people."[134] By September, Tory backing had sagged to just 38 percent.[135] Martin and Pickersgill always insisted that the Liberal critique of the government's economic policy had eroded its support. Many Conservatives concurred. Roy Fabish, the astute Tory insider, judged the tactics "immensely effective. Every day: unemployment, unemployment ... unemployment."[136] Justice Minister Davie Fulton agreed. "Unemployment," he recalled, "probably did more than anything else to beat us."[137] Starr moaned that "the opposition kept pounding at us ... It was an everyday occurrence with the 'Four Horsemen.' I remember $35 million [a small sum even then] for the municipal winter works program. They debated it for eight days, eight solid days."[138]

As the government's fortunes declined, Martin shored up his standing in Essex East. Spooked by his close call of 1958, he and Nell re-established a permanent home in Windsor in July 1960. They splashed out $22,000 for a sprawling stone mansion at 2021 Ontario Street in Walkerville, a showpiece built for $130,000 in 1928 by the prosperous rumrunner Harry Low. It was a magnificent house. Designed in the English cottage or Cotswold style, the four-thousand-square-foot building featured a convex facade of several bays, with jerkin-head gables, oriel windows, and an arched recessed entrance. The interior boasted a spiral oak staircase and walnut panelling.[139] Martin himself oversaw the renovations that transformed the cloister, with its twenty-foot ceilings and sixteen feet of bevelled-glass windows, into the kind of library that had awed him as an undergraduate. "Books," he confessed, "are my one extravagance."[140] Nell, who aspired to membership in Windsor's tony Walkerville set, was thrilled. Martin's pleasure was more layered. It rankled a bit that locals dubbed the home the Low-Martin House (rather than Martin-Low), but after a drink, Martin would chuckle with wicked pleasure at the ironic winds of fortune that had cast him up among the "Walkerville snoots."[141]

Windsorites appreciated his return, its significance pointed out by friendly columnists in the *Windsor Star*. Though his power to help Windsor and its citizens was obviously reduced in Opposition, he ensured that he was not forgotten. As always, he kept in touch, with phone calls and short notes of support and congratulations. Quick to champion local causes, he put himself at the head of campaigns for better mail service and improvements to Windsor's harbour and airport.[142] He joined the city's black residents in attacking slipshod regulations that allowed federally subsidized rental housing to bar them on racial grounds.[143]

Whenever he could, he offered more constructive help. For instance, he used his contacts with premiers and officials in the provincial governments of Ontario, New Brunswick, Quebec, and Manitoba to lobby for contracts on behalf of Canadian Bridge Works, a local steel-maker.[144] He appeared before the Board of Transport Commissioners to fight Canadian National Railway's decision to close the train station at Stoney Point, and won.[145] He waged a four-year battle to convince governments in Ottawa and Toronto to collaborate to dredge the Ruscomb River. He developed the case for dredging, convinced both sides to recognize their shared interest, and coaxed them to the table, where they agreed on joint action.[146]

He returned to Ottawa in November 1960, when Diefenbaker finally summoned Parliament to tackle unemployment and the country's sinking economy. Political anxieties and cabinet bickering curdled the mood in the House. "The pressure this session seems to be even greater than usual," Martin confided to a friend, Frank Starr.[147] He faced other unwelcome distractions during the spring. In late March, he had a hernia operation and was confined to a hospital bed for a week. Six weeks later, he was back in Ottawa General with a badly twisted ankle. Nell was sympathetic. "It has been lonesome without you," she wrote wistfully from Windsor.[148] Paul Jr. struck a different note, teasing his father for his recent weight gain – "with a centre deck like yours it is impossible to fall" – and accusing him of wanting to "try out in Opposition every hospital."[149]

His daughter, Mary Anne, represented a different kind of distraction. Like many other postwar teenagers, she chafed rebelliously under the expectations of her ambitious parents. She had long wanted out, and as she neared the end of grade twelve in April 1960, she urged her parents (and her brother) to allow her to train as a nurse. "It will be a great disappointment to you and Paul," she acknowledged. But, she added hopefully, "I think you'd rather have me a big success in what I want rather than study for something that doesn't appeal to me ... And Dad, I'd rather do that and feel a greater sense of achievement than having an honours BA with all firsts."[150] Her parents were not convinced. Mary Anne was defiant and finished the year with a bang, failing three of her six subjects. "And," she reflected later, "I couldn't have cared less."[151]

She started over at Walkerville Collegiate Institute the following September, but the new city and the school left her just as unhappy, and as the year ended in the spring of 1961 she and a friend sought their own escape. While Martin and Nell were attending Paul's graduation from St. Mike's at the University of Toronto, the two girls borrowed the family car and headed for Manhattan. Understandably, Martin was frantic with worry, later breaking into tears in the House of Commons. The girls were not gone long, however. With help from the FBI, the US embassy in Ottawa, and friends in New York, they were soon back in Windsor, writing their exams. Mary Anne remained a source of worry.

Back in Ottawa, Martin soon tripped over more evidence of the government's incompetence – its strained relationship with Bank of Canada governor James Coyne. Smart, austere, and arrogant, Coyne was a tight money man whose controversial speeches on monetary policy cut across the government's expansionist fiscal program and distressed cabinet. When ministers discovered that he would qualify for an enriched $25,000 pension, they used it as an excuse to fire him, implying that he had acted improperly. The implication was outrageous, but Finance Minister Donald Fleming refused to seek a settlement, and Coyne went public to defend his integrity. Tipped off by a friendly journalist, Martin asked Fleming on 13 June whether the government had demanded Coyne's resignation. Surprised, Fleming turned "red as a beet" and awkwardly ducked the question.[152]

The government was within its rights to fire Coyne, but his pension ought not to have been the issue. Next day, Fleming was wrong-footed from the start as he tried to explain his side of the story. He compounded his error in early July by refusing to let Coyne testify in his own defence before a House committee. Before packed and tense government benches, stirred into a frenzy by a three-line Tory whip, Pearson, Martin, and Pickersgill excoriated Fleming and Diefenbaker for their assault on Coyne's right to a fair hearing. In one "powerful" speech, Martin likened the government's bill of dismissal to a Tudor bill of attainder, a notorious device that was designed to deprive the accused of a fair trial.[153]

When the bill moved to the Senate on 10 July, its Liberal majority gave Coyne his hearing. For three days, he released a flood of documents that highlighted the government's economic ineptitude. According to Coyne, it had neither a fiscal nor a monetary policy, and its actions violated International Monetary Fund rules. There were stories of feuds between Finance and Trade and Commerce, and of one Bank of Canada director who was "a political henchman of the Minister of Finance."[154] The Senate turned back the bill, and Coyne resigned in triumph, collecting his pension as he went. Fleming was ruined, and the government's economic policies were exposed to ridicule. "This whole Coyne affair," Martin later reminisced, "laid the foundation for the fall of the ... Diefenbaker government."[155]

The exhausted parliamentarians recessed for their summer break on 13 July, returned in September to prorogue the House, and scattered until the new year. Parliament reassembled in January 1962, anticipating an election. A desultory debate on the Throne Speech dragged into late February before an empty House, as backbenchers and ministers slipped away to their ridings, and the prime minister dallied. In March, Diefenbaker and his allies in the Tory press flayed the Liberals for obstructionism; a month later, he called an election for 18 June.

The government's defeat seemed inevitable. Cabinet was divided, and the Liberals were ahead in the May polls, 45 to 38 percent.[156] Worse, alarming evidence of the government's economic bungling burst into full view early in the campaign. Fleming's efforts in 1961 to talk down the value of the Canadian dollar from its high of US$1.06 had unsettled international bankers and investors. They wondered, too, about the growth of program spending, up almost 7 percent since 1961, a rising deficit, and the sharp decline in Canada's reserves, which dropped almost $1 billion during the first six months of 1962.[157] To forestall a run on the dollar, Ottawa was forced to peg its value at US92.5 cents in May. Gleeful Liberal workers papered the country in "Diefenbucks" and "Diefendollars," decorated with the prime minister's likeness and worth just 92.5 cents. As one young Torontonian recalled, campaign offices served "Diefen-drinks" – "Canada on the rocks."[158]

Martin's campaign started at home, with a swing through southwestern Ontario and his usual nomination convention on 8 May. The faithful gathered in St. Gilbert's Hall in the heart of Essex East for another "old-time political rally." The Liberal star candidate for York West, Toronto Maple Leaf hockey great Red Kelly, was on hand to autograph souvenir programs for all. "I shook so many hands," he complained, "I had to take my ring off because my fingers were getting raw."[159] Windsor Liberals loved it, for the first time chanting, "Oom Paul, Paul, Oom Paul, Paul." The nickname Oom

Paul, applied by *Windsor Star* columnist Richard Harrison some time during the 1950s, echoed the affectionate Afrikaans diminutive of Oom or Uncle Paul Kruger, the former Transvaal president. It stuck.

Democratic pollster Lou Harris, up from the United States to help, told Liberal campaign managers to play down Pearson, who left voters cold, and emphasize his more popular team. They followed his instructions, and Martin spent the next week campaigning from Manitoba to British Columbia, where the party hoped to pick up seats. He was tired and edgy to start, dismaying party workers in Manitoba with a "tantrum" over travel arrangements.[160] He relaxed as the trip unfolded. There were ample Tory shortcomings to highlight, especially unemployment and the Coyne affair. Martin attacked Diefenbaker for "Madison Avenue government" – more publicity than substance – and offered voters an updated Liberal platform, speaking easily on its proposals for better contributory pensions and comprehensive health care.[161]

The signs of success on Martin's Western tour were good. In Vancouver, 2,300 people turned out to hear him. In Saskatoon, he drew almost 1,000 voters, where he had attracted fewer than 100 four years earlier.[162] But his confidence ebbed as he travelled through eastern and northern Ontario in May, and into the Maritimes. By then, it was clear that a Liberal triumph was slipping away. Polls in early June showed the party's lead over the government narrowing to 38–36 percent as Réal Caouette's Social Credit surged ahead in rural Quebec, denying Pearson the seats he needed for victory. When the votes were counted, Diefenbaker clung to power, reduced to minority standing with 116 seats. The Liberal Opposition claimed 100 seats, with the balance held by Social Credit, who elected 30 members, and the NDP with 19.

Amid dashed Liberal hopes, there was some good news. Five Progressive Conservative cabinet ministers had been defeated, and the Liberals had gained strength in the House. Allan MacEachen and Arthur Laing, defeated in 1958, were back. They were joined by an impressive group of novice MPs, including Edgar Benson, Jack Davis, Walter Gordon, John Turner, Charles "Bud" Drury, Larry Pennell, and Maurice Sauvé. Martin, who won his own riding with an outright majority, also returned to Ottawa with his standing enhanced. "I must say that the result in [southwestern Ontario] was especially gratifying," he wrote one supporter. "It will be a great satisfaction to me to return to Parliament with five colleagues from the district, whereas before I was the only Member for that area."[163]

He retreated to the Colchester cottage for the summer. In September, he and Nell would celebrate their twenty-fifth wedding anniversary and there were festive plans to be made. Politics rarely intruded. Shaken by the election and faced with a divided cabinet, Diefenbaker governed without Parliament. In late June, he cut spending to restore confidence in the dollar. In September, he headed off to the Commonwealth Prime Ministers' Conference in London to crusade against Britain's entry into the European Common Market. Both topics provided Martin with ammunition for a short, sharp salvo against the government when he spent a day campaigning in the Stormont by-election. With his hair plastered against his skull and sweat streaming down his face in the July heat, he disputed Diefenbaker's right to rule without Parliament's confidence.[164] The local conservative newspaper, the *Ottawa Journal*, sent him packing, sneering that the "smiling and ruthless Liberal" was "playing politics and politics will not help Canada in her situation."[165]

But it was all politics now. When the House of Commons gathered on 27 September, the parties schemed and jockeyed for advantage. The Opposition slashed angrily at the government, skirted confidence votes, and waited for the perfect issue to defeat the Tories and bring on an election. Martin loved it. "I am up to my neck in Parliament," he thrilled to a constituent.[166] The new Speaker, Marcel Lambert, was a popular target for Opposition wrath, and Martin enjoyed baiting him. Diefenbaker, with no legislative agenda, played for time.

Time was not his ally. Over the weekend of 20–21 October, rumours reached Ottawa that Soviet missiles were stationed in Fidel Castro's Cuba. On Monday afternoon, 22 October, American president John F. Kennedy informed Diefenbaker of plans to quarantine the island and asked for Canada's support. As Canada was a member of NATO and a partner in NORAD, its support should have been automatic. It was not. Distrustful of the younger man, Diefenbaker hesitated. His half-hearted support for Washington alarmed Canadians, who resolutely backed Kennedy throughout the thirteen-day crisis.

The brush with nuclear war brought Canada's own simmering nuclear weapons debate to a boil. Diefenbaker had embraced joint North American air defence and accepted tactical nuclear weapons for NATO in 1957. His government seemed to grasp the implications of its choices, deciding to equip its forces in Europe and North America with nuclear-armed CF-104s, as well as with Honest John and Bomarc B missiles, which depended on nuclear warheads for their effectiveness. Talks with Washington on acquiring these weapons began well but stalled in 1960. A fervid champion of nuclear disarmament, External Affairs Minister Howard Green blocked progress. American frustrations increased steadily.

In Opposition, Liberal policy was equally ambiguous. The 1961 National Rally rejected nuclear weapons, and Martin had assured campaign audiences in May 1962 that the Liberal Party would not accept nuclear weapons "at this time." Of course, he had added, "if the US feels nuclear arms are necessary," a Liberal government would be "prepared to examine" any American plan.[167] That ambiguity ended abruptly in January 1963, when Pearson declared that a Liberal government would take the weapons and shoulder Canada's alliance responsibilities. Virtually alone among senior Liberals, Martin was not consulted. That hurt, but he rallied loyally and philosophically. Ultimately, he conceded, the decision was Pearson's to make.[168]

The shift in Liberal policy forced the government to clarify its own position. Diefenbaker tried. On 25 January, before packed and anxious House of Commons benches, he insisted on the logic of his policy in a speech so "equivocal" that, as Donald Fleming later wrote, "it surpassed Mackenzie King at his best."[169] Diefenbaker claimed to have abandoned no commitments, insisting that a nuclear role in NATO and NORAD was not needed. Alliance ministers, he said, would resolve Canada's role in NATO at their May meeting, and the country's place in NORAD was the subject of ongoing talks with Washington. The Americans were not amused, and the State Department issued a press release to challenge Diefenbaker's facts. Defence Minister Harkness was initially pleased with his prime minister's statement, then confused, and finally disgusted. He resigned on 3 February. Two days later, the government collapsed in disarray, calling an election for 8 April 1963.

8

SAVING THE WORLD,
1963–64

The election of 1963 defined an era. Down by a dozen points in the February polls, battered Progressive Conservative prime minister John Diefenbaker found his footing as the campaign unfolded. Firmly rejecting the nuclear weapons that had prompted the election, he hung them "like an albatross around Mr. Pearson's neck."[1] He offered Canadians an apparently stark choice between his vision of an authentic, independent Canada and a Liberal future bound to the sleek but hollow modernism of Imperial America. In Martin's view, Pearson and the youthful advisors who surrounded campaign chairman Walter Gordon played into his hands. Liberal gimmicks – homing pigeons that never arrived, a childish and insulting colouring book, and a controversial Truth Squad that dogged the Conservative leader – were US imports that lent weight to Diefenbaker's sinister interpretation. Amplified by academics and pundits over the next decade, Diefenbaker's Manichean vision narrowed the scope of Canadian foreign policy during the 1960s, seducing the naive and unwary with nationalist fantasies of unfettered independence.

That would soon matter for Paul Martin. The campaign was significant for him in other ways, too. It was an unwelcome reminder of his own ambiguous relations with Pearson and his lonely standing in the party. He urged the leader to consult with his most experienced colleagues on election strategy but was ignored.[2] Yet, it was hard for party brass to overlook his effectiveness and popularity as a platform speaker. He delivered the keynote pep talk at Gordon's own nomination meeting in January 1963, and the party gave him a major role on the national campaign trail.[3]

Martin opened and closed the campaign in Windsor, where he spent most weekends. His victory there was certain. The Social Credit candidate, Frank Gignac, scarcely exaggerated when he joked that "I don't think the Lord himself could beat Paul Martin here."[4] Martin spent much of his time on the road, touring the Maritimes and eastern Ontario, Alberta and British Columbia, and Quebec, which he visited twice. He plucked bits and pieces of his party's platform to build speeches on the theme of national unity, responding to worries of regional economic inequality and to Quebec's assertive drive toward a novel progressive social order. The veteran campaigner promised a department of industry, regional planning and investment, and a renewed federalism. "This concept of equality of rights and advantages," he promised voters in tiny Alma, Quebec, "of equality of responsibilities and obligations between the two groups – French and English – will inspire all actions of the next Liberal government."[5]

He encountered Diefenbaker only once. Their paths crossed in Alberta, where Martin greeted the prime minister with a cheeky full-page ad in the *Calgary Herald* that savaged his recent record and demanded a response.[6] Diefenbaker chortled derisively. He alone had salvaged his party's fortunes, driving Liberal poll numbers down to minority territory by late March, and Martin's hijinks couldn't hurt him. Diefenbaker's platform performances had a mystical quality that spring, and he beguiled the voters who flocked to hear him. Marvelling as he watched the Chief dance and weave around the nuclear issue, journalist Charles Lynch reported that the "Old Conjuror" delivered "a wizard performance."[7] Many Canadians thought so, too. On 8 April, though the Liberals won the election, the Tories retained 95 seats, enough to deny Pearson his majority. With 129 seats, the new Liberal government fell 4 seats short. The balance of power was held by Social Credit and the New Democratic Party, with 24 and 17 seats respectively.

Martin was unfazed by the challenges ahead. On 22 April, a perfect spring day in Ottawa, warm and sunny, he almost skipped up the driveway of Rideau Hall to be sworn into cabinet as secretary of state for external affairs – Canada's foreign minister. His colleague Jack Pickersgill, slated for secretary of state and House leader, urged him to slow down. "We've lots to do, Jack," Martin refused.[8] Pearson had saddled the government with a rash campaign promise of "60 Days of Decision," and Martin knew that voters and pundits would be looking for action. More importantly, his own appointment fulfilled a long-standing ambition. He had matured in depression and war, and he embraced foreign policy as a vital activity with real implications for Canadian lives. He was anxious to make a difference in his new portfolio. Doubtless, too, at sixty years old, he was conscious that his generation was aging, its moment passing. His last chance to realize his ultimate ambition, the prime ministership, lay just ahead, sometime in the next few years. There was no time to waste.

THERE WERE FEW surprises in Pearson's first cabinet and none in the portfolios that overlapped with Martin's. Walter Gordon, whose strident nationalism and political judgment Martin distrusted, became minister of finance. Mitchell Sharp headed Trade and Commerce. Martin respected him more but remained wary of the cautious bureaucratic values that Sharp had developed as a deputy minister under C.D. Howe and in his more recent role as a Bay Street insider. He was most comfortable with National Defence Minister Paul Hellyer. A scrappy straight-shooting reformer, Hellyer had been around for more than a decade and was soon absorbed in refashioning his department from the ground up.

Press reaction to the new cabinet was positive but hardly enthusiastic. Editorial writers described it as experienced and moderate, a "cabinet of experts."[9] However, a vague sense of youthful hopes disappointed hung about it. The Liberal *Ottawa Citizen* described it rather wistfully as the triumph of "experience over youth and service over promise."[10] Views of Martin were equally ambivalent. He was typically seen as an "admirable choice" whose appointment made "suitable use of the talents of a veteran."[11] But a note of reserve and implicit criticism crept into the press coverage. The *Toronto Star*, normally an admirer, characterized him blandly as "a solid administrator" who "should do well." To be on the safe side, it added, "we hope Prime Minister Pearson will exercise his unique talents in this field."[12] Martin and his colleagues would need to impress.

Martin was familiar with his new department, which was housed in the neo-Gothic splendour of Parliament Hill's East Block. His majestic office, Room 201, was situated on the building's southwest corner and had once belonged to Sir John A. Macdonald. Outfitted with high arching windows, dark wood panelling, and a handsome Victorian fireplace, it came with a heavy oak desk and dark leather chairs and sofa. Martin's boss, the watchful prime minister, sat a dozen offices away, at the end of a hall that ran directly north. The deputy minister, or under-secretary, occupied Room 263, at the far end of the southern corridor, which also accommodated the department's assistant under-secretaries. Cynical staff dubbed the passage Killer's Row, "where bright ideas went to die."[13] Martin had worked closely with Canada's small foreign service in its influential "Golden Age" of the 1940s and 1950s, and knew many of these men well. He "idealized" the department and generously judged its staff, many sporting the Oxbridge credentials that he so admired, to be "exceptionally able."[14]

External Affairs and its world were changing. The department's workload had grown sharply during the previous decade. Canada maintained diplomatic relations with eighty-four countries, up from forty-one in 1953, and staffed seventy-seven foreign missions, an increase of twenty-four. Consular and passport work were up by 130 percent. Over the past decade, the department's personnel had increased from 1,514 to 2,149, eroding its close-knit sense of community.[15] Money was scarce, and diplomatic assignments, often in the newer posts of Africa and Asia, were less attractive than they once were. External Affairs struggled to keep up, while its morale sagged. "I discovered that 'moaning and groaning' was an External mantra," wrote one recruit to the ministry in 1963, "the not surprising consequence of many reportedly bright people in search of something more to do with less."[16]

The department's operating environment had become more complex and taxing as well. As Europe and the Far East recovered from the Second World War, and post-colonial Africa and Asia pushed to the forefront, Canada's relative standing declined, and with it the scope for meaningful diplomacy. West Germany and France jostled for a bigger role in NATO, raising questions about Canada's place in the alliance. Third World nations added race and economics to Commonwealth and UN agendas, pushing aside traditional Canadian worries about peacekeeping, stability, and global governance. The intensifying East-West struggle for the developing South, which flared most acutely in Southeast Asia and Vietnam, defied the mediatory diplomacy that Canada had patented during the 1950s.

There were novel domestic pressures as well. Increased social spending on health care, pensions, and post-secondary education diverted money away from defence and diplomacy, and complicated relations with Washington and other allies. Ottawa also faced demands from Quebec. Swept up in a nationalist "quiet revolution" of political and economic awakening, the province's educated elite demanded a new diplomacy that embraced its francophone heritage. All of this occurred as the press that had fawned on Canada's postwar diplomats gave way to the skeptical spirit of the 1960s and its rising tide of youthful protest. The change in tone was highlighted early on in *Saturday Night*, the brainy monthly magazine for Canada's liberal elite. Donald Gordon, a former CBC London correspondent turned political scientist, fired a salvo across Martin's bow in October: "Warning: Our Halo Abroad Is Slipping."[17]

Pearson's government was determined to restore the diplomatic credibility that Diefenbaker had squandered. During its election campaign, the Liberal Party had promised improved relations with the United States, Britain, and Canada's other NATO allies. Martin shared these broad priorities. A product of the Great Depression and the Second World War, he remained a staunch liberal internationalist. His foreign policy would aim for the moderate selflessness of the responsible middle power. He strongly backed collective security at the United Nations and NATO, the mainstay of the US-led Western alliance. He brought to the East Block his own short-term priorities, which he liked to lay out during his first year in office. His list shifted a little as headlines changed, but he consistently cited cultivating closer relations with France, tackling the North-South divide, joining the Organization of American States, and seating communist China in the United Nations among his most important objectives.[18]

He adopted his own diplomatic style. He was aware of the quickening pace of global change and the decade's youthful voices raised to welcome it. His daughter, Mary Anne, now nineteen, personified the questing protest culture of the 1960s. However, Martin was ill-equipped to embrace fully these pressures. He was more cautious than he had been earlier. This reflected his personality and a natural unwillingness to engage in risky behaviour that might jeopardize his front-runner status in the race to succeed Pearson. Just as importantly, it was a product of his view that foreign policy was deeply rooted in long-standing historical and geographic forces.

Change was naturally slow. "Foreign policy," he contended, "is not something to be chopped and changed. Foreign policy evolves, and fundamental reversals or changes are not easy to come by and they are so often counterproductive ... Outright change is seldom wise in cause or productive in consequence."[19]

To the chagrin of his professional advisors, he placed enormous emphasis on personal diplomacy and direct contact with his political counterparts. "The only real instrument a foreign minister has is discussion," he remarked, "and while you have reports ... from your ambassador, you must remember that those are not more than reports. I think the good active foreign minister is the man who tries to get at the source of things. There is no better source than the man who makes the policy."[20] In an age of cheap long-distance calling and booming jet travel, Martin sensed the foreign minister's central importance as both architect and instrument of policy.

He was not an original foreign policy thinker, but he read voraciously, even as a busy minister. When he travelled, he took the latest histories and biographies with him, as well as books and journals from the emerging field of international relations, and he teased staff and colleagues for wasting their time on trashy best-sellers.[21] He was well briefed and thoughtful, and his political counterparts were usually willing to hear him out. He treasured the yearly cycle of spring and fall NATO ministerial meetings and delighted in the rituals of the annual UN General Assembly, when foreign ministers from across the globe held court in New York. He met as many as he could, sometimes issuing spur-of-the-moment invitations to visit Ottawa or Windsor. He remained a tireless negotiator, always ready to talk and review well-trodden ground in search of an opening. "It is hard to single out why a meeting is useful," he once explained. "The very fact that it is held means that it is good. You talk about problems in which you have an interest."[22]

Martin's unbounded faith in his own diplomacy made him an easy target for cynics, who suspected that his leadership ambitions lurked behind his every meeting. That was unfair, though his desire to succeed Pearson burned fiercely during the 1960s. Ambition helped to forge his style. Sensitive to charges that he was too political to become Liberal leader, he worked at shedding his partisan combativeness and striking a statesmanlike pose. "The bi-partisan nature of foreign policy has to be re-established," he declared in early 1964.[23] When pressed by a Social Credit member on a partisan issue, he peevishly snapped, "I'm not interested in political matters."[24] Challenged, he sought refuge in vagueness and long impenetrable sentences that were designed to capture the complexity of the task and give him the freedom to manoeuvre.

Both tactics hurt him. When he stood apart from the bitter parliamentary debates over Gordon's budget in 1963 and government scandals in 1964, he was accused of "not pulling his weight."[25] Beleaguered Liberals asserted that "Paul has to forget about saving the world and come give us a hand."[26] His non-political posturing was both untrue to his character and detrimental to his credibility. His rhetorical tricks, verbal sleights of hand that had usually generated admiration and respectful ribbing in the 1950s, were viewed warily during the 1960s, an era that valued "telling it like it is." When he dodged a question at an early press conference, younger reporters responded with "jeers and laughter."[27] Within a few years, even his hometown paper, the *Windsor Star*, could not resist labelling him the "Most Confusing Man of the Year."[28]

Martin leaned heavily on his political and bureaucratic advisors for help. His office remained lively and chaotic, filled with a hurried, often good-humoured, parade of officials and politicians, lobbyists and diplomats, and endless visitors from Windsor. His team was a little older and more cautious than the one he had assembled at Health and Welfare a decade earlier. It was larger and more hierarchical as well. It lacked the broad range of opinion that his former deputy ministers Donald Cameron and George Davidson offered, and it was much less united in search of a common goal. Its heart remained Marjorie Frank, his long-time private secretary. She managed his constantly changing schedule and personal affairs, helped by the popular and witty Anne-Marie Hamon, his assistant private secretary.

He had two principal political assistants, though neither obtained the level of influence enjoyed by their earlier counterparts. Isobel Quenneville, who had organized Windsor youth and women for Martin during the 1950s, filled Don Emerson's role as a constituency aide in Essex East. Duncan Edmonds was Martin's executive assistant in Ottawa. A top graduate of the University of Toronto, he had won a Mackenzie King scholarship to pursue a PhD at the London School of Economics (LSE) in the late 1950s. Edmonds was attracted by Martin's lofty progressivism at the 1958 Liberal convention, where the two first met. Ambitious and idealistic, he had his own agenda, which emphasized foreign aid and youth engagement. Working for Martin proved a disappointment. Edmonds resented filling the "gofer" role that Martin demanded of his staff and scorned his tolerance for Windsor politics.[29] Their relationship was not as close and productive as it ought to have been.

Martin enjoyed better relations with his early senior departmental advisors, mid-career bureaucrats who helped him manage the vast flow of External Affairs paper. He got along well with his first advisor, Mac Bow, whom he inherited from his predecessor. An able and hard-working graduate from the University of Alberta, Bow had been in the minister's office since 1962 and wanted out of the high-pressure job. Despite Martin's reluctance to see him go, he insisted and was rewarded with an appointment as ambassador to Czechoslovakia in early 1964.

Martin replaced him with John Hadwen. The minister's new advisor had fought in Italy and northwestern Europe during the Second World War, before studying at the University of Toronto and the LSE in the 1940s. He joined External Affairs in 1950 and spent the next decade moving up the diplomatic ranks, through postings in Ottawa, Pakistan, New York, and Oslo. A large, fearless man with a quirky and outsized sense of humour, Hadwen thrived in Martin's bustling office. He frequently travelled with him and shared his capacity for hard work, "24-hour stuff." He liked and admired Martin but stopped short of being his champion, a decision that won him the department's trust. Hadwen understood the political imperatives that drove his minister and was able to give foreign service officers a "sympathetic fix" on what Martin wanted from them.

That was important since many Canadian diplomats, including the two men who served as Martin's under-secretaries, were suspicious of his strong political instincts and motives. This was true of his first under-secretary, Norman Robertson, who had watched him skeptically since he had first struggled to promote his name as a young parliamentary secretary at the International Labour Organization in 1945. Despite their differing perspectives, the two men worked well together. Robertson was a legend in Ottawa. Prime Minister King had handed him the under-secretary's mantle at the age of thirty-eight, following the sudden death in 1941 of the department's main architect, O.D. Skelton. Robertson eventually served as high commissioner in London for two terms, ambassador to Washington, and clerk of the Privy Council. He was reappointed under-secretary in 1958. Martin always responded generously to experience and accomplishment, and the veteran mandarin had little trouble with the rookie foreign minister. Historian J.L. Granatstein asserts that Martin "was clearly dazzled by Robertson's range, by his ability to discourse at length and with fluency on the telegrams and the issues," but this patronizing judgment almost certainly overstates the case.[30]

Robertson's tenure with Martin was brief. He was fifty-nine in 1963, worn out by five years in harness. In January 1964, as he and Martin pondered his next assignment, the chain-smoking deputy minister was diagnosed with lung cancer. He told Martin that he wanted Marcel Cadieux, his longtime protege, to succeed him.

There was no doubt that Cadieux possessed the requisite resumé. Born in 1915, he was educated as a lawyer at the classical Collège André Grasset, pursuing graduate studies in law at the Université de Montréal and McGill. He joined External Affairs in 1941, serving abroad in wartime London and postwar Europe. He later worked at NATO headquarters during the height of the Cold War and on peacekeeping duties in Indochina in 1954-55.

In Ottawa, Cadieux divided his time between personnel and legal work. He enjoyed a reputation as a skilled and caring administrator, and thought hard about what it meant to be a Canadian diplomat. He proved a fine lawyer, too, rising to assistant under-secretary and legal advisor in 1956. Cadieux was promoted to deputy under-secretary in 1960.

Cadieux possessed a widely admired sense of humour, though he did not suffer fools gladly. As his irritation mounted, he would pull at his tightening collar, his face suffused with blood, until he erupted with a roar. As Robertson explained to Martin, he was a smart and experienced official, with good judgment and sound conservative views. Moreover, as a French Canadian who had championed francophone rights in Ottawa since the 1940s, he would reinforce the department's capacity to respond to a changing Quebec.[31]

Martin was not persuaded. Retired diplomat Escott Reid, whom he had befriended in the 1930s and whose progressive worldview still impressed him, was sniffing about for a final shot at the top job in External Affairs.[32]

NATO ambassador George Ignatieff was also rumoured to be a candidate.[33] From his hospital bed, Robertson lobbied for Cadieux's appointment, summoning Cabinet Secretary Gordon Robertson for help and sending his wife, Jetty, to see their old friend, Lester B. Pearson. The prime minister told Jetty that they would do "whatever Norman wanted."[34] Despite Martin's lingering doubts, Cadieux was chosen as acting under-secretary in January 1964. The appointment was confirmed in May.

Martin was always careful handling Cadieux, who was backed by powerful Ottawa insiders and enjoyed a sterling reputation around town. He told Cadieux that the appointment was his idea, a claim he later maintained.[35] He openly proclaimed his "greatest admiration" for his under-secretary, but the assessment in his memoirs was cooler, simply acknowledging Cadieux's "moral support" and "sound advice."[36] He adopted an even more critical tone in private. He found Cadieux haughty, aristocratic, and "jerky in his political judgements."[37] Specifically, as he told an interviewer, "the under-secretary was not fully aware of the need ... for more effective communication between the department and the people."[38]

This was a legitimate concern. Martin had worried since the early 1950s that External Affairs did a poor job of explaining its work to Canadians, and he wanted that fixed. But Cadieux held strong, almost metaphysical, views on the nature and role of the diplomat. In his world, politics and foreign policy, the rarefied product of dispassionate study and tranquil reflection by professional diplomats abroad, should rarely meet. The foreign service, he argued in his primer *The Canadian Diplomat,* was part of a superior "priesthood" that was trusted with the welfare of the state. Its members were certainly not cheap flacks who churned out press releases and statements for ambitious ministers. "The truth of the matter," Cadieux concluded in his diary, "is that the Minister seems unable, deliberately or otherwise, to grasp the true character of the diplomatic craft."[39] This critical insight shaped Cadieux's view of Martin.

He unhelpfully viewed Martin's reluctance to rotate good personnel and his caution over budget submissions – hallmarks of his ministerial career in the 1950s – as treasonous assaults on External Affairs itself. Cadieux made no effort to develop much sympathy for the politicians whom he served and could be utterly tone deaf to political context. The under-secretary smirked at Martin's political difficulties and viewed his tradecraft – the quick, reassuring smile at the TV cameras and the white lie to supplicants and office-seekers – as evidence of a fundamental dishonesty. He reacted with adolescent self-righteousness when he learned that Martin was quarrelling with other ministers over the choice of an architect for the department's new headquarters. "I finally understood," he fussed, "it was all about a hateful, disgusting, shitty patronage deal."[40] In the privacy of his diary, Cadieux contemptuously dismissed his minister as self-seeking and ambitious, indiscreet and untrustworthy, disloyal and ignorant.

Yet the two men carried on. Until they quarrelled in 1966 over including Cadieux's wife on a visit to Eastern Europe, a clear departure from government policy, Martin often strolled down to his deputy's Sandy Hill home after Sunday Mass for lunch and a casual review of the week's events. There were practical reasons for making the partnership work. As historian Robert Bothwell argues, Cadieux's backing was clearly essential if Martin hoped to make good on his plans to strengthen the department's francophone element and bolster relations with France. Cadieux, who had ambitions of his own, aspired to head the embassy in Paris. He knew that Martin, a prospective prime minister, could help fulfill this objective.

A careful reading of Cadieux's diary reveals that he also grudgingly acknowledged Martin's political skills and his diplomatic heft. More importantly, the two men shared a fundamentally similar worldview. They were both Catholics and strong anti-communists, deeply committed to Western liberal values and the US-led alliances that protected them. At a minimum, the system expected them to collaborate, and as consummate professionals, they did. Indeed, Cadieux sometimes seemed to hew so closely to Martin and his priorities that Pearson eventually regretted the appointment. "Cadieux has not turned out to be a good under-secretary," he confided to a friend. "With a high political minister like Martin, he should act on his own – the way I did."[41]

THE SUMMER OF 1963 was busy and hectic for Martin and Nell. Governing meant a full-time return to Ottawa, so the Martins set up house on the edge of exclusive Rockcliffe, in the Champlain Towers, a fashionable new high-rise. Ottawa real estate developer and Liberal supporter Robert Campeau combined two apartments into a single suite on the twelfth floor, with a striking view over the city. Delighted by the building's indoor pool, Martin regularly swam there, sometimes accompanied by advisors and diplomats who paced on the deck, snatching a few minutes of his time as he paddled along.

Nell was less happy about the move. In Opposition, she had settled easily into Windsor, her hometown. Ottawa was different. Her children were both absent: Paul, heading into third-year law in Toronto, was away all summer, working on a ship off the coast of South America. Mary Anne was waiting tables in Banff, planning to start at the University of Windsor in the fall. Alone, Nell found cold comfort in the formal social life of the diplomatic circuit. "The people you meet are extremely interesting," she explained, "but you miss the opportunity of getting to know them well, of making close friends. And you miss the community life which to most women is a necessity."[42] The pressure of public life weighed heavily on the older Nell. "I can't even say thank you without shaking all over," she complained.[43] Increasingly, she skipped her husband's diplomatic and political functions, fleeing to Windsor whenever she could, treasuring her time there as a "reprieve."[44]

As Nell managed the move back to Ottawa, Martin divided his attention between Windsor and the demands of his portfolio. After six years in Opposition, Essex Liberals were anxious to enjoy the benefits of government. "It has become more apparent than ever," wrote Martin's neighbouring MP, Eugene Whelan, "that we must do everything in our power to make sure there is something in the estimates for Essex County."[45] Indeed, there would be. Martin pressed Agriculture Minister Harry Hays to boost spending at the Harrow Experimental Farm and demanded higher deficiency payments for the region's tobacco farmers.[46] There were more explicit debts to pay. As Martin reminded campaign chairman Walter Gordon, Plant Advertising had handled Liberal accounts in Windsor and southwestern Ontario for three decades: "The time has arrived to do something for this company."[47]

Martin also had business with Postmaster General Azellus Denis.[48] There were jobs to fill in postal substations 16 and 31, and voters in rural Tecumseh and St. Clair Beach were clamouring for home mail delivery. The new post office in Kingsville needed an architect, and painters were required for hundreds of the familiar red and green post boxes scattered across the Border City. Martin also found time to wage a successful battle on behalf of the Windsor Chamber of Commerce for Canada's first genuine Christmas stamp, which the business group hoped would promote cross-border tourism. "There is no doubt that your longstanding popularity is due to the personal attention you are always willing to give local matters," wrote Murray Elder of the Greater Windsor Industrial Commission.[49] Elder was grateful for help in tackling the region's high freight rates.

Windsor lawyers had reason to be thankful as well. As a senior Ontario minister, Martin reviewed most judicial appointments in the province. When asked about a new citizenship judge for southwestern Ontario, he promptly decided to move the court from London to Windsor. It was more convenient that way.[50] There were other perks for his legal supporters. His key local allies, Don Emerson and law partner Keith Laird, managed a roster of Essex lawyers who were ready to act on Crown business.[51] They were helped by Herb Gray, MP for nearby Essex West. Gray had been active on Martin's behalf since the mid-1950s, backing him at the 1958 leadership convention. Martin supported Gray for the Liberal nomination in 1962, adopting him as a protege, and he increasingly relied on his younger colleague to safeguard his interests in Essex County. Gray got the job done. When Martin's office sought a lawyer to staff a UN observer team in Mauritius a few years later, Laird replied that he "knew of no one in our riding to propose ... Our lawyers are being well looked after."[52]

Few local projects escaped Martin's notice. He arranged for new lights on the Belle River docks and sent the entire file to the *Windsor Star*.[53] On behalf of city council, he resumed his campaign, suspended in 1957, for longer runways at Windsor airport.[54] He also encouraged Transport Minister George McIlraith to maintain dredging operations in Port Burwell and to reopen ship inspection offices in Windsor, closed by the Tories in 1959. "Prepare a good letter to George & get this done," he snapped to an aide. "It will be good for Windsor."[55] At the end of the summer, back in Windsor to take his place in the annual Labour Day Parade, he was the confident and high-spirited master of all he surveyed. He kidded a friend who flagged on the march, boasting that "I felt as good at the end as I did in the beginning."[56]

He was a little slower to grasp his new portfolio. Pearson snapped up the early headlines with fence-mending visits to British prime minister Harold Macmillan in London and American president John F. Kennedy at his retreat in Hyannis Port. Martin had wanted to go on both trips, but he was not invited. "I have so much work to do here," he explained to skeptical Ottawa reporters in April.[57] His claim was true soon enough. In preparation for his trip to Hyannis Port, Pearson asked him in May to get the stalled Canada-US treaty on the Columbia River moving again. Martin tried to decline the tricky job, which he thought belonged to BC ministers, but Pearson insisted. The Columbia River Treaty loomed as an early test of his government's capacity to tackle tough foreign policy issues, and he wanted progress. For the next six months, the Columbia River headed Martin's East Block agenda.

The fourth-largest river in North America, the mighty Columbia tumbled almost three thousand feet from its origins high in the Canadian Rockies to the sea at Astoria, Oregon. Canadian and American engineers had dreamed of taming its erratic floodwaters and harnessing its vast potential for power since the 1940s. After more than a decade of study, the International Joint Commission (IJC), the Canada-US body that was responsible for managing cross-boundary waters, concluded in 1959 that shared development of the Columbia basin would maximize the river's potential and that its benefits should be equally divided between the two countries. By January 1961, Canadian and American negotiators had hammered out a treaty that did just that. British Columbia, which owned the resource, would build dams at Mica, High Arrow, and Duncan to trap the Columbia's waters and regulate its flow. In exchange, the province would receive half of the additional power generated downstream in the United States as a result of the improved flow. It would also receive half the value of the estimated flood damage averted during the treaty's sixty-year lifespan.

The US Senate ratified the deal in March 1961, but the accord ran into difficulty in Canada. BC premier W.A.C. Bennett favoured developing the Peace River basin and wanted to sell the Columbia's downstream power, surplus to his needs, back to the Americans. Diefenbaker tried, but his government failed to secure terms that pleased Bennett, leaving the unpredictable premier in a testy mood. The treaty stalled.

In addition to dealing with Bennett, Pearson's shaky minority government faced further pressures. Many BC Liberals, both federal and provincial, wanted the treaty reopened. The Vancouver Liberal MP Jack Davis called it a "fiasco" and a "sell out of our resources."[58] Nationalists of several stripes, including the highly respected former IJC chair, Andrew McNaughton, the NDP, and left-Liberals such as Walter Gordon, feared that the treaty gave Americans too much control over a Canadian resource. In May 1962, Pearson himself described it as "a very sad story," promising to recruit McNaughton to revise it.[59] Meanwhile, American plans for dams and power plants in the Pacific Northwest moved ahead. They eroded the value of Canada's downstream benefit and reduced its leverage, even as Washington made it clear that its patience was running out. Speedy action was required, and Pearson wanted Martin to deliver.

Flanked by three senior civil servants, Martin summoned Davis, representing the West Coast Liberal doubters, to his office in early May 1963 to determine the government's policy. Martin's main advisor was Gordon Robertson, the deputy minister of northern affairs and natural resources. The two men went back to the 1940s and their collaboration on the Citizenship Act. Martin trusted Robertson, accepting his judgment that the treaty was good for Canada and could not be reopened without jeopardizing the advantages already gained.

Under Martin's reassuring guidance, bureaucrats and politicians agreed to seek a protocol to meet the major nationalist criticisms without upsetting the treaty's main elements. The device would be worked out with British Columbia, negotiated with Washington, and presented to Parliament along with the treaty for approval. The group drafted a paper for Pearson, illustrating the kinds of issues that Ottawa wished to address. Its five provisions clarified the sale of the downstream benefit and Canada's rights over flood control and power generation. Crucially, Davis, who was assured that there would be time to craft even more improvements, signed on to the plan.[60] The tentative policy was approved by cabinet on 9 May and outlined to President Kennedy during Pearson's Hyannis Port visit a few weeks later.[61] Progress on the Columbia helped signal a renewed North American partnership.

While Pearson arranged for Bennett to visit Ottawa in early June for talks on a common Canadian position, Martin held together an unstable consensus among the governing Liberals. Davis persisted in questioning the treaty's value, finding an ally in Gordon, who sat on a cabinet committee set up under Martin to monitor the file's progress. Opponents worried about the long-term sale of power, the treaty's short-term costs, and

Canada's right to divert water from the basin for its own purposes.[62] These concerns were aired in committee and again in cabinet, before Pearson brought the discussion to a close by backing Martin.[63]

Martin tackled Bennett in early June. He liked the populist BC premier, with his impish sense of humour and strong pragmatic streak, whom he had met during the federal-provincial health talks of the 1950s. According to the treaty's historian, the two politicians developed an "extraordinarily close working relationship."[64] They discussed the protocol and a draft agreement between Canada and British Columbia that was intended to remove any possible misunderstanding about their respective roles. The drafting, which was careful and precise, took up most of June. Martin participated actively. He reviewed the final six-page text, clause by clause, with the BC deputy attorney general, Gilbert Kennedy, and negotiated the final compromises with Bennett by phone. Pearson was generous with his praise, telling cabinet that this was "excellent work under great pressure."[65]

Through July, as officials finished their work on the draft protocol, Martin sought to neutralize domestic opposition to the treaty. He met often with McNaughton to review his concerns, and he patiently addressed Saskatchewan's worries about water diversion rights. Davis posed the greatest challenge, insisting again that BC Liberals, including provincial leader Ray Perrault and Arthur Laing, minister of northern affairs, expected to "substantially renegotiate" the treaty.[66] That was impossible, Martin told him bluntly, and reminded him that he had backed the government's policy in early May.[67] But to appease the BC caucus, he added three points to the protocol. The most important of these ensured that American demands for flood control would not be allowed to unilaterally shortchange Canada's power needs.[68] The Liberal consensus held.

In early August, Canadian and American negotiators assembled in Ottawa for talks on the protocol. Martin, who led the Canadian team, and career diplomat Ivan White of the US embassy, made quick work of the draft.[69] Settling on a price for the downstream benefits was much harder. The Americans maintained their 1962 offer to purchase a guaranteed block of power (the downstream benefit supplemented by extra BC power if needed) at a rate of 3.75 mills per kilowatt hour. The province itself would have to market the power to municipalities and corporate consumers across the western states. Bennett insisted that he would sell only surplus power that was generated downstream and would not add BC power to the mix. Moreover, he would sell that power only to a single US buyer at a price of 5.0 mills per kilowatt hour for advance payments covering the cost of constructing the three storage dams.[70]

There were talks in September, and again in December, as the sides weighed the value of the downstream power benefit. In addition to Martin, the Canadian team included Laing, provincial cabinet ministers R.W. Bonner and R.G. Williston, and Hugh Keenleyside, the chair of BC Hydro. White led the three Americans. Calculating the project's construction costs, the Canadians demanded Cdn$400.0 million for British Columbia's power entitlement for thirty years, plus Cdn$69.0 million for it's flood control services. The Americans were stunned. Basing his offer on the estimated value of the power, White proposed a total payment of Cdn$332.6 million for the sixty-year life of the treaty.[71]

Martin proved a "splendid negotiator."[72] Doubtless terrified of disappointing Bennett, R.G. Williston was obdurate and the negotiations were often "vituperative." But Martin, flexible and cajoling, kept them on track. "His keenness of mind, ready humour, and voluptuous turn of phrase," recalled Keenleyside, "helped us through sticky patches."[73] The Canadians held their ground, and the Americans slowly retreated. During a recess, they adjusted their basis for calculating water flow and sharing power from the Grand Coulee Dam in Montana. It was not enough, replied the Canadians. By the end of day two, a gap of Cdn$28 million remained, and the talks verged on collapse. As tempers flared, Martin intervened with a bad joke. "Every time I look at that lovely face," he told the homely White, "I have more loving kindness for you than I have ever had for any alien before."[74] The group broke up in good humour, reassembling first thing next morning to split the difference. Pearson was elated, saluting Martin in cabinet for "a big job well done."[75]

MARTIN SCORED OTHER victories during those first six months. Canada's foreign aid had declined through the late 1950s and was hit hard by Tory cutbacks following the 1962 exchange crisis. According to figures compiled by the Organisation for Economic Co-operation and Development,

Canada's contribution for 1962 totalled a meagre 0.2 percent of GNP, the "poorest" in the organization and well short of the average Western aid allocation of 0.7 percent GNP.[76] The amount was clearly "inadequate," and Canada's allies expected more.[77]

Martin valued aid. His 1956 Asian tour had convinced him of its importance on both humanitarian and political grounds. As secretary of state for external affairs, he was responsible for Canada's small External Aid Office, and he turned to its director general, Herb Moran, for help in restoring Canada's aid budget. Moran was a blunt private-sector lawyer-turned-bureaucrat, whom Martin found tight-fisted, unimaginative, and hard to work with. He knew his subject, however, and came with proposals to expand Canada's annual aid budget to $400.0 million or 0.7 percent of GNP, and to ease its hard conditions.[78] Martin backed Moran's plans for aid, hounding him all summer for the details.[79]

The plan that Martin circulated for his colleagues' approval in September retained as its ultimate objective an aid target of $400.0 million (or 0.7 percent GNP) by 1969-70. It focused, however, on just the next three years. Martin recommended restoring bilateral aid in each of those years to $48.5 million, adding new funds for the mammoth Indus Basin project and food aid, and bumping up expenditures for multilateral assistance and international relief. The centrepiece of the plan involved a $150 million fund for low-interest development loans. Under the scheme, Canada's aid budget would increase from $120.5 million (or 0.3 percent of GNP) in 1963-64 to $182.6 million in 1964-65 to $265.6 million (or 0.5 percent of GNP) in 1966-67.[80]

Naturally, Finance Minister Walter Gordon objected. Canada, he warned, could not possibly afford these costs as it wrestled with deficits, adverse balance of payments, and high unemployment. Trade Minister Mitchell Sharp, who liked the new food aid program, sided with Martin.[81] The three ministers conferred with Pearson in search of compromise. Martin did well. Cabinet adopted the entire plan in principle, though it agreed that Martin would announce the expenditures for 1964-65 alone, postponing the other increases until future economic circumstances were clearer.[82] "This is a great victory you have won," wrote former deputy under-secretary Escott Reid from Washington, where he occupied a senior position with the World Bank. "I know you yourself must feel very happy about it."[83]

Martin did, but his sights were already set on new goals. After a short Christmas break at home, he and Nell joined Pearson and his wife, Maryon, aboard a government plane bound for Paris and the Élysée Palace of the imperious French president, Charles de Gaulle. Since the death in 1959 of nationalist premier Maurice Duplessis, Quebec's conservative old order had crumbled. Under Liberal premier Jean Lesage, the province shed its insular Catholic ideologies, urgently embracing previously unimagined pathways to social, political, and economic modernity. Quebec opened itself to the world and wondered why its country's foreign policy revolved so exclusively around anglophone Washington and London. The astounding transformation made relations with France and other French-speaking countries, long neglected, a vital government priority.

Martin had kept his eye on Franco-Canadian relations since taking office in April. By December, he had already met French foreign minister Maurice Couve de Murville three times, and his new aid program boosted spending in French-speaking Africa. He had encouraged External Affairs to speed up its work on a small cultural affairs program for francophone states and instructed staff to unearth new ideas to expand relations with Paris. His August keynote address to the annual meeting of the Canadian Institute of International Affairs, the country's only and rather modest foreign policy think-tank, reminded its mostly English-speaking members that Canada's foreign policy would have to reflect the "history and traditions of the two main groups in Canada."[84]

He had found the run-up to the Paris visit taxing and Pearson unhelpful. "He was not particularly happy about that initiative," Martin later complained, "not because he did not think it was important, but he just was not at home with French people."[85] Martin had hoped that Trans-Canada Airlines would purchase the new French Caravelle and was upset when Pearson allowed the government airline to opt for an American jet instead.[86] In October, he was dismayed at Pearson's cool reception of André Malraux, the great novelist and Résistance hero who served as de Gaulle's cultural minister. "I don't think Pearson had any idea who Malraux was," he reflected. The Malraux-Pearson meeting had been "a disaster."[87] He was more distressed when Pearson delayed for almost two months before answering de Gaulle's formal invitation to visit. "France is a great power," he begged his boss to reply, "and will become increasingly so. It is important that [the] Prime Minister of Canada be regarded as a friend as indeed you are."[88]

The Paris visit went well. Press coverage was "heavy and good," and the banquets at the Élysée and Canada's embassy glittered appropriately.[89] De Gaulle was charming. He grasped the revolutionary changes unfolding in Quebec, sympathized with Ottawa's efforts to respond, and endorsed Canadian unity. "We do not intend to interfere in your national life," he assured Pearson and Martin. "We will not get mixed-up in Canada's affairs."[90] His North American guests were delighted. As they left, Pearson told him that "he had made many official visits in various capacities, but he had never had a happier one than this."[91] Martin, who had kept out of Pearson's way for most of the visit, was equally pleased. He met with Malraux for an update on cultural exchanges, visited UNESCO director-general René Maheu, and held talks with Couve de Murville at his Quai d'Orsay headquarters.

Martin was especially gratified with the plans for regular bilateral consultations that were announced at the end of the visit. Though they fell short of the full-blown ministerial committee that he wanted, the high-level meetings ensured him a prominent role in bilateral relations with his French counterpart, Couve de Murville. The two were an unlikely pair: the elegant and sophisticated European technocrat and the populist politician from Windsor. At least one observer, Quebec's delegate in Paris, Jean Chapdelaine, judged them woefully mismatched. Chapdelaine, who blamed Martin for ruining his career at External Affairs, spitefully portrayed him perched with "his mouth open, as if swallowing flies, in reverential admiration as M. Couve de Murville does the talking."[92]

Most evidence suggests a genuine and more equal friendship. Couve generally sympathized with Martin's North American sensibilities, and though Martin admitted that the Frenchman "was a cold fish," he always insisted that "our relations were very close."[93] That judgment was echoed by John Hadwen, who watched the two ministers together countless times. "They really liked each other," the veteran diplomat insisted. "It was very clear that there was a chord."[94] Canada's ambassador in Paris, Jules Léger, agreed. "Over the past few years," he assured Martin, "you have successfully established close relations with your French counterpart, which eases our work at every level. From an ambassador's perspective, this friendship is very precious."[95] Marcel Cadieux was more skeptical, though even he acknowledged that "on political questions, Messrs. Martin and Couve de Murville have close official and personal relations."[96] Indeed, soon after Martin arrived home, Couve wrote with considerable warmth: "We were very happy with the visit ... It has left us with lasting and sympathetic memories. Beyond these personal considerations, we must also consider our respective national aspirations and interests. These, too, were very well served and will lead to fruitful results in the future."[97]

No early success meant more to Martin than creating a UN peacekeeping force for Cyprus. The United Nations appeared infrequently on his agenda during his first six months in office. He had flown to New York in May 1963 for a brief introductory meeting with UN secretary-general U Thant. He liked the retiring Burmese statesman, whom he judged a good and sincere man, if perhaps overly cautious as a diplomat.[98] In the fall, he was back in New York for the annual General Assembly, with Nell by his side. They thrived in the great American city. "Far from being the living image of a stuffed shirt at the UN," a friendly reporter observed later, "Mr. Martin was more like a living doll. He exuded confidence, good spirits, and back-slapping friendliness ... He was obviously not only very well-known, but also very well-liked."[99] Though Martin relished the experience, especially the chance to renew old friendships with ambassadors and foreign ministers whom he had known since the 1940s, he was not the star attraction. Pearson headed the delegation and gave Canada's keynote address, a re-affirmation of Canadian faith in the United Nations and all its works, especially its peacekeeping operations.

The extent and nature of the government's commitment to UN peace-keeping was worked out during the fall and winter in the course of its long-promised defence policy review. Paul Hellyer, the energetic and ambitious defence minister, seized on the exercise as a chance to make his mark. He hoped to overhaul his department's impenetrable bureaucracy and align Canadian forces with renewed NATO doctrine that called for a more flexible response to Soviet aggression.[100] But his first draft of a policy white paper was wholly inadequate. He clung to established thinking, rejecting prospects for East-West détente, minimizing post-colonial instability in

Africa and Asia, and ignoring UN peacekeeping. Instead, he favoured Canada's traditional NATO role in Western Europe.

Howls of protest ensued. Finance Minister Walter Gordon and Bud Drury, the minister of industry, accused Hellyer of overlooking domestic policy considerations. Upset by Hellyer's outdated grasp of global developments, Martin savaged him for emphasizing Canada's NATO functions while failing to take into account Europe's renewed capacity to defend itself. More importantly, he argued, Hellyer had overlooked the threat to global order posed by decolonization and ignored the role that Canada was already playing in the Middle East, the Congo, and Indochina. "Throughout the paper," he charged, "there is a basic misconception of the role performed by the UN as a versatile instrument for the preservation of peace and security."[101]

The prime minister agreed.[102] In early February, he summoned interested ministers and their senior advisors to his Sussex Drive residence to hash out a revised draft, placing a much stronger emphasis on Canada's potential contribution to UN peacekeeping. By the time they were done, and the White Paper on Defence was published in late March 1964, the clash between Turkey and Greece over the tiny Mediterranean island of Cyprus had tested the government's faith in UN peacekeeping.

Cyprus constituted precisely the kind of threat to global order that Martin and his diplomats feared. A former British colony, it had gained its independence in 1960 under a complex constitution that was designed to protect the rights of its Turkish Cypriot minority, which represented about 20 percent of its 600,000 people, from its larger Greek Cypriot majority.

The new state hobbled along for almost three years until the frustrated president, Greek Cypriot leader archbishop Makarios, tried to amend the constitution unilaterally in late 1963. Turkish Cypriots protested, Greek Cypriots rioted, and a full-blown crisis exploded. When Turkey threatened to intervene to defend the Turkish Cypriot minority, raising the prospect of war with Greece – both countries were NATO members – Britain grudgingly increased its forces on the island and imposed a truce. Engaged in its headlong retreat from empire, Britain had no appetite for colonial adventure and quickly looked about for help.

Wary of Makarios's links with UN non-aligned members and anxious to prevent Moscow from meddling in NATO's eastern flank, London favoured a NATO force. Through January 1964, Martin and his officials followed Anglo-American efforts to scrape the force together. They were not inclined to be helpful and tried to forestall an invitation to join. Canada was engaged in five other UN missions, and Cyprus was a tough nut to crack. Moreover, as Canadian diplomats declared in London and Washington, the island was a European problem, and European countries were "well able to assume responsibility in this area, one of direct concern to them."[103] No one paid much attention, and late in the afternoon of 31 January, British and US diplomats arrived at Martin's office with an aide-memoire that invited Canada to join a NATO peacekeeping force for Cyprus.[104]

The plan collapsed within days, rejected by Makarios, who insisted on linking the force with the UN Security Council. Nonetheless, the invitation convinced Martin and Pearson that, should a force materialize, Canadian participation was all but inevitable.[105] In early February, Martin told NATO capitals that Ottawa would give "sympathetic consideration" to any force that the Cyprus government requested.[106] Meantime, with one ear carefully cocked for murmurs of domestic discontent, he focused his attention on Anglo-American efforts to craft a UN peacekeeping force acceptable to Makarios, Greece, and Turkey.

As British and American diplomats flirted with various UN formulas and combinations, the mood in External Affairs grew edgy. Arnold Smith, an assistant under-secretary, and Geoff Murray, who had worked closely with Martin in New York during the 1950s and headed the UN division, fretted that the force lacked clear political objectives. They suspected the British of scheming to maintain political control while shifting the military burden onto others. More critically, they warned that the mission would assume imperialist overtones it if lacked an unimpeachable link with the United Nations, leaving Canada "out in the cold with the neo-colonialists."[107]

Martin shared these concerns and was irked when his efforts to engage Washington and London were ignored. "Both US and British [sic]," he complained, "are acting without too much prior consultation with Canada & the others."[108] He was even more irritated a few days later, during the visit of British prime minister Alec Douglas-Home and his foreign secretary, R.A. Butler. After Martin dodged a reporter's question on Canada's possible contribution, Butler cheerfully admitted that Britain wanted a thousand Canadian soldiers. He also played up the Commonwealth connection, a sensitive issue for Quebec ministers, who feared accusations that Ottawa might simply serve as Britain's colonial chore-boy.[109] The British minister did nothing to ease Martin's discomfort when he met later with the entire cabinet. Butler said little, recalled the embarrassed Canadian. He "sat back on a reclining chair with his feet on the cabinet table," leaving a "very bad impression."[110]

To offset that impression and clear up any confusion about the Canadian role, Martin agreed to issue a full statement on Canadian policy. It would serve, minuted Arnold Smith, "as a warning to U Thant & our friends that they do not [sic] take us for granted."[111] The job fell to Pearson, who assured the House on 19 February that no decision on Canadian participation had yet been reached. And none would be until Ottawa was happy with the force's composition and its terms of reference.[112]

But his statement had little impact. Credible rumours continued to surface in New York and London that Canada was about to join Britain in fielding a force, which would come solely from the two countries. From his bed, recovering from a respiratory infection, Martin told Smith to scotch the stories, insisting that Canada would not join a UN force unless it included at least one other significant UN member.[113] Before the force took final shape, he wanted a UN advisory committee to give Ottawa a voice in its political policies. And he encouraged the UN to develop a broadly based mediatory mechanism that would provide a long-term solution for Cyprus.[114] He was also anxious to ensure that funding for the force would not undermine the disputed principle that peacekeeping was a core UN duty whose costs were a collective responsibility.[115]

None of these issues were resolved by 4 March, when the Security Council finally passed a resolution creating a UN peacekeeping force for Cyprus. U Thant quickly invited Canada, Sweden, Finland, Ireland, and Brazil to participate. As he issued his invitation, he made it clear that he expected Canada to serve, an assumption shared in chancelleries and editorial offices around the world. Martin, with backing from Pearson and cabinet, refused to be rushed.[116] In addition to his earlier worries about consultation and mediation, he had legitimate questions about the force's duties and terms of reference. Crucially, would the small force of seven thousand be ordered to disarm Greek Cypriot paramilitaries who totalled almost twice its number? Armed with a list of twenty-one specific questions, Paul Tremblay, Canada's UN ambassador, and Arnold Smith, whom Martin dispatched to London, set out in search of answers.[117]

Smith found the British evasive and inconclusive. They resented the effort to define the force's mandate more precisely, dismissing this as a delaying tactic. They stressed the "over-riding importance of heading off possible conflict between Greece and Turkey."[118] Tremblay found U Thant more accommodating. Though he refused to adopt a formal consultative mechanism and interpreted the UN mediatory role rather narrowly, he assured Tremblay that he would consult with contributing countries "if and when necessary" on both general policy and his mediation efforts. More importantly, though U Thant refused to answer Tremblay's questions on engaging with guerrillas, senior UN officials indicated that UN force commanders would not try to disarm Cypriot irregular forces.[119]

Though the UN position fell short of Canadian desiderata, the pressure to act was becoming unbearable. Renewed rioting racked Cyprus, as Greek Cypriots surged forward to capture Turkish Cypriot territory in anticipation of a UN-imposed halt. Pearson's government faced an escalating barrage of criticism from the Progressive Conservative and New Democratic Opposition, which pinned the delay on Liberal obstructionism. When Martin reassured them that "Canada will not shirk its responsibility," the press pounced.[120] In a mocking editorial titled "'Not Shirking' Duty but …," the *Toronto Star* accused him of "double talk."[121] The *Toronto Globe and Mail* echoed the charge, reproaching Martin for being "less than forthcoming with his answers" and demanding "Why the delay?"[122]

Martin played for time. On 10 March, he summoned the ambassadors of Sweden, Finland, and Ireland to his East Block office, where he assured them that Canadian forces were ready to go. The delay was not Canada's fault. To the consternation of his advisors, who watched the last bit of Canadian leverage slip away, he explained that the decision in principle had been made months earlier. Canada, he insisted, simply wanted clear answers to its questions about the force's role and its prospects. He intended to get them.[123]

As the demand for action intensified during the next thirty-six hours, this stance became difficult to maintain. There were warnings from New York of escalating communal riots in Cyprus, Turkish threats to intervene, and hints from Britain that it could not hold on alone.[124] These were confirmed on the evening of 11 March, when Britain's deputy high commissioner, John Wakely, handed Martin an urgent message from Secretary of State for Commonwealth Relations Duncan Sandys. Unless speedy progress was made, Sandys threatened, London would review its Cyprus commitment as early as 12 March. He pressed Canada "to announce immediately its willingness to participate in a UN force in the hope that it would lead others to follow suit."[125] Tired and cranky under the pressure, Martin was not optimistic. "The financial straits of the UN were deplorable and the size of the UN force inadequate," he complained, adding that he "did not know where the Secretary-General was going to find the necessary international forces." A week would pass before anything could be done, he predicted. "Things would not move quickly."[126]

He was wrong. Next morning, as he left Ottawa for speaking engagements in London, Ontario, Tremblay reported that the dynamics in New York were shifting. Though the Irish, who were in no hurry to help the British, could not be counted on for an early decision, the news from other potential contributors was promising. Finland would not take a final decision until its president returned to Helsinki on 14 March, but its foreign minister estimated the odds of approval at 99 percent. This was thought to be enough to satisfy Sweden's desire for another neutral in the force, and Stockholm was reportedly ready to indicate its acceptance on 13 March.

The Swedish announcement would fulfill Canada's requirement for an "international force" but would come too late for the British, who insisted on assurances by 12 March "that there was a reasonable prospect of an international force materialising." As Tremblay's reports arrived in Ottawa, Martin and Pearson conferred by phone, agreeing that Canada would take the risk of being the first to act. While Pearson hurried to update the House, Martin cancelled his remaining appointments and turned his government JetStar south, toward New York and the United Nations.[127]

For almost an hour, the small plane circled New York until a break in the fog and snow allowed it to land. Late for his appointment with U Thant, Martin rushed downtown to inform him that Canada was ready to join a

UN force "if and when such a force was constituted by the UN."[128] He was pleased with U Thant's promise that UN peacekeepers would not be involved in disarming irregular forces but was astonished to learn that U Thant could not assure him that Sweden had agreed to participate. U Thant insisted that he could do nothing to hasten Sweden's commitment. "His passivity amazed me," Martin wrote later. "The whole shebang was on the brink of collapse and U Thant did not realize it. When he claimed that he could not move because of lack of funds, I replied abruptly, 'We cannot act like shopkeepers.'"[129]

The stunned Canadians returned to Ottawa in a "gloomy" mood. Next morning, Martin gathered in his office with Cadieux and Ross Campbell, a smart and outspoken assistant under-secretary whom he liked and trusted. They marvelled at U Thant's unwillingness "to use his great office to persuade the Swedes and the others to join the force."[130] Perhaps, Martin wondered aloud, Canada should simply ignore the United Nations and encourage the Europeans itself. Someone suggested sending a message through the Swedish and Finnish ambassadors. Maybe, Martin asked, he should call the Swedish and Finnish foreign ministers? Cadieux said no, but Campbell liked the idea. "We had nothing to lose," he argued, "and everything to gain."[131]

With a glass of milk and a sandwich at his elbow, Martin happily began to work the phones, calling his counterparts in Dublin, Stockholm, and Helsinki. This was the kind of personal diplomacy that he loved, drawing on the shared "political bond between foreign ministers."[132] The Swedes, it turned out, were skeptical of the Finnish pledge and were reluctant to act. After securing a conditional commitment from Ireland, Martin could assure Stockholm of another neutral participant in the force.[133] It was enough. On the basis of his transatlantic calls, he told his cabinet colleagues early in the afternoon of 13 March, Ireland and Sweden would definitely join the force.[134] As the House of Commons gathered that evening in emergency session to debate and approve the dispatch of 1,200 Canadian peacekeepers, an advance contingent of 29 officers raced toward Cyprus, signalling the end of the acute phase of its crisis.

As Martin feared, Cyprus would remain a headache. The uncertain mandate, the political deadlock, and the hefty Canadian role meant regular drubbings from the Opposition during the next twelve months. For the moment, however, he savoured his triumph. As peacekeeping historian Alan James suggests, it was perhaps immodest of him to claim in his memoirs that the force came into being solely as a result of his phone calls and that he was its author.[135] Sweden and Finland were already moving toward agreement. As Martin himself conceded to the press at the time, "I really didn't do that much."[136] But with British and Turkish deadlines looming, he forced the pace and gained a day when minutes mattered. For that, he deserved the shower of praise and favourable press coverage that rained on him during the spring of 1964.

The Liberal caucus cheered his "matchless job" and asked Jim Walker, its chief whip, to pass along its "keen appreciation for your efforts and success in the Cyprus dilemma."[137] The *Toronto Globe and Mail* enthused about "the quite fantastic diplomacy that Mr. Martin displayed." Its respected foreign affairs correspondent, Fred Nossal, hailed him for "restoring Canada's voice," and reporter Robert McKeown profiled him in the paper's *Weekend Magazine*.[138] Bruce Hutchison, a fading voice from the postwar era, hoped that the crisis heralded a new foreign policy and described Martin's performance as "outstanding."[139]

The theme was echoed by *Time* magazine, which welcomed Martin's bold effort "to restore the old glow of Canadian pride in the Department of External Affairs. For here was Canada back at the old stand."[140] Even Martin's perennially hostile critic, Blair Fraser, managed to find a kind word for the minister, who was finally pulling his weight at Pearson's "right hand."[141] There was perhaps a hint of nostalgia for the Pearsonian "golden age" among the tributes, but no one cared very much. Most significantly, the prime minister was happy. "You are doing a fine job, Paul," he wrote to mark Martin's birthday in June, "and you know how much this means to me. I am more grateful than I can say for all your cooperation and assistance during this past year."[142]

The praise echoed through Martin's spring and summer. The long stretch of relative calm began with a trip to Geneva in late March for the first UN Conference on Trade and Development (UNCTAD), a novel effort to improve the terms of trade between the rich North and the impoverished South. The excursion was a relaxed affair. Geneva was packed with global figures, including U Thant and US under-secretary of state

George Ball, all of whom greeted Martin with effusive thanks and praise.[143] There was time to reminisce about the 1930s with a visit to the League of Nations archives and to call on old friends. Martin expected little from the gathering but thought his presence was important as a gesture of Canada's strong support for global development. "I think we got the most out of the few days at our disposal," he wrote Canada's UN ambassador in Geneva, Saul Rae. "I enjoyed very much the evenings we had together."[144]

External Affairs left less time for Windsor, though Martin took care that globetrotting headlines did not create the impression that he had forgotten his home. "Never mind that stuff," he dismissed the world's hotspots in a chat with his *Windsor Star* confidant Maurice Jefferies. "I've got something *really* important for you – we're going to get a nice brick veneer on that post office in Emeryville."[145] Yet post offices, docks, and river dredging, the normal currency of votes in Essex County, were on few minds that spring. What really mattered was hockey. Windsor's local professional club, the first-place Detroit Red Wings, faced the Chicago Black Hawks in the National Hockey League's Stanley Cup semi-finals, and CBC Television was not carrying the games. With NHL support, Detroit had imposed a television blackout in Windsor, in hopes of boosting ticket sales. Windsorites were outraged. "I was getting 600 telegrams a day," Martin protested. "And one of them was from my wife."[146]

This was monopoly, Martin bristled, and he rounded up Herb Gray and Eugene Whelan to press Justice Minister Guy Favreau for an inquiry under the Combines Investigation Act. They wanted Maurice Lamontagne, the minister responsible for the CBC, to do something as well. And they marched Windsor druggist Fred Holmes, Martin's old friend and a recent appointment to the industry's regulatory Board of Broadcast Governors, down to the *Windsor Star* to denounce the NHL. When he failed to find legal grounds for action, Martin tackled the tough NHL president, Clarence Campbell, and finally persuaded him to allow local radio station CKWW to broadcast the games. The response was overwhelming. The station received two thousand letters of thanks and had to call telephone operator Bell Canada four times to get its switchboard unblocked. CKWW program director Geoff Stirling knew whom to thank. "As soon as our newsroom in Ottawa is established," he promised Martin, "we will arrange for any special recordings you want to be fed directly into this area as a public service of this Station."[147]

Martin's mood soared during the summer of 1964. With Pearson away in London, he played at prime minister for two weeks in July, indulgently dodging Tory taunts that he was superior to the incumbent.[148] His weekends were filled with excursions home. He spent one at the Bali-Hi Motor Hotel with the Southwest Ontario Liberal Association and another in Michigan, where he collected an honorary degree from Wayne State University. On Dominion Day, he marched with local mayors and his friend, former Michigan governor Soapy Williams, in the International Freedom Festival. A week-long celebration of the postwar liberalism, unionism, and prosperity that joined Windsor and Detroit, the festival hinted at the quickening tempo of the region's economy. These were short stopovers, but as he assured a friend who had encouraged him to make the trip from Ottawa, "I always enjoy even a brief visit to Windsor."[149]

His annual holidays began in August with another cross-border gathering, an international lay retreat in Detroit, where he gave a keynote address. This, too, was a celebration, welcoming the radical theology that the Second Vatican Council was ushering into the conservative Catholic Church. Martin later realized that he had failed fully to grasp the council's far-reaching significance, but at the time he instinctively embraced its liberating transformation of the closed and shuttered church of his youth. His talk, with its theme of "one world," struck just the right note, and he urged his audience to embrace the "new mood of hope based on fundamental religious faith and respect for fundamental human rights."[150]

He spent part of August with Nell in Colchester, sometimes hustling down to the corner store payphone to keep in touch with his department. Mostly, they were alone. Paul Jr. was in Europe, interning with the European Coal and Steel Community. Mary Anne, enrolled at the University of Windsor, spent the summer in Africa, volunteering with Crossroads International. "Oom Paul," approved the *Windsor Star*, "has good reason to be proud of his daughter."[151] Martin's stock had rarely been higher. He had scored a series of diplomatic triumphs since the election of 1963 and stood impregnable in southwestern Ontario and his Windsor redoubt. When a provincial by-election was called in early September for Windsor-

Sandwich, Progressive Conservative premier John Robarts, along with much of his cabinet and his backroom boys, descended on Essex. "We're throwing everything we've got into this one," remarked a Tory campaign worker. "We're fighting Paul Martin's machine and we know it."[152]

9

DEALING WITH WASHINGTON, 1964–65

Paul Martin ended his Colchester holiday early, catching a flight to Tokyo on 29 August for a round of ministerial talks. Canada's polite but distant ties with Japan held little interest for him, but amid the dreary meetings, he found time for a quiet visit to Hiroshima and a grim chat on Pacific affairs with Blair Seaborn, Canada's senior diplomat in war-torn Southeast Asia. By mid-September, he was back in Windsor to welcome US secretary of state Dean Rusk. The proconsular visit was intended to celebrate the renewed Canada-US partnership and affirm Martin's standing with a key American powerbroker. Canadian media obligingly featured photos of Paul and Nell, with Rusk between them, strolling cheerfully across the lawn of Martin's mock Cotswold cottage. Privately, the mood in Windsor was somber, and Martin returned to Ottawa at the end of the month, trailing worries. There was unrest in his riding and Liberal scandal brewing in Parliament. He also feared for several policy initiatives, which were slowly stalling as governing reduced his room to manoeuvre and sapped cabinet's courage. Above all, he fretted about Washington. The escalating conflict in Vietnam was veering dangerously beyond American control, unsettling relations with Canada. A bilateral scrap over North America's auto industry sent spasms of fear through Canada's industrial heartland in southwestern Ontario. So much, Martin knew, depended on relations with Washington.

His troubles began in Windsor. They had taken root almost a year earlier, when a Senate seat for Ontario had opened up. Don Emerson, Martin's chief organizer, and Keith Laird, his law partner and main fundraiser, both aspired to the position, their ambitions quietly encouraged by Martin himself during years of collaboration. The contest tore at the local party as each candidate's supporters pressed Martin for his backing. The lawyers and Windsor establishment favoured Laird. So did Martin, who assured Laird's supporters that "I am doing all I can."[1]

Party workers and rural members sided with Emerson, whom Martin tried to appease with a diplomatic appointment, only to encounter stern opposition from Cadieux.[2] He had no luck either in convincing the Canadian Maritime Commission to hire Emerson as its executive director.[3] He offered Emerson the chairmanship of the local refugee board, but this was part-time work and clearly insufficient.[4] "I am afraid we are losing Don," warned Alice Shanahan, who had remained Martin's principal rural supporter since 1935. "I can't interest him in anything like it used to be," she wrote Martin accusingly. Unable to hide her disappointment, she added, "After working with you for over 30 years & this is the first time I had to write to you this way [sic]."[5]

The crisis simmered quietly until November when Pearson abruptly appointed Toronto businessman John Aird to the seat. Liberal Windsor exploded. "Cambodia isn't Essex East," screamed the *Windsor Star*. "Windsor was robbed! ... And by Oom Paul himself!"[6] Elton Plant, a prominent Liberal, was blunt: "Mr. Martin had a decision to make and he didn't make it in favour of Essex County."[7] Local provincial member Art Reaume was more graphic: "Every time I think of the appointment, it makes me sick to my stomach."[8]

The furor dampened the mood at the Essex East Liberal Women's dinner honouring Martin the next week. He had wisely disappeared from sight as the story broke, but he turned in a strong performance at the event, reassuring his audience of opportunities to come.[9] Though his efforts calmed Windsor Liberals, he returned to Ottawa in a worried frame of mind. "I am very anxious," he wrote his friend Maurice Strong, "to sit down and chat with you at the earliest opportunity about my situation."[10] Next weekend, at the annual Paul Martin Dance, he made more progress with his voters. Attendance was good, and Liberals cheered when, in tribute to her devotion, Martin presented Shanahan with one of the pens that President Lyndon Johnson had used to sign the Columbia River Treaty.[11] It joined the rose from King's casket and the ticket from Kennedy's funeral among her most valued possessions and signalled an end to the disturbing breech in party unity.

But trouble arose in Ottawa, too. The bitter debate over Pearson's new Canadian flag had stoked parliamentary tempers to a fever pitch, and the mood in the House of Commons was vicious. Amid dark rumours of Liberal graft, Canadians wondered how Hal Banks, a corrupt union organizer with ties to the governing party, had escaped justice after a decade of thuggery. Erik Nielsen, the gaunt Progressive Conservative member from the Yukon, whose deep-set eyes hid the cold rage of the born crusader, had part of the answer. When the Department of Justice estimates came up for debate in November, he began peeling back the layers of a bribery scandal that reached deep into the offices of Justice Minister Guy Favreau and Prime Minister Pearson.[12]

For a week, the press and the Opposition – Conservative leader John Diefenbaker actually salivating with glee – hammered at Favreau. Pearson, who maintained that he had not learned of the allegations until days before Nielsen revealed them, slipped out of town, leaving Martin in charge. In fact, Favreau had warned Pearson of the accusations ten weeks earlier. Distraught, he insisted on a royal commission to clear his name. Cabinet obliged, and Martin undertook the delicate task of drafting terms of reference that reconciled the preservation of Favreau's dignity with Opposition demands for wide latitude. His defence of Favreau even won the grudging admiration of his under-secretary, Marcel Cadieux.[13]

And then, suddenly, it was Martin's turn in the spotlight. On 30 November, Diefenbaker drew attention to an old Ontario Police Commission complaint that Ottawa had failed to answer its questions about a handful of dangerous immigrants, one of whom was Onofrio Minaudo. Convicted of murder in his native Sicily, Minaudo had fled to the United States in the 1920s, settling in Detroit and adding extortion, bootlegging, and prostitution to his criminal resumé. The Mafia lieutenant moved to nearby Windsor in 1960, opened a bakery, and applied for landed immigrant status. Though he was ordered deported in 1961, the order was not carried out until March 1964, when Ottawa's hand was forced by Ontario police. Intrigued by the delay, the NDP justice critic, Andrew Brewin, asked in December if anyone had lobbied on Minaudo's behalf. Three names turned up: defeated Tory MP Richard Thrasher from Essex South, retired Liberal MP Dan Brown from Essex West, and Paul Martin from Essex East.[14]

Martin asserted his innocence. Panicked, he claimed that he had not known of Minaudo's background until news reports broke in 1963. Through December and January, he called his political staff every morning, "frantic" with worry about the next question. "For the last six weeks, he has barely lived," Cadieux noted in his diary on 12 January 1965. "He thinks of nothing except this business."[15] Martin's assertions of blamelessness were undercut by Immigration Department correspondence, which showed that he had been warned of Minaudo's character in 1960 but had persisted in his lobbying. Admittedly, he had not dealt directly with Minaudo; his calls to the office of Progressive Conservative immigration minister Ellen Fairclough were based on an affidavit supplied by the mobster's lawyer.

The distinction between acting as an MP and as a lawyer was a murky one, as Martin well knew from his experiences in the 1930s and 1940s. The fact that he had foolishly failed to declare as income the $500 "honorarium" he received for his efforts made the situation even murkier. Worse, as ministerial aide Duncan Edmonds confessed to Cadieux, Minaudo had helped out in Martin's constituency and had once purchased a hundred tickets to the annual Paul Martin Dance.[16]

Like many observers, Cadieux thought the worst of Martin, and he suspected that there might be more to the story. Edmonds was more forgiving. "Martin was totally innocent," he later insisted, attributing his involvement to "naivety, lack of due diligence ... There was no lack of integrity ... [only] lack of wisdom."[17]

There are strong grounds for accepting this judgment. The porous Canada-US border tempted organized crime, which seeped into the political fabric throughout southwestern Ontario. Essex was unexceptional. Moreover, Martin's sins were typically venial, not mortal. He ran ridiculous risks for paltry stakes, sometimes skirting the law but never breaking it. This pattern, which began during the 1930s with his inflated bill at the Brantford municipal railway hearings, continued in his income tax arrears and immigration work later in the decade, and resurfaced in the 1950s as he and prominent Tory senator W.R. Brunt chased down TV stations for Paul Nathanson. In 1960, he joined the board of Latin American Mines Limited, whose stock promptly soared on a "pump and dump" scam.[18] He also jauntily dodged paying income tax on the annual director's fees that he received as a result of his stake in a small chain of vocational schools.[19] As a cabinet minister, he nurtured his ties with penny-stock mining promoter "Wild Bill" Richardson, though he had little to gain from them. "I know you don't take time to consider all aspects of your personal affairs," Marjorie Frank, his secretary warned, "but I do think you should consider the propriety of Mr. Richardson's free use of your name and your association with his enterprises."[20] He did, but he was slow to sever relations, charmed by the eccentric and entertaining Richardson.

A similar casualness undoubtedly characterized his decision to take up Minaudo's cause, rather than any involvement with the mobster or his activities. At most, he was guilty of a financial misdemeanor, which he rectified with a cheque for the receiver general. When Minaudo refused to talk to the RCMP, Martin's Progressive Conservative critics, who were equally implicated, quietly let the matter drop. Pearson said little, though close advisors Tom Kent and Walter Gordon were outraged by Martin's behaviour.[21] The Minaudo affair cast an unfortunate shadow over Martin's relations with Pearson as 1964 ended.

There were other reasons for disquiet in Martin's office. His fight to bring Canada into the Organization of American States (OAS) had clearly ended. This was a cause close to his heart, and he had pressed the case for membership since he was a freshman MP in 1935. Admission into the international organization would have given Canada a greater voice in regional affairs and enhanced its political and economic links with Latin America. But the opposite case, favoured by the prime minister and the diplomats, was equally strong. They worried that membership in the US-dominated body might complicate Canada's relations with Washington and the South American republics, with whom Ottawa enjoyed cordial if superficial relations. Moreover, many Canadians saw the OAS as a tool of American foreign policy or as a threat to Canada's vanishing Commonwealth ties.[22] By November 1964, after a year of prodding reluctant officials and ministers to act, Martin had become resigned to his defeat. "You are right when you say that public opinion here is not yet as conscious as it should be of Latin America generally," he wrote an ally, Senator John Connolly. "Perhaps our task now is to direct our efforts to encouraging informed public discussion in Canada."[23]

Another setback followed. It had long bothered Martin that mainland China remained barred from the United Nations, despite his successful 1955 campaign for universal membership in the world body; China was represented instead by the tiny pro-Western island of Taiwan. By the summer of 1963, he was aware that, by a comfortable margin of 53 to 35 percent, Canadians favoured seating communist China in the United Nations.[24] In July 1963, he had promised the House of Commons Special Committee on Defence that a new policy was coming, one that would include more cultural contacts, more trade, and the "exchange of diplomatic missions."[25] Pearson squelched an early initiative, but Martin raised the idea of sponsoring a "two-China resolution" to seat both Beijing and Taiwan at the UN General Assembly in the fall of 1964. This option would please no one and might even lead to US economic retaliation, his dubious officials warned. Canada should consult more and do nothing. Martin was unconvinced. "The gist of all this," he noted, "is that we move cautiously (always good) – but that we take no initiative. Is this wise?"[26]

Confident in his assessment of American society and politics, Martin doubted that Washington would retaliate. Moreover, he was certain that cabinet and the public expected movement.[27] He pushed ahead and discussed the idea with US secretary of state Dean Rusk in December. Though taken aback by the strength of Rusk's violent opposition, Martin was undeterred and told his colleagues that he was moving forward. But cabinet had heard enough. Transport Minister Jack Pickersgill, who feared offending Washington, led the charge. His blunt advice was that Canada should "recognize China the day after the Americans do."[28] Pearson and Trade Minister Mitchell Sharp piled on. They worried that action by Canada, when the United States was faced with an increasingly difficult situation in Vietnam, would invite reprisals. Martin, they insisted, had badly overestimated pro-China sentiment in Canada. Soundly rebuked, he shelved this project, too, in December 1964.[29]

Another Martin initiative was also in trouble with the Prime Minister's Office by early 1965. Since taking on the External Affairs portfolio two years before, he had worried about the growing gulf between Paris and Washington. French president Charles de Gaulle resented American power, which challenged France's claims to European leadership, and he lashed out at US-led NATO, where American efforts to craft a multilateral nuclear force (MNF) seemed deliberately designed to crimp French influence.[30] Western solidarity was important to Martin, and so were relations with France. He hoped that Canada might heal the breech. "Canadians love France," he told CBC News shortly after his first NATO ministerial meeting in May 1963. "They love her culture, they admire her statesmanship and I think they understand her problems and I would hope that we might in this area of relations be able to play some part in making better known the objectives of our immediate neighbour and of France."[31] When they realized that he was serious, the French and American ambassadors in Ottawa erupted in fury at his impertinence.[32]

Their sneers stung, but Martin persevered. As his concern over France's tense relations with NATO mounted in 1964, he moved Canada into a prominent role as an intermediary. "It is Canadian policy," he reminded his ambassadors in North Atlantic capitals in June, "to do everything possible to ensure that France is not pushed into taking extreme positions."[33] At the December NATO ministerial meeting, he rallied support for a proposal to find common ground with Paris by establishing "a set of principles or general guidelines which could form the basis for an examination of the future of the [NATO] Alliance."[34] He also sided with Paris to defeat American plans for an MNF, demonstrating that France was not alone. When the White House protested, it was reminded "that Canada was torn between her fervent belief in Atlantic integration and her necessary concern to avoid seeming to join in isolating France."[35]

Though Martin's preoccupation with France irritated the United States, Britain, and other NATO allies, he was quick to insist that Canada's traditional attachment to NATO remained unchanged. This was no longer true of Pearson. He worried about tensions within NATO and its capacity to respond to the era's signs of East-West détente. He was concerned by the continued unhappiness of francophone ministers about his 1963 decision to accept nuclear weapons. He faced pressure from colleagues such as Finance Minister Walter Gordon, who doubted the practical value of Canada's NATO contribution, given Europe's recovery, and questioned

Washington's dominant role in the alliance. "Canada," Pearson agreed, "was in danger of being overwhelming by U.S. influence in a variety of ways."[36]

Pearson asked whether Canada's efforts should be concentrated elsewhere, answering his own question during a speech to the Ottawa branch of the Canadian Club in February 1965. "We may have to consider new arrangements," he told the businessmen and diplomats who were packed into the Chateau Laurier, "by which Europe takes responsibility for the security of one side of the Atlantic, North America for the other, with interlocking cooperative arrangements for mutual assistance in case of attack."[37] His views alarmed Canada's allies, whose diplomats were soon knocking on Martin's door for an explanation. Sensing Pearson's "implicit criticism," Martin was obviously angry, and he shot off a note to remind the prime minister that Canada's recent initiative on the future of NATO would surely be undermined by "any indication that the Canadian Government may have doubts about the alliance."[38]

By early March 1965, there were rumours in Ottawa that Pearson wanted to be rid of Martin. The two men, friends and rivals, differed sharply over policy toward the Americas, communist China, and NATO. Cadieux thought that Martin had been badly damaged by the Minaudo embarrassment, and he wondered if Pearson's recent refusal to approve a list of routine diplomatic appointments might be a tactic to force him out.[39] Among ministers, Gordon, unhappy in Finance, was already campaigning to replace his colleague in External Affairs.[40] Against this increasingly strained backdrop, during the winter and spring of 1965, Martin and Pearson faced their most significant diplomatic test yet: the American war in Vietnam.

INDOCHINA WAS NOT a government priority in April 1963, when the Liberals settled into office. Nevertheless, Martin and Pearson were already familiar with the region and its problems. For almost a decade, Canada had served with communist Poland and non-aligned India on the International Control Commission (ICC), which had been established in 1954 to oversee ceasefire agreements in Cambodia, Laos, and Vietnam. The fragile settlement imposed at the 1954 Geneva Conference left Vietnam divided under communist leader Ho Chi Minh in the north and President Ngô Đình Diệm in the south. As the Western representative on the ICC, Canada had watched with mounting frustration as Poland and India conspired to let communist insurgents undermine the peace with impunity. A generation of Canadian diplomats grimly held on, while backing American efforts to right the balance with a stream of arms and military advisors in support of a stable, independent, and non-communist government in South Vietnam. Like their foreign policy advisors, Pearson and Martin shared the view that the Viet Cong insurgency in South Vietnam was largely inspired and supported by communist Hanoi.

Pearson was more skeptical than his minister about the American role in Asia, but this difference hardly mattered early on. At that point, the conflict rarely drew Martin's attention. He was briefly distressed in August 1963 as Buddhist riots in Saigon threatened Diệm's repressive government, and he offered the embattled leader his "close and sympathetic interest."[41] He was spooked at the NATO ministerial meeting that December, when Rusk wondered aloud about sending US troops to Vietnam, and he dispatched two teams of Canadian diplomats to Washington in search of reassurance.[42] They found it on Christmas Eve, the capital ablaze and working overtime in the wake of President Kennedy's assassination just a month earlier. Thus, despite the wave of military coups that rattled South Vietnam in early 1964, Martin remained confident that Washington could be trusted to handle the situation. "The USA attitude on Vietnam," Canada's embassy in Washington reported calmly, "appears to be characterized by a mixture of caution, patience, and determination."[43] Provided the United States did not extend the war, Martin approved of American plans to resist communism in South Vietnam with more advisors, more money, and more arms. Saigon was too weak to negotiate, he thought, and talks would simply turn South Vietnam over to Hanoi, along with its 800,000 Catholic refugees. "Any sign of compromise with the Communists," he insisted, "is unthinkable."[44]

Canada and Martin were drawn more deeply into Vietnam in 1964. With an election approaching, President Lyndon Johnson was anxious to avoid either a showdown with Hanoi or a humbling retreat from South Vietnam. This might be achieved, the White House concluded, by convincing North Vietnam of US resolve not to allow communist forces to defeat Saigon. Canada, a close American ally with ready access to Hanoi through the ICC, was the logical choice to deliver this message. In late April 1964, Rusk flew to Ottawa to ask Pearson and Martin for their help.[45]

Rusk struck a cautious note. He assured the Canadians that Washington was anxious to retain the framework established in Geneva and had no plans to push the war into North Vietnam. Rather, he explained, it hoped to convince Hanoi "that it would be wrong for the Viet Minh to expect that the United States were getting discouraged and were thinking of pulling out. It was important for them to realise that if they didn't put a stop to their operations they would be in deep trouble."[46] Rusk asked the Canadians to send Blair Seaborn, who was slated to replace Gordon Cox as Canada's representative on the ICC, to Vietnam as quickly as possible, authorizing him to act as a secret intermediary between Washington and Hanoi. Pearson and Martin agreed.

Canadian support had its limits, however, and these were spelled out as Seaborn's mission was finalized. On 28 May, Pearson met secretly with Johnson and his national security advisor, McGeorge Bundy in New York's Hilton Hotel, where he warned the president that "any drastic escalation would give rise to great problems both in Canada and internationally."[47] Meanwhile, William Sullivan, Rusk's special advisor on Vietnam and head of the interagency Vietnamese Coordinating Agency, travelled to Ottawa to meet with Martin and his diplomats. They agreed on Seaborn's main objective – to establish a "dialogue" with Hanoi to "see whether there are any grounds for carroting them or whether the threat of sticks produces any movement." They worked out the basic rules for the operation: all communications with Seaborn would pass through Ottawa, and the Canadians promised to transmit the messages "faithfully," even if they did not agree with their content.[48]

Sullivan found Martin "a little nervous," which was hardly surprising, given his quickly growing doubts about US strategy.[49] He was irritated and suspicious at the lapse of time since Rusk's April visit to launch the exercise, and he wondered whether it had already been left too long. He thought that the "carrots" and "sticks" were too imprecise, and he feared losing control of the mission. He insisted on Seaborn's complete "independence," though he promised Sullivan that Seaborn would act as a "friend." More importantly, he was dubious of the US effort to occupy an untenable middle ground between war and peace. The real choice, he rightly argued, was between "direct intervention" and a conference with a negotiated solution. He favoured a conference, and twice during the encounter, he emphasized the Canadian domestic problems that would ensue should the Americans decide to expand the war. "The Opposition tended to be suspicious of US policy in Indochina," he explained, warning that "he would find it difficult to condone ... direct [US] intervention."[50]

The success of Seaborn's first mission to Hanoi in June briefly eased Martin's concerns. Though Seaborn detected no hint of retreat in Prime Minister Pham Van Dong, Martin was pleased that North Vietnam seemed ready to maintain the channel and continue the dialogue. His joy was short-lived, however. He was disconcerted to learn in July that Washington appeared to have no ideas for the next step.[51] When questioned, Bundy assured the Canadian ambassador in the United States, Charles Ritchie, that the Seaborn connection remained "vital," though Washington was not ready to pursue the dialogue lest it appeared too anxious to bargain.[52] Coupled with State Department efforts to dampen Washington gossip about carrying the war north and a new emphasis on local responses to Viet Cong activity, the delay hinted at a shift in the American approach. "We ourselves," Canadian officials told their baffled minister, "are confused now about the likely direction of US policy."[53] Before leaving Ottawa for his Colchester holiday, Martin told his diplomats to sound out the Americans.

But events overtook his orders. In early August, North Vietnamese gunboats reportedly attacked the USS *Maddox* and the USS *Turner Joy*, American destroyers that were deployed in international waters in the Gulf of Tonkin. Johnson retaliated with air strikes against North Vietnam and sought a congressional resolution authorizing him to use military force in Asia. The response struck Pearson, who handled the crisis in Martin's absence, as moderate. Martin shared this view, describing the action as "appropriate to [the] seriousness of [the] challenge posed."[54] At the same time, the canny politician sensed the faint stirrings of popular alarm and worried about supporting the tougher American posture, which did not include a negotiating option. "The long-term western position," he cabled Canada's NATO ambassador, George Ignatieff, "is not well understood and is causing some uneasiness among public ... [It] shows signs of being considered too negative through its opposition to further conference."[55]

His fears were confirmed during the next few weeks. In mid-August, there was another request to send Seaborn north. The awkward July delay and clumsy efforts by US diplomats to brief Seaborn directly in Saigon were worrisome enough. The message, post-Tonkin, was simply a tough reiteration of the American position. Martin was disappointed, complaining that "the US points did not amount to much."[56] He grew more concerned about US inflexibility after meeting with Rusk in Windsor. He felt close to the American, whom he admired and respected greatly. He found him able and honourable, if sometimes a little too cautious and rigid.[57] Though US officials distrusted Martin's political instincts, Rusk seemed to like him and was always ready to hear him out.[58] But this particular visit began poorly, when Rusk was delayed in Washington, dealing with yet another failed coup in Saigon. The Asian crisis hung over the Windsor summit, as Rusk spoke of his "forebodings" and "discouragement." Clearly shaken by his demeanour, Martin hurried back to Ottawa, warning Pearson that "Vietnam is deeply worrying to the USA authorities."[59]

Perhaps, he wondered that fall, it was time for Canada to cut and run. After three months on the job, Seaborn certainly thought so. The crisis in Vietnam, he argued, was entering a phase of increasingly direct conflict between Hanoi and Washington; had Ottawa foreseen this possibility in 1954, it would never have agreed to serve on the ICC. Constantly stymied by Poland and India, who sought to appease their communist friends, Canada could do little through the ICC to prove that "subversion and infiltration [were] an ever mounting threat to South Vietnam."[60] Indeed, Seaborn insisted, the ICC was slowly being reduced to a propaganda instrument for both North and South, with harmful consequences for Canada's reputation as a peacekeeper, both at home and abroad. "We are deluding ourselves if we think that by our participation in the ICC we are making any contribution ... to peace and stability in this part of Southeast Asia, to a truer knowledge of what is happening, or to restraint upon the parties," Seaborn contended. "If we are not doing anything really useful, why do we not pull out, if need be, unilaterally?"[61]

Martin was tempted. He even told Rusk that Canada might relinquish its place to Japan. On reflection, however, he found good reasons to stay.

He doubted that Canadians, attached to their role as peacekeepers, would support unilateral withdrawal. Moreover, Canada's presence on the ICC ensured a Western channel to Hanoi. Perhaps most importantly, Martin himself was loath to risk losing his and Canada's voice in any eventual Asian settlement by too hasty a departure. Canada would hang on for the endgame. Meantime, Seaborn should focus on making the ICC work. "You should seize every available opportunity," Martin urged him, "to take account of communist infringements ... and build up a record of meaningful findings."[62] Seaborn was told to abandon the ICC's consensual methods, accelerate its work, and, even at the risk of isolating Canada, force formal votes so that the record documented the irredeemably biased nature of the ICC.

Even as Seaborn began to work harder to defend South Vietnam's cause within the ICC, Martin fretted over obdurate American policy and Washington's unwillingness to talk. Through October and November, he watched US interest in the Seaborn channel decline, though he remained hopeful that the Americans would prove more talkative after the presidential vote. Yet Johnson's victory produced no change in US policy. Undeterred, Martin convinced Washington in December to send a third message to Hanoi. However, the Americans added nothing new to this message and even diminished its significance by insisting that Seaborn present it as his own estimate of American determination to persevere. When asked if Seaborn might solicit Hanoi's views on a personal basis, Bundy replied with an "emphatic negative."[63] This unhelpful and patronizing response left Martin discouraged as the year ended.[64]

Pearson was growing even more doubtful of American policy in Vietnam, and that meant complications for his relations with Martin. Their varied reactions to their excursion to the president's Texas ranch in January 1965 heralded a difficult spring. The visit was an informal affair. Dressed as a Texas cowhand, Johnson greeted the Canadians, who sported the dark suits and starched white shirts typical of postwar diplomacy. They left the ranch's airstrip on a golf cart: Johnson driving, Pearson beside him, and the president's beagle Him tucked between them. Rusk and Martin squeezed into the back. At the rustic ranch house, the entourage piled into three cars – the principals, "the ladies," and "the press" – for a whirlwind tour of the estate. Along the way, Johnson dispensed drinks and non-stop observations on ranching, domestic and White House politics, and international affairs. Dinner was just as chaotic; steak and catfish on the same plate, served amid the constant clanging of telephones.

The visit rattled Pearson, prompting him to question Johnson's temperament and judgment. "General MacArthur would not have approved," he summed up his trip, "nor, I suspect, John Kennedy."[65] Martin loved Texas. He arrived with Rusk from Washington, cherishing the three hours they spent together on the US government plane. Johnson's casual style and frank talk on all subjects fascinated him.[66] He was captivated by the president's easy intimacy; both early risers, the two shared a morning coffee in their pyjamas. Martin identified with the self-made president and judged him "an intriguing and powerful personality ... He had the same kind of drive as me ... LBJ was a strong president."[67] His assessment of the visit could hardly have differed more markedly from Pearson's. "I don't think that you and I," he wrote Rusk warmly, "have ever had more useful or more relaxed meetings than those which occurred during our visit to Washington and to the President's home at the end of last week."[68]

These very different perspectives on Johnson and US leadership mattered more as the war in Vietnam intensified during February 1965, with stepped-up US air strikes in response to Viet Cong attacks on the American base at Pleiku. The "US was now embarked on a hopeless course," Martin told cabinet, "since the Vietnamese had no will to fight and there were no prospects for strong civilian leadership."[69] Despite mounting misgivings in Canada, Martin (and his advisors) remained reluctant to make Ottawa's differences with Washington too public, convinced of the traditional virtues of quiet diplomacy. When India appealed for a halt in the fighting and a Geneva-style conference, Martin and Pearson inched Canada gently alongside. Drafted in External Affairs, Pearson's carefully honed speech to the Canadian Club defended US objectives but noted the lack of popular support in South Vietnam for them and backed India's call for peace talks. It also reminded restless Canadians that "official doubts about certain US foreign policies often should be expressed in private, through the channels of diplomacy."[70] The speech's careful balance was lost on many observers, including the US embassy, which hailed it as "a full understanding of the US position" and missed the point by insisting that Ottawa had "come down strongly in support of US objectives in Vietnam."[71]

It was harder to mistake Canadian views in private, behind the green baize doors of embassies and foreign offices. Martin used Pearson's speech as a basis to probe energetically for diplomatic openings in Washington, Moscow, and, with a little help from the French, Beijing. The *démarche* was brushed aside in Washington, where US national security advisor McGeorge Bundy warned Ambassador Charles Ritchie that the United States did not want to be "rushed into anything that would smack of negotiation."[72] The Soviet Union was equally discouraging, threatening a campaign to vilify Canada if Ottawa persisted in defending American policy.[73]

Canada's man in Moscow, Robert Ford, urged Martin to press on. A reserved intellectual with a national reputation as a poet, Ford was a self-assured political analyst whose verdicts on Soviet domestic and foreign policy were widely admired in Ottawa. Martin had known him as a recruit to External Affairs in 1940 and regarded him as one of the best diplomats in his department. Ford insisted that the global stakes – progress toward the East-West détente that had flourished after the Cuban missile crisis – justified an exceptional effort. "While we should not lose our nerve in the present situation," he cabled, "I think that the advantages of restoring 'détente' in relations with the West, above all USA, are so great that a very determined effort should be made to do so on the part of the West."[74]

Martin agreed, and in late February, he sent Ford's recent reports to Rusk with another message that emphasized Canada's growing concern, its support for the US position, and its desire to make a "constructive contribution."[75] Perhaps, he offered, the Americans would like to make use of Seaborn yet again. Rusk was doubtful. He dismissed Ford's assessments out of hand and asserted that Washington was following Hanoi's every signal. Politeness alone demanded more, however, and Rusk reluctantly agreed to another Seaborn mission. The unhelpful US message simply echoed Washington's uncompromising public posture and was no doubt intended to provoke Hanoi. The pointless exercise annoyed Pearson, Martin, and their advisors.[76]

Vietnam dominated Martin's diplomatic agenda in March as the US bombing campaign escalated into Operation Rolling Thunder and public anxiety about US policy spread. He battled to find a reason for doubtful Canadians to stand by Washington. The ICC provided some help. When it condemned US bombing in March, Canada appended a minority report, placing the air strikes in their fullest context as a justified response to Hanoi's aggressive efforts to subvert and overthrow the Saigon government. The Opposition predictably denounced Martin's efforts. "I do not belong to the school that believes Canada should become the caboose on the US train," insisted Progressive Conservative leader John Diefenbaker.[77] Left-wing NDP speakers mocked Martin for a policy that could be reduced to the slogan "Don't rock the US boat."[78] Editorial reaction showed Martin holding his own. The *Toronto Star* dismissed Opposition attacks as "bleats from the bleachers."[79] Support came from other major newspapers, including the *Montreal Gazette,* the *Ottawa Citizen,* and the *Regina Leader-Post.*

There was American applause as well, but it provided scant solace. Martin privately scolded Rusk for landing Marines in Vietnam and activating the US Seventh Fleet without warning Ottawa. He asked again for encouraging news of an international conference. "We feel we must go a long way publically in indicating support for USA positions in Vietnam," he explained, "but we cannot be expected to do so relatively ill-informed of US intentions."[80]

He held on, defending American policy in public and pushing hard for talks in private. At the end of March, he gave another major speech in Toronto, arguing in support of US policy, and was rumoured to be working on a peace plan with UN secretary-general U Thant.[81] Pearson, however, bowed to the mounting pressure to do something to stop the bombing. U Thant and other global figures had urged him to speak out, confident that he had Washington's ear. American friends, including Vice-President Hubert Humphrey and journalist Marquis Childs, encouraged him to act. Pearson was sensitive to the chorus of opposition to US bombing, especially among the students and young intellectuals whom he had recruited to the Liberal Party. In late March, in a speech that he was slated to deliver at Temple University in Philadelphia, Pearson decided to raise the idea of using a bombing pause to test Hanoi's willingness to talk.[82]

Martin was appalled. "You can't make that speech!" he recalled telling Pearson. "What you're doing is calling upon the president of the United States to stop the bombing. If you publically criticize the United States like this, you're going to discount our influence in Washington and your own forever. And you must not do that."[83] He urged Pearson to abandon his plan and then suggested that it might "be more effective if it were put forward, in the first instance, privately to President Johnson."[84]

When Pearson objected, Martin threatened to resign but withdrew his threat when he saw that it had little impact. On 2 April, after collecting a university peace award, Pearson addressed the black-tie crowd that had turned out for Temple University's glitzy Founder's Dinner. He praised American leadership, acknowledged US sacrifice, and insisted on Canada's continued support for US objectives in Vietnam. Canada hoped to continue that support, he remarked, but it would depend on Washington's willingness to pursue negotiations. As a first step toward that goal, he proposed that bombing be suspended to give Hanoi a chance to talk without doing "so as the direct result of military pressure."[85] The modest suggestion enraged Johnson, who summoned Pearson to Washington. Voice raised and arms aloft, the towering Texan berated the hapless Canadian as they strolled through Camp David while their aides watched through a window.

Martin too was beside himself with anger over Pearson's speech, and when the two Canadians next spoke, they exchanged "some pretty tough words."[86] Their uneasy differences over the war lingered throughout the spring. In public, Martin continued to rally behind US policy, winning grateful thanks from Rusk and the State Department for his statements in May and June.[87] He remained confident of his ability to shape public opinion, and when sixty demonstrators marched up Parliament Hill on a sunny day in May, he met them boldly.[88] In private, he probed for movement toward negotiations, flitting between Ottawa and the United Nations in New York. Pearson made no effort to hide his doubts. As Seaborn headed to Hanoi yet again at the end of May, searching for an opening after a pause in the bombing, Pearson scribbled scornfully on Martin's briefing notes, "I'll wager 1 piastre that no one in Hanoi will talk to him."[89]

He was right, and his scorn turned to anger when he learned that Seaborn's mission had coincided with a French *démarche*, about which Canada was largely uninformed. That wasn't true, Martin protested, but his defensive tone suggested that Pearson's barbs hurt.[90] Within a month, he was even more distressed to hear Rusk and Johnson refer in public to the Seaborn missions, using the setback as grounds to increase the US war effort and scuttling Martin's backdoor channel to Hanoi. Martin raged at these underhanded tactics to justify expanding the war. He said little in public, however, seeking that reasonable balance between cooperation and independence that had been the hallmark of Canada-US relations throughout the postwar era. Vietnam had made it much more difficult to find, and the situation would only get worse. For the moment, however, as the monsoon rains swept South Asia, briefly suspending the war, Vietnam could wait.

VIETNAM WAS NOT the only issue that complicated Canada's relations with Washington during the mid-1960s. Among the most important of Martin's preoccupations in 1965 was the new Canada-US trade agreement on automotive products, the Autopact. He had carefully watched the deal unfold for almost a year. Sheltered behind high protective tariffs, Canada's automotive industry had lumbered along since the 1940s, growing less productive with each passing decade. This did not much bother the three large American companies that dominated the North American industry. Ford, General Motors (GM), and Chrysler were happy to assemble a limited number of models in Canada for the local market, importing parts and extra vehicles from the United States to round out their narrow range of products. By 1960, the industry, which was based in Oshawa and Windsor, accounted for $500 million of the country's $1.2 billion current account deficit and had slipped into deep trouble as costs and unemployment mounted.[91]

After extensive study, Prime Minister Diefenbaker's Progressive Conservative government introduced an experimental plan in 1962 to encourage automotive exports by remitting taxes on imported transmissions that were incorporated into products for re-export. This measure proved so successful that when Liberal ministers Bud Drury and Walter Gordon set out to tackle Canada's current account deficit and high unemployment in the fall of 1963, they decided to expand it to include all automotive parts. Automotive manufacturers would earn the remission of duties on each dollar's worth of dutiable imports for every dollar's worth of new exports. Unveiled in October 1963, the scheme was expected to shift over $200 million worth of production from US plants to Canada.[92]

Economic policy rarely interested Martin, though he easily grasped the significance of the duty remission scheme to the Windsor economy. He was most aware of its worrisome political impact. "I took the position right from the beginning of the negotiations," he recalled, "that I had as much to lose politically as anybody."[93] In the fall of 1963, he insisted that Drury and Gordon meet with Henry Renaud, president of UAW Local 195 and a long-time executive member of his riding association, "to make it clear that we are not over-looking the Unions in our legislative programme."[94] He was in close touch as well with George Burt, the UAW's Canadian director. Burt and Renaud cautiously welcomed the additional production promised by the plan, but they worried about the impact that changes in the industry might have on individual workers and their jobs.[95] Martin shared their "deep concern" and warned Gordon that the government might have to consider some form of transitional assistance to "sweeten the atmosphere."[96]

Apprehensions about the plan were equally deep-rooted in Washington. Many American policy-makers acknowledged Canada's claim to a larger share of North American automotive production but resented Ottawa's unilateral methods to achieve it. Under pressure from American parts manufacturers who stood to lose market share, Presidents Kennedy and Johnson pushed hard for talks in search of a bilateral solution. As foreign minister, Martin played a small role in defending Canadian policy, though most of the talking was done by Gordon and his combative deputy, Simon Reisman. Martin managed the unions. As negotiators for Canada and the United States met in July 1964 to explore a possible settlement, he met again with Burt. Exports under Gordon's plan were already up from $14 million in the first six months of 1963 to $36 million for the same period in 1964.[97] Burt feared that Washington might scupper the duty remission scheme and throw the industry into disarray. Under pressure from union members to take a stand, he proposed issuing a statement that called on Ottawa to hold its ground. Martin was aghast, and he convinced Burt and Walter Reuther, president of the UAW, "to keep out of this matter" and let the negotiators work.[98] "The less publicity," he scribbled on one report from Washington, "the better."[99]

By October, Reisman and his American counterpart, Phil Tresize, had agreed on the substance of a deal to replace the duty remission scheme. Under its terms, Canada and the United States would remove all tariffs on vehicles and automotive products, and the "Big Three" – Ford, GM, and

Chrysler – would negotiate separate agreements with Ottawa to relocate $260 million worth of production north of the border. As details of the pact leaked out, Martin again soothed the qualms of both labour and Canadian parts manufacturers. Burt trusted him and delayed a meeting with Drury and Labour Minister Allan MacEachen until he could attend in late October. The union leader was anxious about the accord's impact on individual workers, "the human element" who stood to lose jobs and pensions, and might be forced to seek retraining or to relocate to find employment. He wanted the same generous transitional support measures that the US Congress planned to offer American auto workers. Martin made no commitments, but he confidently indicated that the prospects looked "reasonably good" for an aid program that was at least as liberal as its American counterpart.[100]

Canada's automotive parts manufacturers were deeply uneasy as well. They met often with Drury, but they also turned to Martin with their anxieties. Some feared that their tariff-protected factories were hopelessly outclassed by more sophisticated operations in the United States.[101] Many independent operators were apprehensive about competing with American "captive plants" that were wholly owned subsidiaries of one of the Big Three.[102] Most worried that the changes would be "not only painful but abrupt."[103] They urged Ottawa to ensure that the plan included Canadian content requirements for vehicles sold in Canada and an adjustment assistance program for industry. Martin was sympathetic.

When the Autopact came up in cabinet, he warned that introducing some measure of transitional assistance might be necessary to win widespread support in the industry and from the unions.[104] Gordon and Drury were doubtful. Their departments insisted that the Autopact represented a huge net gain for Canadian industry. Any disruptions would be "relatively marginal," and the "major difficulty" would be "the shortage of skilled workers." The government's existing labour support programs were entirely adequate.[105] For the moment, then, Martin could only listen sympathetically to labour leaders and local manufacturers, and make encouraging noises. "While I may have a reputation for optimism," he wrote one distressed Windsor company, "I am confident that in this particular case I am being quite realistic when I emphasize the great benefits which this program will bring. Many of the anxieties will turn out to be unfounded and most firms will find their opportunities enhanced if only they are prepared to take full advantage of them."[106]

Pearson and Johnson, with Martin and Rusk at their side, signed the bilateral Autopact at the president's ranch during their January visit, on a rough bench set beneath majestic oaks that swayed in the cold wind of a Texas "norther." Martin pocketed the signature pens for friends in Windsor and returned home to an edgy city. Though parts makers slowly rallied to the plan in February, there were grumblings of monopoly and discrimination, and one spokesman coolly described the prospects as "sunny and shady."[107] There was trouble with labour, too. When he learned that the accord contained no help for displaced workers, Burt attacked it as a "pig in a poke."[108] Squeezed by militant union locals in Windsor and Oshawa, which denounced the Autopact as a sellout to American capitalism, he insisted on worker assistance as the price for UAW support.[109] In March, the Canadian Labour Congress backed him during its annual presentation to cabinet on labour issues.[110]

In Windsor, tensions worsened. UAW workers went out on strike when parts manufacturer Bendix-Eclipse tried to roll back wages and lay off staff to stay competitive with US firms. Rumours swept the city of more layoffs to come. When Martin denied these reports, the UAW and the NDP attacked him for claiming that there would be no dislocations.[111] "A lot of auto men have the jitters," remarked columnist W.L. Clark of the *Windsor Star.*[112]

Martin and MacEachen summoned executives from American Motors and the Big Three to review their labour plans. The results were hardly reassuring. When asked if the industry could work with the UAW and government to minimize labour disruptions, Earl Brownridge of AMC quipped, "Sometimes we can and sometimes we can't."[113] Martin was not amused, and was even less so two weeks later when Ford suddenly announced plans to lay off 1,600 Windsor workers, beginning in June and bringing them back gradually between January and April 1966. The UAW reacted sharply. "Do you still feel there will be no dislocation of jobs in Windsor?" Burt angrily demanded of Martin.[114]

The government's response was swift and effective. While MacEachen hurried from his Cape Breton riding to confer with Pearson in Ottawa, Martin headed straight to Windsor, where he was scheduled to address the Society of Automotive Engineers. Descending from his plane, he made it clear where he stood. "No one likes this layoff," he scowled, "and I don't like the way it came about from the company."[115] On the record, he promised immediate action; off it, he hinted at a government assistance package. He went further that evening, speaking to four hundred engineers who crowded into the Prince Edward Hotel's overflowing banquet rooms. As he strode up to the stage, he stopped to chat with Ron Todgham, president of Chrysler and a close friend. Smiling out at the crowd, he began his speech by revealing that Chrysler had just agreed to hire five hundred Ford workers.[116] Amid the applause, more good news followed. After vigorously defending the Autopact's benefits, Martin announced that "the Government is ready to accept a more than ordinary measure of responsibility to facilitate the adjustments that may be required."[117]

As the transitional assistance package worked its way through cabinet in May and June, there was much discontent in Ottawa. Many officials and ministers were uncomfortable with the prospect of handing out benefits to laid-off auto workers that matched the take-home pay of the average industrial wage earner. They wondered just where the government's responsibility ended.[118] Bad policy perhaps, but great politics. Martin's safe standing in Windsor labour circles was confirmed in May, when Henry Renaud, with a platoon of Essex East Liberals manning his phone-banks, was easily re-elected president of UAW Local 195. A month later, Burt and the Canadian Council of the UAW formally backed the Autopact.

With a key economic victory behind him, Martin could relax a little as he boarded an RCAF Yukon on the first Sunday in May and departed for Europe, accompanied by Nell and Mary Anne. The two-week tour, a welcome break from the Ottawa routine, targeted a handful of his most important priorities. He stopped briefly in Geneva to deliver a speech on disarmament to world veterans and then flew to Cyprus to visit Canadian peacekeepers. He was understandably hesitant to board the squad's UN helicopter, whose doors had all been removed, but he gamely climbed aboard and was eventually rewarded with handshakes from two Windsor soldiers who were posted atop a distant hill.[119]

From Cyprus, he flew to Marseilles to open the new Canadian consulate, a concrete manifestation of the government's ongoing efforts to intensify its relations with France. The Marseilles consulate was a small triumph, for enhancing relations with France had not proved as easy as Martin and Pearson had once hoped. Quebec City was aggressively pressing its claim to a distinct international personality, challenging Ottawa's constitutional prerogatives and its exclusive claims over foreign policy. The province, which had recently won quasi-diplomatic status for its delegate-general in Paris, had surprised Ottawa by independently concluding an educational exchange agreement with France in February 1965. Two months later, its education minister, Paul Gérin-Lajoie, stunned the Montreal consular corps by declaring that Quebec had the right to conclude international agreements in fields where the province had jurisdiction.[120]

The French role in Quebec's ambitious manoeuvring was unclear. Admittedly, there were bilateral irritants. De Gaulle had snubbed Canada's mild-tempered ambassador, Jules Léger, for an imagined slight in the fall, and a battle was brewing over the sale of Canadian uranium to nuclear-armed France. These tensions were offset, however, by assurances from the French foreign ministry and its minister, Maurice Couve de Murville, that Paris wanted to help Ottawa "keep the country united and independent."[121] France was not the problem, Martin told cabinet in April, pointing his finger at Quebec premier Jean Lesage.[122] Favouring a cooperative solution, he proposed negotiating an *accord cadre* with France (and other French-speaking states) that would erect a framework for provinces to act abroad within their limited provincial jurisdictions. He added a little steel to his policy by asking his colleagues to quadruple federal spending on cultural activities, directly confronting Quebec in a field that it regarded as its own.

Martin arrived in Paris confident of stealing a march on his Quebec rivals for France's affections. The visit began poorly, however, when his plane was directed to the edge of the tarmac, where it was greeted by a single minor French official. He laughed off the low-key welcome, but the Canadian media interpreted it as a deliberate snub in the escalating skirmishes between Paris and Ottawa for the loyalties of Quebec.[123] He stayed in the splendid Hôtel Plaza Athénée, but his room overlooked the busy Avenue Montaigne, which was so noisy that he slept poorly and stamped about in a bad temper.

His mood lifted as his program unfolded. It was built around a retreat with the heads of posts from Canada's West European missions. For two days, Martin and his chief European diplomats engaged in the kind of wide-ranging scholarly talk on policy that he always enjoyed. He slipped out for a relaxed lunch with Couve du Murville and a *tour d'horizon* that circled over bilateral relations, NATO, and, of course, the crisis in Vietnam. There was also time for a joyful visit to the Maison Canadienne, the student residence in the Cité Universitaire where he had spent a few days in 1930. He passed along a federal cheque for repairs and hinted at the vastly expanded program of student exchanges to come. "I envy you," he told the young students, his favourite audience, "because you will see and you will experience, I am sure, the great things that France and Canada will do together."[124]

His last stop was London, for the regular spring NATO ministerial meeting. Ottawa's spring budget had improved the prospects for British exports to Canada, and the UK government gave Martin a warm reception. He conferred with his Greek and Turkish counterparts, reported to the North Atlantic Council on his trip to Cyprus, and won praise from NATO secretary-general Manlio Brosio for his efforts to start peace talks on the island.[125] Though his initiative on NATO's future was stalled by bickering among the ministers, Martin was pleased that the council had avoided a direct confrontation with France. "The NATO session was a particularly good one," he later wrote Canadian ambassador George Ignatieff. "Our own objectives were largely achieved to the extent possible and I felt confident that our interests would continue to be advanced ... I can see that Canada's name stands high in NATO circles."[126]

DURING THE SUMMER of 1965, Martin spent more time in Windsor than he had for many years. Despite the tensions that the new Autopact had created, it was a good place to be. Spurred by tax cuts and ramped-up government spending on both sides of the border, the North American economy roared to life in 1965. Overall growth in Canada was pegged at 5 percent, with inflation running at 1.9 percent and unemployment at 4 percent.[127] By June, it was clear that Windsor was booming. In the first three months of the year, new capital investment totalled $70 million, a figure 50 percent greater than in the same months of 1964 and 350 percent better than in 1963. Overall employment was up by 10 percent from 1964 levels; in the high-paying manufacturing sector, it was up 13 percent.[128] Windsor applications for unemployment insurance were at a record low, and labour shortages loomed. During the first six months of the year, Windsor Harbour handled a record cargo of 878,000 tons, and the city welcomed an additional 90,000 cars carrying visitors from Detroit. Everything was up: retail sales by 8.5 percent, housing starts, and local real estate by 63.0 percent.[129] "Yes, sir," smiled Martin's old friend from the Windsor Chamber of Commerce, Harry Lassaline, "things look pretty rosy."[130]

Martin celebrated the city's quickening pace. He was there for his sixty-second birthday in late June to open the new citizenship court and back again the following week for the International Freedom Festival. As guest of honour, he helped hand out the prize for best float to Leamington, the "Tomato Capital of Canada," and picked up a Freedom Award on Pearson's behalf. Along the city's shorelines, the dredgers were hard at work in St. Thomas River and Puce River, and new lighting was being installed in the Belle River Lighthouse and Jackson Park. Small things perhaps, but they mattered to Windsor and thus they mattered to Martin. "Affairs in Viet Nam are of world importance, but the troubles of Jeanette's Creek are also important to Paul," the *Windsor Star* bragged.[131]

There were post offices to open as well, one at Stoney Creek and another at St. Joachim's. The ceremonies unexpectedly extended Martin's stay in town. Rushing to Stoney Creek, he slipped on the stairs, breaking a bone in his lower back. He hobbled onward and cut the traditional white ribbon at a small civic ceremony, the kind of event he valued as a chance to mark each "tangible sign of our country's progress."[132] The pain was too much to continue, however, and he sent Paul Jr. to fill in at St. Joachim's. "I hear the boy did a good job," he joked that evening from his bed in the Hôtel-Dieu Hospital.[133]

Martin was in hospital for a week, during which time he choreographed a parade of couriers and officials. A vacationing Robert Ford and his wife, Thereza, came down from his boyhood home in London, and Cadieux arrived from Ottawa. "You'd think I was dying," Martin happily complained to the press.[134] The medical slowdown gave him a chance to reflect on his first two years in External Affairs. His personal ambitions were well on track. A Gallup poll published on his birthday confirmed that he was still favoured to succeed Pearson. Forty-three percent of voters backed him against 16 percent for Quebec premier Jean Lesage and just 11 percent for the Liberals' leading nationalist, Walter Gordon.[135] His diplomacy scored well, too. A *Toronto Star* editorial of September 1965 offered a balanced but positive assessment. It lamented the "scarcity of innovations and bold initiatives," but this was not Martin's fault. Like many Canadians, the *Star* had begun to wonder whether the country's support for US policies in Vietnam was expressed perhaps a little too strongly. But on the whole, the leading Liberal paper thought that the country's foreign policy was "in much better shape." Canada's standing in NATO was "squared away," and its relations with London were good. Citing the Columbia River Treaty and the Autopact, the paper noted that ties with the United States were now re-established on their "old cordial basis." Repairing these key relationships had been the government's main task in April 1963. "That job," declared the *Star*, "has been done, and done well."[136]

10

VIETNAM AND A MOOD OF PROTEST, 1965–67

There had been election talk all year. It started when Pearson reappointed Walter Gordon as Liberal campaign chair in late December 1964 and gathered steam through the spring. Gordon was certain that the government could win its coveted majority, and for months, he pestered Pearson for an early vote. The economy was sound, allowing a popular tax cut in the spring budget. The auguries were good, too. As the party's new pollster, Oliver Quayle, reported in April 1965, Canadians liked Pearson. Forty-six percent of them wanted him to remain prime minister, up from 33 percent in 1963. In contrast, only 23 percent wanted to see Progressive Conservative leader John Diefenbaker in the top job. Though tempted, Pearson, who disliked elections, hesitated.[1]

By August, the polls were even better. Liberal support was up another tick, and Tory backing was down. It would not be easy, but Quayle guessed that the governing Liberals might pick up ten to fifteen seats, more than enough for a comfortable majority. Gordon was enthusiastic; Martin was doubtful. Despite a thirteen-point lead in the polls, the veteran politician worried that Liberal support was concentrated in Quebec and that a troublesome 22 percent of voters remained undecided. "Elections," he told the press in August, "make me nervous."[2]

Martin spent Labour Day weekend in the streets of Windsor alongside 55,000 unionists celebrating the good fortune created by the postwar bargain between hard-working North American labour and industry.

Meanwhile, the prime minister flip-flopped on the election issue. When he polled his ministers at a cabinet meeting on 8 September, Martin asked to speak last and then refused to join the discussion. The tenor of the meeting encouraged Pearson to call an election for 8 November. Martin later argued that elections were the prime minister's responsibility and that it was unfair of Pearson to shift the burden onto his ministers. His colleagues were unconvinced by his feeble effort to dodge taking sides. Trade Minister Mitchell Sharp called his behaviour "hilariously funny."[3] Gordon snorted, "Typical Martin indecision. He made a fool of himself."[4] The tense exchange was an inauspicious start to the campaign and a reminder of Martin's standing as a cabinet outlier.

He stayed off the campaign trail during the first weeks of the election. Though healing, his back was more painful than he let on, and during early September, he was happy to let vote getting take second place to the marriage of Paul Jr. to Sheila Cowan, the daughter of his law partner and neighbour Bill. The wedding was a triumphant celebration of the value that the Martins attached to family tradition and ties. Celebrated in Windsor's oldest and stateliest Catholic church, Our Lady of Assumption, it was feted at the Beach Grove Golf Club. Martin's mentor from St. Mike's, Father E.J. McCorkell, presided, Mary Anne was maid of honour, and nephew Michael Maloney was best man.

Campaigning remained suspended for most of the next few weeks as Martin flew to New York for the annual UN General Assembly. At his request, External Affairs had scoured the UN agenda for "Bold New Initiatives" during the previous year but had come up empty-handed.[5] The United Nations had changed since Martin's new members initiative in 1955, and the world needed less Canada. With détente, the United States and the Soviet Union were speaking to each other more often and more clearly, and the non-aligned Afro-Asian bloc, stronger and more coherent, pursued its own post-colonial agenda. "It may take us some time to adjust to the fact that the circumstances of the UN have changed in such a way that there are not easy opportunities for us to make headlines as peacekeepers," warned John Hadwen, Martin's departmental assistant.[6] And, Marcel Cadieux added in August, the prospects for UN progress on the big issues – Cyprus, Vietnam, and China – were "dim."[7]

The outlook changed a little in September, when Pearson offered to help resolve renewed Indo-Pakistani hostilities over Kashmir. Martin cheered his prime minister on and was quick to respond to a request from UN secretary-general U Thant for help in staffing a mission to oversee a shaky ceasefire. Speedy action reflected Canada's "strong and loyal" support for UN peacekeeping and its interest in peaceful relations between two long-time Asian partners. With cabinet's blessing, Martin promised the General Assembly a handful of peacekeepers and observer aircraft. He then hurried home to nominate Liberal candidates in St. Catharines and Port Credit, before rushing back to New York with Nell in early October for Pope Paul VI's historic visit to the United Nations. It was worth it. Nell was thrilled, and a photo of the two Pauls did no harm among Essex East's many Catholic voters. Riding stalwart Alice Shanahan noted that the photo "went through 4 schools from one to another in current events & was handed back to me by Sister Edmond at Maidstone."[8]

Martin's election began in earnest with his nomination meeting at St. Gilbert's Hall in Tecumseh on 6 October. It was vintage stuff: a Dixieland band and overflowing venue, red and white hats for all, and a hootenanny featuring the Brothers-in-Law, a popular satirical quartet from Windsor.[9] Polls consistently showed the Liberals cruising to victory, and there was little urgency in their campaign. With only a month to go before polling day, Martin's role in the national campaign was limited. Strapped into his rigid back brace, he toured swing ridings in Halliburton and Peterborough, and then headed west for four days. He touted the Autopact in Winnipeg, boasted of record wheat sales in Weyburn and Estevan, and urged Edmonton to give Canada the stable majority government that Liberals thought it needed.

Vancouver was a tougher sell. Martin arrived in the hip West Coast city as NDP leader Tommy Douglas and foreign affairs critic Andrew Brewin savaged him for adopting Washington's line in Asia. He replied by defending the American struggle against communist aggression in Vietnam and tracing Canada's efforts to find a basis for peace. Two dozen protesters blocked the doors of the ornate Orpheum Theatre, scuffled with police, and punctuated his speech with catcalls and boos. Hecklers were rarely a problem for the veteran minister, and he gave as good as he got. "I came here to speak for an hour and I'm going to speak for an hour," he insisted, cranking up his microphone.[10] When the students baited him – "What's the word from Washington?" – he shot back, a little too smugly for some editorialists, "The last word I had from Washington was on the Autopact."[11]

Martin came home through the Lakehead and spent two late October days campaigning in Cape Breton and Halifax. Mostly, he stayed close to home, and on election day, he easily beat his two opponents, Progressive Conservative David Gourlie and New Democrat Hugh McConville. Across the country, however, Liberal results were disappointing. The writ had inspired the seventy-year-old John Diefenbaker, who pulled together his fractious party and boarded a train to log 36,000 miles criss-crossing Canada. Along the way, he mocked arrogant Liberal demands for a majority government, and he provided his own issue: Liberal corruption and scandal. "We shall get to the bottom of this," he promised, "and assure Canadians that the cobwebs of the Mafia, the wrongdoings of narcotics pedlars and the corruption of public officials does not become a way of life."[12] By the time he was done, Liberal hopes for a majority had fled. On 8 November, the governing Liberals gained just two seats, falling two members short of their goal. The Conservatives dropped two seats, whereas the NDP and the Créditistes/Social Credit retained the balance of power with twenty-one and fourteen seats respectively. As Martin later moaned, "it was 1963 all over again."[13]

Change came in the wake of the election. Walter Gordon, who shouldered the blame for the loss, offered his resignation from cabinet, which, to his surprise, was accepted. His influential allies in the Prime Minister's Office, Tom Kent and Keith Davey, cultural nationalists who had given Martin fits over restricting US publications in 1964, soon followed. Finance went to cautious Mitchell Sharp, whose job at Trade and Commerce was handed to Robert Winters, a former minister from Nova Scotia who had strong ties to Bay Street. Martin had known him since the 1940s, and the two men were friendly. There were younger, reform-minded voices at the table – Jean Marchand took Citizenship and Immigration, Allan MacEachen was promoted to health minister, and Jean-Luc Pepin was given Mines and Technical Surveys – but they were less experienced and more deferential. The new cabinet was older, steadier, and perhaps more conservative, all of which ought to have made Martin's job in External Affairs a little easier.

Increasingly, his problem was with his boss. Pearson had wanted to move him. He had told Walter Gordon in September that Martin was doing "a very poor job at External, where morale is very low," and he told friends and colleagues that foreign policy making had been much harder when he was minister.[14] Others agreed that Martin should move. Journalist and Liberal watcher Gerald Waring, for instance, plumped for Finance. He warned that Martin risked his domestic credentials if he stayed in External Affairs during the struggle for the Liberal leadership that Pearson's slim minority victory had unleashed.[15] "We seldom saw him," Secretary of State Judy LaMarsh later summed up Martin's leadership challenge.[16] Columnist Peter Newman even wondered if the busy and often absent foreign minister qualified as a genuine leadership candidate.[17] But Martin clearly enjoyed External Affairs, and he refused to move. He was hopeful that a diplomatic triumph would guarantee him front-runner status in the undeclared race to succeed Pearson. He redoubled his assault on the one issue that dominated the global agenda in the mid-1960s, the terrible war in Vietnam, which would become an unhappy and damaging obsession.

Bruised by his April 1965 encounter with Johnson, Pearson was inclined to watchful inactivity in Southeast Asia, ready to help ease the US burden in Vietnam but only when asked. He dutifully rallied in late December when Washington extended its Christmas bombing pause and sought his sanction for its diplomatic peace offensive. This was no longer enough for Martin. His brush with youthful protest in Vancouver reflected the emergence of broad domestic opposition to the war in Vietnam, and it worried him. He was embarrassed by Eric Sevareid's exposé in the November issue of *Look* magazine, which detailed American contacts with Hanoi in 1964, about which Ottawa was sadly uninformed.[18] He was also stung by private high-level Soviet charges that Canada had become little more than an American mouthpiece on the International Control Commission (ICC).[19] When he encountered British foreign secretary Michael Stewart in December, he wondered aloud whether "we could stick with the US in defence of its basic purposes, if we did not show that we were taking extraordinary steps towards getting negotiations started."[20]

He pondered the question over Christmas, which he spent with Nell and his close friend Maurice Strong on the warm beaches of Ocho Rios in Jamaica. It was his first real holiday in four years, he told friends, describing the break as "memorable" and "relaxing."[21] Shelving plans for a Latin

American tour, he tackled Vietnam on his return in January. He began by exploring the possibility of an ICC initiative, an idea that had been kicked around in his office since the previous summer. Secretary-General U Thant had tried to use the ICC to reconvene a Geneva-style conference during the US bombing pause but had encountered American and Soviet opposition. Martin's effort was more modest. Perhaps, he proposed, the ICC could probe the public positions of the parties to the conflict to the point where they might be ready to enter into informal contact, and in due course, formal talks. With a string of reporters trailing behind him, he met with Indian and Polish representatives in Ottawa, U Thant and US ambassador Arthur Goldberg in New York, and Secretary of State Dean Rusk in Washington. "While the road to Geneva may be long and hard," encouraged the *Toronto Globe and Mail,* "Canada should continue its patient probing."[22] The Americans and Indians were supportive, but the Poles dismissed the Canadian idea, echoing Hanoi's line that no talks would be held until American bombing was stopped for good.

Martin was sanguine about the setback. The exercise had shown that the ICC was still "open for business," and it provided ready cover for a different unilateral initiative. Over Cadieux's objections, he decided in late January to send retired diplomat Chester Ronning to Beijing and Hanoi, hoping that Ronning might find a way to break the UN deadlock over Chinese representation, convince Beijing to back the cause of peace in Vietnam, and determine whether Hanoi's position had shifted under US bombing. The son of American missionaries to China, Ronning spoke fluent Mandarin and knew members of both the Chinese and North Vietnamese governments. Affable and easygoing, he was a seasoned diplomat. He had managed Canada's mission in Nanking during the Communist Revolution, accompanied Pearson to the Geneva Conference of 1954, and served as high commissioner to India and head of Canada's delegation to the 1962 Laos conference. He seemed the perfect emissary.[23]

Several factors influenced Martin in taking this step. Naturally, he was driven by his ambitions for the Liberal leadership, but his motives were not purely self-serving. He was attracted by the broad domestic political benefits that would accompany success. "Public opinion in Canada would welcome an initiative," he told Pearson, "which could be presented as a contribution to the search for peace in Vietnam."[24] He was also convinced that Johnson's willingness to undertake unconditional negotiations was genuine and that his declarations to this effect represented an invitation to act. He argued that Ronning would fulfil an American need for a mediator and add to Canada's standing in Washington. Pearson was skeptical but allowed Martin his head.

American officials greeted the initiative with undisguised hostility. The timing was awkward. Martin's proposal arrived in Washington the day after White House advisor McGeorge Bundy had told Canadian ambassador Charles Ritchie that the United States had nothing to say to Hanoi. Yet, trapped by President Johnson's continuing peace campaign, the White House could hardly say no, which simply fuelled US resentment. There were other problems with the initiative. State Department officials viewed the left-wing Ronning, who was widely known to be critical of American policy in Asia, with unfriendly suspicion.[25] Martin's sponsoring role was an issue as well. Many American diplomats liked the Canadian, whom an early US assessment had characterized as "hard-working, meticulous, protocol-conscious and fond of publicity."[26] Martin and Rusk got along, dealing with each other frankly and honestly.[27] Nonetheless, American policy-makers distrusted Martin's ambition, worried about his tendency to "politicize everything," and were frustrated by his refusal to back Washington more strongly in multilateral fora.[28] Significantly, Assistant Secretary of State for Far Eastern Affairs William Bundy dismissed him as "pas serieux."[29] Martin's odds of success lengthened when Pearson cruelly hung him out to dry (hoping to shield his own damaged standing in Washington). "Ronning mission was Martin's idea," he told US ambassador Walt Butterworth, adding that "if anything went wrong, his government would disavow any involvement."[30] Rusk dismissed the initiative as inconsequential. "Quite frankly," he assured his ambassador to Saigon, Henry Cabot Lodge Jr., "I attach no importance to his [Ronning's] trip and expect nothing out of it."[31]

Ronning's progress was slow. Beijing officials, on the cusp of launching their Cultural Revolution against creeping Western influences, simply refused to meet him. Their communist partners in Hanoi also proved unyielding. For two days, North Vietnamese representatives insisted that there could be no talks until Washington had accepted Hanoi's entire "Four Point" peace program, which would amount to an ignominious US retreat. Ronning pushed harder and was rewarded late in his visit when Prime Minister Pham Van Dong acknowledged that Hanoi was ready to talk in exchange for an "official declaration" that the United States would "unconditionally" stop its military operations against North Vietnam.[32] Pham added that Hanoi had already made this offer, referring to a 4 January foreign ministry statement that insisted that a settlement could "be envisaged only when the US ... has accepted the 4-point stand of the DRV, has proved this by actual deeds, has stopped unconditionally and for good its air raids and all other acts of war." In linking his offer to Ronning to the January declaration, Pham's concession was dangerously ambiguous.[33]

But Ronning didn't think so. He and Victor Moore, Canada's representative on the ICC, thought that Pham's meaning was perfectly clear. As far as they were concerned, Pham's offer removed the bombing halt from its context in the January statement and made it the sole precondition for negotiations. Martin agreed, and he telephoned Rusk on 18 March to tell him that he was sending Ronning to Washington to brief the State Department on the "unblocking of channels."[34] Bill Bundy was skeptical. Confronted by the Bostonian's unshakeable faith in his own judgment, Ronning's certainty wilted. He admitted that a US bombing halt on Pham's terms might conceivably imply acceptance of the Four Points, and US capitulation. "On balance," Washington concluded, Ronning "did not himself think anything significant had emerged from his visit."[35] The question was closed.

Martin was deeply disappointed by Bundy's lack of enthusiasm and was especially alarmed to learn that his old friend Averell Harriman, a senior White House advisor, knew nothing of Ronning's potential breakthrough. As he waited for Washington to act, he became increasingly anxious. When Bundy finally told Ritchie in late April that there would be no response to Hanoi, Martin called the American diplomat himself, scolding him for failing to pursue Pham's concession. Canada, he reminded Bundy, represented "one of the very few channels which held any promise ... of moving towards some kind of peaceful settlement."[36] Though unrepentant, Bundy agreed to a second Ronning mission to patch up relations with Martin.

The tough American message given to Ronning flatly rejected Pham's offer, proposing either unconditional talks or mutual measures to de-escalate the war.

A chorus of voices urged Martin to retreat. Without new elements, diplomat Victor Moore argued, the mission was bound to fail. Washington knew this and had adjusted its strategy accordingly. "The Americans appear to be putting Hanoi behind the eight-ball again," Moore told his minister, "and to be escalating what was allegedly a serious and practical cease-fire overture into a peace offensive."[37] Copied on the exchange, Pearson was distraught. "It would be a sad ending to our initiative in this matter if we became merely an instrument of USA propaganda or for putting the DRVN [North Vietnam] on the spot," he cabled Martin.[38]

Martin had his own sources of information, one of which was Arthur Goldberg. The American's New Deal liberalism and experience as a labour lawyer echoed Martin's own progressive values and early career. Named a Supreme Court justice in 1962, Goldberg resigned three years later to become Johnson's UN ambassador. On 16 May, he snuck into Ottawa to consult Martin. Over dinner at Martin's Rockcliffe apartment, Goldberg assured him that "we very much welcome your initiative."[39] Reassured by his advisors that Washington was anxious to preserve the Canadian channel, Martin refused to back down. Instead, he refocused the mission on protecting the initiative. Whatever happened, External Affairs told Moore, "Ronning should do everything to keep open the contact, regardless of the result."[40]

Ronning arrived in Hanoi on 14 June. The results were mixed. North Vietnam was happy to keep the Canadian conduit working, but it dismissed Ronning's message as nothing "that has not already been published in the western press."[41] As Martin weighed the options, his relations with Washington soured. He was coy about sharing the negative results with the State Department, and he did his best to protect the Canadian channel by urging Rusk to delay US plans to bomb Hanoi and Haiphong. His tight-lipped tactics were naturally resented in Washington as an effort "to keep us hemmed in on the grounds the channel is still open."[42]

Angry US diplomats replied in kind. When Martin arranged to debrief the Americans, the State Department sent a mid-level official and the deputy chief of mission from its Ottawa embassy. Bristling at the snub,

Martin telephoned Bundy and, according to witnesses, virtually "instructed" him to come to Ottawa.[43] Bundy arrived the next day and spent the afternoon closeted with Martin in his East Block office, before recessing for dinner at a private dining room at the Chateau Laurier. Martin came with a handful of senior experts from External Affairs and allowed them to speak freely. Pleased to note that most of them disagreed with their minister, Bundy was gleefully blunt: "Basically, Hanoi turned Ronning down cold."[44] Bundy tried steering the talk from Vietnam to Indonesia, Japan, and China, but Martin turned it back, repeatedly insisting that the American approach ought to have been more forthcoming. The evening broke up in boozy tears and an exchange of hard words on the hotel's front steps. More recriminations followed. Before month's end, news of Ronning's second mission had leaked and was cited by top American diplomat George Ball to justify the US refusal to stop the bombing. On 29 June, to Martin's dismay, US bombs began to fall on Hanoi and Haiphong.

The Ronning incident and the unseemly bickering between Martin and Bundy gnawed away at Pearson's confidence in his foreign minister, and he made no effort to hide his distress. He told Walter Gordon in March that Martin's views on foreign policy no longer mattered.[45] He later confided to Defence Minister Paul Hellyer that he "wanted to get Paul Martin out of External Affairs ... [He] is getting too involved in the Vietnam thing to the exclusion of our overall relations with the US."[46] According to Martin, Pearson asked him to leave his portfolio in the spring of 1966.

But the prime minister's views counted for less than they once had. The parliamentary session of that spring was among the country's most disgraceful. Opposition critics brought House business to a standstill over the government's treatment of Victor Spencer, a Vancouver postal clerk arbitrarily dismissed as a spy. Justice Minister Lucien Cardin defended as humane the government's decision to fire Spencer, who was dying of cancer, without formally charging him. Outraged at the illiberal presumption of guilt, NDP and Progressive Conservative MPs demanded an inquiry. When Pearson deserted Cardin and caved in to their demands, caucus revolted and challenged his leadership. A handful of angry Quebec ministers threated to resign. Buoyed by his supporters, Cardin lashed out at the Tories with vague accusations of Conservative misdeeds. Slowly, the press fleshed out the titillating details of the long-faded dalliance between

Gerda Munsinger, a cocktail hostess with murky ties to East German intelligence, and former Conservative cabinet minister Pierre Sévigny. Giddy Canadians queued for the parliamentary gallery, as the embittered House erupted in scandalous charges and counter-charges. "An absurd nightmare," wrote rookie MP Gérard Pelletier, "a Kafkaesque sort of labyrinth without any exit."[47]

Martin watched with concern as his beloved House of Commons stumbled along, recklessly discarding the tolerant collegiality that lay close to the core of his own political credo. At one point during the debate, he strode across the centre aisle to plead with his Tory friends: "Think of this place; what are we doing to this place?"[48] As his memoirs reveal, though discreetly, he saw another shot at the chief job as Pearson's leadership teetered during the crisis.[49] But if tempted, he held his hand, and the chance passed as Pearson righted his government. Martin could afford to wait. External Affairs had been good for him, and he was not about to leave or change course. Journalist Peter Newman, who had dismissed Martin's leadership chances as "uncertain" in the previous December revised his opinion upward.[50] "Once the most outrageously partisan figure in Ottawa," he wrote in February 1966, Martin "has, by sheer force of will, become a dignified foreign minister with a style uniquely his own." He would be "written large" on any list of possible successors.[51]

He already was. In a March Gallup poll, 10 percent of respondents named him as the next likely Liberal leader; his nearest rivals were Sharp at 5 percent and Winters at 2 percent.[52] He did even better in May, when voters were asked to choose between the three potential candidates. Thirty-two percent of them backed him, compared to just 13 percent for Sharp and 10 percent for Winters. With Liberal voters, his support rose to a commanding 38 percent.[53] As the leadership beckoned, he changed his staff to reinforce his ties with the press. Executive assistant Duncan Edmonds left for the Centennial International Development Programme and was replaced by Maurice Jefferies. A friend since the 1930s, Jefferies had spent twenty years as the *Windsor Star*'s man in the Ottawa press gallery, where the genial reporter was well regarded and well connected. Even Martin's style became a touch prime ministerial: he no longer took the St. Patrick Street bus to work, opting instead for a sleek, black Chrysler and a chauffeur. As he strode across Parliament Hill – "watching, nodding, smiling benignly" – some of the in-crowd dubbed him "The Presence."[54]

His Ronning initiative spent, Martin turned his attention back to his stalled ICC scheme and the challenge of overcoming communist obstructionism on the peace commission. He had no illusions that this would be easy when he told visiting Soviet premier Dmitry Polyansky that he would accept an invitation to visit the Soviet Union in November. Like many Canadians, he was drawn to Polyansky, who stood out as a different sort of Soviet leader, one perhaps suited to an era of détente, or more relaxed East-West relations. He was lively and sophisticated, and seemed open to "reason and pragmatism."[55] But he was tough and inflexible on Vietnam, both privately and in public. At a Rideau Club dinner for senior officials and parliamentarians, he shocked everyone with a vicious "tirade" – "one of those with blood and killing and how do we like our boys being slaughtered" – denouncing the US bombing of Hanoi.[56] Martin's impromptu defence of American values and aims was equally frank and undiplomatic. His courageous performance drew appreciative nods from the White House and the State Department.

Rusk was also grateful when Martin arrived in Washington in late July for a three-day meeting of the OECD's Development Assistance Committee. Tackling the looming world food shortage was an important US priority, and President Johnson himself had invited ministers from the fifteen member states. Only Martin and one other minister bothered to show up. Food aid was important, but the war in Asia remained at the top of his agenda, and it was largely responsible for his attendance. He made the most of his ready access to Rusk, warning him that Ottawa was reviewing its China policy in search of "a more realistic approach" to Asia.[57] He briefed Rusk on Polyansky's visit to Ottawa and Soviet doubts about US aims in Vietnam, carefully working the discussion around to his own hopes for an ICC initiative. Rusk was noncommittal. He liked the idea of "a conference by accretion," which might start with a few small powers discussing Laos or Cambodia and ultimately lead to broad talks on Vietnam. He was certain that "something was going to break."[58]

That was all the encouragement Martin needed. Amid the normal political highlights of a hot Windsor summer – the Freedom Festival, the

Liberal picnic, the Labour Day Parade – he remained focused on Vietnam. The war interrupted his annual break at the cottage in Colchester, where he hosted British anti-war activist Philip Noel-Baker, a friend from the 1930s, and it drove him out to the Banff conference on world affairs in Edmonton for the last week of his holidays. Through a busy fall, he plotted strategy and tactics for his Soviet mission, which he broadened to include stops in Warsaw and Rome. Nell, who felt the pressures of public life more heavily than ever after a sickly spring and summer, was reluctant to accompany him, but he and John Hadwen coaxed her into changing her mind. Her program would be unstructured and private, Hadwen promised. He assured her "that we are protecting your interests and that everyone is looking forward to your being on this tour."[59] Martin cleared his schedule in September and told his staff that he wanted to spend as much time as possible in New York, meeting key foreign ministers before his visit to Moscow.[60]

For three days in late September, he parked himself in the regal Barclay Hotel to attend the UN General Assembly. He met U Thant, Rusk, Soviet foreign minister Andrei Gromyko, and a dozen lesser foreign ministers during that short period. He returned to the United Nations three times before the end of October, hosted formal visits to Canada by the French and Japanese foreign ministers, and convinced his Belgian and British counterparts to stop by Ottawa for informal chats on their way home. He swapped ideas and probed for openings, and was swept up in efforts to restore the demilitarized zone (DMZ) that had divided North and South Vietnam until the summer. It had been infiltrated by North Vietnamese troops in July and bombed by the United States in August. Martin worked on an Indian plan to re-establish the DMZ, hoping to use the step to create a joint monitoring commission that might lead to contact between the combatants. He convinced Washington to suspend its bombing in the east end of the DMZ for two weeks in September–October but failed to persuade Gromyko to bring Hanoi into line.[61] "All in all," he concluded during a review of his UN efforts for British foreign secretary George Brown, "there was very little discernible progress in any direction."[62]

Nor was there any discernible progress in Warsaw or Moscow. A twelve-hour flight on a battered RCAF Yukon brought Martin, Nell, Cadieux, Hadwen, and External's foremost Asian hands, Klaus Goldschlag and

Blair Seaborn, to Europe. The Eastern European visits were decked out with the usual Cold War trimmings: slender bilateral deals on cultural and consular affairs, and a handful of extra exit visas for family reunification. There were also important political signals that Martin wanted to send home. He made a "special effort" to tour the Warsaw Ghetto and Auschwitz, ensuring, he wrote Saul Hayes of the Canadian Jewish Congress, "that my hosts were aware of my strong feelings with respect to any discrimination against the Jewish people."[63] He attended Mass in Cracow's cathedral, home to Cardinal Stefan Wyszyński, a stirring symbol of Catholic resistance to communist tyranny.

Martin irritated his Soviet experts, especially Ambassador Robert Ford, by ignoring their advice to cast his net widely in search of shared interests that might advance East-West détente. Instead, he focused on the war in Vietnam, trying hard to convince his communist hosts of American bona fides and win their support for an active ICC. The United States was not the aggressor, he repeated, time and again. Although peace did depend on a halt to US bombing, expecting Washington to act alone was neither reasonable nor practical. He promised that the Americans would stop the bombing in exchange for even a tacit agreement that a reciprocal gesture would follow. With Polish and Soviet help, the ICC could broker this deal and oversee a return to the Geneva ceasefire accords. Polish foreign minister Adam Rapacki was unconvinced and Gromyko "tough" and "hard." The "steady refrain" in the communist camp was "that the US must stop bombing unilaterally, unconditionally, and permanently."[64] By the time he left Moscow for two days in Rome, Martin was visibly exhausted.

But he had no chance to rest. He stopped in Ottawa on 15 November and then headed for Windsor, where he had arranged for Zambian president Kenneth Kaunda to be awarded an honorary doctorate at the University of Windsor on 16 November. He was back in cabinet on 18 November, confronting a crisis over China. He was convinced that peace in Asia depended on China, and when Ronning failed to get to Beijing, he opted for more direct action to bring communist China into the United Nations, the forum for global diplomacy. In a plan adopted in June, he proposed abstaining from the annual Albanian resolution to expel Taiwan and back Beijing. Instead, he supported a motion to seat Beijing in New York without mentioning Taiwan.[65] Pearson was doubtful. Washington would see the abstention as a "radical departure," a view echoed by Cadieux and former External Affairs under-secretary Norman Robertson, whom Pearson consulted.[66] Outnumbered, Martin was told to sound out the Americans.

As Pearson surely anticipated, Rusk was strongly opposed, and Martin was forced to retreat. By late October, he had fallen back on a plan for a "one China, one Taiwan" resolution that would seat both Chinese governments in the United Nations.[67] With Pearson's help, he pushed it through cabinet over stiff opposition from younger ministers, who wanted to recognize Beijing (regardless of Taiwan's status) and were ready to break with the United States if necessary. Even this moderate step was too much for Washington, which recoiled at the spectre of a Beijing victory in New York that would encourage more communist meddling in Asia. With Martin in Europe, Rusk went straight to the "boss," warning Pearson that Martin's policy meant trouble. "We would have to oppose your resolution," he threatened. "I need not underscore the seriousness of such a split."[68]

Trapped between cabinet's liberal wing and the Americans (with Pearson working their corner), Martin struggled to craft a winning compromise. This was the kind of diplomatic horse trading that he understood and enjoyed. While still travelling through Eastern Europe, he cabled advice on substance and tactics to Canada's UN ambassador, George Ignatieff. Keeping Washington in line with hints of a possible abstention on the Albanian motion, Ignatieff secured Italian and Belgian support for a deal. The three NATO members would back a UN study committee to examine how mainland China and Taiwan might both be seated at the UN, taking into consideration "the conflicting territorial claims of the two governments [of China] and the need to seek an appropriate solution taking into account ... the political realities of the area."[69] Goldberg liked the proposed study committee, but the White House didn't. It pressed Rome to withdraw its support and sponsor a rival resolution for a more neutral study committee, whose terms of reference would not acknowledge (and thereby legitimize) the claims of mainland China.

Home from Europe, Martin turned to cabinet for advice. His colleagues were hardly helpful. Ministers insisted that he not retreat from the "two Chinas" approach reflected in his proposed study committee, but Pearson refused to let him abstain on the Albanian resolution, the sole lever that might have persuaded the Americans to compromise. He and Nell were back in New York by 20 November. When a last-minute deal with Goldberg was vetoed by Rusk, the vise tightened. Senior advisors in External Affairs, convinced that Canada had achieved all it could with its "two Chinas" resolution, urged Martin to support the Italian study committee, which was preferred by Washington, and to oppose the Albanian motion. Younger delegation members, including parliamentary secretaries Donald Macdonald and Pierre Trudeau, pressed Martin to abstain.[70] "The discomfited Martin would dodge and weave, as [they] twisted their stilettos," the young diplomat Roy MacLaren recalled, "the whole time punctuated by his loud ahems and various irrelevant flutters."[71]

Reluctantly, Martin agreed to back the imperfect Italian study committee, but he refused to decide on the Albanian motion until the vote was imminent. Finally, on the morning of 29 November, he told Pearson that he favoured abstaining, a move that would disarm the government's domestic critics and lend weight to the idea of an independent Canadian policy. He assured the doubtful prime minister that abstention would not greatly anger Washington. He was right. The Americans were philosophical about the Canadian defection, and he and Rusk cleared the air over a brisk lunch. Indeed, just a few weeks later, the two men met privately at the NATO ministerial meeting in Paris, with Asia at the top of their agenda. Martin was hopeful. He had inched closer to China and still had his channel to Hanoi. And he was sure, though Cadieux and his experts disagreed, that Moscow wanted an end to the war in Vietnam.[72] Peace, it seemed, was just an initiative away.

MARTIN AND NELL spent Christmas in Windsor with family before heading south to join Maurice Strong in Jamaica for a rest. The trip was a celebration of sorts. Martin was making significant headway on at least one of his priorities – foreign aid. His motives for improving it were complex. Aid was indisputably a source of considerable patronage, and Martin ensured that companies bidding on External Aid Office (EAO) contracts knew who was picking the winners. He hoped that strong support for aid would counter doubts about his Vietnam policies, especially among the young and idealistic. His commitment was substantive as well. When he took on the External Affairs portfolio, he was conscious of Canada's poor aid performance and critical of Herb Moran, whom he considered too plodding to head the EAO. He had boosted aid spending, which rose sharply from $122 million in 1965–66 to $300 million in 1966–67, but he remained anxious to do more as the United Nations' first decade of development gathered steam.[73] He thrived on the optimism and energy unleashed in the 1960s by the shimmering promise of development in the new nations of Africa and Asia, joining young Windsorites in their local "Miles for Millions" walkathon as they slogged through spring rains to raise money for their Third World neighbours.

But as foreign aid matured during the 1960s, he knew that nickels and dimes were no longer enough. Simple global charity had become development assistance, a complex operation that embraced technical and capital aid, trade and financial policy, and multilateral donor coordination.[74] Martin had been exposed to these considerations first-hand at the UN Conference on Trade and Development in March 1964. At home, he stayed close to individuals who called for reform, one of whom was his daughter, Mary Anne, who had volunteered in Africa in 1964. Another reformer was his former executive assistant Duncan Edmonds, who became executive director of the Centennial International Development Programme in 1965 and retained an active interest in the foreign aid file. Martin also consulted with Roby Kidd, Canada's leading advocate for international adult education, and with Francis Leddy, the Catholic president of the University of Windsor. Despite Herb Moran's hesitations, the four men pushed through funding for the new Canadian University Service Overseas (CUSO) in early 1965.[75] When Moran accepted a post as ambassador to Japan in mid-1966, amid growing criticism of his "lacklustre" aid operation, Martin recruited Maurice Strong to replace him.[76]

Martin and Strong had been good friends since the 1950s. Strong, too, was a self-made outsider, a businessman whose childhood poverty fuelled a desire for both social justice and personal wealth, an unusual combination. Born in 1929 in Oak Lake, Manitoba, Strong left high school early, briefly working in the 1940s as a merchant seaman in Alaska, an apprentice fur trader among the Inuit of Hudson Bay, and a junior clerk at the United Nations in New York. He joined a Winnipeg brokerage firm in 1948, transferring to Calgary as an oil specialist. He flourished in the booming oil fields, but left it all in the early 1950s to explore the world, finding work and a passion for public service through the YMCA in colonial East Africa. On his return to Canada, he remained active in the YMCA's international wing and with other global charities, honing his expertise in development assistance. He rejoined the oil business, taking charge of a small natural gas producer, Ajax Petroleum, in 1959. His success in turning around the troubled company led to bigger roles early in the 1960s, first as executive vice-president and then as president of Power Corporation, one of Canada's most influential investment companies. In 1962, he moved to Montreal.[77]

Though he may have met Martin as early as 1947, they became close only in the 1950s, drawn together by flamboyant prospector "Wild Bill" Richardson, who convinced them to underwrite several of his high-risk mining syndicates. Martin recognized Strong's ambition, as well as his entrepreneurial instincts and financial acumen. He was soon turning to the businessman for investment and political advice, and he helped Strong position Ajax to take over Progas Limited late in the decade. An extraordinary networker, Strong was equally aware of the benefits that flowed from a friendship with a powerful Liberal minister. He cultivated his relations with Paul and Nell with flattering notes, birthday cards, and thank-you flowers.

The connection between Martin and Strong went much deeper. Martin was drawn by Strong's charisma and unconventional romanticism, characteristics he shared with Martin's other close friends Burgon Bickersteth, Paul Nathanson, and Lord Beaverbrook. For his part, Strong enjoyed Martin's genial personality and was impressed by his intellect and wide-ranging interests. He was also moved by his profound Catholicism. The two men shared a faith in public service, a commitment to postwar liberal internationalism, and a humanitarian concern for the poor and the disadvantaged. Their friendship and alliance was ratified when Martin's son, Paul Jr., who had worked for Strong as a summer student, joined Power Corporation as executive assistant to the president in 1966.

Strong joined the EAO in December 1966, armed with assurances from Pearson and Martin that he would enjoy a free hand in reforming Canadian foreign assistance, aligning its operations with multilateral institutions and programs, and finding new partners in Canada's small community of NGOs.[78] He quickly proved his value. By January 1967, he had arranged for outside consultants to conduct a full-scale review of the EAO, an exercise that was intended to shake it up and bring more coherence to its work. He spent February resolving a bitter row between Martin and Pearson over CUSO funding and its governance structure.[79] Within a month of brokering this East Block truce, Strong had won the backing of both men for his visionary scheme to create a think-tank for international development research, with a massive budget that might top $1 billion.[80]

Ottawa's civil service mandarins strongly resisted this move, especially the turf-conscious under-secretary of state for external affairs, Marcel Cadieux. Their differences were partly cultural. A successful private-sector businessman, Strong was not about to be sidetracked by Ottawa's bureaucratic labyrinth or cowed by its established pecking order. "With his background," observed an official who had been bruised by Strong's direct approach, "he does not fully appreciate or understand the reasons for some of the ritualistic procedures of inter-departmental behaviour."[81]

Ideological differences also set Strong apart. He believed that foreign aid ought to focus on the needs of developing countries and argued that development assistance was "a function separate from, but closely related to, foreign policy, trade policy, finance and other elements ... It may be defined as the science (or art) of applying external resources to the induction of economic and social development in lesser developed countries."[82] Cadieux took the opposite view, firmly insisting that "aid was an aspect of foreign policy."[83] He thought that Strong was overreaching with ambitious plans that were much too grandiose for Canada. In his diary, he mocked his rival's "nativity" and "intolerable" tactics, predicting his rapid demise. "Two or three similar moves, and he'll discredit himself with the Ottawa Establishment, I'm sure."[84]

Martin backed Strong. Of course he did, railed Cadieux, who suspected him of supporting aid solely to appease his younger critics. This narrow and unfair view of his minister was typical of Cadieux by 1967. (Hadwen's replacement by foreign service officer Allan McGill, who quickly came to despise Martin, further narrowed the perspective in the minister's office.) Without consulting Cadieux, Martin brought the development research centre to cabinet in July 1967, a virtual fait accompli. In the fall, he happily endorsed Strong's plans to restructure the EAO. The changes collected government aid programs into one agency, organized EAO operations along functional lines, and began recruiting senior managers from the private sector and academic communities. By the new year, Canadians had started to notice what one observer labelled "a quiet revolution."[85] Most of the credit belonged to Strong, though Martin was deservedly proud of his supporting role in renewing Canada's foreign aid program.

THROUGH 1966, MARTIN's friends were concerned by his breakneck pace. Roland Michener, high commissioner in India, had warned in June against "exhausting your strength" and had advised him, "Don't do too much."[86] The fall had undoubtedly been hard on Martin. "Paul is wound up and tired after the Russian trip, the Red China exercise and the NATO meeting in Paris," Jefferies reported in December 1966, adding that "he can spring back quickly and 10 days in Bridgetown should do the trick."[87] But when Martin returned from Jamaica in January, he was too tired and sick to handle even routine riding business, and doctors confined him to bed.[88] It was an inauspicious start to the new year. Nell blamed Strong, whose social program had proved a little too lively. She also blamed External Affairs, and she and Paul Jr. pressed Cadieux to ease Martin's burden as 1967 opened. Cadieux bristled at the implication that External Affairs was responsible. Martin rarely declined invitations to speak, he complained, and when he did, he spent the free time compulsively working the phones.[89]

On reflection, however, Cadieux grudgingly agreed with the family. Martin's workload had grown enormously since 1963. There were novel programs in public diplomacy, vastly expanded aid operations, and 110 missions to manage, up from just 84 in 1963. Despite Cadieux's griping that Martin had failed External Affairs, the department had tripled its annual non-aid budget, which had risen from $24.4 million in the spring of 1963 to over $74.0 million.[90] The country's centennial celebrations in 1967 promised a spate of state visits and heavy entertaining for Martin – and Nell. Above all, there was politics, made more complex than ever by the quickening underground contest to succeed Pearson. Yes, sensed Cadieux in early 1967, there was trouble ahead for Martin and his department.[91]

The year began with changes in cabinet. Walter Gordon had spent much of his year-long backbench exile promoting his nationalist vision of a Canada freed from the shackles of American corporate and political domination. His views were popular on university campuses, and his book, *A Choice for Canada: Independence or Colonial Status*, became a best-seller, retailing twelve thousand copies in six months.[92] He backed Martin's efforts to extricate the United States from Vietnam but disparaged his preference for quiet diplomacy. "This was one of the occasions when Canada should be prepared to risk the displeasure of the United States by speaking out," he wrote, especially "if there is any chance that our speaking out would do some good."[93] But most of his venom was aimed at limiting US investment and ownership in Canada, an idea that was tested and defeated at the Liberal Party's convention in October 1966. When Gordon and his friends mused that the party no longer had room for real progressives, Pearson invited him back into cabinet to reassure the party's liberal wing. Martin avoided the convention battles over foreign investment, spending his time in getting to know his first grandchild, whom parents Paul Jr. and Sheila had sensibly named Paul. When asked, he told Pearson that he accepted Gordon's reappointment on political grounds, but he privately wondered how well Gordon would fit.

Gordon's return to government linked his economic nationalism with growing popular opposition to the Vietnam War and brought it all straight into cabinet. Martin's failure to advance the cause of peace in Hanoi, Moscow, or Beijing left him vulnerable to the growing ranks of nationalist critics. As images of the dead and wounded, soldier and civilian, American and Asian, flickered across the evening news, Canadians demanded action. Almost any action, it sometimes seemed, would do. Martin's painstaking explanation of his careful diplomacy – dismissed as "torturous diplomatic jargon" – seemed unconvincing at best and possibly even disingenuous.[94]

The currents of protest gathered and strengthened, and swept down on the minister in waves throughout the year. The ad hoc campaign began in January, when University of Toronto faculty claimed that Canadian support for a negotiated peace in Vietnam was compromised by the country's military trade with the United States. This was uncomfortably true, but Martin defended the sales, which were good for the country and part of its broader alliance commitments. Controversy lingered, however, when he dodged a subsequent Quaker request to send medical aid to North and South Vietnam by speciously asserting that, according to government policy, aid recipients were required to pay shipping charges. "There is a principle at stake and Mr. Martin shirked it," the Conservative *Toronto Globe and Mail* charged. "The Canadian Government should never refuse a request for humanitarian aid on grounds of political or diplomatic expediency."[95]

Next month, there were further protests. When Martin gave a talk at the Windsor Liberal Club, local students won national headlines by walking out to protest government policy on arms sales to Washington and on shipping Quaker relief.[96] These were the children of his friends and long-time voters; he followed them into the hall and easily charmed them into dialogue and discussion. In Montreal a week later, when boisterous students disrupted his talk to the McGill University Liberal Club with chants and catcalls, he was unable to cast the same spell and snapped back angrily. "Like Wow!" cheered his sister Claire. "Just saw you on the TV news speaking to Montreal university students & boy were you mad. Good for you!"[97]

As the protests surged, Martin probed feverishly for an opening. He dismayed his officials by promising Secretary of State Dean Rusk that he would consider a further ICC initiative.[98] He offered to meet his Polish counterpart, Adam Rapacki, for secret talks anywhere, anytime.[99] And he speculated with Ambassador Arthur Goldberg about sending Chester Ronning back to Hanoi.[100] He even flirted with an unlikely Indian scheme to have the ICC sponsor a conference that was linked to an unconditional US bombing halt.[101] "I've never worked so hard on anything in my life," he insisted to a *Time* magazine reporter, "nor dealt with anything as important."[102]

He inspired hopeful headlines and offered "encouraging" views on the prospects for peace.[103] He tweaked his speeches to reflect the altered mood, reducing his criticism of North Vietnamese and Chinese aggression, and moderating his expressions of sympathy for the US cause. But Canadian policy remained unchanged. Martin defended American objectives, courageously refusing to yield to pressure to publicly condemn the bombing, fearful of losing his standing in Washington and his influence for peace.[104] "There is information in my keeping, and there are views that I should very much like to put before the Canadian public," he explained to Charles Magill, editor of the *Peterborough Examiner*. "But ... by keeping the channel of communication open to both sides we can help achieve the goal we are all seeking – peace in Viet Nam. That channel can only be kept open by quiet diplomacy. Any other course, as tempting as it might seem at times, would be irresponsible."[105] In sum, he wrote a voter, his frustration palpable, "I am doing all one man can do. I am doing the best I can for Canada and peace."[106]

His best was simply not enough for his critics. The war seemed ample evidence that his peacemaking policies had failed, and the cries for a bombing halt increased. As February ended, a faithful ally, the influential *Toronto Star*, mocked Martin's "don't rock the boat" policies, exclaiming, "silence won't win Viet Nam peace."[107] March and April were worse. Martin took a beating in southern Ontario when the *Star* explored his role in blocking the efforts of a prominent Canadian doctor, Gustave Gingras, to establish a children's hospital in Saigon. The paper drew an implicit comparison between Gingras – nicknamed the "Centennial Lifesaver" – and the foreign minister, who emerged with a vaguely unCanadian hue.[108] In April, it turned its gifted narrator Walter Stewart loose on the story, giving him a full-colour spread that featured gruesome photos of "wards and wards of maimed and burned children" in its weekly magazine. "As long as we remain so polite, timid, and diplomatic," Gingras wept, "the children of Vietnam will go on bleeding and dying."[109]

There were national protests in April. The Ottawa Committee to End the War in Vietnam presented Martin with a cross-country petition, signed by almost fourteen thousand Canadians who wanted the Americans out of Vietnam and the bombing stopped. The committee's non-partisan leadership, which was progressive and mainstream, included CBC Television host Laurier Lapierre, Catholic theologian Gregory Baum, NDP leader Tommy Douglas, and Progressive Conservative human rights advocate Gordon Fairweather, all of whom should have been Martin's allies in the search for peace.[110] Two hundred Laval professors sent Martin their own petition.[111] During the next weekend, Canadians marched through the streets of Halifax, Toronto, Regina, and Vancouver in solidarity with anti-war protesters in New York and San Francisco.[112] The *Toronto Star* extolled Canada's "mood of protest."[113]

In April, alarmed by the shift in public opinion, Martin assayed a peacemaking venture of his own. He offered a four-stage plan that began with the restoration of the DMZ and moved by stages to a freeze on current military activities, an end to hostilities, and the implementation of the 1954

Geneva Accords, including the repatriation of POWs and the withdrawal of foreign forces. The response was tepid. "Mr. Martin is trying," the *Edmonton Journal* noted lamely. "We hope he will hang tough."[114] Hanoi dismissed the plan outright as a "crafty scheme of US imperialists."[115] In Washington, where Martin's domestic difficulties were understood, the proposal was given a sympathetic, if skeptical, reception that was intended to remind Canadians that the United States was not the problem.[116] The available evidence suggested otherwise. When Martin slipped into New York at the end of the month, the news from Goldberg was alarming. Moderates like him no longer mattered, the ambassador confessed. The White House was prepared to step up its commitment in Vietnam, even if it cost the president his job.[117]

There was more controversy in May, when Gerald Clark, associate editor of the *Montreal Star*, accused Canadian members of the ICC of spying for Washington. Martin denied the charges. Though the Canadian ICC representatives shared intelligence with the United States, he insisted that they did not break the rules that governed diplomatic behaviour. This was a fine distinction that both Martin, who feared that he might have to resign, and his critics found hard to grasp.[118] The *Toronto Globe and Mail* described the difference as "farcical" and likened Canada's subordinate role in Vietnam vis-à-vis the United States to Poland's status as a Soviet satellite. The important daily joined the chorus of Canadians who thought that Ottawa needed to show some backbone, urging Pearson and Martin "to endorse the renewed call of UN Secretary General U Thant for a halt to the bombing."[119]

Similar pressure for action was building closer to home within the policy-making establishment and cabinet. Geoff Murray, acting high commissioner in London, and Ambassador Jules Léger in Paris, long-time advisors whom Martin liked and trusted, suggested initiatives to convince Washington to suspend the bombing.[120] Martin could ignore Murray and Léger, but critical cabinet ministers were a different matter. In a speech to a Toronto audience on 13 May, Walter Gordon argued that the Americans were trapped in a civil war "which cannot be justified on either moral or strategic grounds." In a spectacular breech of cabinet solidarity, he electrified the Vietnam debate by calling on Martin and Pearson "to press the Americans to stop the bombing."[121] Martin and Pearson were furious.

Despite his later denials, Martin demanded that Gordon be fired, but Pearson refused, eyeing Gordon's obvious support in cabinet and, more broadly, in the party. He reprimanded Gordon in public but kept him in cabinet, handing Martin and his quiet diplomacy a bruising defeat. Back in his East Block office, Martin told Cadieux that he had lost the party's support and would have to come out against the American bombing. Cadieux was unsympathetic. "In my view," he wrote contemptuously in his diary, "this is short-term politics that is not in the interests of the party, the country, or peace in Vietnam."[122]

Martin held his tongue during the spring and summer, but he found no reason to hope that Canada could avoid an open split with Washington over Vietnam. Certainly, Johnson's snap decision to pay a short visit to Expo '67 in late May gave him none. Martin liked Johnson, and he enjoyed his visit. As the Expo carillon chimed "Deep in the Heart of Texas," he escorted the president through the fair and caught a ride in his helicopter to the prime minister's retreat at Harrington Lake. When talk turned to Vietnam, Johnson's passions, unleashed, spilled into the room as he vigorously defended his policies, graphically explaining that when he called a bombing pause, the "blood of Americans and their friends who were killed was 'on my hands ... If our casualties go up from 337 a week to 1037 I am the one who will be responsible.'"[123] Cadieux was enthralled, but the Texan left Pearson and Martin cold. Martin confessed to his friend John Holmes, a former UN advisor, that he "felt quite hopeless about Viet Nam" and could "see no way out."[124]

Nor did top American diplomat Dean Rusk offer Martin any solution to his dilemma when they met at the June NATO ministerial meeting in Luxembourg. Martin spoke out boldly about Washington's refusal to halt the bombing and the hardship that this stance created for its allies, whose domestic audiences were demanding an end to the war. He urged Rusk to stop bombing and start talking. Gordon, who accompanied Martin to learn something of NATO's workings, described the exchange: "It was an excellent presentation and took courage. Dean Rusk replied somewhat superciliously and proceeded to slap Paul down. In doing so, he made it clear that, when it comes to foreign policy, the US see things in blacks and whites; there is nothing in between ... No one else said anything."[125] Martin never forgave the socialist foreign ministers of West Germany and Britain, Willy Brandt and George Brown respectively, for their craven silence.

Vietnam slipped lower on Martin's agenda during the summer of 1967, pushed aside by other crises, centennial celebrations, and endless speculation about Pearson's retirement. He began his summer in Ottawa, stuck in the capital for the Queen's visit and the lavish centennial celebrations that spread across the lawn of Parliament Hill on 1 July. He skipped the lunch to catch the noon flight home to spend Dominion Day, as he usually did, with his friends and supporters in Essex East. The riding had much to celebrate. Fortified by the Autopact, the city's economy had continued booming through 1966 and 1967. Auto production was up, and Windsor could boast another $140 million invested in eight more plants and thirty expanded factories.[126] As workers poured into the region, the *Windsor Star* retooled its aging plant. Grateful publisher Dick Graybiel told Martin that he was determined "that the people of Windsor get their news about your activities on time!"[127] Indeed, just weeks earlier, the *Star* had heralded Martin's latest triumph, a $2.78 million order for eight hundred Kaiser Jeeps, with the first hundred slated for peacekeeping in Cyprus.[128] There were smaller victories, too, but none so important to local Liberals as the appointment of Martin's law partner and local bagman, Keith Laird, to the Senate. Windsor's mood was festive and upbeat when Martin arrived from Ottawa, still in his tux, in time to open Tecumseh's Centennial Pool. Shucking his tie and dropping his pants before his cheering voters, he was among the first into the water, grinning impishly, "I always carry a swimming suit."[129] Summer had arrived.

Martin was again working on Vietnam by August, when Rusk invited him down for consultations before the United Nations gathered in September. Pearson wanted the meeting to be held in New York to lend it a UN flavour, but Martin favoured Washington. When neither man would concede, the meeting was divided between the two cities.[130] The prospects were troubling. Rusk was looking for help from his friends on the Security Council, where Canada held a temporary seat. The Americans wanted a council resolution that urged North Vietnam and the United States to take mutual steps to end the war, giving the White House cover in its battles with domestic critics. Martin was aghast. Over the summer, his own domestic position had continued to weaken, and polls now showed that 41 percent of Canadians wanted the Americans to withdraw from Vietnam. Only 18 percent favoured staying.[131] He warned Rusk that the Soviet Union would amend any resolution so that it called on the United States to stop its bombing unilaterally. With no support at home, Martin would have to vote for the Soviet motion.[132]

Rusk's cynical interest in using the United Nations to protect his government's domestic flank made a shift in Canadian policy easier for Martin to imagine. It helped that Secretary-General U Thant continued to prioritize the bombing halt and that Danish foreign minister Jens Otto Krag's opening speech to the General Assembly had urged Washington to stop the bombing. "It might be necessary for Canada to say something of the same sort," Martin told Japan's foreign minister as he weighed developments from his quarters at the St. Regis-Sheraton Hotel.[133] He hurried home to consult with the Liberal caucus during the weekend and decided that saying something was indeed necessary. Thus, on 27 September, he stood in the vast UN assembly hall and finally called on Washington to halt its bombing. "It seems clear," he began, "that all attempts to bring about talks between the two sides are doomed to failure unless the bombing is stopped."[134] But then he hedged, linking any potential bombing halt to his April peace plan and reciprocal gestures from Hanoi.

Despite its ambiguities, Martin's speech was recognized and evaluated as a significant change in Canadian policy. It captured the shifting balance of world opinion and caused a small stir in New York, where it inspired similar calls from the Netherlands, Norway, and Finland.[135] His careful timing placed Canada safely among a larger group of US critics, ensuring that the speech did no lasting harm in Washington. The White House simply called it "a further edging away from the US position."[136] For similar reasons, the speech won Martin much less acclaim in Canada than he anticipated. Throughout the fall, he swung, campaign-style, through Halifax, Toronto, and Ottawa, repeating his message. He was met with stony silence and dogged by more controversy over inadequate medical aid for Vietnam and the use of Canadian arms there. "A finer example of evasive double-talk," wrote a disappointed *Toronto Star*, "was never seen in any police court."[137] He protested his treatment and compared his own efforts for peace to Pearson's. "No one," he objected, "can honestly call me a warmonger."[138]

He was right, but amid the swirling national emotions that Vietnam unleashed, it no longer mattered much. With Pearson choosing to fade into the background on the issue after 1965, Southeast Asia was clearly Martin's file. He had worked hard to nurture his ties with Washington, responsibly defending Canadian commitments and the US cause, betting that the Americans held the keys to peace in Vietnam. It was not an unreasonable policy, and he pursued it as long and as forcefully as he could. As a result, he was unshakably identified with the US cause in Southeast Asia. By the fall of 1967, it was far too late for him to hope that his diplomacy might escape the charge of being "cautious and negative." Indeed, the *Toronto Star* dismissed it as grounded in the mistake principle that "fear of the US is the beginning of wisdom."[139] Novelist Morley Callaghan had once used Martin to capture the bursting dynamism of Toronto during the 1920s, but now poet Dennis Lee made the hapless foreign minister the target of his generation's wrath:

In a bad time, people, from an outpost of empire I write
bewildered, though on about living. It is to set down a nation's
failure of nerve; I mean complicity, which is signified by the
gaseous stain above us ...
though on about living. It is to set down a nation's
failure of nerve; I mean complicity, which is signified by the
gaseous stain above us ...
And the consenting citizens of a minor and docile colony
are cogs in a useful tool, though in no way
necessary and scarcely
criminal at all and their leaders are
honourable men, as for example Paul Martin.[140]

11

A HARD-PRESSED MINISTER, 1967

"It has been a tough week," Paul Martin sighed on his return to Ottawa from New York in late June 1967.[1] He was tired and discouraged. He had spent his sixty-fourth birthday at a special UN assembly, haggling with other foreign ministers over a path to Middle East peace. The lack of progress was hardly his fault. The war in Vietnam was hardening East-West and North-South divisions everywhere, and gumming up the global institutions that once represented postwar hopes for a new world order. Compromise and accommodation, Martin's favoured tools of the trade, were becoming rare and suspect commodities. While rich and strong Europe and the restless states of post-colonial Africa and Asia flexed their muscle, Vietnam gnawed at American claims to Western leadership. The shifting balance of power made it possible to imagine new forms of organization and alliance, and fresh combinations of global power. In the spring and summer of 1967, Canadian diplomacy collided with sudden demands for change from Egypt and France, and from within Canada itself. Dismayed and even angry, many Canadians, including Pearson and Martin's younger cabinet rivals, wondered if it was time to abandon Canada's postwar liberal internationalism and do things differently. Martin thought not, and he fought, patiently and tenaciously, for the kind of interdependent, multilateral world that he had promoted since his experiences at Geneva in the 1930s. His dogged liberal optimism proved an inadequate response to the hip cynicism of the swinging 1960s.

For Martin, the United Nations and its peacekeeping operations represented the manifestation of his liberal faith in the prospect of slow, steady, and inevitable progress toward world order. But support for the ineffectual world body and its peacekeepers sagged badly in the mid-1960s. The problems were inherited from the 1950s. Peacekeeping, Pearson's key UN innovation, had run into trouble almost from the moment the General Assembly (UNGA) created its first Emergency Force (UNEF) to keep the truce between Arab and Israeli during the Suez Crisis in November 1956. Most states initially viewed keeping the peace as a collective duty, and costs for the force were divided among UN members according to their ability to pay. There were holdouts, of course, from the start. Citing the UN Charter, France and the Soviet Union, both permanent members of the Security Council, insisted that maintaining peace was the council's job. They rejected the General Assembly's right to raise peacekeepers and refused to pay their share.

During the UNEF's early days, this didn't matter much, as other countries covered the shortfall. By 1964, however, most had grown tired of doing so. Moreover, Paris and Moscow were so far in arrears by then that they risked being ejected from the world body under article 19 of the UN Charter for non-payment of dues. Resolving this crisis was complicated by the skepticism expressed by many of the new African and Asian states. They feared that peacekeeping was draining resources from other UN priorities, and they suspected the United Nations' neo-colonial impulses after its interventions in the Congo and Cyprus. The UN's survival hung in the balance. Although the immediate threat was eased in the fall of 1965, when the UNGA tacitly agreed not to invoke article 19, the larger question – how to organize and pay for UN peacekeeping operations – remained unanswered.

This was the kind of challenge that Martin relished, and he urged his diplomats to take a prominent role in the search for solutions. "The gallant Canadians are in the van," cheered the British delegation in New York, "and good luck to them."[2] The main UN working group on peacekeeping, the Committee of 33, met often through the spring of 1966, but new ideas were few, progress was slow, and frustrations multiplied. "I cannot remember one idea [Martin] ever contributed," Canada's UN expert, Bill Barton, unfairly complained.[3] Endlessly pressed by Martin, he sought in vain for agreement on measures for financing by universal assessment. The lack of support, Martin later recalled, especially from the developing world, was "demoralizing."[4]

Yet, when the UNGA opened in the fall of 1966, Martin had his own modest peacekeeping resolution to offer. His draft invited members to tell the United Nations what they could do to support peacekeeping and asked the Security Council to consider establishing a standby force. It was deliberately vague on the subject of financial support. The motion was backed by London and Washington but opposed by Paris and Moscow, which continued to resist constraints on Security Council power. When Martin refused to retreat, Soviet deputy foreign minister Vasili Kuznetsov redoubled his efforts to upset the Canadian initiative. With French support, he campaigned hard to reinforce Afro-Asian doubts and to convince Canada's traditional peacekeeping allies, including Japan, Brazil, Sweden, Denmark, the Netherlands, and Australia, to abstain. Martin's motion squeaked through committee, but it floundered in the General Assembly, where opponents won sufficient support to shunt the draft aside for more study.

The historian of Canada's role with the UNEF suggests that Martin did well to move his resolution as far as he did, but contemporary observers more accurately judged the setback "a clear defeat."[5] One newspaper described the effort as a "debacle" and warned of the obvious gap between the values of Canada and those of the UN majority.[6] Thoughtful analysts spied danger ahead. Progressive Conservative parliamentarian Heath Macquarrie wondered if Canada was "adapting our foreign policy vis-à-vis the UN to an attitude [in support of peacekeeping] which that body has abandoned?"[7]

External Affairs and its minister didn't think so, and their unquestioning faith in UN peacekeeping persisted through early 1967. They discounted repeated warnings from John Starnes, Canada's shrewd ambassador in Egypt, that Egyptian leaders were weighing the UNEF's worth. Canadian diplomats even backed a UN request to increase the size of Canada's UNEF contingent, and they chewed over the voting on Martin's resolution, certain that Canada would get "substantial support" for another initiative at the UNGA's special session on peacekeeping in April.

Martin attended the special session, accompanied by his parliamentary secretary, Donald Macdonald, who carried the load at the UN meeting.

Martin himself had other things to do. Canada had just started its two-year term on the Security Council, and he used the opportunity to arrange a depressing lunch with the council's permanent members to review the war in Vietnam. He spent most of his time, however, on the campus of nearby Columbia University, where he was that year's Jacob Blaustein Lecturer in international affairs. He devoted the first of his three talks to peacekeeping. He was frank about the shortcomings of the UN effort, especially the recent deadlock over financing, but there was no doubt where his hopes lay. He marvelled at how much the United Nations had learned about this novel instrument for peace in the decade since Suez. He described the variety of interventions that the United Nations had encountered and underlined the importance of precise mandates, the need for centralized planning and operations, and the value of mediation. His message was clear: peacekeeping was important and it would last.[8]

His faith was justified, but his timing was off. On 16 May, amid rising Arab-Israeli tensions, Egyptian president Gamal Abdel Nasser ordered UNEF commander general Indar Jit Rikhye to withdraw his peacekeeping force from its forward positions along the border with Israel. When Secretary-General U Thant asked for clarification, Nasser demanded the UNEF's complete withdrawal on 17 May. For U Thant, the main issues were simple. The force was stationed in Egypt with Cairo's permission, so he had no choice but to comply with Nasser's demand. Moreover, since former secretary-general Dag Hammarskjöld alone had negotiated the original arrangement with Nasser in 1956, U Thant insisted that he was not obliged to consult contributors, the Security Council, or the UNGA. The force would be withdrawn, exposing Israel directly to its Arab enemies. Ranged dangerously behind the main antagonists stood their Cold War sponsors with their nuclear arsenals: the Americans backing Tel Aviv, the Soviets supporting Cairo. Without consulting Martin, Canada's surprised UN ambassador, George Ignatieff, protested, urging U Thant not to act until he had consulted the UNGA.[9]

Martin relied heavily on Ignatieff, whom he had known since the 1940s. While working together on NATO issues over the last few years, they had forged a comfortable relationship, and Martin found him diligent and trustworthy.[10] Ignatieff admired Martin's grasp of UN issues and Middle East politics, and welcomed his clear direction. The two men spoke early each morning, when Martin delivered his orders. Confident of his minister's backing, Ignatieff was often prepared to act without instructions. Pearson, too, was active on the UN file. He had won his Nobel Peace Prize a decade earlier for inventing the UNEF to resolve the Suez Crisis. Nasser's snub hurt, and as the crisis deteriorated, Pearson was apt to meddle. "To make things worse," sighed Cadieux, "we have two foreign ministers, each anxious to be the star."[11] So often now, when their paths crossed, Martin and Pearson, the two old Liberal rivals, rubbed uncomfortably against each other.

Martin's main objective was to preserve a UN role in the region. He argued that the world body retained an unavoidable stake in Middle East peace and that the UNEF had helped achieve stability during the past decade. It ought to be maintained. He pressed U Thant by phone and told Ignatieff that, when he met with U Thant and the UNEF's formal advisory committee on the afternoon of 18 May, he was to "bend every effort" to avoid "precipitate" action leading to withdrawal.[12] Backed by Ralph Bunche, the UN peacekeeping expert, and the two non-aligned contributors, India and Yugoslavia, U Thant refused to change his mind: he would acquiesce to Nasser's demand. That evening in Ottawa, with his "face drawn" and "shoulders hunched," Martin summoned the Egyptian and Israeli ambassadors to his Parliament Hill office. In a last-ditch effort to preserve the UNEF, he asked Israel to consider allowing the force to take up positions on its side of the border.[13] But the gesture was hopeless, and he knew it.

Next morning, he persisted. He told Ignatieff to join Denmark's UN ambassador, Hans Taber, and seek an immediate Security Council meeting. But there were doubts in New York about this course of action. British and American diplomats worried that a meeting might force Israel to voice its fears about Nasser's ultimate objective, thus escalating the crisis. U Thant, who was seeking permission from Nasser for his own mad dash to Cairo, asked Ignatieff to desist. Martin agreed, but he felt pressured to act. He complained to aides about Diefenbaker's "tough questions" in the House and his efforts to pin down the government.[14] There were murmurs of discontent in the press. After consulting with Pearson late Friday evening, Martin decided to fly to New York himself, rapping out a terse statement for the media: "I have not abandoned hope."[15] He hopped on the government JetStar at eight o'clock on Saturday morning and was seated in U Thant's office on the thirty-eighth floor of UN headquarters by noon.

News from the Middle East remained discouraging. Egyptian ambassador Mohammed Awed El Kony, whom Martin met to dispel Cairo's increasing suspicions about Canadian policy, was tough and unhelpful. The UNEF, he insisted bluntly, "is finished."[16] Israeli representative Gideon Rafael called on Martin as well and reported that Tel Aviv would not allow the UNEF to be stationed on its territory.[17] Martin was not surprised. His encounter with U Thant was more hopeful, however. U Thant confirmed Martin's view that the UNEF, though already in full retreat, remained legally in existence, possibly providing a slim basis from which to work. The two men also agreed that the small UN Truce Supervisory Organization (UNTSO), established in 1948 to monitor Israel's borders, could be expanded to replace the UNEF and reduce tensions between Israel and its Arab neighbours.[18] Arriving in Windsor near midnight, Martin was tired but reasonably optimistic. "Peacekeeping was not over," he assured graduating students at Waterloo Lutheran University two days later. "It only means we have to work harder to be more effective."[19]

But again his optimism was misplaced. On 23 May, Nasser stepped up his confrontation with Israel. As his troops settled into abandoned UNEF positions in the Sinai and the strategic outpost of Sharm el-Sheikh, he abruptly closed the Straits of Tiran and the Gulf of Aqaba to Israeli shipping. That, shot back Israeli prime minister Levi Eshkol, meant war. In New York, Ignatieff and Hans Taber rushed to arrange an emergency meeting of the Security Council. The council finally gathered the next day under the harsh glare of TV lights to debate a mild Danish-Canadian resolution that urged restraint and endorsed U Thant's mission to Cairo. Tall and dignified, his brow furrowed with worry, Ignatieff was an active presence in the debate and drew the ire of Egypt's delegate. El Kony savaged Canada for calling the meeting and serving as a stooge for British and American imperialists. In the end, the Canadian resolution garnered tepid support from London and Washington, but was easily blocked by Moscow's representative, the scholarly Nikolai Federenko. The council adjourned without taking a vote or choosing a date for its next meeting.

Though shaken by the setback, Ignatieff shrugged it off as just another "rough day." The Canadian press was more outspoken. The Conservative *Toronto Telegram* characterized the raucous UN squabbling as "a black day for Canada and the UN."[20] The *Ottawa Citizen,* a Liberal paper, described the council meeting as one of Canadian diplomacy's "darkest hours."[21] This was clearly not the kind of statecraft that had once won a Nobel Peace Prize, and Southam News columnist Charles Lynch called loudly for "Maestro" Pearson, while fingering Martin for the UN failure. "Martin has developed a flannel tongue," the pundit complained, adding that "the Martin brand of diplomacy falls short."[22] More trouble followed. Enraged by Ottawa's campaign to preserve the UNEF and by its role in summoning the council, Nasser was apoplectic when he learned that Canadian destroyers were steaming toward the Mediterranean to evacuate Canada's UNEF contingent. He ordered Canadians out of Egypt within forty-eight hours. "Canada's Little Dunkirk," wailed the *Toronto Telegram,* overheated as usual.[23] Yet there was a hard kernel of truth in the *Telly's* charge.

As the crisis deepened, Pearson seemed inclined to heed Lynch's summons, a step that seemed all the more likely as attention shifted to action outside the United Nations, bringing other heads of government into the picture. Neither Washington nor London placed much faith in UN diplomacy, and they hoped to forestall a pre-emptive Israeli assault on Egypt with a declaration by the major maritime powers that asserted Israel's right to free passage through the Straits of Tiran and the Gulf of Aqaba. The proposal was silent on the matter of implementation, but the idea carried a strong implication that, if necessary, the signatories would use force to keep the passage open. This was made explicit for Martin on 29 May, when Israel asked Canada and a few other Western states to join a naval force that would keep the international waterway open.[24]

Though he claimed otherwise in his memoirs, Martin opposed both the declaration and the naval force.[25] He doubted that a declaration would deter Nasser and worried that the new states of Africa and Asia would see it as proof of a Western fondness for "gunboat diplomacy." He reminded Pearson that Canada had no direct shipping interests in the region. Looking to the future, he warned that endorsing the declaration might have repercussions for Canadian coastlines, whose waters some states regarded as international. Should Canada's coast ever become the subject of dispute,

Ottawa might wish to retain an unfettered freedom to reject international law. Most importantly, Martin feared for the safety of Canadian troops, who were still in Egypt as part of the departing UNEF. He anticipated pressure from his friends in the Jewish community to support Israel more strongly, and he skipped a Negev tribute dinner for his good friend Lazarus Phillips, to avoid the lobbying that would certainly occur. When Saul Hayes, president of the Canadian Jewish Congress, finally caught up with him on 2 June, he remained unyielding. Although Canada supported Israel and free passage through the straits, Ottawa was unprepared to sign a maritime declaration or join a naval task force. "It remained the Canadian view," Martin explained, unhappily aware that his was a principled but unpopular position, "that despite the slowness of the UN we must seek to exhaust all the possibilities of the organization."[26]

Although Pearson ostensibly favoured this approach as well, he was clearly more open to action outside the world body and perhaps too subtle by half when it came to a maritime declaration. These issues had arisen during President Johnson's surprise visit to Harrington Lake, where Pearson's comments seemed to confuse him. Johnson left town complaining to aides that Canada (like Europe) would not accept its Middle East duties, but a day later, he was confident "that – if it comes to the point – the Canadians will join the party."[27] Pearson's position was just as slippery when he hosted a dinner for British prime minister Harold Wilson at 24 Sussex Drive on 1 June. Martin, who was present for most of the evening, later wrote that Pearson had promised to sign a maritime declaration. Certainly, according to the British record, he did not rule it out: "He was not saying that Canada would not go along with the declaration but it was difficult for them to agree to something which meant sending warships."[28] Nor did he rule it out when he reviewed the matter again by telephone with Johnson on 2 June. It worried Martin that Pearson's position seemed less fixed, more changeable than his own, but he ended his week hopeful of a peaceful solution.

Martin's hope, like so much else, collapsed early in the morning of 5 June, when Israeli forces launched a pre-emptive assault on Egypt, Jordan, and Syria, determined to settle the issue by force. In Ottawa, unseasonably hot and humid even at three in the morning, sleepless Canadian diplomats and military officers hurried to their downtown offices. Unsure who had started the shooting, or who was winning, they waited until 6:00 a.m. to call Pearson and Martin. The two met with Defence Minister Paul Hellyer at 8:30 for a briefing, before issuing a preliminary call for a ceasefire.[29] Martin and Pearson spent the rest of the morning with visiting Australian prime minister Harold Holt, trying to discover what was happening. The two Canadians backed Israel's cause, but they differed on how to respond to the war. Martin looked to the United Nations, telling Holt that "the only obvious move" was a speedy tour of the war zone by U Thant to generate "a state of anticipation and a quick cease-fire." Pearson insisted that the best course lay in a meeting of the heads of government of the permanent members of the Security Council, in either New York or Europe.[30]

This difference in outlook persisted during the short-lived conflict. Martin favoured a quick ceasefire and a renewed UN role, whereas Pearson took a longer view, seeing the crisis as a chance for Israel and the major powers to find a lasting basis for peace in the Middle East. He was un-impressed with Martin's initial efforts to outline possible elements for a settlement, once asking sharply, "What about Palestine refugees?"[31] They continued to talk past each other as the war entered its second day and triumphant Israeli forces marched into the Sinai Peninsula, Gaza and the West Bank, and the Golan Heights. During a cabinet review of Security Council efforts to adopt a resolution urging an end to the fighting, Martin stressed the "immediate goal" of obtaining a ceasefire. Pearson replied that it was "most important" to tackle the Arab refugee problem. "If it could not be solved in the present crisis," he warned, "it would be even more difficult to solve later."[32]

Tensions between minister and prime minister flared uncomfortably on 7 and 8 June as the fighting eased and the scale of Tel Aviv's victory became apparent. Over Martin's objections, Pearson, who remained in close tele-phone contact with British prime minister Wilson, plowed ahead with a message to Moscow, urging Soviet leaders to join in four-power talks.[33] Martin pursued his own diplomacy. On the TV set in his East Block office, he watched with growing frustration as the Security Council considered how to strengthen its calls for a ceasefire. Convinced that the United Nations was "too passive," Martin instructed Ignatieff by phone to table a resolution to send a Security Council or UN representative to the Middle East to broker a truce.[34] Pearson bristled with indignation when he learned of

Martin's independent move and rebuked him openly in cabinet the next day, lest his initiative reduce pressure on the major powers to talk directly.[35] That afternoon, Pearson unveiled his own six-point peace plan in the House of Commons.[36] In taking this step, he had consulted with neither his foreign minister nor the Department of External Affairs.

The crisis failed to shake Martin's faith in either the UN or peacekeeping. But the unhappy episode further strained his relations with Pearson, who did not share his unwavering attachment to the world body. Many other Canadians expressed their growing doubts. Martin's "peacekeeping approach simply doesn't suit the world," a *Windsor Star* columnist observed bitterly. "Canadians in Vietnam have been made useless by events and Canadians in the Middle East have been kicked out."[37] As spring moved into summer, those views settled into corners of External Affairs and were shared among influential policy-makers in all major parties. The prominent Progressive Conservative Dalton Camp complained of Ottawa's willingness to shoulder ineffectual peacekeeping missions and bemoaned the UN's "passive" role.[38] "Canada is not so sure it wants to be an international fire brigade," Gérard Pelletier, Martin's own parliamentary secretary, declared in August, "running about the Middle East and other areas putting out other people's fires."[39] As Pelletier and many of his compatriots pointed out, Canada had its own problems.

WHILE PEARSON PLAYED Middle East peacemaker, Martin was boarding a plane for the NATO spring ministerial meeting in Luxembourg. A huge delegation of almost fifty officials and reporters trailed him across the tarmac of Uplands airbase and onto the familiar RCAF Yukon.[40] Some were doubtless present for NATO, but most were there to backstop, or report on, the next weekend in Paris. The three-day visit to the French capital was jammed with bilateral activities, but its highlight would surely be Martin's encounter with the haughty French president, Charles de Gaulle, who was coming to Canada at the end of July.

During the eighteen months since the 1965 election, Quebec's insistent demands for its own international status had remained a concern in Martin's office. Early auguries had been uncertain, and progress on the tricky file was hard to evaluate. Martin was pleased when Ottawa and Paris had finally settled on terms for their long-awaited *accord cadre*, which provided authority for Canadian provinces, essentially Quebec, to negotiate cultural agreements directly with France. Wreathed in smiles, Martin and the austere French ambassador François Leduc signed the pact in November 1965 in the Commonwealth Room of Parliament Hill's Centre Block. Delivered just in time to legitimize a second Paris–Quebec City deal on artistic exchanges, the accord was welcomed as reassuring evidence that the awkward trilateral relationship was developing as it should. Editorial writers at Quebec City's *Le Soleil* greeted the pact as "a new step forward," while even their more suspicious anglophone colleagues at the *Ottawa Citizen* expressed approval that the "proper international procedures were being followed."[41]

Martin's main advisors on relations with France were less optimistic than their minister. For Canada's ambassador in Paris, Jules Léger, and Deputy Minister Marcel Cadieux, the prospects were undeniably worrying. The *accord cadre* capped an impressive list of bilateral missions, treaties, and projects that had been launched since the government took office, Léger wrote Cadieux in November 1965, but relations with Paris remained lopsided as most of these initiatives had come from Ottawa. The veteran diplomat worried about the absence of the kind of close and intimate exchanges that characterized relations with the United States and Britain. "What must we conclude?" he asked, answering his own question with the discouraging observation that "our achievements, and they are limited, are indeed very little given the stakes at risk. We will have to count on ourselves alone to succeed."[42]

Cadieux agreed. His dour assessment arrived in Paris a few weeks later, after he had watched Quebec ministers Pierre Laporte and Paul Gérin-Lajoie traipse though Paris to sign their province's recent cultural pact with France. In a weekend full of pomp and cool champagne, the two Quebec politicians had seen as many French ministers as their federal counterparts normally saw in a year. That Léger had been excluded from their activities was especially irksome. These small games of "one-upmanship" weakened ties that were already frayed by lingering resentments over the Trans-Canada Airlines affair and the deadlock over safeguarding the uranium that Canada sold to France. Despite Ottawa's best efforts over two years, Cadieux worried, there was "no doubt that our relations with France, though much better and stronger, are still not deeply rooted."[43]

Martin, who saw the exchange between Léger and Cadieux, still hoped fervently to change that, and he seized his chance to add more substance to relations with Paris in early 1966. Anxious to challenge American leadership in Europe and confident that he could progress faster toward détente with Moscow by acting alone, de Gaulle abruptly withdrew France from NATO's military command in March 1966. Pearson reacted angrily at the news that Canadian troops were no longer welcome in France, mordantly asking a senior French official whether Canada should remove its 100,000 war dead as well.[44] Martin's reaction was different, and he quickly made sure that Canada's response was among the most moderate in the NATO alliance. He brushed aside suggestions from Defence Minister Paul Hellyer, echoed by Pearson, that the government should use the crisis to re-examine its military commitment to Europe, rightly fearing that this would undermine Canada's influence.[45]

Now was not the time to experiment, he warned at the end of March, with typical caution. The ongoing Soviet threat, the fragile state of the NATO alliance, and the possibility that the United States and Germany might adopt more nationalist postures should NATO falter demanded Canada's adherence to the status quo.[46] He convinced his colleagues to go to extraordinary lengths to help France and then turned to face NATO's remaining members, who would determine the conditions of the French withdrawal. The British, humiliated in 1963 when de Gaulle had vetoed their bid to join the European market, were itching for revenge, and they had drafted a hard-edged paper to establish a framework for negotiations. In May, the British minister responsible for NATO affairs, George Thomson, arrived in Ottawa to outline his thinking. In addition to tackling the technical issues raised by the French withdrawal, the British paper included an up-to-date justification for the alliance that would be published "to demonstrate that de Gaulle was not right."[47]

Martin was appalled by the British plan to present the French with a set of minimum demands, a tactic likely to provoke only a dangerous clash with a proud nation.[48] He was especially upset at Thomson's rigid statement on détente and East-West relations, and he quickly set out to replace it with one of his own. He instructed Canadian ambassadors in Washington, Brussels, and Bonn, where governments had the British paper, to press his view at senior levels that the alliance badly needed a generous statement on détente to appease Paris. He was back before cabinet in May, seeking support for his own draft on East-West relations, one acknowledging NATO as more than simply a military alliance and welcoming steps to improve relations with the Soviet Bloc. As the talks slated for NATO's spring meeting came into focus, Martin ordered Léger and Canada's NATO delegation to block any final push by the remaining members to reach an agreed position on East-West relations.[49]

NATO's 1966 spring meeting capped a hectic week for Martin. It began on 28 May, when he escorted U Thant from New York to Windsor, where U Thant collected an honorary degree that Martin had arranged through his good friend Francis Leddy, president of the University of Windsor. The locals loved the splashy event. Norm Hull, editor of the *Windsor Star*, was unstinting in his praise. "This was another notable day in Windsor's history," he wrote Martin, "due entirely to our country's outstanding Minister of External Affairs."[50] With daughter Mary Anne in tow, Martin headed next to the University of British Columbia to collect his own honorary doctorate that celebrated his statesmanlike efforts to keep his department above politics. From Vancouver, he and Mary Anne flew directly to The Hague, where he met the influential Dutch foreign minister, Joseph Luns, to discuss alliance relations with France. Favouring a strong American role in Europe and close North Atlantic unity, Luns was unsympathetic.

Martin had better luck in Brussels, where the North Atlantic Council gathered on 6 June. He made little progress with Secretary of State Dean Rusk but was encouraged by his talks with Italian foreign minister Amintore Fanfani and his Belgian counterpart, Pierre Harmel. These were Martin's kind of colleagues. Veteran political pragmatists and committed internationalists, they broadly agreed on the importance of limiting the harm to NATO caused by the French withdrawal and finding a positive role for NATO in East-West relations.[51] The council's debate was tough, even acrimonious. Martin insisted on links with France, and after a long day of talks, he convinced his reluctant colleagues to delay moving NATO headquarters from Paris to Brussels, retaining a symbol of France's continuing political relationship with NATO. "So far, things have been difficult," John Hadwen, his senior aide, wrote Nell that evening, "but [Martin] has personally done very well."[52]

He continued to do well, and his draft statement on East-West relations made it into the final communiqué. However, his support for France irritated many of Canada's allies, especially the British and the Americans, who accused him of "being more royalist than the king."[53] His fervour bothered his advisors, too, who complained to their American colleagues "that Martin's personal position on this issue went well beyond what [they] considered to be necessary even from the stand-point of domestic politics in Canada."[54] But his success pleased Pearson, who cabled him gratefully to acknowledge "the fine work you are doing at the council meeting and the good results achieved in uneasy circumstances."[55] Just as significantly, it pleased the French. Maurice Couve de Murville, who had been dodging an invitation to come to Canada for more than two years, finally promised Martin that he would pay an official visit during the following September. The visit, the first to federal authorities by a French cabinet minister since 1963, was a small coup for Martin.

From his perspective, his efforts to work as closely as possible with the French in NATO's multilateral setting were undoubtedly bolstering bilateral ties. There were senior-level talks on joint aid for francophone Africa in March.[56] When Jean Basdevant, director-general of cultural affairs for the Quai d'Orsay, flew to Quebec City in June, he readily heeded federal advice to broaden his program to include Ottawa and Toronto. In early September, Martin and most of his senior staff spent a productive day in his East Block offices with Roger Seydoux, France's UN ambassador, in the sort of pre-UNGA talks that had long been a fixture in Canada's relations with Britain and the United States. "This innovation," Martin told the French, "confirms Canada's diplomatic opening toward France, the evidence for which has recently multiplied."[57] A few weeks later, he welcomed Couve de Murville to Ottawa.

Planning the visit had not been easy. At the last minute, Couve had insisted on meeting the recently elected Quebec premier, Daniel Johnson, without being accompanied by the usual federal official. When Martin threatened to scupper the visit, the two sides quickly brokered a secret deal. Pleading urgent business, the foreign minister would beg off the encounter, sending instead a mid-level official to hover nearby. "Looking back," Martin wrote in his memoirs, "I feel the incident, with its overtones of cloak and dagger, was rather discreditable."[58] But that was hardly his (or Léger's) view at the time.

The highlight for Martin was clearly the lavish dinner laid on for Couve at the Rideau Club. He seized his chance to showcase his ties with his French counterpart, whom he showered with praise as a "great statesman, eminent diplomat." His "brilliant and diversified gifts," Martin raved, joined a "Cartesian mind with political imagination." Describing the state of relations between France and Canada, he recited a litany of bilateral good works: new missions in France; joint aid for Africa; consultations with Seydoux; forthcoming economic missions and schemes for common defence procurement; and most recently, shared support for Senegalese president Leopold Senghor's new association of French-speaking states, La Francophonie. He admitted that there were differences – over Vietnam and NATO – but these didn't matter much, because the two countries were clearly "united on essentials."[59]

Cadieux and John Halstead, the head of the European Division, reacted much more negatively to the Couve incident. They feared that the election of Daniel Johnson and the Union Nationale a few months earlier had changed the federal-provincial dynamic. Quebec's premier and his nationalist ministers pursued closer relations with France more relentlessly than Jean Lesage's defeated Liberals ever did. They grasped for recognition as autonomous international actors, conscious that every precedent counted. In the slights and insults, amid the growing secrecy and furtive whisperings between Quebec City and Paris, Cadieux and Halstead sensed de Gaulle's malevolent willingness to respond. As a consequence, by late fall, they took a much dimmer view of relations with France than their minister. They thought the French Embassy slow to inform federal authorities of ministerial visitors from France, and they suspected Ambassador Leduc of independently planning visits with scheming Quebec officials.[60]

Most importantly, they were deeply upset by de Gaulle's recent refusal to meet Ottawa's immigration minister, Jean Marchand, one of a tough new breed of federalist Quebecers committed to a future within a united Canada. When Léger approached the Élysée Palace in November 1966 to seek an audience for Marchand, he was told that de Gaulle met only with foreign ministers. This was transparently untrue, but even appeals to senior French policy-makers, including Minister of State Louis Joxe, failed to shift de Gaulle. Léger's conclusion was disheartening: "There are two very different welcomes accorded ministers depending on whether they come from Ottawa or Quebec City." Clearly, Martin told Pearson, who was deeply disturbed by the incident, Ottawa ought to examine its relations with de Gaulle and France.[61] Meanwhile, he promised to raise the matter with the French foreign minister.

Yet he ducked substantive talks on bilateral issues when he met Couve a few weeks later on the margins of the fall NATO ministerial meeting in Paris. He was preoccupied with Vietnam and his recent East European tour.[62] Instead, Canadian diplomats raised the issue only on an official, and much less exalted, level. With Cadieux's encouragement, Halstead called on his counterparts at the Quai d'Orsay to outline federal concerns about French policy and de Gaulle's snub of Marchand. French diplomats were not unsympathetic, but, they shrugged, what could they do? The General saw French Canadians as "a special case" for whom "the normal rules do not apply."[63]

Drafting Pearson's promised review of Canada-France relations within this tense setting exposed the gap that separated Martin and Cadieux. "Mr. Martin," Cadieux told Governor General Georges Vanier in January 1967, "does not entirely agree with the department's interpretation of recent events in Canada, and the steps to be taken."[64] Martin scoffed at the claim, but his under-secretary was right. In contrast to Halstead and Cadieux, who wanted to confront de Gaulle and challenge Premier Johnson, Martin favoured a softer approach. His reasons for doing so were many and complex. In part, they were rooted in temperament and character. He instinctively shied away from confrontation, seeking compromise and negotiation. There was always a touch of the innocent about Martin as well. His long-time collaborator Gordon Robertson, clerk of the Privy Council, insisted that Martin, who would never have schemed to harm France or another friendly state, found it hard to believe that others might not share his scruples.[65]

Martin had more substantive reasons for avoiding a confrontation with France. He shared none of Cadieux's righteous sense of victimhood and ascribed some of the trouble to Pearson, whom he blamed in his memoirs for failing to engage de Gaulle in 1966.[66] He also valued more highly than Cadieux the progress made in bilateral relations since 1963, and he was reluctant to risk it. He agreed with Léger, who thought Cadieux's early, tough drafts of the review had minimized "real progress" in relations with Paris, resulting in a paper that "in its entirety, seems false."[67] More importantly, Martin was loath to pursue a policy that was likely to alienate Quebec. He identified himself as a Laurier Liberal, staunchly committed to murky compromises in defence of French-English unity. Tutored in the cabinets of the ever-ambiguous prime minister Mackenzie King and the accommodating Louis St. Laurent, he had managed the Union Nationale during the 1950s with shared programs in health care and welfare. He could handle Johnson now. As the leading French Canadian candidate to replace Pearson should he resign, Martin refused to squander his political advantage in Quebec by engaging in an unpopular and unwinnable scrap with Johnson.

His memorandum for Pearson, which reached for a positive note, began with the premise that relations with France had made "encouraging progress." Complications had arisen largely because of Quebec, which was exploiting legitimate French interest in Canada to advance its own nationalist goals. As for de Gaulle, Martin insisted that the French president would "keep the lines open to Ottawa and Quebec," and that he "probably does not intend consciously to weaken Canada as a state." The real danger lay in adopting negative policies that would leave genuine Quebec nationalists no option but independence. To avoid this, Martin offered more of the same. His two main conclusions recommended continuing to put "as much substance as possible" into relations with France and other French-speaking states, and remaining "as helpful to the French Government as possible on multilateral issues."[68]

He offered specific suggestions for coping with immediate problems, especially de Gaulle's anticipated visit to Canada for Expo '67. External Affairs would remind diplomatic missions in Ottawa, including that of the French (whose behaviour had so far been "cautious and correct"), that it remained the proper channel for all diplomatic communications. It would also keep close tabs on French supporters of Quebec separatism (though this attracted only "hotheads and students" in France and posed no real danger). The government should seek opportunities to explain to de Gaulle that Ottawa welcomed closer Quebec-France ties within the context of developing France-Canada relations. This might take the form, as Halstead and Cadieux wished, of a forthright letter from Pearson to de Gaulle, though

Léger's view was more cautious. "I think we should always remember," he wrote in a letter extracted in the memorandum,

> that, although many aspects of French policy under General de Gaulle will probably last a long time, he will not … We have more to gain by biding our time than by grasping the nettle. Time is on our side, not on his. Let us defend ourselves, but discreetly and indirectly. Any other policy would, I think, risk more than it could gain.[69]

As Martin surely hoped, Pearson opted for caution. He endorsed the thrust of the memorandum but questioned the value of writing de Gaulle and refused to do so.

Martin exerted a moderating influence on Canadian policy through the spring of 1967, though his was no longer the only important voice advising Pearson. As de Gaulle's visit to Expo '67 loomed larger on the bilateral agenda, control over its planning shifted from External Affairs to senior officials in the Prime Minister's Office (PMO) and the Privy Council Office, who worked directly with the coordinator for state visits, General R.W. Moncel. At the same time, attitudes toward de Gaulle and Quebec were hardening among a group of Quebec lawyers who were close to Pearson. His parliamentary secretary was Pierre Trudeau, one of three strong federalist MPs elected from Quebec in 1965. He was a determined opponent of Quebec's international activities, which he feared would dissolve the ties of Canadian federalism. His views were echoed by Marc Lalonde, a tough Montreal lawyer who became Pearson's chief of staff in May 1967, and by Jean Beetz, a professor of constitutional law at the Université de Montréal who was brought into the PMO as a legal advisor. Their uncompromising outlook echoed Cadieux's, with whom they kept in close touch through Allan Gotlieb, a top lawyer at External Affairs and its leading advisor on federal-provincial relations.[70]

Cadieux met Ambassador Leduc several times in January to review the ground rules on ministerial visits and to plan de Gaulle's program, though the Élysée refused to confirm the visit until after the French elections in March. The talks seemed friendly and forthright, which made things worse when *Le Devoir* reported from Paris in mid-February that de Gaulle had confirmed his attendance at Expo directly with the Quebec delegation.[71]

Cadieux and Gotlieb were incensed. They were suspicious of Leduc's "evasive" replies to questions about a pending French loan to Quebec, and they peered dubiously into the ambassador's trip to the provincial capital as lawmakers there launched a Department of Intergovernmental Affairs, an agency that seemed uncomfortably like a foreign office.[72] Martin forwarded their concerns to Pearson, warning again that they should be assessed against "the very real progress" being made in bilateral relations. Friction would naturally arise as Paris, Ottawa, and Quebec City rebalanced their long-neglected ties, but there was no need to panic. Similarly, when Jean Marchand raised the visit in cabinet, Martin dismissed his concern, insisting that the embassy was firmly in control.[73] "Best results," he told Pearson, "will be secured through a judicious mixture of alertness, firmness, and friendliness, which has served us well to date."[74]

Yet this was daily becoming a tougher course to follow, as anxieties about de Gaulle's unsettled plans turned every misstep into calculated gambits in the scramble for advantage. Tempers flared in March when de Gaulle sent only a middling politician, Claude Hettier de la Boislambert, chancellor of France's Ordre de la Libération, as his representative to Governor General Georges Vanier's funeral.[75] Another crisis threatened when de Gaulle refused to attend commemorations for the fiftieth anniversary of Vimy Ridge, a First World War battle. Pearson, himself a veteran of that war, wanted to challenge de Gaulle and make the row public. "Soon," Cadieux noted with grim satisfaction, "war will be declared between Ottawa and the Élysée."[76]

Martin hoped not, and he counselled patient silence. Pearson and his advisors resented this advice, though they were too mindful of de Gaulle's unpredictable temper to ignore it. When the story finally broke, Martin downplayed the incident as an unfortunate misunderstanding. Even among those who agreed that this was the right approach – and there were many – the effort won him no praise. "Paul Martin," mocked the national columnist Charles Lynch, who backed his stance, "is past master of turning the other cheek, and acting as though every insult were a bouquet."[77]

Tensions mounted through the spring. Anxious to minimize the federal profile and highlight their ties with France, Quebec politicians and officials urged de Gaulle to start his visit in their *belle province,* landing first in Quebec City or Montreal. To the dismay of federal officials, who obviously favoured Ottawa, de Gaulle was ready to oblige. Martin summoned French ambassador Leduc in early April to confirm the news. He warned Leduc that de Gaulle's visit was a source of increasing bilateral tension and expressed the hope that it would begin in Ottawa. When Leduc confirmed that de Gaulle planned to head first to Quebec by warship, Martin protested. "This would cause serious difficulty," he exclaimed, adding "that it was all the more important that he should have a talk with General de Gaulle himself."[78]

Others drew the same conclusion. While officials bickered over the visit's details, Cadieux and Jules Léger, with help from the influential former under-secretary Norman Robertson, cast about for an emissary who could explain Canadian sensitivities to de Gaulle. The best choice, the only choice, the three senior diplomats agreed, was Martin, working through his friend Couve de Murville. "Couve understands and can sometimes make the old Élyséen prophet see reason," Léger argued.[79] Martin needed no convincing, and by mid-April, it was arranged that he would meet Couve and de Gaulle after the NATO ministerial meeting in June.[80] For some officials, this was not soon enough, and unnamed External Affairs aides complained to the press that Martin, who was headed to London for an Anglo-Canadian cabinet meeting the next week, ought to be using his "friendship" with Couve to improve things more quickly.[81] Fair enough, Martin agreed, slotting an April visit to Paris into his agenda.

Martin arrived in Paris, always splendid during April, in an ugly mood. He had caught a nasty head cold in London, where the joint cabinet meetings had gone poorly, and he was angry with Pearson, who insisted that he extend his European tour to attend the funeral of former West German chancellor Konrad Adenauer. His luncheon encounter with Couve proved inconclusive. Although his government was "not ... setting any conditions," Martin began delicately, he hoped that de Gaulle would begin his visit in Ottawa, where he would enjoy a "rousing welcome," one fit for a "world figure in the heart of the nation," with grand speeches from the steps of the Parliament Buildings. He pleaded, too. "If [de Gaulle] had the unity of our country at his heart," he finished, "he should first come to the national capital." Sphinx-like, Couve coolly promised to "do his best."[82]

Martin's efforts were overtaken by discussions in Canada. Citing precedents set by other heads of state, Quebec premier Johnson made it clear to

Pearson when they met on 5 May that he expected de Gaulle to begin his trip in Quebec. Pearson surrendered. In External Affairs, attention shifted to Martin's next meeting with Couve and de Gaulle, slated for June. De Gaulle seemed more ambiguous and paradoxical than ever, a baffled Cadieux briefed his minister. Although the French leader was anxious to promote a vibrant French Quebec, he knew that a fractured Canada, driven deeper into the US orbit, was not in France's interest. Cadieux argued that Johnson's visit to Paris in May, which had passed without incident, seemed proof that de Gaulle was trying to give Quebec every possible support short of crippling Canada. Perhaps, Cadieux suggested, the French president simply did not understand that such initiatives as his direct contacts with Quebec undermined the Canadian state.[83]

As Cadieux explained, Ottawa had three options for dealing with the problem. It could "passively" resign itself to de Gaulle's misbehaviour, putting at risk the country's future as a federal state. Or it could confront de Gaulle with a "rigide et combative" attitude, though this would surely rupture its relations with both Quebec and Paris. Cadieux favoured a third alternative: federal authorities could continue to pursue an intermediate course that would welcome France's special ties to Quebec within the context of closer relations with the whole of Canada. He urged Martin to use Couve to hammer home Canadian concerns to Paris, hopeful that the French minister might persuade de Gaulle to avoid controversial actions and eschew such favourite but dangerous phrases as "État de Quebec" and "Chef du Canada français."[84] As for handling de Gaulle himself, Cadieux advised Martin to keep things light: thank him for the honour of a reception, assure him that Canadians were anxious to greet him, and seek his views on Vietnam and the Middle East.[85]

Martin's June trip to France was packed with activities celebrating Ottawa's commitment to things French and closer ties with France. He arrived from NATO meetings in Luxembourg late on the morning of 15 June and promptly joined French education minister Alain Peyrefitte in laying the cornerstone for a pricey extension at the historic Maison Canadienne. He announced plans to spend another $900,000 on a cultural centre in Paris, and he delivered a keynote address on relations with France at a lunch for the city's diplomatic correspondents, who paid "$9 bucks a whack" for their duck and strawberry melba. "Dammit," grumbled the Canadians among them, "I can hear him for free most afternoons in the House of Commons."[86] He spent the afternoon with Ambassador Léger and six hundred expatriates at an early reception to mark Canada's centennial. In the evening, he returned to the Maison Canadienne for a Centennial Ball.

The highlight of the visit took place next afternoon, when Martin spent thirty-five minutes with de Gaulle. Their encounter was friendly. They began with Vimy, which de Gaulle dismissed as "un malentendu," a misunderstanding. He and Martin spent most of their time on the Middle East and Vietnam, which left no chance to discuss bilateral problems, even if Martin had wanted. But what little he heard was comforting enough. De Gaulle mentioned his visit in passing, vaguely assuring Martin that "everything would go well."[87] This result was better than anyone had imagined, and Martin emerged from the Élysée Palace with a Quebec flag pinned to his lapel and a happy grin on his face. It stayed in place, even as security guards shooed him away from the Élysée steps to make way for incoming Soviet premier Alexei Kosygin.[88]

Martin was reluctant to disturb the upbeat mood that marked his passage through Paris, and when he encountered Couve the following day, he again chose not to air his bilateral grievances. "It might have been possible to raise certain problems," he told Pearson, "but I was not convinced that the timing was right."[89] He returned to Ottawa in high spirits, reassured by his Paris trip. Canadian diplomats, however, were resigned as de Gaulle virtually dictated the terms of his visit. He would arrive in Quebec City on 23 July aboard the *Colbert,* flagship of France's Mediterranean fleet, greet the new governor general, Roland Michener, and spend the next two days alone with his provincial hosts, moving from Quebec City to Montreal. He would finish in Ottawa. Martin had missed his chance to avert a crisis, Halstead complained, and "there is nothing we can effectively do at this point to avoid it."[90] Cadieux despaired: "Mr. Martin is the only one who still does not understand what he [de Gaulle] is up to. He is not convinced that General de Gaulle has any malicious plans."[91]

Martin, Nell, and External Affairs aide Terry Devlin flew to Quebec City early on Saturday morning, 22 July. Stoked by weeks of frenzied media coverage, the province and its capital were feverish with excitement and bursting with nervous anticipation. "The world," Premier Johnson boasted to the gathering media, "will know that we exist."[92] Martin sensed the mood, and his own temper grew fretful as he spent the afternoon tracking down an elusive Couve, with whom he hoped to dine. When finally located, Couve was too busy for dinner, so they met briefly in Martin's room at the Chateau Frontenac to review arrangements for de Gaulle's visit. Martin sought last-minute assurances that the president would avoid controversy. "Of course, he'll behave," Couve snapped – the French were "civilized."[93]

Federal officials were taking no chances, however. Martin, Nell, and Marie-Eve Marchand (whose husband, Immigration Minister Jean Marchand, was grounded by forest fires in Sept-Îles) arrived dockside at 8:15 Sunday morning to ensure a federal presence if de Gaulle slipped ashore earlier than planned. When Premier Johnson and Governor General Michener appeared, Martin retreated to the VIP stand and watched from a distance as de Gaulle disembarked from the *Colbert* to enthusiastic cheers at 9:30 a.m. After national anthems and short formal remarks, Michener and his federal colleagues raced uphill to the official vice-regal residence, the Citadel, where they welcomed de Gaulle on federal territory with a wreath-laying ceremony and a few minutes of chit-chat. Johnson and de Gaulle then hurried away through the streets of Vieux Québec, which were thronged with vibrant, flag-waving crowds, all cheering "de Gaulle, de Gaulle. Vive la France."[94] From across the street, hidden in the doorway of Notre Dame Cathedral, Martin and Nell looked on, uninvited but enthralled, as de Gaulle addressed the city from the steps of the Hôtel de Ville.[95]

Martin rejoined the official program late Sunday afternoon at a reception hosted by de Gaulle aboard the *Colbert*. The atmosphere was convivial, and the event proceeded, "as smoothly as could be expected."[96] Encountering Martin, de Gaulle leaned over and asked of his first day, "How do you think it went?"[97] Assured that everything was fine, he remarked, "You'll see, all will go well in Ottawa too."[98] Yet the portents were already turning sour. Federal and Quebec officials had spent the day bickering over seating arrangements at Premier Johnson's Sunday night banquet, which had no federal presence at the head table. At the last minute, Martin and Nell were placed at either end of the table, but the Marchands were exiled to Table 6, and former prime minister Louis St. Laurent was tucked into a back corner.

De Gaulle's response to Johnson's toast was more disturbing. He celebrated Quebec's historic evolution from "passive resistance" to the present day, when "French Canadians" were about to take "hold of the means of emancipation" and exert their "right to self-determination." France, he emphasized, would stand by Quebec with "all its soul." This, Martin and Cadieux noted sternly, represented interference in Canada's internal affairs. They warned Pearson of de Gaulle's themes but advised him to refrain from comment until he could speak to de Gaulle in Ottawa.[99]

Martin and Nell left Quebec City for Montreal on a private government railway car early Monday morning, eventually halting on a siding near the Queen Elizabeth Hotel. Meanwhile, just after 9:00 a.m., under dull and rainy skies, de Gaulle and Johnson set out in an open convertible down the Chemin du Roy, which stretched along the north shore of the St. Lawrence River from Quebec City to Montreal. Awash with blue-and-white Quebec flags and painted with fleurs-de-lys, the historic route was lined with crowds of cheering Québécois, bused in from across the province. The French president fed off their energy, frequently stopping to develop his emancipatory themes from the night before. "If he continues like that," Johnson quipped, "by the time we get to Montreal we will have separated."[100]

They arrived at Montreal's Hôtel de Ville at 7:30 p.m., as the clouds lifted and the crowds in nearby Jacques-Cartier Square grew larger. Greeted by Mayor Jean Drapeau, de Gaulle's party moved inside to the third-floor reception room, where a balcony overlooked the square. Boisterous and impatient, the crowd of mostly young Montrealers shouted for de Gaulle, waving separatist slogans above their heads. Naturally, he responded: "I am going to tell you a secret that you will not repeat. This evening, here, and all along my route, I found the same kind of atmosphere as that of the Liberation." The crowd bellowed its approval. The general continued, flattering his listeners and their separatist cause: "I noted what an immense effort of progress, of development, and consequently of emancipation you are accomplishing here." Quebec, he assured them, was not alone: "All France knows, sees and hears what goes on here, and I can tell you, it will be the better for it." He ended with a chorus of vivats: "Vive Montréal! Vive Québec!" and after a moment's hesitation, the separatist slogan, "Vive le Québec libre!"[101]

Martin listened to de Gaulle's speech from his railway car outside the Queen Elizabeth Hotel. "Vive le Québec libre," he suggested hopefully to Nell and Devlin, "could have innocent connotations."[102] They didn't think so, and as the broadcast ended, Martin reluctantly admitted that "the General might indeed have ulterior motives." He carefully confirmed this view in telephone calls with Cadieux, whose reaction he described as "violent," and Marchand, who told him that he was "scandalisé." Martin's third call was to a furious Pearson. As a preliminary response, they agreed that no federal representatives would accompany de Gaulle to Expo the next day and that Martin would make an immediate protest to the French. Later that night, Martin heard from Couve through Léger, who urged him to keep cool and not risk Canada-France relations over a few careless words. Martin was inclined to agree.

But emotions in Ottawa were running high. Telegrams, mostly from English Canadians demanding a forceful reaction, poured into the East Block offices of Pearson and Martin.[103] According to Donald Macdonald, Martin's parliamentary secretary, Toronto MPs wanted de Gaulle sent packing. Cadieux's instincts were similar. He told Martin that the government should cancel the visit. If that were not possible, it ought to issue a strong public statement, scale back the visit to Ottawa, and reduce federal participation.[104] By mid-morning, led by Cadieux and Gordon Robertson, senior officials had reached a consensus in favour of issuing a strong statement that would give de Gaulle no grounds to suspend his visit to Expo but would provoke him into cancelling his trip to Ottawa.[105]

Cabinet hashed out the issue at noon. Sharp, Winters, and Drury were cautious but uncertain in their views. The angry prime minister favoured strong action, but Martin urged restraint. "There could be no ambiguity as to what [de Gaulle] meant," he told his colleagues. Indeed, he claimed that "his own first reaction had been to cancel the General's visit."[106] But now he hesitated. The Americans would certainly be pleased to see de Gaulle humiliated, but what of Quebec, where he remained genuinely popular? And what would become of Canada's relations with France? Pearson persisted, backed by Trudeau and Jean Chrétien, a young minister without portfolio. Full of doubts, Marchand and Health Minister Allan MacEachen edged carefully behind Pearson, who adjourned the meeting at 1:00 p.m. to draft his statement.

Cabinet reassembled at 3:45 p.m. to review Pearson's draft. Martin and several colleagues judged it too strong and pressed for amendments. Martin asked that de Gaulle be given time to explain himself, but this was rejected. Others fared better in convincing the prime minister to revise his draft: now it stated that the government still hoped to see de Gaulle in Ottawa.[107] However, any visit would have to be a lower-profile event, so Martin hustled away to revise de Gaulle's program. Shortly after 6 p.m., Pearson summoned the national media. He described de Gaulle's speech as "unacceptable to the Canadian people" and pointedly reminded him that the "people of Canada are free." Pearson added that he hoped to discuss these themes with de Gaulle in Ottawa. To Cadieux's dismay, Martin and Léger informed Couve that the invitation to Ottawa still stood.[108] Ever the optimist, Martin hoped to salvage the visit, but de Gaulle returned to Paris the next day without visiting Ottawa.

The de Gaulle incident hurt Martin. According to historian John English, Marc Lalonde and many French Canadian ministers argued that his preference for compromise had simply encouraged de Gaulle and ultimately caused the crisis.[109] "A hush puppy style may be proper for our diplomats," wrote one of their allies in English Canada, political scientist Stephen Clarkson, "but it is not the manner that our political leaders should adopt ... They could adopt a more assertive stance that makes clear Canada's existence as a bicultural nation."[110] Through the summer and fall, even as de Gaulle reiterated his views and stepped up direct contacts with Quebec, Martin persisted in overlooking French provocations. "My view," he minuted on yet another alarming report, "is that when the General 'goes' so will the problems."[111] The breaking point came in late September, when Quebec and Paris, without federal permission, erected a new youth exchange office that exceeded the scope of the *accord cadre*. Martin minimized the danger, assuring the House of Commons that relations with France remained "normal."[112] His critics demurred. Promoted to justice minister in April 1967, Trudeau knew exactly what Paris was up to, and he circulated a paper bluntly warning that "France is coming dangerously close to recognizing Quebec."[113] An alternative analysis, implying a hard-hitting policy that challenged the external affairs minister, was finally on the table.

SHORTLY AFTER DE GAULLE'S disastrous visit, Martin fled to Windsor and Colchester for a short break. "I slept alot, swam alot, and walked alot," he told local newsmen.[114] The rest helped. "Nell complains I don't know the flowers from the grass," he joked with friends, but "I still mow the grass now and then at our Colchester cottage to keep my figure trim."[115] He spent the Labour Day weekend in Windsor, marching alongside union leader George Burt. He skipped the speeches, however, hurrying back to Ottawa in time to greet King Constantine of Greece, who was visiting the capital on his centennial tour, and to open the new Skyline Hotel. None of this really mattered very much during the first weeks of September. Instead, Martin was focused on his cabinet colleagues, who were reading his briefing notes and preparing themselves for a crucial debate on Canada's role in NATO and NORAD.

Canada's main alliance commitments had given Martin nagging trouble since the 1965 election. American excesses in Vietnam, better East-West relations, and de Gaulle's withdrawal from NATO had chipped away at Canadian support for both it and NORAD, producing persistent demands for change. Popular backing for Canada's nuclear role in NORAD had fallen sharply, and fewer than 35 percent of Canadians approved by June 1966, down from a high of 54 percent in 1962.[116] The students and young academics who crowded Canadian campuses didn't share the wartime and postwar experiences that had shaped Martin's worldview, and they questioned his unwavering support for NORAD and NATO. Skeptics Lloyd Axworthy and John Warnock dismissed NORAD as "useless" and worried that alliance membership linked Canada to US militarism in Asia.[117]

Doubts about Canada's role and relevance in NATO and NORAD piled higher through the turbulent spring of 1967. Opposition critics, who had backed government alliance policy during the 1940s and 1950s, now aired their misgivings. Attuned to the currents of youthful protest, the NDP turned from both alliances and pressed Ottawa to boost its peace-keeping efforts. "We should withdraw our brigade and air divisions from Europe," argued defence critic Andrew Brewin, and concentrate on a "unified, slightly armed, highly mobile force available for peace keeping and other intervention roles."[118] Recently deposed Progressive Conservative leader John Diefenbaker cited the disappearing Soviet bombing threat (replaced with missiles) and questioned the value of continued NORAD membership.[119] When Martin appeared before the Senate Committee on Foreign Affairs in March, Tory senator Grattan O'Leary grilled him on his refusal to consider withdrawing from NATO, though US congressional leaders were exploring the notion.[120] Even the Canadian Federation of University Liberals raised doubts that spring about the government's alliance attachments. "It is time," insisted the London Free Press, "for a clear statement of Canadian defence policy and intentions."[121]

Martin resisted these pressures for as long as he could. But Pearson, who harboured doubts about both NATO and NORAD, pressed him to review Canadian policy after the United States and Britain slashed their European commitments in April 1967. Pearson reprimanded him for the "inflexibility of our position."[122] The language rankled. Martin resented the implication that he was not keeping up with the times, and he refused to be hurried.[123] By May, however, misgivings over NATO and NORAD were raised more often than ever among senior Liberals. Ministers Jean Marchand and Pierre Trudeau, and parliamentary secretaries Gérard Pelletier and Donald Macdonald, had never fully supported Pearson's decision to accept nuclear weapons in 1963, and they found a champion for their views in Walter Gordon, president of the Privy Council.

Canada's alliances topped the cabinet agenda at the end of May. After a decade in force, NORAD was up for renewal. Martin and Hellyer favoured the pact for sound political and practical reasons. It was cheap and efficient at managing bilateral defence relations, and letting it lapse might cause Washington to scrap the lucrative defence production agreements of 1959 and 1963. Although there was little scope for amending what was a basic agreement, Martin appeased treaty opponents by shortening its term and adding a termination clause. At the very least, he and Hellyer pleaded, the government ought to tell Washington whether it intended to help with North American defence.[124]

Anxious to test Gordon's cabinet strength on the eve of the June NATO ministerial meeting, Martin also asked colleagues to approve force levels for Canada's NATO contribution over the next five years. His proposed reductions were small. The existing brigade group would remain unaltered in West Germany, though the number of RCAF squadrons stationed in Europe would drop from six to four. Even this minor change, he warned, was subject to consultation and negotiation with Canada's allies.[125]

The cabinet discussions were deeply disturbing, and Martin later admitted that he had underestimated the strength of his opponents.[126] Opposition to basing Canadian forces in Europe was so strong, especially from Gordon and among Quebec ministers, that Martin withdrew the question rather than face certain defeat. NORAD fared only marginally better. Martin was told to assure US negotiators that Canada would cooperate in the defence of North America though not necessarily in NORAD. This bought Martin time but nothing else.[127]

During the debate, he had challenged Gordon to visit NATO, but Gordon's trip to the Luxembourg meetings did little to reduce his skepticism.[128] En route home, Gordon asked Basil Robinson, recently promoted to associate under-secretary, to meet with him, Trudeau, and Marchand to review NATO and NORAD. The patient and soft-spoken Robinson, who had earlier served as Diefenbaker's diplomatic advisor, was accustomed to dealing with difficult politicians, and he soon found common ground between Gordon and Martin. As Robinson reported, Gordon was not suggesting that Canada withdraw from NATO: he simply thought that Ottawa should be able to cut its contribution to Europe faster than anticipated.[129] Reduced to a question of timing, the consultations gradually relieved Gordon's concerns, and by late July, "Gordon and company" were ready to accept "the idea of an evolutionary approach to the contribution of forces in Europe." Moreover, Cadieux briefed Martin, Gordon "would not oppose a renewal of NORAD provided there was a reservation about ABMs [anti-ballistic missiles] and a suitable termination clause."[130]

Progress slipped a little in August. The outspoken Progressive Conservative Party president, Dalton Camp, drew national headlines with a proposal to abandon NATO, NORAD, and UN peacekeeping as the pillars of Canadian foreign policy. He urged shifting Canada's energy and dollars into disarmament, non-proliferation, and foreign aid.[131] Camp's suggestion won strong backing in progressive circles. The *Toronto Star,* which echoed Gordon's views, called his speech "brilliant." The *Montreal Star* labelled it "stirring and imaginative."[132] Pearson himself was impressed, describing it as "an extremely interesting and thoughtful speech."[133]

Martin responded boldly to his critics. Though increasingly besieged, he was still an articulate and powerful minister, and at the end of August, he flew to Toronto to speak to the Canadian National Exhibition's (CNE) annual International Day luncheon. He spoke strongly in defence of NATO, NORAD, and UN peacekeeping, dismissing calls to shift funds to foreign aid as "the height of irresponsibility."[134] His speech anticipated cabinet's coming discussion on Canada's two alliances, daring his colleagues to repudiate him.

Martin and Hellyer were back before cabinet in September, with four long papers that defended their NATO and NORAD policies. These placed the alliances in their proper context as part of Canada's postwar effort to erect a collective security system in the face of the overwhelming Soviet threat. Alliance membership ensured Canada's defence, reinforced its sovereignty, and gave Ottawa influence in Washington and Europe, where the country's main interests resided. Severing those ties, Martin cautioned, would compromise the effectiveness of Canadian foreign policy.[135]

There was little debate. Martin argued that Canada's small contribution to Europe "carried with it very considerable influence" and warned that withdrawal from the alliance might well cause it to disintegrate.[136] With a nod of support from Finance Minister Mitchell Sharp, he underlined how low Canadian defence expenditures actually were. Gordon alone stood in his way, insisting that the transformed world order demanded changes in Canadian policy. Canada's present contribution, Pearson weighed in, was "the minimum price for club membership." That ended discussion, and ministers moved on to deal with NORAD, authorizing talks to renew the agreement. Martin had won on NATO and NORAD, though his victory was uncertain. Questions about Canada's role in the two US alliances persisted, provoking ripples of concern and public debate for the rest of the year. "Answers, please, on NATO," the *Toronto Telegram* demanded again in December 1967.[137]

ONCE GRASPED AS a sure pathway to the Prime Minister's Office, foreign policy weighed heavily on Martin's hopes by late 1967. The press responded to his CNE speech with undisguised hostility. It only showed, wrote the *Ottawa Journal*, "how much the blurred edges of our international policies need to be sharpened."[138] The *Vancouver Province* summed up Canadian diplomacy as "dull, unimaginative, and boring."[139] The press heaped scorn on Martin's tortuous language. Editorialists for the *Toronto Globe and Mail* mocked him as "the great malapropist."[140] They derided his optimism and equated him with the era's anonymous monotone TV announcer: "Trouble is temporary and in hand, so do not adjust your sets."[141] Vietnam and France had shattered his credibility. The *Toronto Star* derided his references to good relations with France as "a joke."[142] In August and October, critical Progressive Conservative and NDP Opposition MPs demanded a House committee to review Canadian foreign policy.

Unknown to them, a review was in the works. Smarting from the domestic criticism, Pearson had already discussed the idea with Martin and Cadieux in August. He was influenced by his son Geoffrey, a diplomat and frequent participant in the series of seminars on Canada's foreign policy that Toronto academics in the left-wing University League for Social Reform offered in 1966–67.[143] Cadieux was furious. Though Martin soothed his deputy, convincing him that the review was just "propaganda or counter-propaganda," he shared his distress.[144] He later accused Geoffrey of "poisoning" his father against him and denounced his leading Toronto critic, political scientist James Eayrs, as "a damn fool, a crazy man."[145] Martin dropped his objections when the three men settled on Norman Robertson for the task.

Martin, at least, was beginning to feel that he was out of ideas. He had pushed for peace in Vietnam and the recognition of China as far as he could without irresponsibly breaking with Washington. The political and practical case for NATO and NORAD membership remained compelling. And peacekeeping, however frustrating, was so obviously better than the alternatives. He had bent over backward for Quebec and France. He almost despaired when his former UN advisor John Holmes sent him yet another article on Canada's diminishing international stature. "You set forth the problems, pointed out the dangers, and posed the questions with all your customary lucidity," he replied, "but you did not give a hard-pressed External Affairs Minister much comfort on how we can deal with the current crop of problems. How are we to get beyond 'traditional responses,' which you seem to think may no longer prevail, unless we get some constructive suggestions from wise counsellors like yourself?"[146] Holmes, like Martin, had no answers.

DEFEAT AND THE SENATE, 1968–74

By the fall of 1967, Pearson's government was in trouble. The radiant centennial summer was fading quickly, replaced by headaches over inflation and deficits, and renewed conflict with Quebec over constitutional renewal. In the House of Commons, a sudden vigour rejuvenated the Opposition benches. The Progressive Conservative Party had elected a new leader in September, former Nova Scotia premier Robert Stanfield. He was smart, disciplined, and appealingly low-key. The endless speculation about Pearson's successor and the constant subterranean jostling for advantage among Liberal hopefuls, principally Foreign Minister Paul Martin, Finance Minister Mitchell Sharp, and Defence Minister Paul Hellyer, gnawed at party morale. "There is an air of defeatism in the cabinet, in the caucus, and in the Liberal Party," Walter Gordon complained in October, pointing his finger at the prime minister.[1] The situation had become "impossible," Martin confided to Cadieux.[2]

When cabinet assembled on the afternoon of 14 December, Pearson, wilting under the pressure to step aside, announced his retirement. He would remain, he added, until a successor could be elected at a Liberal Party leadership convention in April 1968. Ministers greeted the news with "stunned amazement."[3] Later that afternoon, Pearson telephoned Martin, who was at a NATO meeting in Belgium, to convey the news. Hurrying to dinner when he took the call, Martin was "dumbfounded" by the timing. He suspected that Pearson had delayed his announcement until he himself was out of the country, in hopes of harming his leadership chances.[4] Like so many of their recent exchanges, it left him hurt and upset.

Martin was now sixty-four, and this was his last chance at the top job. He flew back to Ottawa – reporters joked that he didn't bother waiting for his plane – to join the race. "I felt no hesitation," he wrote in his memoirs of his plunge into the contest.[5] Yet the decision was not that simple. Admittedly, he seemed the clear favourite. He had kept his eye on the prize since joining cabinet in April 1963, and his standing, despite Vietnam, de Gaulle, and the Middle East crisis, remained formidable. Many Ottawa insiders thought him unbeatable. Their view was confirmed by a December poll that put him at the top of the heap, with the support of 29 percent of decided Liberals. Sharp was well behind at 13 percent, followed by Hellyer at 11 percent.[6] Indeed, Martin appeared so favoured that some members of the party's progressive wing, including Pearson, Gordon, Trudeau, and Marchand, considered giving him the job for a year or so, while a younger candidate prepared himself for the role. Both sides viewed this scheme dubiously. No one believed that Martin would relinquish the post once he got it, and he was not interested in those terms anyway. Though Pearson raised the idea with him during the fall, it was quickly abandoned.[7]

Martin was also among the best-organized candidates. He had criss-crossed the country for two decades, doing small favours and pocketing IOUs, adding Liberal names to his roster of friends and supporters. He had already made two informal political tours through Western Canada in early 1967, and his campaign literature, a biography by the sympathetic *Windsor Star* reporter Pat Whelan and a collection of foreign policy speeches, *Paul Martin Speaks for Canada,* had been in the works all summer. By October, a small organizing committee was in place. It included Paul Martin Jr., Bruce Laird, son of Martin's law partner Senator Keith Laird, and David McWilliam, a thirty-four-year-old lawyer and Rhodes scholar who was surveying Martin's strength in Western Canada.[8]

The committee grew through November and December. Keith Laird tapped into pools of funding, and Duncan Edmonds assumed his duties as campaign chair. Claude Frenette and J.G. Fredette, who had joined Martin's External Affairs office in November for $18,000 a year, a princely sum in 1967, began quietly to organize Quebec. Defeated Toronto MP David Hahn started on Ontario. He was helped by Mark MacGuigan, a young Toronto law professor whom Martin had recently helped recruit as dean of law for University of Windsor president Francis Leddy. Jack Austin, a rising Vancouver lawyer, was responsible for British Columbia.[9] Early decisions on tactics and timing were hammered out during a day-long session at Toronto's Royal York Hotel in December. A Martin campaign would focus on the need for "strong, ordered, and sustained political leadership" in the face of a federal system that was "under challenge."[10] As they waited for Pearson to go, Martin's workers set up their offices in a drab complex near the corner of Spark and Elgin Streets, a block from Parliament Hill.

Despite the momentum gathering behind him, Martin hesitated. "I had grave doubts," he admitted to an interviewer a few years later.[11] His age was a real liability, and he knew it. In 1966, MacGuigan had warned him of "a powerful sense of frustration and alienation among the under-40 members," who were eager for change.[12] Hugh Faulkner, a young MP for Peterborough drawn by Martin's political skills and experience, gave a bleak assessment of his chances with the caucus:

> At a point in time when everyone looks to younger men to provide [the] dynamism, innovation, and discipline which the political process seems to need, Mr. Martin's age is a serious disadvantage. It's made more so by his whole approach which appears to many MP's to be a by-product of age and too long in the job ... Most MP's I have talked to are not talking about Mr. Martin as a successor to the PM.[13]

Pearson himself had advised Martin not to run, telling him in October that it was time for a younger man and that he would not win. The caution seemed to have registered, and Pearson had come away from their talk thinking that "Martin may decide not to run!"[14] Martin's doubts persisted into November, when he surprised Cadieux by asking what he would do if he did not become leader.[15] "Paul Martin," Pearson and Gordon agreed a week after Pearson's resignation, "can't make up his mind."[16]

Martin and Nell spent the holidays with Maurice Strong in Montego Bay. Strong and Paul Jr. urged Martin to run. "This kind of influence together with the polls," he recalled, "made me do it."[17] He returned to Ottawa on 7 January, rested, tanned, and ready to run.

Over the next few weeks, a parade of Liberal hopefuls joined the fray. Eric Kierans, a brilliant but quixotic member of Quebec's legislative assembly declared first, on 9 January. Young John Turner, the ambitious minister of consumer affairs from Vancouver, and Hellyer, were next. They were followed on 12 January by Allan MacEachen, who had carved out a place for himself on the party's left wing. A week later, on 19 January, the homespun agriculture minister from the Ottawa Valley, Joe Greene, entered the race. Finance Minister Mitchell Sharp from Toronto declared his candidacy at the same time and was widely acknowledged as a front-runner.

The other front-runner, Paul Martin, also joined the contest on 19 January. Buoyed by a strong performance at the Nova Scotia Liberal convention in Halifax the weekend before, he oozed confidence. "Things are going smoothly," he grinned at reporters, chomping his cigar. "That's the way I like to start a campaign, with things going smoothly."[18] Armed with a slick set of briefing notes and switching easily between English and French, he touched all the right bases at his opening press conference. His French and English Canadian heritage, his exposure to the "third force" of ethnic voters, and his long public service left him uniquely equipped to manage Canada's foremost challenge, "the vital and urgent problem of national unity."[19] He promised to revitalize Liberal Party fortunes in Western Canada and to embrace Canada's future as a Pacific nation.[20] He brushed aside questions regarding his age. Canadians, he insisted, "want modern men, yes, and liberal-minded men, but what they want most is experience."[21]

But things did not go smoothly during the next few weeks. Press reaction to Martin's candidacy zeroed in on his age and was harsh and unsympathetic. The most influential voice of Ontario Liberals, the *Toronto Star*, tagged him in an early editorial as a "redoubtable old pro" who "hasn't kept up with the times."[22] Reporters were quick to notice that the streak of grey hair that normally swept back from the candidate's forehead had been dyed black. The press and the Opposition had a field day as Martin fought, stony-faced, to retain his dignity. "He's not the white-haired boy anymore," Stanley Knowles snickered from the Opposition benches in the House of Commons. "Does he or doesn't he?" chortled NDP leader Tommy Douglas in a parody of a popular ad for Miss Clairol hair-colouring.[23] That weekend, Martin's performance at the Manitoba Liberal convention in

Winnipeg's old Marlborough Hotel was flat. "Paul Martin, by his speech," the young Liberal Tom Axworthy reported to Gordon, "did [him]self a lot of harm."[24]

A bigger problem loomed in Quebec. Martin's hopes depended on a good showing there, where his French Canadian heritage made him a favourite. MPs and leading Liberals from the province, however, refused to support any candidate until it was clear that neither Jean Marchand nor Pierre Trudeau would run. Marchand was out, but what about Trudeau? Tough and intelligent, with the cool good looks of a TV star, the justice minister had leapt to national prominence in early December with a bill to modernize Canada's Criminal Code, removing the state from "the bedrooms of the nation." Martin judged him too cold and cerebral to succeed as a politician, but he was dismayed by the sudden prospect of his candidacy.[25] He besieged his parliamentary secretary, Gérard Pelletier, who was a Trudeau confidant, with phone calls and teas, asking about his friend's intentions. Less than a week into the campaign, he sent Paul Jr. to call on Pelletier. His father was anxious to work with the province's "leading wing," the younger man explained, but they were all waiting for Trudeau. "So," he sighed, "who can we work with?"[26]

Trudeau watched from the sidelines, detached and bemused, as his backers marshalled support for him. On 25 January, Marc Lalonde, the Montreal lawyer who worked as an advisor in the Prime Minister's Office (PMO), hosted an informal "committee for Trudeau's candidacy." By the time Quebec federal Liberals gathered in Montreal at the end of the week, Lalonde and Marchand had stacked the deck in Trudeau's favour. They shut down candidates' hospitality suites during conference workshops and made sure that Trudeau was the only speaker during the key session on constitutional issues.[27] Reporter Tom Hazlitt watched as Martin worked the empty lobby of the conference hotel, "disappointed and often alone."[28]

By early February, Trudeau haunted Martin. "The proof," Pelletier recorded in his diary, "he called me Pierre – four times in a row."[29] Behind Lalonde and Trudeau, Martin sensed Pearson's hostile presence, and he raged at the unfairness of it all.[30] Pearson's subtle hand was certainly evident at the federal-provincial Constitutional Conference, which opened in Ottawa on 5 February. Before banks of TV cameras, Pearson sat Trudeau at his right hand, elevating him to the position of chief federal spokesman. Trudeau shone, spurning demands from Quebec premier Daniel Johnson for "special status" and additional powers. The clash between the two Québécois leaders, so different in type and temperament, gripped English Canada, which cheered its federalist saviour.[31]

Martin, too, had something to say to the premiers. In early January, meddlesome French president Charles de Gaulle had tried again to advance Quebec's claim to its own international persona. Paris convinced its former colony of Gabon to invite Quebec, but not Ottawa, to a conference of francophone education ministers. The crisis generated a reprise of the earlier arguments between an inflexible Cadieux and a compromising Martin, and it did their relations no good. When it was clear that Ottawa would not be invited, External Affairs severed relations with Gabon and set to work on a white paper on federal responsibility for international education.[32] As Martin considered when and how to table the paper, Pearson pushed him aside and summarily ordered that it be distributed. Cadieux, disdaining the political skirmishes raging about him, felt so badly about Pearson's shoddy treatment of Martin that he offered to make it up to him by arranging a press conference later that day.[33] The gesture was kindly meant, but neither Martin nor the other candidates could do much to slow Trudeau's momentum. His star firmly in the ascendant, Trudeau announced his candidacy on 16 February.

Martin's campaign stumbled again three days later. With most candidates and their backbench supporters campaigning across the country, Acting Prime Minister Sharp unwisely pressed ahead with a routine vote on a tax bill before an empty House of Commons. The division bells rang for seventy minutes as Opposition members poured into the chamber to vote. When it was over, the government had been defeated on a confidence measure, by eighty-four to eighty-two. Pearson scurried back from his Jamaica holiday, "spitting tacks."[34] Martin had been travelling with two Quebec MPs at the time of the vote, and Pearson castigated him for his absence when he met him at the airport. Martin, whose "distress" at the government's defeat betrayed his fears, defended his right to campaign.[35] "It was the first and only time," he later recorded, "that we ever really lost our cool with one another."[36] The two men, who began to snipe openly at each other, stopped speaking, their relations marred by an "obvious coldness."[37]

Though Pearson rescued his government, the fiasco shaped the leadership race. It crippled Sharp's bid and encouraged Robert Winters, who had earlier ruled out running, to jump back into the contest as the mature voice of fiscal restraint and government efficiency. The crisis hurt Martin. His critics noted that his vote and those of the two Quebec MPs who were travelling with him would have saved the government. Reporters were openly skeptical of his evasive claim to have a Progressive Conservative "pair,"[38] whom he refused to name lest he embarrass him for having voted.[39] Tory wit Dalton Camp took careful aim. Martin, he delighted Conservative crowds, was so shocked by the budget's defeat that his hair turned white again.[40]

The contest was far from over, however. An early poll, taken just before Trudeau entered the race, put Martin in first place, with 26 percent of respondents. Trudeau came second with 12 percent, and the other candidates each drew between 4 and 6 percent.[41] Martin pressed on. Mostly, he stuck to his central theme: "experience not experiment."[42] Along the way, he raised a few new ideas. He "transfixed" one audience with a plan to hold cabinet meetings outside Ottawa.[43] He wanted to revisit and rationalize the welfare state that he had helped build during the 1950s. He urged tax relief to encourage investment and regional development, the twin keys to national unity.[44] He also promised to visit Hanoi in search of peace, an empty gesture that did him little good. Most importantly, though he ruled out "special status" for Quebec, he signalled his willingness to compromise. He insisted that Canada's prime minister must be "a man who has not clouded relations with any prominent government or provincial premier," drawing a sharp contrast with Trudeau and his hard-line federalism.[45]

Making progress was difficult. In Victoria and Vancouver, Martin was dogged by a posse of anti-war protesters, who waved "Paul the Pentagon Puppet" banners and chanted "Hellyer, Martin, LBJ, how many kids did you kill today?"[46] He did well at the Ontario Liberal convention in Toronto, buttonholing three hundred delegates in his hotel suite, but Trudeau did better, his frenzied admirers crowding the lobbies of the Royal York Hotel.[47]

Urban Ontario was largely beyond Martin's reach, and Hellyer was soon edging him out in the western part of the province. Martin even did poorly in the new riding of Essex, carved from the rural polls in his old riding, where he won just half of the available delegates.[48] But the veteran minister held his own across the Prairies and in vote-rich Quebec. For a while, he led in rural Saskatchewan and Alberta, and could marshal supporters across Manitoba. When Turner's backers arrived with 150 Aboriginal Liberals to elect delegates in Selkirk, Martin's people responded with 300 Ukrainians.[49] In Quebec, his conciliatory approach to federalism attracted support from Jean Lesage and his provincial Liberals.[50] Martin raced across the province at a "supersonic pace" in February and returned in early March for a "joyful" blitz through the Eastern Townships, "campaigning 12 hours at a stretch without rest or food."[51]

Reporters applauded his energy. "Paul Martin scrambles," marvelled Allan Fotheringham, "Oh, how he scrambles."[52] But they recoiled at his old-fashioned style and personalized politics, which emphasized his ties to a different age. "Dad, why talk about Laurier?" Paul Jr. pleaded with him. "People don't know who he is."[53] The media ridiculed "The Man with the Mechanical Arm," who grabbed "every hand in sight ... fixing every Liberal in the eye and inquiring solicitously about family and friends back home."[54] They were appalled by his pitch, which often opened by asking delegates who were supporting other candidates, "Why are you working against me?"[55] It struck an uncomfortable note of desperate betrayal.

Television hated Martin. His voice, which had once resonated strongly in union meeting halls, church basements, and radio broadcasts, came across as thin and reedy on TV. "In close shots," observed one reviewer cruelly, "his glasses are distracting and his eyes unmistakeably look two different ways. And the face, alas, looks pudgy, rather than lined with decades of responsibility."[56] His dark, old-fashioned suits made him look "like one of those black-clad baggy doctors out of the old westerns."[57]

By mid-March, it was clear that Martin's support was slipping, as delegates steadily moved to Trudeau, Hellyer, and Winters. Many of the Liberal delegates whom pollster Peter Regenstreif surveyed admired and liked him personally, "but," as one explained, "to be blunt, I wish he were 10 years younger."[58] He was still running second in late March, just behind Trudeau, but he drew his support from older, rural delegates. His age and style alienated younger Liberals, whom he would need to attract if he hoped to increase his support. Those delegates, Regenstreif's polls suggested, would not come to Martin.[59] Cadieux, who overheard Martin campaigning by phone, captured the impact of the changing generations in a transcript of a hopeless, one-sided conversation. "Don't do that, Laura," Martin pleaded with a youthful delegate, whose support was going to a younger man. "He was counting on her support. He knew her father well. Had she discussed it with him? No? Well, Mr. Martin was going to call him."[60]

As Hugh Faulkner had predicted, Martin won few supporters among Liberal MPs. The skeptical response of his independent-minded colleague in Essex South, Eugene Whelan, was typical. Whelan backed Trudeau, who represented a winning combination of youth and charisma. He doubted Martin's claims of caucus support. "Paul," the blunt-spoken farmer retorted when asked for his help, "you don't have any thirty-two [MPs]. You got five." The sad exchange continued: "Then he kind of begged me. He reminded me that we were both from Windsor and of how it would look if his own neighbours didn't support him. He cried at the end. It was a hard meeting."[61] A straw poll of Liberal members released in late March put Martin in fourth place with just eleven supporters in the House of Commons. Trudeau had thirty-eight, Hellyer fifteen, and Winters thirteen.[62] The only cabinet member in Martin's corner was Forestry Minister Maurice Sauvé. Brilliant but impatient and transparently self-serving, Sauvé brought no one with him.

With the race tightening, Martin turned to Maurice Strong for help. The bureaucrat refused to join the campaign, though he continued to fundraise for Martin. Money, splashed out so freely in December and January on staff and offices, on films and publicity, was drying up. Campaign manager Duncan Edmonds called Pelletier in March to negotiate spending limits. Trudeau supporter Jean-Pierre Goyer was ecstatic. "Martin has already spent all the money he had – and it was a lot," he crowed. "Now's he broke and wants everybody to stop spending."[63]

As Martin's support softened, a wave of editorials came out against him in late March. The *Montreal Star,* whose legendary editor Walter O'Hearn had once cheered him on, was among the first. "The tide runs out on Paul Martin," it declared on 19 March. "Paul Martin, both in terms of age and outlook, is too old for our liking."[64] The *Ottawa Citizen* followed at the end of the month. Martin was simply "the worst choice ... Canadians want – and have a right to demand – greater clarity and honesty in public policy. They will not get it from Paul Martin."[65] The *Toronto Star* was kinder. It acknowledged Martin's competence, wisdom, and experience. "If Canada needed a 'safe' compromising leader of the old-fashioned kind," it suggested,

"Mr. Martin could hardly be denied."[66] But this kind of leadership, in the *Star*'s view, was precisely what Canada no longer needed. It endorsed Trudeau.

The final week of the campaign, Edmonds later complained to Martin, was a "nightmare."[67] The trouble had begun on the previous Thursday, when Martin called for a doctor while campaigning in Sudbury. Inaccurate reports of the aging minister's poor health generated national headlines as Liberals were boarding planes and trains and cars for Ottawa. "Can't a fellow catch a cold without all this publicity?" Martin protested.[68] On Tuesday and Wednesday, he retreated to his Ottawa apartment, desperately chasing delegates by phone. "He sat there in an armchair," departmental assistant Allan McGill observed unkindly, "hair tousled, dressing gown gaping over his hairy belly with two telephones, a black one and a white one, constantly on the go ... He told me to go away."[69]

Martin had no time for Edmonds either. The novice political campaigner was left alone on Wednesday, 3 April, to deal with the backlash from an anti-Trudeau smear campaign run by the Canadian Intelligence Service (CIS). The CIS was a rabid anti-communist group, whose March newsletter accusing Trudeau of communist sympathies had been sent to Liberals across Canada. The *Toronto Star* had linked Martin with the newsletter by matching idiosyncrasies in his delegate mailing list with identical quirks in addresses used by the CIS. Edmonds denied the connection. Incredibly, however, he went on to endorse the charges – "this material is a matter of public record and should be available to our delegates" – and attacked Trudeau's office for alerting the press to the story. Neither Trudeau nor Lalonde was amused, and Edmonds wasted his day in abject apologies.[70]

Wednesday brought more bad news. Unable to gain any traction with Liberals following his budget cockup, Sharp withdrew from the race and threw his support to Trudeau. His decision shocked Martin. A series of informal media polls conducted earlier that week had consistently put him in second place, and he counted on attracting the first drop-outs to build momentum and regain his lead.[71] As Trudeau surged ahead, Martin hustled to Hellyer and Winters, anxious to build a coalition against him. But each of them was confident of bagging second place and neither was ready to commit himself before the first ballot.[72] Though shaken, Martin emerged from his apartment on Wednesday evening, "fresh and smiling, radiating confidence."[73] En route to host a convention reception at the Chateau Laurier, he delighted reporters by pausing in the lobby to fix Jean Chrétien, one of Sharp's men, with a "brief and frigid glare."[74]

There were policy workshops on Thursday and a women's lunch hosted by Nell at the Chateau Laurier on Friday. Martin and his claque of supporters – the young women in demure knee-length magenta dresses and pillbox hats, the men in sports coats – attended both, their spirits boosted by a noisy six-piece Dixieland band. Martin smiled calmly and shook hands, and gamely joined in policy debates in half-empty halls, where few bothered to stay and listen. His workers, pencil and paper in hand, sketched out winning scenarios for the press: 240 votes from Ontario plus 150 from Quebec and a handful from elsewhere would keep him in second; when Hellyer and Winters collapsed, they argued, Martin would move past Trudeau. The press was doubtful. "Fading by the moment," judged *Toronto Star* reporter Lotta Dempsey.[75] By Friday afternoon, Brian Stewart, a *Montreal Gazette* journalist who was covering the Martin camp, detected a "subtle sense of panic."[76]

The speeches began on Friday evening. With little to lose, Agriculture Minister Joe Greene was at his relaxed best. He delivered an old-fashioned "barn-burner" that roused the delegates. Hellyer's effort, boring and flat, killed his momentum and cost him his chance at victory. When Trudeau spoke on national unity and his vision for a just society, the crowd hushed to catch his every word, and he electrified his youthful audience.

Martin's speech went badly. He was the first of the major candidates to speak, and he was forced to begin as the crowds were still entering the new Civic Centre at Lansdowne Park. His placard-waving supporters and the brass band that accompanied him to the stage for an opening pep rally left the Liberal crowd cold. The acoustics in the cavernous hockey arena were terrible, and the embarrassing murmur of whispered conversation drowned out his opening comments. His speech repeated familiar campaign themes, prompting the *Toronto Star* to dismiss it as "tired generalities and evasions."[77] Even his friend, Robert Hull of the *Windsor Star,* rated it as "pedestrian ... out of date and touch."[78] It won only mild and polite applause, before the speaker retreated. "Martin's time is over," tolled the syndicated columnist Peter Newman. "He is the victim of its passage and his only choice now is how much grace he can muster for his final exit."[79]

At eleven on Saturday morning, the Civic Centre opened its doors, and delegates and hangers-on, anxious to snag the best seats, rushed into the arena. By noon, the convention site was clogged with television cameras and boom mikes, and thick with a multi-coloured sea of waving placards. The candidates were packed into front-row boxes at the northern and eastern ends of the rink. Martin sat with his family nearby: Nell and Mary Anne, Paul Jr. and his wife, Sheila, and his sisters, Anita, Claire, and his favourite, Lucille. The youngest Martin, grandson Paul, had sent a telegram: "Good luck Grandpa. I still like you best."[80]

At 1:45 p.m., a band struck up "Another Op'nin', Another Show," and delegates headed off to vote. "Well, I cast a good vote," Martin smiled on his way back to his seat.[81] Ninety minutes later, Liberal Party president John Nichol announced the first ballot results:

Trudeau 752
Hellyer 330
Winters 293
Martin 277
Turner 277
MacEachen 165
Greene 169
Kierans 103

There was an audible gasp at Martin's poor fourth-place showing. He sat calmly, eating his roast beef sandwich. He closed his eyes for a moment and bowed his head. Behind him, the magenta signs sagged. He put his arm around Nell, whispering into her ear. Mary Anne hugged him and gave him a kiss, while his supporters burst into "For He's a Jolly Good Fellow." Winters and Hellyer rushed over to seek his support, but he refused. He had decided the night before that he would drop out and release his supporters if he could not win. "He's still the number two man in the country," an aide explained. "It would be too demoralizing for the other candidates if he was to throw his support to one."[82] While Martin signed a letter withdrawing his name, Maurice Sauvé scuttled to Trudeau as the jeering crowd behind him chanted, "Too late, too late, too late."[83]

Tempted as he sometimes was by self-pity, Martin began drafting a statement that opened, "I am a victim of the generation gap." He stifled the urge, however, and turned to the press. "I have learned how important it is to be generous in victory and serene in defeat. This is my mood and composure now," he said.[84] He thanked his workers, released his voters, and pledged his loyalty to the next Liberal leader. From the stage, Nichol announced his withdrawal from the race.

During the next three ballots, Martin sat quietly in his box, three seats from the aisle, between Nell and Paul Jr., sipping a glass of whiskey hidden in a napkin and puffing on a long cigar. When the action paused on the steamy and overcrowded convention floor, Liberal stalwarts made their way to him with their thanks and congratulations for a lifetime of effort.

At the end of the day, as Pearson turned over the Liberal Party to Pierre Trudeau, he generously acknowledged his own debt to Martin. He singled out Martin alone for praise, reminding his audience that he had been "fighting the battles of Liberalism before many of the delegates who are here today were born."[85] The gesture helped to restore relations between the two men.

Other tributes would follow from friends, rivals, and strangers. The most elegant came from author Hugh MacLennan, whose iconic novel of French-English conflict, *Two Solitudes*, reflected the bicultural tensions that Martin had wrestled with for decades: "Along with millions of others who followed the Convention on television, I was moved by the dignity and quietness you so naturally displayed. You set us all an example of how a wise and great public servant can conduct himself under extreme pressure. I think we all know that in these terribly difficult years your loyalty has never wavered."[86]

FRIENDS AND COLLEAGUES worried that the loss would kill him. "It was a hard blow," concluded Marcel Cadieux, with uncharacteristic sympathy.[87] They were wrong. The day after his defeat, Paul and Nell attended Sunday Mass at Notre Dame Cathedral, later joining John Turner, another defeated candidate, and his wife, Geills, for a quiet dinner. The next day, Martin began to rebuild his political life. He told Cadieux on Monday that he would not run again and would accept only the External Affairs portfolio. Anything else would be a "humiliation."[88] At lunch, Pearson suggested the post of government leader in the Senate, but Martin demurred.[89] Next day, Prime Minister Trudeau offered him Justice, but that was impossible. Martin was not running again, and as a Catholic, he wanted no part of the government's plans to liberalize laws that banned abortion and homosexuality.[90] The matter rested for a day or two, until Trudeau offered Martin a cabinet post as government leader in the Senate. Nell told him to do whatever he wanted, but Paul Jr. and Mary Anne were doubtful. Close friends Paul Nathanson and Maurice Strong urged him to stay, to make a difference, even at the fringes of power.[91] Martin himself asked the ailing incumbent, John Connolly, to step aside. On 20 April 1968, he was sworn in to Trudeau's first cabinet. Three days later, an election was called.

As Trudeau and his ministers canvassed voters gone wild with Trudeaumania, Martin stayed home, tending routine government business in Ottawa and offering campaign tips. He briefly swung by Windsor, teaching his wooden successor, Mark MacGuigan, the fine art of mainstreeting and healing the local wounds left by Eugene Whelan's refusal to back him for party leader. "I don't know of any divisions in the Liberal Party in Essex County," he loyally assured the faithful at Whelan's nominating rally.[92] After the Liberals won the election on 25 June, Martin grew his sideburns fashionably long and set his sights on making the Senate younger and hipper, more active and relevant.

His new role profoundly altered the rhythm of his life. The leadership defeat freed his family from politics and the constraints of official life. This was good for Nell, who had grown to dislike Ottawa and yearned for her native Windsor. She greeted the news of Martin's retirement from elective office with quips that she had "poured her last cup of tea and gone to her last campaign supper!"[93] Inevitably, there were questions about her new life, and looking ahead to another stint in Ottawa, she wondered wistfully, "Would we ever be able to get our own home?"[94] But this mattered less in the early 1970s, as she settled into their home in Windsor, leaving Martin to shuttle back and forth to Ottawa alone. She did well enough without him. "Now dear, you go, for Pete's sake," she cheerfully urged him onto another government mission. "You will enjoy it and I can go home and open the cottage."[95] She did well with him, too. "It was fun," she told friends of a get-together with Martin's closest External Affairs colleagues and their wives, old friends from the 1940s. "I got kind of high, all the women did, so happy to be together and relax and say whatever we liked in complete confidence."[96]

Defeat offered a liberating change for Martin's daughter, Mary Anne, as well. At the age of twenty-three, she was under-employed and restless. Poor health had slowed her down, and she had dragged out her degree until 1967, when she briefly worked with a Toronto film company. Mostly, through 1967 and 1968, she was reluctantly drafted to substitute for Nell as Martin's official hostess or to campaign for him. When Nell suggested that Mary Anne join the hordes of postwar Western youth who were discovering the world, she seized her chance.[97] By Christmas 1968, she had crossed Europe and landed in India, where she fell in love with a young American Peace Corps volunteer, Michael Bellamy. They were engaged by April.

Paul and Nell were relieved. Bellamy had two good degrees, hailed from a prominent Catholic family in Cleveland, and enjoyed a faint connection to Martin's old college, St. Mike's, through a brother who had studied there. Martin was less happy when Mary Anne postponed the wedding, refusing to seek the American security clearance that Bellamy's status as a US government employee required of her. They would wait until his contract ended, she told a local wire-service stringer, who sent the story back to Canada, where a blushing Martin scrambled to assure his friend, former US secretary of state Dean Rusk, that no anti-American sentiment was intended.[98] It was probably just as well that by the time Bellamy wrote to invite his prospective in-laws to his December wedding in India, the short notice precluded their attendance.[99] Mary Anne and Michael were wed in the small Carmelite Chapel in Chandigarh on 13 December 1969. Within a year, they were in Madison, Wisconsin, where Michael began a doctorate in English literature, and Mary Anne waitressed to pay the bills. "I finally had my own life," she later recalled with defiant satisfaction, "and I could find my own identity."[100]

Mary Anne and Michael embraced the counter-culture ethos that flourished on North American campuses in the early 1970s. As Martin scornfully put it, the anti-war movement fused with Black Power, feminism, and a host of other causes in a "revolt against everything."[101] The free-spirited Nell responded easily and charitably. "Taking it all and all," she said enthusiastically, "they are a great couple, wonderful company, losing some of their anti-establishment (well!!!! A bit anyhow.)."[102] Martin's relations with Michael Bellamy were more difficult. He itched to sympathize, but the American's radical politics epitomized the youthful revolution that had swept Trudeau to office, and he reacted sharply and personally, often needling his son-in-law to the point of meanness. "He has no program," Martin complained. "As young men we did."[103] He helped with tuition and expenses, but the tensions added distance to his awkward relationship with Mary Anne. As Michael finished his degree, Martin inquired discreetly about the prospects for work, even mobilizing his ties to Wilfrid Laurier University, where he had become chancellor in 1972. "Your career may be impressive to Canada," Mary Anne wrote gratefully, "but this singular action is the one I'll never forget."[104] His stiff, ungracious reply – "I do not feel that I did anything extraordinary. I would do this for anyone" – exposed the hurt he felt at her implication that he might ever have let her down.[105]

Politics also became less important for Paul Jr. in the early 1970s. He had been tempted by his father's vacant seat, but Martin "cautioned" him against running.[106] "I begged him not to," he confided to friends. "I told him to stick to business, make yourself known as an established expert in one field, and then get in."[107] Martin was pleased when Paul did just that, rejoining Power Corporation in 1968 as an aide to its new head, Paul Desmarais, and working as a "corporate firefighter," fixing and disposing of troubled assets.[108] By 1973, he was president of the Power subsidiary, Canada Steamship Lines. "He is a hard worker, and, I believe, innovative," Martin boasted to his friend Burgon Bickersteth. "We are proud of him."[109] He was also pleased by his son's growing family and the arrival of grandsons Jamie in 1969 and David in 1974. "He is a lovely baby," he wrote after meeting David, "as far as baby's [sic] go."[110]

Martin and his son talked almost daily. Paul Jr., who was developing a talent for business, increasingly helped manage his father's money. By 1971, Martin was a wealthy man. The family's holding company, Nellmart Limited, held almost $400,000 in North American securities and had sunk another $149,000 into MNS Investments, a venture capital fund owned by Martin, Nathanson, and Strong. Nellmart held another $85,000 in cash and savings.[111] With a Senate salary of almost $34,000, Martin made more than $98,000 in 1971.[112] Yet money still worried him. "All I seem to be doing is taking it in and paying it out," he complained to his former secretary Marjorie Frank, who continued to handle his personal finances. He kept a sharp eye on his investments, gave sparingly to charity, and nagged Paul Jr. over stock transactions and small bills: "We are not doing so hot are we in a rising market?"[113] He passed along legislative reports, philosophy texts, and autographed ball game programs to Paul Jr. as well. His son responded with good-humoured teasing. "I cannot tell you how much I appreciate your sending me a copy of *The Philosophy of Ludwig Feuerbach,*" he wrote Martin. "Night after night, as I hunt around the house for something to read, I say to myself – 'Oh, if only I could find a copy of the *Philosophy of Ludwig Feuerbach.*'"[114] Their relationship remained close and happy. "More important than his business ability," Martin told his friends, "he is a good husband and father, and this pleases us greatly."[115]

Defeat imprisoned Martin. "I have no rear glass mirror in my make-up," he explained to reporter Jack Best. "What's past is past."[116] But this was not entirely true. The leadership loss was difficult for Martin, and the disappointment lingered, not far from the surface. When tired, or after a drink or two, he sometimes slumped in a chair and surrendered to unseemly self-pity. He raged against his friend and rival, Pearson, and the Anglo-Protestant establishment for conspiring against him on the basis of class and religion.[117] He was hurt when his former cabinet colleague Jack Pickersgill published Prime Minister King's diary, with its mocking references to him, and by the frank comments on his shortcomings in Pearson's memoirs. "I was not too happy about Mike's book," he wrote an assistant about the third volume of Pearson's memoirs. "I do not think it was good of him to speak critically of any colleagues except in general terms. That is something that should be left to the historians."[118] He was indignant when Hart House invited Pearson to celebrate its fiftieth anniversary in 1970 but ignored him. "Of course," he grumbled, "he is an ex-Prime Minister."[119]

He blamed his closest advisors – Paul Jr., Maurice Strong, and even junior aide Jim Peterson – for making him seek the Liberal leadership.[120] He attributed much of his loss to the youth culture that seized the North American political imagination in the mid-1960s, tracing its origins back to President Kennedy's fabled Camelot in the White House. "I am a victim of the change resulting from the generation gap, and on occasion, it makes me somewhat bitter," he confided to Bickersteth. "The Kennedy image, synthetic and false, and sometimes fraudulent as it was, has played its part unwittingly in much that has happened."[121] Without Kennedy, he was always certain, there would have been no Trudeau and no defeat in April 1968.

He blamed himself, too. He regretted his decision to enter politics so early and thought he should have waited until he had established himself elsewhere. Most of all, he regretted his choice to remain in the busy but difficult External Affairs portfolio through the 1960s. "My absorption with External Affairs was too great," he complained.[122] He had lost touch with the dynamic changes that swept the Catholic Church after the Second Vatican Council and had become isolated from the pressing new problems of urbanization and inner cities, the environment and the quality of working-class life. Foreign affairs had distracted him from the domestic heart of political life. "I worked hard all through my public life. I worked like a damned fool," he despaired. "I did some important things when I was foreign minister ... But these things [did] nothing for me politically."[123]

He found comfort in rediscovering and contemplating the changing world about him. He marvelled at the revolution that shook the Catholic Church in the wake of Vatican II after 1965: the diminished insularity, the new roles for women and the laity, the growing ecumenical spirit. "This would not have surprised Newman," he rejoiced at the echoes of his youthful philosophical studies. "He was among the first to encourage laymen to teach in Catholic colleges."[124] He read two of the council's leading theologians, Hans Küng and Gregory Baum. Typically, he worried about the swiftness of the changes but embraced the Catholic future with hope. "I am sure," he predicted, "that something good and wise will settle in."[125]

He also found some smug comfort in watching the evolution of Canadian diplomacy under the new prime minister. When Trudeau came to power in 1968, he was determined to shed Pearson's postwar internationalism in favour of a more modest foreign policy that was rooted explicitly in the national interest. Martin disliked both the new emphasis on interdepartmental committees and Trudeau's willingness to tap the deep talent pool in External Affairs to bolster weaker departments. When Jules Léger left Paris to become deputy minister at the secretary of state's department,

Martin despaired. "All his great experience gone to waste," he protested.[126] He also disliked Trudeau's "exaggerated pragmatism," and he fiercely opposed the government's decision to defy international legal convention by unilaterally extending Canada's control over its Arctic waters in 1970.[127] After storming out of the cabinet debate, Martin crudely recalled, he was so angry with Trudeau that "I went for a major evacuation in the nearest toilet. He got the point."[128]

Pearson resented Trudeau's repudiation of his diplomatic legacy, but Martin discerned in the results an affirmation of his own diplomacy. The drastic reforms that were heralded in the early recognition of communist China, the 1969-70 defence and foreign policy reviews that targeted NATO and NORAD, and the agenda for change laid out in the six slim pamphlets of *Foreign Policy for Canadians* were slow in coming. "Foreign policy is not something you can turn on and off like a tap," he observed, emphasizing its continuities.[129] Canada remained in NORAD, he pointed out, and cuts to its NATO contribution were hardly the first of their kind. Moreover, Trudeau's pursuit of relations with Beijing and of a greater role in Latin America and Africa were all foreshadowed by Martin's policies of the 1960s. His direct participation in the cabinet discussions that shaped Trudeau's foreign policy undoubtedly helped make the changes more palatable. It also helped that he was close to diplomat Geoff Murray, the chief author of *Foreign Policy for Canadians*. "I know he wrote a good bit of it with his tongue in his cheek," Martin grinned, discounting its more extravagant claims.[130] By mid-decade, as Trudeau embraced Canada's Commonwealth ties and better North-South relations, Martin judged him as "no less an idealist" than himself.[131]

The Senate provided Martin with ample time to engage his critics and defend his policies. "I am anxious that there should be a record of my activities and my work," he announced soon after his arrival.[132] A full-scale biography seemed appropriate, and he offered the project to two of his old St. Mike's classmates, archivist Norah Story and Toronto librarian Josephine Phelan. They were a distinguished pair, though they lacked recent experience as political biographers. Phelan enjoyed a strong reputation as a Catholic children's author and had won a Governor General's Award for Non-Fiction in 1951 for *The Ardent Exile*, a biography of Thomas D'Arcy McGee. Story had won the same award for the *Oxford Companion to*

Canadian History and Literature in 1967. "The girls," as Martin called them, went right to work. Tape recorder in hand, the devoted Story planted herself in Martin's Senate office, while he dictated hours of reminiscences, some too hot to retain. Phelan plowed through clippings and his mass of papers, refining the documentation on his family history and unearthing uncomfortable contradictions between his memory and the record. When caught, Martin laughed, "That is the evil of these damn diaries."[133]

It was soon clear to Martin that his diplomatic record required particular care. The raging war in Vietnam and Canada's close US connections remained as controversial as ever. He himself tackled his critics, spending a day with University of Toronto professor Stephen Clarkson, editor of the collection *An Independent Foreign Policy for Canada?* and his contributors. "I am grateful for their interest," he fumed as he prepared himself for the meeting, "but I wish to God they were more sophisticated."[134] Over lunch and dinner, he preached the virtues of "quiet diplomacy" and challenged the book's "absurd thesis" that Washington determined Canadian foreign policy. By his own admission, he lost the fight. He spoke frequently at teach-ins and on campuses in Canada and the United States, defending Canada's role in Vietnam and its membership in US-led alliances. "The young people of today are certainly different," he admitted wryly after one bruising encounter, "but on the whole I find them stimulating – if not always comfortable to be with."[135]

The debate over Canada's role in Southeast Asia grew more heated after June 1971, when leaked US documents lent weight to the view that Martin's diplomacy had aimed to back the American war effort, an interpretation developed most fully in journalist Charles Taylor's 1974 best-seller, *Snowjob: Canada, the United States and Vietnam.* Martin had known Taylor for years, and he liked the reporter, whose writing he admired. Nonetheless, in his *Toronto Globe and Mail* review of the book, he held nothing back. He challenged Taylor's reliance on US sources, listed his "blatant errors and omissions," and mocked his "contrived reality." He dismissed Taylor's charge that Canada was "party to a war-like policy" as "a monstrous allegation in the light of our efforts to bring about peace talks."[136] The truth was more complicated than either man would have admitted, but one thing was clear: Martin's diplomatic legacy, especially in relation to Vietnam, was simply too important to be left to "the girls." He would write it himself.

He engaged two young historians, John Desmarais and Nick d'Ombrain, as assistants and set to work. Story and Phalen were devastated when they learned of the project in July 1973. "I cannot become involved in such a situation without risking a reputation that has taken a lifetime to build," Story stated. "It implies distrust of my ability."[137] She and Phelan tried to come to terms with Martin over the summer but failed. By Christmas, "the girls" were gone. The exercise, however, was undoubtedly therapeutic for Martin. "I am pounding away preparing my 'record' as foreign minister," he wrote cheerfully in October 1973. "It will soon be ready. The more I think of it, the more I think it is a good record."[138] The University of Toronto Press concurred, and it offered to publish the nine-hundred-page transcript, which traced Martin's diplomacy in meticulous and painstaking detail. He refused. Pearson may have settled for Toronto, but he wanted Oxford University Press. In the spring of 1974, he sent the manuscript to the British publisher and waited. The book was not a simple memoir, he insisted, but a "record" of his foreign policy.[139]

THE SENATE, OF course, was Martin's priority. He settled in Room 279, a large panelled corner office in the Centre Block that offered expansive views of Parliament Hill and the East Block. His operation was small and quiet: He kept a driver, and his handful of secretaries was supervised by the efficient Marian Dormer, who replaced Marjorie Frank. He also employed a series of young aides. They were supposed to be legislative assistants, but the expert Jean Sutherland of the Speaker's office did most of the detailed legislative work. Instead, the assistants worked on his schedule, drafted briefing notes and speeches, and dabbled with his memoirs. Tom Brett, a young lawyer with familiar family ties to Pembroke and St. Mike's, joined his office in the fall of 1968 and stayed for eighteen months. He was followed by Nick d'Ombrain and William Dobell. The Senate's pace was leisurely, and Martin was good to his young staff, regaling them with political gossip and rarely losing his temper or making extraordinary demands on their time.

Created in 1867 to safeguard regional interests, the Senate in 1968 had 102 seats, 24 from each of the country's four main regions, with another 6 from Newfoundland. Senators, who were usually nominated by the prime minister in gratitude for notable partisan service, remained in the Senate, virtually unaccountable, until age seventy-five. Their chamber enjoyed the same legal powers as the elected House of Commons, with two exceptions: it could not initiate money bills and it could veto a bill as often as it wished. All legislation required its approval. The Senate had not used its veto since 1939, however, and had focused its efforts on committee hearings, public inquiries, and the clarification of bills. Even these roles taxed an institution that was unrepresentative and rapidly aging. Senate reform, mostly to make it more representative and effective, had become a staple of constitutional bargaining by the late 1960s.

Martin disliked his new job. As he wrote of the experience in 1978, he took each long day as it came, "hoping assignments will open up and something useful will flow therefrom."[140] They rarely did. Senate debates lacked the feverish cut and thrust of the House of Commons, where the stakes really mattered. Routinely rubber-stamping other ministers' legislation was undeniably boring. Yawning and dozing off during one interminable debate, Martin sent a note to Progressive Conservative Grattan O'Leary, urging him "to stand up and give me hell."[141] Worse, individual senators, "beholden to nobody" and rarely interested in political preferment, proved difficult to marshal into a disciplined voting bloc.[142] That often spelled trouble for Martin. "I suppose if I did not have the Senate as a pied-a-terre I would be lost," he wrote Bickersteth glumly. "But I do find the trivialities irritating."[143]

He began his new job with lofty ambitions for a better Senate. "I did not come into this place, this historic chamber," he told his colleagues in his first speech in September 1968, "to preside over the liquidation of the Senate."[144] His speech emphasized the chamber's existing power to review and improve legislation, scrutinize government operations, and study the society around it. It should start, he argued, with Canada's foreign policy, a subject far too important to leave to scholars, journalists, or dissidents. He imagined his Senate, empowered by experience and expertise, playing a role akin to the one fulfilled by the powerful US Senate Committee on Foreign Relations, which ratified US ambassadors and approved their treaties. In this, he was doomed to be disappointed.

He did reasonably well during his first few years at the helm of Canada's upper chamber. His appointment coincided with a burst of Senate activity, and he scooped up the easy credit for its renewed vigour. Maurice

Lamontagne's committee on science policy and Salter Hayden's powerful banking and commerce committee were both hard at work by the time Martin arrived. He joined the Senate's committee on External Affairs, which was soon holding hearings on relations with Latin America, the Caribbean, and the Pacific Rim, all Trudeau priorities. His former Windsor ally, Senator David Croll, began his influential study of Canadian poverty in December 1968, and Keith Davey turned his talents to examining Canada's mass media during the following spring. "I would never work longer or harder in my life than I did for the next two years," Davey recalled of his efforts. "Fifteen hours a day was the norm."[145]

Transforming the Senate's appointment process was more difficult, but here, too, Martin made modest headway. His hopes for a more active Senate demanded a different kind of senator. After governing for twenty-eight of the last thirty-four years, the Liberal Party, with almost seventy senators, was overrepresented in the upper chamber. Liberal newcomers squeezed onto Opposition benches alongside an ever-shrinking group of Conservatives. Of the ninety sitting senators, Martin judged, fewer than half were "relatively active."[146] Eighteen of the ninety were over seventy-five, and only nine were under forty-five. Most came from narrow political and legislative backgrounds. In June 1969, Martin urged Trudeau to appoint younger, non-Liberal senators, drawn from more representative non-political backgrounds.

When Trudeau ignored him, he returned to the charge in October, and again in January 1970. It was time to act, he insisted. He worried that the fourteen vacant Senate seats would discourage and demoralize his few active senators. There were political reasons to move as well. Eight of the vacancies were from Western Canada, where Liberal fortunes were starting to plunge. The longer Trudeau delayed, the higher the cost. "Candidates proliferate, and those not chosen," the experienced politician warned, "will not have enough time to forget their misfortune before the next election."[147] Martin boiled with frustration as the matter dragged into summer. He was finally rewarded, however, when Trudeau announced eight new senators in October 1970. Three were women, and four – progressive academic Eugene Forsey, socialist-feminist Thérèse Casgrain, former Alberta Social Credit premier Ernest Manning, and BC Teamster Edward Lawson – were clearly not Liberals.

It was a start, but only a small one, and though Martin used every trick in his repertoire, his Senate activities and reforms attracted just a polite smattering of applause. A few friends, the columnist Arthur Blakely and writers at the *Toronto Star* and the *Winnipeg Free Press*, made vaguely cheerful noises about "leading with vigour" and "important work."[148] Most press gallery journalists viewed the Senate with "indifference laced with contempt."[149] When they bothered to notice Martin's efforts to change its culture, they smiled tolerantly. "The Senate is showing signs of becoming, if not a hotbed of passion or even passionate politicking," wrote reporter Christina Newman, "at least a living institution bent on stirring itself into important activity after a somnolent century of fat privilege and general lassitude."[150]

Everyone noticed, of course, when there were problems. Martin was conscious of his role as the government's principal spokesman in the Senate and believed that Liberal senators ought to back government policy. But this view sat uncomfortably with his equally strong belief in the value of a hard-working and independent Senate. The uncertainty produced by this contradiction meant trouble. He clashed early with the prickly Croll over appointing an ombudsman to help Canadians keep an eye on the chamber. Neither the government nor Martin was anxious to have an outside watchdog judging the Senate, and they whipped up members to defeat the measure.

There was more controversy the following year. Passage of the government's anti-hate legislation stalled in May 1970, when Ontario Liberal senator Dan Lang, a lawyer, tried to refer the bill to the Supreme Court to test its constitutionality.[151] Martin himself raised cabinet eyebrows when he sent the government's bill on statutory instruments, full of eye-glazing clauses on government regulations and parliamentary committees, to a Senate committee for study in June. In the fall, he and Croll quarrelled again, squabbling publicly over Croll's poverty study, which savaged the Liberal government for its inadequate treatment of the poor in Canada.[152] To cabinet's dismay, Martin's Senate was becoming an unruly and unpredictable source of dissent. In January 1971, restless senators on the Senate's commerce committee even amended Consumer Affairs Minister Ron Basford's hazardous products bill, adding a clause to restrict cabinet's ability to impose regulations without parliamentary oversight. As Martin squirmed before his unhappy cabinet colleague, satisfied senators voted themselves a week's holiday and headed south. "Alas," sighed the *Toronto Globe and Mail*, "business as usual."[153]

During the spring of 1971, Martin suffered a different kind of setback when he renewed his campaign for a better, stronger chamber. Five Progressive Conservatives were soon to retire, and he thought they should all be replaced by Tories. He favoured youth, women, and ethnics. "Both the Government side and the Opposition," he told Trudeau, "urgently need some hard-working Senators."[154] But Liberal loyalists had reacted coolly to Trudeau's earlier round of appointments. (When Eugene Forsey pointed out that he at least sat as a Liberal, Trudeau moaned, "That makes it worse.")[155] Trudeau would not make the same mistake twice, and he ignored Martin's pleas. Of the eight new senators whom he selected that fall, all were Liberals and just one was a woman. Fifteen of the sixteen additional senators who were chosen while Martin remained government leader were also Liberals. Only two were women. This was a bedrock reality of Canadian politics, and try as he might, he could not change it.

That his difficulties in managing the Senate were deep-rooted became apparent in December 1971. After a raucous year-long debate, Finance Minister Edgar Benson had almost pushed his massive bill to reform Canada's income tax system through a hostile House of Commons. As consideration of Benson's measures neared completion, Martin started rounding up Liberal senators for the speedy action needed to meet the government's 1 January deadline. Uneasy Liberal and Opposition senators balked at the government's assumption that they would meekly do as they were told.[156] One of Martin's own nominees, Forsey, led the attack. An acknowledged constitutional expert, he condemned the government's "unreasonableness," urging his colleagues "to take a stand and say it shall not happen again."[157] When the 707-page tax bill landed in the Senate just a week before Christmas, its disgruntled occupants revolted.

The Conservative press, whose readers resented the new tax on capital gains, egged on the recalcitrant senators. "A travesty," shouted the *Sun*, Toronto's upstart tabloid.[158] The *Montreal Gazette* urged senators to resist the bill, and the *Toronto Globe and Mail* accused them of an "an unforgivably bad job."[159] An uncomfortable Martin looked desperately out of his depth. First, he bluffed, feebly warning that cabinet might call a snap election on constitutional grounds if the Senate blocked the popular will as expressed by the House.[160] Amid the guffaws that greeted this sally, he quickly retreated and sent the bill to committee, where Tory members held it hostage during the last weekend before Christmas. Finance Minister Benson himself finally stepped in and bargained with the senators: in exchange for speedy passage of his bill, the government would incorporate their ideas into a bill of amendments to be passed in the spring.[161] His offer succeeded, and the senators quickly passed his bill.

The unruly Senate did Martin no end of harm, especially with key prime ministerial advisor Allan MacEachen. The wily government House leader, who was responsible for Trudeau's legislative agenda, took a "shady" view of the Senate.[162] MacEachen disliked Martin's willingness to tolerate Senate hearings and complained at his lack of control over its members.

MARTIN FLED OTTAWA whenever he could. This suited Trudeau and External Affairs Minister Mitchell Sharp, who often turned to him when they wanted a steady minister for missions abroad. Martin fussed at the imposition and was sometimes irked by the implication that he could be spared from cabinet and Senate business.[163] He was also upset that his earnest diplomacy drew so little notice, though he reported faithfully on his travels to his Senate colleagues. In the press, the ranks of his friends were thinning, and their young replacements were inclined to sneer as he disappeared on "perpetual goodwill visit[s] to countries that no one in Canada has ever heard of."[164] But the routine work of diplomacy, waving the flag at state funerals and inaugurations, needed to be done, and his willingness to lend an experienced hand was valued by his old friends in External Affairs. He mostly cultivated the remoter fringes of Canadian diplomacy, in Eastern Europe or the developing world, where Canadian diplomats often struggled to find ministers who were willing to visit. They welcomed the chance that Martin offered to revive a fading relationship or boost a country's profile among Ottawa policy-makers. His presence, diplomat Vic Moore wrote of his visit to Zambia for a Commonwealth youth ministers' conference in 1973, "has brought a new and very welcome zest and cohesion to the whole operation."[165]

Martin enjoyed his diplomatic travels. Most involved only representational duties, where the pace was relaxed and the workload light. He attended the funerals of Israeli prime minister Levi Eshkol in 1969 and of Egyptian president Gamal Abdel Nasser in 1970, and he cheered democracy's progress at state ceremonies for Mexican president Luis Echeverría in 1972 and President Carlos Andrés Pérez of Venezuela in 1974. He often combined his official travel with personal interests or short vacations and visits to old friends. In July 1971, he secured an invitation to South Korean general Chung-hee Park's inauguration, part of a larger campaign to boost ties with Seoul, which was organized by the Korean embassy and Francis Leddy, whose University of Windsor maintained close ties with schools in Korea. Martin's interest helped push Korea up the government's agenda, prompting Ottawa to open an embassy there in 1973. Similarly, a trip to mark modern Turkey's fiftieth anniversary in November 1973 provided a chance to revisit Rome with Nell and Canadian ambassador Klaus Goldschlag. "My visit was something like a recovery of university days when so long ago I visited Florence and Caserta," Martin wrote Goldschlag wistfully. "It is hard to explain the emotion I experienced."[166]

There were more substantive missions as well. Ottawa's festering row with Paris over Quebec's international status had flared again in the fall of 1968. Federal officials feared that Quebec and Paris were close to arranging separate representation for Quebec at the conference of francophone education ministers that was slated for Congo's capital, Kinshasa, in January 1969. Their misgivings deepened when External Affairs learned that President Hamani Diori of Niger planned to convene a summit to institutionalize a group of French-speaking nations, La Francophonie. When Father Georges-Henri Lévesque invited Trudeau to attend festivities to mark the fifth anniversary of the National University of Rwanda, the prime minister seized the chance to send Martin to Africa.[167]

Martin's objectives were threefold. Trudeau hoped he would convince Congolese president Joseph Mobutu and President Diori of Canada's support for their respective French-speaking initiatives. More significantly, he was to remind them of Ottawa's unique role in the conduct of Canadian diplomacy and to secure assurances from them that a single federal delegation from Canada, with representation from provinces that had a strong francophone presence, would be welcome at their gatherings.[168] Martin was doubtful of success. "I was opposed to the African trip," he recalled soon after his return. "I didn't want to go, because I didn't think it could be done."[169]

Accompanied by diplomat Michel de Goumois, he headed to Africa in late November. Their flight was a miserable experience. Both men were plagued by bad colds, and Martin, anxious about his first real task for Trudeau, was bothered by recent press reports that wondered why he was wasting his time in Africa when there was work to do at home. They landed in Niger early in the morning of 29 November and were soon at work. Martin and Diori talked all morning and again the next day over dinner at the presidential palace, an elegant Moorish building set amid historical gardens. Martin dangled Canadian aid. Engineers were virtually on their way, he promised, along with the twenty thousand tons of prairie wheat that Niger had recently requested. Diori smiled, gracefully falling in with Canada's position.[170] He happily signed a letter to Trudeau, welcoming a Canadian delegation with participation by all provinces with substantial francophone populations.[171]

After paying short courtesy visits to Senegal and the Ivory Coast, the Canadians headed to Rwanda. Father Lévesque's campus was a showpiece for Martin's efforts to expand aid to francophone Africa in the early 1960s, and he and the senator enjoyed a satisfying reunion. The envoys were back in Kinshasa by 10 December. They had breakfast that morning with Congolese foreign minister Justin Bomboko and spent a crucial hour with Mobutu. The general charmed his visitor by recalling an April 1963 trip to Ottawa, during which he had watched Martin in the House of Commons.[172] There was a familiar review of Canadian aid, past and future, and a letter from Trudeau for Mobutu, seeking support. This was forthcoming. Civil wars in the Congo province of Katanga and nearby Nigeria had left Mobutu with little sympathy for separatists, African or otherwise. As Mobutu explained to Trudeau, when he spoke of Canada, he meant the federal government, not some province.[173] Martin had done well in both Niamey and Kinshasa, but his small victories in the long war of attrition over Quebec's status brought him no joy. "Not much has been made of this," he grumbled on his return. "I often wonder what newspapermen in Canada do ... This was an important matter and nobody noticed."[174]

Neither did many Canadians notice when Martin's next big job came up in the spring of 1970. Canada had long enjoyed close relations with the Commonwealth Caribbean. Fish, aid, and tourists flowed south, while rum, molasses, and expensive sugar, guaranteed access to the Canadian market under a duty rebate program, flowed north. But after ratifying a commodity agreement in 1968 to regulate the global sugar trade, Ottawa abruptly cancelled the rebate. Its offer of a $5 million agricultural development fund hardly made up the shortfall.

The cancellation came hard on the heels of measures to restrict oil and textile imports from the Caribbean, and amid lingering racial tensions· over rioting by West Indian students at Sir George Williams University in Montreal. When Commonwealth Caribbean heads of government assembled in April 1970, they ignored the aid offer and erupted with rare "harsh words" for Canada.[175] Startled, cabinet extended the sugar rebate for another year and decided to send an emissary to the region to "create a dialogue."[176] Choosing the right person was trickier than it looked, and cabinet was split. Sending too junior a representative would be resented as an insult; the wrong minister, however, might succumb to pressure for on-the-spot concessions. Sharp settled on Martin.

Martin knew the region well. He had often vacationed there in the 1950s and 1960s, socializing with local leaders and touring Canadian aid projects. He had also attended the 1966 Canada–Commonwealth Caribbean heads of government meeting that established the original rebate program. His mission unfolded in two parts. In September, he and his External Affairs handler, Larry Smith, an old-school diplomat known for his soft-spoken and unflappable manner, swung through the Eastern Caribbean to a warm and enthusiastic welcome. Even the formidable prime minister of Trinidad and Tobago, Eric Williams, was kind, setting aside ninety minutes for talks, hosting a formal lunch, and attending a reception in Martin's honour. The Canadians enjoyed deep-sea fishing, picnics on the beach, and some wonderful swimming. Despite nagging back pain, Martin was in great form, charming prime ministers, governors, and even the protesters who milled about his hotel, denouncing Canada as "a racist institution" in mimeographed pamphlets headlined "Hello, Mr. Martin!"[177]

Martin and Smith were back in the islands by mid-October. This visit was much less pleasant. Martin was deeply discouraged by the October Crisis in Quebec, which had suddenly blown up during his absence, and by the sight of troops with machine guns in the streets of Ottawa and Montreal. The talks were tougher in the Western Caribbean, where sugar was more important, and he endured verbal lashings from Guyanese prime minister Forbes Burnham and Jamaican prime minister Hugh Shearer.[178] Mostly, Martin listened, as he had during his first tour, and what he heard dismayed him. Caribbeans liked Canada. Governors and taxi-drivers alike valued its willingness to treat their region as an equal partner. Canada, they told him, had no imperial ambitions. He learned that many had deep personal connections to Canada, extending from nostalgia for Canadian National Steamship "lady boats" to sons and daughters who lived in Toronto. As he told Sharp, Ottawa's ham-handed diplomacy threatened these ties.[179]

He took his views straight to the top. Smith did most of the drafting, but the recommendations submitted to cabinet were his. He backed Caribbean demands to extend the sugar duty rebate, at least until the end of 1971, and possibly longer. He divided the agricultural development fund between bilateral projects and the Caribbean Development Bank, dodging the thorny question of intra-island politics. He offered a suite of ideas to improve aid flows. Notably, he pressed cabinet to bring Belize and the Bahamas, where there was no formal Canadian presence, under the jurisdiction of Canada's high commissioner in Jamaica and to open a high commission in Barbados.[180] His report was substantive, and he was sure of success. When Smith cautioned against including his detailed country notes, more than seventy single-spaced pages, Martin overruled him: "Put them in as annexes! The PM is interested."[181]

The outcome was not the triumph that Martin had anticipated. External Affairs had changed since his day, and Sharp and his deputy, Ed Ritchie, were uneasy with his directness.[182] The lack of interdepartmental consultation on recommendations related to aid, trade, and the transfer of funds made them nervous. Though they backed the key proposal to extend sugar duty rebates to the end of 1971, they removed any implication that there might be more help later. They were also doubtful about establishing a new post in Barbados. That idea, they decided, would have to go through the new Interdepartmental Committee on External Relations (ICER), where it would be weighed against competing demands for scarce funds in accordance with the prime minister's ideas on rational decision making and public-sector management. Cabinet approved the amended recommendations in December. Yet, even a one-year extension in the context of Martin's goodwill mission was enough to reshape Canada's relations with the Caribbean for the rest of the decade.[183] It was another success, but the press and the pundits ignored it, which left Martin feeling empty and disappointed.

His last major assignment, as head of Canada's delegation to the third UN Conference on Trade and Development (UNCTAD III) in Santiago, Chile, was unhappier still. His memoirs describe the UN gathering in May 1972 as among the "most unsatisfactory" he ever attended.[184] Canadian preparations were dismal and bogged down in interdepartmental squabbling. Though Canadian aid had crept up recently, Canada had not kept its promise made at UNCTAD II to reduce tariffs for less developed countries (LDC) through a generalized system of preferences (GSP). Worried by growing US protectionism and unsettled monetary conditions, Finance blocked all progress.[185] Moreover, Canadian policy-makers, though led at the official level by seasoned trade negotiator Don McPhail, were too junior to overcome the impasse.[186] Worse, trouble was certain to arise with the media and in the church and NGO communities, which were becoming increasingly disenchanted with Canada's failure to address Third World poverty. When Trudeau suspended ministerial travel pending an election, Sharp and Trade Minister Jean-Luc Pepin pressed Martin to take UNCTAD on.

He hesitated. He knew of the unsettled policy surrounding UNCTAD III but was disarmed by the friendly and lively desk officer who was responsible for the conference, Margaret Catley-Carlson.[187] She quickly became a favourite. Martin was also drawn by the high stakes involved at UNCTAD III. He had fond memories of participating in the first UNCTAD in 1964 and was surely conscious of the heightened profile of North-South issues, which moved up the global agenda in the 1970s, the United Nations' second decade of development. Perhaps he hoped to make a real difference one more time. He certainly tried hard, insisting that cabinet clarify Canadian policy on the GSP so that he would have something positive to offer in Santiago. At the end of March, unhappy ministers grudgingly promised to implement the tariff changes "at the earliest feasible date."[188] It wasn't much of a concession, but it was enough to persuade Martin to go.

He stayed for a long week of "complaints from LDCs and polite waffling from developed countries."[189] He chaired Commonwealth consultations with humour and tact, and helped strengthen a last-minute Canadian proposal to boost concessional financing through international aid agencies. However, his speech, with its stale initiatives, made little impression on either the delegates in Santiago or the media in Canada, where it drew only "moderate" coverage.[190] Disappointed, Martin complained to friends that "the press does not really understand or care very much."[191] But the critics did. The Canadian Council of Churches and the Catholic bishops denounced Trudeau for policies that were "non-committal, cynical, closed-fisted, and disruptive."[192] Privately, Martin agreed with this assessment, but good solider that he was, he mounted a podium at his alma mater, St. Michael's College, and defended his government's policies before its church-based detractors.

MARTIN PLAYED ONLY a minor role in the federal election of October 1972. He helped with the party's speakers' bureau in Ottawa and spoke at a handful of Maritime rallies, but the results of the election nonetheless affected him. Trudeau lost his majority and clung to power with the slimmest of margins over Robert Stanfield's Progressive Conservatives. The New Democratic Party (NDP) held the balance of power, tipping the government leftward. Under the heightened scrutiny of a minority government, Martin was a wasting asset. At the age of sixty-nine, he was finding it harder to keep up with the rapidly shifting political values around him. He had difficulty, for instance, with women's rights. "I am not too happy over the strident and unfeminine tones of women's liberation," he told the press, even as he defended government measures to improve the status of women![193]

He also had trouble with the emerging consensus around conflict of interest guidelines for legislators. After a lifetime in politics, he bridled at the implication that legislators would ever allow personal interest to trump government policy.[194] He responded grudgingly when NDP critics forced cabinet to adopt new rules in June 1973, which called on legislators to dispose of their assets or declare them publicly. He retained his role as president of his family's holding company, Nellmart, through the fall, until his name appeared in embarrassing news reports on the "Golden Grits," a network of Liberal and corporate directorships that embraced Deputy Mines Minister Jack Austin, Power Corporation, and Commerce Capital, the newest iteration of MNS Investment.[195] He was rebuked by Trudeau, who insisted that he comply with the guidelines.[196]

The Senate, whose smooth operation was more important than ever in a minority setting, continued its obstreperous ways. Through 1973, it had considered the government's wiretap legislation, amending the bill to make it easier for police to monitor suspected criminals. The Commons rejected the change on privacy grounds, however, and sent the legislation back to the Senate in January 1974. The revised bill was now stuck in the upper chamber while senators debated the merits of amending it a second time, and Martin needed two full days of debates and a rare Saturday sitting to get it passed.[197] MacEachen discontentedly eyed his fouled-up legislative schedule. The syndicated pundit Charles Lynch was dismissive: "The more serious the senators become, the broader the comedy."[198] By March, Ottawa was prey to persistent rumours that Martin was to be shuffled out of cabinet to make way for a younger, more effective Senate leader.[199]

The rumours were true. Following his majority win in the July 1974 election, Trudeau remade his cabinet, dumping Jean Dubé, Herb Gray, Stanley Haidasz, Robert Stanbury – and Martin. One critical journalist dubbed it the "Tuesday Night Massacre."[200] Anxious to bolster the Liberal presence in British Columbia, where incumbent regional minister Jack Davis had lost his election and the party retained just four seats, Trudeau turned to Vancouver senator Ray Perrault. He promoted Perrault to government leader in the Senate, pushing Martin out of cabinet. Martin was livid. He was less than four months shy of King's record as Canada's longest-serving cabinet minister. "The timing was lousy," unnamed aides protested to the press.[201] Unwilling to retire, Martin dug in his heels and refused to go quietly. Trudeau offered him the embassy in Washington, but he demanded the high commission in London. Meeting this request would require some shuffling of recent diplomatic appointments, but Trudeau agreed. On 30 October 1974, Martin resigned his Senate seat and joined Canada's foreign service.

13

LEGACIES, 1974–92

The London appointment delighted Martin's friends. Diplomat-turned-scholar John Holmes called it "imaginative."[1] Under-Secretary of State for External Affairs Ed Ritchie wrote warmly to say, "Welcome back on board."[2] Others were more critical. Disheartened foreign service officers made no secret of their unhappiness at seeing such a plum posting slip into the hands of an aging politician. Canada's outgoing high commissioner, Jake Warren, was popular with the British, who felt that he had "made an outstanding success of his job."[3] Whitehall officials regretted his departure. "I cannot help feeling," observed the Queen's private secretary, Martin Charteris, "that Jake's departure will create a void which Mr. Martin will not be able to fill very successfully."[4]

Journalist Hugh Winsor wondered "what possible debt do we owe Paul Martin?" As he told CBC Radio listeners, Martin was "a political has-been, a reminder of the ambivalent 50's and 60's. He represents the worst traditions in Canadian foreign policy."[5] That kind of criticism lingered, and *Maclean's* marked Martin's second year on the job with a mocking and hurtful attack on Canada's "forgotten man."[6]

These judgments underestimated Martin. Before his departure, his freshly broken arm in a sling, he toured British diplomatic missions in Ottawa, Toronto, and Montreal, sending all the right signals and impressing UK officials from the start. They found him genuinely interested in the work and excited by his posting. "The humanity, humility, conscientiousness

336

and good intentions with which Paul Martin is approaching his new job," observed P.H. Scott, the British consul general in Montreal, "is likely to confound the sceptics."[7]

Paul and Nell threw themselves into London and made the four years there among the happiest of their lives. They found the transatlantic separation from friends and family difficult. "We get very lonesome," Martin wrote his son, "for you and Mary Anne, your wife and your wonderful children. I often wonder why it is that Paul does not phone, but realise that he is so preoccupied with so many things."[8] Diplomatic life, with its predictable annual and daily rhythms, provided ample compensation. There were regular breaks at Christmas, in Canada or southern Europe, and a relaxed summer holiday each year. Nell usually left London in July and returned in September, spending the time at the family cottage in Colchester, often with Mary Anne and Michael Bellamy, and their two young daughters, Catherine and Julia. Martin joined them for a time in August, before visiting Paul Jr. and his family at his corporate retreat in the Saguenay for a few weeks of "fishing and catching up with my soul."[9]

In London, the Martins took to the luxury of living in the well-staffed neo-Georgian elegance of the high commissioner's official residence at 12 Upper Brook Street in the city's central Mayfair district. Martin typically rose at six o'clock and breakfasted on grapefruit and bran flakes, while he and Nell conducted their daily "seminar" on the previous day's events. He swam in the mornings, initially at a neighbour's pool down the street and eventually at the nearby Grosvenor Hotel. Nell passed her days happily entertaining the endless stream of London visitors, old friends from Ottawa or Windsor.

Martin began his day in his office at Macdonald House, the former US embassy where the bulk of the staff were housed. He read the London press and the overnight telegrams, before settling down to dictate his diary, inspired by Canada's great diplomatic diarist, Charles Ritchie. But whereas Ritchie's entries consisted of short, pungent remarks on his daily activities, Martin's diary featured long commentaries on the morning news or developments a world away, all clearly intended for future readers. Editor Bill Young (future librarian of Parliament) would later prune the text mercilessly for publication, lining the margins with sharp comments: "trite," "namedropping," and "news reports."[10]

Martin styled himself an elder statesman, a conceit that sometimes irritated his high commission staff. Excited by his job, he was again a tough boss, and staff made the usual complaints about his demands. Drawn from a dozen departments in Ottawa, the mission's five hundred staff members represented "a miniature government of Canada," scattered between Canada House, Macdonald House in Grosvenor Square, and the immigration offices farther down the street. Martin's managerial burden was not especially heavy. London was a desirable posting, and it attracted strong and capable foreign service officers. André Bissonette, who stayed for a year as his deputy, was followed by Gerry Hardy. Skilled and well-regarded diplomats, both could be trusted to carry out his directions. As always, Martin guarded his staff jealously and was resentful when External Affairs poached one of its stars for a short assignment elsewhere. "How impossible can Ottawa get?" he griped.[11]

He worked during lunch, building and nurturing an outstanding network of politicians, journalists, diplomats, and businessmen, hosting them at the East India Club, or the Travellers Club, or the Athenaeum. "His dinners, with his devoted Nell, were great occasions," wrote diplomat Patrick Reid, "but his lunches, with practical influence peddling the key, were the arena where the master politician was really worth watching."[12] He took his Liberal friends to the Reform Club, where, his eyes twinkling mischievously, he reminded them that William Gladstone became British prime minister at eighty-two and that he himself was just a shade past seventy.[13] "Lunch at the Reform Club," wrote a grateful Jean Chrétien, then trade minister, "sitting before the great Gladstone, and discussing Laurier and our dear Canada, was an unforgettable experience."[14] The high commissioner sometimes snuck back to the residence for a short afternoon nap.

Martin spent the balance of his day calling on British policy-makers and diplomatic contacts, trading gossip and news, and filing reports to Ottawa. Between meetings, he made time to greet the girls in the Richmond Thunderbird Baton and Drum Corps, and the boys from St. Michael's Choir School, as well as countless other groups of Canadians, young and old. He stalked the high commission's library at Canada House on Thursdays, greeting patrons and asking, "Anybody here from Windsor?" He wore a path to Heathrow Airport, where he dutifully met many of his visitors, always curious for the latest news from Ottawa. He faithfully turned out for the city's formal diplomatic occasions – the opening of Parliament, the Guildhall lunches, the Westminster prayers – and he wondered at the diplomats who did not. "Some," he marvelled sadly, "never show up."[15] He would never make a mistake like that.

In the evenings, he and Nell entertained. They escorted friends and visitors to Wimbledon tennis and West End theatres. "This," he said of the great Canadian ballerina Karen Kain, dancing at Covent Garden, "is what is meant when we speak of cultural affairs as a modern instrument of foreign policy."[16] They hosted elaborate dinners for queens and princes, prime ministers and premiers, diplomats and celebrities, but there was always room at the table for old friends from Canada. "We went to a hell of a lot of dinners," he explained. "That's where you did a lot of your work. You went to dinners, or you gave one. And you always learned something."[17] They carried it off well. "I could hardly believe my eyes seeing [renowned author] C.P. Snow across the table," wrote diplomat Dorothy Armstrong. "Best of all, the evenings were fun and the setting, food and wines truly lovely."[18] The Queen Mum was equally pleased. "Oh Canada!" she enthused when a dessert with the Maple Leaf Flag entered the room.[19] "As always, at your home," her aide wrote Martin, "the luncheon was a gastronomic treat of rare quality."[20]

Though British officials found his style "tortuous and long-winded," they admired his tireless capacity to establish connections and admitted that he "impressed all he met by the thoroughness and humility with which he prepared himself for the job."[21] The grumbling in official Ottawa subsided, too. Trudeau, who made a triumphant tour of London in March 1975, was delighted with Martin's careful planning for the visit, praising his "wise political judgement [which] was very much in evidence."[22] Later that year, when France excluded Canada from a gathering of the leading Western industrial nations, Martin's effective diplomacy won further applause. Ross Campbell, head of Atomic Energy of Canada, expressed a widespread consensus when he congratulated Martin for his efforts to win British backing for Canada's participation in the group, the nascent G-7 summit. "Your ability to get through to the Prime Minister and Foreign Secretary at the critical moment could not have been done by many heads of post," he wrote. "I am resultantly forced to concede that a political background has its virtues."[23] Perhaps it did. When External Affairs Minister Don

Jamieson visited London in 1976, Martin knew precisely what was required. According to Derek Burney, the minister's assistant, Jamieson "really had fun in London, and his program there, with its nice mix of business (with some pretty outstanding appointments), pleasure and breathing spaces was held up [in External Affairs] ... as the type of model everyone should follow."[24]

Martin's early success in London clearly reflected his extensive network of political contacts on both sides of the Atlantic. It was also grounded in his deep interest in Britain and Anglo-Canadian relations, indelibly shaped by the blissful days spent as a Cambridge law student in 1929–30 and his easy contacts with Britain's top UN diplomats after 1945. His anglophilia underpinned his view of Britain, even in the 1970s, as "the cross-roads of the world ... the greatest world metropolitan centre."[25] This romantic view, described by his closest friends as "insufferable," was qualified by his sharp appreciation for the calculus of power. As foreign minister in the mid-1960s, Martin knew that the partnership between Canada and Britain was fast disappearing. Disagreements over NATO, over relations with France and Europe, and over trade plagued Anglo-Canadian relations after 1963. "Something was lacking," he wrote of that decade in his memoirs. "I could not put my finger on it, because I knew it had more to do with the appearance than the substance of our political relationship."[26]

A decade later, he encountered a more harmonious but increasingly distant and less dynamic relationship. Yet, amid the disarray that accompanied Britain's ongoing adjustment to its shrinking post-colonial world, there were reassuring signs that Anglo-Canadian relations were "excellent and active," marked by an "ease, informality and frequency of contact." Most importantly, the two countries were headed "in the direction of a more equal relationship as allies, trading partners, and middle powers."[27] This optimistic assessment was shared by the occupants of the Foreign and Commonwealth Office (FCO). "Anglo-Canadian relations," they assured their prime minister in 1975, "are conducted in a frank and friendly manner ... [and] are remarkable for the breadth and frequency of contact between Ministers and officials."[28]

Martin warned against complacency as Britain managed the final phases of its long retreat from empire and addressed priorities closer to home. Soaring inflation, record unemployment, and endless strikes blighted

Britain's economy. The country faced nationalist demands for constitutional reform in Scotland and Wales, as well as growing sectarian violence and terrorism in Northern Ireland. Beyond the British Isles, London was shaking off the last vestiges of empire in Southern Africa, while coming to terms with its recent membership in the European Economic Community. In Martin's view, the implications for Canada were clear:

> They do not automatically think of us when making decisions which may affect us, as they do of their EEC partners or the US. Even when they do think of us, they will not necessarily sacrifice what they perceive to be their interests, even marginally, simply to oblige us. We have to work, and work hard, to ensure that they understand our viewpoint on key issues, and demonstrate to them how their interests and ours can be made to coincide.[29]

For Martin, defending Canada's interests in a context where they might easily be overlooked meant reinforcing and promoting a stronger pro-Canadian constituency in Britain. The impetus behind this effort was partly bureaucratic. He arrived in London just as the Department of External Affairs concluded a two-year exercise, nicknamed the "New Look," to direct extra resources to public affairs activities abroad so that they were large enough "to allow persuasive communication with citizens of foreign countries, who should be influenced in favour of Canada and Canadian policies, and indirectly with their Governments."[30] The program, which promised to triple public affairs spending in key countries, including Britain, was put into place for the fiscal year that began in April 1974.[31] In London, the first step in the New Look involved creating a senior management position at the high commission, which was expected to pull together press relations, academic and Canadian studies, and cultural programs into a "greatly expanded" and "integrated" set of activities.[32]

Martin welcomed the department's interest in public affairs, which reflected his own long-established operating preferences. But even with his strong support, the initial effort to improve London's public affairs activities was troubled. A round of budget cuts announced in October 1975, part of Trudeau's anti-inflation campaign, made initiatives hard to fund. More misfortune followed when the local press officer quit in late

1975, and a replacement was not easily located.[33] As a result of these setbacks, Martin himself took a closer interest in the press operation, promoting his young executive assistant, Lorne Green, to mission press officer. Under Green, the press office was transformed. It expanded and standardized its list of media contacts, reorganized its file system, and stepped up media training for its small group of locally engaged staff. By the end of 1976, the high commission boasted that, for the first time, it had established "consistent and substantial contacts" with foreign editors from all the major British papers.[34]

Martin became even more vigilant about protecting the public affairs program after Premier René Lévesque's separatist Parti Québécois triumphed in a November 1976 provincial election. His faith in Trudeau and federalism remained unshakeable. "The people of Quebec will not leave Canada," he wrote Senator John Connolly in February 1977, adding that "I have no doubt of the outcome."[35] He worked closely with Patrick Reid, director-general of public affairs in External Affairs, to convince his minister, Don Jamieson, and his deputy, Allan Gotlieb, to protect the high commission's public affairs budget as inflation and fiscal restraint reduced its value. The balance of the public affairs program, made up of Canadian studies and cultural affairs, was slowly strengthened during the next few years under diplomat Richard Roberts and then Reid himself. "We think we are justified in claiming," Roberts told Ottawa in the spring of 1978, "that public affairs "have improved the image of the mission as an effective agent of the Canadian Government."[36]

Martin's strong support for public affairs extended to the emerging field of Canadian Studies, a government-led initiative to promote the study of the country on British campuses. He liked mingling with visiting writers and artists, and Canadian Studies provided scope for a small but personally important initiative of his own. He treasured his year as a Cambridge law student, and on a nostalgic visit to Trinity College in September 1976, he wondered how young lawyers might be given a similar chance to step outside "the humdrum of monotony" to encounter the law's "transcendental quality."[37] Cambridge, beginning to scramble for new sources of North American revenue, was intrigued. Two weeks later, a bright and ambitious legal scholar at Trinity, Basil Markesinis, wrote Martin with plans for a summer law school aimed at Canadian lawyers.[38] Markesinis suggested that Cambridge offer a two- or three-week program of specialized lectures on common and international law, British constitutional and administrative law, and Europe's changing legal norms. Fees and an endowment fund of $50,000 to $75,000 would cover the costs. Martin and Cambridge professor D.W. Bowett, the president of Queens' College, met in November, and after setting aside the endowment as unrealistic, agreed to proceed. At once, Martin wrote the deans of Canadian law schools to gauge their support for a Cambridge summer course, beginning in 1979.[39]

The summer school project took shape during 1977. Throughout the spring, Martin wove a network of Canadian supporters by phone, cable, and letter. He won early backing from Barry Strayer, a rising assistant deputy minister in the federal Justice Department. James Kerr of the alumni Cambridge Society of Toronto offered help with identifying donors. Martin also enlisted friends Jack Clyne, a former BC Supreme Court justice, and Nathan Nemetz, BC chief justice, to his cause. Canadian law deans endorsed the plan in May, sending two of their number from Osgoode Hall and Laval University to join Martin's informal organizing committee. At the same time, the group began to solicit funds. Money was clearly on Martin's agenda when Alberta premier Peter Lougheed toured London in late May. As an aide reminded him, "$15,000 is peanuts in Alberta!"[40] A delegation that included Bud Estey, a Supreme Court justice, and senior judges from British Columbia, Alberta, and Ontario nailed down the details with Cambridge in October. The outcome was never in doubt. As the Canadians walked across Trinity's grounds, evensong echoing in their ears, they were swept up in Martin's passion. "I had always felt that Cambridge and what it stands for would emerge as the compelling argument," he wrote contentedly. "This, I think, is what happened."[41] A November 1977 press release formally announced the creation of the Canadian Institute for Advanced Legal Studies.

Though External Affairs turned Martin down when he asked for money, the provincial law associations came through, and by March 1978, the institute's steering committee had the $65,000 it needed to subsidize the summer course.[42] But the Canadian committee was worried by gaps in the curriculum, which persisted all summer, and was dismayed by the unresolved logistical challenges. Cambridge had modern accommodation for only sixty participants and proposed housing the others in student dorms. It still had no plans for feeding the group, or activities for accompanying spouses, and children were not welcome.[43] Queens' College president Bowett had other concerns. He felt hurt and under-appreciated, and was troubled by shifts in the timetable and repeated demands to rewrite the course brochure.[44] The practical problems were made worse by poor personal relations between Jack Clyne and Bowett.[45] "The whole exercise is teetering on the brink," Bud Estey warned in early 1979.[46]

Martin went to work. "We are not going to falter now," he cabled Estey.[47] He recruited Lord Denning, master of the rolls and Britain's top civil court justice, to speak at the summer school. He also hosted a "memorable" dinner for Denning, which drew Home Secretary Merlyn Rees and Attorney General Sam Silken, and attracted promises to encourage British lawyers to attend the course.[48] Martin also sent diplomat Richard Roberts to Cambridge, where the practical and experienced official sorted through the logistical problems, finding the required campus accommodation, loosening the ban on children, and developing a program for spouses.[49] Estey relaxed, and registration picked up through the spring, reaching 150 by June.

The institute's inaugural course, opened on 9 July 1978, was a solid success. The Canadian visitors loved Cambridge. Lord Denning packed the hall for his lecture on administrative law, and the Toronto Globe and Mail sparked excited corridor gossip when it labelled a talk by Quebec's chief justice as "separatist." Sitting at the centre of it all, on his favourite courtyard bench, Martin basked in the praise and the July sunshine. The institute, which would eventually grow to include scholarships, lectures, and a second course in Strasbourg, was a small but valuable strand in the web of fragile ties that bound Canada to its waning British heritage.

No bilateral issue mattered more for Martin than the confrontation with Britain over Air Canada's landing rights at Heathrow Airport. Then as now, Heathrow was badly overcrowded. "Blend the Tower of Babel with the Black Hole of Calcutta, add the complete works of Kafka, and stir," wrote one contemporary observer. "That's Heathrow on a quiet day."[50] Since expansion was not an option, the UK Department of Transport concluded in 1977, London would have to rely on two airports. In April, George Rogers, the Department of Trade's permanent under-secretary of civilian aviation, arrived in Ottawa with news that Air Canada would have to move from Heathrow to remote Gatwick.[51]

Air Canada was distraught. It feared the capital costs of moving and the loss of its passengers and cargo to US carriers that flew directly from American border airports to Heathrow. When Ottawa officials proved unhelpful, Air Canada's European vice-president, David Bryce-Buchanan, turned to Martin for help.

The high commissioner needed no persuading. He pressed Ottawa to re-examine Air Canada's case and consider anew the implications of addressing the issue on the political level.[52] Ottawa met him halfway, agreeing that there would be representations, but that these would not be political. Instead, they would be confined to registering Ottawa's economic interest in "fair and equitable" treatment for the Canadian airline on trade policy grounds.[53]

Martin jauntily ignored Ottawa's strictures, and his representations exceeded his mandate. In an early October meeting with Edmund Dell, the secretary of state for trade, he emphasized the political stakes involved. Canada's national carrier had been a tenant at Heathrow, known the world over as "London's airport," since 1949. A berth at Heathrow entailed a "degree of prestige," he continued, as he warned Dell that moving Air Canada would "cause significant political reaction."[54] Insisting that the issue was political rather than economic, Martin pressed his deputy minister, Allan Gotlieb, and Michael Pitfield, the clerk of the Privy Council, to ask Trudeau to raise it directly with the British prime minister when he visited London in December.[55]

Transport Minister Otto Lang and Claude Taylor, president of Air Canada, disagreed with this approach. Echoing Transport Canada bureaucrats, they wondered if it would be more effective to keep Trudeau's "political ammunition" in reserve.[56] They worried that raising Heathrow to the political level might link the issue to the renegotiation of the 1949 Anglo-Canadian civil aviation agreement, allowing the British to use Heathrow as a lever to secure access to Western Canada, a long-standing interest, without giving any additional benefit to Canada. It was "vital" that Canada not create the impression that Ottawa was ready to trade landing rights at Heathrow for access to Western Canada. These were compelling arguments. Martin was thanked for his help, and Heathrow was struck from the prime ministerial agenda.[57]

But Martin persisted. When Air Canada president Taylor arrived in London just days before Trudeau's visit, Martin cornered him at a reception and persuaded him to "clarify" his position. Air Canada, Martin reported triumphantly to headquarters, had changed its mind and would welcome Trudeau's intervention.[58] He tackled External Affairs Minister Jamieson and Trudeau when they arrived in London a week later, convincing them that Canada should explore the issue with British prime minister James Callaghan and throw the government's weight behind Air Canada. During a long and relaxed dinner with the two prime ministers, Martin raised the move to Gatwick, underlining bwoth its economic impact and its "important political dimension." Callaghan vaguely acknowledged that the British "must avoid discrimination against Canada," a statement that Martin interpreted as indicating that there was some flexibility in the British position.[59] Lang and Jamieson agreed, and on Trudeau's return to Ottawa, the government decided to support formally Air Canada's opposition to the move.[60]

Martin's delight was short-lived. When Air Canada executives met British authorities in January, the latter demonstrated a good deal more resolve than their political masters. George Rogers disputed Martin's version of his conversation with Callaghan, insisting that the decision to move Air Canada was "irrevocable." In response, Canadian Transport officials urged Lang to suspend talks on the bilateral civil aviation agreement and link Air Canada's Heathrow tenancy to Britain's search for access to Western Canada. Martin strongly endorsed these views and went further. Convinced that British officials had misread their political leaders, he argued that the time had come to go public and scotch "this harmful rumour about Canadian passivity in the face of the British decision."[61]

Jamieson hesitated. He had developed a smooth working relationship with the British foreign secretary, David Owen, and he was reluctant to risk it by bringing the Air Canada dispute into the open. Ottawa's hand was forced when Rogers leaked word of the quarrel to the London-based *Financial Times*, underlining Britain's resolve and leaving its ministers no room to retreat. The Canadian reaction was swift and forceful. Jamieson instructed Martin to raise the matter at the political level in the FCO, which Martin accused of "unfriendly behaviour not normally expected from one's best friends."[62] In Ottawa, the government made it clear that as long as Air Canada might be moved to Gatwick, the British would not gain access to Western Canada.[63] The strength of its position was revealed a few days later when former Progressive Conservative prime minister John Diefenbaker, jowls aquiver, urged the House of Commons to pass a resolution "strongly objecting" to British policy.[64] Martin lost no time in alerting UK officials to the growing pressure on Trudeau's government not to back down.

He welcomed the strong signals coming from Ottawa and was also pleased with growing evidence of British uncertainty. In late January, Trade Minister John Smith assured a hostile questioner in the British House of Commons that "the transfer of Canadian services to Gatwick is still under discussion."[65] Later that month, senior British officials confessed to Martin that they were becoming apprehensive about the "potential damage" to UK-Canada bilateral relations.[66] Sir John Ford, the British high commissioner in Ottawa, even suggested suspending discussions for six months to ease tensions.[67] Clearly, Martin cabled Ottawa, this was not the moment to relax the effort.[68]

He maintained the pressure with two public appearances in March, "putting his case as bluntly as a diplomat can."[69] The effort drew quick plaudits from the *Toronto Globe and Mail,* which described it as "both lucid and tough," and a reaction from British foreign secretary Owen.[70] Meeting with Jamieson in New York, Owen wanted to smooth things over with a joint communiqué that affirmed Air Canada's move to Gatwick "in principle" and demonstrated British willingness to help the airline get the best deal possible.[71] This was not nearly enough, insisted Martin, though Owen's invitation to talk convinced him to recommend a pause in the Canadian campaign: "For the moment at least, we should give the British a chance to be our friends rather than assume they will be our enemies."[72]

The break was well timed. Overdue spring elections in both countries produced new governments, which needed time to settle in. Martin soon detected signs that Prime Minister Margaret Thatcher's Conservative government might reverse its predecessor's decision.[73] At the end of the long, hot summer of 1979, he ramped up the pressure again. He called the new Progressive Conservative foreign minister, Flora MacDonald, and Transport Minister Don Mazankowski, and with their backing he gave one final heave on Air Canada's behalf. "We could not move to Gatwick," he told British ministers, "and would not."[74] Armed with his reports, MacDonald herself raised the issue with British foreign secretary Peter Carrington.[75]

Martin pouted when he discovered that MacDonald had played the final round without him, but he was delighted to learn that Carrington was ready to deal. Air Canada's regular flights would remain at Heathrow, whereas extra charters would move to Gatwick. This seemed a sensible solution, and when Martin encountered former trade minister Edmund Dell at lunch at few days later, he crowed happily, "I'm going to win."[76] A week later, the British signalled their climb-down.

By then, it was time for Martin to go. Paul Jr. had urged him to retire a year earlier, but he had refused. The work was still too vital to abandon, and another year would qualify him for supplementary pension benefits. He sensed, however, the shifting order of the landmarks of his life. He had recently handed full control of his holding company, Nellmart, to Paul Jr., and he took leave in February of his sister Aline, the first of his adult siblings to die. His old law firm, Martin, Laird, Easton & Cowan, where he had not practised for decades, dropped his name from its letterhead. By the time Joe Clark's Progressive Conservatives were elected in May, he had already held the post of high commissioner for longer than usual. Clark, whom he admired, was entitled to his own political representative in London. Paul Martin left Britain at the end of October 1979.

PAUL AND NELL retired to their Windsor home on Ontario Street in late 1979. "This city was good to me and I wouldn't have gone anywhere else," he insisted.[77] Nell was happy to be back in her hometown, content to play cards with neighbours or settle down with an ancient "whodunnit" by Mary Roberts Rinehart or Agatha Christie. They rose early, pottered about, and delighted in the antics of Scampy, a little mutt who had overstayed his welcome with Sheila and Paul Jr. Martin, however, found the small city confining, and he escaped when he could. He and his old friends Michael Brogan and Clifford Hatch often drove through southwestern Ontario to attend political speeches and funerals, keeping in touch. They crossed to Detroit, where they browsed the Borders Bookstore, alert for bargains, and they watched the Tigers play baseball. Martin remained active in the Canadian Institute for Advanced Legal Studies at Cambridge, and every two years, he headed to Britain under the discreet but watchful eye of an accompanying friend or grandchild.

He ventured farther afield as well, travelling to China with Paul Jr. in the spring of 1986. Their arrival coincided with a visit by Progressive Conservative prime minister Brian Mulroney, who spotted Martin at an event for Canadian businessmen and showered him with praise. He loved the attention, but he saw through Mulroney's charm. "Of course," he laughed while admiring the prime minister's political skills, "he's full of crap."[78] At eighty-three, Martin was quicker than many to grasp the enormous scale of the pro-market reforms promoted by Chinese leader Deng Xiaoping. "Another revolution is underway," he wrote hopefully to his good friend and former advisor John Holmes. "Mao has not been purged, but corrected … A new liberation is on the way, one that will free the farmers and the millions in the cities."[79]

Martin especially enjoyed spending time with students, who were impressed by his first-hand knowledge of the century's most significant events and actors. He was an adjunct professor of political science at the University of Windsor and often appeared at campus events or hunkered down in the library to read. He gave a regular series of talks in the mid-1980s at McGill University, where he had clashed with anti-war protesters twenty years earlier. "There were no riots?" his son asked mischievously after one talk on the Vietnam War. "Most of them weren't even born," replied Martin.[80]

John Holmes and historian Robert Bothwell invited Martin to the University of Toronto to speak to their classes. University of Waterloo historian John English dispatched doctoral students Stephen Azzi and Angie Sauer to Windsor to discuss their dissertations with him. He quizzed them on Canadian history. When pressed for a speaker to address local gatherings of the Canadian Institute of International Affairs, English often turned to Martin, who was still able to fill an evening with just a few notes jotted on the back of an envelope. His staunch internationalism undimmed, he viewed the growing skepticism about the United Nations and the renewed Cold War of the early 1980s with alarm. "Our ingenuity should be [sic] to change our world so that no government would 'find it profitable to use force' to attain its international goals," he told audiences. "The US, the Soviet Union and others should return to the UN."[81]

Martin spent much of his retirement working on his memoirs, shaping his story and defending the legacy detailed in his massive foreign policy manuscript, "At the Right Hand of Power." During his London tenure, he had resisted pressure from publishers and friends to abandon the project in favour of more conventional memoirs. "The latter is a different book altogether," he maintained. "In the memoirs, I will not hesitate to be opinionated. In the foreign policy book, I write history and what could be more authentic than coming from the External Affairs minister of that period?"[82] By 1978, however, his "history" had been turned down by several major publishers, including Oxford, Macmillan, and Collins. Only Toronto's small Deneau Publishers showed any interest, and its owner, Denis Deneau, also insisted on traditional memoirs. Strongly encouraged by Paul Jr. to change course, Martin reluctantly merged the two projects in 1978, hiring historian Bill Young to help with the research. The aging minister, for whom appearances still mattered, quickly became good friends with the shaggy-haired academic. At home in Windsor, he spent the mornings in his ground-floor study, seated at an antique desk shipped down from Montreal, composing his memoirs in his large, spiky longhand, while Young hunted down references among his papers in Ottawa.

As he hurried to complete his memoirs, Martin knew that others were at work on his place in history. The Historical Division of External Affairs had started a "semi-official" departmental history in 1978, and by the early 1980s, draft chapters by historian Don Page were circulating among an informal academic advisory group. When Martin stumbled across a copy in August 1982 while visiting English in Waterloo, he "hit the roof."[83] His objections were twofold. He believed that interests trumped personality in making foreign policy, and he doubted the value of discussing individual temperaments. He was especially upset at the way in which Page had handled his own personality, which included the outrageous claim that Martin had indecisively allowed Nell to influence policy. He was soon on the phone. He called Holmes, one of the project's advisors, and his other Ottawa contacts. A critical story appeared in the *Ottawa Citizen,* written by columnist Jack Best, an old Martin crony.[84] He also called his Windsor protege, Mark MacGuigan, who was just leaving his post as secretary of state for external affairs. "There is a difference between liberty and licence," MacGuigan reminded Deputy Minister de Montigny Marchand, asking him to speak with Holmes and York University historian Jack Granatstein.[85]

Marchand did more than talk, summoning Ambassador Arthur Blanchette home from Tunis to review the entire project. Blanchette had known Martin since the 1950s and had served as chief historian in the early 1970s. He consulted widely with academics and the leading diplomats of Canada's postwar "Golden Age." No one accepted Martin's view that personalities didn't matter, but most agreed that Page's treatment of them was "unbalanced, unfair at times, and even biting."[86] By the time Martin's former colleague and MacGuigan's successor Allan MacEachen had finished, Page had been replaced by John Hilliker, and a formal editorial board under Holmes had been established to ensure a more balanced and responsible narrative. Martin could hardly have hoped for a better outcome.

Long before Holmes and Hilliker finished with the official account of External Affairs, Martin's own memoirs had begun to appear: the two volumes of *A Very Public Life* were published in 1983 and 1985, followed in 1988 by *The London Diaries*. To the end, Martin resisted the efforts of friends and journalists to persuade him to include the ribald stories from inside politics that made him such an engaging political raconteur over drinks in a faculty lounge or a hotel lobby. "There's too much of that garbage going around," he would reply. "I'm not getting down in the gutter ... It's not my style."[87] Sadly, his style echoed the Victorian-era biographies that had populated his Pembroke childhood. He tracked his every encounter with notable classmates and professors, diplomats and politicians, national and international figures, with a kind word for almost everyone. The memoirs lovingly reproduced lengthy passages from his major speeches on long-forgotten subjects, piling detail on detail and obscuring the urgent passion, liberal ideas, and political ambitions that shaped his career.

The reviews were polite and friendly. His prose was described as "clear and unadorned," and his career was clearly interesting and lively.[88] But reviewers, some refighting earlier long-finished battles, wondered about the lack of material drawn from the sharp end of Martin's political life and his decision to downplay his driving ambitions, prime ministerial and otherwise. His stiff pose in the memoirs and his refusal to lapse into anger or bitterness, deflecting setbacks with self-deprecating humour, confirmed his life-long reputation as a political operator. King's biographer, Blair Neatby, skipped lightly over the absence of politics in Martin's book, generously describing him as "a gentleman from an older school of decorum and civility."[89]

Others were less kind. Business journalist David Olive criticized Martin's "unconvincing guilelessness."[90] The charges were echoed by Montreal political scientist Dale Thomson, who had worked for Louis St. Laurent in the 1950s, and historian Ramsay Cook, who had backed Trudeau in 1968. Cook summed up the second volume as "an unsatisfying book because it leaves the politics out ... Something essential seems to remain unsaid."[91] Jack Pickersgill cruelly punctured Martin's claim to offer an authentic account of his career, warning readers that the memoirs were "not history, but the material of history."[92] Martin shrugged off his critics. His friends liked his memoirs, and he enjoyed flogging copies. The project left him with a genuine sense of accomplishment. "No expenditure of effort on my part was as heavy as what I put into the two volumes of A Very Public Life during the past six years," he sighed happily in a note to Holmes.[93]

Another legacy mattered to Martin – Paul Jr.'s political future. Through the late 1970s, Martin had continued to worry that Paul Jr. might enter politics too soon. "No news could have disturbed us more than that of your thinking of running in the next election," he wrote his son in March 1976, advising him not to do so.[94] He also discouraged Liberal Party members from recruiting his son. "My view is that now is not the time," he wrote MacGuigan, who was fired up by Paul Jr.'s speech to a Liberal policy convention in March 1977. "He ought to wait for a number of years until he is called."[95] For father and son, the subject was a sensitive one. "I will be prepared to be unemotional," Martin promised, raising the issue with Paul Jr. for discussion. "Will you?"[96] Paul Jr. proved more level-headed than his father expected, and the temptations of politics were offset by the attractions of family life and his career with Canada Steamship Lines. As the decade progressed and Martin became increasingly confident of his son's judgment, his fears abated. After discussing Paul Jr.'s ambitions during their annual fishing retreat in August 1979, he resolved to "be less of an obstacle if he points to political life."[97]

Martin backed his son wholeheartedly as he made the transition into Liberal politics during the mid-1980s. "His dedication was unbelievable," recalled John English, whom Martin strongly encouraged to seek the Liberal candidacy in Kitchener.[98] He attended the Liberal policy convention in November 1986 to support his son, who chaired an early-morning session on foreign policy. "He insisted I come," Martin quipped to the press. "I didn't even know it was on, and when I saw the time, I thought he was joking."[99] He turned up for his son's speeches and coached from the sidelines, like many parents. Peering out at his father's waving hands during a speech to Toronto's august Empire Club, Paul Jr. groaned with exasperation, "I don't know if I'm speaking too fast or too slow."[100] Fortified with a new pacemaker, Martin made it down to Montreal, cheering enthusiastically as Paul Jr. was nominated as the Liberal candidate in LaSalle–Émard for the 1988 federal election.

He marshalled all his fading energies and political contacts to support his son's first run for the Liberal Party leadership in 1990. Accompanied by Michael Brogan and Fred Quenneville, who had helped him fight his political battles since the 1940s, he toured southwestern Ontario, signing up new members and talking to key Liberals and potential delegates. The elderly crew was exhausted at the end of a full day of vote getting. "It was wonderful," recalled Quenneville's wife, Barbara, of this last campaign.[101]

The results were mixed. Paul Jr. did poorly in most of southwestern Ontario, except Kitchener–Waterloo. The contest for Windsor was particularly bitter and hard-fought. Martin's riding of Essex East had disappeared in 1968, and after several redistributions, its constituent parts were scattered across Essex Windsor, which included much of former agriculture minister Eugene Whelan's old territory, and Windsor–St. Clair. Paul Jr.'s rivalry with front-runner Jean Chrétien was reinforced by ancient tensions between Martin and Whelan, who backed the favourite. When Chrétien won the Essex Windsor delegates in February, Whelan pointed across the room to Martin and said, "Most of these people here tonight don't even know who he is. I think it's a shame to have him sitting here."[102] The tables turned the next night in Windsor–St. Clair, which elected twelve delegates who were pledged to Paul Jr. "The old riding has stuck with me since 1935," shouted Martin. "Now my riding has stuck by him."[103]

Martin closely followed his son's national campaign as Paul Jr. lost further ground to Chrétien through the winter and spring. He frequently called campaign headquarters, asking the only question that mattered: "Is it getting worse?"[104] It was. On 23 June 1990, his eighty-seventh birthday, Martin sat with English and his wife, Hilde, as he watched his son lose to Jean Chrétien.

·PAUL MARTIN DID not live to see his son's political career revive and flourish. His formidable memory and physical strength were fast disappearing. He was too weak to travel to Ottawa in July 1992, when Prime Minister

Mulroney awarded him the title of "Right Honourable," an honour usually reserved for federal chief justices, governors general, and prime ministers. After breaking a hip in mid-August, he suffered a heart attack a month later and died at Windsor's Hôtel-Dieu Hospital on 14 September 1992. He was eighty-nine.

There were tributes by political leaders from across Canada and warm editorials in the Ontario papers. The *Toronto Star,* a faithful companion in the battles of Liberalism since the 1930s, was unstinting in its admiration, celebrating Martin as "a giant of Canadian politics."[105] A Canadian Forces plane delivered twenty-eight parliamentarians to Our Lady of Assumption Church for the funeral, a last chance to proclaim the values, personal and social, that mattered most to Paul Martin. His family, Nell, Mary Anne, and Paul Jr., the eulogist, were prominent. The federal government was represented by Trade Minister Michael Wilson, and Premier Bob Rae and Lieutenant Governor Hal Jackman represented Ontario. The Catholic Church was there in force: four bishops, a dozen priests, and an honour guard of seventy-five Knights of Columbus, decked out in black suits and red capes. "Mr. Martin was a titan," former Liberal Party leader John Turner remarked on his way into the church. "He really towered above the political process for half a century."[106]

That Turner was right has not always been clear to Canadians. Paul Martin was easy to lampoon, and his dramatic and outsized character generated a stream of amusing anecdotes, which obscured more than they revealed of his true nature and significance. There is no doubt that he was a professional and practical politician. But he celebrated politics as an instrument that could bring individual citizens together to reach shared goals. A member of Canada's French-speaking and Catholic minority, he matured in a culture that embraced accommodation, compromise, and tolerance as key political virtues. He held strong Liberal partisan views but preached and practised a tolerant and civil politics that tried to unite Canadians.

His critics attacked his willingness to compromise and deal, his political ambitions, and his use of patronage and bare-knuckle politics, unfairly casting him as an unprincipled operator. Yet there was nothing shabby or suspect about Martin's political career, which, in the best Catholic tradition, he embraced as a vocation. "I am not afraid to be called a politician," he often declared. "Next to preaching the word of God, there is nothing nobler than to serve one's fellow countrymen in government."[107]

Among the most skilled retail politicians of his age, Martin was also one of its most thoughtful. He inherited a traditional French Canadian attachment to Sir Wilfrid Laurier's Liberal Party. As a student, however, he deliberately rooted his heritage deeply in the Western philosophic tradition, reinforcing it by a lifetime of reading. He drew from the liberalism of John Stuart Mill and the social teachings of the Catholic Church and its leading thinkers, Thomas Aquinas, Pope Leo XIII, and John Henry Newman, to fashion a reformist and liberal politics that summoned the state to reinforce the dignity and value of the individual against both unbridled free-market capitalism and the authoritarian state. Only strong and forceful government action, he insisted, could provide citizens with the necessary framework to protect individual liberty and the rights of workers, to provide ready access to post-secondary education, and to supply pensions and health care. Properly constituted, Martin's ideal government was a progressive mechanism of social equality, citizen engagement, and individual liberation.

He also thought hard about Canada's place in the world, offering Canadians a distinctly liberal view of their country's global obligations. Like individuals, nations ought to be free to work out their own destinies, ultimately sustained by the rule of law and world government. Inspired by this distant and impossible dream during the bleakest years of the dishonest 1930s, Martin backed notions of citizenship that freed Canadians from the vestiges of imperial Britain. He also embraced the postwar ideals of global citizenship. The United Nations promised a world free from war and want, and he believed that Canada had a duty to help build its promised new order. Occasionally naive about the world around him and often tempted to overreach himself, Martin tackled the task with a dogged faith in the value of endless dialogue, patient compromise, and the possibility of progress. This was neither easy nor fashionable, especially in the urgent and passionate 1960s, though his internationalism remained unshakeable to the end.

Simply put, at home and abroad, Paul Martin embodied both his church's call to action and humankind's obligation to fashion a more just and equitable world.

NOTES

PREFACE

1 Quoted in "Peacekeeping Use Not Over," *Regina Leader Post*, 23 May 1967.

CHAPTER 1: SWEET PAUL, 1903–30

1 Research Notes, Martin Papers, vol. 360, file: Martin Family, Library and Archives Canada (LAC).
2 Author interview with Anita Martin and Claire Guay, 17 April 2007; Robert Bothwell and John English interview with Paul Martin, 1 November 1974, Bothwell Papers, University of Toronto Archives (UTA).
3 Martin, *Far from Home*, 27.
4 Bothwell and English interview with Martin, 1 November 1974, Bothwell Papers, UTA.
5 Baedeker, *The Dominion of Canada*, 231–32.
6 Norah Story interview with Paul Martin, [1969–70], Martin Papers, vol. 351, tape 2, side 1, LAC.
7 Tom Hazlitt, "Martin and His Memories Return to Sleepy Pembroke," *Toronto Star*, 6 March 1968.
8 Harold Dingman, "Personality: Paul Martin," *New Liberty*, September 1948, 63.
9 Author interview with Anita Martin and Claire Guay, 17 April 2007.
10 Story interview with Martin, [1969–70], Martin Papers, vol. 354, tape 17, side 2, LAC.
11 "Paul Martin, as Child, Loved to Make Speeches," *Ottawa Journal*, 1 February 1945; author interview with Anita Martin and Claire Guay, 17 April 2007.
12 Story interview with Martin, [1969–70], Martin Papers, vol. 351, tape 1, side 1, LAC.
13 Bothwell and English interview with Martin, 11 November 1974, Bothwell Papers, UTA.
14 Jean-François Pelletier, "Le Saint-Alexandre d'il y a soixante-dix ans." See also Gilbert, *La vie a St-Alexandre*.

15 Martin, *Far from Home*, 19.
16 Martin to Nell Martin, [July 1942], Martin Papers, vol. 184, file: Letters to Mrs P Martin, LAC.
17 Bothwell and English interview with Martin, 1 November 1974, Bothwell Papers, UTA.
18 Story interview with Martin, [1969–70], Martin Papers, vol. 351, tape 2, side 1, LAC.
19 Martin's application for admission, 29 August 1921, UTA.
20 Josephine Phelan, Draft Memoirs, Phelan Papers, box 1, file 9, LAC.
21 Henry Carr, "Playground Changes," in *St. Michael's College Yearbook*, vol. 12, 1921–22, University of St. Michael's College Archives (USMC Archives); McCorkell, *Memoirs*, 57.
22 Norah Story, "Jottings on St Mike's," Martin Papers, vol. 361, LAC.
23 Bothwell and English interview with Martin, 1 November 1974, Bothwell Papers, UTA.
24 McGowan, *The Waning of the Green*, 143–47.
25 McCorkell, *Henry Carr*, 27; Shook, *Catholic Post-Secondary Education*, 134–35.
26 English, *Shadow of Heaven*, 117–18.
27 McGowan, *The Waning of the Green*, 70–80.
28 Hogan, "Salted with Fire."
29 Shook, *Catholic Post-Secondary Education*, 161–62; Owens, *The Philosophical Tradition of St. Michael's College*, 19–21.
30 Owens, *The Philosophical Tradition of St. Michael's College*, 22–23.
31 Martin, *Far from Home*, 31; Phelan, Draft Memoirs, Phelan Papers, LAC.
32 Shook, *Catholic Post-Secondary Education*, 160.
33 Martin, *Far from Home*, 37.
34 Quoted in Michael Higgins, "Cardinal John Henry Newman: A Modern Christian," *Toronto Globe and Mail*, 18 September 2010.
35 Martin, *Far from Home*, 47–48.
36 "The Hon Paul Martin Notes the Timeliness of Newman," *Catholic Record*, 20 and 27 October 1945.
37 *SMC Year Book*, vol. 14, 1922–23, USMC Archives.
38 McCorkell, *Henry Carr*, 29. He probably meant "football."
39 *SMC Year Book*, vol. 15, 1923–24, 123, USMC Archives.
40 *SMC Year Book*, vol. 14, 1922–23, USMC Archives.
41 "Terrible Tragedy Narrowly Averted," *The Varsity*, 18 January 1923; "Changes Take Place in St Mike's Parliament," *The Varsity*, 27 February 1923.
42 Callaghan, *The Varsity Story*, 89.
43 "Varsity Wins Debate at Toronto," *The Varsity*, [February 1923], Martin Papers, vol. 101, Scrapbook, LAC.
44 Callaghan, *The Varsity Story*, 124.
45 *SMC Year Book*, vol. 16, 1924–25, 53–53, USMC Archives.
46 Phelan, Draft Memoirs, 73, Phelan Papers, LAC; Callaghan, *The Varsity Story*, 126.
47 The nickname is used in correspondence between Martin classmates. See "Cal" to Frank Flaherty, 14 February 1932, Flaherty Papers, vol. 24, file: Pers. Corr., LAC; see also *SMC Year Book*, vol. 16, 1924–25, 26, USMC Archives.
48 Martin to Frank Flaherty, 14 April 1930, Flaherty Papers, vol. 24, file: Pers. Corrs., LAC.

49 Phelan, Draft Memoirs, 73, Phelan Papers, LAC; author interview with Gordon Robertson, 5 November 2007.
50 Henry Carr to Martin, 28 April 1947, Martin Papers, vol. 151, file: 1946–47, LAC.
51 Bissell, *The Young Vincent Massey*, 58–62.
52 Callaghan, *The Varsity* Story, 6.
53 Martin, *Far from Home*, 32.
54 Bothwell and English interview with Martin, 1 November 1974, Bothwell Papers, UTA.
55 Burgon Bickersteth to Mother and Father, 2 February 1936, Bickersteth Papers, box 2, UTA.
56 Burgon Bickersteth to W.L.M. King, 8 December 1929, King Papers, microfilm reel C-2308, 135746, LAC.
57 Donald MacRae to Roscoe Pound, 8 September 1928, Martin Papers, vol. 151, file 1946–47, LAC.
58 "Pembroke Student Outlines Views of Present Day University Men," *Pembroke Standard-Observer*, n.d., Martin Papers, vol. 149, clipping in Scrapbook, LAC.
59 Martin, *Far from Home*, 41; "Constitution Still Safe: Varsity Students Approve," *Toronto Telegram*, 12 November 1924.
60 McGowan, *The Waning of the Green*, 13.
61 "Pembroke Student Outlines Views," Martin Papers, LAC.
62 Ibid.
63 Ibid.
64 Fleming, *So Very Near*, 1:53.
65 Bothwell and English interview with Martin, 11 November 1974, Bothwell Papers, UTA.
66 "The Hon Paul Martin Notes the Timeliness of Newman," *Catholic Record*, 20 and 27 October 1945.
67 "Pembroke Boy Led Varsity Team to Brilliant Victory in Debate," *Toronto Globe*, 9 February 1926.
68 *The Torch*, March 1926, UTA.
69 Martin Papers, vol. 149, LAC.
70 "Martin Liberal Nominee," *Ottawa Journal*, 4 June 1928.
71 Story interview with Martin, [1969–70], Martin Papers, vol. 351, tape 1, side 2, LAC.
72 "Service or Self-Interest?," *Toronto Globe*, 5 June 1928.
73 Martin Diary, 5 and 19 June 1928, Martin Papers, vol. 184, file: Diaries and Notebooks, LAC.
74 "Prime Factor in By-Elections Is Wage Situation," *Pembroke Standard-Observer*, 13 June 1928.
75 Martin Diary, 12 and 22 June 1928, Martin Papers, LAC.
76 Quoted in "Warmly Denies He Is Sponsor of Low Wages," *Ottawa Journal*, 16 June 1928.
77 "Did Pembroke's Industries Just Grow Here?," *Pembroke Standard-Observer*, 11 June 1928.
78 "Dunlop Will Be Elected: Everything Points to a Landslide," *Pembroke Standard-Observer*, 26 June 1928; "Paul Martin, as Child."
79 "Dunlop Sweeps North Renfrew – Majority 2112," *Pembroke Standard-Observer*, 28 June 1928.

80 Bothwell and English interview with Martin, 11 November 1974, Bothwell Papers, UTA.

81 Martin Diary, 27–28 June 1928, Martin Papers, LAC.

82 "A Coming Young Man," *Ottawa Journal,* 28 June 1928.

83 Martin Diary, 22 July 1928, Martin Papers, LAC.

84 Story interview with Martin, [1969–70], Martin Papers, vol. 351, tape 3, side 1, LAC; Martin, *Far from Home,* 69.

85 Donald MacRae to Roscoe Pound, 8 September 1928, Martin Papers, vol. 151, file: December 1946 to December 1947, LAC.

86 Ibid., 24 September 1928; and Pound to MacRae, 12 September 1928, Martin Papers, vol. 151, file: December 1946 to December 1947, LAC.

87 Bothwell and English interview with Martin, 11 November 1974, Bothwell Papers, UTA.

88 Martin to Burgon Bickersteth, 28 September 1928, Bickersteth Papers, file 46, UTA.

89 Ibid., [Christmas 1928].

90 Ibid., 28 September 1928.

91 Ibid., [Christmas 1928].

92 Martin, *Far from Home,* 76.

93 Paul Martin's Harvard transcripts, issued to author, 17 September 2009.

94 Burgon Bickersteth to Vincent Massey, 6 March 1929, Bickersteth Papers, file 83, UTA; Burgon Bickersteth, "Statement re Paul Martin," 2 May 1929, Bickersteth Papers, file 46, UTA.

95 Martin to Burgon Bickersteth, 6 March 1929, Bickersteth Papers, file 46, UTA.

96 Although Martin claims otherwise in *Far from Home,* 82–83, suggesting that others propelled him to Cambridge, the correspondence in the Bickersteth Papers, file 46, reveals how closely he was involved in directing the search for a scholarship.

97 Martin to Burgon Bickersteth, [February 1929], Bickersteth Papers, file 46, UTA; Martin to Vincent Massey, 8 March 1929, Bickersteth Papers, box 83, UTA.

98 Martin to Burgon Bickersteth, 1 May 1929, Bickersteth Papers, file 46, UTA.

99 Martin to Frank Flaherty, 24 November 1929, Flaherty Papers, vol. 24, file: Pers. Corrs., LAC.

100 Ibid.

101 Martin Papers, vol. 187, file: Souvenirs, LAC.

102 "The Union Society," *Cambridge Review,* 9 May 1930.

103 Martin to Flaherty, 24 November 1929, Flaherty Papers, LAC.

104 Story interview with Martin, [1969–70], Martin Papers, vol. 351, tape 2, side 1, LAC.

105 Martin, *Far from Home,* 93.

106 Story interview with Martin, [1969–70], Martin Papers, vol. 351, tape 2, side 1, LAC; Rich, "Alfred Zimmern's Cautious Idealism."

107 Martin to Frank Flaherty, 14 April 1930, Flaherty Papers, vol. 24, file: Pers. Corr., LAC.

108 Martin to W.L.M. King, [26] August 1930, King Papers, microfilm reel C-2320, 151630–32, LAC.

109 Story interview with Martin, [1969–70], Martin Papers, vol. 351, tape 3, side 1, LAC.

110 Paul Martin, "Philosophy of Internationalism" (paper presented at the ninth annual meeting of the American Catholic Philosophical Association, Duquesne University, Pittsburgh, 28 December 1933), 1, 4, and 13.

CHAPTER 2: THE YOUNG POLITICIAN, 1930–39

1 Price and Kulisek, *Windsor*, 91.
2 Gervais, *The Rumrunners*.
3 Price and Kulisek, *Windsor*, 98.
4 Robert Bothwell interview with Paul Martin, 16 November 1974, Bothwell Papers, University of Toronto Archives (UTA). Population statistics from Historydetroit.com, "Detroit History: Statistically Speaking," n.d., http://historydetroit.com/statistics/.
5 Norah Story interview with Paul Martin, [1969–70], Martin Papers, vol. 351, tape 1, side 1, Library and Archives Canada (LAC).
6 Robert Bothwell and John English interview with Paul Martin, 11 November 1974, Bothwell Papers, UTA.
7 Martin to Frank Flaherty, 11 December 1930, Flaherty Papers, vol. 24, file: Pers. Corr., LAC.
8 Ibid., 17 October 1931.
9 Martin impressed Macphail, both for the forum's "openness" and as "a brilliant young lawyer." See Pennington, *Agnes Macphail*, 143.
10 "Mr. Guthrie Tonight," *Windsor Daily Star*, 31 November 1931.
11 For examples of Martin's positions, see "The Problems of War Debts," transcript of an address on CKCK Radio, 22 January 1933, Martin Papers, vol. 102, LAC; "Belief in Collective System Is Only Remedy for Bruised World," *London Advertiser*, 18 February 1933; "Blames Britain and USA for Re-Armament," *Sarnia Canadian Observer*, 15 May 1934.
12 "Dionne Row Ironed Out," *Windsor Daily Star*, 28 February 1935.
13 "Prepared to Fight," *Windsor Daily Star*, 23 February 1935.
14 Quoted in Bissell, *The Young Vincent* Massey, 217.
15 Story interview with Martin, [1969–70], vol. 351, tape 3, side 2, LAC.
16 Bissell, *The Young Vincent* Massey, 216.
17 W.L.M. King Diary, 5 August 1932, LAC.
18 Ibid., 20 July 1933.
19 Martin to W.L.M. King, 4 October 1935; and W.L.M. King to Martin, 4 October 1935, King Papers, C-2330–31, LAC; Martin to W.L.M. King, 28 February 1933; and W.L.M. King to Martin, 3 March 1935, King Papers, C-3674–75, LAC.
20 King Diary, 7 October 1935, LAC.
21 Saywell, *'Just Call Me Mitch,'* 51–52, 55.
22 Ibid., 57.
23 Quoted in ibid., 107.
24 Quoted in "More Disclosures on Bonds Forecast," *Toronto Mail and Empire*, 11 April 1933.
25 "Liberal Predicts New Revelations," *Toronto Globe*, 10 April 1933.
26 "Chick Challenged on Wages Paid," *Windsor Daily Star*, [June 1934].
27 "Big Sum to Defeat Clark," *Windsor Daily Star*, 14 June 1934. See also Saywell, *'Just Call Me Mitch,'* 153n31.
28 Martin, *Far from Home*, 130.
29 "Nomination Battles Seen," *Windsor Daily Star*, 6 February 1935.

30 Quoted in "Enthusiastic Support Is Tendered Paul Martin," *Windsor Daily Star*, 7 June 1935.
31 Quoted in "Dr Gardner Openly Accuses Paul Martin," *Windsor Daily Star*, 7 June 1935.
32 "Enthusiastic Support."
33 "Grit Candidates Go to the Mat at House Meeting," *Windsor Daily Star*, [April 1935].
34 "Paul Martin Liberal Candidate in Essex," Canadian Press Report, *Windsor Daily Star*, 8 June 1935.
35 "Paul Martin Wins Grit Nomination on Third Ballot," *Windsor Daily Star*, 10 June 1935.
36 R.F. Benoit to W.L.M. King, 8 June 1935, King Papers, microfilm reel C-3678, 174507, LAC; E.A. Pickering to Mr King, 11 June 1935 and 13 June 1935; W.L.M. King's marginal note; and draft letter, W.L.M. King to Martin, 10 June 1935, King Papers, microfilm reel C-3682, 179747–51, LAC.
37 Quoted in "Retirement Plan Derided," *Windsor Daily Star*, 13 September 1935.
38 Quoted in "Must Pay Attention to Needs of Youth States Paul Martin," *Windsor Daily Star*, 30 July 1935; "Puts Query to His Opponent," *Windsor Daily Star*, 4 October 1935.
39 Quoted in "Hecklers Are Busy at Conservative-Liberal Debate," *Windsor Daily Star*, 7 October 1935.
40 Quoted in "Tory Scorns New Parties," *Windsor Daily Star*, 3 October 1935.
41 "Mr Martin Shows Ability to Take It"; "Paul Waits on Last Poll"; "Four Candidates Lose Deposits," *Windsor Daily Star*, 15 October 1935.
42 Vincent Massey Diary, 24 October 1935, Massey Papers, vol. 30, UTA.
43 Burgon Bickersteth to Mother and Father, 20 October 1935, Bickersteth Papers, vol. 2, UTA.
44 Bothwell interview with Paul Martin, 1 November 1974, Bothwell Papers, UTA.
45 Story interview with Martin, [1969–70], Martin Papers, vol. 351, tape 1, side 2, LAC.
46 Ibid.
47 Martin to F.D. Austin, 6 July 1937, Martin Papers, vol. 1, file: Roseland Post Office, 1936–45, LAC.
48 Author interview with Trevor Price, 2 September 2007.
49 Ibid.
50 Confidential interview.
51 Author interview with Gordon Robertson, 5 November 2007.
52 Author interview with Barbara Quenneville, 20 August 2007.
53 Martin, *Far from Home*, 212. See also Martin to Edgar Markham, 2 November 1935, Martin Papers, vol. 1, file: Belle River Post Office, 1935–38, LAC.
54 Martin to C.D. Howe, Minister of Transport, 27 July 1936, Martin Papers, vol. 1, file: Gordon, C.B., LAC; on contracts, see also Martin to J.C. Hunter, Deputy Minister of Public Works, 11 January 1936; Martin to P.J.A. Cardin, Minister of Public Works, 12 August 1936; and Martin to D.M. Allan, Private Secretary to the Minister of Agriculture, 6 July 1937, Martin Papers, vol. 1, file: Gordon, C.B., LAC.
55 Martin to Keystone Contractors, 29 May 1936, Martin Papers, vol. 1, LAC.
56 Martin to H.F. Bennett, 28 June 1940, Martin Papers, vol. 3, file: Public Works, 1938–1940, LAC. See also Martin to H.F. Bennett, 29 June 1940; and Martin to J.D. Renaud, 6 July and 22 July 1939, Martin Papers, vol. 3, file: Public Works, 1938–1940, LAC.

57 Edgar Markham to Martin, 15 October 1935, Martin Papers, vol. 1, file: Belle River Post Office, 1935–38, LAC.

58 See correspondence in Martin Papers, vol. 3, file: Maidstone Post Office, LAC.

59 "Gives Opinions on Commuting," *Windsor Daily* Star, 5 November 1935; "Pleased," *Windsor Daily Star*, 12 November 1935; "Inquiry to Be Resumed Next Month," *Windsor Daily Star*, 21 November 1935.

60 "Up to Motor Industry Now," *Windsor Daily Star*, 22 November 1935.

61 "Corn Growers Assail South African Treaty," *Windsor Daily Star*, 30 October 1935; "To Undertake Corn Probe," *Windsor Daily Star*, 16 December 1935; "Dr. Grisdale Stresses Need for Organization," *Windsor Daily Star*, 7 February 1936.

62 Martin to Brooke Claxton, 20 February 1936, Claxton Papers, vol. 19, file: Nominal Correspondence, 1931–39, LAC.

63 Canada, *House of Commons Debates* (18 June 1936), 3879–85.

64 "Gaining a Semi-Convert," *Windsor Daily Star*, 25 June 1936; "A Brilliant Maiden Speech," *Windsor Daily Star*, 25 June 1936.

65 W.L.M. King to Martin, 18 June 1936, Martin Papers, vol. 121, Scrapbooks, 82, LAC.

66 Macphail to Martin, 18 June 1936, Martin Papers, vol. 121, Scrapbooks, 83, LAC.

67 Story interview with Nell Martin, 8 April 1969, Martin Papers, vol. 351, tape 4, side 2, LAC; author interview with Michael Maloney, 21 August 2007; Joanne Strong, "The Informal Nell Martin," *Toronto Globe and Mail*, 18 June 1973; Paul Martin Jr., *Hell or High Water*, 1–2.

68 Story interview with Nell Martin, 8 April 1969, Martin Papers, vol. 351, tape 4, side 2, LAC.

69 Martin to Nell Martin, [13 June] 1938, Martin Papers, vol. 184, file: Letters to Mrs Paul Martin, LAC.

70 Ibid., [June] 1938.

71 Ibid., 9 June 1938.

72 Story interview with Nell Martin, 8 April 1969, Martin Papers, vol. 351, tape 4, side 2, LAC.

73 Author interview with Barbara Quenneville, 20 August 2007.

74 Paul Martin Jr., *Hell or High Water*, 9–10.

75 M.J. Coldwell, Draft Memoirs, Coldwell Papers, vol. 58, file: Memoirs 17–32, LAC.

76 "Essex East Member Is Moving Up," *Canadian Business Magazine*, [1943].

77 Author interview with Basil Robinson, 15 July 2006.

78 Quoted in Strong, "The Informal Nell Martin."

79 George Davidson to Martin, 15 June 1951, Martin Papers, vol. 11, LAC.

80 Martin to Inspector of Income Tax, 20 February 1935, Martin Papers, vol. 421, LAC.

81 Lumina Martin to Nell Martin, 2 July 1938, Martin Papers, vol. 184, file: Letters to Mrs Paul Martin, LAC.

82 Martin to Nell Martin, [summer 1938], vol. 184, file: Letters to Mrs Paul Martin, LAC.

83 Exchange with C.D. Howe, Canada, *House of Commons Debates* (24 February 1938), 783–84; exchange with Charles Dunning, Canada, *House of Commons Debates* (12 April 1939), 2716–18.

84 Canada, *House of Commons Debates* (10 February 1939), 823–33, and (23 March 1939), 2185.

85 Ibid. (16 March 1938), 1383–90.
86 On appeals to the Privy Council, see ibid. (8 April 1938), 2186–96; on the amendment to the Post Office Act, see ibid. (23 May 1938), 4435–36.
87 Ibid. (17 June 1938), 3992–94.
88 Bothwell and English interview with Martin, 11 November 1974, Bothwell Papers, UTA.
89 Neatby, *William Lyon Mackenzie King*, 174–76.
90 King Diary, 28 September 1936, LAC.
91 Martin, "King: The View from the Backbench," 33.
92 W.L.M. King Diary, 28 September 1936, LAC.
93 Ibid., 29 September 1936.
94 Martin to W.L.M. King, [1 October 1938], King Papers, microfilm reel C-3691, 191215, LAC.
95 W.L.M. King to Martin, 5 October 1936, King Papers, microfilm reel C-3691, 191216, LAC.
96 Martin, *So Many Worlds*, 188.
97 Martin to J.W. Dafoe, 28 October 1936, Dafoe Papers, July-December 1936, microfilm reel M-77, LAC.
98 Canada, *House of Commons Debates* (9 February 1937), 700.
99 Martin to Howard Henry (King's private secretary), 19 July 1937 and attachment, King Papers, microfilm reel C-3727, 204672–75, LAC.
100 Canada, *House of Commons Debates* (25 March and 1 April 1938), 1732–37 and 1922–30. See also Martin, *Far from Home*, 197–98, which offers a badly distorted view of this speech. On Reid's article, see Granatstein, "Becoming Difficult," 18.
101 King Diary, 25 March 1938, LAC.
102 "Party Health Seen in Bickerings of King and Hepburn," *Toronto Globe and Mail*, 19 April 1938.
103 King Diary, 21 April 1938, LAC.
104 Ibid.
105 Martin to W.L.M. King, 18 July 1938, King Papers, microfilm reel C-3776, 217141, LAC.
106 King Diary, 27 July 1938, LAC; E.J. Tarr to W.L.M. King, 27 July 1938; and W.L.M. King to E.J. Tarr, 27 July 1938, King Papers, microfilm reel C-3740, 222193–95, LAC; Martin to W.L.M. King, 3 November 1938, King Papers, microfilm reel C-3775, 217148–51, LAC.
107 Martin to Nell Martin, 27 September 1938, Martin Papers, vol. 184, LAC.
108 Ibid., [October 1938].
109 Martin to W.L.M. King, 25 October 1938, King Papers, microfilm reel C-3736, 217148–49, LAC.
110 Martin to Nell Martin, 8 June 1939, Martin Papers, vol. 184, LAC.

CHAPTER 3: A CONQUERED WORLD, 1939–45

1 Martin to Nell Martin, [12 September 1939], Martin Papers, vol. 184, Library and Archives Canada (LAC).
2 Ibid., [6 September 1939].
3 Ibid., [7 September 1939].

4 Quoted in Bothwell and Kilbourn, *C.D. Howe*, 123.

5 Granatstein, *Canada's War*, 28–35.

6 Bothwell and Kilbourn, *C.D. Howe*, 126.

7 Martin to Russell Simon, 24 February 1940, Martin Papers, vol. 2, file: Post Office Roseland, 1936–41, LAC.

8 Quoted in "Paul Martin in Challenge," *Windsor Daily Star*, 6 March 1940. This paragraph also draws on the following *Windsor Daily Star* articles: "Says Rival Desperate," 2 March 1940; "Tory 'Trick' Is Assailed," 5 March 1940; "Tells about Youth Aid," 7 March 1940; "Martin Sees Tory Split," 8 March 1940; "Sees Neglect of Promises," 8 March 1940; "Aid to Youth Commended," 9 March 1940; "Country Corn Aid Is Cited," 9 March 1940; "Hall Jammed in Tecumseh," 12 March 1940; "Urges Sound Pay Security," 22 March 1940.

9 For the national results, see Beck, *The Pendulum of Power*, 238–39.

10 Martin to Nell Martin, [May 1940], Martin Papers, vol. 184, LAC.

11 Ibid.

12 "Programme of Immediate Canadian Action Drawn Up by a Group of Twenty Canadians," 17–18 July 1940, Records of the League of Nations Society, vol. 11, file: Copies of Articles, Reports, Speeches, etc. 1939–41, LAC. I would like to thank Boris Stipernitz for insisting on this meeting's importance.

13 Austin Cross, "From Lennoxville to Parliament Hill," *Canada's Weekly*, 12 December 1947.

14 Martin, *Far from Home*, 263.

15 Martin to Nell Martin, 8 July 1940, Martin Papers, vol. 184, LAC.

16 Granatstein, *Canada's War*, 106–7.

17 Martin to Art Reaume, 27 November 1950, Martin Papers, vol. 415, file: 204 Roselawn, LAC.

18 Confidential interview.

19 Martin tax returns, Martin Papers, vol. 418, LAC.

20 F.J. Buck, Bank of Montreal, to Martin, 23 March 1943, Martin Papers, vol. 415, LAC.

21 Canada, *House of Commons Debates* (26 November 1940), 412–17; Canada, *House of Commons Debates* (4 June 1941), 3498–3502.

22 "Will Meet Paul Martin," and "No Questionnaires," *Windsor Daily Star*, 10 April 1941.

23 "Hi-Jacking Says Howe," *Windsor Daily Star*, 1 October 1941.

24 Quoted in "Martin Calls for Sacrifice," *Windsor Daily Star*, 20 October 1941.

25 "Put the Members to Work," *Windsor Daily Star*, 10 June 1941.

26 Martin to Nell Martin, [November 1941], Martin Papers, vol. 184, LAC.

27 Ibid.

28 See, for instance, Canada, *House of Commons Debates* (19 and 26 March 1942), 1453–55 and 1678–79.

29 W.L.M. King to Martin, 15 June 1942, King Papers, microfilm reel C-6809, 280613, LAC.

30 L.B. Pearson, cited in Brennan, *Reporting the Nation's Business*, 63.

31 Martin to W.L.M. King, 24 April 1942; and W.L.M. King's marginal note to Mr. Turnbull, 2 May 1942, King Papers, microfilm reel C-8609, 280610–11; Martin to Nell Martin, [May 1942], Martin Papers, vol. 184, LAC.

32 Martin to Nell Martin, 28 June 1942, Martin Papers, vol. 184, LAC.

33 Pickersgill, *The Mackenzie King Record*, 375–76.

34 W.L.M. King Diary, 24 September 1942, LAC.

35 Canada, *House of Commons Debates* (20 April 1943), 2345.

36 See, for example, the Canadian Press report reprinted in "Paul Martin Is Mentioned," *Windsor Daily Star*, 11 February 1943.

37 "Cabinet Assistants," *Windsor Daily Star*, 21 April 1943; see also "Sharing the Load," *London Free Press*, 6 May 1943.

38 Quoted in Saywell, *"Just Call Me Mitch,"* 506.

39 Martin to W.L.M. King, 1 May 1943, King Papers, microfilm reel C-7041, 298058–59, LAC.

40 W.L.M. King to Martin, 4 May 1943, King Papers, microfilm reel C-7041, 298060, LAC.

41 King Diary, 7 May 1943, LAC.

42 Martin, *Far from Home*, 358.

43 "Essex East Member Is Moving Up," reprinted from *Canadian Business Magazine* [1943], Martin Papers, vol. 150, file: Clippings, 1939–46; "Well Up the Political Ladder," *Saturday* Night, 31 July 1943.

44 Figures cited in Lewis, *The Good Fight*, 209.

45 Granatstein, *Canada's War*, 279.

46 Martin to W.L.M. King, 26 August 1943, King Papers, microfilm reel C-7041, 298063–63A; King Diary, 28 August 1943, LAC.

47 J.W. Pickersgill to Martin, 17 December 1943, King Papers, microfilm reel C-7041, 298090, LAC.

48 See, for example, "Democratic System Aim," *Le Devoir* (Montreal), 6 July 1943; "Dans le monde ouvrir," *Le Devoir*, 20 September 1943.

49 Quoted in "New Approach to Labour," *Toronto Globe and Mail*, 16 November 1943.

50 See, for example, "Paul Martin Reviews War Labor Policies," *Windsor Daily Star*, 20 January 1944.

51 For statistics, see "Government Alive to Labor's Needs," *Regina Leader-Post*, 15 December 1943; see also, "First Postwar Aim Is Public Welfare," *Montreal Gazette*, 30 November 1943; "Foreshadows New Rights for Labor," *Winnipeg Free Press*, 21 January 1944.

52 "Resources to Determine Peace: Martin," *Toronto Globe and Mail*, 11 December 1943; "World League Required to Avoid Future Wars," *Brantford Expositor*, 21 January 1944; "Urges Using Charter Model," *Ottawa Journal*, 20 February 1944.

53 See "Mr Martin, M.P., on Labour Problems," *The Canadian Register*, 30 September 1944; "Is This True?," *Ottawa Evening Journal*, 3 April 1944.

54 Norman Robertson's marginalia on London to Ottawa, Tel. No. 173, 18 January 1945, reprinted in Hilliker, *Documents on Canadian External Relations*, 1101n6.

55 King Diary, 26 July 1944, LAC. For Martin's speech, see Canada, *House of Commons Debates* (26 July 1944), 402–6. The debate was continued on 28 July 1944.

56 "Un homme neuf," *La Presse* (Montreal), [29 May] 1943 (author's translation); original: "un magnifique et trop rare effort ... M. Martin s'est révélé comme un parlementaire de forte envergure."

57 "Man of the Year," *Montreal Standard*, 20 May 1944. He shared the honour with Brooke Claxton.

58 "The Royal City of Windsor, Ontario," *Montreal Labour World*, [spring 1944].
59 "Offer Is Called a Pretext by the CIO," *Toronto Star*, 24 April 1944.
60 John Mainwaring, "Memorandum for the Minister of Labour," 23 May 1944, Martin Papers, vol. 1, file: ILO, Philadelphia, 1944, LAC.
61 "International Counsels Forward Step: Martin," *Toronto Globe and Mail*, 12 February 1945.
62 Martin to Nell Martin, [January 1945], Martin Papers, vol. 360, LAC.
63 Nell Martin to W.L.M. King, 5 January 1945; W.L.M. King to Nell Martin, 13 January 1945, King Papers, microfilm reel C-9877, 347525–27, LAC.
64 Martin to W.L.M. King, 5 February 1945; W.L.M. King to Martin, 5 February 1945, King Papers, microfilm reel C-9173, 369378-81, LAC.
65 Martin to W.L.M. King, [February 1945]; W.L.M. King to Martin, 15 February 1945, King Papers, microfilm reel C-9874, 347464–88, LAC.
66 Paul Gravelle, Secretary of the Western Ontario Liberal Association, to W.L.M. King, 24 March 1945, King Papers, microfilm reel C-9874, 342807–8, LAC.
67 Brooke Claxton, Memorandum for the Prime Minister, 5 March 1945; W.L.M. King to Martin, 8 March 1945, King Papers, vol. 304, file P-659, LAC.
68 Brooke Claxton to W.L.M. King, 11 April 1945, King Papers, microfilm reel C-9872, 330789–90, LAC (emphasis in original).
69 King Diary, 13 April 1945, LAC. For Martin's account of the campaign biography, see his *Far from Home*, 373–74.
70 King Diary, 13 April 1945, LAC.
71 Ibid., 17 April 1945.
72 John English interview with Paul Martin, 17 December 1974, Bothwell Papers, University of Toronto Archives.
73 Martin to Nell Martin, [1941], Martin Papers, vol. 184, LAC.
74 Ibid., [July 1942].
75 Author interview with Michael Maloney, 21 August 2007.
76 Martin to Nell Martin, January 1946, Martin Papers, vol. 184, LAC.
77 Nell Martin to Martin, 15 January 1946, Martin Papers, vol. 152, LAC.

CHAPTER 4: APPRENTICE MINISTER, 1945–48

1 "Parade Honors Secretary of State Prior to His Nomination," *Windsor Daily Star*, 25 April 1945; "Essex East Convention Unanimous," *Windsor Daily Star*, 30 April 1945; Martin, *Far from Home*, 364–65.
2 Granatstein, *Canada's War*, 408–9; Bercuson, *True Patriot*, 134–37.
3 Quoted in R.M. Harrison, "Now," *Windsor Daily Star*, 7 June 1945.
4 MacPherson, "The 1945 Collapse of the CCF," 197.
5 "Byrne Says Martin and Reds Linked," *Windsor Daily Star*, 7 June 1945. The evidence is laid out in Whitaker, *The Government Party*, 160, 499n79. Martin denied the charge in *Far from Home*, 375.
6 W.L.M. King to Martin, 6 July 1944, King Papers, microfilm reel C-9877, 347505, Library and Archives Canada (LAC).

7 W.L.M. King to Martin, 19 January 1946, King Papers, microfilm reel C-9173, 369377, LAC.

8 "Hope Staggered Hours in CS Will Disappear," *Ottawa Citizen*, 5 October 1945.

9 Austin Cross, "Cross Town with Cross," *Ottawa Citizen*, 11 February 1946.

10 Martin to W.L.M. King, 11 September 1945, King Papers, microfilm reel C-9877, 347514, LAC; "CS Group Laud Nelson's Appointment," *Ottawa Journal*, 6 October 1945.

11 Martin to "Dear Colleagues," 9 September 1945, King Papers, microfilm reel C-9173, 369450, LAC.

12 W.L.M. King Diary, 9 October 1945, LAC; see also Brooke Claxton to Martin, 16 October 1945, Claxton Papers, vol. 90, file: Correspondence – Martin, LAC.

13 Martin to W.L.M. King, 19 March 1946, King Papers, microfilm reel C-9173, 369385, LAC; Martin to J.W. Pickersgill, 19 October 1946, King Papers, microfilm reel C-9173, 369454, LAC.

14 King Diary, 19 July 1945, LAC.

15 "Martin to See Mitchell," *Windsor Daily Star*, 24 September 1945; "Group to Go to Toronto," *Windsor Daily Star*, 25 September 1945; "Ford Strike Parley Off," *Montreal Daily Star*, 1 October 1945.

16 Quoted in "Factory Is Now Completely Closed," *Windsor Daily Star*, 9 October 1945.

17 Colling, *Ninety-Nine Days*, 56.

18 Canada, *House of Commons Debates* (9 October 1945), 872.

19 "Commission Reveals Plan as Union Members Gather," *Windsor Daily Star*, 2 November 1945; "Tense Feeling in City as Ont and RCMP Forces Confront Pickets," *St. Thomas Times Journal*, 3 November 1945; "18,500 Now Idle in Windsor," *Ottawa Morning Journal*, 5 November 1945.

20 Colling, *Ninety-Nine Days*, 83. "Martin, Reaume, Essex MP's Urge Strike Violence Avoided," *Windsor Daily Star*, 5 November 1945.

21 Canada, *House of Commons Debates* (5 November 1945), 1845. See also "Martin, Reaume, Essex MP's"; "MP's and Mayor Meet Authorities," *Windsor Daily Star*, 6 November 1945.

22 Kaplan, *Canadian Maverick*, 191-92.

23 Colling, *Ninety-Nine Days*, 138.

24 Quoted in Moulton, "Ford Windsor 1945," 145-46.

25 "UAW Thanks Paul Martin for Helping Settle Ford Strike," *Windsor Daily Star*, 16 March 1946; "UAW Thanks Paul Martin," *Windsor Daily Star*, 25 February 1946.

26 Norah Story interview with Paul Martin, [1969–70], Martin Papers, vol. 351, tape 1, side 2, LAC.

27 Martin, *Far from Home*, 441.

28 Story interview with Martin, [1969–70], Martin Papers, vol. 351, tape 9, side 2, LAC.

29 Robertson, *Memoirs of a Very Civil Servant*, 62.

30 Martin, *Far from Home*, 441.

31 John Marshall, "Citizenship Changes Proposed," *Windsor Daily Star*, 25 August 1945; Torchy Anderson, "May Grant Canadians Legal Right to Call Themselves Canadians," *Ottawa Evening Journal*, 25 August 1945; Cabinet Conclusions, 5 September 1945, PCO Records, LAC.

32 High Commission in the UK to SSEA, Tel. No. 2947, 10 October 1945, RG 25, vol. 3302, file 8204-40, LAC; UK High Commissioner in Ottawa to Dominions Office, 29 November 1945, Foreign Office Records (FO) 372/4303, National Archives (NA).

33 Cabinet Paper (45) 287, 16 November 1945, FO 372/4303, NA.

34 John Read to Norman Robertson, 18 October 1945, RG 25, vol. 3302, file 8204-40, LAC.

35 "Other Incidents," *Ottawa Evening Citizen*, 24 October 1945. For general reaction outside the House, see "What It Means to Be Canadian," *Montreal Gazette*, 24 October 1945; "La citoyennete canadienne sera bientot un fait," *Montreal Matin*, 23 October 1945; and "Qui a droit au titre de Canadien," *La Presse* (Montreal), 23 October 1945; more ambivalent, but still supportive, "Une loi plus precise sur la nationalité canadienne," *Le Devoir* (Montreal), 26 October 1945.

36 Martin to Nell Martin, [9 January 1946], Martin Papers, vol. 184, LAC.

37 Ibid.

38 Nell Martin to Martin, 15 January 1946, Martin Papers, vol. 152, LAC.

39 Martin to Nell Martin, 30 January 1946, Martin Papers, vol. 184, LAC.

40 Ibid., 7 February 1946.

41 Ibid., 13 January 1946.

42 Ibid., 7 February 1946.

43 Ibid., 11 January 1946.

44 Dominions Office to UK High Commissioner in Ottawa, 14 December 1945, FO 372/4303, NA; Norman Robertson to John Read, 29 December 1945, with attached correspondence from Stephen Holmes, Deputy UK High Commissioner to Robertson, 29 November and 29 December 1945; and High Commissioner in the UK to SSEA, 15 January 1946, RG 25, vol. 3302, file 8204-80, LAC.

45 Canada, *House of Commons Debates* (2 April 1946), 509.

46 Ibid. (5 April 1947), 598.

47 Ibid., 619.

48 Martin to Gordon Robertson, 15 November 1945; and Martin to Robertson, 25 October 1945, RG 25, vol. 3302, file 8204-40, LAC.

49 A.L. Jolliffe to Martin, 13 November 1945; and A.L. Jolliffe to Martin, 9 April, 12 April, 15 April, and 29 April 1945, RG 76, microfilm reel 10615, LAC.

50 Pickersgill, *Seeing Canada Whole*, 286.

51 Quoted in "'Paul Martin Day' in Pembroke Revives Old Memories," *Ottawa Journal*, 8 March 1946.

52 "Easter Parade at Ottawa," *London Free Press*, 19 April 1946.

53 Paul Martin Jr., *Hell or High Water*, 15. See also Martin, *Far from Home*, 459-60; Martin to Brooke Claxton, 20 August 1946, Claxton Papers, vol. 90, file: Correspondence – Martin, LAC.

54 New York to SSEA, Tel. No. CG-586, 12 September 1945, and SSEA to New York, Tel. No. 436, 25 September 1946, reprinted in Page, *Documents on Canadian External Relations*, 936-37 *(DCER)*.

55 Holmes, *Shaping of Peace*, 1:42.

56 Hugh Keenleyside to L.B. Pearson, 20 November 1946; and Escott Reid to Louis St. Laurent, 11 December 1946, reprinted in Page, *DCER*, 832-36.

57 Washington to New York, 9 December 1946, Martin Papers, vol. 152, LAC.

58 English, *Shadow of Heaven*, 299.
59 Quoted in [Blair Fraser], "Backstage at Ottawa: Johnny Canuck, Diplomat," *Maclean's*, 15 January 1947.
60 Martin to Nell Martin, 31 December 1945, Martin Papers, vol. 184, LAC.
61 Martin to Brooke Claxton, 20 September 1946, Claxton Papers, vol. 90, file: Correspondence – Martin, LAC.
62 King Diary, 4 September 1946, LAC.
63 "List Abbott for Finance, Claxton Foreign Minister," *St. John's Evening Telegram*, 6 September 1946; "Canada's Foreign Service," *Saskatoon-Star Phoenix*, 6 September 1946; "Quebec Meets Hon Lionel Chevrier," *Quebec Chronicle* (Quebec City), 25 September 1946.
64 [Blair Fraser], "Backstage at Ottawa," *Maclean's*, 15 September 1946.
65 King Diary, 26 February, 31 October, and 12 December 1946, LAC.
66 Ibid., 12 December 1946; "Claxton Goes to Defence Department and Martin to Health," *Ottawa Citizen*, 13 December 1946.
67 Martin, *So Many Worlds*, 35–36.
68 King Diary, 12 December 1946, LAC.
69 Martin to W.L.M. King, 13 December 1946, Martin Papers, vol. 152, LAC; King Diary, 12 and 13 December 1946, LAC.
70 Canada, Department of National Health and Welfare, *Annual Report for 1947*, 5–6, 139.
71 Dan Wallace to Martin, 7 May 1954, Martin Papers, vol. 11, file: Asian Trip, LAC.
72 Confidential interviews; "Union Man Appointed," *Hamilton Citizen*, 24 August 1945; Dempson, *Assignment Ottawa*, 41.
73 "Dan Wallace," *Ottawa Citizen*, 14 May 1954.
74 "Deputy Minister of Health Retires," *Ottawa Journal*, [2 September 1965], clipping in possession of Donald Cameron Jr., interviewed by author on 26 March 2009.
75 The term is Martin's, from his *So Many Worlds*, 34.
76 Brooke Claxton to W.L.M. King, 23 July 1946, quoted in Bercuson, *True Patriot*, 141.
77 Details of Davidson's early life are in Splane, *George Davidson*. This sketch of Davidson is drawn from the author's interviews with Gordon Robertson, 5 November 2007; Basil Robinson, 7 June 1994; and Michael Hicks, 5 September 2010, as well as Ian Stewart's interviews with R.B. Bryce, 2 May 1989 and 22 May 1990, Ottawa Decides, 1945–71, LAC.
78 Bercuson, *True Patriot*, 130.
79 George Davidson to Harry Cassidy, 12 March 1943, quoted in Splane, *George Davidson*, 110.
80 Author interview with Arthur Menzies, 26 June 2006.
81 L.B. Pearson to A.D.P. Heeney, 1 February 1954, Pearson Papers, vol. 5, LAC.
82 Confidential interviews.
83 Martin, *Far from Home*, 432.
84 Brooke Claxton, "Note on Health and Welfare, 1946," Claxton Papers, vol. 224, file: Memoir Notes 1940–46, LAC.
85 John English interview with Paul Martin, 17 December 1974, Bothwell Papers, University of Toronto Archives.

86 George Davidson to Martin, 23 June 1965, Martin Papers, vol. 275, file: Birthday 1965, LAC.

87 The figures on inflation are from Sharp, *Which Reminds Me*, 36. On labour, see Bothwell and Kilbourn, *C.D. Howe*, 206.

88 Michael Hicks interview with R.B. Bryce, 2 May 1989, Ottawa Decides, 1945–1971, LAC.

89 Max Freedman, Memorandum from Ottawa, 6 February 1947, Dexter Papers, box 4, file 1947, Queen's University Archives (QUA).

90 Bryden, *Old Age Pensions*, 95–97.

91 Martin to W.L.M. King, 18 January 1947, King Papers, microfilm reel C-11039, 387048–52, LAC.

92 Cabinet Conclusions, 22 and 23 January 1947, PCO Records, LAC; King Diary, 22 and 23 January 1947, LAC.

93 "Memorandum on Old Age and Blind Pensions for Cabinet Consideration," 5 March 1947, RG 29, vol. 166-A, file 230-4-13, LAC; Cabinet Conclusions, 20 March 1947, PCO Records, LAC.

94 Cabinet Conclusions, 20 March 1947, PCO Records, LAC.

95 "MP's Pity Aged; Living Cost so High," *Windsor Daily Star*, 25 April 1947.

96 Quoted in "Liberal MP's Join Pensions Bill Protest," *Ottawa Citizen*, 20 June 1947.

97 "Minister Defends Old Age Pension Proposal," *Halifax Chronicle*, 26 June 1947; "Bracken Spikes Charge Called Drew on Pensions – Forces Martin to Retract," *Evening Telegram*, 26 June 1947.

98 Irving, "Harry Cassidy," 54–55.

99 Max Freedman to Grant Dexter, 14 January 1948, Dexter Papers, box 5, folder 32, QUA.

100 Harry Cassidy, "A Canadian Program of Social Security," 16 December 1947, RG 19, vol. 440, file 108-8-1, LAC. Technically, Cassidy's first priority was bolstering the Department of National Health and Welfare so that it had the resources to administer the health grants.

101 Martin to W.L.M. King, 5 January 1948, RG 29, vol. 1063, file 502-1-1, LAC.

102 Ibid.

103 Max Freedman to Grant Dexter, 14 January 1948, Dexter Papers, box 5, folder 32, QUA.

104 Michael Hicks interview with R.B. Bryce, 2 May 1989, Ottawa Decides, 1945–1971, LAC.

105 Paul Martin, Memorandum on Health Insurance, Cabinet Document 659, 20 April 1948, RG 2, vol. 66, file C-20-5, LAC.

106 Cabinet Conclusions, 21 April 1948, PCO Records, LAC.

107 King Diary, 22 June 1948, LAC.

108 Ibid., 24 June 1948.

109 Ibid., 12 May 1948.

110 Ibid.

111 Ibid., 13 May 1948.

112 Bothwell and Kilbourn, *C.D. Howe*, 221.

113 Thomson, *Louis St Laurent*.

114 Max Freedman to Grant Dexter, 14 October 1947, Dexter Papers, box 4, file 1947, QUA.

115 Ralph Maybank Diary, 27 January 1948, Maybank Papers, box 5, file 91-1948, Manitoba Archives.

116 Pickersgill told Maybank of this discussion; see ibid. Martin's memoirs, *So Many* Worlds, 4, contains a competing account of this exchange: Martin quotes St. Laurent as saying, "Now is the time for you. This will be the *only* time" (emphasis in original).

117 Maybank Diary, 27 January 1948, Maybank Papers, Manitoba Archives.

118 "Confusion about Liberal Leadership," *Sherbrook Record*, 24 January 1948.

119 Story interview with Martin, [1969–70], Martin Papers, vol. 352, tape 9, side 1, LAC.

120 Power and Ward, *A Party Politician*, 395.

121 Robert Taylor, "Paul Martin Next Leader Brantford Liberals Hope," *Toronto Daily Star*, 19 June 1948; "To Select Successor to Mr Mackenzie King," *Mimico Advertiser*, 9 July 1948; "Draft Martin Move," *Chatham Daily News*, 15 July 1948.

122 "Sinclair Favours Martin for Liberal Leadership," *Windsor Daily Star*, 30 June 1948.

123 "St. Laurent Supporters Preparing for a Real Fight," *Vancouver Daily Province*, 10 July 1948; "Draft Martin Move Begun by Toronto Liberal Group," *Toronto Daily Star*, 16 July 1948; see also Alex Fisher to Don Emerson, 19 July 1948; and Herb Daly to Paul Martin, 3 August 1948, Martin Papers, vol. 18, file 270, LAC.

124 Brooke Claxton to Terry MacDermot, 26 July 1948, Claxton Papers, vol. 52, file: Terry MacDermot, LAC.

125 Quoted in "Paul Martin in the Field," *Ottawa Evening Citizen*, 19 July 1948.

126 Martin to Helen Holden, 16 July 1948, Martin Papers, vol. 18, file 270, LAC.

127 Harold Dingman, "Inside Ottawa," *Oshawa Daily Times Gazette*, 28 July 1948.

128 Martin to Lum Clark, 11 August 1948, Martin Papers, vol. 19, file 270, LAC. This letter may have been judged too frank, since it is labelled "draft" and does not appear to have been sent.

129 "Western Ontario Liberals Want Martin as Federal Chief," *Ottawa Evening Journal*, 4 August 1948; "Move to Draft Martin Launched," *Windsor Daily Star*, 4 August 1948.

130 King Diary, 4 August 1948, LAC.

131 Ibid., 5 August 1948.

132 Camp, *Gentlemen, Players and Politicians*, 2.

133 Quoted in "Five Liberals May Enter Race Today," *Ottawa Evening Citizen*, 7 August 1948.

134 [Blair Fraser], "Backstage at Ottawa: Harsh Words at the Liberal Love Feast," *Maclean's*, 15 September 1948, 15–16, 79.

CHAPTER 5: A LIBERAL IN A HIGH-TORY CABINET, 1948–52

1 Allan McLean to Martin, 2 November 1948, Martin Papers, vol. 151, file: Personal, Library and Archives Canada (LAC).

2 Author interview with Michael Hicks, 5 September 2010.

3 Quoted in Wardhaugh, *Behind the Scenes*, 347.

4 Michael Hicks interview with R.B. Bryce, 2 May 1989, Ottawa Decides, 1945–1971, LAC.

5 Martin to Louis St. Laurent, 17 March 1949, Martin Papers, vol. 15, file 50-1-2, LAC.

6 Ibid., 5 April 1949.

7 Cabinet Conclusions, 8 April and 25 April 1949, PCO Records, LAC.

8 Quoted in Martin, *So Many Worlds*, 85.

9　"500 Vets' Homes in First Project," *Windsor Daily Star*, 17 March 1949; "RCAF Plane Brings Defence Minister," *Windsor Daily Star*, 2 May 1949; Pickersgill, *Seeing Canada Whole*, 325.

10　"In Essex East," *Windsor Daily Star*, 2 May 1949.

11　See, for example, "Conservative Candidates," *Windsor Daily Star*, 21 April 1949; "Now," *Windsor Daily Star*, 20 April 1949.

12　"4,000 Turn Out for Paul Martin Nomination," *Windsor Daily Star*, 17 May 1949; "Essex East Grits Show Enthusiasm," *Windsor Daily Star*, 17 May 1949.

13　"Martin Opens Four-Day Tour in NFL," *Ottawa Morning Citizen*, 18 May 1949; "Fantastic Conflict in Promises Cost Drew Support, Says Martin," *Toronto Daily Star*, 28 May 1949; "Unsavoury Drew Alliance," *Toronto Daily Star*, 31 May 1949; "Martin Asks Drew Describe Alliance with Duplessis," *Ottawa Evening Journal*, 8 June 1949; "Martin Claims Canada at Threshold of Health Insurance," *Ottawa Morning Journal*, 11 June 1949.

14　"The People's Mandate," *Toronto Star Weekly*, 16 July 1949.

15　"Job for Western Liberals," *Vancouver Sun*, 4 July 1949.

16　Quoted in Martin, *So Many Worlds*, 67.

17　Harold Dingman, "Report to the Nation," *Liberty Magazine*, [September 1947].

18　Quoted in "Membership in UN Is Cornerstone of Foreign Policy," *Ottawa Evening Citizen*, 3 October 1949.

19　See, for example, "Canada Asks World Court Rule on Aim of Russian Satellites," *Ottawa Evening Journal*, 5 October 1949.

20　Quoted in "Soviet Foreign Minister's Talk Fatigues Paul Martin," *Kitchener Waterloo Record*, 13 October 1949.

21　Canada, Department of External Affairs, "Daily Airmail Bulletin," 27 October 1949, Martin Papers, vol. 131, file: UN 4th Session, 1949, LAC.

22　Quoted in "Canada Makes Crushing Reply to Russia," *Montreal Daily Star*, 15 November 1949.

23　"Plain Talk," *Victoria Daily Times*, 17 November 1949.

24　"Mr. Martin's Great Speech," *Toronto Daily Star*, 17 November 1949.

25　Minutes of the Cabinet Committee on the Dominion-Provincial Conference, 28 October 1949, RG 19, vol. 92, file 135-0-167, LAC.

26　Donald Cameron, Memorandum to the Director of Health Insurance Studies, 18 November 1949; and M.W. Sharp to Donald Cameron, 21 November 1949, RG 29, vol. 1061, file 500-3-4; see also Gordon Robertson, Memorandum for Mr. Mackenzie, 28 December 1949, RG 2, vol. 187, file 5-60, LAC.

27　Bercuson, *True Patriot*, 205–6.

28　Memorandum by Defence Liaison Division, 20 February 1950, reprinted in Donaghy, *Documents on Canadian External Relations*, 16:892.

29　Bruce Hutchison to Grant Dexter, [February 1950], Dexter Papers, box 6, folder 37, Queen's University Archives (QUA).

30　Minutes of the Second Meeting of the Interdepartmental Working Committee on Health Insurance, 9 December 1949, RG 29, vol. 1061, file 500-3-4, LAC.

31　Minutes of the Third Meeting of the Interdepartmental Working Committee on Health Insurance, 22 December 1949, RG 29, vol. 1061, file 500-3-4, LAC.

32 F.W. Jackson to J.A. Macdonald, 3 June 1950, RG 29, vol. 1061, file 500-3-4, LAC.
33 Minutes of the Interdepartmental Committee on Social Security, 30 December 1949, RG 19, vol. 92, file 135-0-167; see also George Davidson, Memorandum to the Minister: Old Age Security, [early 1950], Martin Papers, vol. 40, file: Old Age Security Committee, 1950, LAC.
34 Cabinet Minutes, 8 February 1950, LAC; see also Paul Martin, Notes on the Joint Committee, Martin Papers, vol. 40, file: Old Age Pensions, LAC.
35 Fleming, So Very Near, 1:187.
36 Mann-Trofimenkoff, Stanley Knowles, 111.
37 Bryden, Old Age Pensions, 123.
38 Ibid., 124–25; Mann-Trofimenkoff, Stanley Knowles, 111–12; Blair Fraser, "Backstage at Ottawa: Wartime Taxes? Not Yet," Maclean's, 15 September 1950.
39 Donaghy, "The Road to Constraint," 189–212.
40 "Old Age Pensions," Winnipeg Free Press, 8 July 1950.
41 "Korean War Hits Old Age Pensions," Winnipeg Free Press, 19 July 1950; see also "Places to Prune," Winnipeg Free Press, 16 October 1950.
42 "No Pension Delay," Windsor Daily Star, 25 July 1950.
43 Bruce Hutchison, Memorandum on Talk with Mike Pearson, 25 October 1950, box 6, folder 38, QUA.
44 Figures in Table H19-34: Federal Government Budgetary Expenditure, Classified by Function, 1867 to 1975, in Statistics Canada, Historical Statistics of Canada, http://www.statcan.gc.ca/pub/11-516-x/sectionh/4057752-eng.htm#1.
45 Cabinet Conclusions, 16 August 1950, PCO Records, LAC.
46 H.D. Clark, Memorandum for W.C. Clark, re: Report of the Working Committee on Health Insurance, 18 August 1950, RG 19, vol. 92, file 135-0-167(A), LAC.
47 Bruce Hutchison to Grant Dexter, 17 October 1950; see also Bruce Hutchison to Grant Dexter, 12 October 1950; and Bruce Hutchison to Grant Dexter, 14 October 1950, Dexter Papers, box 5, folder 38, QUA.
48 "Places to Prune," Winnipeg Free Press, 16 October 1950.
49 Fiscal Conference Committee: Minutes of the Fourth Meeting, 6 November 1950, RG 29, vol. 3354, file 2101-5-2, LAC.
50 Minutes of the Interdepartmental Committee on Social Security, 2 and 13 November 1950, RG 19, vol. 3430, file S-13-1, LAC; Minutes of the Cabinet Committee on Federal-Provincial Relations, 7 and 23 November 1950, Martin Papers, vol. 4, file: Committee and Conferences 1950, LAC.
51 Fiscal Conference Committee: Minutes of the Second Meeting, 19 October 1950, RG 29, vol. 3354, file 2101-5-2, LAC.
52 Ibid.
53 Minutes of the Cabinet Committee on Federal-Provincial Relations, 23 November 1950, Martin Papers, vol. 4, file: Committee and Conferences 1950, LAC.
54 Donald Cameron, Health Insurance Proposal, 4 November 1950, RG 29, vol. 1061, file 500-3-4, LAC; Departmental Report on Health Insurance, 27 November 1950, RG 19, vol. 92, file 135-Q-167(A), LAC.
55 Donald Cameron, Memorandum to the Minister, 27 November 1950, RG 29, vol. 1061, file 500-3-4, LAC.

56 Minutes of the Cabinet Committee on Federal-Provincial Relations, 30 November 1950, Martin Papers, vol. 4, file: Committee and Conferences 1950, LAC.

57 Nell Martin to Martin, 11 January 1951, Martin Papers, vol. 11, file: Personal Letters, LAC.

58 Martin to A.J.P. Taylor, 29 August 1972, Martin Papers, vol. 512, file: Letters T, LAC.

59 Martin to George Carty, [1956], Martin Papers, vol. 17, file 260-10 Lord Beaverbrook, LAC.

60 Martin to Lord Beaverbrook, 20 February 1952, Martin Papers, vol. 153, LAC.

61 Martin to Lord Beaverbrook, 14 April 1953, Martin Papers, vol. 12, file: Beaverbrook, LAC.

62 Martin to Nell Martin, 31 December 1950, Martin Papers, vol. 360, file: Correspondence, 1945-50, LAC.

63 Nell Martin to Martin, 30 December 1950, Martin Papers, vol. 11, file: Personal Letters, 1951-57, LAC.

64 Author interview with Mary Anne Bellamy, 22 August 2007.

65 Nell Martin to Martin, 11 January 1951, Martin Papers, vol. 11, file: Personal Letters, 1951-57, LAC; Paul Martin Jr. to Nell Martin, March 1950, Martin Papers, vol. 151, LAC.

66 Paul Martin Jr., *Hell or High Water,* 3.

67 George Drew to Martin, [June 1950]; and Martin to George Drew, [June 1950], Martin Papers, vol. 151, LAC.

68 Nell Martin to Martin, 11 January 1951, Martin Papers, vol. 11, file: Personal Letters, 1951-57, LAC.

69 "Bombs and Worry," *Saturday Night,* 6 March 1951; "Ottawa Appears to Recognize Welfare Aspects of Civil Defence," *Toronto Telegram,* 27 February 1951.

70 Major-General Frank Worthington to J.J. Wadsworth, 7 March 1951, Worthington Papers, file 3, Department of National Defence (DND).

71 Quoted in Burtch, *Give Me Shelter,* 42.

72 Canada, House of Commons, *Debates* (9 May 1951), 2861.

73 Verbatim Minutes of the Joint Canada-US Civil Defence Meeting, 7 August 1951, Martin Papers, vol. 4, file: Civil Defence Misc, LAC.

74 Quoted in Worthington, '*Worthy,*' 227-28.

75 Burtch, "If We Are Attacked," 82.

76 Editorial, *Victoria Daily Colonist,* 18 September 1951.

77 Martin, *So Many Worlds,* 146-47.

78 F.F. Worthington, Diary Files, passim, Worthington Papers, file 4, DND.

79 Quoted in Burtch, *Give Me Shelter,* 55.

80 Bruce Hutchison, "A Pain Square in the Neck," *Regina Leader-Post,* 10 November 1951.

81 "An Opportunistic Expedient," *Toronto Telegram,* 30 July 1951.

82 Quoted in Michael Young, "The Heat Is on 'Purse Control,'" *Saturday Night,* 3 July 1951.

83 "Industry's Problems," *Windsor Daily Star,* 4 August 1951; "Windsor, Ottawa Map Unemployment Talks," *London Free Press,* 21 August 1951.

84 "Committee to Solve Windsor Unemployment Problem," *Windsor Daily Star,* 30 August 1951; see also Victor Mackie to Grant Dexter, 7 September 1951, Dexter Papers, box 6, file 40, QUA.

85 Cabinet Conclusions, 9 September 1951, PCO Records, LAC.

86 Ibid., 26 September 1951.

87 Ibid., 13 October 1951; Paul Pelletier to W.C. Clark, 17 October 1951, RG 19, vol. 327, file 101-81G, LAC.

88 This account is from Ian Stewart's interview with J.W. Pickersgill, Gordon Robertson, R.B. Bryce, Mitchell Sharp, and Louis Rasminsky, 25 May 1989, Ottawa Decides, 1945–71, LAC. The quotation is from Sharp, *Which Reminds Me*, 43. Martin almost certainly did not use the term "medicare," which was not coined until the early 1960s.

89 Victor Mackie to Grant Dexter, 7 February 1952, Dexter Papers, box 6, folder 41, QUA; see also Victor Mackie to Grant Dexter, 7 September 1951, Dexter Papers, box 6, folder 40, QUA; Blair Fraser, "Health Insurance on the Horizon," *Maclean's*, 15 August 1951.

90 Bruce Hutchison to Grant Dexter, 28 January 1952, Dexter Papers, box 6, folder 41, QUA.

91 See, for example, F.W. Jackson to Donald Cameron, 12 February 1952, RG 29, vol. 1062, file 500-3-7, LAC; Dan Wallace, Memorandum for the Minister, 12 February 1952, Martin Papers, vol. 28, file: Health Insurance – General, LAC.

92 Mackie to Dexter, 7 September 1951, Dexter Papers, QUA.

93 Chester Bloom, "New Inflation Fears Force Ottawa to Put Off Health Insurance Plan," *Vancouver News Herald*, 19 November 1951.

94 Bruce Hutchison to Grant Dexter, 18 February 1952, Dexter Papers, box 6, folder 41, QUA.

95 Ibid., 20 March 1952.

96 Ibid.

97 Cabinet Conclusions, 19 February 1952, PCO Records, LAC.

98 Ibid.; Martin, *So Many Worlds*, 222.

99 Quoted in Bruce Hutchison to Grant Dexter, 14 April 1952, Dexter Papers, box 6, folder 41, QUA.

100 Figures in Table H19-34: Federal Government Budgetary Expenditure, Classified by Function, 1867 to 1975, http://www.statcan.gc.ca/pub/11-516-x/sectionh/4057752-eng.htm.

101 Martin to Vincent Massey, [February 1952], Martin Papers, vol. 127, LAC.

102 Lumina Martin to Martin, [date stamped 16 January 1952], Martin Papers, vol. 153, LAC (emphasis in original).

103 *Canada: Nation on the March*, xi.

104 Canada, Statistics Canada, *Historical Statistics of Canada* (Ottawa: Statistics Canada, 1983), Series A350, F1–13, E49–59, D223–235.

105 Quoted in Bothwell and Kilbourn, *C.D. Howe*, 261-62.

106 Cited in Bruce Hutchison to Grant Dexter, 14 April 1952, Dexter Papers, box 6, folder 41, QUA.

107 Quoted in "'Just Like at U of T, You Hate to See My Name Ahead,' Martin Twits Tory," *Toronto Daily Star*, 6 June 1952.

108 Mary Anne Martin to Martin, [June 1952], Martin Papers, vol. 153, LAC.

109 "Among Canada's Best Dressed Men," *Goderich Signal*, 12 February 1953.

110 "Visa Racket at Border Exposed," *Windsor Daily Star*, 9 August 1952; "Fake Visa Charge Faces 100 Canadians," *Toronto Globe and Mail*, 9 August 1952.

111 "Wrote Out False Assets Statements for 100 Canadians," *Windsor Daily Star*, 13 August 1952.

112 Keith Laird to Martin, 13 April 1939, Martin Papers, vol. 11, file: Tannenbaum-Americo Dean, LAC.

113 Martin to Robert Easton, 4 October 1946, Martin Papers, vol. 11, file: Tannenbaum-Americo Dean, LAC.

114 Dan Wallace, Memorandum for the Minister, 25 March 1948, Martin Papers, vol. 11, file: Tannenbaum-Americo Dean, LAC.

115 Reverend W.L. Langlois to Martin, 11 August 1949, Martin Papers, vol. 10, file 250-7-13, LAC.

116 D.G. Emerson, Memorandum to Miss Betty Neill, 26 January 1949; and Martin to Gerald Mokama, Martin Papers, vol. 10, file 250-7-13, LAC.

117 O'Leary's son, Brian, relayed the threat to Martin. See Brian O'Leary to Martin, [May 1952], vol. 11, file: Tannenbaum-Americo Dean, LAC.

118 Emerson's handwritten notes for Martin, 15 August 1952, Martin Papers, vol. 10, file 250-7-13, LAC.

119 "Second Windsorite Tied to Visa Deal," *Windsor Daily Star*, 18 August 1952.

120 *Le Soleil* (Quebec City), 25 August 1952.

121 Anita Martin to Martin, 18 August 1952, Martin Papers, vol. 10, file 250-7-13, LAC.

122 Marie Martin to Martin, 5 March 1953, with enclosures from Aline Wald to Marie Martin, Martin Papers, vol. 10, file 250-7-13, LAC.

123 Bruce Hutchison, "'Time for a Change' in Canada?" *The Reporter*, 20 January 1953.

124 Martin to Paul Nathanson, 27 January 1953, Martin Papers, vol. 450, LAC.

CHAPTER 6:
THE GREATEST COUNTRY IN THE WORLD, 1953–56

1 Martin to Lord Beaverbrook, 14 April 1953, Martin Papers, vol. 12, Library and Archives Canada (LAC).

2 Nell Martin to Martin, [13/14 February 1952], Martin Papers, vol. 153, LAC.

3 Grant Dexter to Bruce Hutchison, 21 December 1952, Dexter Papers, box 6, folder 42, Queen's University Archives (QUA).

4 Martin to Louis St. Laurent, 3 November 1952, Martin Papers, vol. 6, file 40-8, LAC; Martin, Memorandum to Cabinet, 13 November 1952, PCO Records, vol. 213, file C-205, LAC.

5 Martin to Lord Beaverbrook, 12 June 1953, Martin Papers, vol. 12, LAC.

6 Pickersgill, *My Years with Louis St. Laurent*, 194.

7 Whitaker, *The Government Party*, 249.

8 "Martin Hits PC Pledges," *Windsor Daily Star*, 14 July 1953.

9 Ibid.

10 Whitaker, *The Government Party*, 246.

11 "Paul Martin Hits Windsor with Boogie Beat," *Ottawa Evening Journal*, 27 July 1953.

12 Quoted in ibid.

13 Quoted in "Essex East PC's Pick Al Kennedy," *Windsor Daily Star*, 18 June 1953.

14 Robert Bothwell, Conversation with Carl Goldenberg and J.W. Pickersgill, 1 December 1976, Bothwell Papers, University of Toronto Archives.

15 Quoted in "Essex Votes Drop 10,000," *Windsor Daily Star,* 11 August 1953.

16 John Bird, "The Mellowing Men," *Edmonton Journal,* 28 September 1953.

17 Mildred Roberts to Martin, 1 February 1955, Martin Papers, vol. 212, LAC.

18 Alice Shanahan to Martin, 26 January 1956, Martin Papers, vol. 212, file: Alice Shanahan, LAC.

19 Charles Woodsworth, "How Is the Cabinet Fixed for Orators?" *Toronto Daily Star,* 8 September 1955.

20 Quoted in "Hoedown for 'Our Paul,'" *Windsor Daily Star,* 5 November 1955.

21 On Martin's mailing list, see Martin Papers, vol. 18, file 270: Essex East, 1946–57, LAC.

22 "Martin at Mass in Morning, Negro Vespers in Evening," *Ottawa Evening Journal,* 29 July 1953.

23 Betty Neill to Mr. Carty, 10 October 1955, Martin Papers, vol. 12, file 8, LAC.

24 Quoted in "Rinfret Praises Blending of Races in This Area," *Windsor Daily Star,* 5 March 1951.

25 Martin Papers, vol. 15, file 130, LAC; Martin Papers, vol. 16, file 130, LAC.

26 Martin Papers, vol. 14, files 5-3-11 and 5-3-12, LAC.

27 Ibid., file 45-6-4, LAC.

28 Whitaker, *The Government Party,* 187, 231.

29 See Martin Papers, vol. 15, file 130, LAC; Martin Papers, vol. 16, file 130, LAC.

30 Canada, Department of National Health and Welfare, *Annual Report for 1948,* 119–20.

31 Canada, Department of National Health and Welfare, *Annual Report for 1956,* 144.

32 Richard Needham, "Timber of Two Principal Parties Analyzed for Cabinet Positions," Martin Papers, vol. 127, clipping file: January to December 1953, LAC.

33 Author interview with Arthur Menzies, 26 June 2006.

34 "Oratory," *Montreal Gazette,* 18 September 1954.

35 Woodsworth, "How Is the Cabinet Fixed for Orators?"

36 George Carty to Morley Scott, 7 March 1953, Martin Papers, vol. 12, file 3, LAC.

37 Margaret Aitken, "Between You and Me," *Toronto Telegram,* 26 January 1956.

38 Quoted in "St Laurent and Party Greeted at Bermuda," *Ottawa Journal,* 25 March 1957.

39 George Carty to Martin, 11 March 1953, Martin Papers, vol. 12, file 3, LAC.

40 Bird, "The Mellowing Men."

41 Austin Cross to Martin, 18 November 1952, Martin Papers, vol. 12, LAC.

42 Patrick Nicholson to Martin, [November 1954], Martin Papers, vol. 12, LAC.

43 Alex Hume to Martin, 11 May 1956, Martin Papers, vol. 172, LAC.

44 Frank Ahearn to Martin, 8 October 1956, Martin Papers, vol. 175, LAC.

45 Martin to Lord Beaverbrook, 12 June 1953, Martin Papers, vol. 12, LAC; Martin to Paul Nathanson, 27 January 1953, Martin Papers, vol. 450, LAC.

46 Don Emerson to Bill Tubman, 29 April 1950, Martin Papers, vol. 21, file 300-71, LAC.

47 Frances Godsoe to Betty Neill, 28 September 1954, Martin Papers, vol. 12, LAC.

48 Quoted in "Van Horne," *Time* (Canadian edition), 28 January 1957.

49 Woodsworth, "How Is the Cabinet Fixed for Orators?"

50 Margaret Aitken, "Between You and Me," *Toronto Telegram,* 13 April 1956.

51 Malcolm Taylor, *Health Insurance,* 205.

52 Martin, *So Many Worlds*, 104–5.
53 On his problems with his officials, see Fred Jackson to Donald Cameron, 22 April 1954; Donald Cameron, Memorandum for the Minister, 24 June 1954; Martin to Donald Cameron, 25 June 1954; and K.C. Charron to Donald Cameron, 28 June 1954, Martin Papers, vol. 14, file 45-1-1, LAC; on relations with provincial ministers, see H.L. Pottle to Martin, 29 October 1954; George Davidson, Memorandum for the Minister, 12 November 1954; Martin to H.L. Pottle, 15 November 1954; and Martin to F.C. Bell, 1 December 1954, Martin Papers, vol. 14, file 45-1-4, LAC; see also Martin to T.J. Bentley, 9 December 1954; and Martin to W.A. Goodfellow, 1 February 1955, Martin Papers, vol. 14, file 45-1-1, LAC. On cabinet worries, see Cabinet Conclusions, 29 April, 18 November, and 23 November 1954, PCO Records, LAC.
54 Robert Winters to Martin, 1 April 1955; Marcel Inkel, private secretary to the minister of veterans affairs, to Don Emerson, 9 June 1955; Arthur Pigott, President of the Welfare Council of Toronto, to Martin, 16 September 1955; Jean Lesage to Martin, 8 November 1955; and Samuel Balcom MP to Martin, 28 November 1955, Martin Papers, vol. 14, LAC.
55 Martin, Memorandum for George Davidson, 27 December 1955, Martin Papers, vol. 14, file 5-8-1, LAC.
56 "A Blueprint Comes First," *Toronto Globe and Mail*, 30 April 1954; "Too Much Dallying," *Regina Leader-Post*, 28 June 1954.
57 Quoted in "Civil Defence Program Attacked, Victoria Staff Fired," *London Free Press*, 8 October 1954.
58 Jules Léger, Memorandum for the SSEA, 8 June 1955, reprinted in Donaghy, *Documents on Canadian External Relations (DCER)*, 21:71–72; Canada, *House of Commons Debates* (1955), 2:1864; see also "Martin to Give Facts on Radiation," *Ottawa Citizen*, 31 March 1955.
59 "The Spectre Still Stalks," *Kingston Whig-Standard*, 14 April 1955.
60 Donald Cameron to Martin, 21 April, 11 May, 17 May, and 18 May 1955, Martin Papers, vol. 4, file: Radiation 1955, LAC.
61 Martin to Paul Nathanson, 22 July 1955, Martin Papers, vol. 450, LAC.
62 Department of National Health and Welfare, "Polio Vaccine," [summer 1955], Martin Papers, vol. 32, LAC.
63 Donald Cameron, Memorandum for the Minister, 23 March 1955, RG 29, vol. 1201, file 311-P11-26, LAC.
64 Donald Cameron, Memorandum for the Minister, 29 April 1955, Martin Papers, vol. 32, LAC.
65 Health and Welfare, "Polio Vaccine," Martin Papers, LAC.
66 Martin, *So Many Worlds*, 74–75.
67 "Canadian Paul Martin Showed Imagination," *The New Republic*, 23 May 1955.
68 "The Canadian Vaccine Story," *New York Post*, 20 May 1955.
69 Mark Gayn, "Polio: Canada's Way," *Nation Magazine*, 4 June 1955.
70 "The US Vaccine Mess," *Toronto Daily Star*, 25 May 1955.
71 Martin to Paul Nathanson, 22 July 1955, Martin Papers, vol. 450, LAC.
72 For details, see Donaghy, "Blessed Are the Peacemakers," 134–46.

73 "Martin Emerges as Seasoned Negotiator at UN Meetings," *Chatham Daily News*, 7 November 1952. See also I. Norman Smith, "All This UN Talk, Talk, Talk, Is Vitally Important Work," *Ottawa Evening Journal*, 8 November 1952; Mark Harrison, "Canada Rescues UN from 'I-Dotting' Yanks, 'Legal-Minded' British," *Toronto Daily Star*, 28 November 1952; Walter O'Hearn, "Canada's Delegate Is Frank," *Montreal Star*, 28 November 1952.

74 Jules Léger to Martin, 31 December 1952, Martin Papers, vol. 10, file: Personal Letters, LAC (author's translation); original: "l'une des expériences les plus enrichissantes de 1952 ... J'en garde un souvenir ému à cause de l'amitié que vous avez bien voulu m'y manifester."

75 Martin to Percy Phillips, 3 November 1954, Martin Papers, vol. 12, LAC.

76 Ottawa to Geneva, Tel. No. 118, 11 October 1954, reprinted in Donaghy, *DCER*, 20:247.

77 Martin, *So Many Worlds*, 163.

78 NATO (Pearson) to Ottawa (Martin), Tel. No. 846, 21 October 1954, reprinted in Donaghy, *DCER*, 20:270.

79 Donald Cameron to Martin, 28 October 1954, Martin Papers, vol. 12, LAC.

80 Holmes, *Shaping of Peace*, 2:317.

81 L.B. Pearson to Martin, 1 December 1954, Pearson Papers, vol. 9, File 7, LAC.

82 Quoted in "Martin Says Russia May Be Sincere," *Winnipeg Free Press*, 24 November 1954.

83 "Martin Hints Russia Plans Major Changes," *Toronto Daily Star*, 16 May 1955.

84 Quoted in Holmes, *Shaping of Peace*, 2:339.

85 Jules Léger, Memorandum for the Minister, 5 August 1955, reprinted in Donaghy, *DCER*, 21:16–19.

86 Washington to Ottawa, Tel. No. WA-1376, 12 August 1955; and Washington to Ottawa, Tel. No. WA-1502, 1 September 1955, DEA file 5475-CR-40, LAC.

87 Washington to Ottawa, Tel. No. WA-1551, 12 September 1955, DEA file 5475-CR-40, LAC.

88 L.B. Pearson, Memorandum to Cabinet, 14 September 1955, reprinted in Donaghy, *DCER*, 21:3.

89 Draft Memorandum from Canadian Embassy to State Department, [December 1955]; and Washington to Ottawa, Tel. No. 1605, 20 September 1955, DEA file 5475-CR-40, LAC.

90 New York to Ottawa, Tel. No. 16, 22 September 1955; and New York to Ottawa, Tel. No. 29, 27 September 1955, reprinted in Donaghy, *DCER*, 21:22–23 and 21:23–24. Pearson had little sympathy for this view. On a telegram from France, he minuted that "surely the UN was not formed to protect colonial powers." See Paris to Ottawa, Tel. No. 473, 20 September 1955, DEA file 5475-CR-40, LAC.

91 Geoffrey Murray, unpublished memoirs.

92 New York to Ottawa, Tel. No. 184, 25 October 1955, reprinted in Donaghy, *DCER*, 21:26–27.

93 Ottawa to New York, Tel. No. V-96, 31 October 1955, reprinted in Donaghy, *DCER*, 21:30–31.

94 Stursberg, *Agreement in Principle*, 225.

95 Peter Stursberg, "Canada Seeking Universality," *Montreal Star*, 2 November 1955.
96 Marcel Cadieux, Memorandum for the Under-Secretary of State for External Affairs, 3 November 1955, DEA file 5475-CR-40, LAC.
97 Ottawa to London, Tel. No. V-1864, 10 November 1955; and New York to Ottawa, Tel. Nos. 269, 270, and 271, 11 November 1955, reprinted in Donaghy, *DCER*, 21:36–43.
98 Selwyn Lloyd to Harold Macmillan, Foreign Secretary, 5 October 1955, Foreign Office Records 371/117399, National Archives (NA).
99 Sir Pierson Dixon to Selwyn Lloyd, 6 January 1956, Prime Minister's Office Records 11/1681, NA.
100 Telegram from the Mission at the United Nations to the Department of State, 26 October 1955, reprinted in US Department of State, *Foreign Relations of the United States (FRUS)*, 11:316–17.
101 Telegram from the Secretary of State to the Department of State, 13 November 1955, reprinted in US Department of State, *FRUS*, 11:355–56.
102 Telegram from the Mission at the United Nations to the Department of State, 15 November 1955, reprinted in US Department of State, *FRUS*, 11:359–61.
103 William R. Frye, "18-17-16 – and We Lost the Game," *The Reporter*, 26 January 1956, 16.
104 Geoffrey Murray, unpublished memoirs.
105 Telegram from the Mission at the United Nations to the Department of State, 21 November 1955, reprinted in US Department of State, *FRUS*, 11:385.
106 Washington to Ottawa, Tel. No. 1941, 23 November 1955, reprinted in Donaghy, *DCER*, 21:52–53.
107 Martin, *So Many Worlds*, 198.
108 Telegram from the Mission at the United Nations to the Department of State, 23 November 1955, reprinted in US Department of State, *FRUS*, 11:393.
109 Geoffrey Murray, unpublished memoirs (emphasis in original).
110 Martin, undated memorandum, Martin Papers, vol. 33, file 9, LAC.
111 Draft Memorandum from the Canadian Embassy to the State Department, [December 1955], DEA file 5475-CR-40, LAC. See also Martin, *So Many Worlds*, 198.
112 Japan was admitted to the United Nations during the eleventh General Assembly in 1956. Outer Mongolia joined in 1961.
113 John Holmes to Martin, 4 January 1956, Martin Papers, vol. 167, LAC. Holmes's judgment remained unchanged forty years later, when he described it as "one of the most remarkable feats in the history of the General Assembly." Holmes, *Shaping of Peace*, 2:327.
114 Vincent Massey to Martin, 31 December 1955, Martin Papers, vol. 167, LAC.
115 Gerald Waring, "Ottawa Report," *Montreal Herald*, 3 December 1955; see also Pat Nicholson, "Ottawa Report: Sees Paul Martin as Liberal Heir Apparent," *Daily Sentinel Review* (Woodstock, ON), 10 November 1955; Austin Cross, "Nominates Paul Martin Canada's Man of the Year," *Ottawa Citizen*, 22 December 1955.
116 Malcolm Taylor, *Health Insurance*, 107–9, 123.
117 Quoted in "Speaking Notes for Paul Martin," [September 1955], Martin Papers, vol. 18, file 270, LAC. Pickersgill claimed that he had been misquoted. Malcolm Taylor, *Health Insurance*, 125.

118 Cabinet Conclusions, 18 March 1955, PCO Records, LAC.
119 In his memoirs, Martin claimed that he was not consulted on the federal position. Martin, *So Many Worlds*, 235. The cabinet minutes show that he had an opportunity to comment on St. Laurent's opening remarks, and his papers reveal that he did so. See his marginalia on St. Laurent, draft Opening Remarks, [April 1955], Martin Papers, vol. 15, file 95-1-1, LAC.
120 "Health Insurance Up to Provinces," *Hamilton Daily News*, 21 February 1955; "Provincial Agreements Needed for Health Plans," *London Free Press*, 20 March 1955; "Health Insurance Hinges on Provincial Backing," *London Free Press*, 15 April 1955.
121 "The National Role in Health Insurance," *Ottawa Citizen*, 19 April 1955.
122 "Government Heads Speed Plans to Effect New Jobless Aid," *Winnipeg Free Press*, 26 April 1955.
123 Quoted in George Bain, "Ottawa Letter," *Toronto Globe and Mail*, 30 April 1955.
124 Martin, *So Many Worlds*, 232.
125 Grant Dexter to Tom Kent, 25 October 1956, Dexter Papers, box 1, file: Memos 1956, QUA.
126 Meeting of Provincial Health Officials and Advisors, 4 July 1955, RG 19, vol. 3890, file 5535094/H434(55), LAC.
127 "Report to the Chairman of the Preparatory Committee for the Federal-Provincial Conference," 29 July 1955, Martin Papers, vol. 6, file 40-5, LAC.
128 Fred Jackson to Martin, 6 September 1955, Martin Papers, vol. 15, file 95-1-1, LAC; see also "Informal Discussion concerning Health Insurance," 25 August 1955, RG 19, vol. 3890, file 5535094/H434(55), LAC.
129 Grant Dexter to Tom Kent, 5 February 1956, Dexter Papers, box 1, QUA.
130 R.B. Bryce to Donald Cameron, 8 September 1955; Donald Cameron to R.B. Bryce, 9 September 1955; and Donald Cameron, Memorandum for the Minister, 16 September 1955, RG 29, vol. 1132, file 504-5-6, LAC. See also Grant Dexter to Tom Kent, 1 March 1956, Dexter Papers, box 1, file: Memos 1956, QUA.
131 Bothwell and Kilbourn, *C.D. Howe*, 279; Blair Fraser, "Will Walter Harris Be Our Next Prime Minister?" *Maclean's*, 15 August 1954; Maurice Jefferies, "Today in Ottawa," *Windsor Daily Star*, 2 July 1954; Grant Dexter to Tom Kent, 18 December 1954, Dexter Papers, box 1, file: Memos 1956, QUA.
132 Martin to Walter Harris, 1 September 1955, Martin Papers, vol. 15, file 95-1-1, LAC.
133 Cabinet Conclusions, 28 September 1955, PCO Records, LAC.
134 Quoted in Malcolm Taylor, *Health Insurance*, 212.
135 George Davidson to Martin, handwritten note, [September 1955], Martin Papers, vol. 8, file 40-5-NHW, LAC.
136 Ibid. (emphasis in original).
137 Taylor, *Health Insurance*, 212.
138 Ibid., 130.
139 George Carty, Memorandum for the Minister, 1 December 1955, Martin Papers, vol. 15, file 95-1-1, LAC.
140 George Carty, Memorandum for the Minister, 20 December 1955, Martin Papers, vol. 8, file 40-5-NHW, LAC; Donald Cameron, Memorandum for the Minister, 12 January 1956, RG 29, vol. 1062, file 500-3-8, LAC.

141 Donald Cameron, Memorandum for the Minister, 12 January 1956, RG 29, vol. 1062, file 500-3-8, LAC.
142 Ibid., 9 January 1956; George Davidson, Memorandum to Mr. Deutsch, 17 January 1956, RG 19, vol. 3890, file 135-0-167, LAC.
143 Cabinet Conclusions, 18 and 20 January, PCO Records, LAC.

CHAPTER 7: DISAPPOINTMENT AND OPPOSITION, 1956–63

1 Malcolm Taylor, *Health Insurance*, 216.
2 Quoted in "'Agreement' Near on Health Plan," *Windsor Daily Star*, 25 January 1956.
3 "Fine Federal Health Offer," *Toronto Star*, 27 January 1956.
4 Reg Hardy, "Provinces Expected to Approve Scheme Proposed by Ottawa," *Hamilton Spectator*, 27 January 1956.
5 Clark Davey, "Ottawa Willing to Pay Half Cost of Health Plan," *Toronto Globe and Mail*, 27 January 1956.
6 Quoted in Margaret Aitken, "Between You and Me," *Toronto Telegram*, 20 February 1956.
7 Quoted in Arthur Blakely, "Ottawa: Day by Day," *Montreal Gazette*, 31 January 1956.
8 Norah Story interview with Paul Martin, [1969–70], Martin Papers, vol. 351, tape 3, side 1, LAC.
9 "Public Right Disregarded," *Edmonton Journal*, 30 July 1956.
10 Martin, *So Many Worlds*, 256.
11 Escott Reid to L.B. Pearson, 9 May 1956, Pearson Papers, vol. 12, file: Escott Reid, LAC.
12 Martin to Escott Reid, 8 December 1956, Martin Papers, vol. 517, file: Asia Tour, LAC.
13 "Nell Going with Paul," *Toronto Globe and Mail*, 18 October 1956, Martin Papers, vol. 168, LAC.
14 Betty Neill to the Office, 18 November 1956, Martin Papers, vol. 11, file: Personal Letters, LAC.
15 Author interview with Arthur Menzies, 26 June 2006.
16 Nell Martin, Circular Letter No. 6, 10 December 1956, Martin Papers, vol. 11, file: Personal Letters, LAC.
17 Escott Reid, *Radical Mandarin*, 292–93.
18 Author interview with Menzies, 26 June 2006.
19 Martin to Louis St. Laurent, 25 November 1956, Martin Papers, vol. 23, file: Asian Tour, LAC.
20 Between his visit to Indonesia in late November and his time in Burma, three weeks later, his perspective shifted radically. Compare Martin to Louis St. Laurent, 29 November 1956, with Martin to Louis St. Laurent, 20 December 1956, Martin Papers, vol. 23, file: Asian Tour, LAC.
21 Martin to St. Laurent, 20 December 1956, Martin Papers, LAC.
22 Canada, *House of Commons Debates* (17 January 1957), 2606.
23 Donald Cameron to Martin, 5 December 1956, Martin Papers, vol. 23, file: Asian Tour, LAC; Cabinet Conclusions, 19 December 1956, PCO Records, LAC.
24 Cabinet Conclusions, 17 and 22 January 1957, PCO Records, LAC.

25 Malcolm Taylor, *Health Insurance*, 222–26; Graham, *Old Man Ontario*, 327–28.
26 Cabinet Conclusions, 7 and 21 March 1957, PCO Records, LAC.
27 English, *The Worldly Years*, 185.
28 Quoted in Richard Jackson, "$6 Old Age Pension Boost Bothering Liberals Most," *Ottawa Journal*, 22 May 1957.
29 "Hot Meeting in Winkler," *Winkler Progress*, 22 May 1957.
30 "Might as Well Go Home Paul, You Can't Win," *Saskatoon Star-Phoenix*, 27 May 1957.
31 Quoted in Richard Jackson, "Ottawa Offbeat," *St. Thomas Times-Journal*, 1 June 1957.
32 Quoted in English, *The Worldly Years*, 194.
33 Ibid., 195.
34 W.A. Fraser to C.D. Howe, 11 September 1957, Howe Papers, vol. 108, file 5, LAC.
35 Ibid.
36 C.D. Howe to W.A. Fraser, 25 September 1957, Howe Papers, vol. 108, file 5, LAC.
37 Bruce Hutchison to Grant Dexter, 10 September 1957, Dexter Papers, box 1, file: Memos 1957, Queen's University Archives (QUA).
38 Paul Jefferies to Martin, 10 September 1957, Martin Papers, vol. 205, file: Leadership, LAC.
39 Martin to Burgon Bickersteth, 18 February 1958, Bickersteth Papers, B2005-113/00105, University of Toronto Archives (UTA).
40 Martin, *So Many Worlds*, 312.
41 Martin to Paul Nathanson, 21 October 1957, Martin Papers, vol. 450, file: Nathanson, LAC.
42 Robert Bothwell interview with Fraser Bruce, 18 February 1976, Bothwell Papers, B79-0055/002, UTA.
43 Robert Bothwell interview with Walter Harris, 27 October 1975, Bothwell Papers, B79-0055/002, UTA.
44 Confidential interview.
45 Peter Stursberg interview with Lionel Chevrier, 6 January 1977, Stursberg Papers, vol. 28, LAC.
46 Bruce Hutchison to Grant Dexter, 10 September 1957, Dexter Papers, box 1, file: Memos 1957, QUA.
47 Bothwell and Kilbourn, *C.D. Howe*, 336.
48 Quoted in "250 Supporters Cheer Statement," *Windsor Daily Star*, 14 December 1957.
49 Richard Jackson, "Ottawa Offbeat," *Daily Times Journal* (Fort William), 1 February 1958.
50 Peter Stursberg interview with Keith Davey, 27 January 1977, Stursberg Papers, vol. 28, LAC.
51 Peter Stursberg interview with James Coutts, 22 April 1977, Stursberg Papers, vol. 28, LAC.
52 T.E. Keyes to Martin, 30 December 1957, Howe Papers, vol. 228, file 62, LAC.
53 Stursberg interview with Davey, 27 January 1977, Stursberg Papers, LAC.
54 Martin, *So Many Worlds*, 314.
55 "Mrs. Paul Martin Is No Politician," *Montreal Star*, 14 January 1958.
56 Tim Creery, "Individuality Stamps Pearson, Martin Drives for Liberal Leadership," *Montreal Daily Star*, 14 January 1958.

57 Robert Bothwell and John English interview with Paul Martin, 11 November 1974, Bothwell Papers, UTA.

58 Quoted in Arthur Blakely, "Ottawa Day by Day," *Montreal Gazette,* 16 January 1958.

59 Pickersgill, *The Road Back,* 16.

60 Quoted in "I Back Mike – Martin," *Montreal Gazette,* 17 January 1958.

61 Quoted in Robert Hanley, "Says Martin's Feelings Hurt by Liberals' Firm Rejection," *Hamilton Spectator,* 17 January 1958.

62 Nielsen, *The House Is Not a Home,* 86.

63 Canada, *House of Commons Debates* (20 January 1958), 3515. Green's comment precedes Pearson's resolution but faithfully reflects the raucous debate.

64 Quoted in Stursberg, *Diefenbaker: Leadership Gained,* 88–89.

65 Author interview with Trevor Price, 2 September 2007.

66 Quoted in "Tory Trade Policies 'Bennett Over Again' – Predict Dire Result," *Toronto Daily Star,* 6 March 1958.

67 Quoted in Harold Hilliard, "Tory Times Tough Right Back to '90's, Paul Martin Claims," *Toronto Daily Star,* 5 March 1958.

68 Martin to Frank Ahearn, 26 February 1958, Martin Papers, vol. 189, LAC.

69 Richard Jackson, "Ottawa Offbeat," *Sudbury Daily Star,* 12 April 1958.

70 Ibid.

71 "Cheers ... Near Tears ... Then Cheers Again," *Windsor Daily Star,* 1 April 1958.

72 Don Emerson to Martin, 20 July 1960, Martin Papers, vol. 250, file: Emerson, LAC.

73 Quoted in Walter Pitman, "Men Who Matter in Parliament," *Peterborough Examiner,* 5 October 1961.

74 Grant Dexter to Tom Kent, [October 1957], Dexter Papers, vol. 1, file: Memos 1957, QUA.

75 B.T. Richardson, "He's the Leader Nagged by a Doubt," *Toronto Telegram,* 10 August 1960.

76 Story interview with Martin, [1969–70], Martin Papers, vol. 351, tape 4, side 1, LAC.

77 Frank Ahearn to Martin, 4 January 1959, Martin Papers, vol. 189, LAC.

78 H.R. Lawson to Martin, 14 February 1957, Martin Papers, vol. 356, file: Evolution of Holdings, LAC.

79 McDonald, "Blind Trust."

80 Moore, "Nathan L. Nathanson," 22–45.

81 Martin to Paul Nathanson, 7 August 1956, Martin Papers, vol. 418, LAC.

82 Maxwell Cummings to Martin, 24 October 1956; and J.C. Wrangham to Martin, 22 January 1957, Martin Papers, vol. 418, LAC; Martin to Paul Nathanson, 25 February 1957, Martin Papers, vol. 450, LAC.

83 Martin to Paul Nathanson, 21 October 1957, Martin Papers, vol. 450, LAC.

84 Author interview with Paul Martin Jr., 24 May 2012.

85 J. Ros Ker to Martin, 13 December 1957, Martin Papers, vol. 210, LAC.

86 Income tax returns, Martin Papers, vol. 418, LAC.

87 Story interview with Martin, [1969–70], Martin Papers, vol. 351, tape 10, side 1, LAC.

88 Author interview with Paul Hellyer, 30 July 2006.

89 Pearson, *Mike,* 3:39.

90 Author interview with Tom Kent, 23 August 2007.
91 Lester B. Pearson to Martin, 31 March 1958, Martin Papers, vol. 223, file 5, LAC.
92 Ralph Hyman, "For Paul Martin – High Hopes of a Place at the Top," *Toronto Globe and Mail Magazine*, 12 November 1960; see also Maurice Jefferies, "Big Job Offers Won't Lure Martin from Public Life," *Windsor Daily Star*, 29 January 1959.
93 Ralph Maybank to L.B. Pearson, and enclosure, 8 July 1962, Pearson Papers, Series N2, vol. 22, LAC.
94 Author interview with Kent, 23 August 2007. On this point, see also Blair Fraser, "Split-Level Cabinet," *Maclean's*, 4 April 1964.
95 Story interview with Martin, [1969–70], Martin Papers, vol. 352, tape 9, side 2, LAC.
96 Quoted in Hyman, "For Paul Martin – High Hopes."
97 Grant Dexter to File, 5 April 1962, Dexter Papers, box 1, file: Memos 1957, QUA.
98 Chubby Power to Grant Dexter, 17 June 1957, Dexter Papers, box 1, file: Memos 1957, QUA.
99 English, *The Worldly Years*, 208.
100 This and the next few paragraphs draw heavily on Azzi, *Walter Gordon*, 75–84; English, *The Worldly Years*, 218–32; Kent, *A Public Purpose*, 89–110; McCall-Newman, *Grits*, 36–42.
101 McCall-Newman, *Grits*, 36.
102 Story interview with Martin, [1969–70], Martin Papers, vol. 351, tape 3, side 2, LAC.
103 Quoted in English, *The Worldly Years*, 219.
104 Quoted in McCall-Newman, *Grits*, 46.
105 Story interview with Martin, 13 May 1971, Martin Papers, vol. 351, tape 2, side 1, LAC.
106 Author interview with Kent, 23 August 2007.
107 Nielsen, *The House Is Not a Home*, 86–88; Walker, *Fun along the Way*, 173–73.
108 Richard Jackson, "Unofficially Leads Ottawa Liberals?" *Sudbury Daily Star*, 31 March 1959.
109 Holt, *The Other Mrs. Diefenbaker*, 307–10.
110 Stursberg, *Diefenbaker: Leadership Gained*, 71–72.
111 Quoted in Goodman, *Life of the Party*, 107.
112 Author interview with Basil Robinson, 15 July 2006.
113 Richard Jackson, "Ex-Minister, as Pro Politician, Keeps Parliament in Turmoil," *Sudbury Star*, 31 March 1959.
114 Arthur R. Ford, "Commons Lacks Old-School Orators," *London Free Press*, 14 November 1959.
115 Sévigny, *This Game of Politics*, 122.
116 Patrick Nicholson, "Color Abundant in Parliament," *Quebec Chronicle-Telegraph*, 9 June 1961.
117 W.L. Clark, "As We See It," *Windsor Star*, 20 July 1960.
118 Nell Martin to Marjorie Frank, [August 1958], Martin Papers, vol. 206, file: Middle East, LAC.
119 Ibid., 2 September 1958.
120 "Notes on Mr. Martin's Trip to the Middle East," 10 October 1958, Martin Papers, vol. 206, file: Middle East, LAC.

121 Ibid.

122 Nell Martin to Marjorie Frank, 12 September 1958, Martin Papers, vol. 206, file: Middle East, LAC.

123 "Notes on Mr. Martin's Trip to the Middle East," 10 October 1958; and Martin to Sidney Smith, 24 November 1958, Martin Papers, vol. 206, file: Middle East, LAC.

124 Martin, *So Many Worlds*, 335–36.

125 Quoted in Tom Hazlitt, "Martin and His Memories Return to Sleepy Pembroke," *Toronto Star,* 6 March 1968.

126 Patrick Nicholson, "Martin Denies Retirement Plan," Ottawa report, publication and date unknown [c. first week of February 1959], Martin Papers, vol. 223, file 3, LAC.

127 Canada, *House of Commons Debates* (23 March 1959), 2134.

128 See Canada, *House of Commons Debates* (10 April 1959), 2568 (Douglas Harkness); (20 April 1959), 2849 (Frank McGee); (7 April 1960), 2989 (Michael Starr); see also Ken Kelly, "'Old Pro' Martin 'Expert Needler,'" *Ottawa Journal,* 15 March 1960.

129 Quoted in Harry Bruce, "Angry MP's Shake Fists at Martin," *Ottawa Journal,* 30 May 1959.

130 Canada, *House of Commons Debates* (2 February, 12 February, and 19 February 1960), 650, 1022, 1232, and 1241.

131 Ibid. (2 February 1960), 646.

132 See Canada, *House of Commons Debates* (29 January 1960), 495–96 (Paul Martin, Michael Starr); (1 February 1960), 551–52 (Paul Martin, Michael Starr); (2 February 1960), 646–48 (Paul Martin); (5 February 1960), 766–67 (Michael Starr); see Canada, *Report of the Committee on Unemployment Statistics* (Ottawa: Queen's Printer, 1960), [ii], 19.

133 Quoted in Lee Bellard, "Architect with a Needle," *Toronto Daily Star,* 29 March 1960.

134 Canada, *House of Commons Debates* (28 July 1960), 7153.

135 Saywell, *Canadian Annual Review (CAR) for 1960,* 58–60.

136 Quoted in Stursberg, *Diefenbaker: Leadership Gained,* 211.

137 Ibid., 210.

138 Ibid., 212-13.

139 Keith Laird to Martin, 20 July 1960, Martin Papers, vol. 418, file: Windsor House, LAC.

140 Quoted in Hyman, "For Paul Martin – High Hopes."

141 Author interview with Mary Anne Bellamy, 22 August 2007.

142 See, for instance, Martin to Mayor M.J. Patrick, 4 April 1962, Martin Papers, vol. 217, LAC; "Time for Decision. Take a Standing Tomorrow," [May 1962], Martin Papers, vol. 197, file: Federal Election 1962, LAC.

143 See, for example, Canada, *House of Commons Debates* (19 January 1960), 127; (11 March 1960), 1999–2001; (20 June 1960), 5111; and (5 July 1960), 5739–40.

144 Martin to Premier L.J. Robichaud, and related correspondence, 24 March 1961, Martin Papers, vol. 214, file: Transmission Towers, LAC.

145 Martin to Friends, 10 July 1959; and Martin to H. Markham, 4 March 1960, Martin Papers, vol. 214, file: Transport, LAC.

146 See correspondence in Martin Papers, vol. 210, files: Ruscomb River Dredging, 1959–60, and Ruscomb River Public Works, 1959–63, LAC.

147 Martin to Frank Starr, 28 March 1961, Martin Papers, vol. 214, LAC.

148 Nell Martin to Martin, [May 1961], Martin Papers, vol. 223, LAC.
149 Paul Martin Jr. to Martin, 12 May 1961, Martin Papers, vol. 214, LAC.
150 Mary Anne Martin to Martin, 19 April 1960, Martin Papers, vol. 516, LAC.
151 Author interview with Bellamy, 22 August 2007.
152 Martin, *So Many Worlds*, 348.
153 This account of the Coyne affair is drawn from Granatstein, *Canada, 1957–67*, 78–83; English, *The Worldly Years*, 233–34; Smith, *Rogue Tory*, 393–413; Saywell, *CAR for 1961*, 13–19.
154 Quoted in Saywell, *CAR for 1961*, 16.
155 Quoted in Granatstein, *Canada, 1957–67*, 78.
156 English, *The Worldly Years*, 239; Smith, *Rogue Tory*, 441.
157 Muirhead, *Against the Odds*, 194–49.
158 Author interview with Norman Hillmer, 27 November 2013.
159 Quoted in "Just an Amateur Again," *Windsor Star*, 9 May 1962.
160 C.M. Bowman to D.G. Blair, 13 May 1962, Martin Papers, vol. 220, LAC.
161 See, for instance, "Martin Hits Govt. Fight with Coyne," *Winnipeg Free Press*, 12 May 1962; "Promise, Performance Contrast Will Be Issue," *Regina Leader-Post*, 14 May 1962.
162 "Diefenbaker 'Defendant,'" *Windsor Star*, 14 May 1962; "Martin Accorded Ovation at Mammoth Liberal Rally," *Vancouver Sun*, 15 May 1962.
163 Martin to J.W. Hefferman, 25 July 1962, Martin Papers, vol. 197, file: Federal Election 1962, LAC.
164 "Paul Asks Parliament Be Called," *Windsor Star*, 13 July 1962.
165 "Paul Martin Rejects Mackenzie King's View," *Ottawa Journal*, 13 July 1962.
166 Martin to Joseph Zagel, 18 October 1962, Martin Papers, vol. 239, file: Aetna Maintenance, LAC.
167 Quoted in "Martin Takes Poke at N-Testing Stand," *Winnipeg Tribune*, 11 May 1962.
168 Martin, *So Many Worlds*, 366.
169 Fleming, *So Very Near*, 2:583.

CHAPTER 8: SAVING THE WORLD, 1963–64

1 Charles Lynch, "Prime Minister's Starring Role: Defence Doubletalk," *Ottawa Citizen*, 2 April 1963.
2 Martin, *So Many Worlds*, 368–69.
3 "Says Prime Minister No Longer in Control," *Windsor Star*, 28 January 1963.
4 Quoted in "Martin's Opponents Glum," *Windsor Star* clipping, Martin Papers, vol. 197, file: 1963 Election, Library and Archives Canada (LAC).
5 Quoted in "Martin Warns Quebec: Socreds Tory Accomplices," *Windsor Star* clipping, Martin Papers, vol. 197, file: 1963 Election, LAC.
6 "An Open Letter to the Prwime Minister from the Hon. Paul Martin," *Calgary Herald*, 23 March 1963.
7 Lynch, "Prime Minister's Starring Role."
8 Quoted in "The Prime Minister," *Time*, 3 May 1963.
9 "Pearson Selects Cabinet of Experts," *London Free Press*, 23 April 1963.

10 "Mr. Pearson Ignores Glamour," *Ottawa Citizen*, 23 April 1963.

11 "Skilful Blending of Talent," *Regina Leader-Post*, 23 April 1963; "The New Cabinet: The Persons," *Montreal Gazette*, 23 April 1963.

12 "The New Pearson Team," *Toronto Star*, 23 April 1963.

13 Hilliker and Barry, *Canada's Department of External Affairs*, 49.

14 Martin, "At the Right Hand," iv.

15 Canada, Department of External Affairs, *Annual Report for 1963*, 48–49.

16 Burney, *Getting It Done*, 11.

17 Donald Gordon, "Warning: Our Halo Abroad Is Slipping," *Saturday Night*, October 1963, 23–25.

18 See Peter Stursberg, "Paul Martin: The Man and His Policy," *Saturday Night*, November 1963, 15–20; Peter Newman, "Paul Martin: Quiet Style and New Politics for Canadian Foreign Affairs," *Maclean's*, 22 February 1964.

19 Martin, "At the Right Hand," 9.

20 Norah Story interview with Paul Martin, [1969–70], Martin Papers, vol. 353, tape A-7, side 1, LAC.

21 Author interview with Herb Gray, 8 August 2007.

22 Story interview with Martin, [1969–70], Martin Papers, vol. 353, tape A-7, side 1, LAC.

23 Quoted in Newman, "Paul Martin: Quiet Style."

24 Quoted in Peter Jackman, "Parliament: Repatriating Paul for Duty on the Home Front," *Ottawa Journal*, 18 December 1964.

25 See Stursberg, "Paul Martin: The Man," 15.

26 Jackman, "Parliament: Repatriating Paul."

27 See Stursberg, "Paul Martin: The Man," 15.

28 "Now," *Windsor Star*, 31 December 1965.

29 Sawatsky, *The Insiders*, 65–66.

30 Granatstein, *A Man of Influence*, 358.

31 Bothwell, "Marcel Cadieux"; Hilliker and Barry, *Canada's Department of External Affairs*, 258–60.

32 Escott Reid, Conversation with L.B. Pearson, 27 August 1964, Reid Papers, vol. 33, file 22, LAC.

33 Don Page, "Interview with Paul Martin, 19 March 1979," Department of Foreign Affairs, Trade and Development (DFATD) Oral History Project.

34 Granatstein, *A Man of Influence*, 362–63.

35 Page, "Interview with Paul Martin, 19 March 1979," DFATD Oral History Project.

36 Michel de Goumois to author, 31 July 2013; Martin, *So Many Worlds*, 379.

37 Author interview with Duncan Edmonds, 12 November 2007.

38 Story interview with Martin, [1969–70], Martin Papers, vol. 353, tape A-16, side 1, LAC.

39 Marcel Cadieux Diary, 10 April 1964, Cadieux Papers, vol. 12, file 10, LAC (author's translation); original: "La vérité des choses est que le Ministre ne semble pas, à dessin ou autrement, à se rendre compte du caractère véritable du métier de diplomate."

40 Ibid., 2 July 1964 (author's translation); original: "J'ai fini par comprendre – il s'agit d'une odieuse, d'une dégoutante, d'une merdeuse affaire de patronage."

41 Escott Reid, Memorandum of Conversation with L.B. Pearson, 30 January 1967, Reid Papers, vol. 35, file 31, LAC.

42 Quoted in "They Also Serve," *Windsor Star*, 12 September 1964.

43 Quoted in "Mrs. Paul Martin Speaks Candidly about Home, Politics, Elections," *Oshawa Times*, 20 March 1968.

44 "They Also Serve."

45 Eugene Whelan to Martin, 3 September 1963, Martin Papers, vol. 232, file 27-1, LAC.

46 Martin to Harry Hays, 6 September 1963; and Harry Hays to Martin, 18 September 1963, Martin Papers, vol. 232, file 27-I, LAC.

47 Martin to Walter Gordon, 24 October 1963, Martin Papers, vol. 232, file: Finance, LAC.

48 This paragraph is based on the correspondence in Martin Papers, vol. 234, file 3, LAC.

49 Murray Elder to Martin, 16 July 1963, Martin Papers, vol. 234, file 88, LAC.

50 Guy Favreau to Martin, 17 June 1963; and Herb Gray to Guy Favreau, 6 August 1963, Martin Papers, vol. 231, file: Justice, LAC.

51 Herb Gray to Martin, 3 June 1963, Martin Papers, vol. 233, file: Justice, LAC.

52 Maurice Jefferies to Martin, 14 July 1966, Martin Papers, vol. 251, file: External Affairs, LAC.

53 Martin to Th. Chevalier, 30 July 1963; and Martin to Aline Pritchard, 19 August 1963, Martin Papers, vol. 241, file: Belle River, LAC.

54 George McIlraith to Martin, 21 June 1963, and subsequent correspondence, Martin Papers, vol. 234, file 88, LAC.

55 Martin's marginal note on Keith Laird to Martin, 9 September 1963, Martin Papers, vol. 232, file 88, LAC.

56 Martin to Henry Renaud, 3 September 1963, Martin Papers, vol. 237, file 28-1-R, LAC.

57 Quoted in "These Are the Keys to Success of Pearson Government," *Toronto Star*, 22 April 1963.

58 Quoted in Swainson, *Conflict over the Columbia*, 246, 248.

59 Ibid., 227–28.

60 Paul Martin, Memorandum for the Prime Minister, 7 May 1963, RG 25, vol. 5181, file 5724-2-40, LAC.

61 Cabinet Conclusions, 9 May 1963, PCO Records, LAC.

62 Jack Davis to Prime Minister, 14 May 1963; Minutes of a Meeting of the Cabinet Committee on the Columbia River, 29 May 1963; Jack Davis to Ed Ritchie, 30 May 1963; and Jack Davis to Walter Gordon, 30 May 1963, RG 25, vol. 5181, file 5724-2-40, LAC.

63 Cabinet Conclusions, 30 May 1963, PCO Records, LAC.

64 Swainson, *Conflict over the Columbia*, 266.

65 Martin, Memorandum for Cabinet: Discussions with British Columbia, 5 June 1963; and Martin, Memorandum for Cabinet: Agreement with British Columbia, 26 June 1963, RG 25, vol. 5181, file 5724-2-40, LAC; Cabinet Conclusions, 6 June 1963, PCO Records, LAC.

66 Jack Davis to Martin, 3 July 1963, RG 25, vol. 5181, file 5724-2-40, LAC.

67 Martin to Jack Davis, 5 July 1963, RG 25, vol. 5181, file 5724-2-40, LAC.

68 A.E. Ritchie, Memorandum for the Minister, 17 July 1963, RG 25, vol. 5181, file 5724-2-40, LAC.

69 Draft Joint Summary Record of Discussion and Conclusions, 1–2 August 1963, RG 25, vol. 5181, file 5724-2-40, LAC.

70 Swainson, *Conflict over the Columbia*, 261.

71 Draft Joint Summary Record of Discussion and Conclusion, 9-11 December 1963, RG 25, vol. 5181, file 5724-2-40, LAC.

72 Sherman, *Bennett*, 279.

73 Keenleyside, *On the Bridge of Time*, 513.

74 Quoted in Sherman, *Bennett*, 279.

75 Cabinet Conclusions, 11 December 1963, PCO Records, LAC.

76 Briefing Note for Visit of Prime Minister Pearson: Foreign Aid, 3 May 1963, NSF, Country Files: Canada, Box 19, John F. Kennedy Library.

77 US Department of State, Position Paper: Canadian Aid Program, 13 September 1963, RG 40, Acc. NN#-40-87-1, box 1, file: Joint Canada-US Committee, United States National Archives.

78 Herb Moran, Memorandum for the Minister, 22 April 1963, RG 25, vol. 5591, file 12881-2-40, LAC.

79 Herb Moran to Mac Bow, 19 June 1963; and Herb Moran to John Read, 30 July 1963, RG 25, vol. 5591, file 12881-2-40, LAC.

80 Herb Moran, Memorandum for the Minister and attached draft Memorandum for Cabinet, 10 September 1963, RG 25, vol. 5591, file 12881-2-40, LAC.

81 Walter Gordon to Martin, 10 October 1963; and Martin to L.B. Pearson, 19 October 1963, RG 25, vol. 5591, file 12881-2-40, LAC.

82 Cabinet Conclusions, 14 November 1963, PCO Records, LAC.

83 Escott Reid to Martin, 18 November 1963, Martin Papers, vol. 236, file 28-1-R, LAC.

84 Quoted in Norman Robertson, Memorandum for the Minister, 30 August 1963, RG 25, vol. 10097, file 20-1-2-France, LAC.

85 Story interview with Martin, [1969-70], Martin Papers, vol. 351, tape 2, side 2, LAC.

86 Jean Fournier, Memorandum for the USSEA, 9 September 1963, RG 25, vol. 10097, file 20-1-2-France, LAC; Orme Dier to Norman Robertson, 16 September 1963, RG 25, vol. 10101, file 20-Canada-9-Pearson, LAC.

87 Story interview with Martin, [1969-70], Martin Papers, vol. 351, tape 8, side 1, LAC.

88 Paris to Ottawa, Tel. No. 1362, 17 November 1963, RG 25, vol. 10101, file 20-Canada-9-Pearson, LAC.

89 Ottawa to Paris (for Minister), Tel. No. W-8, 16 January 1964, RG 25, vol. 10101, file 20-Canada-9-Pearson, LAC.

90 Ottawa to Paris, Tel. No. S-33, 30 January 1964, RG 25, vol. 10101, file 20-Canada-9-Pearson, LAC (author's trasnslation). Original: "Nous n'avons pas l'intention de gêner votre vie nationale. Nous ne nous mélerons pas des affaires Canadiennes."

91 Paris to Ottawa, Tel. No. SVC-23, 22 January 1964, RG 25, vol. 10101, file 20-Canada-9-Pearson, LAC.

92 Quoted in Meren, *With Friends Like These*, 117.

93 Story interview with Martin, [1969-70], Martin Papers, vol. 353, tape 15, side 1, LAC.

94 Author interview with John Hadwen, 12 July 2007.

95 Jules Léger to Martin, 14 June 1966, Martin Papers, vol. 229, file 40, LAC (author's translation); original: "Au cours des dernières années, vous avez réussi à établir une intimité avec votre homologue français qui facilite le travail à tous les niveaux. En termes de métier, cette amitié est très précieuses."

96 Cadieux Diary, 12 January 1967, Cadieux Papers, vol. 12, file 9, LAC (author's translation); original: "En matiere politique, M. Martin et Couve de Murville ont des relations personnelles et officielles étroites."
97 Maurice Couve de Murville to Martin, 2 February 1964, Martin Papers, vol. 226, file 14: Misc. Correspondence, LAC (author's translation); original: "Nous avons nous-mêmes été particulièrement heureux de la visite ... Nous en garderons un souvenir durable et particulièrement sympathique. Au-delà des sentiments personnels, ils y a les sentiments de nos nations respectives et leurs intérêts bien compris. Tous cela a été excellement servi et les conséquences en seront fructueuses dans l'avenir."
98 Story interview with Martin, [1969–70], Martin Papers, vol. 353, tape 7-A, LAC.
99 "At UN Martin Becomes a Star Performer," *Hamilton Spectator*, [September 1965].
100 Hellyer, *Damn the Torpedoes*, 2–4, 32–39.
101 Martin to Paul Hellyer, 21 December 1963, Raymont Papers, file 768, Directorate of History and Heritage (DHIST), Department of National Defence; see also Ross Campbell to Air Chief Marshall Frank Miller, 6 February 1954, with attached draft, Raymont Papers, file 759, DHIST.
102 Kent, *A Public Purpose*, 312.
103 Arnold Smith, Memorandum for the Minister, 29 January 1964, RG 25, vol. 10130, file 21-14-1-Cyprus, LAC; Martin, "At the Right Hand," 422.
104 Ross Campbell, Memorandum for the Acting Under-Secretary, 1 February 1964, RG 25, vol. 10130, file 21-14-1-Cyprus, LAC.
105 Cabinet Conclusions, 4 February 1964, PCO Records, LAC.
106 Ottawa to Tel Aviv et al., Tel. No. S-56, 6 February 1964, RG 25, vol. 10130, file 21-14-1-Cyprus, LAC.
107 G.S. Murray to Arnold Smith, 12 February 1964; and Arnold Smith to File, 24 February 1964, RG 25, vol. 10130, file 21-14-1-Cyprus, LAC.
108 Martin marginal note on Ross Campbell, Memorandum for the Minister, 8 February 1964, RG 25, vol. 10130, file 21-14-1-Cyprus, LAC.
109 "Troops? 1,000 Troops? Butler Springs Big Surprise," *Windsor Star*, 11 February 1964.
110 Story interview with Martin, [1969], Martin Papers, vol. 351, tape 8, side 1, LAC.
111 Arnold Smith's marginal note on his Memorandum for the Minister, 18 February 1964, RG 25, vol. 10130, file 21-14-1-Cyprus, LAC.
112 Canada, *House of Commons Debates* (19 February 1964), 6.
113 Arnold Smith, Memorandum for File, 24 February 1964, RG 25, vol. 10130, file 21-14-1-Cyprus, LAC.
114 Ottawa to New York, Tel. No. G-22, 25 February 1964; and Ottawa to London, Tel. No. S-88, 1 March 1964, RG 25, vol. 10130, file 21-14-1-Cyprus, LAC.
115 Marcel Cadieux, Memorandum for the Minister, 3 March 1964; and Ottawa to New York, Tel. No. V-66, 3 March 1964, RG 25, vol. 10137, file 21-14-6-UNFICYP-9, LAC.
116 Cabinet Conclusions, 5 March 1964, PCO Records, LAC.
117 Ottawa to New York, Tel. No. S-99, 4 March 1964, RG 25, vol. 10130, file 21-14-1-Cyprus, LAC.
118 London to Ottawa, Tel. No. 837, 10 March 1964, RG 25, vol. 10130, file 21-14-1-Cyprus, LAC.

119 New York to Ottawa, Tel. No. 356, 10 March 1964, RG 25, vol. 10130, file 21-14-1-Cyprus, LAC.

120 "Canada Gets Force Ready, Waits Word," *Montreal Gazette*, 7 March 1964.

121 "'Not Shirking' Duty but ...," *Toronto Star*, 9 March 1964.

122 "Cyprus: Why the Delay?" *Toronto Globe and Mail*, 10 March 1964.

123 Mac Bow to Mr. Cadieux, 11 March 1964, RG 25, vol. 10130, file: 21-14-1-Cyprus, LAC; Martin, "At the Right Hand," 422.

124 New York to Ottawa, Tel. No. 359, 10 March 1964; and New York to Ottawa, Tel. No. 368, 11 March 1964, RG 25, vol. 10130, file 21-14-1-Cyprus, LAC.

125 Ross Campbell, Memorandum for the USSEA, 12 March 1964, RG 25, vol. 10130, file 21-14-1-Cyprus, LAC.

126 Ibid.

127 Ibid.; "Martin Spurred Cyprus Force Decision," *Toronto Star*, 14 March 1964.

128 New York to Ottawa, Tel. Nos. 374 and 387, 12 March 1964, RG 25, vol. 10130, file 21-14-1-Cyprus, LAC.

129 Martin, *So Many Worlds*, 547.

130 Martin, "At the Right Hand," 435.

131 Ibid.

132 Ibid.

133 Ross Campbell, Memorandum to Mr. Martin, 13 March 1964, RG 25, vol. 10130, file 21-14-1-Cyprus, LAC. As an anonymous External Affairs source explained to the Ottawa press, "Ireland triggered Sweden. Actually, the Irish agreement was a bit of a surprise." Quoted in "Martin Spurred Cyprus Force Decision."

134 Cabinet Conclusions, 13 March 1964, PCO Records, LAC.

135 Alan James, *Keeping the Peace*, 110–11.

136 Quoted in "Martin Spurred Cyprus Force Decision."

137 Jim Walker to Martin, 25 March 1964, Martin Papers, vol. 251, file: EA, LAC.

138 Quoted in Saywell, *Canadian Annual Review for 1964*, 231; see also Fred Nossal, "Focus on Paul Martin," *Toronto Globe and Mail*, 16 May 1964; Robert McKeown, "There's a New Paul Martin," *Toronto Globe and Mail Weekend Magazine*, 30 May 1964.

139 Bruce Hutchison, "Canada's New Foreign Policy," *Winnipeg Free Press*, 19 May 1964.

140 "Brilliance Written with a Quill Pen," *Time*, 27 April 1964.

141 Blair Fraser, "Split-Level Cabinet," *Maclean's*, 4 April 1964.

142 L.B. Pearson to Martin, 22 June 1964, Martin Papers, vol. 275, file: Birthday Greetings, LAC.

143 Geneva to Ottawa, Tel. No. 282, 23 March 1964; and Geneva to Ottawa, Tel. No. 299, 25 March 1964, RG 25, vol. 10130, file 21-14-1-Cyprus, LAC.

144 Martin to Saul Rae, 30 March 1964; and Martin to Ken Menzies, 30 March 1964, Martin Papers, vol. 237, LAC.

145 Quoted in Richard Jackson, "Hill Talk," *Ottawa Journal*, 18 April 1964 (emphasis in original).

146 Quoted in Jack Dulmage, "Between Whistles," *Windsor Star*, 17 June 1964.

147 Geoff Stirling to Martin, 1 April 1964, Martin Papers, vol. 291, file: NHL, LAC.

148 John Walker, "Political Knife in Back for PM," *Ottawa Citizen*, 15 July 1964.

149 Martin to Frank Wansbrough, 2 July 1964, Martin Papers, vol. 230, file 25-10, LAC.
150 Quoted in "Martin at Retreat," *Windsor Star,* 3 August 1964.
151 "Now," *Windsor Star,* 18 July 1964.
152 Quoted in Fraser Kelly, "Testing Martin's Machine," *Toronto Telegram,* 9 September 1964.

CHAPTER 9: DEALING WITH WASHINGTON, 1964–65

1 Martin to Clarence Nichols, 20 April 1964, Martin Papers, vol. 279, file: N, Library and Archives Canada (LAC).
2 Marcel Cadieux Diary, 14 April 1964, Cadieux Papers, vol. 12, file 1, LAC.
3 Martin to Alexander Watson, Chairman of the Canadian Maritime Commission, 6 April 1964, Martin Papers, vol. 250, file: Don Emerson, LAC.
4 Martin to Don Emerson, 8 July 1964, Martin Papers, vol. 250, file: Don Emerson, LAC.
5 Alice Shanahan to Martin, 22 August 1964, Martin Papers, vol. 297, file: Mrs. Tom Shanahan, LAC.
6 "Now," *Windsor Star,* 11 November 1964.
7 Quoted in "Many Grits Blame Paul for 'Snub,'" *Windsor Star,* 14 November 1964.
8 Ibid.
9 "Paul Ranges Far, Wide in Talk," *Windsor Star,* 16 November 1964.
10 Martin to Maurice Strong, 19 November 1964, Martin Papers, vol. 250, file: Don Emerson, LAC.
11 "Martin, Reaume Honoured," *Windsor Star,* 26 November 1964.
12 Nielsen, *The House Is Not a Home,* 139–43.
13 Kent, *A Public Purpose,* 325–26; Cadieux Diary, 1 December 1964, Cadieux Papers, vol. 12, file 1, LAC.
14 Gwyn, *The Shape of Scandal,* 56–57; Newman, *The Distemper of Our Times,* 279–80.
15 Cadieux Diary, 12 January 1965, Cadieux Papers, vol. 12, file 9, LAC (author's translation); original: "Depuis un mois et demi, il ne vit pas. Il ne pense qu'a cette affaire."
16 Ibid., 20 January 1965.
17 Author interview with Duncan Edmonds, 12 November 2007.
18 "Latin American Stock Suspended, TSE Cites Working Capital Lack," *Toronto Globe and Mail,* 19 January 1967.
19 Martin to Paul Martin Jr., 21 February 1966, Martin Papers, vol. 295, file: RETS, LAC.
20 Marjorie Frank to Martin, [June 1965], Martin Papers, vol. 296, file: Bill Richardson, LAC.
21 Kent, *A Public Purpose,* 330.
22 The arguments are outlined in N.A. Robertson, Memorandum for the Minister, 6 May 1963, and attachments, Memorandum: Canada and the OAS, 1 May 1963, and Canada and the OAS, 3 May 1963, RG 25, vol. 5044, file 2226-40, LAC.
23 Martin to Senator John Connolly, 20 November 1964, Martin Papers, vol. 12, file 12-2, LAC.
24 Gallup Poll, 27 November 1963, Canadian Institute of Public Opinion (CIPO) Archives.

25 "Martin Asks Closer Ties with China," *Ottawa Journal,* 25 July 1963.

26 Martin's marginalia on Marcel Cadieux, Memorandum for the Minister, 29 October 1964, RG 25, vol. 9325, file 20-China-14, LAC.

27 Martin's marginalia on ibid.

28 Pickersgill quoted in Donald Page to File, 6 October 1982, CIH-330, file 7-5-2-7, Department of Foreign Affairs, Trade and Development (DFATD).

29 Cabinet Conclusions, 22 December 1964, PCO Records, LAC. See also Martin, *So Many Worlds,* 513–14.

30 Donaghy, "Domesticating NATO," 447–48.

31 Transcript, CBC NATO Special, 24 May 1963, Martin Papers, vol. 230, file 25-11(1), LAC.

32 Martin, *So Many Worlds,* 575.

33 Circular Documents, No. A7/64, 25 June 1964, RG 25, vol. 10288, file 27-4-NATO-12-1964-Spring, LAC.

34 Ottawa to NATO Paris, Tel. No. DL-2256, 10 November 1964, RG 25, vol. 10300, file 27-4-NATO-12-1964-Spring, LAC.

35 McGeorge Bundy, Memorandum for A/Secretary of State George Ball, 16 December 1964, National Security Files, Country file: Canada, vol. 2, box 165, LBJ Library.

36 Quoted in Bothwell, *Alliance and Illusion,* 224.

37 L.B. Pearson, "Extracts from an Address by the Rt. Hon. L.B. Pearson to the Canadian Club of Ottawa," 10 February 1965, DFATD, *Statements and Speeches,* No. 63/3.

38 Marcel Cadieux, Memorandum for the Minister, 18 February 1965, RG 25, vol. 10288, file 27-4-NATO-1, LAC. See also Cadieux Diary, 3 March 1965, Cadieux Papers, vol. 12, file 9, LAC.

39 Cadieux Diary, 3 March 1965, Cadieux Papers, vol. 12, file 9, LAC.

40 Escott Reid, Confidential Note, March 1965, Reid Papers, vol. 33, file 22, LAC.

41 Ottawa to Saigon, Tel. No. Y-289, 1 August 1963, RG 25, vol. 4639, file 50052-A-1-40, LAC.

42 Memorandum of Conversation: North Vietnam, 24 December 1963, Harriman Papers, box 519, file: Vietnam General: December 1963, LAC.

43 Washington to Ottawa, Tel. No. 1002, 16 March 1964, RG 25, vol. 10113, file 20-22-Viets-2-1, LAC.

44 Martin, Memorandum for the Prime Minister, 28 April 1964, RG 25, vol. 14151, file 35-4-5-1-1964, LAC.

45 Preston, "Balancing War and Peace," 73–111.

46 Minutes of Rusk-SSEA Meeting, 30 April 1964, RG 25, vol. 10113, file 20-22-Viets-2-1, LAC. See also telegram from the Department of State to the Embassy in Vietnam, 1 May 1964, in US Department of State, *Foreign Relations of the United States (FRUS),* 1:281–82.

47 US Department of State, *FRUS,* 1:395.

48 Quoted in Preston, "Balancing War and Peace," 76. See also Record of Conversation: Visit of Messrs Sullivan and Cooper to the Department, 3 June 1964, RG 25, vol. 10113, file 20-22-Viets-2-1, LAC.

49 US Department of State, *FRUS,* 1:395n5.

50 Record of Conversation: Visit of Messrs Sullivan and Cooper, 3 June 1964, RG 25, LAC.

51 Washington to Ottawa, Tel. No. 2250, 22 June 1964, RG 25, vol. 10113, file 20-22-Viets-2-1, LAC.
52 Washington to Ottawa, Tel. No. 2518, 14 July 1964, RG 25, vol. 10113, file 20-22-Viets-2-1, LAC.
53 Louis Rogers, Memorandum for the USSEA, marginal notes and attached memorandum, 31 July 1964, RG 25, vol. 10113, file 20-22-Viets-2-1, LAC.
54 Ottawa to NATO Paris, Tel. No. Y-609, 14 August 1964, RG 25, vol. 10113, file 20-22-Viets-2-1, LAC.
55 Ibid.
56 Martin's marginalia on Marcel Cadieux, Memorandum for the Minister, 12 August 1964, RG 25, vol. 10113, file 20-22-Viets-2-1, LAC.
57 Martin, "At the Right Hand," 108.
58 Author interview with Basil Robinson, 15 July 2006.
59 Martin, Memorandum for the Prime Minister, 14 September 1964, RG 25, vol. 8795, file 20-1-2-USA, LAC.
60 Blair Seaborn to SSEA, Dispatch No. 332, 1 September 1964, RG 25, vol. 10113, file 21-13-Viet-ICSC-11, LAC.
61 Ibid.
62 Ottawa to Saigon, Tel. No. Y-682, 28 September 1964, RG 25, vol. 10113, file 21-13-Viet-ICSC-11, LAC.
63 Washington to Ottawa, Tel. No. 4190, 3 December 1964, RG 25, vol. 10113, file 20-22-Viets-2-1, LAC.
64 Delworth, "A Study of Canadian Policy," 23.
65 Pearson, *Mike*, 126–27.
66 Martin, Memorandum for File, 18 January 1965, Martin Papers, vol. 226, file 22, LAC.
67 Martin, "At the Right Hand," 396.
68 Martin to Dean Rusk, 18 January 1965, Martin Papers, vol. 226, file 14, LAC.
69 Cabinet Conclusions, 9 February 1965, PCO Records, LAC.
70 Pearson, "Extracts from an Address," 10 February 1965, in DFATD, *Statements and Speeches*, No. 63/3.
71 American Embassy Ottawa to State Department, Airgram A-616, 15 February 1965, RG 59, box 1989, file: POL 15-1 CAN, United States National Archives.
72 Washington to Ottawa, Tel. No. 485, 17 February 1965, RG 25, vol. 9394, file 20-22-Viets-2, LAC.
73 Moscow to Ottawa, Tel. No. 175, 16 February 1965, RG 25, vol. 9394, file 20-22-Viets-2, LAC.
74 Moscow to Ottawa, Tel. No. 210, 25 February 1965, RG 25, vol. 9394, file 20-22-Viets-2, LAC.
75 Ottawa to Washington, Tel. No. Y-157, 25 February 1965, RG 25, vol. 9394, file 20-22-Viets-2-1, LAC.
76 Delworth, "A Study of Canadian Policy," 31.
77 Canada, *House of Commons Debates* (8 March 1965), 12069.
78 Ibid., 12071.
79 "Bleats from the Bleachers," *Toronto Star*, 10 March 1965; see also "Groping for Answers in Vietnam," *Montreal Gazette*, 10 March 1965; "The Nation: A Reliable Friend Now,"

Ottawa Citizen, 10 March 1965; "The Minority Report," *Regina Leader-Post,* 10 March 1965.

80 Ottawa to Washington, Tel. No. Y-189, 13 March 1965, RG 25, vol. 9394, file 20-22-Viets-2, LAC.

81 "Martin: Subversion Must Be Stopped," *Windsor Star,* 27 March 1965.

82 Donaghy, *Tolerant Allies,* 127–30.

83 Quoted in Stursberg, *Lester Pearson,* 218.

84 Paul Martin, Memorandum for the Prime Minister, 29 March 1965, RG 25, vol. 10101, file 20-Canada-9-Pearson, LAC.

85 Quoted in Pearson, *Mike,* 138–39.

86 Quoted in Stursberg, *Lester Pearson,* 218.

87 Washington to Ottawa, Tel. No. 1890, 8 June 1965; and Dean Rusk to Martin, 8 June 1965, RG 25, vol. 11487, file 20-22-Viets-2-1, LAC.

88 "60 Demonstrators March on Hill," *Vancouver Sun,* 15 May 1965.

89 Pearson's marginal notes on Arnold Smith, Memorandum for the Minister, 31 May 1965, RG 25, vol. 11487, file 20-22-Viets-2-1, LAC.

90 Martin, Memorandum for the Prime Minister, 11 June 1965, RG 25, vol. 11487, file 20-22-Viets-2-1, LAC.

91 Beigie, *Canada-U.S. Automotive Agreement,* 12–19.

92 Donaghy, *Tolerant Allies,* 29–30.

93 Gerry Wright interview with Paul Martin, [1971–72], Martin Papers, vol. 354, tape A-19, side 2, LAC.

94 Martin to Walter Gordon and Bud Drury, 24 October 1963, Martin Papers, vol. 233, file: Finance, LAC.

95 Henry Renaud to Martin, 16 October 1963; George Burt to Martin, 10 October 1963; and Martin to George Burt, 25 October 1963, Martin Papers, vol. 241, file: Auto Industry, LAC.

96 Simon Reisman, Dictated Note for Mr. Martin, 13 November 1963, Martin Papers, vol. 233, file: Finance, LAC.

97 "Canada Exports to US of Cars, Parts Surge," *Wall Street Journal* (New York), 22 September 1964.

98 George Burt to Martin, 20 July 1964, RG 25, vol. 14272, file 37-7-1-USA-2, LAC.

99 Martin's marginal notes on Washington to Ottawa, Tel. No. 2652, 23 July 1964, RG 25, vol. 14272, file 37-7-1-USA-2, LAC.

100 Ottawa to Washington, Tel. No. E-2146, 28 October 1964; and Economic Division to Ed Ritchie, 28 October 1964, RG 25, vol. 14272, file 37-7-1-USA-2, LAC.

101 R.H. Long, President of Bendix-Eclipse of Canada, to Martin, 16 December 1964, RG 25, vol. 14272, file 37-7-1-USA-2, LAC.

102 T.H. Eansor, General Manager, Fabricated Steel Products, to Martin, 22 December 1964, RG 25, vol. 14272, file 37-7-1-USA-2, LAC.

103 Marcel Cadieux, Memorandum for the Minister, 24 November 1964, RG 25, vol. 14272, file 37-7-1-USA-2, LAC.

104 Cabinet Conclusions, 21 December 1964, PCO Records, LAC.

105 Ed Ritchie, Memorandum for the Minister, 17 March 1965, RG 25, vol. 14272, file 37-7-1-USA-2, LAC.

106 Martin to R.M. Foote, Automotive Specialities Manufacturing Ltd., 15 January 1965, Martin Papers, vol. 241, file: Auto Industry, LAC.
107 "New Auto Deal Worries Parts Men," *Windsor Star*, 24 February 1965; "Car Group Approves Auto Pact," *Windsor Star*, 4 February 1965.
108 George Burt to Martin, 30 December 1964, RG 25, vol. 14272, file 37-7-1-USA-2, LAC.
109 On intra-union politics, see Anastakis, *Auto Pact*, 112–15.
110 "CLC Asks Cut in Auto Prices," *Windsor Star*, 10 March 1965.
111 "Martin Says Auto Rumors 'Aren't True,'" *Windsor Star*, 20 March 1965; UAW press release, 26 March 1965; and Mrs. M.E. Dale to Martin, 5 April 1965, RG 25, vol. 14272, file 37-7-1-USA-2, LAC.
112 W.L. Clark, "As We See It," *Windsor Star*, 22 March 1965.
113 Minutes of a Meeting concerning the Manpower Situation in the Automobile Industry, 9 April 1965, RG 25, vol. 14272, file 37-7-1-USA-2, LAC.
114 George Burt to Martin, 22 April 1964, RG 25, vol. 14272, file 37-7-1-USA-2, LAC.
115 Quoted in "Federal Aid in Layoffs Promised," *Windsor Star*, 23 April 1965.
116 "Chrysler Might Absorb 500," *Windsor Star*, 24 April 1965.
117 Martin, Speech to the Society of Automotive Engineers, 23 April 1965, RG 25, vol. 14272, file 37-7-1-USA-2, LAC.
118 See, for example, G.G. Brooks to Bill Dymond, 4 May 1965; and Jim Langley to Ed Ritchie, 17 May 1965, RG 25, vol. 14272, file 37-7-1-USA-2, LAC.
119 Author interview with Basil Robinson, 15 July 2006.
120 Thomson, *Vive le Québec libre*, 144–47.
121 Marcel Cadieux, Memorandum for the Minister, 13 November 1964, RG 25, vol. 10097, file 20-1-2-France, LAC.
122 Cabinet Conclusions, 29 April 1965, PCO Records, LAC.
123 A.E. Ritchie to Mr. Hadwen, 12 May 1965, Martin Papers, vol. 230, file 25-11, LAC.
124 "Notes pour la visite de L'Hon. Paul Martin à la Maison Canadienne," 6 May 1965, Martin Papers, vol. 229, file 39, LAC (author's translation); original: "Je vous envie, car vous verrez, et vous vivrez, j'en suis sûr, de grandes choses que la France et le Canada vont faire ensemble."
125 London to Ottawa (Martin to Pearson), Tel. No. 1662, 12 May 1965, Martin Papers, vol. 225, file 5, LAC.
126 Martin to George Ignatieff, 14 May 1965, Martin Papers, vol. 230, file 25-13, LAC.
127 Figures cited in English, *The Worldly Years*, 305.
128 Figures cited in Martin, Speech to the Society of Automotive Engineers, 23 April 1965, RG 25, vol. 14272, file 37-7-1-USA-2, LAC.
129 Figures cited in "1965 – The Year of No Doldrums for Windsor," *Toronto Globe and Mail*, 10 August 1965.
130 Quoted in Frank Rasky, "Windsor: The City That Wouldn't Die," *Canadian Weekly*, 21 August 1965.
131 "As We See It: Keeping Eye on Constituents," *Windsor Star*, 11 March 1965.
132 "Paul Martin Presides as Post Office Opens," *Windsor Star*, 10 July 1965.
133 Quoted in "Wrapped in Corset, on Hospital Bed, Martin Maintains Busy Pace," *London Free Press*, 12 July 1965.
134 Ibid.

135 Gallup Poll, 23 June 1965, CIPO Archives.

136 "Foreign Affairs: The Main Task Done Well," *Toronto Star,* 22 September 1965.

CHAPTER 10: VIETNAM AND A MOOD OF PROTEST, 1965–67

1 English, *The Worldly* Years, 304–5.

2 Quoted in Martin, *So Many Worlds,* 491.

3 Sharp, *Which Reminds Me,* 126.

4 W.L. Gordon, Memo of Conversation with Mike re: The Election Decision, 12 September 1965, Gordon Papers, vol. 16, file: Memos to L.B. Pearson, Library and Archives Canada (LAC).

5 Andrew, *The Rise and Fall,* 73.

6 John Hadwen, Memorandum for the USSEA, 7 December 1964, Martin Papers, vol. 226, file 21: UN, LAC.

7 Marcel Cadieux, Memorandum for the Minister, 9 August 1965, Martin Papers, vol. 226, file 21: UN, LAC.

8 Alice Shanahan to Martin, 17 July 1964, Martin Papers, vol. 297, file: Mrs. Tom Shanahan, LAC.

9 "Paul Picked – Naturally," *Windsor Star,* 6 October 1965.

10 Quoted in "Martin Fixes Hecklers," *Toronto Star,* 16 October 1965.

11 Quoted in ibid.

12 Quoted in Saywell, *Canadian Annual Review (CAR) for 1966,* 91.

13 Martin, *So Many Worlds,* 495.

14 Walter Gordon, Memorandum of Conversation with Mike: re The Election Decision, 12 September 1965, Gordon Papers, vol. 16, file: Memos to L.B. Pearson, LAC; author interview with Richard O'Hagan, 30 June 2012.

15 Gerald Waring, "Let Sharp Go to External and Martin to Finance," *Vancouver Sun,* 3 December 1965.

16 LaMarsh, *Memoirs of a Bird,* 313.

17 Peter C. Newman, "Fight for Control of Liberal Party Now Under Way," *Ottawa Journal,* 16 December 1965.

18 George Bain, "Ottawa and Hanoi's Offer," *Toronto Globe and Mail,* 1 December 1965.

19 The accusation was made to Ford by Acting Foreign Minister Vasili Kuznetsov, and reported by Martin in Moscow to Ottawa, Tel. No. 1688, 15 December 1965, RG 25, vol. 11487, file 20-22-Viets-2-1, LAC. Martin noted on the telegram, "I don't like this charge – what are your comments?"

20 "Conversation between Paul Martin and Michael Stewart, London, 10 December 1965," 29 December 1965, RG 25, vol. 11487, file 20-22-Viets-2-1, LAC.

21 Martin to Kenny Strong, 18 January 1966, Martin Papers, vol. 285, LAC; Martin to Mike Cole, 19 January 1966, vol. 283, LAC.

22 "Canada Carries the Latest Frail Vietnam Hope," *Toronto Globe and Mail,* 1 March 1966.

23 Evans, "Ronning and Recognition."

24 Martin, Memorandum for the Prime Minister, 20 January 1966, RG 25, vol. 9397, file 20-22-Viets-2-1-1, LAC.

25 State Department to American Consul Hong Kong, cited in Herring, *The Secret Diplomacy*, 173.

26 Embassy Ottawa to Department of State, Tel. No. 1366, 22 April 1963, RG 59, box 3852, file Pol 15-1, United States National Archives.

27 Author interview with Basil Robinson, 15 July 2006.

28 Author interview with U. Alexis Johnson, 8 June 1992. For an utterly unbalanced assault on Martin, see Ottawa to Department of State, Airgram A-667, 6 January 1967, Mandatory Review 93-408, LBJ Library.

29 Quoted in Bothwell, *Alliance and Illusion*, 217.

30 Quoted in Herring, *The Secret Diplomacy*, 171.

31 Quoted in ibid., 179.

32 Saigon to Ottawa, Tel. No. 184, 11 March 1966, RG 25, vol. 9404, file 20-22-Viets-2-1-1, LAC.

33 Quoted in Donaghy, *Tolerant Allies*, 134–35.

34 Martin's marginalia on Marcel Cadieux, Memorandum for the Minister, 18 March 1966, RG 25, vol. 9404, file 20-22-Viets-2-1-1, LAC.

35 Quoted in Herring, *The Secret Diplomacy*, 179.

36 Ottawa to Washington, Tel. No. Y-288, 22 April 1966, RG 25, vol. 9404, file 20-22 -Viets-2-1-1, LAC.

37 Ottawa to NATO Paris, Tel. No. M-99, 6 June 1966, RG 25, vol. 9404, file 20-22-Viets-2-1-1, LAC.

38 Ottawa to Brussels, Tel. No. Y-405, 6 June 1966, RG 25, vol. 9404, file 20-22-Viets-2-1-1, LAC.

39 "Conversation between the SSEA and Ambassador Goldberg, May 16, 1966," Martin Papers, vol. 227, file: Vietnam, LAC.

40 Ottawa to Saigon, Tel. No. Y-425, 9 June 1966, RG 25, vol. 9404, file 20-22-Viets-2-1-1, LAC.

41 Saigon to Ottawa, Tel. No. 524, 18 June 1966, RG 25, vol. 9404, file 20-22-Viets-2-1-1, LAC.

42 Walt Rostow, Memorandum for the President, 8 June 1966, National Security Files, Memoranda to the President, vol. 5, box 8, LBJ Library.

43 Delworth, "A Study of Canadian Policy."

44 Herring, *The Secret Diplomacy*, 197.

45 English, *The Worldly Years*, 357. See also Walter Gordon, Memorandum: Lunch with LBP, 30 March 1966, Gordon Papers, vol. 16, file: Memos to L.B. Pearson, LAC.

46 Hellyer, *Damn the Torpedoes*, 209.

47 Quoted in Saywell, *CAR for 1966*, 15.

48 Ibid., 14.

49 Martin, *So Many Worlds*, 609.

50 Newman, "Fight for Control of Liberal Party."

51 Peter Newman, "Strange Case of Paul Martin: A Politician Turns to Statecraft," *Vancouver Sun*, 5 February 1966.

52 Gallup Poll, 31 March 1966, Canadian Institute of Public Opinion (CIPO) Archives.

53 Gallup Poll, 28 May 1966, CIPO Archives.

54 Richard Jackson, "Plot and Counter-Plot and Double Agents," *St. John's Evening Telegram*, 16 November 1966.

55 Talking Points – Polyansky Visit, 15 July 1966, Martin Papers, vol. 227, file 26, LAC. Soviet president Leonid Brezhnev would later tell Martin that "we call him [Polyansky] the Canadian. If he can get elected, you can have him." Quoted in Rudd, *The Constant Diplomat*, 76.

56 Thereza Ford's diary, quoted in Rudd, *The Constant Diplomat*, 68.

57 Washington to Ottawa, Tel. No. 2181, 26 July 1966, Martin Papers, vol. 227, file: Development Assistance, LAC.

58 Ibid.

59 John Hadwen to Nell Martin, 12 September 1966; and Ottawa to Moscow, Tel. No. S-809, 8 September 1966, Martin Papers, vol. 229, file 43, LAC.

60 John Hadwen, Memorandum for Mr. Martin, 8 September 1966, Martin Papers, vol. 227, file 25, LAC.

61 New York to Ottawa, Tel. No. 1731, 26 September 1966; New York to Ottawa, Tel. No. 1760, 27 September 1966; Notes for Use in Talk with Secretary-General: Vietnam DMZ, 7–8 October 1966; and Martin to Dean Rusk, 26 October 1966, Martin Papers, vol. 227, file 25, LAC.

62 Ottawa to London, Tel. No. Y-701, 11 October 1966, Martin Papers, vol. 227, file 25, LAC.

63 Martin to Saul Hayes, 21 December 1966, Martin Papers, vol. 236, file 28-1-H, LAC.

64 Ottawa to New York, Tel. No. S-1124, 22 November 1966, Martin Papers, vol. 227, file 25, LAC.

65 Martin, Memorandum for the Prime Minister, 28 June 1966, RG 25, vol. 9325, file 20-China-14, LAC.

66 Mary MacDonald to J.E. Hadwen, 11 July 1966; and Marcel Cadieux, Memorandum for the Minister, 22 July 1966, RG 25, vol. 9325, file 20-China-14, LAC.

67 [P.A. McDougall], Chinese Representation: Notes on Three Possible Courses of Action, 21 October 1966, RG 25, vol. 9325, file 20-China-14, LAC.

68 Dean Rusk to L.B. Pearson, 9 November 1966, Pearson Papers, vol. 7, file 821/C359.1.Conf., LAC.

69 Basil Robinson, Memorandum for the Minister, 17 November 1966, RG 25, vol. 9325, file 20-China-14, LAC.

70 St. Amour, "Sino-Canadian Relations," 120.

71 MacLaren, *The Fundamental Things Apply*, 77.

72 Peter McKellar, Memorandum from the Office of the SSEA to Far Eastern Division, 20 December 1966, RG 25, vol. 9398, file 20-22-Viets-2-1, LAC.

73 Figures cited in David Morrison, *Aid and Ebb Tide*, 8. See also Martin, *Canada and the Quest for Peace*, 80.

74 David Morrison, *Aid and Ebb Tide*, 57–58.

75 John Hadwen to File: Peace Corps, 25 February 1965; and Martin to Herb Moran, 24 February 1965, Martin Papers, vol. 225, file: Foreign Aid, LAC. See also Brouwer, *Canada's Global Voice*, 24–27.

76 In a 1966 account of this development, Martin called Strong with news of the opening, adding "You wouldn't want to take it, would you?" Well, came the quick reply, "If that

was an offer, the answer was yes!" Stapells, Introduction to Maurice Strong, 172. In a later version of the offer, told near the end of Strong's career, he kept silent with Martin, saving his reply for his boss, Prime Minister Pearson. See Strong, *Where on Earth*, 99.

77 Elaine Dewar, "Mr. Universe," *Saturday Night*, June 1992, 17–21, 73–83.

78 Strong, *Where on Earth*, 100.

79 L.B. Pearson to Martin, 27 January and 21 February 1967; and John Hadwen to Martin, 24 February 1967, Martin Papers, vol. 225, file: Foreign Aid, LAC.

80 Marcel Cadieux Diary, 15 March 1967, Cadieux Papers, vol. 12, file 9, LAC.

81 Larry Smith to Marcel Cadieux, 7 March 1969, quoted in Stockdale, "Pearsonian Internationalism," 13.

82 Record of the External Aid Board, 8 February 1967, quoted in Stockdale, "Pearsonian Internationalism," 17.

83 Ibid.

84 Cadieux Diary, 15 March, Cadieux Papers, vol. 12, file 9, LAC (author's translation); original: "Deux ou trois opérations de ce genre et j'ai bien l'impression qu'il va se discréditer au sein de 'l'établissement' à Ottawa."

85 William Robb, "New Face on External Aid," *Canadian Business*, May 1968, 12–13.

86 Roland Michener to Martin, 23 June 1966, Martin Papers, vol. 284, file 28–1, LAC.

87 Maurice Jefferies to Duncan Edmonds, 28 December 1966, Martin Papers, vol. 250, file: Duncan Edmonds, LAC.

88 "More Rent Talks Set with MPs," *Windsor Star*, 11 January 1967.

89 Cadieux Diary, 13 January 1967, Cadieux Papers, vol. 12, file 9, LAC.

90 Figures drawn from Canada, Department of External Affairs, *1963 Bulletin*, 329; and Canada, Department of Finance, *Public Accounts*.

91 Cadieux Diary, 30 January 1967, Cadieux Papers, vol. 12, file 9, LAC.

92 Azzi, *Walter Gordon*, 138.

93 Gordon, *A Choice for Canada*, 10.

94 "Working for Peace," *Vancouver Sun*, 13 January 1967.

95 "Talking around a Principle," *Toronto Globe and Mail*, 26 January 1967.

96 "Pickets Walk Out," *Vancouver Sun*, 4 February 1967.

97 Claire and Mel Guay to Martin, 10 February 1967, Martin Papers, vol. 287, file 28-G-1, LAC.

98 Washington to Ottawa, Tel. No. 3569, 25 November 1966, RG 25, vol. 9398, file 20-22-Viets-2-1, LAC.

99 Ottawa to Warsaw, Tel. No. Y-165, 9 February 1967, RG 25, vol. 9398, file 20-22-Viets-2-1, LAC.

100 Martin, Memorandum for File: Vietnam, 21 February 1967, Martin Papers, vol. 227, file: Vietnam, 1964–67, LAC.

101 Martin's marginalia on Marcel Cadieux, Memorandum for the Minister, 8 March 1967, RG 25, vol. 9398, file 20-22-Viets-2-1, LAC.

102 Quoted in "The Bridge on the River Ben Hai," *Time*, 10 March 1967, 13.

103 See, for example, "Martin Sees Peace Hopes in Vietnam," *Ottawa Citizen*, 30 December 1966; "Working for Peace," *Vancouver Sun*, 13 January 1967.

104 George Bain, "Tougher Vietnam Line?" *Toronto Globe and Mail*, 15 February 1967.

105 Martin to Charles Magill, 20 February 1967, Martin Papers, vol. 287, file M, LAC.

106 Martin to Vic Hooey, 16 January 1967, Martin Papers, vol. 287, file 28-H-1, LAC.

107 "Silence Won't Win Viet Nam Peace," *Toronto Star,* 28 February 1967.

108 Richard Snell, "How Red Tape Killed a Centennial Lifesaver," *Toronto Star,* 13 March 1967.

109 Quoted in Walter Stewart, "Forgotten Children," *Toronto Star Weekly,* 1 April 1967.

110 "Martin Given Vietnam Petition," *Ottawa Citizen,* 14 April 1967.

111 "Peacemakers Role Urged," *Toronto Star,* 15 April 1967.

112 "Canadians Demonstrate against Vietnam War," *Quebec Chronicle Telegraph,* 17 April 1967.

113 "The Mood of Protest," *Toronto Star,* 15 April 1967.

114 "Stick with It, Mr. Martin," *Edmonton Journal,* 21 April 1967.

115 "New Bid Spurned by North Vietnam," *New York Times,* 17 April 1967.

116 Ed Ritchie to Marcel Cadieux, and attachment, 20 April 1967, RG 25, vol. 9399, file 20-22-Viets-2-1, LAC.

117 New York to Ottawa, Tel. No. 1087, 28 April 1967, RG 25, vol. 9399, file 20-22-Viets-2-1, LAC.

118 Cadieux Diary, 11 May 1967, Cadieux Papers, vol. 12, file 12-9, LAC.

119 "Too Much Like Poland," *Toronto Globe and Mail,* 12 May 1967.

120 London to Ottawa, Tel. No. 2385, 3 May 1967, RG 25, vol. 9399, file 20-22-Viets-2-1, LAC.

121 Gordon, *A Political Memoir,* 281–82.

122 Cadieux Diary, 17 May 1967, Cadieux Papers, vol. 12, file 12-9, LAC (author's translation); original: "A mon avis, il s'agit d'une politique à courte vue qui dessert à longue échéance non seulement les intérêts du Parti et du Canada mais aussi de là paix au Vietnam."

123 Quoted in Washington to Ottawa, Tel. No. 1982, 26 May 1967, RG 25, vol. 9399, file 20-22-Viet-2-1, LAC; see also Pearson, *Mike,* 144–47, and R.P. Davis, Memorandum of Conversation: President's Conversation with Prime Minister Pearson, 25 May 1967, in *FRUS,* 12:715–19.

124 John Holmes, Memorandum to File, 30 May 1967, Holmes Papers, box 75, file 7, Trinity College Archives.

125 Quoted in Smith, *Gentle Patriot,* 325.

126 Figures in "Open Letter from Paul Martin," reprinted in *North Essex News,* 23 February 1967.

127 Richard Graybiel to Martin, 21 February 1966, Martin Papers, vol. 236, file 28-G-1, LAC.

128 "Big Defence Order for Kaiser," *Windsor Star,* 1 June 1967.

129 Quoted in "Black Tie to Dogpaddle," *Windsor Star,* 3 July 1967.

130 John Hadwen, Memorandum for UN Division, 21 August 1967, Martin Papers, vol. 229, file 41: UN, LAC.

131 English, *The Worldly Years,* 379.

132 Ottawa to New York, Tel. No. Y-537, 8 September 1967, RG 25, vol. 9399, file 20-22-Viets-2-1, LAC.

133 New York to Ottawa, Tel. No. 2490, 22 September 1967, RG 25, vol. 9399, file 20-22-Viets-2-1, LAC.

134 Martin, "Canada and the Universal Forum for Peace," address to the UN General Assembly in New York, 27 September 1967, in Department of Foreign Affairs, Trade and Development, *Statements and Speeches*, No. 67/30.
135 Fred Nossal, "Martin's Halt-the-Bomb Plea Reflects an International Mood," *Toronto Telegram*, 10 October 1967.
136 Briefing Paper for Mr. Walt Rostow ad Mr. Ernest Goldstein, [19 October 1967], National Security Files, Country File: Canada, Box 167, LBJ Library.
137 "Don't Need Hypocrisy on Vietnam Arms," *Toronto Star*, 18 November 1967.
138 Quoted in "Vietnam Intervention Wrong: Martin," *Toronto Star*, 14 November 1967.
139 "Can the Liberals Turn Left for a Leader?," *Toronto Star*, 3 August 1967.
140 Lee, "Third Elegy."

CHAPTER 11: A HARD-PRESSED MINISTER, 1967

1 Martin to Ross Campbell, 26 June 1967, Martin Papers, vol. 286, file 28-I-C, Library and Archives Canada (LAC).
2 Carroll, *Pearson's Peacekeepers*, 75.
3 Quoted in McGill, *My Life as I Remember It*, 232.
4 Martin, *So Many Worlds*, 538.
5 UNEF historian Michael Carroll's assessment is in his *Pearson's Peacekeepers*, 96–97; Saywell, *Canadian Annual Review (CAR) for 1966*, 219.
6 "The Defeat of Canada's Resolution at the UN," *St. John's Evening Telegram*, 3 January 1967.
7 Canada, *House of Commons, Debates* (10 February 1967), 12909.
8 Martin, *Canada and the Quest for Peace*, 1–32.
9 Marcel Cadieux, Memorandum for the Minister, 18 May 1967, RG 25, vol. 10642, file 21-14-6-UNEF-1, LAC.
10 Martin, *So Many Worlds*, 463.
11 Marcel Cadieux Diary, 8 June 1967, Cadieux Papers, vol. 12, file 12-9, LAC (author's translation); original: "Pour arranger les choses, nous nous trouvons avec deux ministeres des affaires étrangères qui cherchent tous les deux à tenir le premier rôle."
12 Ottawa to New York, Tel. No. DL-1206, 18 May 1967, RG 25, vol. 10642, file 21-14-6-UNEF-1, LAC.
13 "Martin Still Resisting – Thant Orders Pull-Out," *Windsor Star*, 19 May 1967.
14 Author interview with Eric Bergbusch, 14 June 2010.
15 Quoted in "Martin Pressing to Retain Forces," *Charlottetown Evening Post*, 20 May 1967.
16 New York to Ottawa, Tel. No. 1380, 20 May 1967, Martin Papers, vol. 225, file 13, LAC.
17 Ottawa to Tel Aviv, Tel. No. V-385, 23 May 1967, Martin Papers, vol. 225, file 13, LAC.
18 New York to Ottawa, unnumbered Tel., 20 May 1967, Martin Papers, vol. 225, file 13, LAC. See also Telegram from the Mission at the UN to Department of State, 20 May 1967, reprinted in US Department of State, *Foreign Relations of the United States (FRUS)*, 19:37.
19 Quoted in "Peacekeeping Use Not Over," *Regina Leader-Post*, 23 May 1967.

20 Arthur Cole, "A Black Day for Canada and the UN," *Toronto Telegram*, 25 May 1967.

21 Quoted in Saywell, *CAR for 1967*, 222.

22 Charles Lynch, "Time for the Maestro in Quiet Diplomacy," *London Free Press*, 26 May 1967.

23 Ron Collister, "Cairo: Dependents Fly Out," *Toronto Telegram*, 29 May 1967.

24 Ottawa to Tel Aviv, Tel. No. ME-467, 29 May 1967, RG 25, vol. 13343, file 20-1-2-Israel, LAC; Cabinet Conclusions, 29 May 1967, PCO Records, LAC.

25 Martin, *So Many Worlds*, 644. To emphasize the strength of his opposition, Martin added by hand on his Memorandum for the Prime Minister that "we certainly should not agree to this declaration until we have seen the Norwegian formula" (1 June 1967, RG 25, vol. 13434, file 25-3-2-Arab-Israel, LAC).

26 Thomas Carter, Memorandum for the USSEA, 2 June 1967, RG 25, vol. 13434, file 25-3-2-Arab-Israel, LAC.

27 President's Daily Diary, 25 May 1967, extracted in US Department of State, *FRUS*, 19:102n7; Message from President Johnson to Prime Minister Wilson, 25 May 1967, reprinted in US Department of State, *FRUS*, 19:106-7.

28 Meeting between the PM and the PM of Canada, 1 June 1967, Prime Minister's Office Records 13/1906, National Archives.

29 Richard Jackson, "Calls for End to Firing," *Ottawa Journal*, 5 June 1967; Robert Hull, "How Ottawa Reacted to War," *Windsor Star*, 6 June 1967.

30 Commonwealth to Middle Eastern Division, 5 June 1967, RG 25, vol. 13434, file 25-3-2-Arab-Israel, LAC.

31 Pearson's marginalia on Martin, Memorandum for the Prime Minister, 5 June 1967, RG 25, vol. 13434, file 25-3-2-Arab-Israel, LAC.

32 Cabinet Conclusions, 6 June 1967, PCO Records, LAC.

33 Martin, Memorandum for the Prime Minister, 7 June 1967, RG 25, vol. 13434, file 25-3-2-Arab-Israel, LAC.

34 Basil Robinson, Memorandum for File, 10 June 1967, RG 25, vol. 13434, file 25-3-2-Arab-Israel, LAC.

35 Cabinet Conclusions, 8 June 1967, PCO Records, LAC.

36 Canada, *House of Commons Debates* (8 June 1967), 1293-95.

37 "Now," *Windsor Star*, 29 May 1967.

38 Quoted in Saywell, *CAR for 1967*, 231.

39 Quoted in Dave McIntosh, "Martin Irked over Speech by Deputy," *Vancouver Sun*, 29 August 1967.

40 Patrick Nicholson, "Paris No Outing for Paul," *Quebec Chronicle Telegraph*, 22 June 1967.

41 "Accord-cadre France-canadien," *Le Soleil* (Quebec City), 20 November 1965 (author's translation); original: "un nouveau pas en avant." "Basis for Cultural Exchanges," *Ottawa Citizen*, 23 November 1965.

42 Jules Léger to Marcel Cadieux, 2 November 1965, RG 25, vol. 10097, file 20-1-2-France, LAC (author's translation); original: "Faut-il conclure? Que ce qui a fait est bien peu en comparaison de l'importance de l'enjeu, que même cela est fragile, et que nous ne devons compter que sur nous-mêmes pour réussir."

43 Marcel Cadieux to Jules Léger, 6 December 1965, RG 25, vol. 10097, file 20-1-2-France, LAC (author's translation); original: "Aucune doute que nos relations avec la France,

bien qu'elles se soient grandement améliorées et renforcés, n'ont pas encore pris racine fermement dans l'actualité." On a more hopeful note, Cadieux added, that "the base already established is becoming stronger and can withstand some shocks, but not too many, please!" (author's translation); original: "La base déjà établie prend une forme plus nette et peut déjà résister à certain chocs, mais pas trop nombreux, de grâce!"

44 Pearson, *Mike*, 264.

45 Basil Robinson, Memorandum for File, 17 March 1966; and Paul Hellyer to Martin, 14 March 1966, RG 25, vol. 10289, file 27-4-NATO-1, LAC.

46 Draft Memorandum for Cabinet, 29 March 1966; and Record of Cabinet Decision, 31 March 1966, DEA file 27-4-NATO-3-1-France, RG 25, vol. 10295, LAC.

47 NATO Paris to Ottawa, Tel. No. 939, 3 May 1966; and Ottawa to NATO Paris, Tel. No. DL-1359, 18 May 1966, RG 25, vol. 8839, file 27-4-NATO-12-1966-Spring, LAC.

48 Discussion between SSEA and British Minister for NATO Affairs, 18 May 1966, Martin Papers, vol. 226, LAC.

49 Ottawa to NATO Paris, Tel. No. DL-1518, 2 June 1966, RG 25, vol. 10301, file 27-4-NATO-12-1966-Spring, LAC.

50 Norman Hull to Martin, 20 June 1966, Martin Papers, vol. 284, LAC.

51 Brussels to Ottawa, Tel. No. 406, 6 June 1966; and NATO Del to Ottawa, Tel. No. 416, 6 June 1966, Martin Papers, vol. 226, file 17: NATO, LAC.

52 John Hadwen to Nell Martin, 6 June 1966, Martin Papers, vol. 225, file 12: Personal, LAC.

53 Dean Rusk for the President, 9 June 1966, National Security Files, Rostow Memoranda for the President, vol. 5, box 8, LBJ Library.

54 Ibid.

55 Ottawa to Paris (Pearson to Martin), Tel. No. PM-106, 7 June 1966, Martin Papers, vol. 225, file 12: Personal, LAC.

56 Jean Basdevant, Note for the Secretary General, 18 March 1966, America, Canada, box 245, Archives Diplomatiques Francaises.

57 Roger Seydoux to the Minister of Foreign Affairs, Letter 1119/NU, 23 September 1966, America, Canada, box 245, ADF (author's translation); original: "Cette innovation confirme ouverture vers la France de la politique étrangère canadienne, dont les signes se sont récemment multipliés."

58 Martin, *So Many Worlds*, 587.

59 Speech by the Hon. Paul Martin at a Dinner in Honour of Mr. Couve de Murville, 28 September 1966, RG 25, vol. 10077, file 20-France-9, LAC.

60 For the list of federal complaints, see John Halstead, Memorandum for Marcel Cadieux, 16 December 1966, RG 25, vol. 10097, file 20-1-2-France, LAC.

61 Quoted in Martin, Memorandum for the Prime Minister, 8 December 1966, RG 25, vol. 10097, file 20-1-2-France, LAC (author's translation); original: "Il y a bien deux poids et deux mesures pour l'accueil qu'on réserve aux Ministres selon qu'ils viennent d'Ottawa ou de Québec."

62 NATO Paris to Ottawa, Tel. No. 3011, 14 December 1966, Martin Papers, vol. 225, file: France, LAC.

63 John Halstead, Memorandum for the USSEA, 16 December 1966, RG 25, vol. 10097, file 20-1-2-France, LAC.

64 Cadieux Diary, 12 January 1967, Cadieux Papers, vol. 12, file 12-9, LAC (author's translation); original: "M. Martin n'était pas tout à fait d'accord avec le Ministère au sujet de l'interprétation à donner à certains incidents au Canada et aux mesures à prendre."

65 Author interview with Gordon Robertson, 5 November 2007.

66 Martin, *So Many Worlds,* 584–86.

67 Paris to Ottawa, Tel. No. 126, 16 January 1967 (author's translation); original: "dans son ensemble nous semble fausse"; and Cadieux Diary, 16 January 1967, Cadieux Papers, vol. 12, file 9, LAC.

68 Martin, Memorandum for the Prime Minister, 24 January 1967, RG 25, vol. 10045, file 20-1-2-France, LAC.

69 Quoted in ibid.

70 Hilliker and Barry, *Canada's Department of External Affairs,* 397.

71 Marcel Cadieux, Memorandum for the Minister, 25 January 1967; and Ottawa to Paris, Tel. No. S-2, 11 February 1967, RG 25, vol. 10045, file 20-1-2-France, LAC.

72 John Halstead, Memorandum for the USSEA, 17 February 1967; and Marcel Cadieux, Memorandum for the Minister, 1 March 1967, RG 25, vol. 10045, file 20-1-2-France, LAC.

73 Cabinet Conclusions, 14 February 1967, PCO Records, LAC.

74 Martin, Memorandum for the Prime Minister, 24 February 1967, RG 25, vol. 10045, file 20-1-2-France, LAC.

75 Chris Eberts, Memorandum for the Minister, 14 March 1967, RG 25, vol. 10045, file 20-1-2-France, LAC.

76 Cadieux Diary, 27 February 1967, Cadieux Papers, vol. 12, file 12-9, LAC (author's translation); original: "Il est évident qu'à l'avenir la guerre va être déclaré entre Ottawa et l'Élysée."

77 Charles Lynch, "For French Gall, Try de Gaulle," *Vancouver Province,* 6 April 1967.

78 John Halstead, Memorandum for the Under-Secretary of State for External Affairs, 5 April 1967, RG 25, vol. 10045, file 20-1-2-France, LAC.

79 Paris to Ottawa, Tel. No. 815, 29 March 1967, RG 25, vol. 10045, file 20-1-2-France, LAC (author's translation); original: "Couve comprend et peut parfois faire entendre raison au vieux prophète Élyséen."

80 Paris to Ottawa, Tel. No. 918, 7 April 1967; and Ottawa to Paris, Tel. No. S-456, 14 April 1967, RG 25, vol. 10045, file 20-1-2-France, LAC.

81 Alan Harvey, "A Weekend in Paris for Mr. Martin?" *Toronto Globe and Mail,* 15 April 1967.

82 Paris (from Martin) to Ottawa, Tel. No. 1127, 23 April 1967, Martin Papers, vol. 225, file 12: France, LAC.

83 Marcel Cadieux, Memorandum for the Minister, 6 June 1967, RG 25, vol. 10045, file 20-1-2-France, LAC.

84 Ibid.

85 Ibid., 14 June 1967.

86 Nicholson, "Paris No Outing for Paul."

87 Martin, Memorandum for the Prime Minister, 19 June 1967, RG 25, vol. 10045, file 20-1-2-France, LAC (author's translation); original: "tout allait bien se passer."

88 "Martin Calls on French President," *Quebec Chronicle Telegraph,* 17 June 1967.

89 Martin, Memorandum for the Prime Minister, 19 June 1967, RG 25, vol. 10045, file 20-1-2-France, LAC (author's translation); original: "Il aurait peut-être été possible de soulever certains problèmes, mais j'étais convaincu que l'occasion n'était pas propice."

90 Quoted in Meren, *With Friends Like These*, 118.

91 Cadieux Diary, 12 July 1967, Cadieux Papers, vol. 8, file 15, LAC (author's translation); original: "Le seul qui ne comprend pas encore de quoi il retourne est M. Martin. Il n'est pas persuadé que le Général de Gaulle ait de mauvaises intentions."

92 Quoted in English, *The Worldly Years*, 340.

93 Quoted in Thomson, *Vive le Québec libre*, 199.

94 English, *The Worldly Years*, 341.

95 In addition to published sources, this account relies heavily on a memorandum prepared by John Hadwen and Terry Devlin, which traces Martin's movements. John Hadwen and Terry Devlin, Memorandum to File, 14 August 1967, Martin Papers, vol. 225, file: France, LAC.

96 Ibid.

97 Ibid. In other accounts, recorded much later, de Gaulle remarks, "Well, Martin, this is going well." See English, *The Worldly Years*, 341.

98 Quoted in Thomson, *Vive le Québec libre*, 201. The account by Hadwen and Devlin does not record Martin's reply to this comment.

99 Martin to L.B. Pearson, 24 July 1967, Martin Papers, vol. 225, file: France, LAC.

100 Quoted in Thomson, *Vive le Québec libre*, 203.

101 Ibid., 207.

102 This paragraph is based on Hadwen and Devlin, Memorandum for File, 14 August 1967, Martin Papers, vol. 225, file: France, LAC.

103 Unless otherwise indicated, this paragraph is based on ibid.

104 These views were expressed in Cadieux Diary, 25 and 26 July 1967, Cadieux Papers, vol. 8, file 15, LAC.

105 Hadwen and Devlin, Memorandum for File, 14 August 1967, Martin Papers, vol. 225, file: France, LAC; and Cadieux Diary, 25 July 1967, Cadieux Papers, vol. 8, file 15, LAC.

106 Cabinet Conclusions, 25 July 1967, 12:00 p.m. meeting, PCO Records, LAC.

107 Cabinet Conclusions, 25 July 1967, 3:45 p.m. meeting, PCO Records, LAC.

108 Cadieux Diary, 26 July 1967, Cadieux Papers, vol. 8, file 15, LAC.

109 English, *The Worldly Years*, 347.

110 Clarkson, "Conclusion," 257.

111 Martin's minute on Memorandum for the Prime Minister, 2 October 1967, RG 25, vol. 10045, file 20-1-2-France, LAC.

112 Canada, *House of Commons Debates* (5 October 1967), 2835.

113 Ivan Head to Minister of Justice, 2 October 1967, RG 25, vol. 10045, file 20-1-2-France, LAC.

114 Quoted in "Be It Ever so Humble," *Windsor Star*, 24 August 1967.

115 Martin to Vern DeGreer, 16 November 1967, Martin Papers, vol. 286, file 28-D-1, LAC.

116 Byers, "Canadian Foreign Policy."

117 Axworthy, "Canada and the World Revolution," 31–33; Warnock, "Canada and the Alliance System," 36–39.

118 Quoted in Saywell, *CAR for 1967*, 263.

119 Saywell, *CAR for 1967*, 264.

120 "NATO Pullout Is Rejected by Martin," *Toronto Globe and Mail,* 16 March 1967.
121 "Canada's Future in NATO – Is What?" *London Free Press,* Martin Papers, vol. 337, Clippings File: NATO, 1966-67, LAC.
122 L.B. Pearson, Memorandum for the Hon. Paul Martin, Pearson Papers, MG 26, N4, vol. 280, file 832 Secret, LAC.
123 Martin, Memorandum for the Prime Minister, 6 May 1967, Pearson Papers, MG 26, N4, vol. 280, file 832 Secret, LAC.
124 Martin, Memorandum to Cabinet, 31 May 1967, RG 25, vol. 10361, file 27-14-NORAD-1, LAC.
125 Memorandum to the Cabinet, 31 May 1967, RG 25, vol. 10301, file 27-4-NATO-12-1967-Spring, LAC.
126 Norah Story interview with Paul Martin, [1969–70], Martin Papers, vol. 352, tape 8, side 2, LAC.
127 Basil Robinson, Memorandum for Defence Liaison (1) Division, 1 June 1967, RG 25, vol. 10289, file 27-14-1, LAC.
128 Martin, *So Many Worlds,* 480. Gordon recalls this episode differently in *A Political Memoir,* 286.
129 Basil Robinson, Memorandum for the Under-Secretary, 2 July 1967, RG 25, vol. 10289, file 27-4-NATO-1, LAC.
130 Jim Nutt to Basil Robinson, 28 July 1967, RG 25, vol. 10361, file 27-14-NORAD-1, LAC; Gordon, *A Political Memoir,* 287. Martin claims that the views Gordon expressed at the time were more favourable to NATO. Martin, *So Many Worlds,* 480.
131 Cited in Saywell, *CAR for 1967,* 266.
132 Quoted in ibid.
133 Quoted in "Questions, Please," *Vancouver Province,* 31 August 1967.
134 Paul Martin, "Contribution to International Peace and Development," Speech at the International Day Luncheon of the Directors of the Canadian National Exhibition, Toronto, 26 August 1967, Department of Foreign Affairs, Trade and Development, *Statements and Speeches,* 67/27.
135 Memorandum for the Cabinet, 5 September 1967, Pearson Papers, MG 26, N4, vol. 280, file 830 Secret, LAC.
136 Cabinet Conclusions, 12 September 1967, PCO Records, LAC.
137 "Answers, Please, on NATO," *Toronto Telegram,* 12 December 1967.
138 "On the Side of Angels Is Not Enough," *Ottawa Journal,* 31 August 1967.
139 "Questions, Please."
140 "Sayings for a Safe Place," *Toronto Globe and Mail,* 30 December 1967.
141 Doug Fisher and Harry Crowe, "Canada's Frustrating Foreign Policy," *Toronto Telegram,* 27 October 1967.
142 "Paul Martin Speaks for Canada," *Toronto Star,* 16 November 1967.
143 Hilliker and Barry, *Canada's Department of External Affairs,* 407–8.
144 Marcel Cadieux to Paul Tremblay, 19 September 1967, Cadieux Papers, vol. 8, file 8-15, LAC.
145 On Pearson, see Cadieux Diary, 8 April 1967, Cadieux Papers, vol. 8, file 15, LAC; Story interview with Martin, [1969–70], Martin Papers, vol. 351, tape 3, side 1, LAC.
146 Martin to John Holmes, 3 November 1967, Martin Papers, vol. 226, file 16: NATO, LAC.

CHAPTER 12: DEFEAT AND THE SENATE, 1968–74

1 W.L. Gordon, Notes for Discussion at Cabinet, 23 October 1967, Gordon Papers, vol. 16, file: LBP, Library and Archives Canada (LAC).
2 Marcel Cadieux Diary, 21 November 1967, Cadieux Papers, vol. 12, file 9, LAC.
3 Hellyer, *Damn the Torpedoes*, 260.
4 Martin, *So Many Worlds*, 606.
5 Ibid., 615.
6 Figures cited in Granatstein, *Canada: The Years of Uncertainty*, 305–6.
7 W.L. Gordon, Memoranda for File, 8 November and 17 November 1967, Gordon Papers, vol. 16, file: LBP, LAC; Hellyer, *Damn the Torpedoes*, 256–57; Martin, *So Many Worlds*, 612.
8 Agenda for Meeting, 30 October 1967, Martin Papers, vol. 273, file: Leadership, LAC.
9 Agenda for the Toronto Meeting, 3 December 1967, Martin Papers, vol. 273, file: Leadership, LAC.
10 Hugh Faulkner to Paul Martin Jr., 10 December 1967, and attachment, Martin Papers, vol. 273, file: Leadership, LAC.
11 Norah Story interview with Paul Martin, [c. 1970], Martin Papers, vol. 351, tape 5, side 2, LAC.
12 Mark MacGuigan to Paul Martin Jr., 5 April 1966, Martin Papers, vol. 273, file: Leadership, LAC.
13 Hugh Faulkner to Paul Martin Jr., 10 December 1967, Martin Papers, vol. 273, file: Leadership, LAC.
14 W.L. Gordon, Memorandum for File, 24 October 1967, Gordon Papers, vol. 16, file: LBP, LAC.
15 Cadieux Diary, 21 November 1967, Cadieux Papers, vol. 8, file 15, LAC.
16 W.L. Gordon, Memorandum for File, 19 December 1967, Gordon Papers, vol. 16, file: LBP, LAC.
17 Norah Story interview with Martin, [1969–70], Martin Papers, vol. 351, tape 5, side 2, LAC.
18 Quoted in "Martin Jaunty on Visit," *Toronto Globe and Mail*, 19 January 1968.
19 "Martin, Sharp, Hats in Ring," *Winnipeg Free Press*, 19 January 1968.
20 "Martin, Sharp Seek Leadership," *Vancouver Sun*, 19 January 1968.
21 Quoted in "Martin Enters Leader Battle," *Montreal Star*, 19 January 1968.
22 "Paul Martin: A Redoubtable Old Pro," *Toronto Star*, 20 January 1968. A *Toronto Globe and Mail* editorial, "Mr. Martin Tries Again," 20 January 1968, reminded readers that Martin "has been in politics a long, long time, long enough to have made a lot of friends, but also a lot of enemies." The syndicated columnist Peter Newman was clearly one of the latter. "Alas, Poor Martin," read the banner atop his *Vancouver Sun* column on 20 January, "We Know Him Too Well."
23 Quoted in Robert Miller, "Does He or Doesn't He? MPs Gibe as Gray Paul Changes Hue," *Toronto Star*, 23 January 1968.
24 Tom Axworthy to W.L. Gordon, 25 January 1968, Gordon Papers, vol. 13, file: Leadership Convention, LAC.
25 Story interview with Martin, [1969–70], Martin Papers, vol. 353, tape 15, side 2, LAC.

26 Quoted in Gérard Pelletier, *Years of Choice*, 259.

27 Hellyer, *Damn the Torpedoes*, 268–69.

28 Tom Hazlitt, "Would-Be Leaders Lonely, Forgotten in 'Trudeau Town,'" *Toronto Star*, 29 January 1968.

29 Gérard Pelletier, *Years of Choice*, 270.

30 Story interview with Martin, [1969–70], Martin Papers, vol. 353, tape 15, side 1, LAC.

31 English, *Citizen of the World*, 455–58.

32 Gendron, *Towards a Francophone Community*, 133–34.

33 Cadieux Diary, 7 February 1968, Cadieux Papers, vol. 8, file 14, LAC.

34 Martin, *So Many Worlds*, 618.

35 Martin's "distress" during the crisis is examined in Blair Fraser, "Back Stage in Ottawa: How Some Grits Managed to Keep Their Cool," *Maclean's*, March 1968, 2.

36 Martin, *So Many Worlds*, 618.

37 "'Impatient' Successor Sparks Pearson Gibe," *Montreal Star*, 22 March 1968.

38 A "pair" is an MP on the other side of the House who promises not to vote when you are absent.

39 "The Big Losers in 'Black Monday' Are Sharp, Martin, MacEachen," *Toronto Star*, 21 February 1968; Hellyer, *Damn the Torpedoes*, 270.

40 "The Hopefuls and How They Stack Up Now," *Windsor Star*, 24 February 1968.

41 Gallup Poll, 28 February 1968, Canadian Institute of Public Opinion Archives.

42 "Man-to-Man Campaign: Martin's Personal Tack," *Windsor Star*, 10 February 1968.

43 "Safer to Stay Home," *Toronto Globe and Mail*, 29 March 1968.

44 "Martin Joyful after Blitz of 25 Ridings in Quebec," *Toronto Star*, 4 March 1968.

45 "Special Status Out – Martin," *Montreal Star*, 16 March 1968.

46 "Demonstrators Anger Martin," *Quebec Chronicle Telegraph*, 1 February 1968; Wilf Bennett, "Paul Goes Looking for Western Gold," *Windsor Star*, 7 February 1968.

47 "Man-to-Man Campaign."

48 "Harrow Spikes Martin Drive," *Windsor Star*, 1 March 1968; Peter Regenstreif, "Hellyer Has Edge on the First Ballot in Western Ontario," *Toronto Star*, 12 March 1968.

49 Gerald Waring, "They'd Fly 100 Miles for One of Your Smiles," *Vancouver Sun*, 14 March 1968; Peter Regenstreif, "Trudeau Leads in Rural Alberta," *Toronto Star*, 15 March 1968; Peter Regenstreif, "The Prairies: Martin, Hellyer in Lead," *Toronto Star*, 20 March 1968.

50 Dominique Clift, "Lesage Liberals Back Martin to Hurt Trudeau," *Toronto Star*, 15 March 1968.

51 John Gray, "Paul's Quebec Caper," *Montreal Star*, 23 February 1968; "Martin Joyful after Blitz."

52 Allan Fotheringham, "In Politics, He's a Craftsman," *Vancouver Sun*, 26 March 1968.

53 Martin Diary, 8 August 1979, MG 35, A292, box 13, LAC.

54 Ibid.; Geoffrey Stevens, "A Man for All Seasons Sought by Liberals, Left, Right and Centre," *Toronto Globe and Mail*, 12 February 1968.

55 Quoted in Fraser, "Back Stage in Ottawa: How Some Grits."

56 "Paul Martin," *Toronto Globe and Mail*, 30 March 1968.

57 Ibid.

58 Quoted in Regenstreif, "Hellyer Has Edge."

59 Peter Regenstreif, "Clear Lead over Opponents for Two Ballots," *Halifax Chronicle Herald*, 23 March 1968.
60 Cadieux Diary, 11 March 1968, Cadieux Papers, vol. 8, file 14, LAC (author's translation); original: "'Ne fais pas cela, Laura.' Il avait compté sur son appui. Il avait bien connu son père. Avait-elle discuter l'affaire avec lui. No? M. Martin allait l'appeler."
61 Whelan and Archbold, *Whelan*, 113.
62 Peter Newman, "MP's Reveal Preferences," *Montreal Star*, 23 March 1968.
63 Quoted in Gérard Pelletier, *Years of Choice*, 288.
64 "The Tide Runs Out on Paul Martin," *Montreal Star*, 19 March 1968.
65 "After Pearson, Who?" *Ottawa Citizen*, 28 March 1968.
66 "Trudeau: The Best Choice for Canada," *Toronto Star*, 28 March 1968.
67 Duncan Edmonds to Martin, 22 May 1970, Martin Papers, vol. 466, file: Private Correspondence, 1968 to 1973, LAC.
68 Quoted in "Martin Angrily Denies Reports His Health Poor," *Toronto Star*, 30 March 1968.
69 McGill, *My Life as I Remember It*, 237.
70 Quoted in Ron Haggart, "Martin Office Mail List Aided Smear: Trudeau Men," *Toronto Star*, 3 April 1968; Duncan Edmonds to Martin, 22 May 1970, Martin Papers, vol. 466, file: Private Correspondence, 1968 to 1973, LAC; McCall-Newman, *Grits*, 115; Sawatsky, *The Insiders*, 66–67.
71 "New Poll of Delegates Shows Trudeau Far in Front," *Montreal Gazette*, 3 April 1968.

	Canadian Press poll (1,045 delegates)	CBC poll (all delegates)	*Montreal Gazette* poll (all delegates)
Trudeau	328	606	708
Martin	166	346	389
Hellyer	165	329	357
Winters	110	213	254
Turner	80	224	161
MacEachen	77	163	54
Sharp	65	139	142

72 Hellyer, *Damn the Torpedoes*, 275.
73 Pat Whelan, "Martin Camp Shaken ... but Still Confident," *Windsor Star*, 4 April 1968.
74 Tom Hazlitt, "Waning Martin Insists He'll Be Victor," *Toronto Star*, 4 April 1968.
75 Lotta Dempsey, "Everybody's in Love with Trudeau," *Toronto Star*, 4 April 1968.
76 Brian Stewart, "The Pace Steps Up – The Way It Was," *Montreal Gazette*, 6 April 1968.
77 "A Leader Must Inspire – But to What End?" *Toronto Star*, 6 April 1968.
78 Robert Hull, "Two 'New' Men Hold Spotlight," *Windsor Star*, 6 April 1968.
79 Peter Newman, "Voices from the Rostrum," *Montreal Star*, 6 April 1968.
80 Paul William Martin to Martin, 6 April 1968, Martin Papers, vol. 273, file: Leadership, LAC.
81 Quoted in Scott Young, "The Bitter Pill Martin Took Like a Man When His Dream Was Shattered," *Toronto Globe and Mail*, 8 April 1968.

82 Quoted in Marjorie Nichols, "Martin – The Final Defeat Accepted with Calm," *Ottawa Journal*, 8 April 1968.

83 Quoted in Anthony Westall and Geoffrey Stevens, "71/2 Hours of Chaos, and an Enigma Chosen Next PM," *Toronto Globe and Mail*, 8 April 1968.

84 Quoted in Tom Hazlitt, "Martin Bows Out with Dignity, Grace," *Toronto Star*, 8 April 1968.

85 Quoted in "It Was Trudeau from the Start," *Ottawa Journal*, 8 April 1968.

86 Hugh MacLennan to Martin, 7 April 1968, Martin Papers, vol. 273, file: Leadership, LAC.

87 Cadieux Diary, 8 April 1968, Cadieux Papers, vol. 8, file 13, LAC (author's translation); original: "Le coup a été dur."

88 Ibid.

89 Story interview with Martin, [1969–70], Martin Papers, vol. 351, tape 6, side 2, LAC.

90 Cadieux Diary, 9 April 1968, Cadieux Papers, vol. 8, file 13, LAC; Story interview with Martin, Martin Papers, [1969–70], vol. 351, tape 6, side 2, LAC.

91 Story interview with Martin, [1969–70], Martin Papers, vol. 351, tape 6, side 2, LAC.

92 Quoted in "Grit Split Rumours Sunk, Whelan by Acclamation," *Windsor Star*, 11 May 1968.

93 Martin, *So Many Worlds*, 632.

94 Nell Martin to Martin, [fall 1968], Martin Papers, box 466, file: Private Correspondence, LAC.

95 Nell Martin to Martin, [May 1969], Martin Papers, box 455, file: Strasburg, LAC.

96 Nell Martin to Alison Ignatieff, [January 1971], Ignatieff Papers, box 6, file 6, Trinity College Archives.

97 Author interview with Mary Anne Bellamy, 22 August 2007.

98 "US Security Irks Paul Martin's Daughter," *Toronto Telegram*, 22 September 1969.

99 Michael Bellamy to Martin, 28 October 1969, Martin Papers, box 450, file: Martin, LAC.

100 Author interview with Bellamy, 22 August 2007.

101 Story interview with Martin, [1969–70], Martin Papers, vol. 352, tape 12, side 1, LAC.

102 Nell Martin to Alison Ignatieff, [January 1971], Ignatieff Papers, box 6, file 6, Trinity College Archives.

103 Story interview with Martin, [1971], Martin Papers, vol. 353, tape A-5, side 2, LAC.

104 Mary Anne Bellamy to Martin, 9 November 1973, Martin Papers, vol. 494, file: Martin, LAC.

105 Martin to Mary Anne Bellamy 15 November 1973, Martin Papers, vol. 494, file: Martin, LAC.

106 Story interview with Martin, [1970], Martin Papers, vol. 351, tape 3, side 2, LAC.

107 Ibid., Martin Papers, vol. 353, tape 15, side 1, LAC.

108 Paul Martin Jr., *Hell or High Water*, 41–51.

109 Martin to Burgon Bickersteth, 22 April 1974, Martin Papers, box 508, LAC.

110 Martin to Rosa Binder, 19 July 1974, Martin Papers, box 508, LAC.

111 Nellmart Ltd. Portfolio Analyses, Martin Papers, vol. 513, file: Nellmart Portfolio Listings, 1967–69, LAC.

112 Martin tax return, 1971, Martin Papers, vol. 513, file: Income Tax Returns, LAC.

113 Martin to Paul Martin Jr., 20 July 1976, Martin Papers, vol. 398, file D-28, LAC.

114 Paul Martin Jr. to Martin, 8 November 1973, Martin Papers, vol. 494, file: Martin, LAC.

115 Martin to B. Easton, 23 January 1974, Martin Papers, vol. 508, LAC.

116 Jack Best interview with Paul Martin, [1971], Martin Papers, vol. 354, tape A-22, side 1, LAC.

117 See, for example, Story interview with Martin, [1969–70], Martin Papers, vol. 351, tape 1, side 1, LAC.

118 Martin to Nick D'Ombrain, 16 December 1975, Martin Papers, vol. 369, LAC. Martin described the King diaries as "disasters." Martin to Josephine Tessier, 11 May 1978, Martin Papers, vol. 398, LAC.

119 Martin to Burgon Bickersteth, 13 May 1970, Martin Papers, vol. 441, LAC.

120 Story interview with Martin, [1969–70], Martin Papers, vol. 351, tape 5, side 2, LAC.

121 Martin to Burgon Bickersteth, 17 September 1969, Martin Papers, vol. 441, LAC.

122 Story interview with Martin, [1969–70], Martin Papers, vol. 354, tape A-20, side 1, LAC.

123 Ibid., Martin Papers, vol. 351, tape 1, side 2, LAC.

124 Ibid., Martin Papers, vol. 353, tape A-14, side 1, LAC.

125 Martin to Burgon Bickersteth, 8 July 1970, Martin Papers, vol. 441, LAC.

126 Story interview with Martin, [1969–70], Martin Papers, vol. 353, tape A-16, side 1, LAC.

127 Martin Diary, 25 March 1978, Martin Papers, vol. 519, LAC.

128 Ibid., 2 June 1979, Martin Papers, MG 35, A292, box 13, LAC.

129 Best interview with Martin, [1971], Martin Papers, vol. 354, tape A-22, side 1, LAC.

130 Story interview with Martin, [1969–70], Martin Papers, vol. 353, tape A-16, side 1, LAC. Secretary of State for External Affairs, *Foreign Policy for Canadians* (Ottawa: Information Canada, 1970).

131 Martin Diary, 25 March 1979, Martin Papers, vol. 519, LAC.

132 Martin to Burgon Bickersteth, 17 September 1969, Martin Papers, vol. 441, LAC.

133 Story interview with Martin, [1969–70], Martin Papers, vol. 351, tape 2, side 1, LAC.

134 Ibid., [1969–70], Martin Papers, vol. 351, tape 3, side 1, LAC.

135 Martin to Jules Léger, 13 January 1971, Martin Papers, vol. 449, LAC.

136 Martin, Review of *Snowjob*, by Charles Taylor, *Toronto Globe and Mail*, 14 September 1974.

137 Norah Story to Martin, 31 July 1973, Martin Papers, vol. 365, file: Correspondence 1972, LAC.

138 Martin to Josephine Phelan, 11 October 1973, Martin Papers, vol. 365, file: Correspondence 1972, LAC.

139 R.I.K. Davidson to Martin, 16 January 1974; and Martin to R.I.K. Davidson, 25 February and 13 May 1974, Martin Papers, vol. 365, file: Correspondence 1972, LAC.

140 Martin Diary, 17 April 1978, Martin Papers, vol. 519, LAC.

141 Martin, *So Many Worlds*, 641.

142 Ibid., 638.

143 Martin to Burgon Bickersteth, 17 September 1969, Martin Papers, vol. 441, LAC.

144 Canada, *Senate of Canada Debates* (18 September 1968), 42.

145 Davey, *The Rainmaker*, 143.

146 Tom Brett, Senate Appointments, 27 August 1969, Martin Papers, vol. 464, LAC.

147 Martin to Pierre Trudeau, 21 January 1970, Martin Papers, vol. 464, LAC.

148 See, for example, Arthur Blakely, "Senate Coming to Life," *Ottawa Citizen,* 29 November 1971; "The Old Promise," *Winnipeg Free Press,* 14 March 1970; John Gray, "Martin Puts Some Life into Senate," *Toronto Star,* 26 March 1970.

149 John Hay to author, 31 July 2013.

150 Christina Newman, "The Body Politic," *Chatelaine,* February 1971.

151 "Senate Refuses to Refer Hate Bill to Supreme Court," 13 May 1970, Martin Papers, vol. 483, file: Personal Clippings, LAC.

152 "Croll Hits Speculation on Report," *Ottawa Journal,* 13 November 1970.

153 "Alas, Business as Usual," *Toronto Globe and Mail,* 16 February 1971.

154 Martin to Pierre Trudeau, 21 June 1971, Martin Papers, vol. 464, LAC.

155 Forsey, *A Life on the Fringe,* 152.

156 Gerard McNeil, "Senators Face Holiday Debate," *Ottawa Citizen,* 8 December 1971.

157 "A Cavalier Treatment of the Senate," *Ottawa Journal,* 13 December 1971.

158 "Senators Invited to Commit Suicide," *Toronto Sun,* 15 December 1971.

159 "A Test of the Senate," *Toronto Globe and Mail,* 16 December 1971, and "Right of Senate," *Montreal Gazette,* 16 December 1971.

160 Arthur Blakely, "Election Call Threatened on Tax Bill," *Ottawa Citizen,* 16 December 1971.

161 "Senate Committee Clears Way for Tax Bill's Passage," *Ottawa Citizen,* 21 December 1971.

162 Martin Diary, 20 September 1977, Martin Papers, vol. 519, LAC.

163 See, for example, Martin to Mitchell Sharp, 24 June 1971, RG 25, vol. 9283, file 20-Canada-9-Martin, LAC.

164 Geoffrey Stevens, "Tissue Paper Tinsel and a Hearty Ho, Ho," *Toronto Globe and Mail,* 25 December 1973.

165 Victor Moore to Martin, 23 January 1973, Martin Papers, vol. 490, file: Commonwealth Youth Ministers, LAC.

166 Martin to Klaus Goldschlag, 6 November 1973, Martin Papers, vol. 490, LAC.

167 "Voyage du Sénateur Martin en Afrique," n.d., RG 25, vol. 9282, file 20-Canada-9-Martin, LAC.

168 Pierre Trudeau to Martin, 8 November 1968, RG 25, vol. 10101, file 20-Canada-9-Martin, LAC.

169 Story interview with Martin, [1969–70], Martin Papers, vol. 351, tape 4, side 1, LAC.

170 Dakar to Ottawa (Flash for Prime Minister), Tel. No. 734, 2 December 1968, RG 25, vol. 9282, file 20-Canada-9-Martin, LAC.

171 President Hamani Diori to P.E. Trudeau, [29 November 1968], Martin Papers, vol. 455, file: Africa Trip, LAC.

172 Kinshasa to Ottawa, Tel. No. 1038, 11 December 1968, RG 25, vol. 9282, file 20-Canada-9-Martin, LAC.

173 Joseph Mobutu to Pierre Trudeau, 11 December 1968, Martin Papers, vol. 455, file: Africa Trip, LAC.

174 Best interview with Martin, Martin Papers, vol. 358, tape 22-A, side 1, LAC.

175 Mitchell Sharp to Martin, 2 September 1970, RG 25, vol. 9282, file 20-Canada-9-Martin, LAC.

176 Cabinet Conclusions, 21 May 1970, PCO Records, LAC.

177 Port-of-Spain to Ottawa (Martin for Sharp), Tel. No. 1335, 15 September 1970; and Port-of-Spain to Ottawa (Martin for Sharp), Tel. No. 1359, 18 September 1970, RG 25, vol. 9282, file 20-Canada-9-Martin, LAC.

178 Kingston to Ottawa (Martin for Sharp), Tel. No. 766, 13 October 1970; and Kingston to Ottawa (Martin for Sharp), Tel. No. 768, 14 October 1970, RG 25, vol. 9283, file 20-Canada-9-Martin, LAC.

179 Martin to Mitchell Sharp, 5 October 1970, RG 25, vol. 9283, file 20-Canada-9-Martin, LAC.

180 Martin, Draft Memorandum for Cabinet, 9 November 1970, RG 25, vol. 9283, file 20-Canada-9-Martin, LAC.

181 Larry Smith to Martin, 10 November 1970, and Martin's marginal notes, Martin Papers, vol. 450, LAC.

182 Ed Ritchie, Memoranda for the Minister, 23 November and 4 December 1970, RG 25, vol. 9283, file 20-Canada-9-Martin, LAC.

183 Carmichael, *Passport to the Heart*, 74–75.

184 Martin, *So Many Worlds*, 669.

185 Mitchell Sharp, Memorandum for Cabinet, 3 March 1972; and Briefing Note for President Nixon's Visit, 4 April 1972, RG 25, vol. 13887, file 37-9-UNCTAD-12-1972, LAC.

186 Ken Wardroper to Under-Secretary Ed Ritchie, 23 March 1972, RG 25, vol. 13887, file 37-9-UNCTAD-12-1971, LAC.

187 David Morrison, *Aid and Ebb Tide*, 222–24.

188 Ed Ritchie, Memorandum for the Minister, 21 March 1972; and Ken Wardroper to Michel Dupuy, 7 April 1972, RG 25, vol. 13887, file 37-9-UNCTAD-12-1972; Cabinet Conclusions, 30 March 1972, PCO Records, LAC.

189 Santiago to Ottawa, Tel. No. UN-19, 18 April 1972, RG 25, vol. 13887, file 37-9-UNCTAD-12-1972, LAC.

190 Ottawa to Santiago, Tel. No. ECD-439, 18 May 1972, RG 25, vol. 13887, file 37-9-UNCTAD-12-1972, LAC.

191 Martin to Arnold Smith, 30 May 1972, Martin Papers, vol. 492, file: UNCTAD, LAC.

192 Quoted by Heath MacQuarrie in Canada, *House of Commons* Debates (29 May 1972), 2629.

193 Quoted in "Martin Urges Senate Support for Status of Women Report," *Toronto Star*, 21 April 1971.

194 Notes on Senate, n.d., Martin Papers, vol. 458, file: Conflict of Interest, LAC.

195 James Ferrabee, "Family Ownership a Problem for Liberal Senator Martin," *Ottawa Citizen*, 9 November 1973; "Is Putting Part of Personal Holdings in a Blind Trust Satisfactory Answer?" *Ottawa Citizen*, 9 November 1973; Doug Fisher, "Maurice, Bill, Jack & Junior," *Toronto Sun*, 16 November 1973.

196 Pierre Trudeau to Martin, 28 December 1973, Martin Papers, vol. 515, file: Prime Minister, LAC.

197 "Senators Struggle with Bill," *Ottawa Citizen,* 12 January 1974; "Senators Continue," *Ottawa Journal,* 12 January 1974.
198 Charles Lynch, "Senate Let Down," *Windsor Star,* 12 January 1974.
199 Peter Thomson, "Pressure Mounts for Trudeau to Shuffle His Cabinet," *Ottawa Journal,* 30 March 1974.
200 Lubor Zink, "Trudeau's Cabinet Shuffle," *Toronto Sun,* 9 August 1974.
201 Jack Best, "Aides Angry: Martin Ousted Near Historic Hill Milestone," *Ottawa Citizen,* 14 August 1974.

CHAPTER 13: LEGACIES, 1974–92

1 John Holmes to Martin, 3 February 1975, Martin Papers, vol. 372, Library and Archives Canada (LAC).
2 Ed Ritchie to Martin, 8 August 1974, Martin Papers, vol. 382, file: Appointment to London, LAC.
3 E.D. O'Mahony to Mr. Neil Smith, 1 November 1974, Foreign and Commonwealth Office Records (FCO) 82/407, National Archives (NA).
4 Martin Charteris to Sir Thomas Brimelow, 21 September 1974, FCO 82/407, NA.
5 Transcript of a Commentary by Hugh Winsor, 10 October 1974, FCO 23/92, NA.
6 Marci McDonald, "The Forgotten Man," *Maclean's,* 9 August 1976, 22–27.
7 P.H. Scott to Sir John Johnston, 16 December 1974, FCO 82/407, NA.
8 Martin to Paul Martin Jr., 13 January 1976, Martin Papers, vol. 397, LAC.
9 Martin to Robert Bothwell, 24 July 1979, Martin Papers, vol. 367, LAC.
10 See, for example, Martin Diary, 3 October 1978, Martin Papers, MG 35, A292, box 9, LAC.
11 Ibid., 30 September 1977, Martin Papers, MG 35, A292, box 9, LAC.
12 Patrick Reid, *Wild Colonial Boy,* 235.
13 Author interview with Jim Coutts, 12 December 2011.
14 Jean Chrétien to Martin, 20 December 1976, Martin Papers, vol. 373, LAC (author's translation); original: "Pour moi, déjeuner au Reforme Club, assi devant le portrait du grand Gladstone et parlant de Laurier et de notre cher Canada fut une expérience inoubliable."
15 Martin, *The London Diaries,* 393.
16 Martin Diary, 13 July 1979, Martin Papers, MG 35, A292, box 9, LAC.
17 Quoted in Maureen Garvie, "Notebook," *Kingston Whig Standard,* 24 December 1988.
18 Dorothy Armstrong to Martin, 14 December 1976, Martin Papers, vol. 366, LAC.
19 Author interview with Norman Hillmer, 27 November 2013.
20 Sir Martin Gilliat to Martin, 14 June 1979, Martin Papers, vol. 370, LAC.
21 Biographical Briefing Note for the Secretary of State, [22 January 1975], FCO 82/527, NA; Biographical Briefing Note for the Prime Minister, 2 December 1976, Prime Minister's Office Records 16/1531, NA.
22 Pierre Trudeau to Martin, 25 March 1975, Martin Papers, vol. 391, file: PM Visit 1975, LAC.

23 Ross Campbell to Martin, 15 January 1976, Martin Papers, vol. 368, LAC.

24 Christian Hardy to Martin, 5 January 1977, Martin Papers, vol. 373, LAC.

25 Martin to Lucille Martin, Marie Martin, and Claire Guay, 17 February 1975, Martin Papers, vol. 397, LAC.

26 Martin, *So Many Worlds*, 407. See also Hilliker and Donaghy, "Canadian Relations with the United Kingdom," 25–46.

27 "Canada-UK Relations," [1975]; and "Bilateral Relations – Canada – United Kingdom," 16 July 1978, RG 25, vol. 8125, file 20-1-2-BRIT, LAC.

28 "Visit of the Prime Minister of Canada: Steering Brief," 6 March 1975, CAB [Cabinet Records] 133/447, NA.

29 High Commissioner in the UK to SSEA, Numbered Letter 97, 27 January 1975, RG 25, vol. 8125, file 20-1-2-BRIT, LAC.

30 Circular Document, No. 24/72 (FAI), 31 October 1972, RG 25, vol. 13172, file 56-1-2-New Look, LAC.

31 F.A.B. Roger, "An Overview of Information Services Development, or What the 'New Look' Looks Like," [January 1974], RG 25, vol. 13172, file 56-1-2-New Look, LAC.

32 L.A.D. Stephens to GEP, 18 March 1974, RG 25, vol. 13170, file 56-1-2-BRIT, LAC.

33 Patrick Reid to Christian Hardy, 4 June 1976, RG 25, vol. 16160, file 56-1-2-BRIT, LAC.

34 Christian Hardy to the SSEA, Letter 1322, 22 October 1976, RG 25, vol. 16160, file 56-1-2-BRIT, LAC.

35 Martin to John Connolly, 21 February 1977, Martin Papers, vol. 368, LAC.

36 High Commission in the UK (Roberts) to SSEA, Letter 278, 22 March 1978, RG 25, vol. 13170, file 56-1-2-BRIT, LAC.

37 Martin, Notes for an Address to the Canadian Institute for Advanced Legal Studies, Cambridge, July 1979, Martin Papers, vol. 384, file: CIALS, LAC.

38 Basil Markesinis to Martin, 20 September 1976, Martin Papers, vol. 384, file: CIALS, LAC.

39 Martin to Law Deans, 3 December 1976, Martin Papers, vol. 384, file: CIALS, LAC.

40 Ottawa to London, Tel. No. 539, 3 May 1977, and Richard Roberts' marginal notation, Martin Papers, vol. 384, file: CIALS, LAC.

41 Martin, *The London Diaries,* 303.

42 Ottawa to London, Tel. No. 568, 13 June 1977; and Nathan Nemetz to Martin, 21 March 1978, Martin Papers, vol. 384, file: CIALS, LAC.

43 Jack Clyne to Martin, 5 October 1978, Martin Papers, vol. 384, file: CIALS, LAC.

44 Derek Bowett to Jack Clyne (cc. Martin), [October 1978], Martin Papers, vol. 384, file: CIALS, LAC.

45 Author interview with Douglas Carruthers, 27 March 2009.

46 Ibid.

47 London to Ottawa (Martin for Estey), Tel. No. 335, 30 January 1979, Martin Papers, vol. 384, file: CIALS, LAC.

48 Martin, *The London Diaries,* 479; Lord Denning to Martin, 18 March 1979, Martin Papers, vol. 384, file: CIALS, LAC.

49 Richard Roberts, Report on a Visit to Cambridge, [February 1979], Martin Papers, vol. 384, file: CIALS, LAC.

50   Quoted in Norman Webster, "Air Canada Set to Win U.K. Dispute," *Toronto Globe and Mail*, 9 October 1979.

51   London to Ottawa, Tel. No. 664, 28 March 1977; and London to Ottawa, Tel. No. 752, 6 April 1977, RG 25, vol. 14847, file 42-8-3-1-BRIT, LAC.

52   London to Ottawa, Tel. No. 6762, 15 September 1978, RG 25, vol. 14847, file 42-8-3-1-BRIT, LAC.

53   Ottawa to London, Tel. No. EBS-1772, 21 September 1978, RG 25, vol. 14847, file 42-8-3-1-BRIT, LAC.

54   Meeting between the Rt. Hon. Edmund Dell and Mr. Paul Martin, 3 October 1978, RG 25, vol. 14847, file 42-8-3-1-BRIT, LAC.

55   Martin Diary, 25 November 1978, Martin Papers, MG 35, A292, box 9, LAC.

56   A.E. Gotlieb, Memorandum for the Minister, EBS-2328, 23 November 1978, RG 25, vol. 14847, file 42-8-3-1-BRIT, LAC.

57   Briefing Note: Prime Minister Trudeau's Visit to the UK: Bilateral Air Negotiations, 29 November 1978, RG 25, vol. 14847, file 42-8-3-1-BRIT, LAC.

58   London to Ottawa, Tel. No. 2413, 30 November 1978, RG 25, vol. 14847, file 42-8-3-1-BRIT, LAC.

59   London to Ottawa, Tel. No. 131, 10 January 1979, RG 25, vol. 14847, file 42-8-3-1-BRIT, LAC.

60   Ottawa to London, Tel. No. EBS-0089, 5 January 1979, RG 25, vol. 14847, file 42-8-3-1-BRIT, LAC.

61   W.M. McLeish, Memorandum to the Minister of Transport, 10 January 1979, and attachment, RG 25, vol. 14847, file 42-8-3-1-BRIT, LAC.

62   London to Ottawa, Tel. No. 262, 19 January 1979, RG 25, vol. 14847, file 24-8-3-a, LAC.

63   A.E. Gotlieb, Memorandum for the Minister, 19 January 1979, RG 25, vol. 14847, file 42-8-3-1, LAC; Canada, *House of Commons Debates* (24 January 1979), 2514.

64   Canada, *House of Commons Debates* (26 January 1979), 2597–98.

65   United Kingdom, *Parliamentary Debates*, Commons (22 January 1979).

66   London to Ottawa, Tel. No. 331, 29 January 1979, RG 25, vol. 14847, file 42-8-3-1, LAC.

67   Memorandum to Under-Secretary, EBS-386, 6 February 1979, RG 25, vol. 14847, file 42-8-3-1, LAC.

68   London to Ottawa, Tel. No. 331, 29 January 1979, RG 25, vol. 14847, file 42-8-3-1, LAC.

69   Norman Webster, "Martin Gets Tough Over British Proposal to Move Air Canada," *Toronto Globe and Mail*, 7 March 1979, 12.

70   Editorial, "And There We'll Stay," *Toronto Globe and Mail*, 15 March 1979, 6.

71   New York to Ottawa (copied to London), Tel. No. 497, 19 March 1979, RG 25, vol. 14847, file 42-8-3-1, LAC.

72   London to Ottawa, Tel. No. 770, 27 March 1979, RG 25, vol. 14847, file 42-8-3-1, LAC.

73   London to Ottawa, Tel. No. 1777, 20 July 1979, RG 25, vol. 14847, file 42-8-3-1, LAC.

74   Martin Diary, 7 September 1979, Martin Papers, MG 35, A292, box 13, LAC.

75   A.E. Gotlieb, Memorandum for the Minister, 19 September 1979, and MacDonald's marginal note of 24 September 1979, RG 25, vol. 14847, file 42-8-3-1, LAC.

76   Martin Diary, 1 October 1979, Martin Papers, MG 25, A292, box 13, LAC.

77   Quoted in Stevie Cameron, "Didn't You Used to Be ...?" *Toronto Globe and Mail*, 28 August 1987.

78 Quoted in Paul McKeague, "Paul Martin Sr. Was Unique: Cantankerous, Fun, Idealistic," *Kitchener-Waterloo Record,* 17 September 1992.
79 Martin to John Holmes, 15 April 1986, Holmes Papers, box 68, file 6, Trinity College Archives.
80 Paul Martin Jr., "Concluding Remarks," 43.
81 Martin to John Holmes, 4 April 1985, Holmes Papers, box 54, file 5, Trinity College Archives.
82 Martin to John English, 6 June 1979, Martin Papers, vol. 399, LAC.
83 John Holmes to Basil Robinson, 12 October 1982, Holmes Papers, box 37, file 6, Trinity College Archives.
84 Jack Best, "External Affairs Decides to Sanitize, Not Publicize, Anniversary Book," *Ottawa Citizen,* 12 November 1982.
85 Mark MacGuigan to de Montigny Marchand, 24 September 1982, "History," Historical Section, Department of Foreign Affairs, Trade and Development (DFATD).
86 De Montigny Marchand, Memorandum for the Minister, 14 December 1982, "History," Historical Section, DFATD.
87 Quoted in Olive, "Paul Martin: The Vaulting Ambition," 32.
88 Blair Neatby, "Political Animal," *Saturday Night,* February 1984, 65.
89 Ibid.
90 Olive, "Paul Martin: The Vaulting Ambition," 32.
91 Ramsay Cook, "A Paradise Sadly Denied," *Toronto Globe and Mail,* 14 December 1985; Dale Thomson, "Paul Martin Shows Politics Still 'the Greatest Adventure,'" *Montreal Gazette,* 21 December 1985.
92 J.W. Pickersgill, "Candid Recollection by a Great Parliamentarian," *Ottawa Citizen,* 16 November 1985.
93 Martin to John Holmes, 15 April 1986, Holmes Papers, box 68, file 6, Trinity College Archives.
94 Martin to Paul Martin Jr., 11 March 1976, Martin Papers, vol. 397, file: Paul Martin, LAC.
95 Martin to Mark MacGuigan, 30 March 1977, Martin Papers, vol. 376, Nominal file, LAC.
96 Handwritten note on Martin to Paul Martin Jr., 11 March 1976, Martin Papers, vol. 397, file: Paul Martin, LAC.
97 Martin, *The London Diaries,* 549.
98 Author interview with John English, 16 August 2013.
99 Quoted in "Liberals' War-Horse Up at First Light for Session," *Toronto Star,* 29 November 1986.
100 Quoted in "Parting Shots of Clark Aide Left Tory Old Boys Chortling," *Toronto Globe and Mail,* 23 January 1986.
101 Author interview with Barbara Quenneville, August 2007.
102 Quoted in "Proud Paul Martin Delivers Old Riding to Son," *Toronto Star,* 18 February 1990.
103 Ibid.
104 David Herle, "After the Carnage, Some Muted Optimism," *Toronto Globe and Mail,* 21 December 2009.

105 "Paul Martin (1902–92)," *Toronto Star,* 15 September 1992.
106 Quoted in "Canada's Political Elite Attend Martin's Funeral," *Hamilton Spectator,* 18 September 1992.
107 Quoted in R.M. Harrison, "Now," *Windsor Daily Star,* 7 June 1945.

BIBLIOGRAPHY

PRIMARY SOURCES

CANADA

Canadian Institute of Public Opinion Archives, Toronto
Department of National Defence – Directorate of History and Heritage, Ottawa (DND)
    Robert Raymont Papers
    Frank Worthington Papers
Library and Archives Canada, Ottawa (LAC)
    D.C. Abbott Papers
    Marcel Cadieux Papers
    Brooke Claxton Papers
    M.J. Coldwell Papers
    J.W. Dafoe Papers
    Department of External Affairs Records (RG 25)
    Department of Finance Records (RG 19)
    Department of Immigration Records (RG 76)
    Department of Labour Records (RG 27)
    Department of National Health and Welfare Records (RG 29)
    Department of Secretary of State Records (RG 6)
    Frank Flaherty Papers
    Walter Gordon Papers
    Walter Harris Papers
    C.D. Howe Papers
    Robert Inch Papers
    Institute for Research in Public Policy Papers
    William Lyon Mackenzie King Papers
    League of Nations Society of Canada Papers
    Paul Martin Papers

Lester B. Pearson Papers
Josephine Phelan Papers
Lazarus Phillips Papers
Privy Council Office Records (PCO Records, RG 2)
Escott Reid Papers
Louis St. Laurent Papers
Peter Stursberg Papers
Manitoba Archives
Ralph Maybank Papers
Queen's University Archives
Grant Dexter Papers
Tom Kent Papers
Trent University Archives
Trent University Sound and Video Recordings Collection. Box 1: Donald Cameron
Interview. 1973
Trinity College Archives, Toronto
John Holmes Papers
George Ignatieff Papers
University of St. Michael's College Archives (USMC Archives)
Fr. Henry Carr Papers
Fr. E.J. McCorkell Papers
St. Michael's College Yearbooks, 1921–27
University of Toronto Archives (UTA)
Burgon Bickersteth Papers
Robert Bothwell Papers
Faculty of Arts and Science Records
Hart House Records
Vincent Massey Papers
University of Waterloo Archives
John English Papers

UNITED KINGDOM

National Archives, Kew (NA)
Dominions Office Records (DO)
Foreign and Commonwealth Office Records (FCO)
Foreign Office Records (FO)
Prime Minister's Office Records

UNITED STATES

Harvard University Archives
Student Records
Lyndon Baines Johnson Library (LBJ Library)
National Security Files
White House Confidential Files

John F. Kennedy Library
  National Security Files

INTERVIEWS

Mary Anne Bellamy. Colchester, Ontario. 22 August 2007.
Eric Bergbusch. Ottawa, Ontario. 14 June 2010.
E.P. Black. Ottawa, Ontario. 9 November 1994.
Tom Brett. Toronto, Ontario. 15 August 2013.
Michael Brogin. Windsor, Ontario. 20 August 2007.
Donald Cameron Jr. Peterborough, Ontario. 26 March 2009.
Douglas Carruthers. Toronto, Ontario. 27 March 2009.
Joe Clark. Rockcliffe, Ontario. 31 May 2012.
Jim Coutts. Toronto, Ontario. 12 December 2011.
Craig Davidson. Telephone. 21 August 2010.
Tom Delworth. Ottawa, Ontario. 14 March 1997; Telephone. 6 August 2012.
Duncan Edmonds. Iroquois, Ontario. 12 November 2007.
Gar Emerson. Ottawa, Ontario. 29 September 2010.
John English. Toronto, Ontario. 16 August 2013.
Doug Fisher. Ottawa, Ontario. 7 December 2008.
John Fraser. Ottawa, Ontario. 9 June 1994.
Allan Gotlieb. Toronto, Ontario. 4 July 2013.
Herb Gray. Ottawa, Ontario. 8 August 2007.
John Hadwen. Rockcliffe, Ontario. 12 July 2007.
Paul Hellyer. Walker's Point, Ontario. 30 July 2006.
Michael Hicks. Ottawa, Ontario. 5 September 2010.
Norman Hillmer. Ottawa, Ontario. 27 November 2013.
U. Alexis Johnson. Telephone. 8 June 1992.
Tom Kent. Kingston, Ontario. 23 August 2007.
Otto Lang. Telephone. 27 July 2013.
Peyton Lyon. Ottawa, Ontario. 12 November 2008.
A.J. MacEachen. Ottawa, Ontario. 28 November 2005.
Michael Maloney. Simcoe, Ontario. 21 August 2007.
Anita Martin and Claire Guay. Pembroke, Ontario. 18 April 2007.
Frederic S. Martin. Ottawa, Ontario. 15 June 2010.
Paul Martin Sr. Windsor, Ontario. 15 June 1992.
Paul Martin Jr. Ottawa, Ontario. 2 May 2007 and 24 May 2012; Montreal, Quebec. 10
  September 2013.
Sheila Martin. Montreal, Quebec. 10 September 2013.
Arthur Menzies. Rockcliffe, Ontario. 26 June 2006.
Joan Bissett Neiman. Telephone. 29 July 2013.
Richard O'Hagan. Huntsville, Ontario. 30 June 2012.
Jerry Philip. Colchester, Ontario. 21 August 2007.
Trevor Price. Telephone. 2 September 2007.
Barbara Quenneville. Windsor, Ontario. 20 August 2007.

Gordon Robertson. Ottawa, Ontario. 5 November 2007.
Basil Robinson. Rockcliffe, Ontario. 7 June 1994, 16 November 2003, 15 July 2006.
Richard Splane. Telephone. 26 February 2007.
John Turner. Telephone. 1 April 2009.
William Young. Ottawa, Ontario.

BOOKS, ARTICLES, AND THESES

Acheson, Dean. *Present at the Creation: My Years in the State Department.* New York: W.W. Norton, 1969.
Anastakis, Dmitry. *Auto Pact: Creating a Borderless North American Auto Industry, 1960–1971.* Toronto: University of Toronto Press, 2005.
Andrew, Arthur. *The Rise and Fall of a Middle Power: Canadian Diplomacy from King to Mulroney.* Toronto: James Lorimer, 1993.
Axworthy, Lloyd. "Canada and the World Revolution." *Canadian Dimension* 3 (March–April 1966): 31–33.
Azzi, Stephen. *Walter Gordon and the Rise of Canadian Nationalism.* Montreal and Kingston: McGill-Queen's University Press, 1999.
Baedeker, Karl. *The Dominion of Canada: Handbook for Travellers.* 3rd rev. ed. Leipzig: Karl Baedeker, 1907.
Beck, J.M. *The Pendulum of Power.* Scarborough: Prentice Hall Canada, 1968.
Beigie, Carl. *The Canada-U.S. Automotive Agreement: An Evaluation.* Quebec City: Canada-American Committee, 1970.
Belliveau, John Edward. *The Headliners: Behind the Scenes Memoirs.* Hantsport, NS: Lancelot Press, 1984.
Bercuson, David J. *True Patriot: The Life of Brooke Claxton, 1898–1960.* Toronto: University of Toronto Press, 1993.
Bissell, Claude. *The Imperial Canadian: Vincent Massey in Office.* Toronto: University of Toronto Press, 1986.
–. *The Young Vincent Massey.* Toronto: University of Toronto Press, 1981.
Bothwell, Robert. *Alliance and Illusion: Canada and the World, 1945–1984.* Vancouver: UBC Press, 2007.
–. "Marcel Cadieux: The Ultimate Professional." In *Architects and Innovators: Building the Department of Foreign Affairs and International Trade, 1909–2009,* ed. Greg Donaghy and Kim Richard Nossal, 207–22. Montreal and Kingston: McGill-Queen's University Press, 2009.
Bothwell, Robert, and William Kilbourn. *C.D. Howe: A Biography.* Toronto: McClelland and Stewart, 1979.
Breacher, Michael. *India and World Politics: Krishna Menon's View of the World.* London: Oxford University Press, 1968.
Brennan, Patrick. *Reporting the Nation's Business: Press-Government Relations during the Liberal Years, 1935–1957.* Toronto: University of Toronto Press, 1994.
Brouwer, Ruth Compton. *Canada's Global Voice: CUSO in Development, 1961–86.* Vancouver: UBC Press, 2013.

Bryden, Kenneth. *Old Age Pensions and Policy-Making in Canada*. Montreal and Kingston: McGill-Queen's University Press, 1974.

Buckner, Phillip, ed. *Canada and the End of Empire*. Vancouver: UBC Press, 2005.

Burney, Derek H. *Getting It Done: A Memoir*. Montreal and Kingston: McGill-Queen's University Press, 2005.

Burtch, Andrew. *Give Me Shelter: The Failure of Canada's Cold War Civil Defence*. Vancouver: UBC Press, 2012.

–. "If We Are Attacked, Let Us Be Prepared: Canada and the Failure of Civil Defence, 1945–1963." PhD diss., Carleton University, 2009.

Byers, R.B. "Canadian Foreign Policy and Selected Attentive Publics." Paper prepared for Defence (1) Liaison Division, 8 December 1967. Mimeograph, Department of Foreign Affairs, Trade and Development Library.

Callaghan, Morley. *The Varsity Story*. Toronto: Macmillan, 1948.

Camp, Dalton. *Gentlemen, Players and Politicians*. Toronto: McClelland and Stewart, 1970.

Canada: Nation on the March. Toronto: Clarke, Irwin, 1953.

Canada. *House of Commons Debates, 1935–79*.

–. *Senate of Canada Debates, 1968*.

–. Department of External Affairs. *Annual Report for 1963*. Ottawa: Queen's Printer, 1964.

–. Department of External Affairs. *Annual Report for 1967*. Ottawa: Queen's Printer, 1968.

–. Department of External Affairs. *1963 Bulletin*. Ottawa: Queen's Printer, 1964.

–. Department of Finance. *Public Accounts, 1966–67*. Ottawa: Queen's Printer, 1967.

–. Department of National Health and Welfare. *Annual Report for 1947*. Ottawa: King's Printer, 1947.

–. Department of National Health and Welfare. *Annual Report for 1948*. Ottawa: King's Printer, 1948.

–. Department of National Health and Welfare. *Annual Report for 1956*. Ottawa: Queen's Printer, 1956.

–. Statistics Canada. *Historical Statistics of Canada*. Ottawa: Statistics Canada, 1983.

Carmichael, Trevor A. *Passport to the Heart: Reflections on Canada-Caribbean Relations*. Kingston, JA: Ian Randle, 2000.

Carroll, Michael. *Pearson's Peacekeepers: Canada and the United Nations Emergency Force, 1956–67*. Vancouver: UBC Press, 2009.

Chapnick, Adam. *Canada's Voice: The Public Life of John Wendell Holmes*. Vancouver: UBC Press, 2009.

Clarkson, Stephen. "Conclusion." In *An Independent Foreign Policy for Canada?*, ed. Stephen Clarkson, 253–69. Toronto: University League for Social Reform, 1968.

Colling, Herb. *Ninety-Nine Days: The Ford Strike in Windsor, 1945*. Toronto: NC Press, 1995.

Davey, Keith. *The Rainmaker: A Passion for Politics*. Toronto: Stoddart, 1986.

Delworth, Thomas. "A Study of Canadian Policy with Respect to the Vietnam Problem, 1962–1966." Unpublished mimeograph. Historical Section, Department of Foreign Affairs, Trade and Development.

Dempson, Peter. *Assignment Ottawa: Seventeen Years in the Press Gallery.* Toronto: Ryerson Press, 1968.

Donaghy, Greg. "Blessed Are the Peacemakers: Canada, the United Nations, and the Search for a Korean Armistice, 1952–53." *War and Society* 30, 2 (August 2011): 134–46.

–, ed. *Documents on Canadian External Relations.* Vol. 16, *1950.* Ottawa: Supply and Services Canada, 1996.

–, ed. *Documents on Canadian External Relations.* Vol. 20, *1954.* Ottawa: Minister of Public Works and Government Services, 1997.

–, ed. *Documents on Canadian External Relations.* Vol. 21, *1955.* Ottawa: Canada Communication Group, 1999.

–. "Domesticating NATO: Canada and the North Atlantic Alliance, 1963–68." *International Journal* (Toronto) 52, 3 (Summer 1997): 445–63.

–. "The Road to Constraint: Canada and the Korean War, June-December 1950." In *Diplomatic Documents and Their Users,* ed. John Hilliker and Mary Halloran, 189–212. Ottawa: Department of Foreign Affairs and International Trade, 1995.

–. *Tolerant Allies: Canada and the United States, 1963–1968.* Montreal and Kingston: McGill-Queen's University Press, 2002.

Donaghy, Greg, and Stéphane Roussel, eds. *Escott Reid: Diplomat and Scholar.* Montreal and Kingston: McGill-Queen's University Press, 2004.

English, John. *Citizen of the World: The Life of Pierre Elliott Trudeau.* Vol. 1, *1919–1968.* Toronto: Alfred A. Knopf Canada, 2006.

–. *Shadow of Heaven: The Life of Lester B. Pearson.* Vol. 1, *1987–1948.* Toronto: Lester and Orpen Dennys, 1989.

–. *The Worldly Years: The Life of Lester B. Pearson.* Vol. 2, *1949–1972.* Toronto: Alfred A. Knopf Canada, 1992.

English, John, and John Stubbs, eds. *Mackenzie King: Widening the Debate.* Toronto: Macmillan, 1977.

Evans, Brian. "Ronning and Recognition: Years of Frustration." In *Reluctant Adversaries: Canada and the People's Republic of China,* ed. Brian Evans and Bernie Frolic, 148–67. Toronto: University of Toronto Press, 1991.

Fleming, Donald. *So Very Near: The Political Memoirs of the Honourable Donald M. Fleming.* Vol. 1, *The Rising Years.* Toronto: McClelland and Stewart, 1985.

–. *So Very Near: The Political Memoirs of the Honourable Donald M. Fleming.* Vol. 2, *The Summit Years.* Toronto: McClelland and Stewart, 1985.

Forsey, Eugene. *A Life on the Fringe: The Memoirs of Eugene Forsey.* Toronto: Oxford University Press, 1990.

Garton, Harold. *Hockey Town Canada.* Carp, ON: Creative Bound, 1992.

Gendron, Robin. *Towards a Francophone Community: Canada's Relations with France and French Africa, 1945–1968.* Montreal and Kingston: McGill-Queen's University Press, 2006.

Gervais, Marty. *The Rumrunners – A Prohibition Scrapbook.* Thornhill, ON: Firefly Books, 1980.

Gilbert, Alphonse. *La Vie a St-Alexandre.* Limbour, QC: College St-Alexandre, 1953.

Goodman, Eddie. *The Life of the Party: The Memoirs of Eddie Goodman.* Toronto: Key Porter Books, 1988.

Gordon, Walter. *A Choice for Canada: Independence or Colonial Status.* Toronto: McClelland and Stewart, 1966.

–. *A Political Memoir.* Toronto: McClelland and Stewart, 1977.

Graham, Roger. *Old Man Ontario: Leslie M. Frost.* Toronto: University of Toronto Press for the Ontario Historical Studies Series, 1990.

Granatstein, J.L. "Becoming Difficult: Escott Reid's Early Years." In *Escott Reid: Diplomat and Scholar,* ed. Greg Donaghy and Stéphane Roussel, 11–22. Montreal and Kingston: McGill-Queen's University Press, 2004.

–. *Canada: The Years of Uncertainty and Innovation, 1957–1967.* Toronto: McClelland and Stewart, 1986.

–. *Canada's War: The Politics of the Mackenzie King Government, 1939–45.* Toronto: Oxford University Press, 1975.

–. *A Man of Influence: Norman A. Robertson and Canadian Statecraft, 1929–68.* Toronto: Deneau, 1981.

Gwyn, Richard. *The Shape of Scandal: A Study of a Government in Crisis.* Toronto: Clarke, Irwin, 1965.

Hellyer, Paul. *Damn the Torpedoes: My Fight to Unify Canada's Armed Forces.* Toronto: McClelland and Stewart, 1990.

Herring, George C. *The Secret Diplomacy of the Vietnam War: The Negotiating Volumes of the Pentagon Papers.* Austin: University of Texas Press, 1983.

Hilliker, John, ed. *Documents on Canadian External Relations.* Vol. 11, *1944–1945.* Ottawa: Supply and Services Canada, 1990.

Hilliker, John, and Donald Barry. *Canada's Department of External Affairs.* Vol. 2, *Coming of Age, 1946–1968.* Montreal and Kingston: McGill-Queen's University Press, 1995.

Hilliker, John, and Greg Donaghy. "Canadian Relations with the United Kingdom at the End of Empire, 1956–73." In *Canada and the End of Empire,* ed. Phillip Buckner, 25–46. Vancouver: UBC Press, 2005.

Hillmer, Norman, and J.L. Granatstein. *Empire to Umpire: Canada and the World to the 1990s.* Toronto: Copp Clark Longman, 1994.

Hogan, Brian. "Salted with Fire: Studies in Catholic Social Thought and Action in Ontario, 1931–1961." PhD diss., University of Toronto, 1986.

Holmes, John. *The Shaping of Peace: Canada and the Search for World Order, 1943–57.* 2 vols. Toronto: University of Toronto Press, 1979 and 1982.

Holt, Simma. *The Other Mrs. Diefenbaker: A Biography of Edna May Brower.* Toronto: Doubleday Canada, 1982.

Igartua, José E. *The Other Quiet Revolution: National Identities in English Canada, 1945–71.* Vancouver: UBC Press, 2006.

Irving, Allan. "Harry Cassidy." In *Encyclopaedia of Canadian Social Work,* ed. Francis J. Turner, 54–55. Waterloo: Wilfrid Laurier University Press, 2005.

James, Alan. *Keeping the Peace in the Cyprus Crisis of 1963–64.* London: Palgrave, 2002.

James, Warren. *The People's Senator: The Life and Times of David A. Croll*. Toronto: Douglas and McIntyre, 1990.

Johnson, U. Alexis. *The Right Hand of Power: The Memoirs of an American Diplomat*. Englewood Cliffs, NJ: Prentice Hall, 1984.

Kaplan, William. *Canadian Maverick: The Life and Times of Ivan C. Rand*. Toronto: University of Toronto Press, 2009.

Keenleyside, Hugh L. *On the Bridge of Time: The Memoirs of Hugh L. Keenleyside*. Vol. 2. Toronto: McClelland and Stewart, 1982.

Kent, Tom. *A Public Purpose: An Experience of Liberal Opposition and Canadian Government*. Montreal and Kingston: McGill-Queen's University Press, 1988.

LaMarsh, Judy. *Memoirs of a Bird in a Gilded Cage*. Toronto: McClelland and Stewart, 1968.

Lee, Dennis. "Third Elegy (Nathan Phillips Square, Toronto)." *Canadian Dimension* 4, 6 (September-October 1967): 32–33.

Legault, Albert, and Michel Fortmann. *The Diplomacy of Hope: Canada and Disarmament, 1945–1988*. Montreal and Kingston: McGill-Queen's University Press, 1992.

Legree, Joseph C. *Lift Up Your Hearts: A History of the Roman Catholic Diocese of Pembroke*. Pembroke: privately published, 1988.

Lewis, David. *The Good Fight: Political Memoirs, 1909–58*. Toronto: Macmillan, 1981.

MacDowell, Laurel Sefton. *Renegade Lawyer: The Life of J.L. Cohen*. Toronto: University of Toronto Press for the Osgoode Society for Canadian Legal History, 2001.

MacLaren, Roy. *The Fundamental Things Apply: A Memoir*. Toronto: University of Toronto Press, 2010.

MacPherson, Ian. "The 1945 Collapse of the CCF in Windsor." *Ontario History* 61 (December 1969): 197–212.

Mallon, J. Francis. *My Student Days at St. Michael's*. Toronto: University of St. Michael's College, 1990.

Mann-Trofimenkoff, Susan. *Stanley Knowles: The Man from Winnipeg North Centre*. Saskatoon: Western Producer Prairie Books, 1982.

Markwell, D.J. "Zimmern, Sir Alfred Eckhard (1879–1957)." *Dictionary of National Biography*. http://dx.doi.org/10.1093/ref:odnb/37088.

Martin, Paul. "At the Right Hand : A Record of Canadian Foreign Policy, 1963–1968." Typed manuscript, author's possession.

–. *Canada and the Quest for Peace*. New York: Columbia University Press, 1967.

–. *Far from Home*. Vol. 1 of *A Very Public Life*. Toronto: Deneau, 1983.

–. "King: The View from the Backbench and the Cabinet Table." In *Mackenzie King: Widening the Debate*, ed. John English and John Stubbs, 30–39. Toronto: Macmillan, 1977.

–. *The London Diaries, 1975–1979*. Ed. William Young. Toronto: University of Toronto Press, 1988.

–. *Paul Martin Speaks for Canada: A Collection of Speeches on Foreign Policy*. Toronto: McClelland and Stewart, 1968.

–. *So Many Worlds*. Vol. 2 of *A Very Public Life*. Toronto: Deneau, 1985.

Martin, Paul, Jr. "Concluding Remarks." In *Paul Martin and Canadian Diplomacy,* ed. Ryan Touhey, 41–45. Waterloo: Centre on Foreign Policy and Federalism, 2001.

–. *Hell or High Water: My Life In and Out of Politics.* Toronto: McClelland and Stewart, 2008.

McCall-Newman, Christina. *Grits: An Intimate Portrait of the Liberal Party.* Toronto: Macmillan, 1982.

McCorkell, E.J. *Henry Carr: Revolutionary.* Toronto: Griffin Press, 1969.

–. *Memoirs.* Toronto: Basilian Press, 1975.

McDonald, Marci. "Blind Trust: How Much Do We Really Know about Canada's Next Prime Minister?" *The Walrus,* October 2003. http://thewalrus.ca/blind-trust/.

–. "The Forgotten Man." *Maclean's,* August 1976, 22–27.

McGill, Allan S. *My Life as I Remember It.* Vancouver: Granville Island, 2004.

McGowan, Mark. *The Waning of the Green: Catholics, the Irish, and Identity in Toronto, 1887–1922.* Montreal and Kingston: McGill-Queen's University Press, 1998.

Meren, David. *With Friends Like These: Entangled Nationalisms and the Canada-Quebec-France Triangle, 1944–1970.* Vancouver: UBC Press, 2012.

Moore, Paul. "Nathan L. Nathanson Introduces Canadian Odeon: Producing National Competition in Film Exhibition." *Canadian Journal of Film Studies* 12, 2 (Fall 2003): 22–45.

Morrison, David R. *Aid and Ebb Tide: A History of CIDA and Canadian Development Assistance.* Waterloo: Wilfrid Laurier University Press, 1998.

Morrison, Neil F. *Garden Gateway to Canada: 100 Years of Windsor and Essex County, 1854–1954.* Toronto: Ryerson Press, 1954.

Moulton, David. "Ford Windsor 1945." In *On Strike: Six Key Labour Struggles in Canada, 1919–1949,* ed. Irving Abella, 129–53. Toronto: James Lewis and Samuel, 1974.

Muirhead, Bruce. *Against the Odds: The Public Life and Times of Louis Rasminsky.* Toronto: University of Toronto Press, 1999.

Nash, Knowlton. *Microphone Wars: A History of Triumph and Betrayal at the CBC.* Toronto: McClelland and Stewart, 1994.

Neatby, Blair. "Political Animal." *Saturday Night,* February 1984, 65.

–. *William Lyon Mackenzie King.* Vol. 3, *1932–1939, The Prism of Unity.* Toronto: University of Toronto Press, 1976.

Newman, Peter C. *The Distemper of Our Times: Canadian Politics in Transition, 1963–1968.* Toronto: McClelland and Stewart, 1968.

Nielsen, Erik. *The House Is Not a Home.* Toronto: Macmillan, 1989.

Olive, David. "Paul Martin: The Vaulting Ambition of a True Grit." *Quill and Quire* 50, 8 (August 1984): 32.

Owens, Joseph. *The Philosophical Tradition of St. Michael's College.* Toronto: USMC Archives, 1979.

Page, Donald, ed. *Documents on Canadian External Relations.* Vol. 12, *1946.* Ottawa: Supply and Services Canada, 1977.

Pearson, Lester B. *Mike: The Memoirs of the Rt. Hon. Lester B. Pearson.* Vol. 3, *1957–1968.* Ed. J.A. Munro and A.I. Inglis. Toronto: University of Toronto Press, 1975.

Pelletier, Gérard. *Years of Choice, 1960–68.* Trans. Alan Brown. Toronto: Methuen, 1987.

Pelletier, Jean-François. "Le Saint-Alexandre d'il y a soixante-dix ans." http://www. college-stalexandre.qc.ca/spip.php?article42.

Pennington, Doris. *Agnes Macphail: Reformer.* Toronto: Simon Pierre, 1990.

Pickersgill, J.W. *The Mackenzie King Record.* Vol. 1, *1939–44.* Toronto: University of Toronto Press, 1960.

–. *My Years with Louis St. Laurent: A Political Memoir.* Toronto: University of Toronto Press, 1975.

–. *Seeing Canada Whole: A Memoir.* Markham, ON: Fitzhenry and Whiteside, 1994.

Power, C.G., with Norman Ward. *A Party Politician: The Memoirs of Chubby Power.* Toronto: Macmillan, 1966.

Preston, Andrew. "Balancing War and Peace: Canadian Foreign Policy and the Vietnam War, 1961–1965." *Diplomatic History* 27, 1 (January 2003): 73–111. http://dx.doi.org/ 10.1111/1467-7709.00340.

Price, Trevor, and Larry Kulisek. *Windsor, 1892–1992: A Centennial Celebration.* Windsor: Chamber, 1992.

Reid, Escott. *Radical Mandarin: The Memoirs of Escott Reid.* Toronto: University of Toronto Press, 1989.

Reid, Patrick. *Wild Colonial Boy: A Memoir.* Vancouver: Douglas and McIntyre, 1995.

Rich, P. "Alfred Zimmern's Cautious Idealism: The League of Nations, International Education and the Commonwealth." In *Thinkers of the Twenty Years' Crisis: Interwar Idealism Reassessed,* ed. D. Long and P. Wilson, 79–99. Oxford: Clarendon Press, 1995.

Robertson, Gordon. *Memoirs of a Very Civil Servant: Mackenzie King to Pierre Trudeau.* Toronto: University of Toronto Press, 2000.

Ruud, Charles. *The Constant Diplomat: Robert Ford in Moscow.* Montreal and Kingston: McGill-Queen's University Press, 2009.

Sawatsky, John. *The Insiders: Government, Business and the Lobbyists.* Toronto: McClelland and Stewart, 1987.

Saywell, John, ed. *Canadian Annual Review for 1960.* Toronto: University of Toronto Press, 1961.

–, ed. *Canadian Annual Review for 1961.* Toronto: University of Toronto Press, 1962.

–, ed. *Canadian Annual Review for 1963.* Toronto: University of Toronto Press, 1964.

–, ed. *Canadian Annual Review for 1964.* Toronto: University of Toronto Press, 1965.

–, ed. *Canadian Annual Review for 1965.* Toronto: University of Toronto Press, 1966.

–, ed. *Canadian Annual Review for 1966.* Toronto: University of Toronto Press, 1967.

–, ed. *Canadian Annual Review for 1967.* Toronto: University of Toronto Press, 1968.

–, ed. *Canadian Annual Review for 1968.* Toronto: University of Toronto Press, 1969.

–. *"Just Call Me Mitch": The Life of Mitchell F. Hepburn.* Toronto: University of Toronto Press, 1991.

Sévigny, Pierre. *This Game of Politics.* Toronto: McClelland and Stewart, 1965.

Sharp, Mitchell. *Which Reminds Me ... A Memoir.* Toronto: University of Toronto Press, 1994.

Sherman, Paddy. *Bennett.* Toronto: McClelland and Stewart, 1966.

Shook, Laurence. *Catholic Post-Secondary Education in English-Speaking Canada.* Toronto: University of Toronto Press, 1971.

Smith, Denis. *Gentle Patriot: A Political Biography of Walter Gordon*. Edmonton: Hurtig, 1973.

–. *Rogue Tory: The Life and Times of John G. Diefenbaker*. Toronto: Macfarlane, Walter and Ross, 1995.

Splane, Richard B. *George Davidson: Social Policy and Public Policy Exemplar*. Ottawa: Canadian Council on Social Development, 2003.

St. Amour, Norman. "Sino-Canadian Relations, 1963–1968: The American Factor." In *Reluctant Adversaries: Canada and the People's Republic of China*, ed. Brian Evans and Bernie Frolic, 106–29. Toronto: University of Toronto Press, 1991.

Stapells, Bredin. Introduction to Maurice Strong, "International Development – Canada's Centennial Challenge." In *The Empire Club of Canada Addresses, 1966–67*, 172–86. Toronto: Empire Club, 1967.

Stockdale, Peter. "Pearsonian Internationalism in Practice: The International Development Research Centre." PhD diss., McGill University, 1995.

Strong, Maurice. *Where on Earth Are We Going?* Toronto: A.A. Knopf, 2000.

Stursberg, Peter. *Agreement in Principle*. Toronto: Longmans, Green, 1961.

–. *Diefenbaker: Leadership Gained, 1956–62*. Toronto: University of Toronto Press, 1975.

–. *Diefenbaker: Leadership Lost, 1962–67*. Toronto: University of Toronto Press, 1976.

–. *Lester Pearson and the American Dilemma*. Toronto: Doubleday, 1980.

Swainson, Neil A. *Conflict over the Columbia: The Canadian Background to an Historic Treaty*. Montreal and Kingston: McGill-Queen's University Press, 1979.

Taylor, Charles. *Snowjob: Canada, the United States and Vietnam (1954–1973)*. Toronto: House of Anansi Press, 1974.

Taylor, Malcolm G. *Health Insurance and Canadian Public Policy: The Seven Decisions That Created the Health Insurance System and Their Outcomes*. 2nd ed. Montreal and Kingston: McGill-Queen's University Press, 2009.

Thomson, Dale C. *Louis St Laurent, Canadian*. Toronto: Macmillan, 1967.

–. *Vive le Québec libre*. Toronto: Deneau, 1988.

US Department of State. *Foreign Relations of the United States, 1964–68*. Vol. 1, *Vietnam 1964*. Washington, DC: US Government Printing Office, 1992.

–. *Foreign Relations of the United States, 1955–1957*. Vol. 11, *United Nations and General International Matters*. Washington, DC: US Government Printing Office, 1988.

–. *Foreign Relations of the United States, 1952–1954*. Vol. 15, Part 1, *Korea*. Washington, DC: US Government Printing Office, 1984.

–. *Foreign Relations of the United States, 1964–1968*. Vol. 12, Western Europe. Washington, DC: US Government Printing Office, 2001.

–. *Foreign Relations of the United States, 1964–1968*. Vol. 19, *Arab-Israeli Crisis and War, 1967*. Washington, DC: US Government Printing Office, 2004.

Walker, David James. *Fun along the Way: Memoirs of Dave Walker*. Toronto: Robertson Press, 1989.

Wardhaugh, Robert. *Behind the Scenes: The Life and Work of W.C. Clark*. Toronto: University of Toronto Press, 2010.

Warnock, John. "Canada and the Alliance System." *Canadian Dimension* 3 (March–April 1966): 36–39.

Whelan, Eugene, with Rich Archbold. *Whelan: The Man in the Green Stetson*. Toronto: Irwin, 1986.

Whitaker, Reg. *The Government Party: Organizing and Financing the Liberal Party of Canada, 1930–58*. Toronto: University of Toronto Press, 1977.

Worthington, Larry. *"Worthy": A Biography of Major-General F.F. Worthington*. Toronto: Macmillan, 1961.

ILLUSTRATION CREDITS

1 Martin's grade seven class at Pembroke Separate School, 1915. Library and Archives Canada (LAC), PA 149121.

2 Martin's graduation photo, 1925. LAC, e011093069.

3 Martin campaigning in Windsor in the early 1930s. LAC, e011093068.

4 Gordon Graydon, Louis St. Laurent, and Martin arrive at UN General Assembly meeting, 1946. Canadian Army Photo, LAC, PA 129002.

5 Prime Minister W.L.M. King and Martin at Citizenship Court ceremonies, 1947. National Film Board, LAC, e011093066.

6 Martin at meeting of Interprovincial Old Age Pension Board, 1948. Department of National Health and Welfare, LAC, e011093064.

7 Martin with Dr. Donald Cameron and Dr. Fred Jackson in his Ottawa office, 1950. Capital Photo, LAC, PA 143199.

8 Maj. Richard Bingham, Martin, and Brig. J.C. Jefferson at a launch for a civil defence display, c. 1952. National Health and Welfare, LAC, e011093065.

9 Martin addressing a meeting of the Political Committee at the UN, 1952. UN Photo, LAC, 39114.

10 Martin's family, 1953. LAC, e011093067

11 Martin, Nell, and Lord Beaverbrook sailing in Montego Bay, Jamaica, 1954. LAC, e011093070.

12 Martin consults with Hammarskjöld during debate on the admission of new members at the UN, 1955. Leo Rosenthal (photographer), LAC, e011093073.

13 Martin shares a hookah with a villager in East Punjab, India, 1957. Robert McKeown (photographer), LAC, e011093080.

14 Martin and Alan Hodges on the set at CKCO TV Kitchener, 1957. Ray Parks (photographer), LAC, e11093078.

15 Martin and Louis St. Laurent greet Pearson on his return from Norway, 1958. Duncan Cameron (photographer), LAC, PA-114542.

16 Martin supporters carry him around the hall during the Liberal Party Leadership Convention, 1958. AP Photo.

17 Martin and new MPs Herb Gray and Eugene Whelan shortly after the 1962 election. *Windsor Star*, used with permission.

18 Martin listens to a voter in his Essex East riding during the 1963 election campaign. Horst Ehricht (photographer), LAC, e011093191.

19 Martin and Nell in the library at the Lowe-Martin House, Windsor, 1963. Horst Ehricht (photographer), LAC, e011093063.

20 Martin and Couve de Murville meet in Paris on 16 January 1964. Paris Préfecture de Police, LAC, PA-88364.

21 Martin with Pearson, George Ignatieff, and Dirk Stikker at NATO Headquarters in Paris, 1964. NATO Photo.

22 Martin meets with UN Secretary-General U Thant in New York to discuss crisis in Cyprus, 1964. UN Photo 84156, LAC, e011093061.

23 Martin and Douglas Dillon at a meeting of the Canada-US Joint Ministerial Committee on Trade and Economic Affairs, Ottawa, 1964. Duncan Cameron (photographer), LAC, PA 113495.

24 Martin and Dean Rusk chat at ministerial meeting of the North Atlantic Council in The Hague, 1964. NATO Photo.

25 Martin and Pearson bid farewell to President Johnson at his Texas ranch, 1965. Yoichi Okamoto (photographer), LBJ Library.

26 Martin sits in the stands with Paul Martin Jr. at the 1968 leadership convention. Peter Bregg (photographer), CP Photo.

27 Martin with Marc Rochon and Don McPhail at the UN Conference on Trade and Development, Chile, 1972. LAC, e011093079.

28 Martin and Nell relaxing at the family cottage in Colchester, 1976. LAC, PA 164958.

29 Martin addresses a political science class at Wilfrid Laurier University, 1986. James Hertel (photographer), Wilfrid Laurier Archives, U57-4289.

30 Martin and Paul Martin Jr. at the Lowe-Martin House in Windsor, c. 1990. Photograph by Deborah Samuel.

ACKNOWLEDGMENTS

I am deeply grateful to a large number of people for their support with this project over the last several years. I am particularly thankful to the Right Honourable Paul Martin Jr. and his wife, Sheila, who backed this project from the start. Mr. Martin answered my questions forthrightly, rummaged about in his files for papers and phone numbers, and refrained from interfering. His assistant, Therese Horvath, responded to my inquiries with exceptional efficiency and kindness.

In my research, I have been helped by several invaluable assistants: Ryan Touhey, Joel Kropf, and Nathan Hoeppner. My longtime friend and colleague, Christopher Cook, also provided exceptional research help over the years, particularly in my search for photographs. Martin Helle helped keep my records straight, before heading to Windsor himself. Loretta Barber of Library and Archives Canada, Sylvia Lassam of Trinity College Archives, and Cindy Preece of Wilfrid Laurier University Archives made working with the records under their custody a genuine pleasure. Rafael Eskenazi, director of the University of Toronto's access to information office, unlocked Martin's student records, inspired by the lofty but often unrealized ideals behind access to information legislation.

The Department of Foreign Affairs, Trade and Development recognized the importance of this project to my scholarly career and was steadfast in its support. My divisional directors since 2006 – Ariel Delouya, Weldon Epp, and Alan Bowman – stickhandled the arrangements for unpaid leave without complaint. My historian colleagues Mary Halloran, Janice Cavell, and Hector Mackenzie graciously met the challenges created by my absences. John Hilliker, former head of the department's historical section, made his judicious counsel freely available. Pat Belanger and Archie Campbell provided great and ready help with sources. Of course, the views expressed in this book are mine alone and do not represent the views of my department or the Government of Canada.

This book would not have been possible without the support of three exceptional historians, who have been friends and teachers at every step in my career: Robert Bothwell, John English, and Norman Hillmer. They shared sources and papers, provided historical advice and guidance, and read and commented on the entire manuscript. I am greatly indebted to them. I owe an important vote of thanks as well to Michael Stevenson, who also read the manuscript and provided helpful advice on Diefenbaker's nuclear weapons policy.

The editorial team at UBC Press was patient and kind. Senior editor Emily Andrew skillfully guided the manuscript through the assessment process before handing it over to the tender mercies of Deborah Kerr, my copy-editor, and Holly Keller, the production manager. All contributed to making it a better book.

A community of friends and family shared research and ideas, provided encouragement, and most importantly, supplied diverting distractions: Stephen Azzi, Eric Bergbusch, Richard Bingham, Mike Carroll, Adam Chapnick, Richard Daly, Xavier Gelinas, John Hay, John Meehan, Galen Perras, Dave Meren, Stéphane Roussel, Annette Ryan, Boris Stipernitz, Peter Stockdale, Mako Watanabe, and David Webster.

Finally, I am especially grateful for the constant support of my entire family, without whom this project would not have been finished. Ron and Dawn Shephard have long shown a genuine and supportive interest in my work. June Day, Colm Donaghy, and Geraldine Byrne generously housed, fed, and entertained me on several research trips to London. For decades, John and Margaret Flynn have provided a summer refuge from the archival grind. My mother, Maureen Donaghy, supervised my kids during research trips and lent her unwavering support in thousands of other small and not-so-small ways. My sisters, Mary and Fionnuala, and my late brother, Tom, and their families, have always encouraged my projects, though with far too much unnecessary kidding.

My children, Katherine, Michael, and Stephen, cheerfully made space for Paul Martin and the biography in their busy lives. My wife, Mary, patiently juggled their schedules and her own successful career to make time for my work. This book is dedicated to her.

INDEX

Printed and bound in Canada by Friesens

Set in Alternate Gothic, Perpetua, and Minion
by Artegraphica Design Co. Ltd.

Text design: Irma Rodriguez

Copy editor: Deborah Kerr

Proofreader: Frank Chow

Indexer: Dianne Tiefensee